Kubernetes Management Design Patterns

With Docker, CoreOS Linux, and Other Platforms

Deepak Vohra

Apress®

Kubernetes Management Design Patterns: With Docker, CoreOS Linux, and Other Platforms

Deepak Vohra
White Rock, British Columbia
Canada

ISBN-13 (pbk): 978-1-4842-2597-4 ISBN-13 (electronic): 978-1-4842-2598-1
DOI 10.1007/978-1-4842-2598-1

Library of Congress Control Number: 2017930815

Cover image designed by Freepik.
Managing Director: Welmoed Spahr
Lead Editor: Steve Anglin
Development Editor: Matthew Moodie
Technical Reviewer: Massimo Nardone
Coordinating Editor: Mark Powers
Copy Editor: James A. Compton
Compositor: SPi Global
Indexer: SPi Global
Artist: SPi Global

Distributed to the book trade worldwide by Springer Science+Business Media New York, 233 Spring Street, 6th Floor, New York, NY 10013. Phone 1-800-SPRINGER, fax (201) 348-4505, e-mail orders-ny@springer-sbm.com, or visit www.springeronline.com. Apress Media, LLC is a California LLC and the sole member (owner) is Springer Science + Business Media Finance Inc (SSBM Finance Inc). SSBM Finance Inc is a **Delaware** corporation.

For information on translations, please e-mail rights@apress.com, or visit http://www.apress.com/us/services/rights-permission.

Apress titles may be purchased in bulk for academic, corporate, or promotional use. eBook versions and licenses are also available for most titles. For more information, reference our Print and eBook Bulk Sales web page at http://www.apress.com/bulk-sales.

Any source code or other supplementary material referenced by the author in this book is available to readers for download or cloning at Github via the book's product page, located at www.apress.com/9781484225974. For more detailed information, please visit http://www.apress.com/source-code.

Printed on acid-free paper

Contents at a Glance

Contents

About the Author

Deepak Vohra is a consultant and a principal member of the NuBean software company. Deepak is a Sun-certified Java programmer and Web component developer. He has worked in the fields of XML, Java programming, and Java EE for over seven years. Deepak is the coauthor of *Pro XML Development with Java Technology* (Apress, 2006). Deepak is also the author of *JDBC 4.0* and *Oracle JDeveloper for J2EE Development, Processing XML Documents with Oracle JDeveloper 11g, EJB 3.0 Database Persistence with Oracle Fusion Middleware 11g*, and *Java EE Development in Eclipse IDE* (Packt Publishing). He also served as the technical reviewer on *WebLogic: The Definitive Guide (O'Reilly Media, 2004)* and *Ruby Programming for the Absolute Beginner* (Cengage Learning PTR, 2007).

About the Technical Reviewer

Massimo Nardone has more than 22 years of experiences in Security, Web/Mobile development, Cloud and IT Architecture. His true IT passions are security and Android.

He has been programming and teaching how to program with Android, Perl, PHP, Java, VB, Python, C/C++ and MySQL for more than 20 years.

He holds a Master of Science degree in Computing Science from the University of Salerno, Italy.

He has worked as a Project Manager, Software Engineer, Research Engineer, Chief Security Architect, Information Security Manager, PCI/SCADA Auditor and Senior Lead IT Security/Cloud/SCADA Architect for many years.

Technical skills include: Security, Android, Cloud, Java, MySQL, Drupal, Cobol, Perl, Web and Mobile development, MongoDB, D3, Joomla, Couchbase, C/C++, WebGL, Python, Pro Rails, Django CMS, Jekyll, Scratch, etc.

He currently works as Chief Information Security Office (CISO) for Cargotec Oyj.

He worked as visiting lecturer and supervisor for exercises at the Networking Laboratory of the Helsinki University of Technology (Aalto University). He holds four international patents (PKI, SIP, SAML and Proxy areas).

Massimo has reviewed more than 40 IT books for different publishing company and he is the coauthor of *Pro Android Games* (Apress, 2015).

About the Technical Reviewer

Introduction

Docker was made available as open source in March 2013 and has become the most commonly used containerization platform. Kubernetes was open-sourced in June 2014 and has become the most widely used container cluster manager. The first stable version of CoreOS Linux was made available in July 2014 and since has become the most commonly used operating system for containers. My first book, *Kubernetes Microservices with Docker* (Apress, 2016), is an introduction to creating microservices with Kubernetes and Docker. This book, *Kubernetes Management Design Patterns,* takes container cluster management to the next level and discusses all or most aspects of administering and configuring Kubernetes on CoreOS and applying suitable design patterns such as ConfigMaps, autoscaling, resource quotas, and high availability. Kubernetes is a cluster manager for Docker and rkt containers, but this book discusses Kubernetes in the context of Docker only. A cluster manager for Docker containers is needed because the Docker engine by itself lacks some functionality, such as the ability to scale a cluster of containers, schedule pods on nodes, or mount a certain type of storage (such as an AWS Volume or Github repo) as volumes. Docker Engine 1.12 integrates the Docker Swarm cluster manager and Docker Swarm does overcome some of the earlier limitations of Docker by providing replication, load balancing, fault tolerance, and service discovery, but Kubernetes provides some features suitable for developing object-oriented applications. The Pod abstraction is the atomic unit of deployment in Kubernetes. A Pod may consist of one or more containers. Co-locating containers has several advantages as containers in a Pod share the same networking and filesystem and run on the same node. Docker Swarm does not support autoscaling directly. While Docker Swarm is Docker native, Kubernetes is more production-ready having been used in production at Google for more than 15 years.

Kubernetes Design Patterns

> *A software design pattern is a general reusable solution to a commonly occurring problem within a given context in software design.*
>
> Wikepedia

A Docker image includes instructions to package all the required software and dependencies, set the environment variables, and run commands, and it is a reusable encapsulation of software for modular design. The atomic unit of modular container service in Kubernetes is a *pod,* which is a group of containers with a common filesystem and networking. The Kubernetes pod abstraction enables design patterns for containerized applications similar to object oriented design patterns. Pod, service, replication controller, deployment, and ConfigMap are all types of Kubernetes objects. Further, because containers interact with each other over HTTP, making use of a commonly available data format such as JSON, Kubernetes design patterns are language and platform independent. Containers provide some of the same benefits as software objects such as modularity or packaging, abstraction and reuse. Kubernetes has described three classes or types of patterns.

- Management design patterns
- Patterns involving multiple cooperating containers running on the same node
- Patterns involving containers running across multiple nodes

Some of the benefits of modular containers are as follows:

- The container boundary is an encapsulation or abstraction boundary that can be used to build modular, reusable components.
- The reusable containers may be shared between different applications and agile developer teams.
- Containers speed application development.
- Containers are suitable for agile team development.
- Containers can be used to encapsulate a best design or implementation.
- Containers provide separation of concerns

The design patterns are introduced in the publication Design Patterns For Container-Based Distributed Systems, by Brendan Burns and David Oppenheimer (`https://www.usenix.org/node/196347`). In this book we shall be using some of these and other design patterns.

Kubernetes Architecture

A Kubernetes cluster consists of a single *master node* (unless a high-availability master is used, which is not the default) and one or more *worker nodes* with Docker installed on each node. The following components run on each master node:

- *etcd* to store the persistent state of the master including all configuration data. A high-availability etcd cluster can also be used.
- An *API Server* to serve up the Kubernetes REST API for Kubernetes objects (pods, services, replication controllers, and others).
- *Scheduler* to bind unassigned pods on nodes.
- *Controller manager* performs all cluster level operations such as create and update service endpoints, discover, manage and monitor nodes. The replication controller is used to scale pods in a cluster.

The following components are run on each worker node:

- *kubelet* to manage the pods (including containers), Docker images, and volumes. The kubelet is managed from the API Server on the master node.
- *kube-proxy* is a network proxy and load balancer to serve up services.

The Kubernetes architecture is shown in Figure I-1.

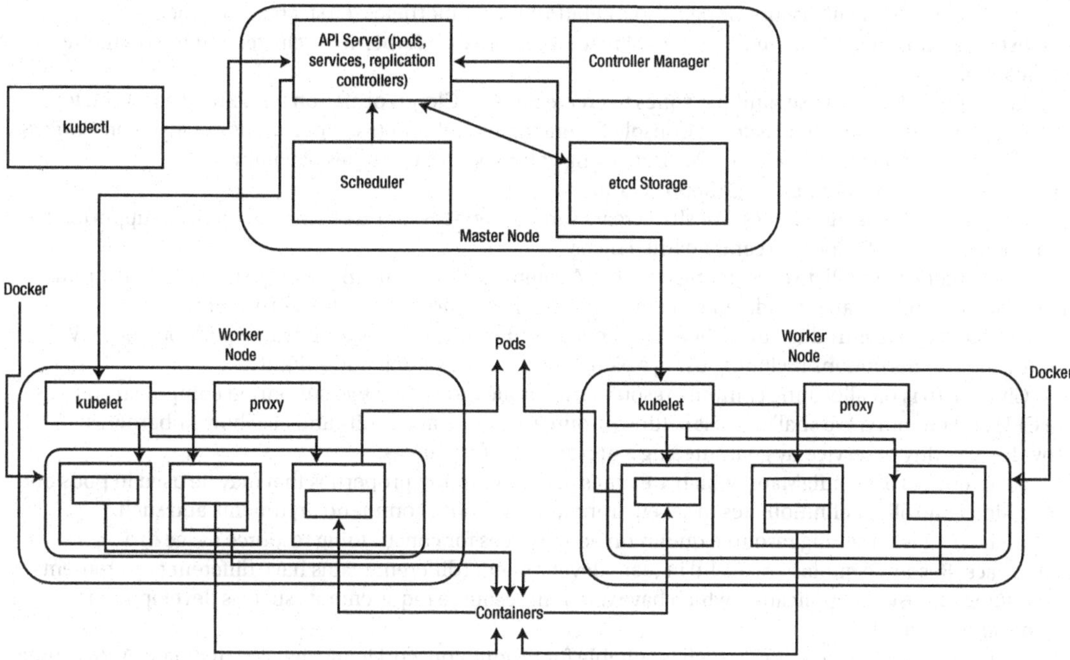

Figure I-1. *Kubernetes Architecture*

Why CoreOS?

CoreOS is the most widely used Linux OS designed for containers, not just Docker containers but also rkt (an implementation of the APP Container spec) containers. Docker and rkt are pre-installed on CoreOS out-of-the-box. CoreOS supports most cloud providers including Amazon Web Services (AWS) Elastic Compute Cloud (EC2), Google Cloud Platform, and virtualization platforms such as VMWare and VirtualBox. CoreOS provides Cloud-Config for declaratively configuring for OS items such as network configuration (flannel), storage (etcd), and user accounts. CoreOS provides a production-level infrastructure for containerized applications including automation, security and scalability. CoreOS has been leading the drive for container industry standards and in fact founded appc. CoreOS is not only the most widely used operating system for containers but also the most advanced container registry, Quay. CoreOS provides server security with Distributed Trusted Computing. CoreOS also provides Tectonic Enterprise for enterprise-level workloads without operational overhead and an out-of-the-box Kubernetes cluster and a user-friendly dashboard.

Chapter Description

In Chapter 1 we shall install Kubernetes on Amazon Web Services (AWS), create a sample deployment and service, and subsequently invoke the service. Kubernetes installation on AWS requires almost no configuration to spin-up a multi-node cluster.

In Chapter 2 we shall install Kubernetes on CoreOS, which is the main platform we shall use for most of the chapters. We'll first create an AWS EC2 instance from Amazon Linux AMI, which has the AWS Command Line Interface (CLI) preinstalled. We'll then SSH log in to the EC2 instance and install Kube-aws. Then we will launch a CloudFormation for a Kubernetes cluster with one controller node and three worker nodes and SSH log in to the controller instance and install kubectl binaries to access the API server.

In Chapter 3 we shall discuss Google Cloud Platform for Kubernetes. First, create a project and a VM instance. Subsequently connect to the VM instance to create a Kubernetes cluster and test a sample application.

In Chapter 4 we shall use multiple zones to create an AWS CloudFormation for a Kubernetes cluster.

Chapter 5 introduces the Tectonic Console for managing Kubernetes applications deployed on CoreOS.

Chapter 6 is on volumes. We demonstrate using volumes with two types of volumes: awsElasticBlockStore volume and gitRepo volume.

Chapter 7 is on using services. We shall create sample services for three kinds of services supported by Kubernetes: ClusterIP, NodePort and LoadBalancer.

In Chapter 8 we shall discuss rolling updates. A rolling update is the mechanism by which a running replication controller can be updated to a newer image or specification while it is running.

In Chapter 9 we introduce the scheduling policy used by Kubernetes to schedule pods on nodes. We discuss the various options including using a NodeSelector, and setting node affinity.

Chapter 10 is on allocating compute resources to applications. The two supported compute resources are CPU and memory. We shall discuss setting resource requests and limits and also how Kubernetes provides a quality of service by guaranteeing a preset level of resources.

Chapter 11 is on ConfigMaps, which are maps of configuration properties that may be used in pods and replication controller definition files to set environment variables, command arguments and such.

Chapter 12 is on setting resource quotas on namespaces for constraining resource usage in a namespace. Resource quotas are useful in team development (different teams have different requirements) and different phases of application which have different resource requirements such as development, testing, and production.

Chapter 13 is on autoscaling, which is suitable for production workloads that can fluctuate. Autoscaling of a deployment, replica set, or replication controller scales the number of pods in a cluster automatically when the load fluctuates.

Chapter 14 is on logging. The default logger is discussed in addition to cluster-level logging using Elasticsearch, Fluentd, and Kibana.

In Chapter 15 OpenShift, a PaaS platform for Kubernetes, is discussed to create a high availability master Kubernetes cluster using Ansible. Ansible is an automation platform for application deployment, configuration management, and orchestration.

In Chapter 16 a high availability web site is developed using AWS Route 53 for DNS failover.

PART I

Platforms

CHAPTER 1

Kubernetes on AWS

Kubernetes is a cluster manager for Docker (and rkt) containers. The Introduction outlines its basic architecture and relationship to CoreOS and Amazon Web Services (AWS). In this chapter we'll spin up a basic cluster without configuration.

Note *Kubernetes Microservices with Docker* (Apress, 2016) covers installing Kubernetes on single-node and multi-node clusters.

Problem

Installing Kubernetes by installing its individual components (Docker, Flannel, Kubelet, and Service Proxy) separately is an involved process that requires many commands to be run and files to be configured.

Solution

AWS provides a legacy tool called `kube-up.sh` to spin up a Kubernetes cluster without requiring any configuration. Only an AWS account, the AWS Command Line Interface (CLI), and access to the AWS APIs are required. Kubernetes and other tools such as Elasticsearch (used to index and store logs), Heapster (used to analyze compute resource usage), Kibana (a GUI dashboard used to view the logs), KubeDNS (used to resolve DNS names for services), Kubernetes-dashboard, Grafana (used for metrics visualization), and InfluxDB are all installed with a single command.

Overview

In this chapter we will create a multi-node cluster (consisting of one master and multiple minions) on Amazon Elastic Compute Cloud (EC2) using the AWS Command Line Interface. The stages are as follows:

Setting the Environment

Starting a Cluster

Testing the Cluster

Configuring the Cluster

Stopping the Cluster

D. Vohra, *Kubernetes Management Design Patterns*, DOI 10.1007/978-1-4842-2598-1_1

Setting the Environment

Because we're using Amazon EC2, an AWS account is required. Also, to configure AWS you need to obtain security credentials. Select Security Credentials for a user account. In the Your Security Credentials screen, select the Access Keys node and click Create New Access Key as shown in Figure 1-1 to create a new access key.

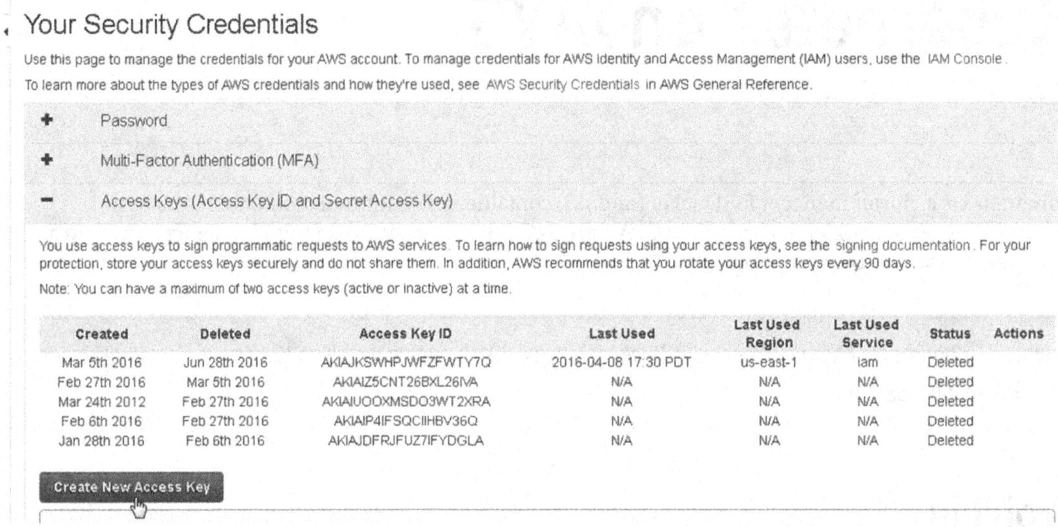

***Figure 1-1.** Creating a new access key*

A new security access key is created and the Access Key ID and Secret Access Key are listed.

Copy the Access Key ID and Secret Access Key to be used later to configure AWS. The Access Key ID and Secret Access Key will be different for different users.

```
AWS_ACCESS_KEY_ID  AKIAISQVxxxxxxxxxxxxxxx
AWS_SECRET_ACCESS_KEY  VuJD5gDxxxxxxxxxxxxxxxxxxxx
```

Because the AWS Command Line Interface is required, create an EC2 instance of the Amazon Linux Amazon Machine Image (AMI), which has the AWS CLI preinstalled. Click on Launch Instance as shown in Figure 1-2 to create a new instance.

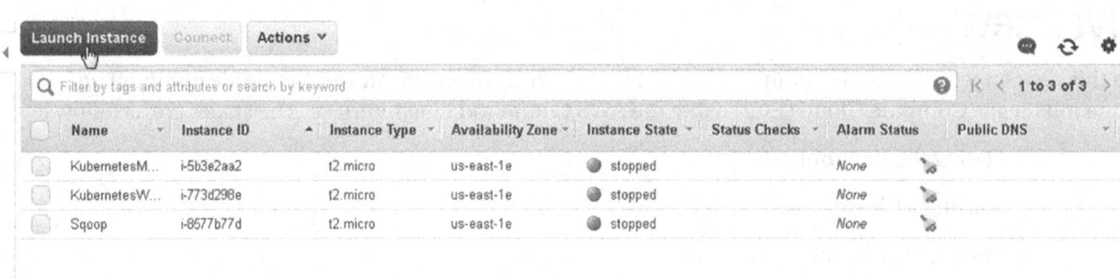

***Figure 1-2.** Launching an EC2 instance*

In the next screen, select the Amazon Linux AMI (64 bit) as shown in Figure 1-3.

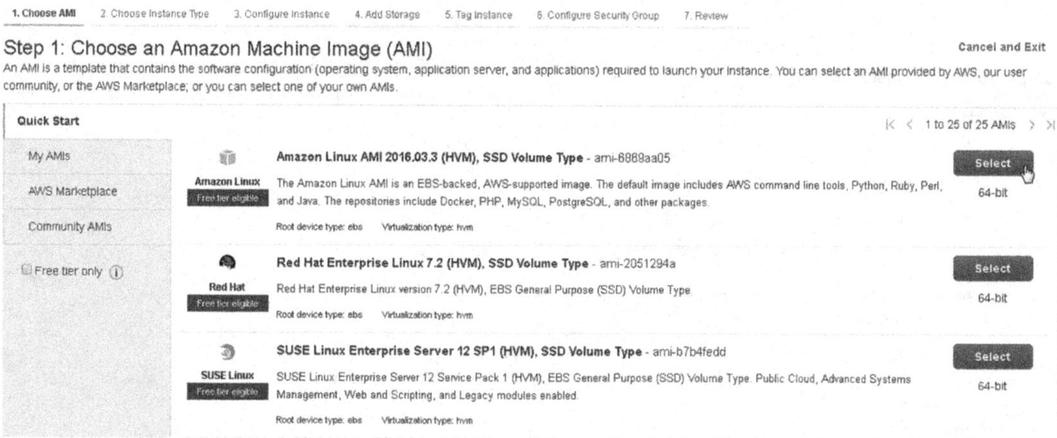

Figure 1-3. *Selecting Amazon Linux AMI*

For the Instance Type, select a relatively large Instance size (m4.xlarge) as shown in Figure 1-4, because the default (Free Tier) micro size may not provide sufficient memory or disk space to install Kubernetes. Some of the instance types such as m4.xlarge may only be launched in a virtual private cloud (VPC). When you are ready, click Next:Configure Instance Details.

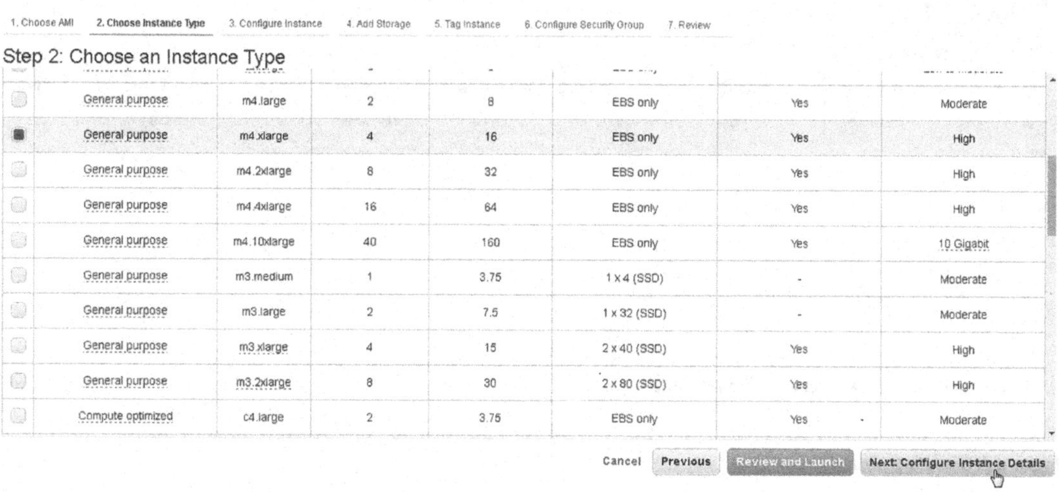

1. Choose AMI
2. Choose Instance Type
3. Configure Instance
4. Add Storage
5. Tag Instance
6. Configure Security Group
7. Review
Step 2: Choose an Instance Type
General purpose m4.large 2 8 EBS only Yes Moderate
General purpose m4.xlarge 4 16 EBS only Yes High
General purpose m4.2xlarge 8 32 EBS only Yes High
General purpose m4.4xlarge 16 64 EBS only Yes High
General purpose m4.10xlarge 40 160 EBS only Yes 10 Gigabit
General purpose m3.medium 1 3.75 1 x 4 (SSD) - Moderate
General purpose m3.large 2 7.5 1 x 32 (SSD) - Moderate
General purpose m3.xlarge 4 15 2 x 40 (SSD) Yes High
General purpose m3.2xlarge 8 30 2 x 80 (SSD) Yes High
Compute optimized c4.large 2 3.75 EBS only Yes Moderate
Cancel
Previous
Review and Launch
Next: Configure Instance Details

Figure 1-4. *Choosing an instance type*

Specify the instance details such as Network VPC and Subnet as shown in Figure 1-5. When finished, click Next: Add Storage.

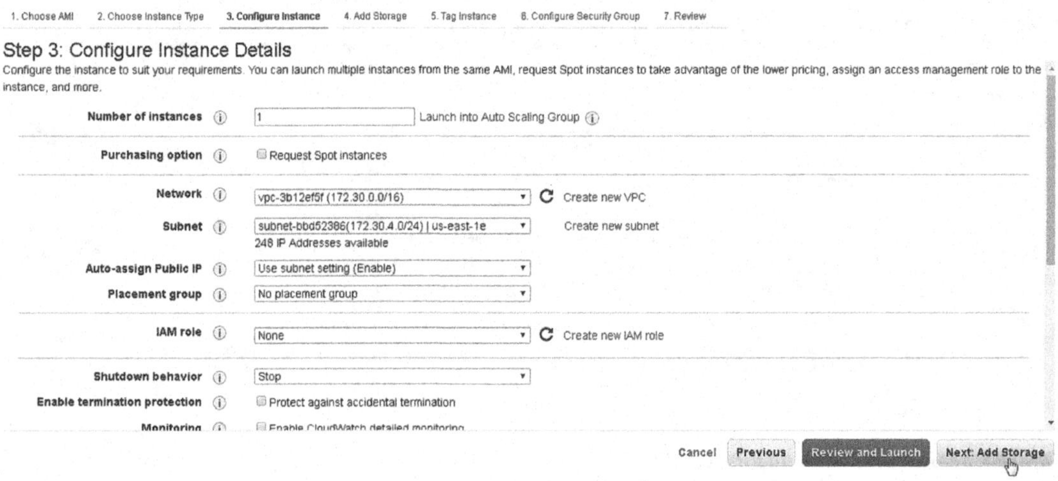

Figure 1-5. *Configuring instance details*

A new EC2 instance is created. Obtain the Public DNS for the instance as shown in Figure 1-6.

Figure 1-6. *The public DNS*

Using the private key that was specified when the instance was created, SSH log in to the instance:

```
ssh -i "docker.pem"  ec2-user@ec2-52-3-250-193.compute-1.amazonaws.com
```

The Amazon Linux command prompt is displayed as shown in Figure 1-7.

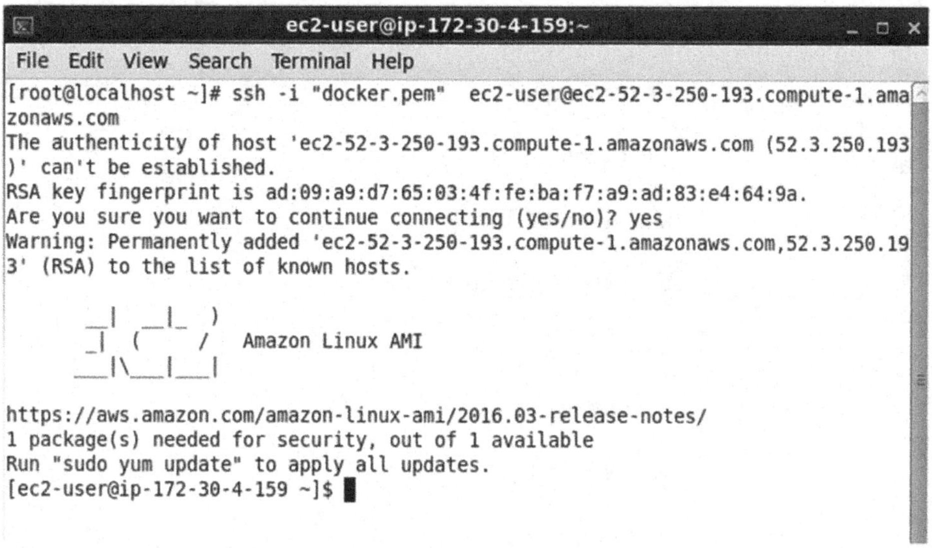
ec2-user@ip-172-30-4-159:~
File Edit View Search Terminal Help
[root@localhost ~]# ssh -i "docker.pem" ec2-user@ec2-52-3-250-193.compute-1.ama
zonaws.com
The authenticity of host 'ec2-52-3-250-193.compute-1.amazonaws.com (52.3.250.193
)' can't be established.
RSA key fingerprint is ad:09:a9:d7:65:03:4f:fe:ba:f7:a9:ad:83:e4:64:9a.
Are you sure you want to continue connecting (yes/no)? yes
Warning: Permanently added 'ec2-52-3-250-193.compute-1.amazonaws.com,52.3.250.19
3' (RSA) to the list of known hosts.
Amazon Linux AMI
https://aws.amazon.com/amazon-linux-ami/2016.03-release-notes/
1 package(s) needed for security, out of 1 available
Run "sudo yum update" to apply all updates.
[ec2-user@ip-172-30-4-159 ~]$

Figure 1-7. *Amazon Linux AMI command prompt*

Configuring AWS

When a Kubernetes cluster is started on AWS EC2, a new VPC is created for the master and minion nodes. The number of VPCs that may be created in an AWS account has a limit, which can vary for different users. Before starting the cluster, delete the VPCs that are not being used so that the limit is not reached when a new VPC is created. To begin, select VPC in the AWS Services as shown in Figure 1-8.

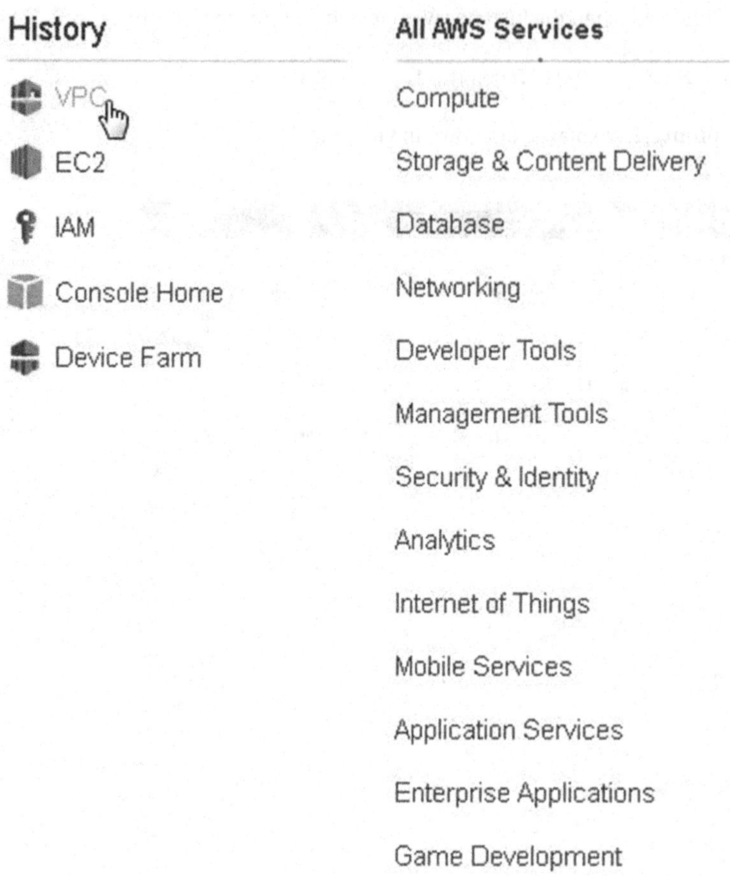

Figure 1-8. *Selecting the VPC console*

Click on Start VPC Wizard as shown in Figure 1-9 to list and delete VPCs if required.

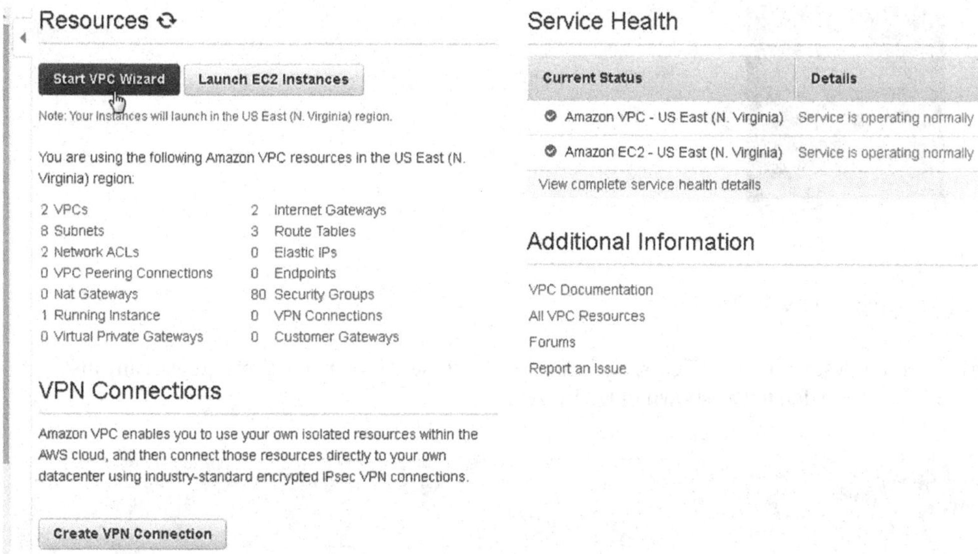

Figure 1-9. *Starting the VPC Wizard*

The VPCs already available are listed as shown in Figure 1-10.

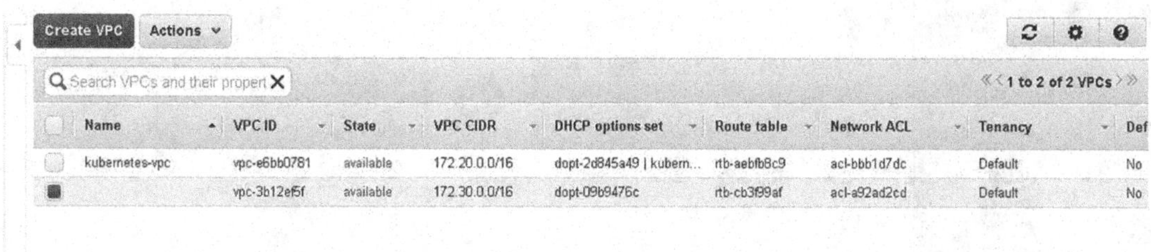

Figure 1-10. *Available VPCs*

To delete a VPC, select the VPC and click Actions ➤ Delete VPC, as shown in Figure 1-11.

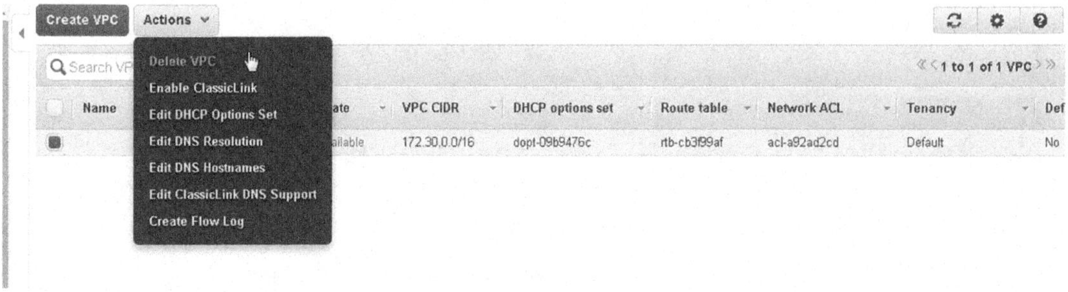

Figure 1-11. *Selecting Actions ➤ Delete VPC*

In the confirmation screen that appears, click Yes, Delete. If the VPC is not associated with any instance, the VPC should start to be deleted as shown in Figure 1-12.

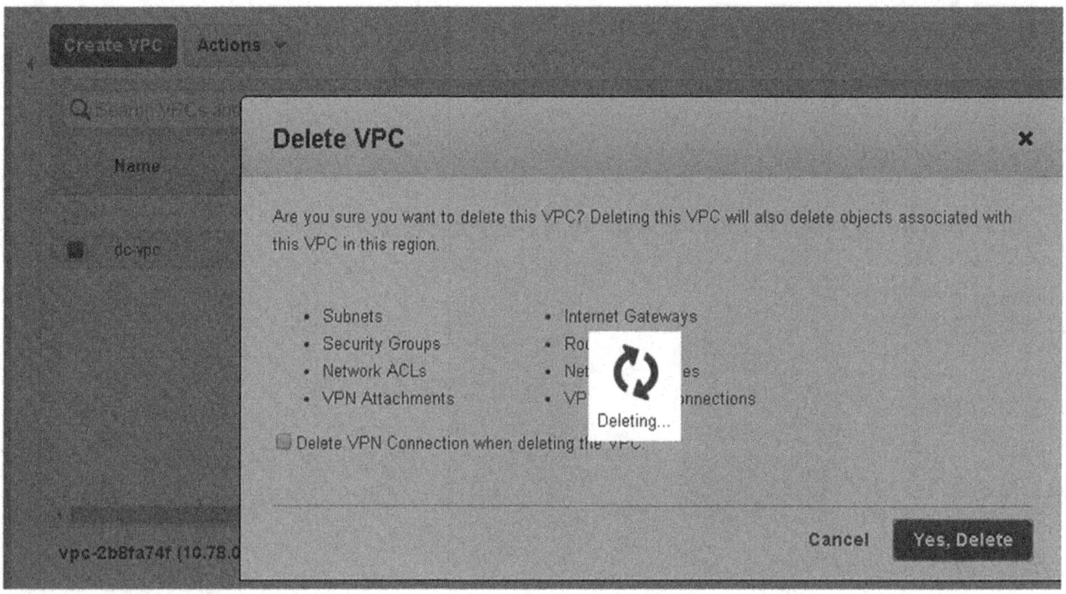

Figure 1-12. *Deleting a VPC*

If a VPC is associated with any instance, then it is not deletable and the Yes, Delete button is unavailable, as shown in Figure 1-13.

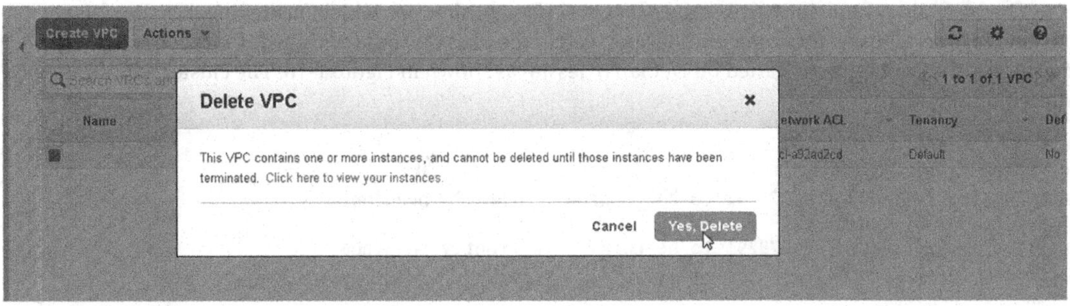

Figure 1-13. *The message for a nondeletable VPC*

Next, configure AWS on the Amazon Linux instance using the following command:

```
aws configure
```

When prompted, specify the AWS Access Key ID and AWS Access Key. Also specify the default region name (`us-east-1`) and the default output format (`json`) as shown in Figure 1-14.

```
[ec2-user@ip-172-30-4-159 ~]$ aws configure
AWS Access Key ID [None]: AKIAISQVST
AWS Secret Access Key [None]: VuJD5gD
Default region name [None]: us-east-1
Default output format [None]: json
[ec2-user@ip-172-30-4-159 ~]$
```

Figure 1-14. *Configuring AWS*

Starting the Kubernetes Cluster

Now that you have configured AWS, run the following command to install Kubernetes:

```
export KUBERNETES_PROVIDER=aws; wget -q -O - https://get.k8s.io | bash
```

This command starts the Kubernetes installation process as shown in Figure 1-15.

```
[ec2-user@ip-172-30-4-159 ~]$ aws configure
AWS Access Key ID [None]: AKIAISQVST
AWS Secret Access Key [None]: VuJD5g
Default region name [None]: us-east-1
Default output format [None]: json
[ec2-user@ip-172-30-4-159 ~]$ export KUBERNETES_PROVIDER=aws; wget -q -O - https
://get.k8s.io | bash
```

Figure 1-15. *Installing Kubernetes*

The preceding command invokes the `cluster/kube-up.sh` script, which further invokes the `cluster/aws/util.sh` script using the configuration specified in the `cluster/aws/config-default.sh` script. One master and four minions are started on Debian 8 (jessie) as shown in Figure 1-16. The cluster initialization is started subsequently.

```
Sleeping for 3 seconds...
Waiting for instance i-04978291 to be running (currently pending)
Sleeping for 3 seconds...
Waiting for instance i-04978291 to be running (currently pending)
Sleeping for 3 seconds...
 [master running]
Attaching IP 50.112.79.71 to instance i-04978291
Attaching persistent data volume (vol-c026ee75) to master
2016-06-28T18:42:25.708Z        /dev/sdb        i-04978291      attaching       v
ol-c026ee75
cluster "aws_kubernetes" set.
user "aws_kubernetes" set.
context "aws_kubernetes" set.
switched to context "aws_kubernetes".
user "aws_kubernetes-basic-auth" set.
Wrote config for aws_kubernetes to /home/ec2-user/.kube/config
Creating minion configuration
Creating autoscaling group
 0 minions started; waiting
 0 minions started; waiting
 0 minions started; waiting
 0 minions started; waiting
 0 minions started; waiting
 4 minions started; ready
Waiting for cluster initialization.

  This will continually check to see if the API for kubernetes is reachable.
  This might loop forever if there was some uncaught error during start
  up.

...........
```

Figure 1-16. *Starting master and minions*

The cluster is started and validated, and the components installed are listed. The URLs at which the Kubernetes master, Elasticsearch, Heapster, and other services are running are listed as shown in Figure 1-17. The directory path at which the Kubernetes binaries are installed is also listed.

```
Flag --api-version has been deprecated, flag is no longer respected and will be
deleted in the next release
Validate output:
NAME                 STATUS    MESSAGE              ERROR
scheduler            Healthy   ok
controller-manager   Healthy   ok
etcd-1               Healthy   {"health": "true"}
etcd-0               Healthy   {"health": "true"}
Cluster validation succeeded
Done, listing cluster services:

Kubernetes master is running at https://50.112.79.71
Elasticsearch is running at https://50.112.79.71/api/v1/proxy/namespaces/kube-sy
stem/services/elasticsearch-logging
Heapster is running at https://50.112.79.71/api/v1/proxy/namespaces/kube-system/
services/heapster
Kibana is running at https://50.112.79.71/api/v1/proxy/namespaces/kube-system/se
rvices/kibana-logging
KubeDNS is running at https://50.112.79.71/api/v1/proxy/namespaces/kube-system/s
ervices/kube-dns
kubernetes-dashboard is running at https://50.112.79.71/api/v1/proxy/namespaces/
kube-system/services/kubernetes-dashboard
Grafana is running at https://50.112.79.71/api/v1/proxy/namespaces/kube-system/s
ervices/monitoring-grafana
InfluxDB is running at https://50.112.79.71/api/v1/proxy/namespaces/kube-system/
services/monitoring-influxdb

Kubernetes binaries at /home/ec2-user/kubernetes/cluster/
You may want to add this directory to your PATH in $HOME/.profile
Installation successful!
[ec2-user@ip-172-30-4-159 ~]$
```

Figure 1-17. *Kubernetes and components started*

The one kubernetes-master and four kubernetes-minion nodes started are listed in the EC2 console as shown in Figure 1-18.

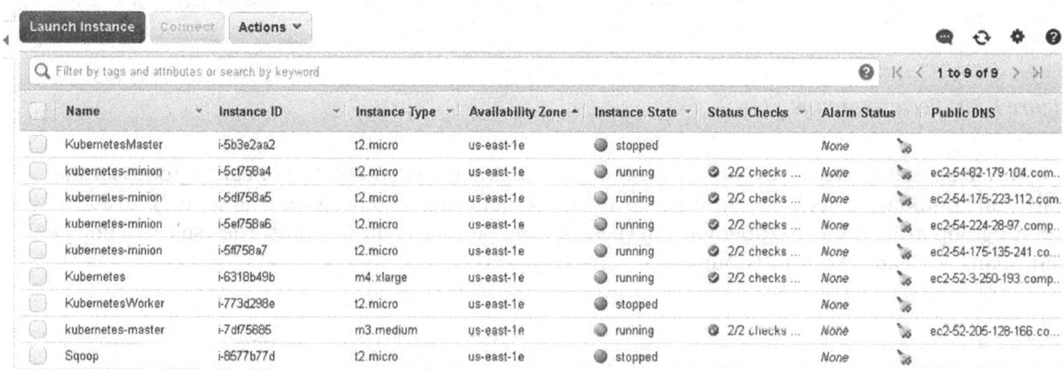

Name	Instance ID	Instance Type	Availability Zone	Instance State	Status Checks	Alarm Status	Public DNS
KubernetesMaster	i-5b3e2aa2	t2.micro	us-east-1e	stopped		None	
kubernetes-minion	i-5cf758a4	t2.micro	us-east-1e	running	2/2 checks ...	None	ec2-54-82-179-104.com..
kubernetes-minion	i-5df758a5	t2.micro	us-east-1e	running	2/2 checks ...	None	ec2-54-175-223-112.com.
kubernetes-minion	i-5ef758a6	t2.micro	us-east-1e	running	2/2 checks ...	None	ec2-54-224-28-97.comp..
kubernetes-minion	i-5ff758a7	t2.micro	us-east-1e	running	2/2 checks ...	None	ec2-54-175-135-241.co...
Kubernetes	i-6318b49b	m4.xlarge	us-east-1e	running	2/2 checks ...	None	ec2-52-3-250-193.comp..
KubernetesWorker	i-773d298e	t2.micro	us-east-1e	stopped		None	
kubernetes-master	i-7df75885	m3.medium	us-east-1e	running	2/2 checks ...	None	ec2-52-205-128-166.co...
Sqoop	i-8577b77d	t2.micro	us-east-1e	stopped		None	

Figure 1-18. *kubernetes-master and kubernetes-minion EC2 instances*

The cluster information may be obtained with the kubectl cluster-info command, as shown in Figure 1-19.

```
[ec2-user@ip-172-30-4-159 ~]$ kubectl cluster-info
Kubernetes master is running at https://52.205.128.166
Elasticsearch is running at https://52.205.128.166/api/v1/proxy/namespaces/kube-system/services/elasticsearch-logging
Heapster is running at https://52.205.128.166/api/v1/proxy/namespaces/kube-system/services/heapster
Kibana is running at https://52.205.128.166/api/v1/proxy/namespaces/kube-system/services/kibana-logging
KubeDNS is running at https://52.205.128.166/api/v1/proxy/namespaces/kube-system/services/kube-dns
kubernetes-dashboard is running at https://52.205.128.166/api/v1/proxy/namespaces/kube-system/services/kubernetes-dashboard
Grafana is running at https://52.205.128.166/api/v1/proxy/namespaces/kube-system/services/monitoring-grafana
InfluxDB is running at https://52.205.128.166/api/v1/proxy/namespaces/kube-system/services/monitoring-influxdb
[ec2-user@ip-172-30-4-159 ~]$
```

Figure 1-19. *Running the kubectl cluster-info command*

The different instances need to access each other. A security group is created for each of the instance types, master and minion, as shown in Figure 1-20.

Figure 1-20. *Security groups*

To add all traffic between the instances, add the default security group to the security groups for the master and minion; the default security group allows all traffic of all protocols from all sources. To add a security group to an instance (kubernetes-master, for example) select the instance. Then select Actions ➤ Networking ➤ Change Security Groups as shown in Figure 1-21.

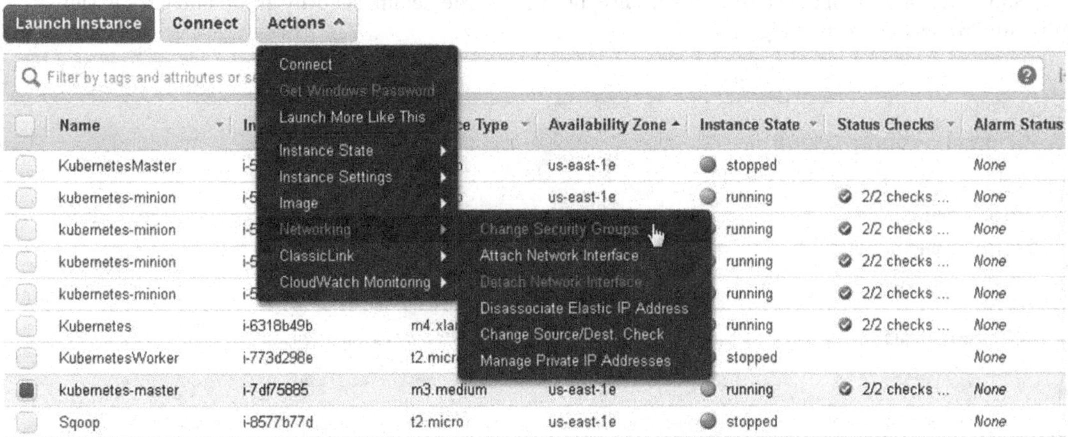

Figure 1-21. *Selecting Actions ➤ Networking ➤ Change Security Groups*

In the Change Security Groups screen, select the default security group in addition to the security group assigned to the master node and click Assign Security Groups as shown in Figure 1-22.

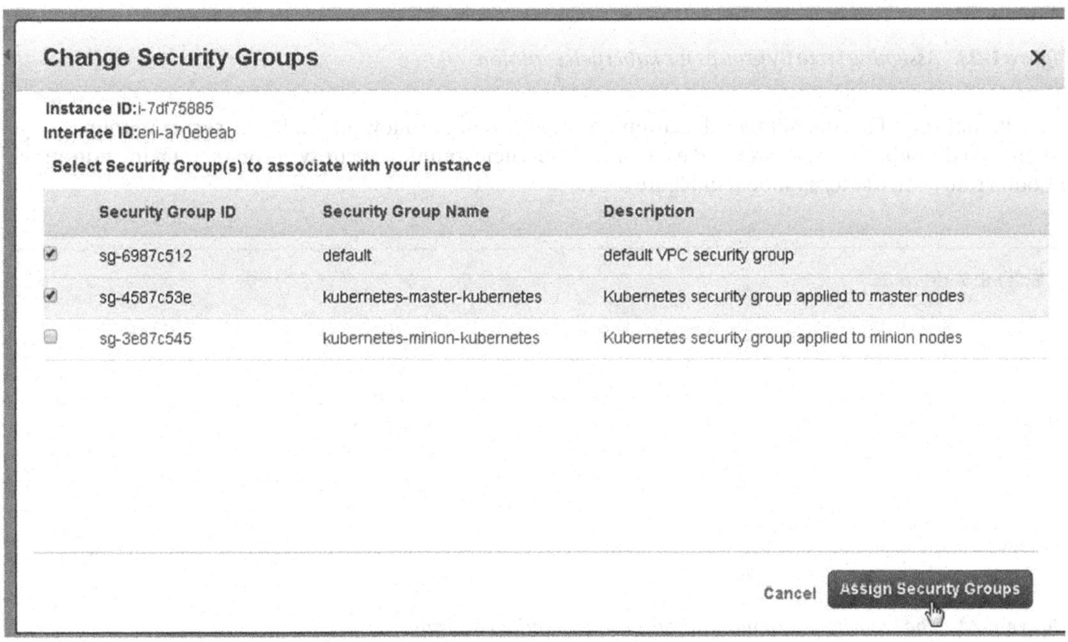

Figure 1-22. *Assigning security groups for kubernetes-master*

Similarly, for each of the kubernetes-minion nodes, add the default security group and click Assign Security Groups as shown in Figure 1-23.

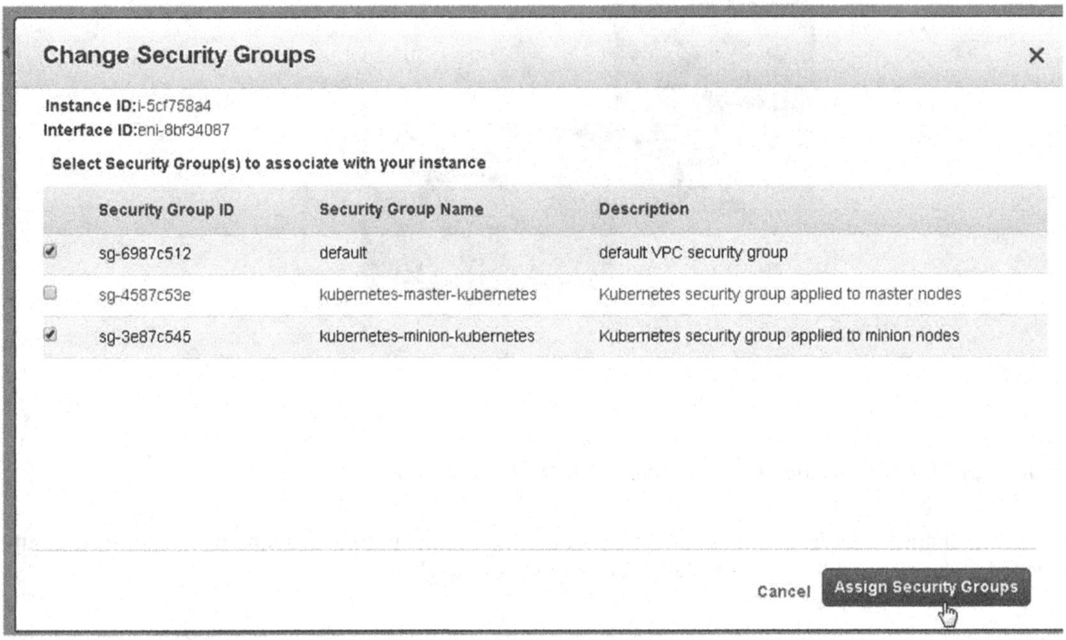

Figure 1-23. *Assigning security groups for kubernetes-minion*

Alternatively, if the default security group was modified not to allow all traffic, the security group assigned to the kubernetes-master and each of the kubernetes-minion security groups should include an inbound rule to all traffic, as shown in Figure 1-24.

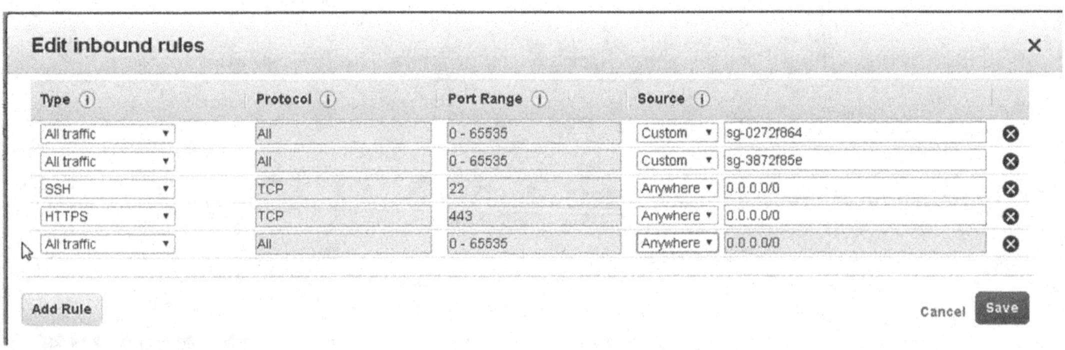

Figure 1-24. *The security group with inbound rules to allow all traffic*

Testing the Cluster

Next, we will test the Kubernetes cluster. First, we need to add the directory path in which the Kubernetes binaries are installed to the environment variable PATH.

```
export PATH=/home/ec2-user/kubernetes/platforms/linux/amd64:$PATH
```

Subsequently echo the PATH environment variable as shown in Figure 1-25.

```
[ec2-user@ip-172-30-4-159 kubernetes]$ export PATH=/home/ec2-user/kubernetes/pla
tforms/linux/amd64:$PATH
[ec2-user@ip-172-30-4-159 kubernetes]$ cd ~
[ec2-user@ip-172-30-4-159 ~]$ echo $PATH
/home/ec2-user/kubernetes/platforms/linux/amd64:/usr/local/bin:/bin:/usr/bin:/us
r/local/sbin:/usr/sbin:/sbin:/opt/aws/bin:/home/ec2-user/.local/bin:/home/ec2-us
er/bin
```

Figure 1-25. *Setting the PATH environment variable*

To test the cluster, run a Docker image such as the nginx image to create three pod replicas:

```
kubectl run nginx --image=nginx --replicas=3 --port=80
```

List the pods:

```
kubectl get pods
```

List the deployments:

```
kubectl get deployments
```

Create a service of type LoadBalancer for the deployment:

```
kubectl expose deployment nginx --port=80 --type=LoadBalancer
```

List the services:

```
kubectl get services
```

List the pods across the cluster

```
kubectl get pods -o wide
```

If Kubernetes has installed correctly, all the previous commands should run correctly and generate the output to indicate that a pod cluster has been created, as shown in Figure 1-26.

```
[ec2-user@ip-172-30-4-159 ~]$ kubectl run nginx --image=nginx --replicas=3 --por
t=80
deployment "nginx" created
[ec2-user@ip-172-30-4-159 ~]$ kubectl get pods
NAME                     READY     STATUS    RESTARTS   AGE
nginx-198147104-de6gq    1/1       Running   0          23s
nginx-198147104-q322k    1/1       Running   0          23s
nginx-198147104-u3sah    1/1       Running   0          23s
[ec2-user@ip-172-30-4-159 ~]$ kubectl get deployments
NAME     DESIRED   CURRENT   UP-TO-DATE   AVAILABLE   AGE
nginx    3         3         3            3           45s
[ec2-user@ip-172-30-4-159 ~]$ kubectl expose deployment nginx --port=80 --type=L
oadBalancer
service "nginx" exposed
[ec2-user@ip-172-30-4-159 ~]$ kubectl get services
NAME         CLUSTER-IP     EXTERNAL-IP   PORT(S)   AGE
kubernetes   10.0.0.1       <none>        443/TCP   55m
nginx        10.0.165.153                 80/TCP    22s
[ec2-user@ip-172-30-4-159 ~]$ kubectl get pods -o wide
NAME                     READY     STATUS    RESTARTS   AGE       NODE
nginx-198147104-de6gq    1/1       Running   0          2m        ip-172-20-0-175
.us-west-2.compute.internal
nginx-198147104-q322k    1/1       Running   0          2m        ip-172-20-0-174
.us-west-2.compute.internal
nginx-198147104-u3sah    1/1       Running   0          2m        ip-172-20-0-175
.us-west-2.compute.internal
[ec2-user@ip-172-30-4-159 ~]$ 
```

Figure 1-26. *Creating a pod cluster for* `nginx`

Configuring the Cluster

The default configuration settings used to start a new cluster are specified in the `cluster/aws/config-default.sh` file. The default configuration includes settings for AWS zone, number of nodes, master size, node size, AWS S3 region, AWS S3 Bucket, and instance prefix.

```
export KUBE_AWS_ZONE=eu-west-1c
export NUM_NODES=3
export MASTER_SIZE=m3.medium
export NODE_SIZE=m3.medium
export AWS_S3_REGION=eu-west-1
export AWS_S3_BUCKET=mycompany-kubernetes-artifacts
export INSTANCE_PREFIX=k8s
```

The `config-default.sh` file may be opened in a `vi` editor:

```
sudo vi /home/ec2-user/kubernetes/cluster/aws/config-default.sh
```

The configuration settings are listed as shown in Figure 1-27.

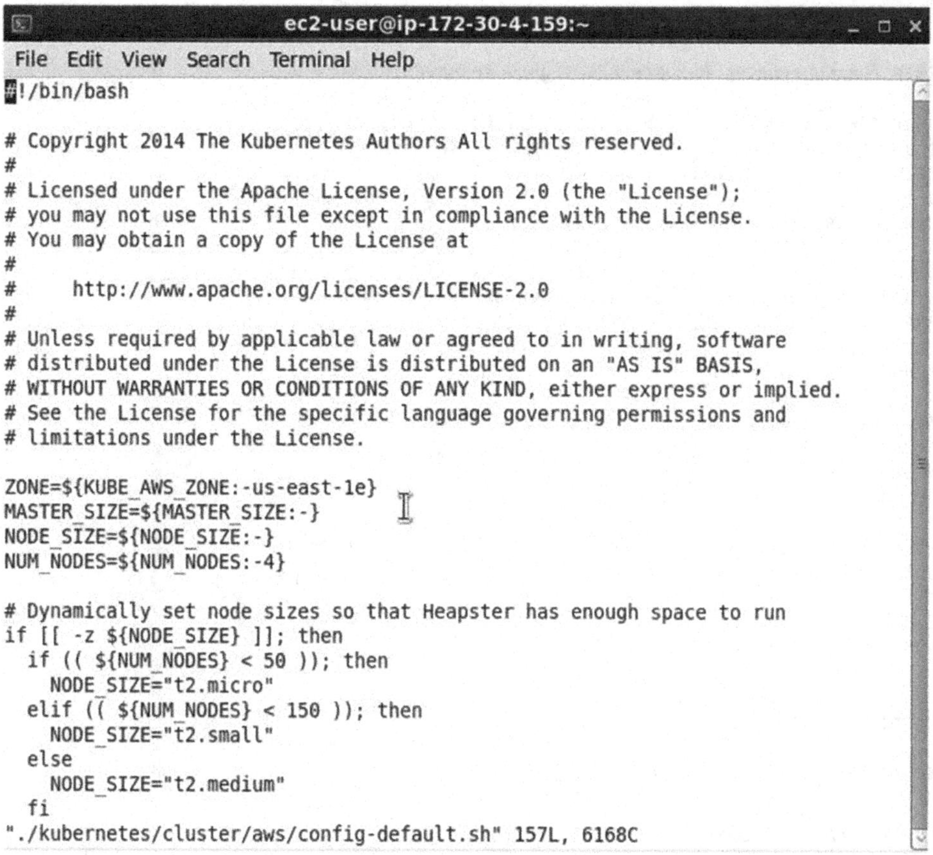


```
#!/bin/bash

# Copyright 2014 The Kubernetes Authors All rights reserved.
#
# Licensed under the Apache License, Version 2.0 (the "License");
# you may not use this file except in compliance with the License.
# You may obtain a copy of the License at
#
#     http://www.apache.org/licenses/LICENSE-2.0
#
# Unless required by applicable law or agreed to in writing, software
# distributed under the License is distributed on an "AS IS" BASIS,
# WITHOUT WARRANTIES OR CONDITIONS OF ANY KIND, either express or implied.
# See the License for the specific language governing permissions and
# limitations under the License.

ZONE=${KUBE_AWS_ZONE:-us-east-1e}
MASTER_SIZE=${MASTER_SIZE:-}
NODE_SIZE=${NODE_SIZE:-}
NUM_NODES=${NUM_NODES:-4}

# Dynamically set node sizes so that Heapster has enough space to run
if [[ -z ${NODE_SIZE} ]]; then
  if (( ${NUM_NODES} < 50 )); then
    NODE_SIZE="t2.micro"
  elif (( ${NUM_NODES} < 150 )); then
    NODE_SIZE="t2.small"
  else
    NODE_SIZE="t2.medium"
  fi
"./kubernetes/cluster/aws/config-default.sh" 157L, 6168C
```

Figure 1-27. *Listing the default configuration settings*

As an example, change the AWS zone from `us-east-1e` to `us-west-2a` as shown in Figure 1-28.

```
#!/bin/bash

# Copyright 2014 The Kubernetes Authors All rights reserved.
#
# Licensed under the Apache License, Version 2.0 (the "License");
# you may not use this file except in compliance with the License.
# You may obtain a copy of the License at
#
#     http://www.apache.org/licenses/LICENSE-2.0
#
# Unless required by applicable law or agreed to in writing, software
# distributed under the License is distributed on an "AS IS" BASIS,
# WITHOUT WARRANTIES OR CONDITIONS OF ANY KIND, either express or implied.
# See the License for the specific language governing permissions and
# limitations under the License.

ZONE=${KUBE_AWS_ZONE:-us-west-2a}
MASTER_SIZE=${MASTER_SIZE:-}
NODE_SIZE=${NODE_SIZE:-}
NUM_NODES=${NUM_NODES:-4}

# Dynamically set node sizes so that Heapster has enough space to run
if [[ -z ${NODE_SIZE} ]]; then
  if (( ${NUM_NODES} < 50 )); then
    NODE_SIZE="t2.micro"
  elif (( ${NUM_NODES} < 150 )); then
    NODE_SIZE="t2.small"
  else
    NODE_SIZE="t2.medium"
  fi
"/home/ec2-user/kubernetes/cluster/aws/config-default.sh" 157L, 6168C
```

Figure 1-28. *Modifying the AWS zone*

Shut down the cluster after making any modifications:

```
/home/ec2-user/kubernetes/cluster/kube-down.sh
```

Restart the cluster:

```
/home/ec2-user/kubernetes/cluster/kube-up.sh
```

The cluster should be started in the `us-west-2a` zone as shown in Figure 1-29.

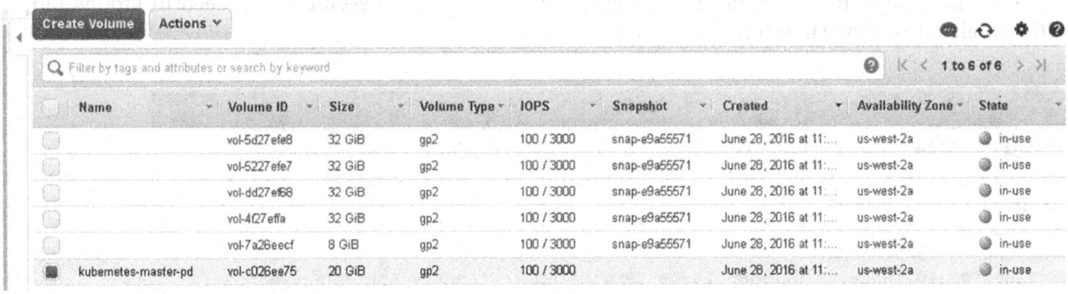

Name	Volume ID	Size	Volume Type	IOPS	Snapshot	Created	Availability Zone	State
	vol-5d27efe8	32 GiB	gp2	100 / 3000	snap-e9a55571	June 28, 2016 at 11:...	us-west-2a	in-use
	vol-5227efe7	32 GiB	gp2	100 / 3000	snap-e9a55571	June 28, 2016 at 11:...	us-west-2a	in-use
	vol-dd27ef68	32 GiB	gp2	100 / 3000	snap-e9a55571	June 28, 2016 at 11:...	us-west-2a	in-use
	vol-4f27effa	32 GiB	gp2	100 / 3000	snap-e9a55571	June 28, 2016 at 11:...	us-west-2a	in-use
	vol-7a26eecf	8 GiB	gp2	100 / 3000	snap-e9a55571	June 28, 2016 at 11:...	us-west-2a	in-use
kubernetes-master-pd	vol-c026ee75	20 GiB	gp2	100 / 3000		June 28, 2016 at 11:...	us-west-2a	in-use

Figure 1-29. *Restarted Kubernetes cluster with nodes in the new AWS zone*

Stopping the Cluster

To stop the cluster, run the kube-down.sh command:

```
/home/ec2-user/kubernetes/cluster/kube-down.sh
```

As the output in Figure 1-30 indicates, the ELBs in the VPC are deleted, the instances in the VPC are deleted, and the auto-scaling groups and the auto launch configuration are deleted.

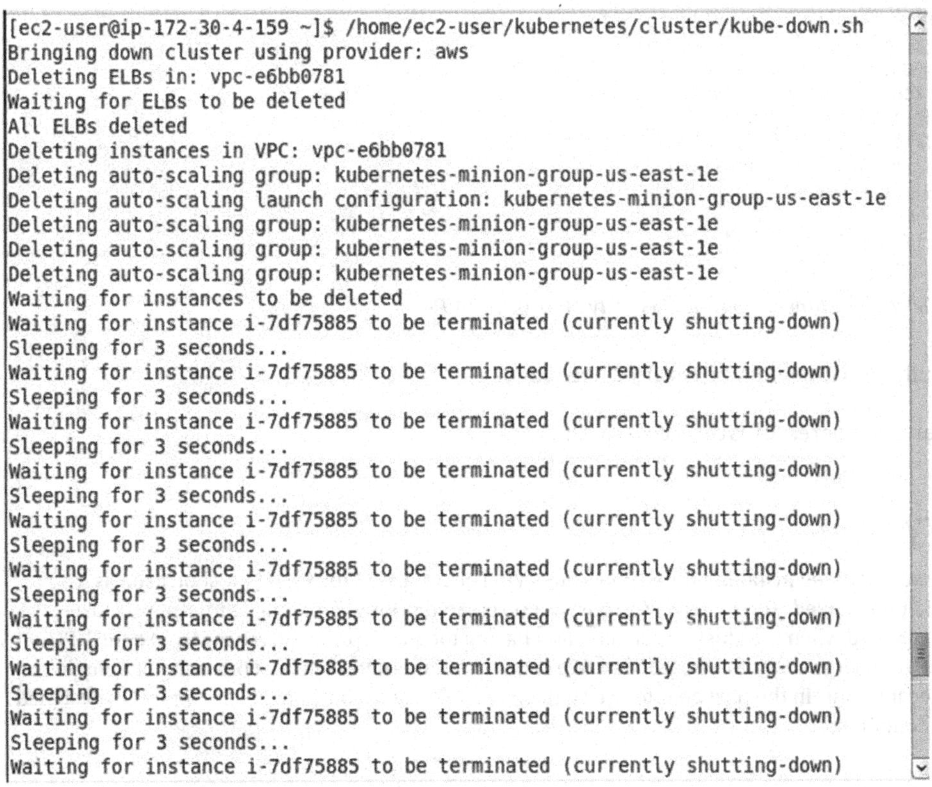

```
[ec2-user@ip-172-30-4-159 ~]$ /home/ec2-user/kubernetes/cluster/kube-down.sh
Bringing down cluster using provider: aws
Deleting ELBs in: vpc-e6bb0781
Waiting for ELBs to be deleted
All ELBs deleted
Deleting instances in VPC: vpc-e6bb0781
Deleting auto-scaling group: kubernetes-minion-group-us-east-1e
Deleting auto-scaling launch configuration: kubernetes-minion-group-us-east-1e
Deleting auto-scaling group: kubernetes-minion-group-us-east-1e
Deleting auto-scaling group: kubernetes-minion-group-us-east-1e
Deleting auto-scaling group: kubernetes-minion-group-us-east-1e
Waiting for instances to be deleted
Waiting for instance i-7df75885 to be terminated (currently shutting-down)
Sleeping for 3 seconds...
Waiting for instance i-7df75885 to be terminated (currently shutting-down)
Sleeping for 3 seconds...
Waiting for instance i-7df75885 to be terminated (currently shutting-down)
Sleeping for 3 seconds...
Waiting for instance i-7df75885 to be terminated (currently shutting-down)
Sleeping for 3 seconds...
Waiting for instance i-7df75885 to be terminated (currently shutting-down)
Sleeping for 3 seconds...
Waiting for instance i-7df75885 to be terminated (currently shutting-down)
Sleeping for 3 seconds...
Waiting for instance i-7df75885 to be terminated (currently shutting-down)
Sleeping for 3 seconds...
Waiting for instance i-7df75885 to be terminated (currently shutting-down)
Sleeping for 3 seconds...
Waiting for instance i-7df75885 to be terminated (currently shutting-down)
Sleeping for 3 seconds...
Waiting for instance i-7df75885 to be terminated (currently shutting-down)
```

Figure 1-30. *Stopping a Kubernetes cluster*

After all instances have been deleted, the elastic IP is released, and eventually the security groups and VPC are deleted as shown in Figure 1-31.

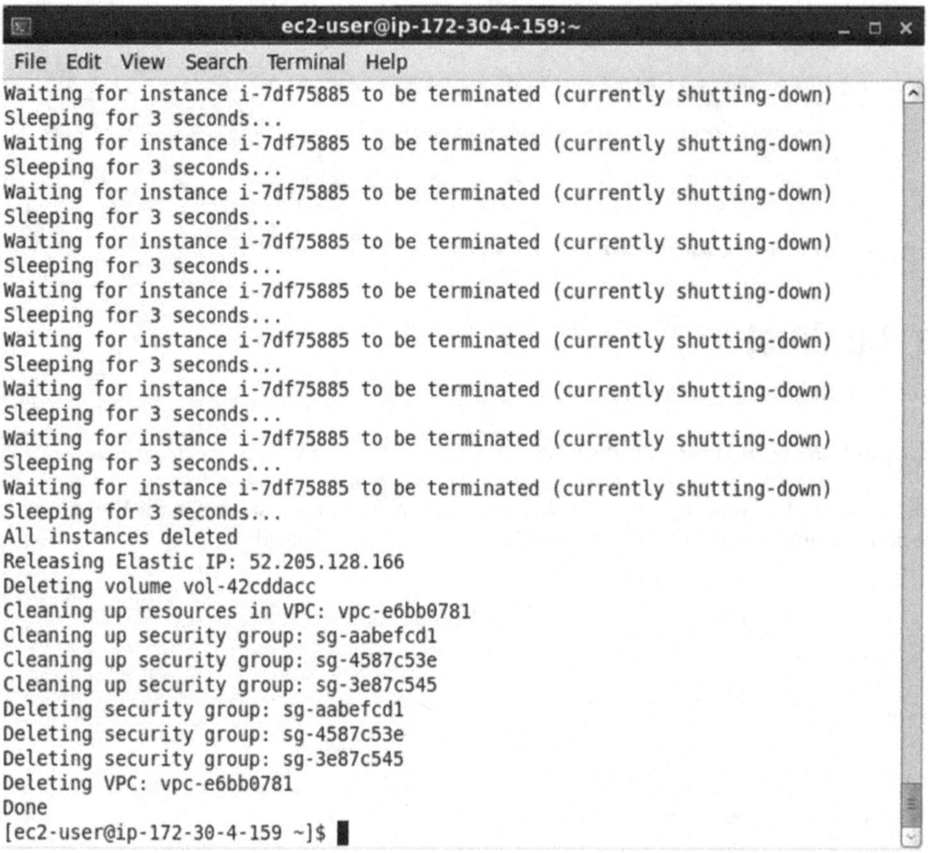
ec2-user@ip-172-30-4-159:~
File Edit View Search Terminal Help
Waiting for instance i-7df75885 to be terminated (currently shutting-down)
Sleeping for 3 seconds...
Waiting for instance i-7df75885 to be terminated (currently shutting-down)
Sleeping for 3 seconds...
Waiting for instance i-7df75885 to be terminated (currently shutting-down)
Sleeping for 3 seconds...
Waiting for instance i-7df75885 to be terminated (currently shutting-down)
Sleeping for 3 seconds...
Waiting for instance i-7df75885 to be terminated (currently shutting-down)
Sleeping for 3 seconds...
Waiting for instance i-7df75885 to be terminated (currently shutting-down)
Sleeping for 3 seconds...
Waiting for instance i-7df75885 to be terminated (currently shutting-down)
Sleeping for 3 seconds...
Waiting for instance i-7df75885 to be terminated (currently shutting-down)
Sleeping for 3 seconds...
Waiting for instance i-7df75885 to be terminated (currently shutting-down)
Sleeping for 3 seconds...
All instances deleted
Releasing Elastic IP: 52.205.128.166
Deleting volume vol-42cddacc
Cleaning up resources in VPC: vpc-e6bb0781
Cleaning up security group: sg-aabefcd1
Cleaning up security group: sg-4587c53e
Cleaning up security group: sg-3e87c545
Deleting security group: sg-aabefcd1
Deleting security group: sg-4587c53e
Deleting security group: sg-3e87c545
Deleting VPC: vpc-e6bb0781
Done
[ec2-user@ip-172-30-4-159 ~]$

Figure 1-31. *Deleting instances, volumes, security groups, and VPC*

Subsequently, the cluster may be restarted if required.

```
/home/ec2-user/kubernetes/cluster/kube-up.sh
```

Summary

In this chapter we discussed installing Kubernetes on AWS. The Amazon Linux AMI must be used as it has the AWS CLI preinstalled. Too many VPCs must not be created prior to creating a Kubernetes cluster, as a new VPC is created when the cluster is created and having too many prior VPCs could make the VPC quota allocated to a user account to be exceeded. We spun up a Kubernetes cluster consisting of a single master and three minions. In the next chapter we shall install Kubernetes on CoreOS, the Linux OS designed specifically for containers.

CHAPTER 2

Kubernetes on CoreOS on AWS

Kubernetes is usually used with a cloud platform, as the hardware infrastructure required for a multi-node Kubernetes cluster is best provisioned in a cloud environment. In Chapter 1 we used the kube-up tool to spin up a cluster without requiring any configuration.

Problem

The kube-up tool does not create a production-ready cluster. One of the limitations of kube-up is that it does not support CoreOS. Docker has to be installed, even though the Docker installation is preconfigured.

Solution

Docker is installed out-of-the-box on CoreOS. The CoreOS tool kube-aws can be used to spin up a production-ready Kubernetes cluster on CoreOS nodes on EC2 without much configuration. The kube-aws tool makes use of AWS CloudFormation to create a cluster of EC2 instances running CoreOS. AWS CloudFormation is a service to provision AWS resources such as EC2 instances, Auto Scaling Groups, and Elastic Load Balancing load balancers, all using a template. Using a single cluster configuration file to provision an AWS CloudFormation for a Kubernetes cluster is a management design pattern. The same cluster template may be reused to provision other Kubernetes clusters. Figure 2-1 shows an AWS CloudFormation that consists of a Kubernetes Master node and three Kubernetes worker nodes, along with an Auto Scaling Group and a Launch Configuration.

D. Vohra, *Kubernetes Management Design Patterns*, DOI 10.1007/978-1-4842-2598-1_2

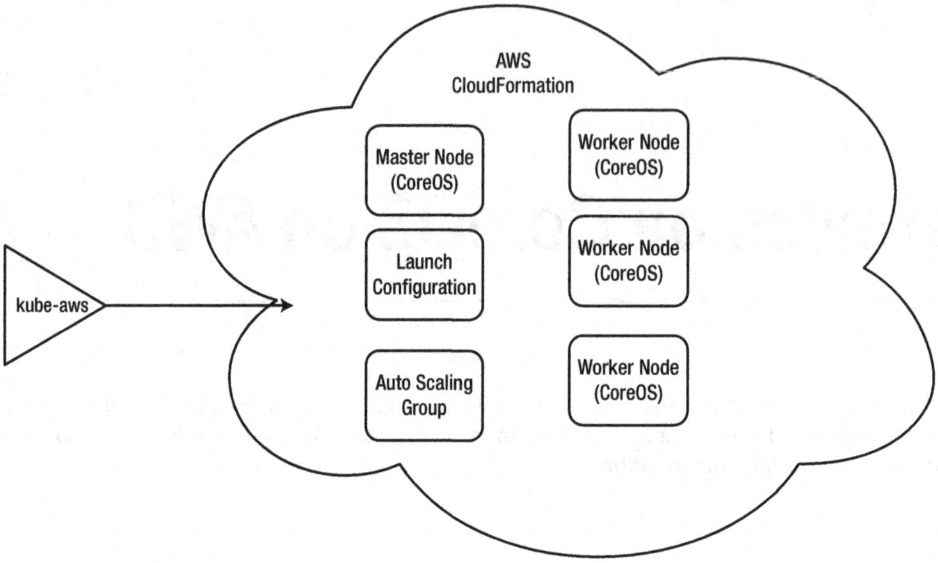

Figure 2-1. *AWS CloudFormation for a Kubernetes cluster*

Overview

AWS CloudFormation provisions a collection of AWS resources based on a template, which defines the resources and the dependencies. In this chapter we shall deploy an AWS CloudFormation for a cluster of CoreOS instances running Kubernetes. We shall use an AWS Launch Configuration and a Scaling Group for automatically launching and scaling the CloudFormation. The `kube-aws` CloudFormation generator CLI tool is used to create the CloudFormation stack from a template. The stages we'll explore are as follows:

Setting the Environment

Configuring AWS Credentials

Installing `kube-aws`

Setting Up Cluster Parameters

Creating a KMS Key

Setting Up an External DNS Name

Creating the Cluster CloudFormation

Creating an Asset Directory

Initializing the Cluster CloudFormation

Rendering Contents of the Asset Directory

Customizing the Cluster

Validating the CloudFormation Stack

Launching the Cluster CloudFormation

Configuring DNS

Accessing the Cluster

Testing the Cluster

Setting the Environment

The following software is required for this chapter:

- AWS Command Line Interface (CLI)
- `kube-aws` CloudFormation Generator

To set up your environment, first create an Amazon EC2 instance from Amazon Linux AMI (`ami-7172b611`), which has the AWS CLI preinstalled. Modify the Inbound/Outbound rules to allow all traffic for all protocols in port range 0–65535 from any source and to any destination. Obtain the Public IP of the EC2 instance. SSH Log in to the EC2 instance:

```
ssh -i  kubernetes-coreos.pem  ec2-user@54.86.194.192
```

The Amazon Linux command prompt is displayed. You're now ready to go.

Configuring AWS Credentials

We need to create a set of AWS Security credentials, which we will use to configure the EC2 instance from which the CloudFormation stack is launched. The AWS Security credentials used in Chapter 1 may be used if not deleted. To create new AWS Security credentials click on Security Credentials for the user account and click on Create New Access Key to create an access key. Copy the Access Key ID and the access key. In the Amazon Linux instance run the following command to configure the instance with the AWS credentials:

```
aws configure
```

Specify the access key ID and access key when prompted. Specify the default region name (`us-east-1`) and the output format (`json`).

Installing Kube-aws

CoreOS applications on GitHub and packaged into AppC images are signed with the CoreOS Application Signing Key. So that you'll be able to distribute your own work, import the CoreOS Application Signing Key, as shown here:

```
gpg2 --keyserver pgp.mit.edu --recv-key FC8A365E
```

Next, validate the key:

```
gpg2 --fingerprint FC8A365E
```

Figure 2-2 shows the output from this command. As you can see, the key fingerprint is `18AD 5014 C99E F7E3 BA5F 6CE9 50BD D3E0 FC8A 365E`, which is the correct key fingerprint; the value is a constant.

```
[ec2-user@ip-172-30-1-188 ~]$ gpg2 --keyserver pgp.mit.edu --recv-key FC8A365E
gpg: directory `/home/ec2-user/.gnupg' created
gpg: new configuration file `/home/ec2-user/.gnupg/gpg.conf' created
gpg: WARNING: options in `/home/ec2-user/.gnupg/gpg.conf' are not yet active dur
ing this run
gpg: keyring `/home/ec2-user/.gnupg/secring.gpg' created
gpg: keyring `/home/ec2-user/.gnupg/pubring.gpg' created
gpg: requesting key FC8A365E from hkp server pgp.mit.edu
gpg: /home/ec2-user/.gnupg/trustdb.gpg: trustdb created
gpg: key FC8A365E: public key "CoreOS Application Signing Key <security@coreos.c
om>" imported
gpg: no ultimately trusted keys found
gpg: Total number processed: 1
gpg:               imported: 1  (RSA: 1)
[ec2-user@ip-172-30-1-188 ~]$ gpg2 --fingerprint FC8A365E
pub   4096R/FC8A365E 2016-03-02 [expires: 2021-03-01]
      Key fingerprint = 18AD 5014 C99E F7E3 BA5F  6CE9 50BD D3E0 FC8A 365E
uid       [ unknown] CoreOS Application Signing Key <security@coreos.com>
sub   2048R/3F1B2C87 2016-03-02 [expires: 2019-03-02]
sub   2048R/BEDDBA18 2016-03-08 [expires: 2019-03-08]
sub   2048R/7EF48FD3 2016-03-08 [expires: 2019-03-08]

[ec2-user@ip-172-30-1-188 ~]$ █
```

Figure 2-2. *Importing and validating the CoreOS application signing key*

Donwload the latest release tarball and detached signature (`.sig`) for kube-aws from `https://github.com/coreos/coreos-kubernetes/releases`:

```
wget https://github.com/coreos/coreos-kubernetes/releases/download/v0.7.1/kube-aws-linux-
amd64.tar.gz
wget https://github.com/coreos/coreos-kubernetes/releases/download/v0.7.1/kube-aws-linux-
amd64.tar.gz.sig
```

Validate the tarball's GPG signature.

```
gpg2 --verify kube-aws-linux-amd64.tar.gz.sig kube-aws-linux-amd64.tar.gz
```

The primary key fingerprint should be `18AD 5014 C99E F7E3 BA5F 6CE9 50BD D3E0 FC8A 365E`, as shown in Figure 2-3.

```
[ec2-user@ip-172-30-1-188 ~]$ ls -l
total 4552
-rw-rw-r-- 1 ec2-user ec2-user 4655969 Jun  4 00:32 kube-aws-linux-amd64.tar.gz
-rw-rw-r-- 1 ec2-user ec2-user     287 Jun  6 21:36 kube-aws-linux-amd64.tar.gz.
sig
[ec2-user@ip-172-30-1-188 ~]$ gpg2 --verify kube-aws-linux-amd64.tar.gz.sig kube
-aws-linux-amd64.tar.gz
gpg: Signature made Mon 06 Jun 2016 09:32:47 PM UTC using RSA key ID BEDDBA18
gpg: Good signature from "CoreOS Application Signing Key <security@coreos.com>"
[unknown]
gpg: WARNING: This key is not certified with a trusted signature!
gpg:          There is no indication that the signature belongs to the owner.
Primary key fingerprint: 18AD 5014 C99E F7E3 BA5F  6CE9 50BD D3E0 FC8A 365E
     Subkey fingerprint: 55DB DA91 BBE1 849E A27F  E733 A6F7 1EE5 BEDD BA18
[ec2-user@ip-172-30-1-188 ~]$ ▌
```

Figure 2-3. *Validate the tarball's GPG signature*

Extract the binary from the tar.gz file:

```
tar zxvf  kube-aws-linux-amd64.tar.gz
```

Add kube-aws to the path:

```
sudo mv linux-amd64/kube-aws /usr/local/bin
```

The kube-aws CloudFormation generator is installed. You can display information about its usage with the kube-aws -help command.

Setting Up Cluster Parameters

Before initializing and launching the AWS CloudFormation cluster we need to create or define the following cluster parameters:

- EC2 key pair
- KMS key
- External DNS name

Before creating a key pair we need to configure an AWS region; we already did that with the aws configure command. Run the following command to create a key pair called kubernetes-coreos and save it as kubernetes-coreos.pem:

```
aws ec2 create-key-pair --key-name kubernetes-coreos --query 'KeyMaterial' --output text >
kubernetes-coreos.pem
```

Modify the access permissions of the key pair using the mode 400, which sets access permissions to read by owner.

```
chmod 400 kubernetes-coreos.pem
```

The key pair is created and access permissions are set as shown in Figure 2-4.

```
[ec2-user@ip-172-30-1-188 ~]$ aws ec2 create-key-pair --key-name kubernetes-core
os --query 'KeyMaterial' --output text > kubernetes-coreos.pem
[ec2-user@ip-172-30-1-188 ~]$ chmod 400 kubernetes-coreos.pem
```

Figure 2-4. *Creating the key pair*

On the AWS console the kubernetes-coreos key pair should be listed, as shown in Figure 2-5.

Figure 2-5. *Listing the key pair in the EC2 console*

Creating a KMS Key

Next, create a KMS key, which is used to encrypt and decrypt cluster TLS assets and is identified by an Amazon Resource Name (ARN) string. Use the aws CLI to create a KMS key for region us-east-1.

```
aws kms --region=us-east-1 create-key --description="kube-aws assets"
```

A KMS key is created as shown in Figure 2-6. Copy the KeyMetadata.Arn string arn:aws:kms:us-east-1:672593526685:key/b7209ba2-cb87-4ccf-8401-5c6fd4fb9f9b to be used later to initialize the cluster CloudFormation.

```
[ec2-user@ip-172-30-1-188 ~]$ aws kms --region=us-east-1 create-key --descriptio
n="kube-aws assets"
{
    "KeyMetadata": {
        "KeyId": "b7209ba2-cb87-4ccf-8401-5c6fd4fb9f9b",
        "Description": "kube-aws assets",
        "Enabled": true,
        "KeyUsage": "ENCRYPT_DECRYPT",
        "KeyState": "Enabled",
        "CreationDate": 1467655082.654,
        "Arn": "arn:aws:kms:us-east-1:672593526685:key/b7209ba2-cb87-4ccf-8401-5
c6fd4fb9f9b",
        "AWSAccountId": "672593526685"
    }
}
[ec2-user@ip-172-30-1-188 ~]$ ▌
```

Figure 2-6. *Creating a KMS key*

Setting Up an External DNS Name

Next you need to register a domain name with a domain registrar, as we shall be using the domain's external DNS name to make the cluster API accessible. We have used the external DNS name `NOSQLSEARCH.COM`. The `NOSQLSEARCH.COM` domain is not usable for all users, and different users would need to register a different domain name with a domain registry. Or, use a domain that is already registered.

Creating the Cluster

Creating a cluster requires the following procedure:

1. Create an asset directory.
2. Initialize the CloudFormation stack.
3. Render the contents of the asset directory.
4. Customize the cluster optionally in the `cluster.yaml` file.
5. Validate the CloudFormation stack and the cloud-config user data files.
6. Launch the CloudFormation stack.

We shall discuss each of these stages next.

Creating an Asset Directory

Create a directory on the Amazon Linux EC2 instance for the generated assets. Then cd (change directory) to the asset directory:

```
mkdir coreos-cluster
cd coreos-cluster
```

Initializing the Cluster CloudFormation

Using the Amazon EC2 key pair, KMS Key ARN string, and external DNS name, initialize the CloudFormation stack:

```
kube-aws init --cluster-name=kube-coreos-cluster
--external-dns-name=NOSQLSEARCH.COM
--region=us-east-1
--availability-zone=us-east-1c
--key-name=kubernetes-coreos
--kms-key-arn="arn:aws:kms:us-east-1:672593526685:key/b7209ba2-cb87-4ccf-8401-5c6fd4fb9f9b "
```

The CloudFormation stack assets are created; the main configuration file is `cluster.yaml`, as shown in Figure 2-7.

```
[ec2-user@ip-172-30-1-188 ~]$ mkdir coreos-cluster
[ec2-user@ip-172-30-1-188 ~]$  cd coreos-cluster
[ec2-user@ip-172-30-1-188 coreos-cluster]$   kube-aws init --cluster-name=kube-c
oreos-cluster --external-dns-name=NOSQLSEARCH.COM --region=us-east-1 --availabil
ity-zone=us-east-1c --key-name=kubernetes-coreos --kms-key-arn="arn:aws:kms:us-e
ast-1:672593526685:key/b7209ba2-cb87-4ccf-8401-5c6fd4fb9f9b"
Success! Created cluster.yaml

Next steps:
1. (Optional) Edit cluster.yaml to parameterize the cluster.
2. Use the "kube-aws render" command to render the stack template.
[ec2-user@ip-172-30-1-188 coreos-cluster]$ █
```

Figure 2-7. *Creating CloudFormation stack assets*

Rendering Contents of the Asset Directory

Next, render (generate) the cluster assets (templates and credentials), which are used to create, update, and interact with the Kubernetes cluster.

```
kube-aws render
```

The CloudFormation template `stack-template.json` is created (as shown in Figure 2-8); it will be used to create the Kubernetes cluster. The `cluster.yaml`, userdata files for the Kubernetes controller and the worker, and `stack-template.json` could optionally be customized.

```
[ec2-user@ip-172-30-1-188 coreos-cluster]$ kube-aws render
Success! Stack rendered to stack-template.json.

Next steps:
1. (Optional) Validate your changes to cluster.yaml with "kube-aws validate"
2. (Optional) Further customize the cluster by modifying stack-template.json or
files in ./userdata.
3. Start the cluster with "kube-aws up".
[ec2-user@ip-172-30-1-188 coreos-cluster]$ █
```

Figure 2-8. *Rendering clustering assets*

Customizing the Cluster

Customizing the cluster is optional, and the CloudFormation stack could be launched with its defaults. Among the reasons to customize are to use a different cloud provider region and external DNS name than specified when rendering the cluster assets and to use nondefault settings for other parameters. Some of the configuration settings in `cluster.yaml` are discussed in Table 2-1.

Table 2-1. *Cluster.yaml Configuration Settings*

Configuration setting	Description	Default Value
`clusterName`	Name of Kubernetes cluster. If more than one cluster are to deployed in the same AWS account, Kubernetes cluster name must be unique within the AWS account. For the example cluster, set this to `kube-coreos-cluster`.	
`externalDNSName`	DNS name routable to the Kubernetes controller nodes from worker nodes and external clients. Configure the `createRecordSet` and `hostedZone` options below if you'd like `kube-aws` to create a Route53 record sets/hosted zones for you. Otherwise the deployer is responsible for making this name routable. For the example cluster, set this to `NOSQLSEARCH.COM`.	
`releaseChannel`	CoreOS release channel to use. Currently supported options: [`alpha`, `beta`]	alpha
`createRecordSet`	Set to true if you want `kube-aws` to create a Route53 A Record for you.	false
`hostedZone`	The name of the hosted zone to add the `externalDNSName` to, such as "`google.com`". This needs to already exist; `kube-aws` will not create it for you.	""
`hostedZoneId`	The ID of hosted zone to add the externalDNSName to. Either specify `hostedZoneId` or `hostedZone`, but not both.	""
`keyName`	Name of the SSH keypair already loaded into the AWS account being used to deploy this cluster. For the example cluster, set to `kubernetes-coreos`.	
`region`	Region to provision Kubernetes cluster. For the example cluster, set to `us-east-1`.	
`availabilityZone`	Availability zone to provision Kubernetes cluster when placing nodes in a single availability zone (not highly-available) Comment out for multi availability zone setting and use the `subnets` section instead. For the example cluster set to `us-east-1c`.	
`controllerInstanceType`	Instance type for controller node.	m3.medium
`controllerRootVolumeSize`	Disk size (GiB) for controller node.	30
`workerCount`	Number of worker nodes to create.	1.
`workerInstanceType`	Instance type for worker nodes.	m3.medium

(continued)

Table 2-1. *(continued)*

Configuration setting	Description	Default Value
`workerRootVolumeSize`	Disk size (GiB) for worker nodes.	30
`vpcId`	ID of existing VPC to create subnet in. Leave blank to create a new VPC.	
`routeTableId`	ID of existing route table in existing VPC to attach subnet to. Leave blank to use the VPC's main route table.	
`vpcCIDR`	CIDR for Kubernetes VPC. If vpcId is specified, must match the CIDR of existing vpc.	"10.0.0.0/16"
`instanceCIDR`	CIDR for Kubernetes subnet when placing nodes in a single availability zone (not highly-available) Leave commented out for multi availability zone setting and use the `subnets` section instead.	"10.0.0.0/24"
`subnets`	Kubernetes subnets with their CIDRs and availability zones. Differentiating availability zone for two or more subnets result in high-availability (failures of a single availability zone won't result in immediate downtimes).	
`controllerIP`	IP Address for the controller in Kubernetes subnet. When we have two or more subnets, the controller is placed in the first subnet and controllerIP must be included in the instanceCIDR of the first subnet. This convention will change once CoreOS supports H/A controllers.	10.0.0.50
`serviceCIDR`	CIDR for all service IP addresses.	"10.3.0.0/24"
`podCIDR`	CIDR for all pod IP addresses.	"10.2.0.0/16"
`dnsServiceIP`	IP address of Kubernetes dns service (must be contained by `serviceCIDR`).	10.3.0.10
`kubernetesVersion`	Version of hyperkube image to use. This is the tag for the hyperkube image repository.	v1.2.4_coreos.1
`hyperkubeImageRepo`	Hyperkube image repository to use.	quay.io/ coreos/ hyperkube
`useCalico`	Whether to use Calico for network policy. When set to "true," `kubernetesVersion` must also be updated to include a version tagged with CN,I e.g. `v1.2.4_coreos.cni.1`.	false
`stackTags: Name`	AWS Tag for CloudFormation stack resources.	"Kubernetes"
`stackTags: Environment:`	AWS Tag for CloudFormation stack resources.	"Production"

By default one Kubernetes controller and one Kubernetes worker are launched. As an example, we shall modify the number of Kubernetes workers to 3. Open `cluster.yaml` in the `vi` editor:

```
sudo vi cluster.yaml
```

Set `workerCount` to 3 as shown in Figure 2-9 and save the `cluster.yaml` file.

```
# The ID of hosted zone to add the externalDNSName to.
# Either specify hostedZoneId or hostedZone, but not both
#hostedZoneId: ""

# Name of the SSH keypair already loaded into the AWS
# account being used to deploy this cluster.
keyName: kubernetes-coreos

# Region to provision Kubernetes cluster
region: us-east-1

# Availability Zone to provision Kubernetes cluster when placing nodes in a sing
le availability zone (not highly-available) Comment out for multi availability z
one setting and use the below `subnets` section instead.
availabilityZone: us-east-1c

# ARN of the KMS key used to encrypt TLS assets.
kmsKeyArn: "arn:aws:kms:us-east-1:672593526685:key/b7209ba2-cb87-4ccf-8401-5c6fd
4fb9f9b"

# Instance type for controller node
#controllerInstanceType: m3.medium

# Disk size (GiB) for controller node
#controllerRootVolumeSize: 30

# Number of worker nodes to create
workerCount: 3

# Instance type for worker nodes
:wq
```

Figure 2-9. *Modifying cluster.yaml to set Worker Nodes to 3*

Customizing the `cluster.yaml` does not require the assets to be re-rendered, but if the user data files or the stack template is modified, the cluster assets must be rerendered (we don't need to re-render):

```
kube-aws render
```

Validating the CloudFormation Stack

After modifying any file (`stack-template.json` or the user data files), the CloudFormation stack must be validated:

```
kube-aws validate
```

As indicated by the output in Figure 2-10, the user data and the stack template are valid.

```
[ec2-user@ip-172-30-1-188 coreos-cluster]$ kube-aws validate
Validating UserData...
UserData is valid.

Validating stack template...
Validation Report: {
  Capabilities: ["CAPABILITY_IAM"],
  CapabilitiesReason: "The following resource(s) require capabilities: [AWS::IAM
::InstanceProfile, AWS::IAM::Role]",
  Description: "kube-aws Kubernetes cluster kube-coreos-cluster"
}
stack template is valid.

Validation OK!
[ec2-user@ip-172-30-1-188 coreos-cluster]$ █
```

Figure 2-10. *Validating the CloudFormation stack*

Launching the Cluster CloudFormation

Launch the CloudFormation stack with the following command:

```
kube-aws up
```

It could take a few minutes for the cluster to be launched and for the Kubernetes controller and workers to become available. The preceding command does not complete until the cluster has launched. The controller IP is listed when the cluster is lauched. The cluster status may be found with the following command:

```
kube-aws status
```

As the output from the preceding commands in Figure 2-11 indicates, the cluster is launched.

```
[ec2-user@ip-172-30-1-188 coreos-cluster]$  kube-aws up
Creating AWS resources. This should take around 5 minutes.
Success! Your AWS resources have been created:
Cluster Name:    kube-coreos-cluster
Controller IP:   23.22.192.55

The containers that power your cluster are now being dowloaded.

You should be able to access the Kubernetes API once the containers finish downl
oading.
[ec2-user@ip-172-30-1-188 coreos-cluster]$ kube-aws status
Cluster Name:    kube-coreos-cluster
Controller IP:   23.22.192.55
```

Figure 2-11. *Launching the cluster and validating status*

The EC2 console should list the controller and worker instances as running or initializing, as shown in Figure 2-12.

Name	Instance ID	Instance Type	Availability Zone	Instance State	Status Checks	Alarm Status	Public D
kube-coreos-cluster-kube-aws-controller	i-73ac32f5	m3.medium	us-east-1c	running	Initializing	No Data	ec2-23-2
kube-coreos-cluster-kube-aws-worker	i-edad336b	m3.medium	us-east-1c	running	Initializing	*None*	ec2-54-1
kube-coreos-cluster-kube-aws-worker	i-f2ad3374	m3.medium	us-east-1c	running	Initializing	*None*	ec2-54-1
kube-coreos-cluster-kube-aws-worker	i-f3ad3375	m3.medium	us-east-1c	running	Initializing	*None*	ec2-54-8

Figure 2-12. *Listing the controller and worker nodes*

An EC2 security group, a scaling group, and a launch configuration are also created.

Configuring DNS

Next, we need to configure the external DNS, `NOSQLSEARCH.COM` in the example, to add an A record for the public IP address of the controller. Obtain the public IP address of the controller from the EC2 console as shown in Figure 2-13.

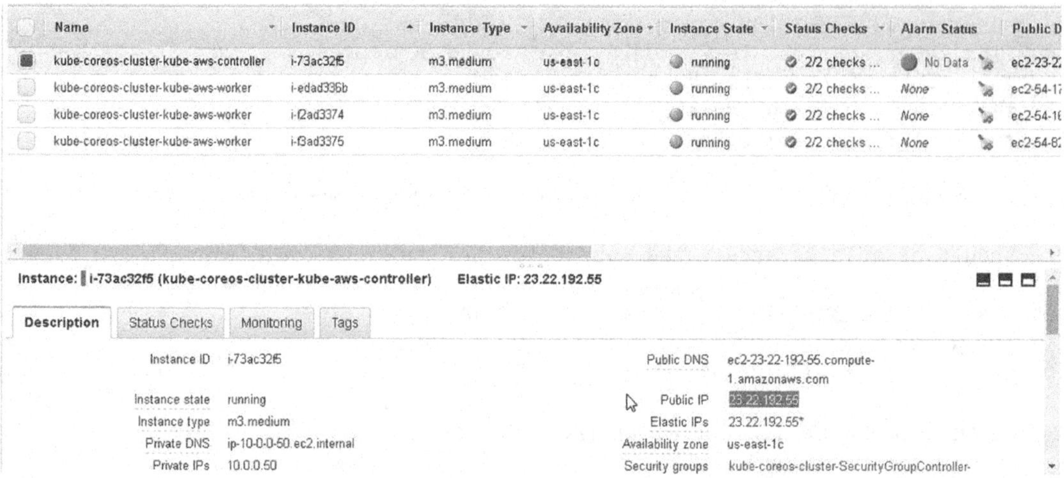

Figure 2-13. *Obtaining the public IP address*

The procedure for adding an A record could be slightly different for different domain registries. In the DNS Zone File for the external DNS NOSQLSEARCH.COM, choose Edit Record as shown in Figure 2-14 to modify the A record.

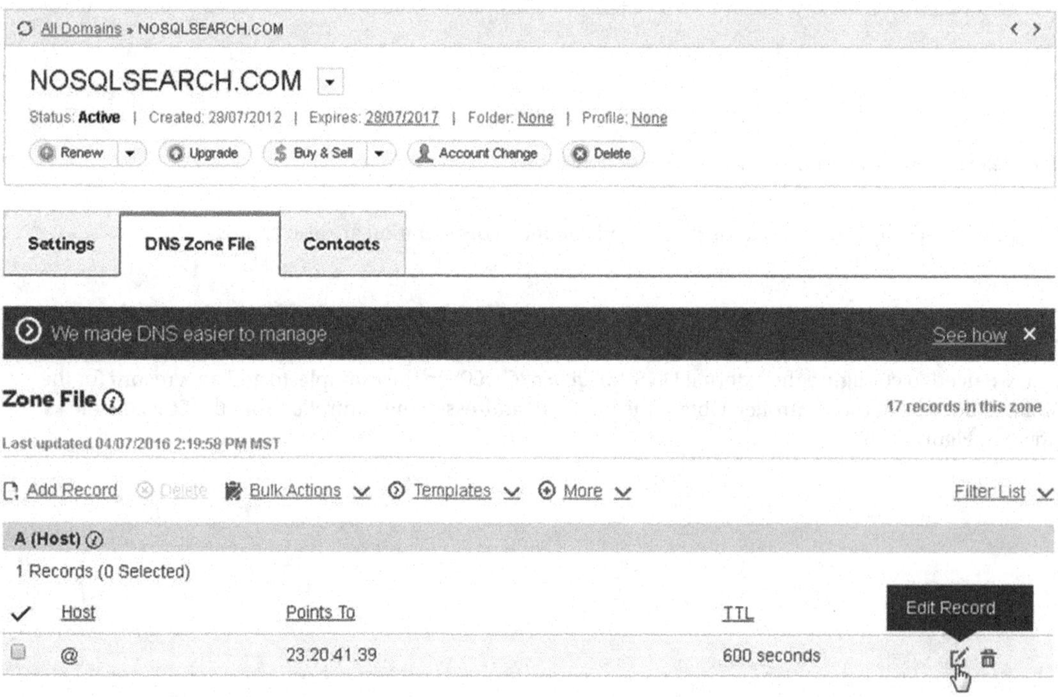

Figure 2-14. *Editing the A record*

In the Edit Zone Record screen, specify the public IP address in the Points To field and click Finish as shown in Figure 2-15.

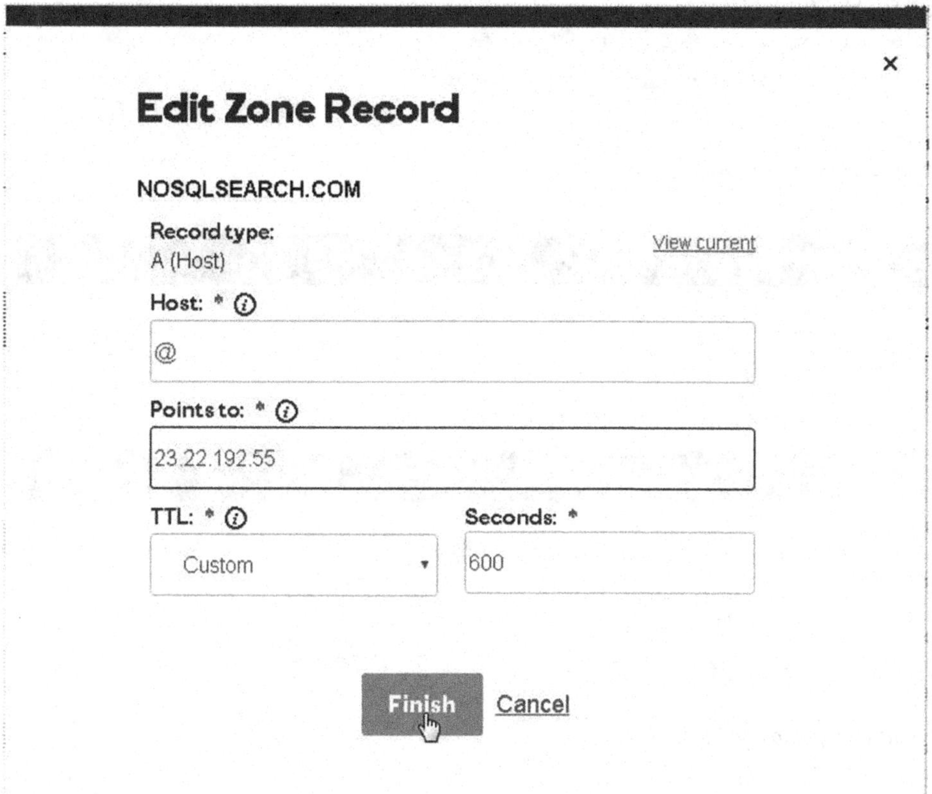

Figure 2-15. *Adding an A record*

Click on Save Changes to save the modifications to the A record as shown in Figure 2-16.

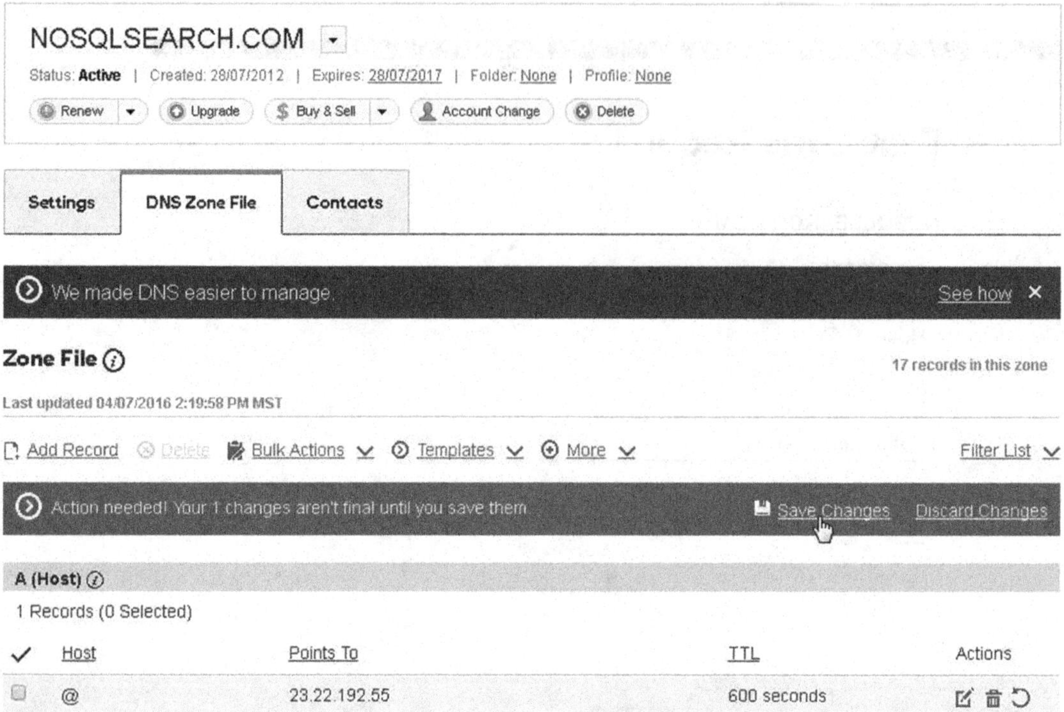

Figure 2-16. *Saving changes to the A record*

The A record should list the Points To as the public IP address of the controller instance as shown in Figure 2-17.

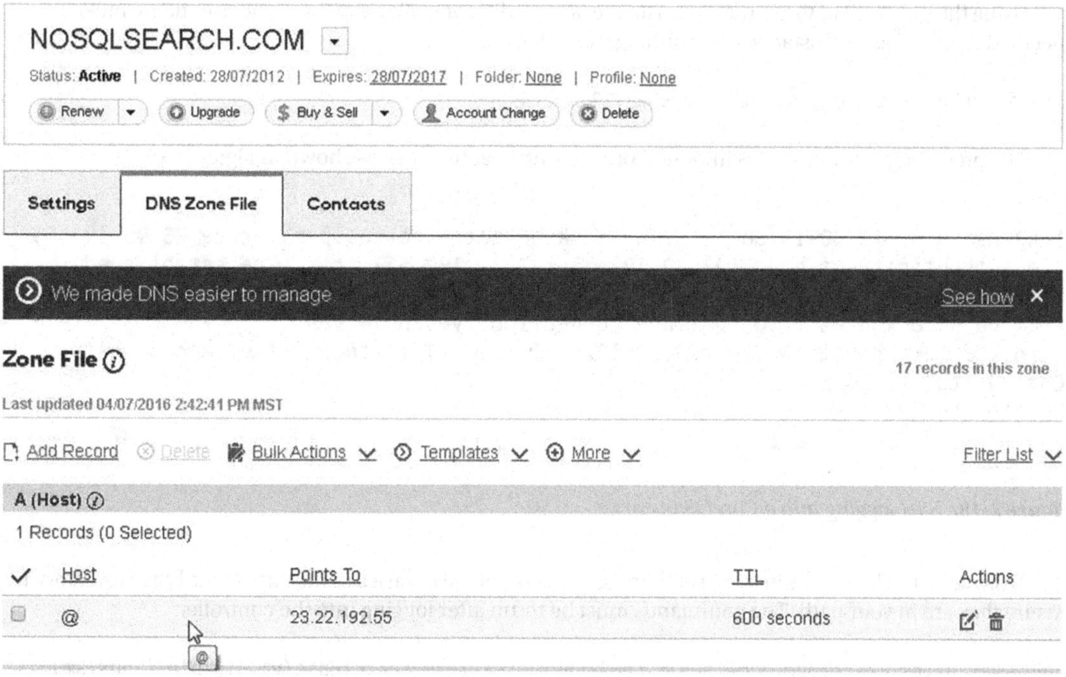

Figure 2-17. *The updated A record*

Accessing the Cluster

Download the kubectl binaries, which are used to manage the Kubernetes cluster. Set access permissions to the kubectl binaries to make them executable, and move the kubectl binaries to /usr/local/bin, which is in the path:

```
sudo wget https://storage.googleapis.com/kubernetes-release/release/v1.3.0/bin/linux/amd64/
kubectl
sudo chmod +x kubectl
sudo mv kubectl /usr/local/bin/
```

Using the kubectl config file access the cluster to list the nodes. The one controller node and the three worker nodes should be listed as shown in Figure 2-18. The controller node is not schedulable by default, which implies that pods cannot be run on the node.

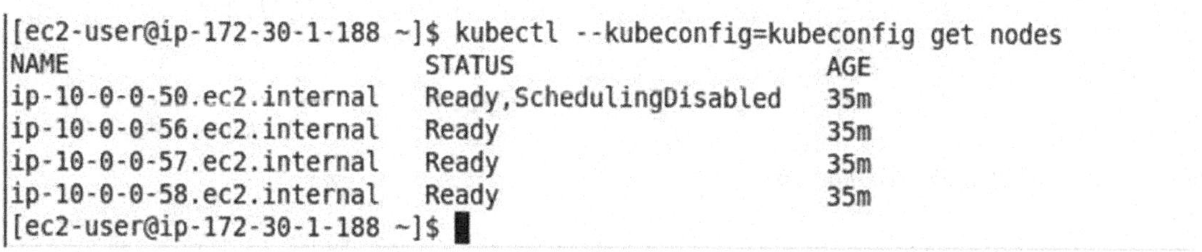

[ec2-user@ip-172-30-1-188 ~]$ kubectl --kubeconfig=kubeconfig get nodes
NAME STATUS AGE
ip-10-0-0-50.ec2.internal Ready,SchedulingDisabled 35m
ip-10-0-0-56.ec2.internal Ready 35m
ip-10-0-0-57.ec2.internal Ready 35m
ip-10-0-0-58.ec2.internal Ready 35m
[ec2-user@ip-172-30-1-188 ~]$

Figure 2-18. *Listing the Kubernetes cluster nodes*

Using the public IP of the controller instance, access the controller instance. The user name must be specified as "core" as the instances are running CoreOS.

```
ssh -i "kubernetes-coreos.pem"  core@23.22.192.55
```

The preceding command logs into the CoreOS controller instance as shown in Figure 2-19.

```
[ec2-user@ip-172-30-1-188 ~]$ ssh -i "kubernetes-coreos.pem"  core@23.22.192.55
The authenticity of host '23.22.192.55 (23.22.192.55)' can't be established.
ECDSA key fingerprint is 95:f2:5e:04:60:a7:e7:fe:26:7d:c6:76:b2:6c:95:12.
Are you sure you want to continue connecting (yes/no)? yes
Warning: Permanently added '23.22.192.55' (ECDSA) to the list of known hosts.
CoreOS stable (1010.6.0)
Update Strategy: No Reboots
core@ip-10-0-0-50 ~ $
```

Figure 2-19. *SSH logging into a CoreOS instance*

Download the kubectl binaries, set permissions, and move binaries to the /usr/local/bin directory to ensure they are in your path. The commands must be rerun after logging into the controller.

```
sudo wget https://storage.googleapis.com/kubernetes-release/release/v1.3.0/bin/linux/amd64/
kubectl
sudo chmod +x kubectl
sudo mv kubectl /usr/local/bin/
```

The kubectl binaries are installed as shown in Figure 2-20.

```
core@ip-10-0-0-50 ~ $ sudo wget https://storage.googleapis.com/kubernetes-releas
e/release/v1.3.0/bin/linux/amd64/kubectl
--2016-07-04 21:45:12--  https://storage.googleapis.com/kubernetes-release/relea
se/v1.3.0/bin/linux/amd64/kubectl
Resolving storage.googleapis.com... 209.85.144.128, 2607:f8b0:400d:c04::80
Connecting to storage.googleapis.com|209.85.144.128|:443... connected.
HTTP request sent, awaiting response... 200 OK
Length: 56515944 (54M) [application/octet-stream]
Saving to: 'kubectl'

kubectl              100%[===================>]  53.90M  53.4MB/s    in 1.0s

2016-07-04 21:45:14 (53.4 MB/s) - 'kubectl' saved [56515944/56515944]

core@ip-10-0-0-50 ~ $ sudo chmod +x kubectl
core@ip-10-0-0-50 ~ $ sudo mv kubectl /usr/local/bin/
```

Figure 2-20. *Installing Kubectl binaries*

List the nodes:

```
kubectl get nodes
```

The single controller node and the three worker nodes are listed as shown in Figure 2-21.

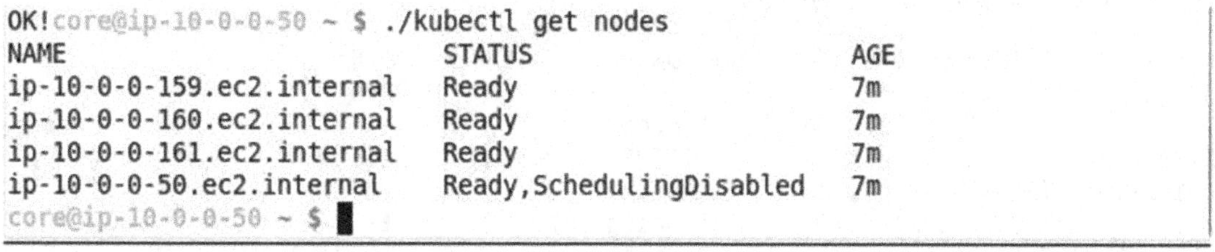

OK!core@ip-10-0-0-50 ~ $ ./kubectl get nodes
NAME STATUS AGE
ip-10-0-0-159.ec2.internal Ready 7m
ip-10-0-0-160.ec2.internal Ready 7m
ip-10-0-0-161.ec2.internal Ready 7m
ip-10-0-0-50.ec2.internal Ready,SchedulingDisabled 7m
core@ip-10-0-0-50 ~ $

Figure 2-21. *Listing the Kubernetes cluster nodes*

Testing the Cluster

To test the cluster, run some example application, such as the `nginx` server. Run three pod replicas of the `nginx` application:

```
./kubectl -s http://localhost:8080 run nginx --image=nginx  -replicas=3 --port=80
```

List the replication controllers:

```
./kubectl get rc
```

List the services:

```
./kubectl get services
```

List the deployments:

```
./kubectl get deployments
```

List the pods:

```
./kubectl get pods
```

Create a service for the `nginx` deployment:

```
./kubectl expose deployment nginx --port=80 --type=LoadBalancer
```

List the services again, and the `nginx` service should be listed:

```
./kubectl get services
```

Figure 2-22 shows the output from the preceding commands.

```
core@ip-10-0-0-50 ~ $ ./kubectl -s http://localhost:8080 run nginx --image=nginx
  --replicas=3 --port=80
deployment "nginx" created
core@ip-10-0-0-50 ~ $ ./kubectl get rc
core@ip-10-0-0-50 ~ $ ./kubectl get services
NAME          CLUSTER-IP   EXTERNAL-IP   PORT(S)   AGE
kubernetes    10.3.0.1     <none>        443/TCP   5m
core@ip-10-0-0-50 ~ $ ./kubectl get deployments
NAME      DESIRED   CURRENT   UP-TO-DATE   AVAILABLE   AGE
nginx     3         3         3            3           39s
core@ip-10-0-0-50 ~ $ ./kubectl get pods
NAME                     READY     STATUS    RESTARTS   AGE
nginx-198147104-2u7b4    1/1       Running   0          1m
nginx-198147104-c8o3n    1/1       Running   0          1m
nginx-198147104-x0ah0    1/1       Running   0          1m
core@ip-10-0-0-50 ~ $ ./kubectl expose deployment nginx --port=80 --type=LoadBal
ancer
service "nginx" exposed
core@ip-10-0-0-50 ~ $ ./kubectl get services
NAME          CLUSTER-IP   EXTERNAL-IP        PORT(S)   AGE
kubernetes    10.3.0.1     <none>             443/TCP   7m
nginx         10.3.0.127   a1a2ad2f44231...   80/TCP    9s
core@ip-10-0-0-50 ~ $ ▌
```

Figure 2-22. *Creating a deployment and service for* `nginx`

Next, describe the `nginx` service:

```
./kubectl describe svc nginx
```

The service description lists its endpoints, as shown in Figure 2-23.

```
core@ip-10-0-0-50 ~ $ ./kubectl describe svc nginx
Name:                   nginx
Namespace:              default
Labels:                 run=nginx
Selector:               run=nginx
Type:                   LoadBalancer
IP:                     10.3.0.127
LoadBalancer Ingress:   a1a2ad2f4423111e6848d0a928873259-235290971.us-east-1.elb
.amazonaws.com
Port:                   <unset> 80/TCP
NodePort:               <unset> 31531/TCP
Endpoints:              10.2.29.3:80,10.2.32.2:80,10.2.32.3:80
Session Affinity:       None
Events:
  FirstSeen     LastSeen        Count   From                    SubobjectPath   T
ype             Reason                  Message
  ---------     --------        -----   ----                    -------------   -
-------- ------                 -------
  38s           38s             1       {service-controller }                   N
ormal           CreatingLoadBalancer    Creating load balancer
  36s           36s             1       {service-controller }                   N
ormal           CreatedLoadBalancer     Created load balancer


core@ip-10-0-0-50 ~ $ █
```

Figure 2-23. *Service description lists the service endpoints*

Invoke a service endpoint:

```
curl 10.2.29.3
```

The HTML markup for the `nginx` server application is output as shown in Figure 2-24.

```
core@ip-10-0-0-50 ~ $ curl 10.2.29.3
<!DOCTYPE html>
<html>
<head>
<title>Welcome to nginx!</title>
<style>
    body {
        width: 35em;
        margin: 0 auto;
        font-family: Tahoma, Verdana, Arial, sans-serif;
    }
</style>
</head>
<body>
<h1>Welcome to nginx!</h1>
<p>If you see this page, the nginx web server is successfully installed and
working. Further configuration is required.</p>

<p>For online documentation and support please refer to
<a href="http://nginx.org/">nginx.org</a>.<br/>
Commercial support is available at
<a href="http://nginx.com/">nginx.com</a>.</p>

<p><em>Thank you for using nginx.</em></p>
</body>
</html>
core@ip-10-0-0-50 ~ $
```

Figure 2-24. *Invoking the service endpoint with curl*

Similarly invoke another endpoint:

```
curl 10.2.32.2
```

The nginx application HTML markup is listed, as shown in Figure 2-25.

```
core@ip-10-0-0-50 ~ $ curl 10.2.32.2
<!DOCTYPE html>
<html>
<head>
<title>Welcome to nginx!</title>
<style>
    body {
        width: 35em;
        margin: 0 auto;
        font-family: Tahoma, Verdana, Arial, sans-serif;
    }
</style>
</head>
<body>
<h1>Welcome to nginx!</h1>
<p>If you see this page, the nginx web server is successfully installed and
working. Further configuration is required.</p>

<p>For online documentation and support please refer to
<a href="http://nginx.org/">nginx.org</a>.<br/>
Commercial support is available at
<a href="http://nginx.com/">nginx.com</a>.</p>

<p><em>Thank you for using nginx.</em></p>
</body>
</html>
core@ip-10-0-0-50 ~ $
```

Figure 2-25. *Invoking another service endpoint*

To be able to invoke the `nginx` service endpoint in a browser, we need to set port forwarding from a local machine. Copy the key pair `kubernetes-coreos.pem` to the local machine:

```
scp -i docker.pem ec2-user@ec2-54-85-83-181.compute-1.amazonaws.com:~/kubernetes-coreos.pem
~/kubernetes-coreos.pem
```

Using the key pair, set port forwarding from the local machine to a service endpoint on the controller instance:

```
ssh -i kubernetes-coreos.pem -f -nNT -L 80:10.2.29.3:80 core@ec2-23-22-192-55.compute-1.
amazonaws.com
```

Port forwarding from a local machine to the service endpoint is set as shown in Figure 2-26.

```
[root@localhost ~]# scp -i docker.pem ec2-user@ec2-54-85-83-181.compute-1.amazon
aws.com:~/kubernetes-coreos.pem ~/kubernetes-coreos.pem
The authenticity of host 'ec2-54-85-83-181.compute-1.amazonaws.com (54.85.83.181
)' can't be established.
RSA key fingerprint is be:cf:d6:dd:44:d4:39:b0:d9:1d:d0:8e:30:4e:1b:3a.
Are you sure you want to continue connecting (yes/no)? yes
Warning: Permanently added 'ec2-54-85-83-181.compute-1.amazonaws.com' (RSA) to t
he list of known hosts.
kubernetes-coreos.pem                          100% 1675     1.6KB/s   00:00
[root@localhost ~]# ssh -i kubernetes-coreos.pem -f -nNT -L 80:10.2.29.3:80 core
@ec2-23-22-192-55.compute-1.amazonaws.com
The authenticity of host 'ec2-23-22-192-55.compute-1.amazonaws.com (23.22.192.55
)' can't be established.
RSA key fingerprint is ad:bd:41:b9:ae:f9:12:47:52:0e:2f:fe:8f:ed:80:8e.
Are you sure you want to continue connecting (yes/no)? yes
Warning: Permanently added 'ec2-23-22-192-55.compute-1.amazonaws.com,23.22.192.5
5' (RSA) to the list of known hosts.
[root@localhost ~]# 
```

Figure 2-26. *Setting port forwarding*

Invoke the service endpoint on the local machine browser to display the `nginx` application output as shown in Figure 2-27.

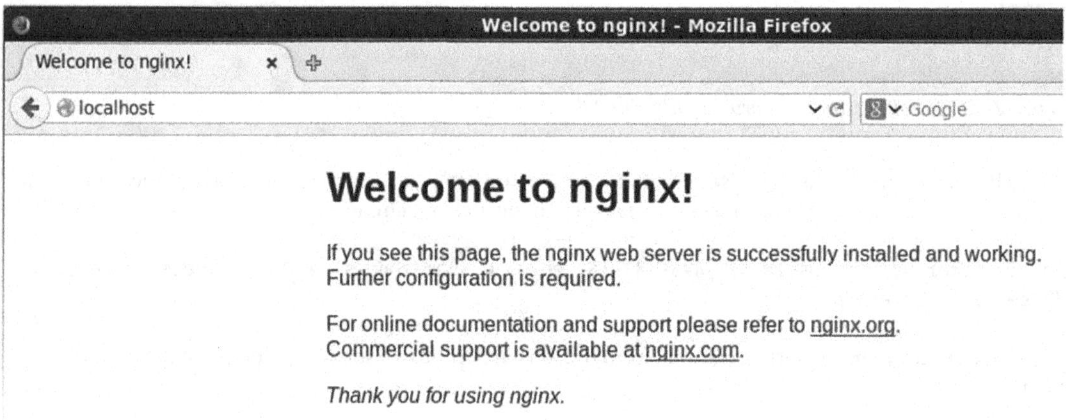

Figure 2-27. *Invoking the service in a browser*

Exit the controller instance as shown in Figure 2-28.

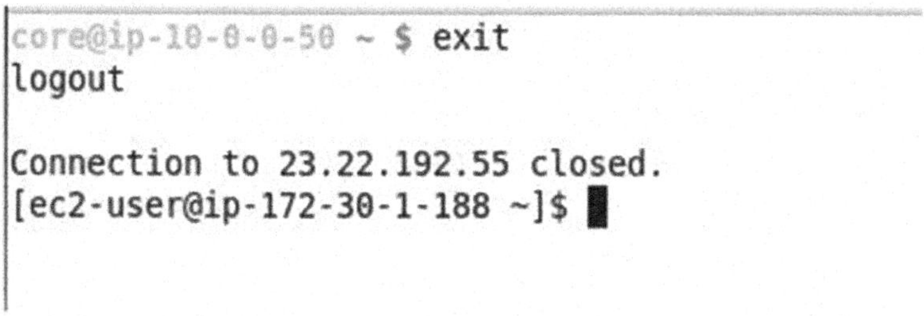
core@ip-10-0-0-50 ~ $ exit
logout
Connection to 23.22.192.55 closed.
[ec2-user@ip-172-30-1-188 ~]$

Figure 2-28. *Exiting CoreOS instance*

Summary

In this chapter we launched an AWS CloudFormation stack for a Kubernetes cluster on CoreOS instances. The procedure we followed was this: First, install kube-aws. Next, set up the cluster parameters, such as creating a KMS key and setting up an external DNS name. To create the cluster CloudFormation, create an asset directory, initialize the cluster CloudFormation, render contents of the asset directory, customize the cluster, validate the cluster and launch the cluster. After the cluster has been launched, access the cluster and create an `nginx` application pod cluster.

In the next chapter we will install Kubernetes on the Google Cloud platform.

CHAPTER 3

Kubernetes on Google Cloud Platform

Google Cloud Platform is a public cloud computing platform that includes database services and infrastructure on which applications and websites may be hosted on managed virtual machines. This integrated PaaS/IaaS is a collection of services that may be categorized into Compute, Storage and Databases, Networking, Big Data, and Machine Learning, to list a few.

Problem

While Docker is pre-installed on CoreOS, Kubernetes is not. As discussed in Chapter 2 Kubernetes has to be installed on CoreOS.

Solution

The service category of most interest for using Kubernetes is Compute, which includes a Compute Engine for running large-scale workloads on virtual machines hosted on Google's infrastructure, an App Engine for developing scalable web and mobile apps, and a Container Engine for running Docker containers on Kubernetes on Google's infrastructure. Google Container Engine is a Kubernetes based cluster manager for Docker containers and thus does not require installation of Kubernetes. We shall use the Google Container Engine, a Google managed service for Kubernetes. Google Container Engine has Docker preinstalled and provides built-in support for Google Cloud Platform, which as stated is both an Infrastructure as a Service (IaaS) and a Platform as a Service (PaaS). Google Cloud Platform is an alternative to Amazon Web Services (AWS), which is the cloud provider we use in most other chapters.

Overview

The design patterns discussed in subsequent chapters may be used on Google Cloud Platform as well, though the configuration could be different. In this chapter we will use the Google Compute Engine to create a virtual machine instance, install Kubernetes on it using binaries, and subsequently create a sample Kubernetes application and service. We shall also discuss using the Google Container Engine, which is Kubernetes based cluster manager for Docker containers. The steps we'll take are as follows:

- Setting the Environment
- Creating a Project on Google Cloud Platform
- Enabling Permissions

D. Vohra, *Kubernetes Management Design Patterns*, DOI 10.1007/978-1-4842-2598-1_3

Enabling the Compute Engine API

Creating a VM Instance

Connecting to the VM Instance

Reserving a Static Address

Creating a Kubernetes Cluster

Creating a Kubernetes Application and Service

Stopping the Cluster

Using Kubernetes with Google Container Engine

Setting the Environment

To create a Kubernetes cluster and deploy an application on it we will use the following procedure on Google Cloud Platform:

1. Create a project.
2. Enable the Compute Engine API.
3. Enable permissions.
4. Create and connect to a Virtual Machine instance.
5. Reserve a static address.
6. Create a Kubernetes cluster.
7. Create a sample Kubernetes application and service.

The only prerequisite is to install SSH for Google Cloud Platform as shown in Figure 3-1.

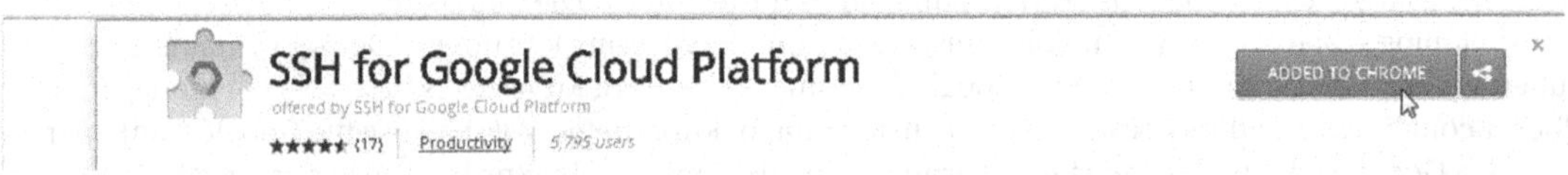

Figure 3-1. *Installing SSH for Google Cloud Platform*

We also need to create a new Billing Account at `https://console.cloud.google.com/billing`. Before we can use the Compute Engine API, the billing needs to be enabled for a project. Most of the Google Cloud Platform artifacts may also be created and/or managed with the command-line tool `gcloud`. We have used the Google Cloud Platform console for most of the chapter except for setting some configurations. These include configuring `kubectl` to use a particular project, to push a Docker image to Google Container Registry, and to delete a Google Container Engine cluster.

Creating a Project on Google Cloud Platform

To create a project, navigate to the Google Cloud Platform console at `https://console.cloud.google.com/start`. The Google Cloud Platform console is displayed as shown in Figure 3-2.

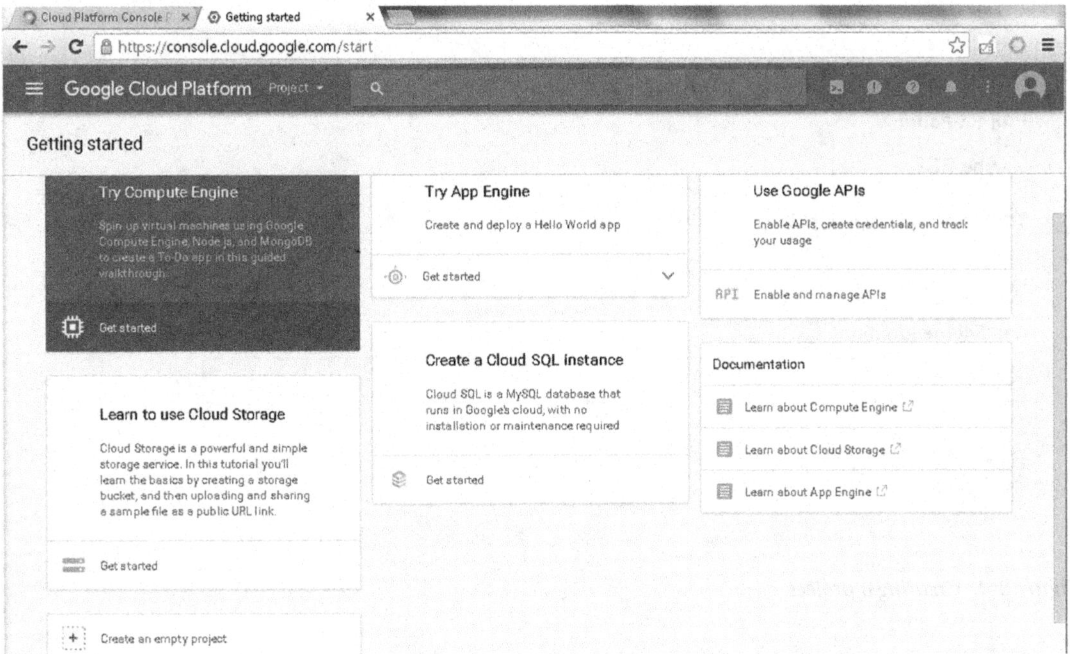

Figure 3-2. *Displaying the Google Cloud Platform console*

Select the Project dropdown and click Create Project as shown in Figure 3-3.

Figure 3-3. *Selecting Create Project to begin project creation*

In the New Project dialog, specify a Project name (Kube-GCE for example) and optionally select an App Engine location in the advanced options. Click on Create as shown in Figure 3-4.

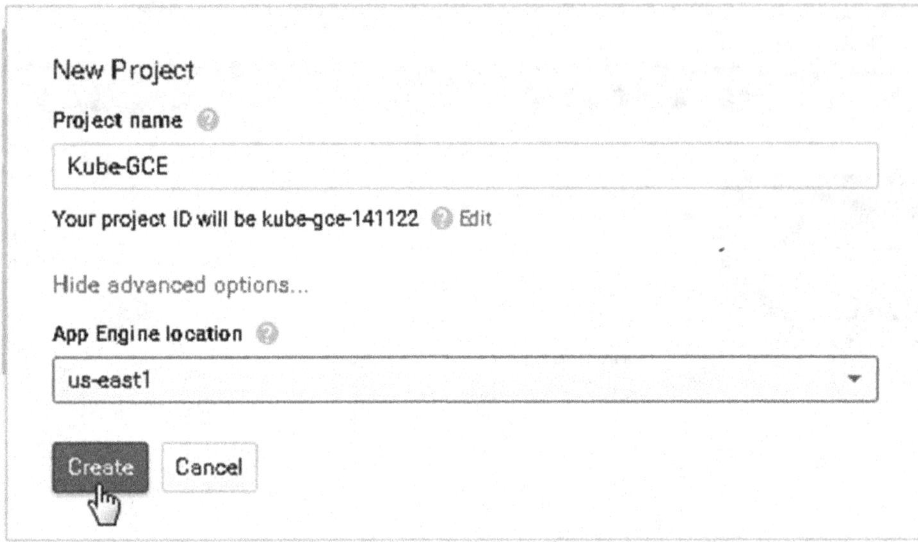

Figure 3-4. *Creating a project*

The message `Creating project "Kube-GCE"` is displayed, as shown in Figure 3-5.

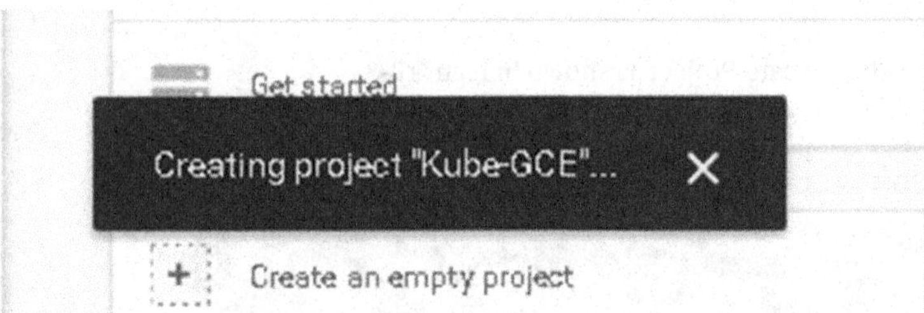

Figure 3-5. *Creating a project "Kube-GCE" message*

The new project is added in the Projects on the Dashboard as shown in Figure 3-6.

Figure 3-6. *The new project is added*

The Kube-GCE project may be selected from the project list to display its details as shown in Figure 3-7, or you can create another project with Create Project.

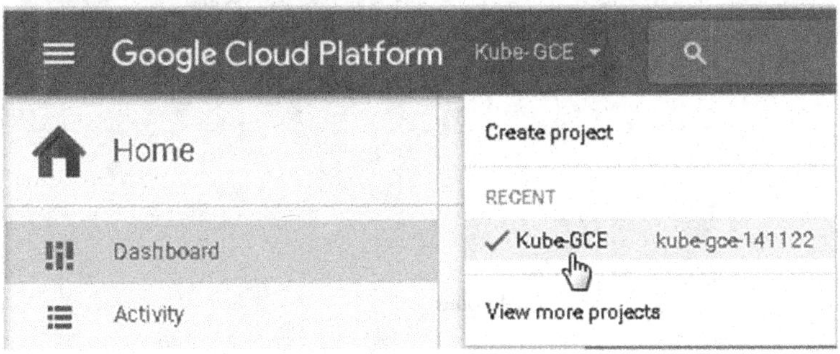

Figure 3-7. *Selecting a project*

The Dashboard can be accessed at `https://console.cloud.google.com/projectselector/home/dashboard`. The project Kube-GCE should be listed on the Dashboard as shown in Figure 3-8.

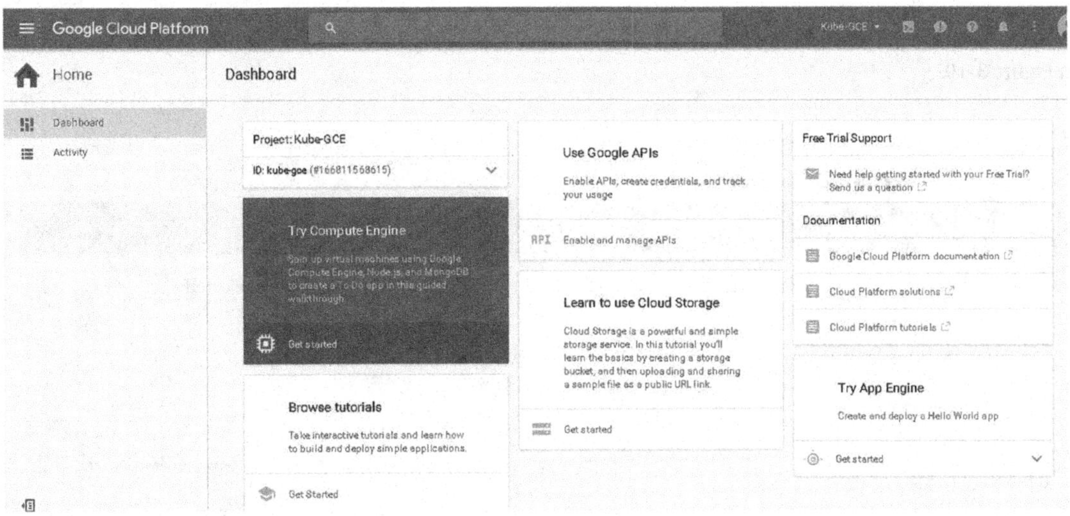

Figure 3-8. *Project description on dashboard*

If no project exists yet, the Dashboard URL `https://console.cloud.google.com/projectselector/home/dashboard` displays a dialog prompt to create a project as shown in Figure 3-9.

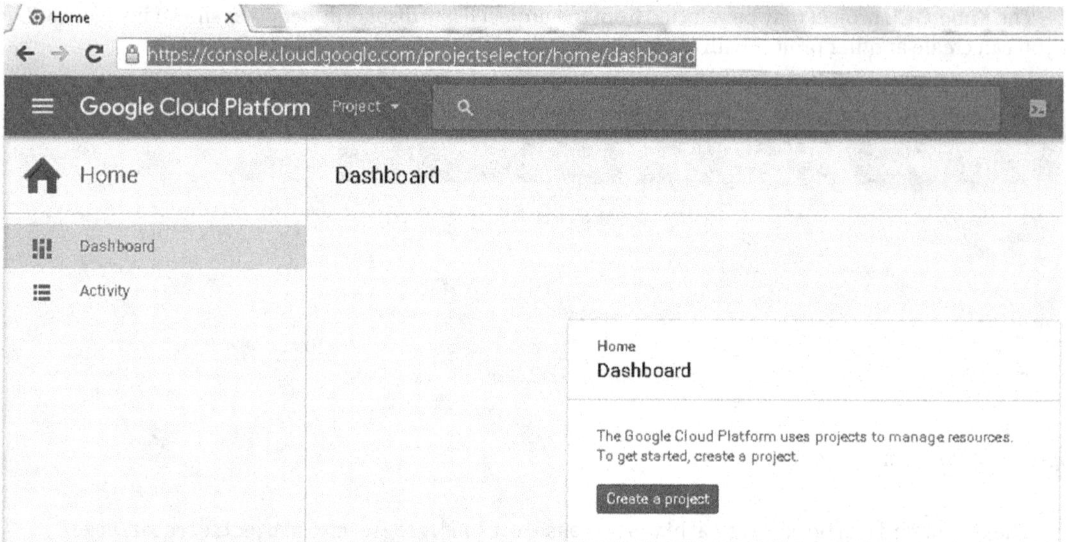

Figure 3-9. *The Create a Project link in the Dashboard dialog*

The projects may be managed at `https://console.cloud.google.com/iam-admin/projects`, as shown in Figure 3-10.

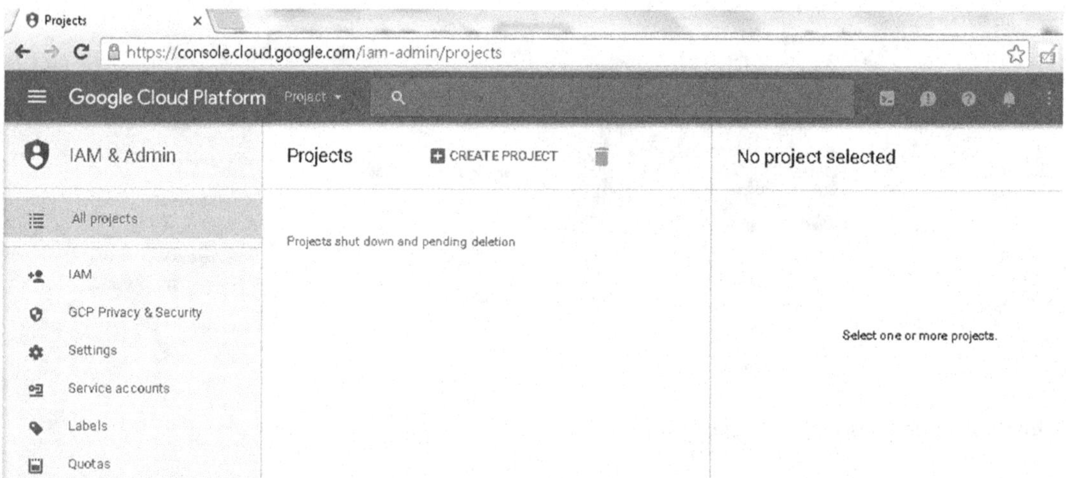

Figure 3-10. *Managing projects at All Projects*

Enabling Permissions

To enable permissions for a project, navigate to the Projects page at `https://console.cloud.google.com/iam-admin/projects`. Select the Kube-GCE project as shown in Figure 3-11.

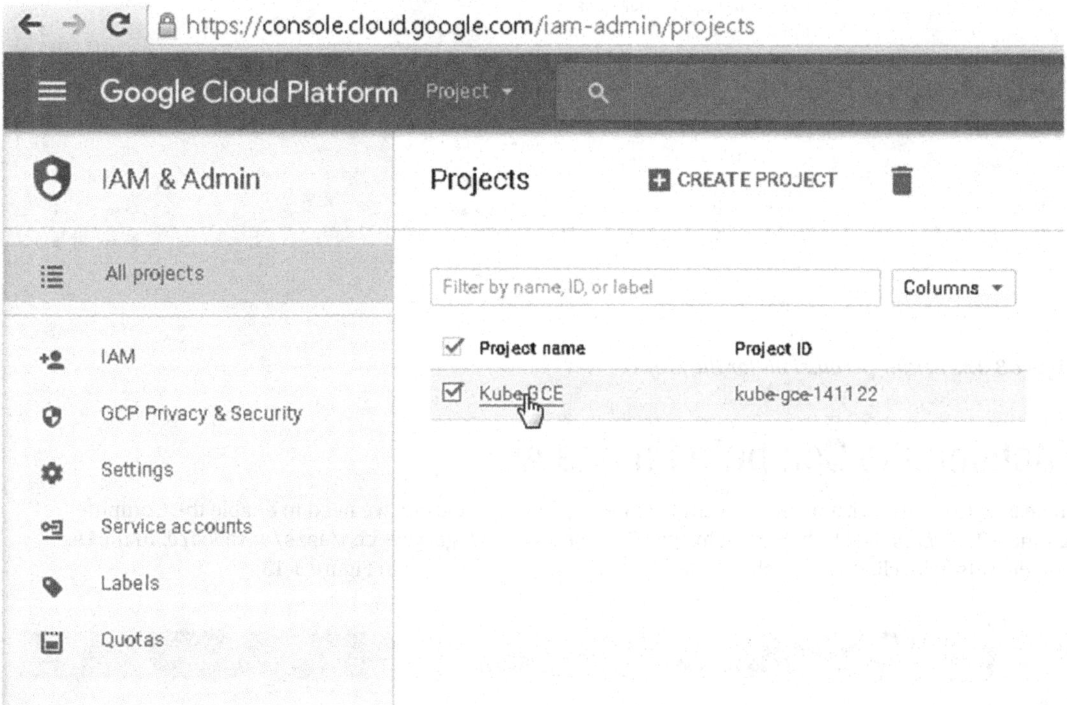

Figure 3-11. *Selecting a project*

Permissions for the project resources are displayed. Modify all permissions to "Owner" as shown in Figure 3-12.

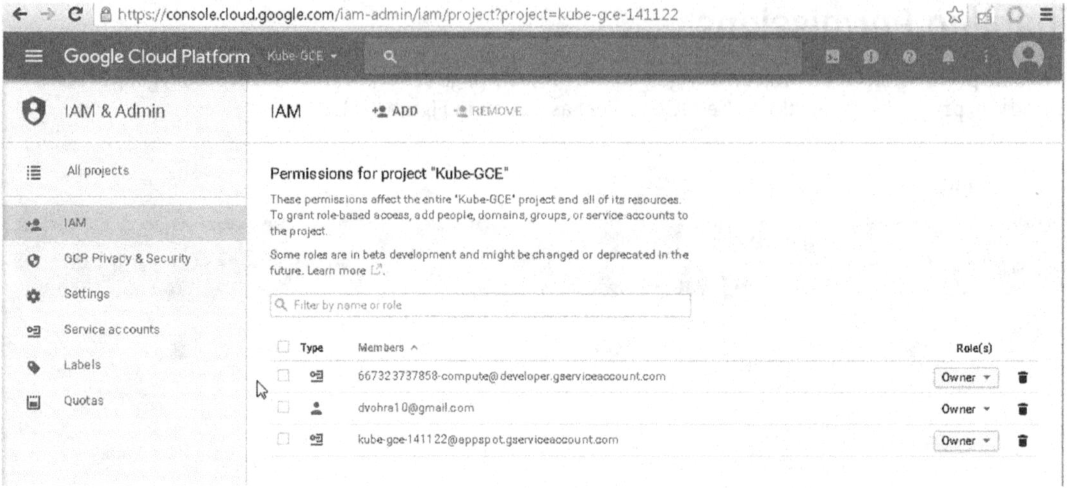

Figure 3-12. *Setting permissions for the project*

Enabling the Compute Engine API

To be able to create a virtual machine and create a Kubernetes cluster, we need to enable the Compute Engine API. Access the Dashboard at `https://console.cloud.google.com/apis/dashboard`. In the Use Google APIs field, click the Enable and Manage APIs link in as shown in Figure 3-13.

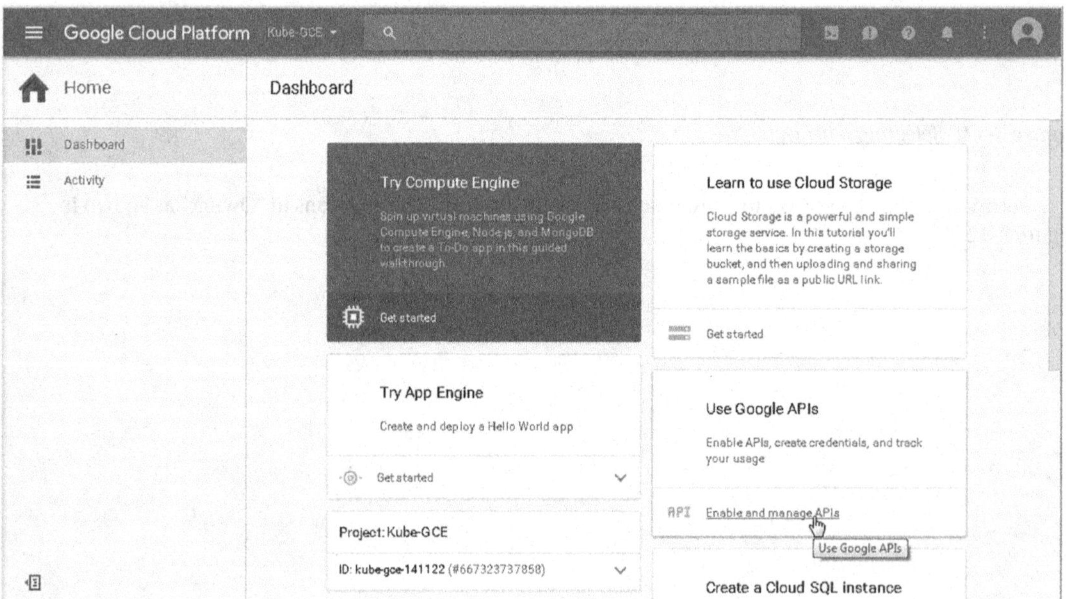

Figure 3-13. *Selecting the Enable and Manage APIs link*

The Compute Engine API is not listed by default for a new project, as shown in Figure 3-14.

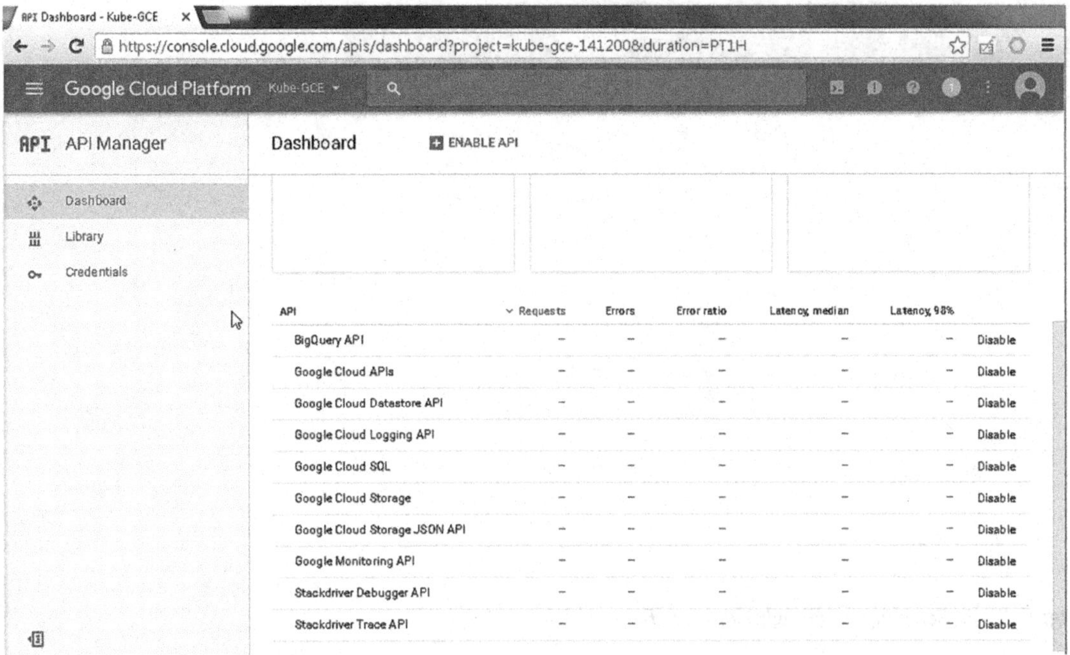

Figure 3-14. *Listing the Enabled and Disabled APIs*

To fix that, click ENABLE API as shown in Figure 3-15.

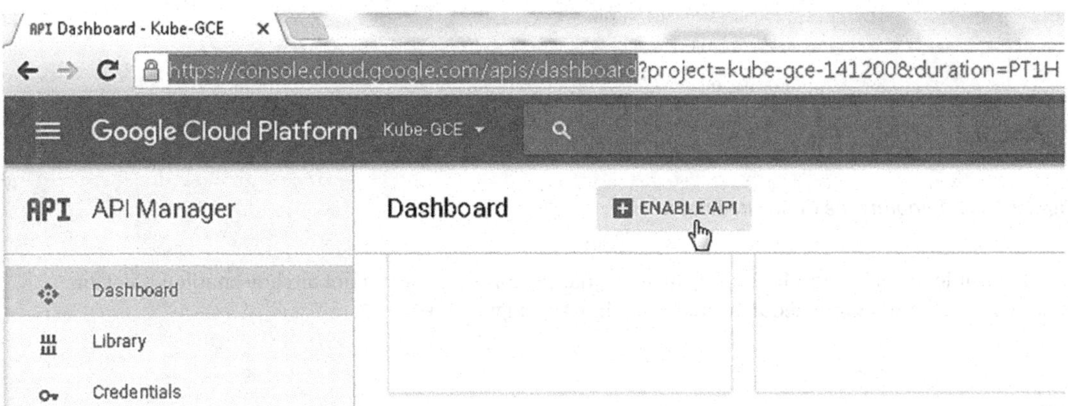

Figure 3-15. *Clicking on ENABLE API*

Then select the Compute Engine API, as shown in Figure 3-16.

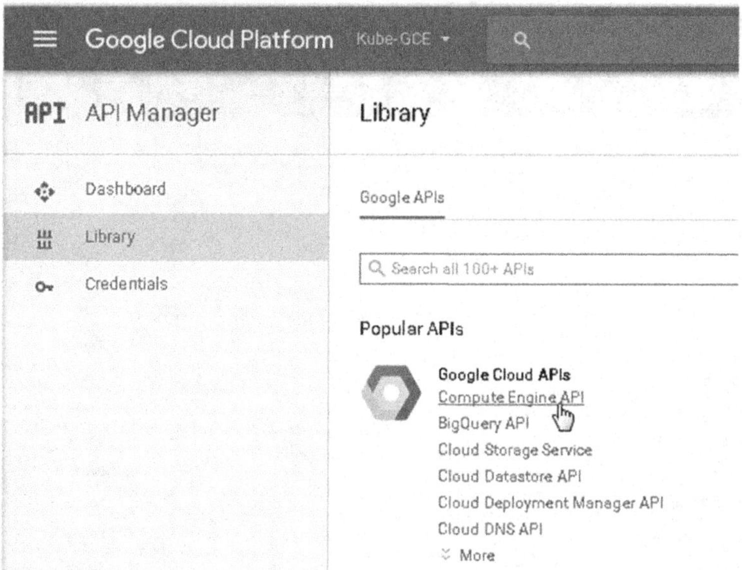

Figure 3-16. *Selecting the Google Compute Engine API*

The Compute Engine API is selected. Click ENABLE as shown in Figure 3-17.

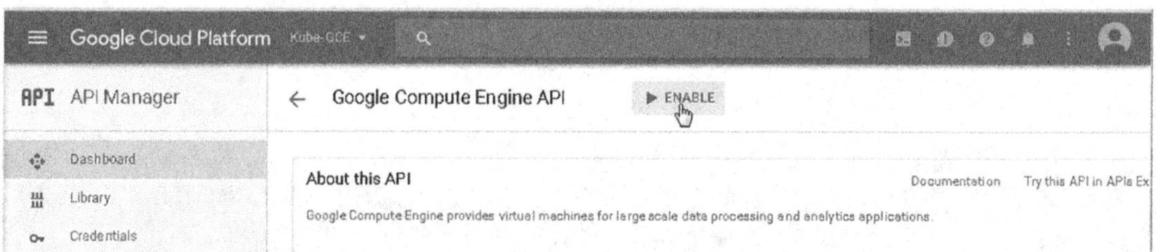

Figure 3-17. *Enabling the Compute Engine API*

To be able to enable an API, Billing must be enabled for the project if not already enabled. Click on Enable Billing in the Billing Required dialog as shown in Figure 3-18.

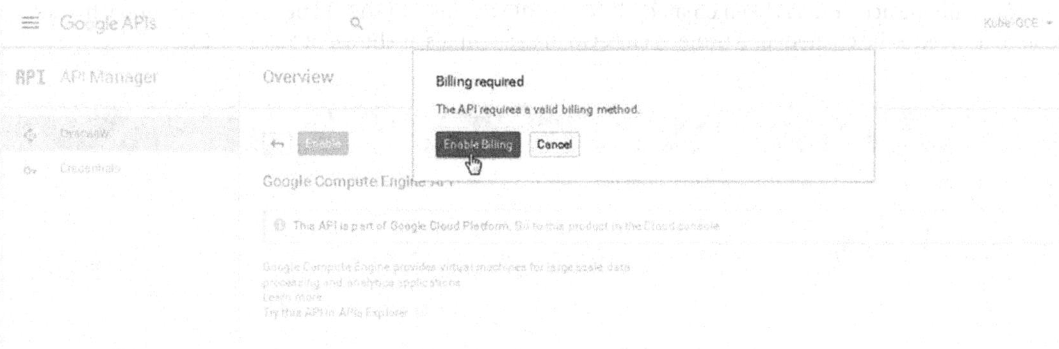

Figure 3-18. *Enabling billing*

An ENABLING message is displayed, as shown in Figure 3-19.

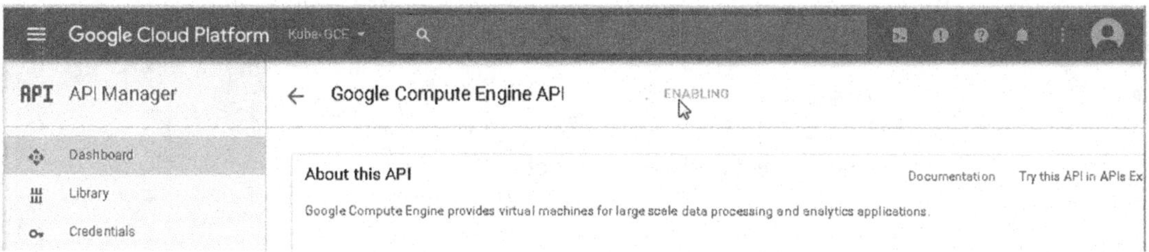

Figure 3-19. *Google Compute Engine API being enabled*

If a Billing Account does not exist, click Create Billing Account in the Enable Billing for Project dialog as shown in Figure 3-20.

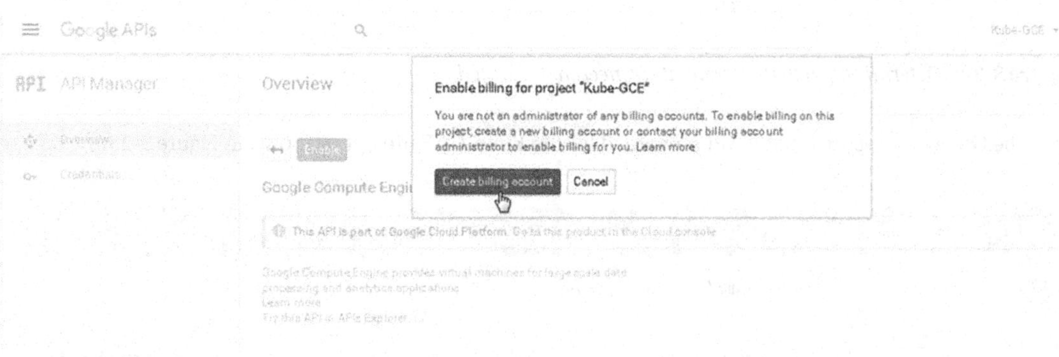

Figure 3-20. *Creating a Billing Account*

After a Billing account has been created, the Compute Engine API should be enabled. To find whether credentials need to be created for a project, click Go to Credentials as shown in Figure 3-21.

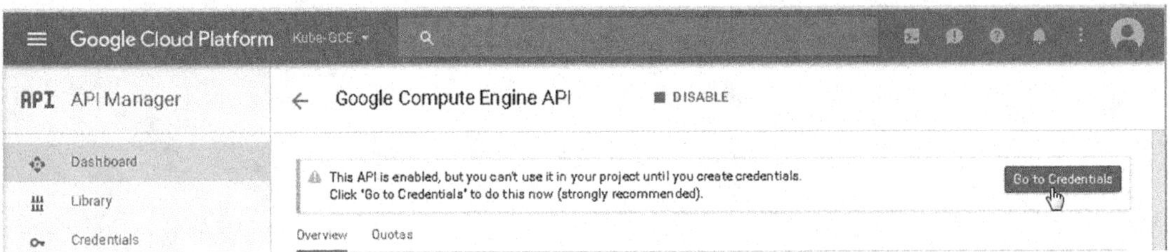

***Figure 3-21.** Navigating to the Credentials page*

As indicated in the Credentials page, new credentials don't need to be created and the Application Default Credentials may be used. Click on Cancel as shown in Figure 3-22.

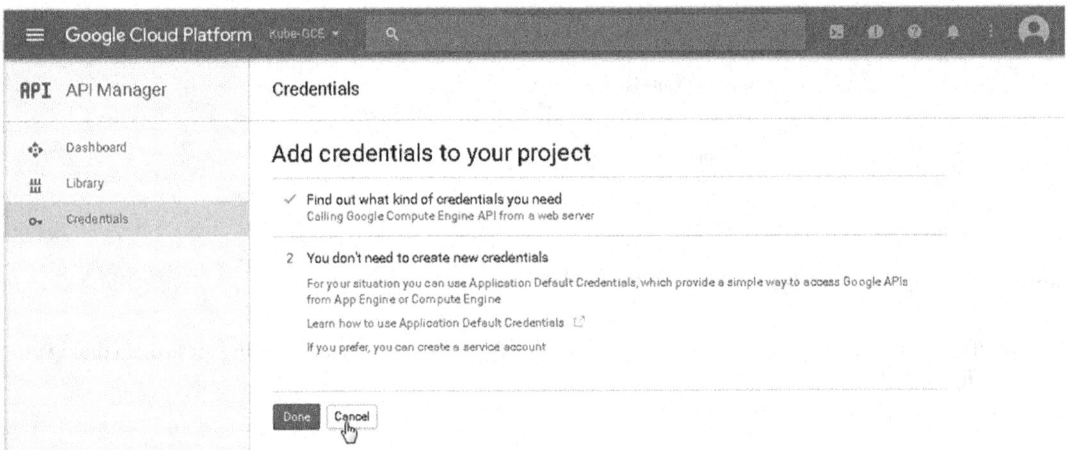

***Figure 3-22.** Determining whether credentials need to be added*

The Google Compute Engine API is enabled for the Kube-GCE project as shown in Figure 3-23.

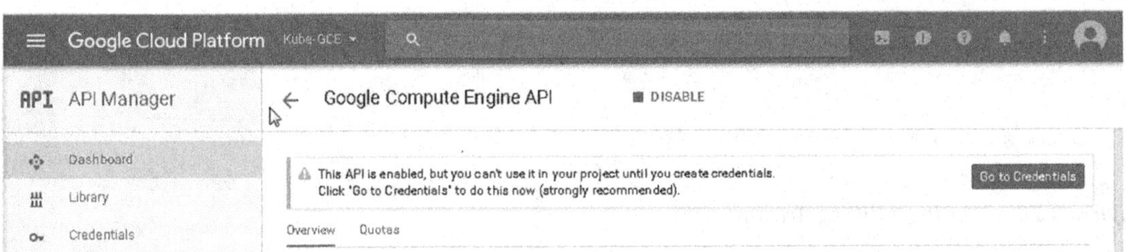

***Figure 3-23.** Google Compute Engine API enabled*

The Google Compute Engine API should be listed in the Dashboard as shown in Figure 3-24.

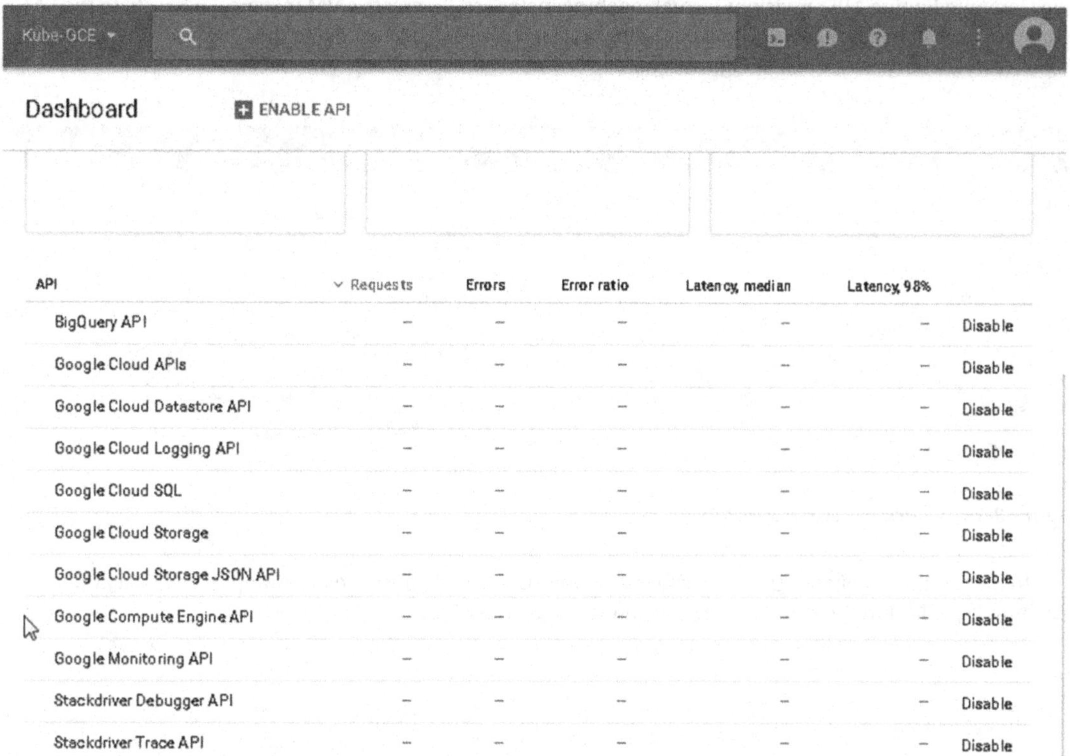

Figure 3-24. *Google Compute Engine API listed as Enabled*

As indicated by the message A project is needed to enable APIs in Figure 3-25, to enable the Google Compute Engine API a project is required.

Figure 3-25. *A project is needed to enable APIs*

Creating a VM Instance

The Compute Engine API provisions virtual machine instances. To create a VM instance, navigate to the VM Instances page at `https://console.cloud.google.com/compute/instances`. In the Compute Engine dialog, click Create Instance as shown in Figure 3-26.

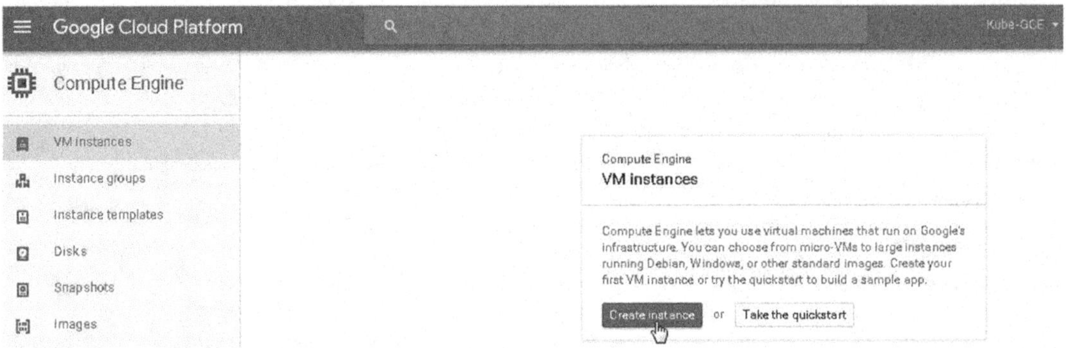

Figure 3-26. *Clicking on Create Instance*

In the Create an instance page, specify an instance name (`vm-kube-gce` for example). Select a Zone, Machine Type, Identity, and API Access as shown in Figure 3-27.

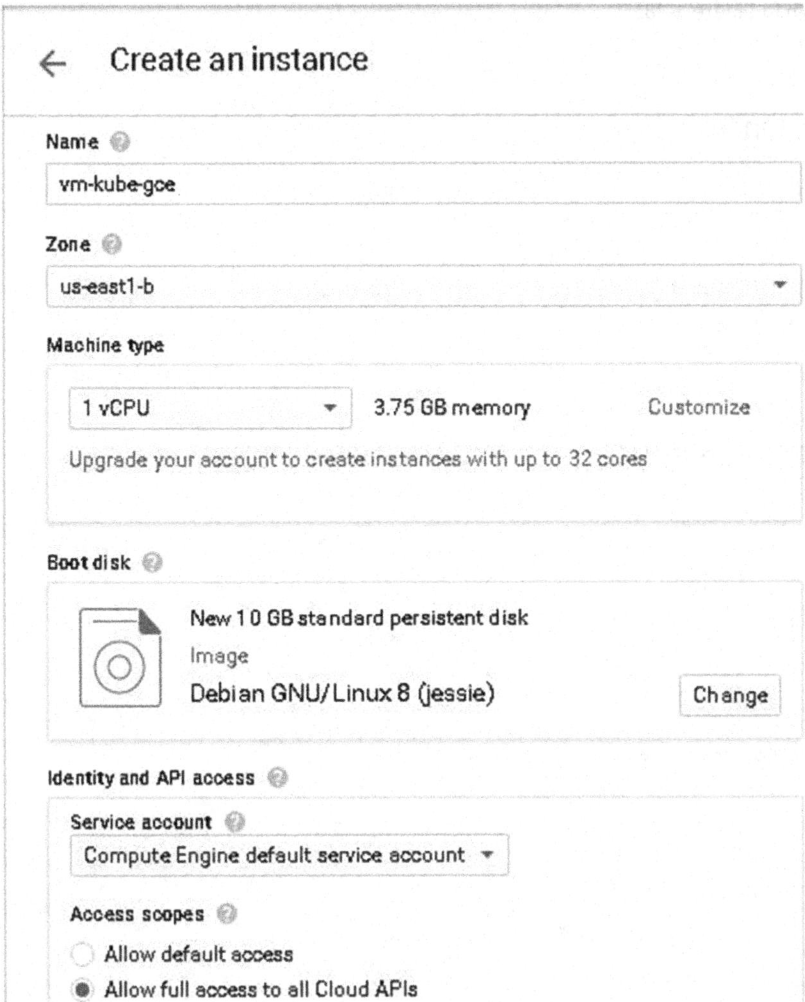
Create an instance
Name
vm-kube-gce
Zone
us-east1-b
Machine type
1 vCPU
3.75 GB memory
Customize
Upgrade your account to create instances with up to 32 cores
Boot disk
New 10 GB standard persistent disk
Image
Debian GNU/Linux 8 (jessie)
Change
Identity and API access
Service account
Compute Engine default service account
Access scopes
Allow default access
Allow full access to all Cloud APIs

Figure 3-27. *The Create an Instance page*

Click on Create as shown in Figure 3-28.

Figure 3-28. *Clicking on Create*

A new VM instance is created, as shown in Figure 3-29.

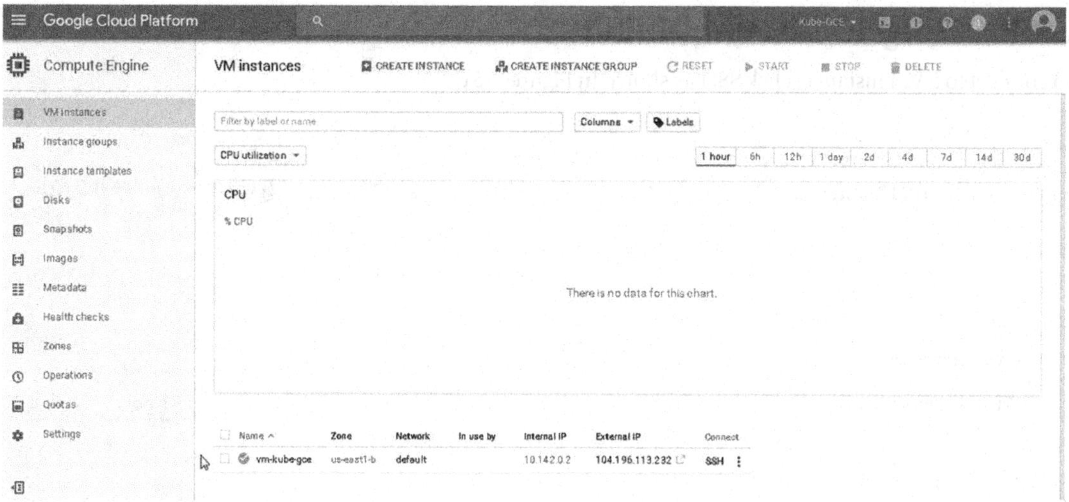

Figure 3-29. *A new VM instance*

Select the VM instance to lists its stats, such as CPU Utilization as shown in Figure 3-30. Initially the chart may have no data.

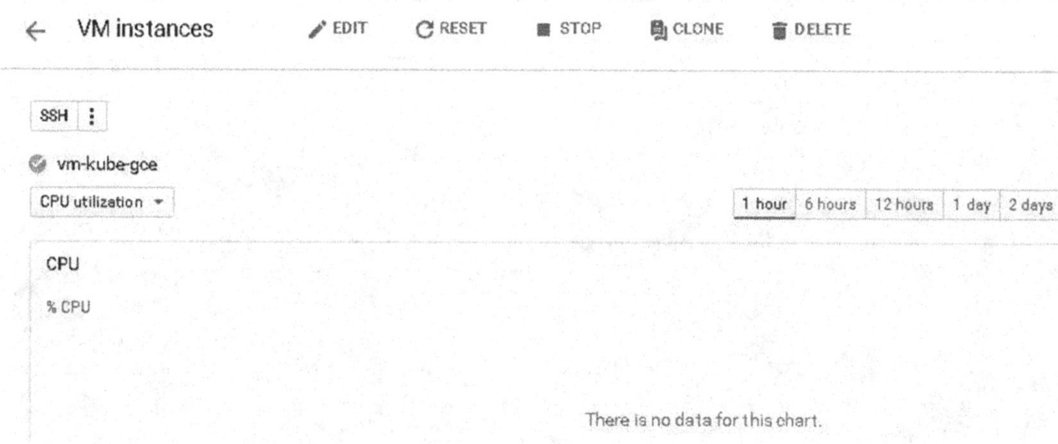

Figure 3-30. *Listing a VM's CPU utilization*

Connecting to the VM Instance

To connect to a VM instance, click SSH as shown in Figure 3-31.

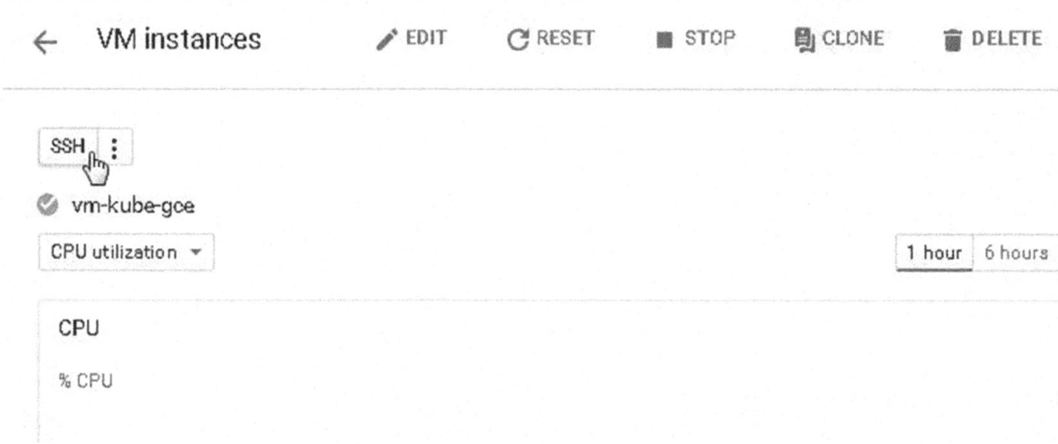

Figure 3-31. *Clicking SSH to begin connecting to the VM instance*

A `Connecting...` message should be displayed as shown in Figure 3-32.

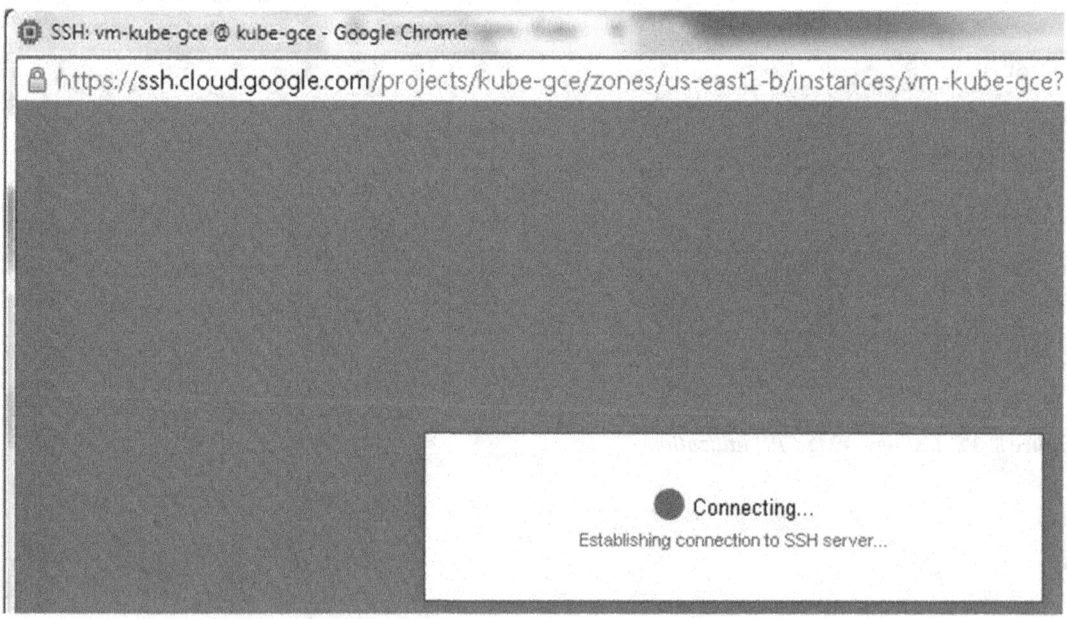

Figure 3-32. *Connecting to a VM instance*

The VM instance is connected to and a command prompt is displayed.

Reserving a Static External IP Address

Each VM instance is assigned an internal IP address, which is used to communicate with other VM instances on the same network. To be able to communicate outside the network, with the Internet to download Kubernetes binaries for example, we need to assign a static external IP address to the VM instance. Navigate to the URL `https://console.cloud.google.com/networking/addresses` to create a static external IP address.

In the Reserve a Static Address page, click Regional and specify a Region. In the Attached To field, select the VM instance created earlier. Click on Reserve as shown in Figure 3-33.

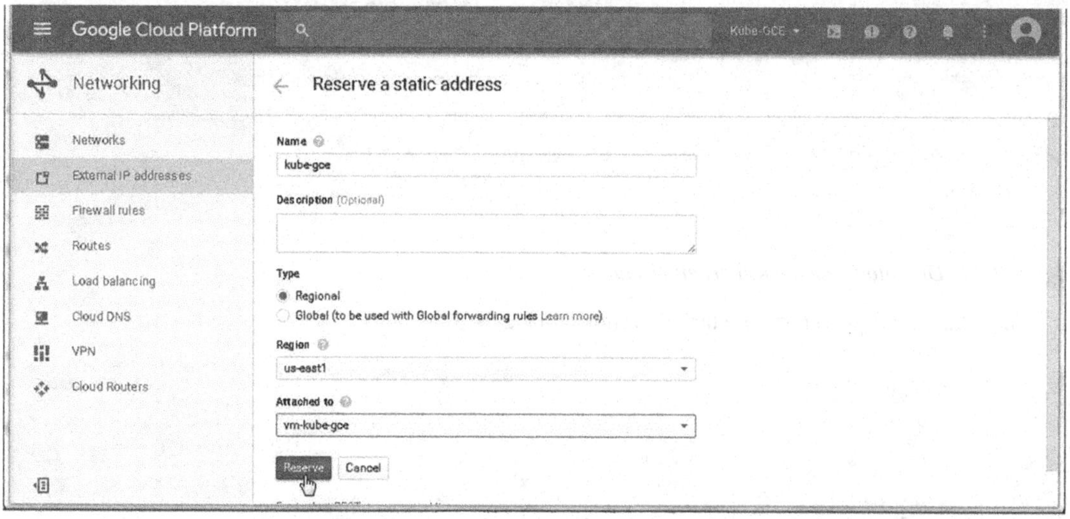

Figure 3-33. *Clicking on Reserve to reserve a static address*

A static external IP Address is reserved for the VM instance.

Creating a Kubernetes Cluster

To create a Kubernetes cluster, run one of the following commands in the shell for the VM instance.

```
curl -sS https://get.k8s.io | bash
```

or

```
wget -q -O - https://get.k8s.io | bash
```

The Kubernetes binaries are downloaded as shown in Figure 3-34.

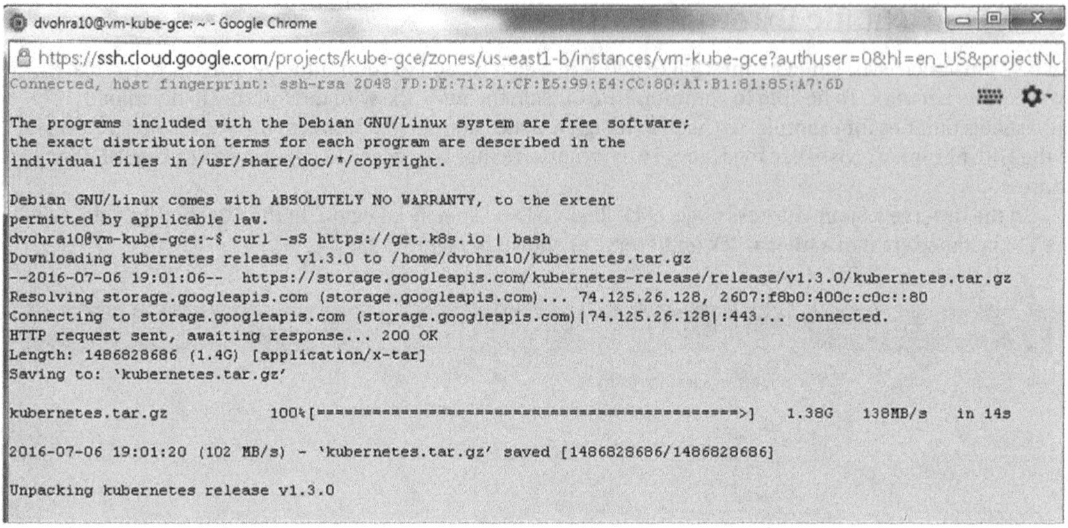

```
dvohra10@vm-kube-gce: ~ - Google Chrome
https://ssh.cloud.google.com/projects/kube-gce/zones/us-east1-b/instances/vm-kube-gce?authuser=0&hl=en_US&projectNu
Connected, host fingerprint: ssh-rsa 2048 FD:DE:71:21:CF:E5:99:E4:CC:80:A1:B1:81:85:A7:6D

The programs included with the Debian GNU/Linux system are free software;
the exact distribution terms for each program are described in the
individual files in /usr/share/doc/*/copyright.

Debian GNU/Linux comes with ABSOLUTELY NO WARRANTY, to the extent
permitted by applicable law.
dvohra10@vm-kube-gce:~$ curl -sS https://get.k8s.io | bash
Downloading kubernetes release v1.3.0 to /home/dvohra10/kubernetes.tar.gz
--2016-07-06 19:01:06--  https://storage.googleapis.com/kubernetes-release/release/v1.3.0/kubernetes.tar.gz
Resolving storage.googleapis.com (storage.googleapis.com)... 74.125.26.128, 2607:f8b0:400c:c0c::80
Connecting to storage.googleapis.com (storage.googleapis.com)|74.125.26.128|:443... connected.
HTTP request sent, awaiting response... 200 OK
Length: 1486828686 (1.4G) [application/x-tar]
Saving to: 'kubernetes.tar.gz'

kubernetes.tar.gz          100%[===============================================>]   1.38G   138MB/s   in 14s

2016-07-06 19:01:20 (102 MB/s) - 'kubernetes.tar.gz' saved [1486828686/1486828686]

Unpacking kubernetes release v1.3.0
```

Figure 3-34. *Downloading the Kubernetes binaries*

Then the Kubernetes cluster is started as shown in Figure 3-35.

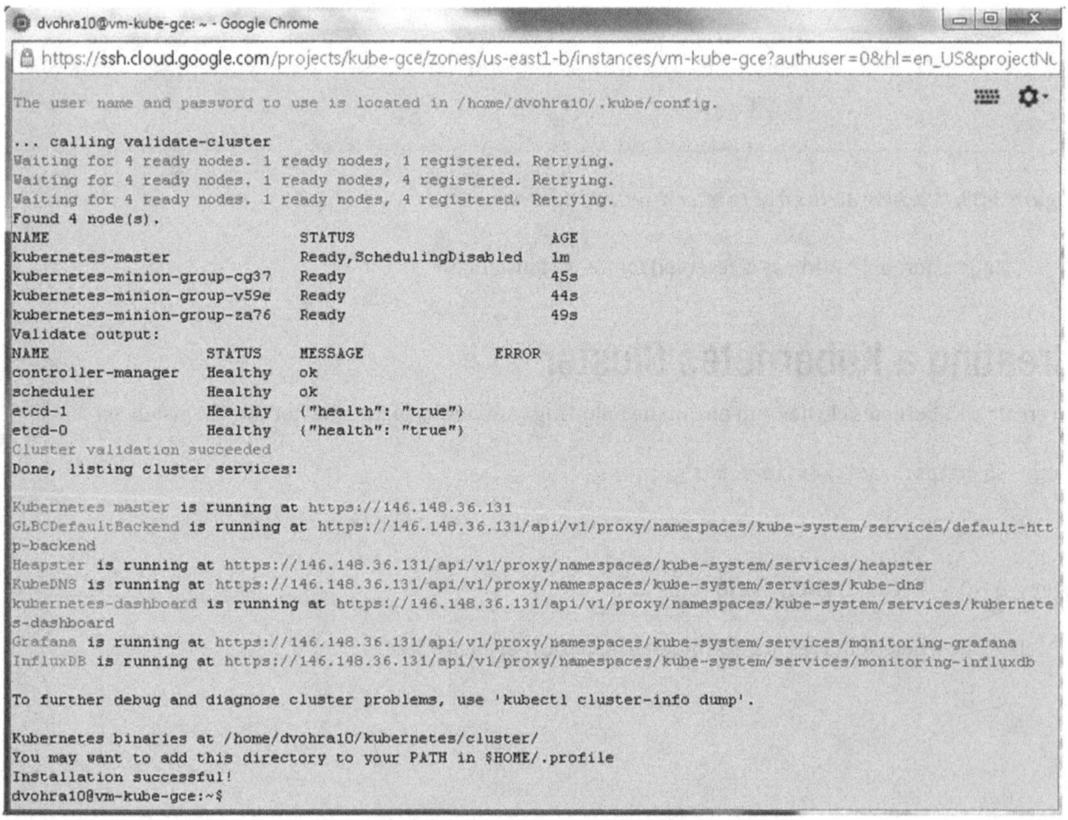

```
dvohra10@vm-kube-gce: ~ - Google Chrome
https://ssh.cloud.google.com/projects/kube-gce/zones/us-east1-b/instances/vm-kube-gce?authuser=0&hl=en_US&projectNu
The user name and password to use is located in /home/dvohra10/.kube/config.

... calling validate-cluster
Waiting for 4 ready nodes. 1 ready nodes, 1 registered. Retrying.
Waiting for 4 ready nodes. 1 ready nodes, 4 registered. Retrying.
Waiting for 4 ready nodes. 1 ready nodes, 4 registered. Retrying.
Found 4 node(s).
NAME                             STATUS                     AGE
kubernetes-master                Ready,SchedulingDisabled   1m
kubernetes-minion-group-cg37     Ready                      45s
kubernetes-minion-group-v59e     Ready                      44s
kubernetes-minion-group-za76     Ready                      49s
Validate output:
NAME                 STATUS    MESSAGE              ERROR
controller-manager   Healthy   ok
scheduler            Healthy   ok
etcd-1               Healthy   {"health": "true"}
etcd-0               Healthy   {"health": "true"}
Cluster validation succeeded
Done, listing cluster services:

Kubernetes master is running at https://146.148.36.131
GLBCDefaultBackend is running at https://146.148.36.131/api/v1/proxy/namespaces/kube-system/services/default-htt
p-backend
Heapster is running at https://146.148.36.131/api/v1/proxy/namespaces/kube-system/services/heapster
KubeDNS is running at https://146.148.36.131/api/v1/proxy/namespaces/kube-system/services/kube-dns
kubernetes-dashboard is running at https://146.148.36.131/api/v1/proxy/namespaces/kube-system/services/kubernete
s-dashboard
Grafana is running at https://146.148.36.131/api/v1/proxy/namespaces/kube-system/services/monitoring-grafana
InfluxDB is running at https://146.148.36.131/api/v1/proxy/namespaces/kube-system/services/monitoring-influxdb

To further debug and diagnose cluster problems, use 'kubectl cluster-info dump'.

Kubernetes binaries at /home/dvohra10/kubernetes/cluster/
You may want to add this directory to your PATH in $HOME/.profile
Installation successful!
dvohra10@vm-kube-gce:~$
```

Figure 3-35. *Starting a Kubernetes Cluster with four nodes*

To list the services, run the following command:

```
kubectl.sh get --all-namespaces services
```

The services are listed as shown in Figure 3-36.

```
dvohra10@vm-kube-gce:~$ kubectl.sh get --all-namespaces services
NAMESPACE     NAME                    CLUSTER-IP     EXTERNAL-IP   PORT(S)            AGE
default       kubernetes              10.0.0.1       <none>        443/TCP            8m
kube-system   default-http-backend    10.0.17.225    <nodes>       80/TCP             7m
kube-system   heapster                10.0.220.227   <none>        80/TCP             7m
kube-system   kube-dns                10.0.0.10      <none>        53/UDP,53/TCP      7m
kube-system   kubernetes-dashboard    10.0.94.209    <none>        80/TCP             7m
kube-system   monitoring-grafana      10.0.198.75    <none>        80/TCP             7m
kube-system   monitoring-influxdb     10.0.218.95    <none>        8083/TCP,8086/TCP  7m
dvohra10@vm-kube-gce:~$
```

Figure 3-36. *Listing the services in All Namespaces*

To list all the pods, run the following command:

```
kubectl.sh get --all-namespaces pods
```

All the pods in all the namespaces are listed, as shown in Figure 3-37.

```
dvohra10@vm-kube-gce:~$ kubectl get --all-namespaces pods
-bash: kubectl: command not found
dvohra10@vm-kube-gce:~$ kubectl.sh get --all-namespaces pods
NAMESPACE     NAME                                                READY   STATUS    RESTARTS   AGE
kube-system   etcd-server-events-kubernetes-master                1/1     Running   0          9m
kube-system   etcd-server-kubernetes-master                       1/1     Running   0          9m
kube-system   fluentd-cloud-logging-kubernetes-master             1/1     Running   0          8m
kube-system   fluentd-cloud-logging-kubernetes-minion-group-cg37  1/1     Running   0          8m
kube-system   fluentd-cloud-logging-kubernetes-minion-group-v59e  1/1     Running   0          8m
kube-system   fluentd-cloud-logging-kubernetes-minion-group-za76  1/1     Running   0          8m
kube-system   heapster-v1.1.0-527143062-t57xt                     4/4     Running   0          7m
kube-system   kube-addon-manager-kubernetes-master                1/1     Running   0          9m
kube-system   kube-apiserver-kubernetes-master                    1/1     Running   1          9m
kube-system   kube-controller-manager-kubernetes-master           1/1     Running   0          8m
kube-system   kube-dns-v17-yz76j                                  3/3     Running   0          8m
kube-system   kube-proxy-kubernetes-minion-group-cg37             1/1     Running   0          8m
kube-system   kube-proxy-kubernetes-minion-group-v59e             1/1     Running   0          8m
kube-system   kube-proxy-kubernetes-minion-group-za76             1/1     Running   0          8m
kube-system   kube-scheduler-kubernetes-master                    1/1     Running   0          8m
kube-system   kubernetes-dashboard-v1.1.0-4u2lq                   1/1     Running   0          8m
kube-system   l7-default-backend-v1.0-1norr                       1/1     Running   0          8m
kube-system   l7-lb-controller-v0.7.0-kubernetes-master           1/1     Running   0          9m
kube-system   monitoring-influxdb-grafana-v3-spgl8                2/2     Running   0          8m
kube-system   node-problem-detector-v0.1-0lzvh                    1/1     Running   0          8m
kube-system   node-problem-detector-v0.1-5fw5i                    1/1     Running   0          8m
kube-system   node-problem-detector-v0.1-8sl7g                    1/1     Running   0          8m
kube-system   node-problem-detector-v0.1-jn5r2                    1/1     Running   0          8m
dvohra10@vm-kube-gce:~$
```

Figure 3-37. *Listing all the pods*

To list all the nodes, run the following command:

```
kubectl.sh get nodes
```

One controller node and three minion nodes are listed, as shown in Figure 3-38.

```
dvohra10@vm-kube-gce:~$ kubectl.sh get nodes
NAME                              STATUS                       AGE
kubernetes-master                 Ready,SchedulingDisabled     10m
kubernetes-minion-group-cg37      Ready                        9m
kubernetes-minion-group-v59e      Ready                        9m
kubernetes-minion-group-za76      Ready                        9m
dvohra10@vm-kube-gce:~$
```

Figure 3-38. *Listing the Kubernetes cluster nodes*

List all the namespaces with the following command:

```
kubectl.sh get namespaces
```

The two namespaces `default` and `kube-system` are listed, as shown in Figure 3-39.

```
dvohra10@vm-kube-gce:~$ kubectl.sh get namespaces
NAME          STATUS    AGE
default       Active    15m
kube-system   Active    15m
dvohra10@vm-kube-gce:~$
```

Figure 3-39. *Listing the namespaces*

The CPU utilization of the VM instance may be displayed in the console as shown in Figure 3-40.

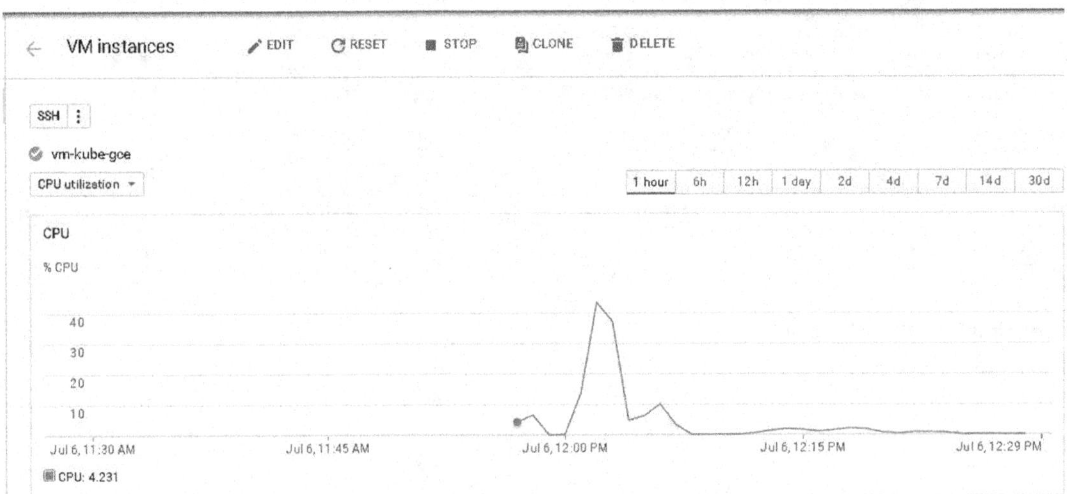

Figure 3-40. *Displaying the graph for CPU Utilization*

The VM Instances also lists the controller and minion instances started for the Kubernetes cluster, as shown in Figure 3-41.

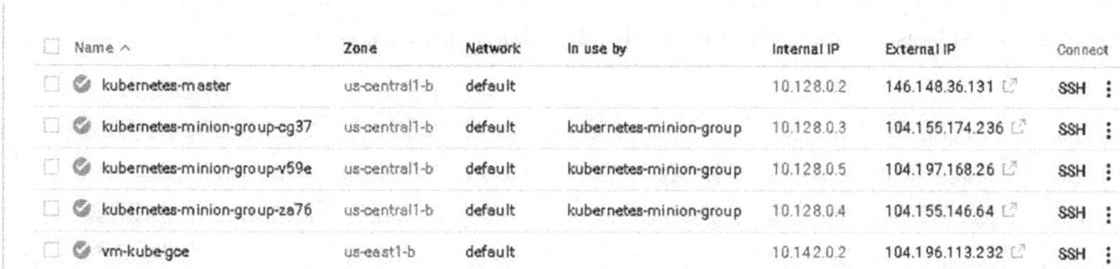

Name ^	Zone	Network	In use by	Internal IP	External IP	Connect
kubernetes-master	us-central1-b	default		10.128.0.2	146.148.36.131	SSH
kubernetes-minion-group-cg37	us-central1-b	default	kubernetes-minion-group	10.128.0.3	104.155.174.236	SSH
kubernetes-minion-group-v59e	us-central1-b	default	kubernetes-minion-group	10.128.0.5	104.197.168.26	SSH
kubernetes-minion-group-za76	us-central1-b	default	kubernetes-minion-group	10.128.0.4	104.155.146.64	SSH
vm-kube-gce	us-east1-b	default		10.142.0.2	104.196.113.232	SSH

***Figure 3-41.** Listing the Kubernetes controller and minion instances*

Select the External IP Addresses tab to list all the external IP addresses, including those for the controller and minion instances, as shown in Figure 3-42.

***Figure 3-42.** Listing the external IP addresses*

Creating a Kubernetes Application and Service

In this section we'll create a sample Kubernetes application using the Docker image `nginx`. The following command creates a deployment for the `nginx` Docker image.

```
kubectl.sh --namespace=default run nginx --image=nginx -replicas=3 -port=80
```

Deployment "`nginx`" is created as shown in Figure 3-43.

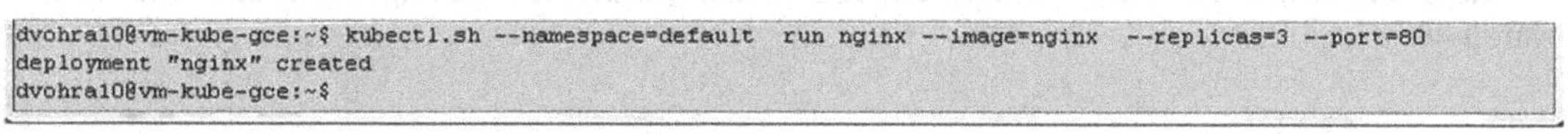

***Figure 3-43.** Creating a deployment `nginx`*

List the pods, including the nodes the pods run on:

```
kubectl.sh get pods -o wide
```

The three pod replicas including the node are listed as shown in Figure 3-44.

```
dvohra10@vm-kube-gce:~$ kubectl.sh --namespace=default  run nginx --image=nginx  --replicas=3 --port=80
deployment "nginx" created
dvohra10@vm-kube-gce:~$ kubectl.sh get pods -o wide
NAME                     READY     STATUS    RESTARTS   AGE       IP           NODE
nginx-2032906785-a9b1g   1/1       Running   0          27s       10.244.1.5   kubernetes-minion-group-za76
nginx-2032906785-lyig2   1/1       Running   0          27s       10.244.3.4   kubernetes-minion-group-v59e
nginx-2032906785-qnc10   1/1       Running   0          27s       10.244.2.5   kubernetes-minion-group-cg37
dvohra10@vm-kube-gce:~$
```

Figure 3-44. *Listing the node replicas*

List the deployments:

```
kubectl.sh get deployments
```

Create a service for type LoadBalancer:

```
kubectl.sh expose deployment nginx --port=80 --type=LoadBalancer
```

List the services:

```
kubectl.sh get services
```

The output from the preceding commands is shown in Figure 3-45.

```
dvohra10@vm-kube-gce:~$ kubectl.sh get deployments
NAME      DESIRED   CURRENT   UP-TO-DATE   AVAILABLE   AGE
nginx     3         3         3            3           59s
dvohra10@vm-kube-gce:~$ kubectl.sh expose deployment nginx --port=80 --type=LoadBalancer
service "nginx" exposed
dvohra10@vm-kube-gce:~$ kubectl.sh get services
NAME         CLUSTER-IP     EXTERNAL-IP   PORT(S)   AGE
kubernetes   10.0.0.1       <none>        443/TCP   31m
nginx        10.0.213.175   <pending>     80/TCP    10s
dvohra10@vm-kube-gce:~$
```

Figure 3-45. *Listing the deployments and services*

Describe the nginx service:

```
kubectl.sh describe svc nginx
```

The service description, including the service endpoints and any error messages, is listed as shown in Figure 3-46.

```
dvohra10@vm-kube-gce:~$ kubectl.sh describe svc nginx
Name:                   nginx
Namespace:              default
Labels:                 run=nginx
Selector:               run=nginx
Type:                   LoadBalancer
IP:                     10.0.213.175
Port:                   <unset> 80/TCP
NodePort:               <unset> 31882/TCP
Endpoints:              10.244.1.5:80,10.244.2.5:80,10.244.3.4:80
Session Affinity:       None
Events:
  FirstSeen     LastSeen        Count   From                    SubobjectPath   Type            Reason          M
essage
  ---------     --------        -----   ----                    -------------   --------        ------          -
------
  1m            36s             5       {service-controller }                   Normal          CreatingLoadBala
ncer            Creating load balancer
  1m            36s             5       {service-controller }                   Warning         CreatingLoadBala
ncerFailed      Error creating load balancer (will retry): Failed to create load balancer for service default/ng
inx: failed to ensure static IP : error creating gce static IP address: googleapi: Error 403: Quota 'STATIC_ADDR
ESSES' exceeded. Limit: 1.0, quotaExceeded


dvohra10@vm-kube-gce:~$
```

Figure 3-46. *Listing the service description*

Next, we shall invoke a service endpoint. Copy a service endpoint as shown in Figure 3-47.

```
dvohra10@vm-kube-gce:~$ kubectl.sh describe svc nginx
Name:                   nginx
Namespace:              default
Labels:                 run=nginx
Selector:               run=nginx
Type:                   LoadBalancer
IP:                     10.0.213.175
Port:                   <unset> 80/TCP
NodePort:               <unset> 31882/TCP
Endpoints:              10.244.1.5:80,10.244.2.5:80,10.244.3.4:80
Session Affinity:       None
Events:
  FirstSeen     LastSeen        Count   From                    SubobjectPath   Type            Reason          M
essage
```

Figure 3-47. *Obtaining a service endpoint*

Invoke the service endpoint with `curl`.

```
curl 10.244.1.5
```

The HTML markup for the service is listed as shown in Figure 3-48.

```
dvohra10@vm-kube-gce:~$ curl 10.244.1.5
<!DOCTYPE html>
<html>
<head>
<title>Welcome to nginx!</title>
<style>
    body {
        width: 35em;
        margin: 0 auto;
        font-family: Tahoma, Verdana, Arial, sans-serif;
    }
</style>
</head>
<body>
<h1>Welcome to nginx!</h1>
<p>If you see this page, the nginx web server is successfully installed and
working. Further configuration is required.</p>

<p>For online documentation and support please refer to
<a href="http://nginx.org/">nginx.org</a>.<br/>
Commercial support is available at
<a href="http://nginx.com/">nginx.com</a>.</p>

<p><em>Thank you for using nginx.</em></p>
</body>
</html>
dvohra10@vm-kube-gce:~$
```

Figure 3-48. *Invoking a service endpoint*

Similarly, invoke another service endpoint:

```
curl 10.244.2.5
```

The second service endpoint is also invoked, as shown in Figure 3-49.

```
dvohra10@vm-kube-gce:~$ curl 10.244.2.5
<!DOCTYPE html>
<html>
<head>
<title>Welcome to nginx!</title>
<style>
    body {
        width: 35em;
        margin: 0 auto;
        font-family: Tahoma, Verdana, Arial, sans-serif;
    }
</style>
</head>
<body>
<h1>Welcome to nginx!</h1>
<p>If you see this page, the nginx web server is successfully installed and
working. Further configuration is required.</p>

<p>For online documentation and support please refer to
<a href="http://nginx.org/">nginx.org</a>.<br/>
Commercial support is available at
<a href="http://nginx.com/">nginx.com</a>.</p>

<p><em>Thank you for using nginx.</em></p>
</body>
</html>
dvohra10@vm-kube-gce:~$
```

Figure 3-49. *Invoking another service endpoint*

Stopping the Cluster

To stop the VM instances, select the instances in the console and click Stop as shown in Figure 3-50.

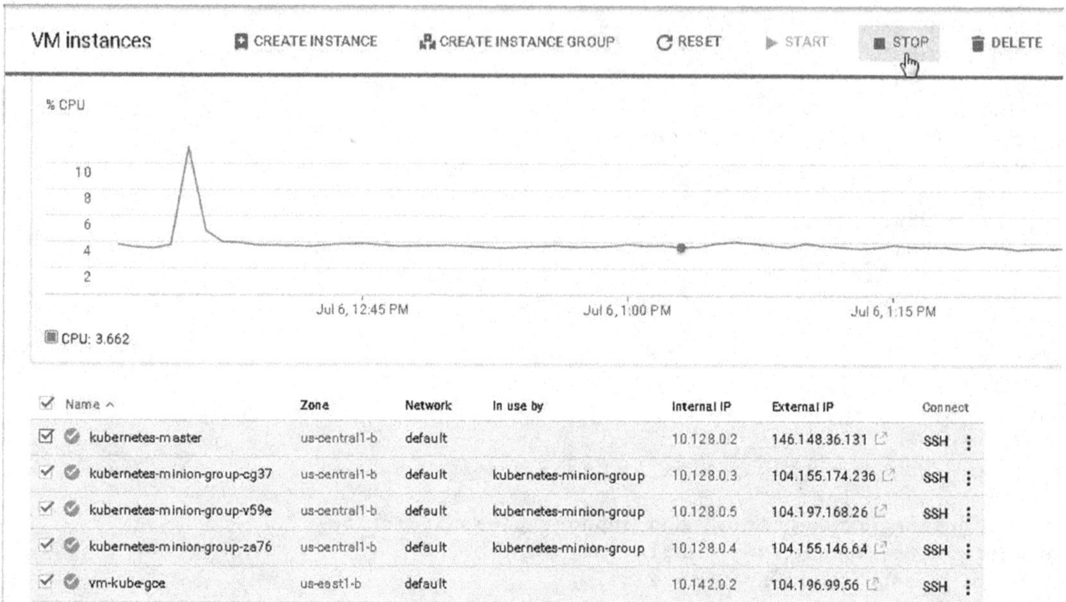

Figure 3-50. *Selecting all nodes and clicking on Stop*

In the verification dialog, choose Stop as shown in Figure 3-51.

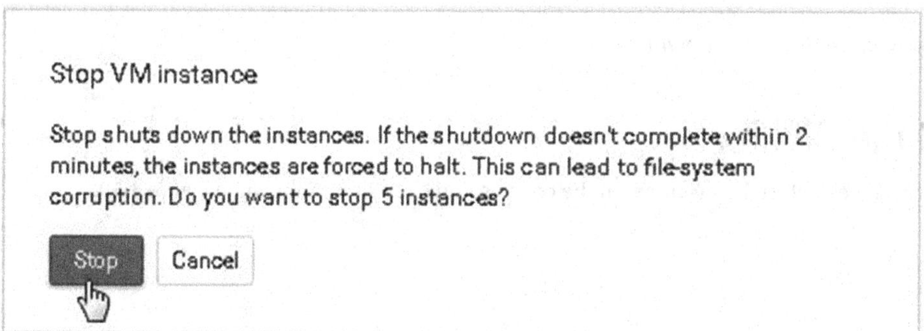

Figure 3-51. *Stopping a VM instance*

The VM Instances are stopped as shown in Figure 3-52.

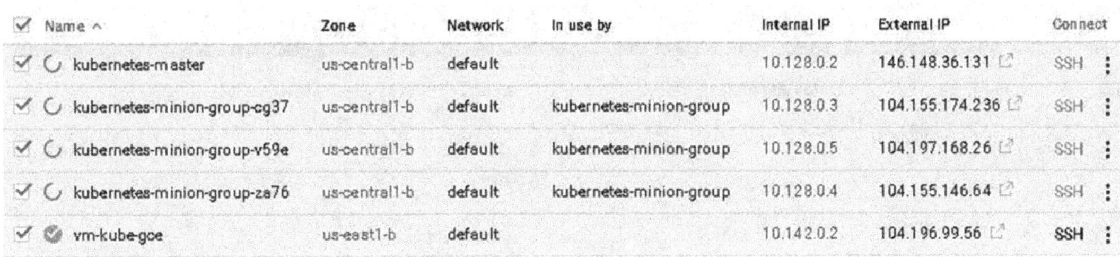

Name
Zone
Network
In use by
Internal IP
External IP
Connect
kubernetes-master
us-central1-b
default
10.128.0.2
146.148.36.131
SSH
kubernetes-minion-group-cg37
us-central1-b
default
kubernetes-minion-group
10.128.0.3
104.155.174.236
SSH
kubernetes-minion-group-v59e
us-central1-b
default
kubernetes-minion-group
10.128.0.5
104.197.168.26
SSH
kubernetes-minion-group-za76
us-central1-b
default
kubernetes-minion-group
10.128.0.4
104.155.146.64
SSH
vm-kube-gce
us-east1-b
default
10.142.0.2
104.196.99.56
SSH

Figure 3-52. *VM instances being stopped*

Using Kubernetes with Google Container Engine

Google Container Engine is Google-managed service for Kubernetes clusters running Docker containers. Google Container Engine is a component of the Google Cloud Platform. It fully manages and orchestrates the cluster, including scheduling the containers and running them based on specified CPU and memory requirements. Google Container Engine provides the flexibility of using a private, public, or hybrid cloud, and it provides auto-scaling of clusters based on resource utilization. Google services such as Google Cloud Logging, Google Cloud VPN, Google Container Registry, and Google accounts and role permissions are integrated with Google Container Engine.

To run a Kubernetes application on Google Container Engine, the following procedure is used.

1. Create a Billing Account if one does not already exist.
2. Create a Project on Google Cloud Platform.
3. Enable Permissions for the project.
4. Enable Billing for the project.
5. Enable Google Compute Engine and Google Container Engine APIs.
6. Create a Google Container Cluster.
7. Connect to the Google Cloud Shell.
8. Configure `kubectl` for the container cluster.
9. Test the Kubernetes cluster.

We have discussed steps 1 through 5 earlier in this chapter, except that Google Container Engine API also needs to be enabled. In this section we shall discuss step 6 onward. We have used a project called `Kube-GKE`.

Creating a Google Container Cluster

Select the project in which a Google Container Cluster is to be created on the Google Container Engine at URL `https://console.cloud.google.com/kubernetes`. A URL similar to `https://console.cloud.google.com/kubernetes/list?project=kubernete-gke` is invoked. In Container Clusters, click on Create a Container Cluster as shown in Figure 3-53.

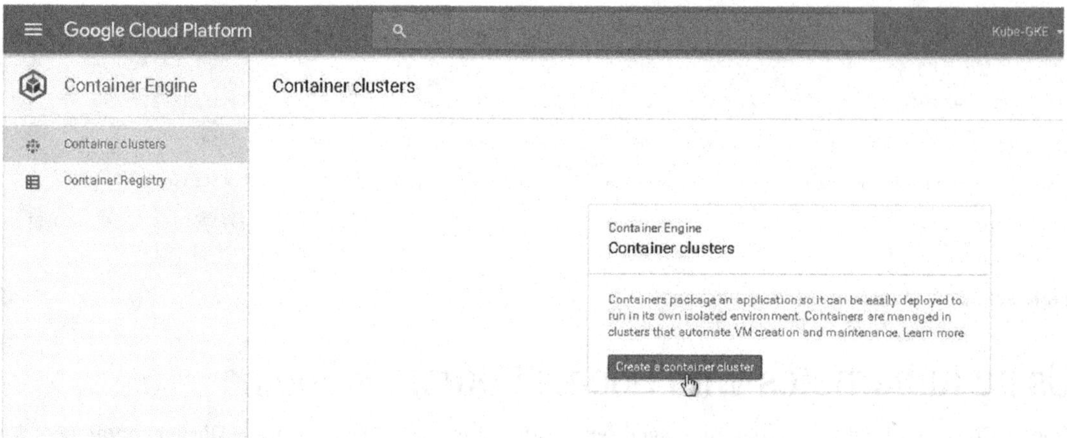

Figure 3-53. *Clicking on Create a Container Cluster*

The URL `https://console.cloud.google.com/kubernetes/add?project=kubernetes-gke` (the URL could be slightly different) is invoked, and an input form is displayed to specify the container cluster detail as shown in Figure 3-54.

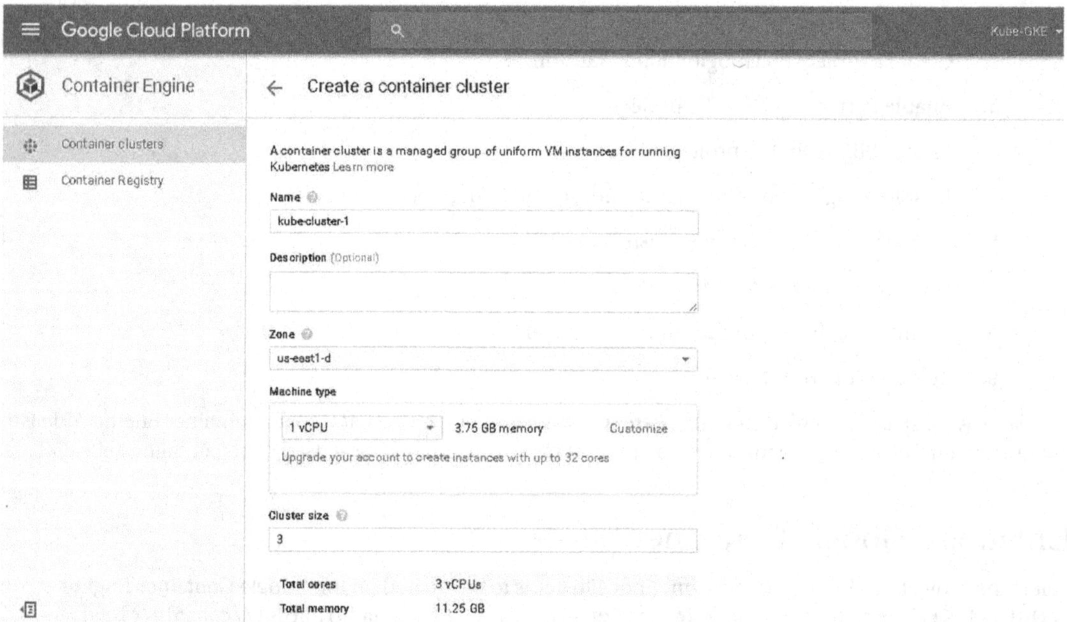

Figure 3-54. *Specifying Cluster Name, Zone and Machine Type*

Specify a cluster name or keep the default cluster name (for example kube-cluster-1). Select a Zone, for example us-east1-d. Select the Machine type as the number of CPU cores. For example, select 1 vCPU, which has 3.75 GB memory. Specify a Cluster size, 3 for example. Keep the "default" setting for Subnetwork. Optionally select Logging and monitoring options and click on Create as shown in Figure 3-55.

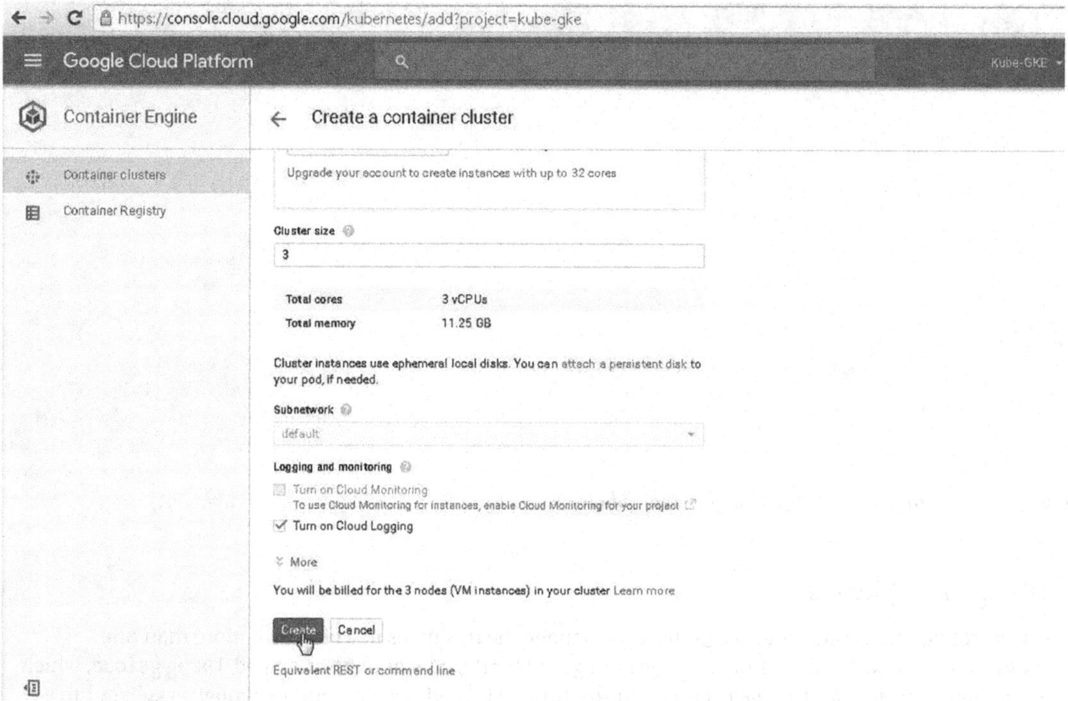

***Figure 3-55.** Creating a container cluster*

A container cluster is created as shown in Figure 3-56.

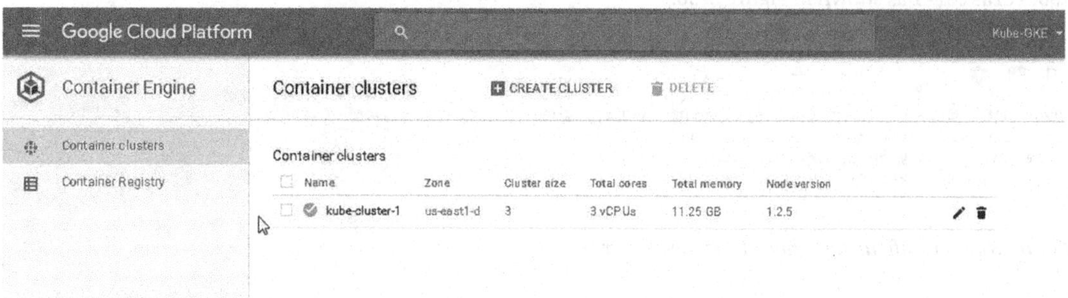

***Figure 3-56.** Container cluster kube-cluster-1*

Connecting to the Google Cloud Shell

To connect to the Google Cloud Shell, click the ➤ icon as shown in Figure 3-57. A message `Welcome to Cloud Shell` and the command prompt for the Cloud Shell should be displayed.

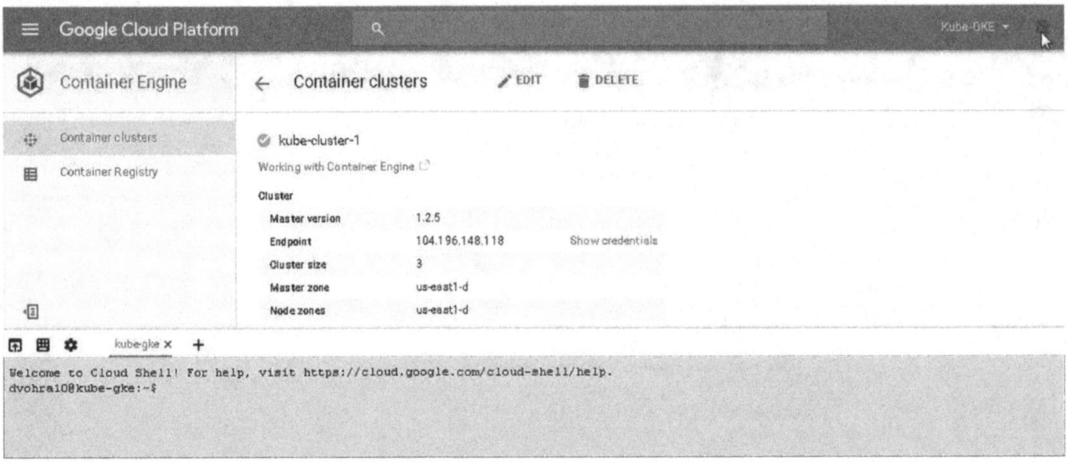

Figure 3-57. Connecting to the Google Cloud Shell

Configuring kubectl

The `kubectl` command-line interface is used to manage the resources in a cluster. If more than one container clusters exist, `kubectl` needs to be configured for the cluster to be managed. Using `gcloud`, which is a command-line tool for Google Cloud Platform, run the following command to configure `kubectl` to a specific cluster. The zone must be included in the command, with the `-zone` option:

```
gcloud container clusters get-credentials  kube-cluster-1 --zone us-east1-d
```

The cluster endpoint and auth data are fetched, and a `kubeconfig` entry is generated for `kube-cluster-1` as shown in Figure 3-58.

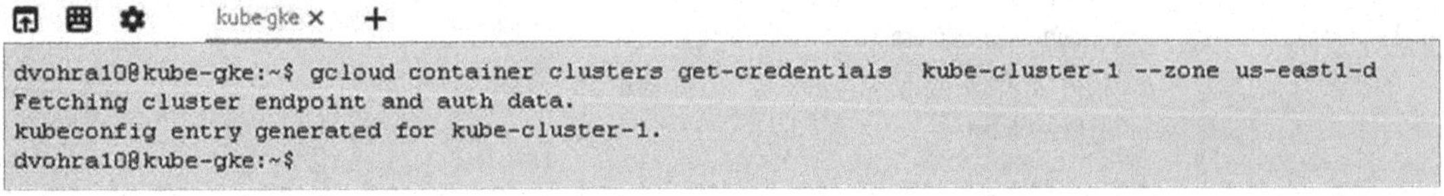

Figure 3-58. Configuring `kubectl` for the cluster

Testing the Kubernetes Cluster

The cluster info may be listed with the following command:

```
kubectl cluster-info
```

As shown in Figure 3-59, the Kubernetes master and other cluster components are running.

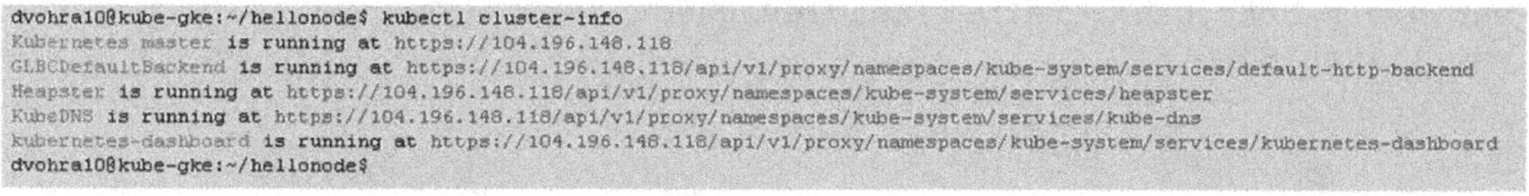

dvohra10@kube-gke:~/hellonode$ kubectl cluster-info
Kubernetes master is running at https://104.196.148.118
GLBCDefaultBackend is running at https://104.196.148.118/api/v1/proxy/namespaces/kube-system/services/default-http-backend
Heapster is running at https://104.196.148.118/api/v1/proxy/namespaces/kube-system/services/heapster
KubeDNS is running at https://104.196.148.118/api/v1/proxy/namespaces/kube-system/services/kube-dns
kubernetes-dashboard is running at https://104.196.148.118/api/v1/proxy/namespaces/kube-system/services/kubernetes-dashboard
dvohra10@kube-gke:~/hellonode$

Figure 3-59. *Listing cluster info*

Next, we shall create a Node application to test the cluster. Create a folder called `hellonode` (or some other folder name). In the `hellonode` folder create a Node file `server.js` with the `vi` editor as shown in Figure 3-60.

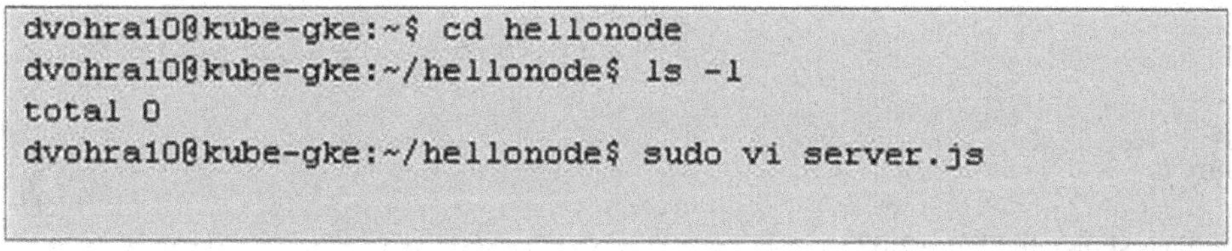

dvohra10@kube-gke:~$ cd hellonode
dvohra10@kube-gke:~/hellonode$ ls -l
total 0
dvohra10@kube-gke:~/hellonode$ sudo vi server.js

Figure 3-60. *Creating a Node script server.js*

The Node script `server.js` responds to any request with the response `Hello World!`.

```
var http = require('http');
var handleRequest = function (request, response) {
  response.writeHead(200);
  response.end('Hello World!');
};
var www = http.createServer(handleRequest);
www.listen(8080);
```

The `server.js` is shown in a `vi` editor in Figure 3-61.

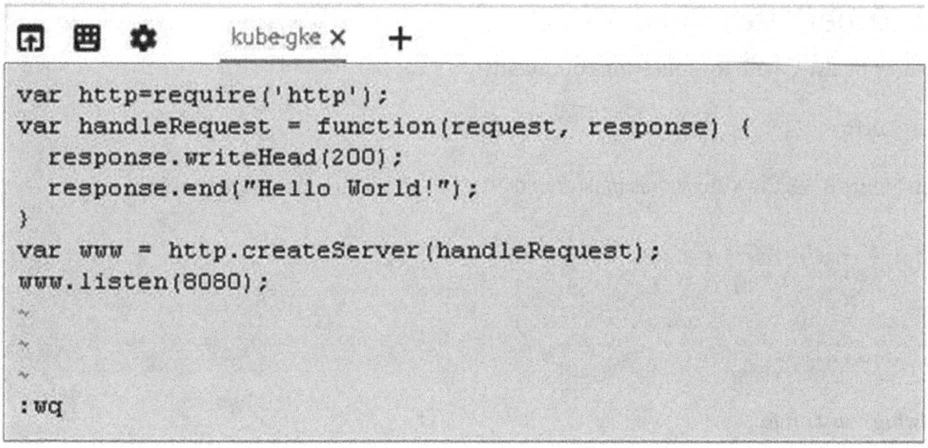
kube-gke
var http=require('http');
var handleRequest = function(request, response) {
response.writeHead(200);
response.end("Hello World!");
}
var www = http.createServer(handleRequest);
www.listen(8080);
:wq

Figure 3-61. *The server.js Node Script*

Next, create a Docker file, also in the `hellonode` folder, to describe the Docker image to build including the port the application listens on.

```
FROM node:4.4
EXPOSE 8080
COPY server.js .
CMD node server.js
```

The Docker file is shown in Figure 3-62.

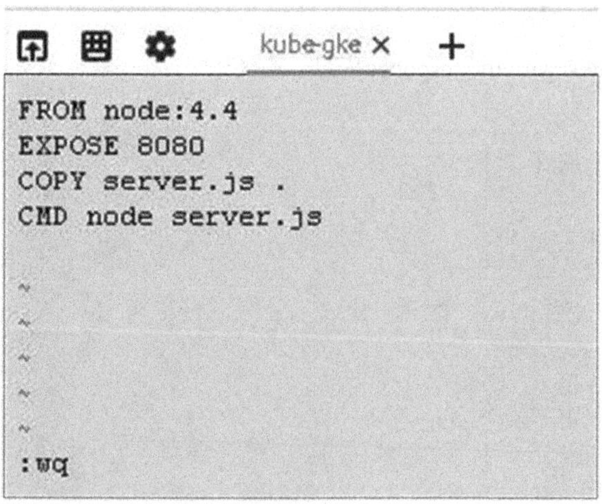
kube-gke
FROM node:4.4
EXPOSE 8080
COPY server.js .
CMD node server.js
:wq

Figure 3-62. *The Dockerfile*

Next, build a Docker image using the `docker build` command.

```
docker build -t gcr.io/kube-gke/hello-node:v1.
```

The Docker image `node:4.4`, from which the image `gcr.io/kube-gke/hello-node:v1` is built, is pulled as shown in Figure 3-63.

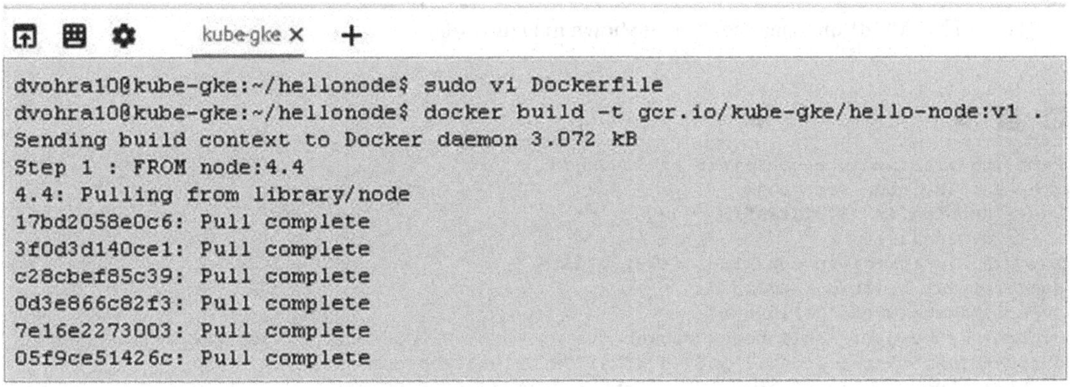

kube-gke
dvohra10@kube-gke:~/hellonode$ sudo vi Dockerfile
dvohra10@kube-gke:~/hellonode$ docker build -t gcr.io/kube-gke/hello-node:v1 .
Sending build context to Docker daemon 3.072 kB
Step 1 : FROM node:4.4
4.4: Pulling from library/node
17bd2058e0c6: Pull complete
3f0d3d140ce1: Pull complete
c28cbef85c39: Pull complete
0d3e866c82f3: Pull complete
7e16e2273003: Pull complete
05f9ce51426c: Pull complete

Figure 3-63. *Running the `docker build` command*

The Docker image is built as shown in Figure 3-64.

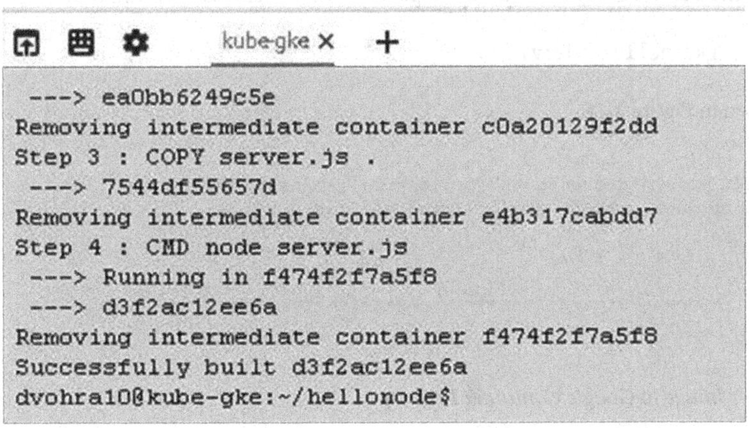

kube-gke
---> ea0bb6249c5e
Removing intermediate container c0a20129f2dd
Step 3 : COPY server.js .
---> 7544df55657d
Removing intermediate container e4b317cabdd7
Step 4 : CMD node server.js
---> Running in f474f2f7a5f8
---> d3f2ac12ee6a
Removing intermediate container f474f2f7a5f8
Successfully built d3f2ac12ee6a
dvohra10@kube-gke:~/hellonode$

Figure 3-64. *The Docker image built*

Run the Docker image with the `docker run` command:

```
docker run -d -p 8080:8080 gcr.io/kube-gke/hello-node:v1
```

Invoke the application with the `curl` command:

```
curl http://localhost:8080
```

The `Hello World!` message is output as shown in Figure 3-65.

kube-gke
Removing intermediate container e4b317cabdd7
Step 4 : CMD node server.js
---> Running in f474f2f7a5f8
---> d3f2ac12ee6a
Removing intermediate container f474f2f7a5f8
Successfully built d3f2ac12ee6a
dvohra10@kube-gke:~/hellonode$
dvohra10@kube-gke:~/hellonode$ docker run -d -p 8080:8080 gcr.io/kube-gke/hello-node:v1
d5f534401bbc5a5afe5e7f5401212c644d08574177786b919331eb44dcb54a76d
dvohra10@kube-gke:~/hellonode$ curl http://localhost:8080
Hello World!dvohra10@kube-gke:~/hellonode$

Figure 3-65. *Running and Invoking the hello-node Application*

The Docker image may be pushed to the Google Container Registry, with the following command:

```
gcloud docker push gcr.io/kube-gke/hello-node:v1
```

The command output is shown in Figure 3-66.

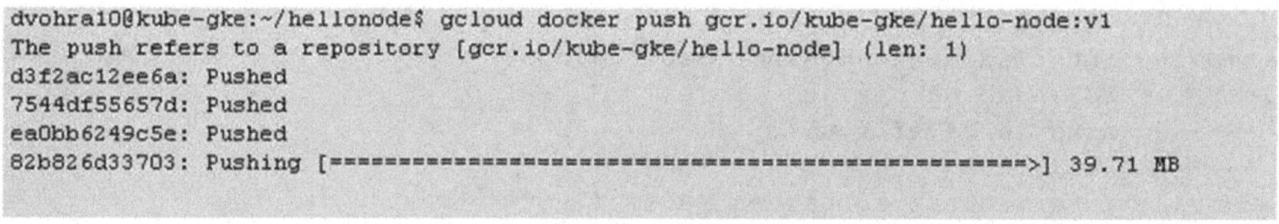
dvohra10@kube-gke:~/hellonode$ gcloud docker push gcr.io/kube-gke/hello-node:v1
The push refers to a repository [gcr.io/kube-gke/hello-node] (len: 1)
d3f2ac12ee6a: Pushed
7544df55657d: Pushed
ea0bb6249c5e: Pushed
82b826d33703: Pushing [==>] 39.71 MB

Figure 3-66. *Uploading the Docker Image to Google Container Registry*

The Docker image is pushed to the repository as shown in Figure 3-67.

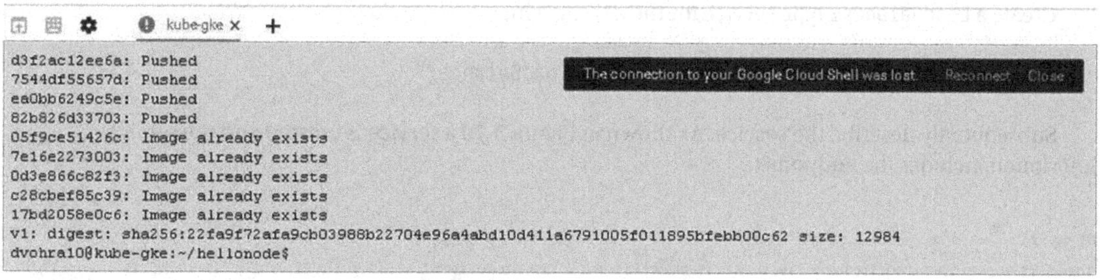

```
d3f2ac12ee6a: Pushed
7544df55657d: Pushed
ea0bb6249c5e: Pushed
82b826d33703: Pushed
05f9ce51426c: Image already exists
7e16e2273003: Image already exists
0d3e866c82f3: Image already exists
c28cbef85c39: Image already exists
17bd2058e0c6: Image already exists
v1: digest: sha256:22fa9f72afa9cb03988b22704e96a4abd10d411a6791005f011895bfebb00c62 size: 12984
dvohra10@kube-gke:~/hellonode$
```

Figure 3-67. *Docker Image Uploaded to Repository*

The repository image may be used to create a Kubernetes deployment and Service. Run the `kubectl run` command to create a deployment:

```
kubectl run hello-node --image=gcr.io/kube-gke/hello-node:v1 --port=8080
```

The deployment `hello-node` is created as shown in Figure 3-68.

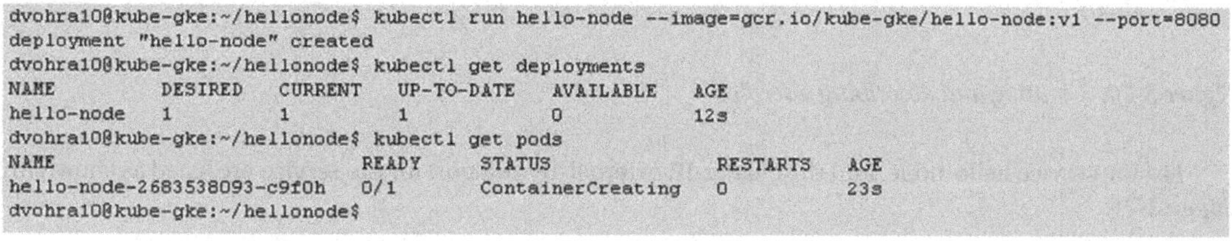

```
dvohra10@kube-gke:~/hellonode$ kubectl run hello-node --image=gcr.io/kube-gke/hello-node:v1 --port=8080
deployment "hello-node" created
dvohra10@kube-gke:~/hellonode$ kubectl get deployments
NAME         DESIRED   CURRENT   UP-TO-DATE   AVAILABLE   AGE
hello-node   1         1         1            0           12s
dvohra10@kube-gke:~/hellonode$ kubectl get pods
NAME                          READY     STATUS              RESTARTS   AGE
hello-node-2683538093-c9f0h   0/1       ContainerCreating   0          23s
dvohra10@kube-gke:~/hellonode$
```

Figure 3-68. *Creating a deployment*

List the deployments and the pods as shown in Figure 3-69, and you'll see a `hello-node` deployment and a `hello-node` prefixed pod listed.

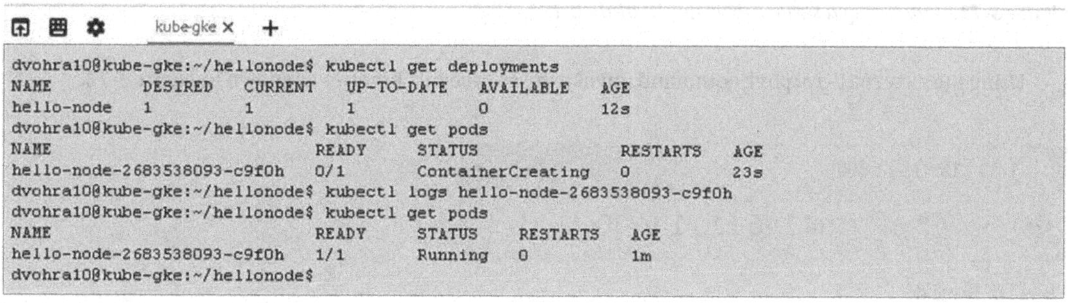

```
dvohra10@kube-gke:~/hellonode$ kubectl get deployments
NAME         DESIRED   CURRENT   UP-TO-DATE   AVAILABLE   AGE
hello-node   1         1         1            0           12s
dvohra10@kube-gke:~/hellonode$ kubectl get pods
NAME                          READY     STATUS              RESTARTS   AGE
hello-node-2683538093-c9f0h   0/1       ContainerCreating   0          23s
dvohra10@kube-gke:~/hellonode$ kubectl logs hello-node-2683538093-c9f0h
dvohra10@kube-gke:~/hellonode$ kubectl get pods
NAME                          READY     STATUS    RESTARTS   AGE
hello-node-2683538093-c9f0h   1/1       Running   0          1m
dvohra10@kube-gke:~/hellonode$
```

Figure 3-69. *Listing the deployment and pod*

Create a LoadBalancer type service for the deployment:

```
kubectl expose deployment hello-node --type="LoadBalancer"
```

Subsequently describe the service. As shown in Figure 3-70 a service is created and the service description includes the endpoints.

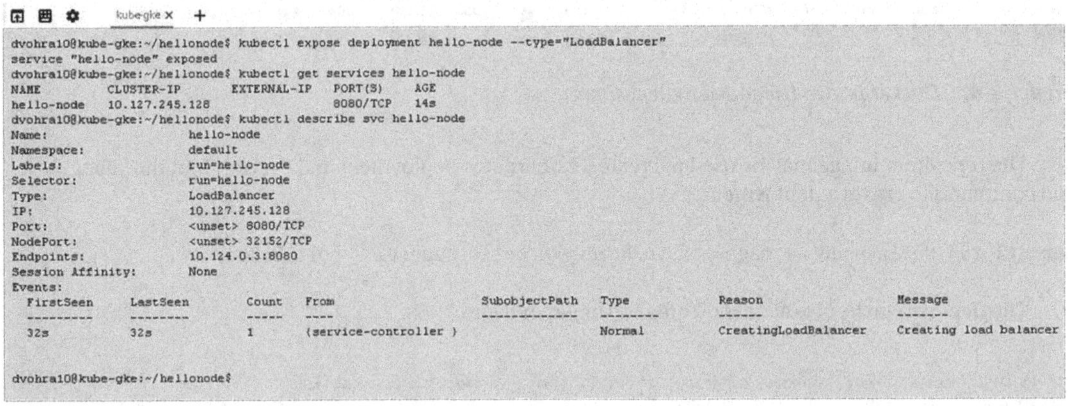

Figure 3-70. *Creating and describing a service*

List the service hello-node, and the cluster-IP, external-IP, and port for the service are listed as shown in Figure 3-71.

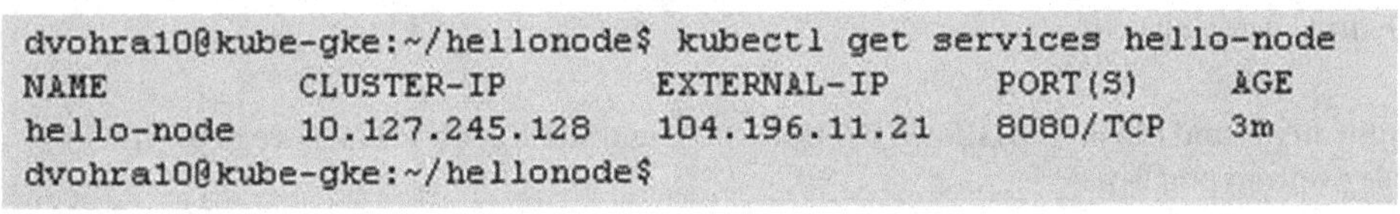

Figure 3-71. *Obtaining a service external IP and port*

Using the external-ip:port command, invoke the service in a browser as shown in Figure 3-72.

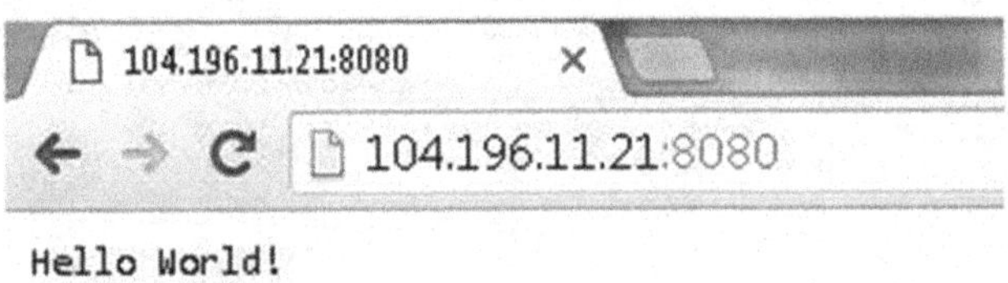

Figure 3-72. *Invoking the service in a browser*

The service and deployment can now be deleted:

```
kubectl delete service,deployment hello-node
```

The service `hello-node` and the deployment `hello-node` are deleted, as shown in Figure 3-73.

```
dvohra10@kube-gke:~/hellonode$ kubectl get services hello-node
NAME         CLUSTER-IP       EXTERNAL-IP     PORT(S)    AGE
hello-node   10.127.245.128   104.196.11.21   8080/TCP   14m
dvohra10@kube-gke:~/hellonode$ kubectl delete service,deployment hello-node
service "hello-node" deleted
deployment "hello-node" deleted
```

Figure 3-73. *Deleting deployment and service*

The container cluster `kube-cluster-1` may also be deleted:

```
gcloud container clusters delete kube-cluster-1 --zone us-east1-d
```

Specify Y to delete the cluster when prompted, as shown in Figure 3-74.

```
dvohra10@kube-gke:~/hellonode$
dvohra10@kube-gke:~/hellonode$ gcloud container clusters delete kube-cluster-1 --zone us-east1-d
The following clusters will be deleted.
 - [kube-cluster-1] in [us-east1-d]

Do you want to continue (Y/n)?  Y
```

Figure 3-74. *Deleting the cluster*

Summary

In this chapter we discussed creating a Kubernetes cluster on Google Cloud Platform. The procedure was as follows: First, create a project in the Google Cloud Platform console. Subsequently, enable the Compute Engine API and permissions. Create and connect to a virtual machine instance and reserve a static address. Create a Kubernetes cluster and test the cluster by creating an application. We also discussed using Kubernetes on Google Container Engine. In the next chapter we shall discuss using multiple zones for a Kubernetes cluster.

PART II

Administration and Configuration

CHAPTER 4

Using Multiple Zones

High availability in a Kubernetes cluster is implemented using various parameters. High availability of master controllers would provision multiple master controllers. High availability of etcd would provision multiple etcd nodes. High availability of public DNS would provision multiple public DNSes. In a cloud-native application, availability of a cluster would depend on the availability of the region or zone in which the nodes are run. AWS provides various high-availability design patterns, such as Multi Region Architecture, Multiple Cloud Providers, DNS Load Balancing Tier, and Multiple Availability Zones. In this chapter we will discuss the Multiple Availability Zones design pattern as implemented by Kubernetes. Amazon AWS availability zones are distinct physical locations with independent power, network and security and insulated from failures in other availability zones. Availability zones within the same region have low latency network connectivity between them.

Problem

If all the nodes in a Kubernetes cluster are run in the same cloud provider zone (as defined by Amazon AWS and Google Cloud Platform), failure of a single zone would bring down the whole Kubernetes cluster as shown in Figure 4-1.

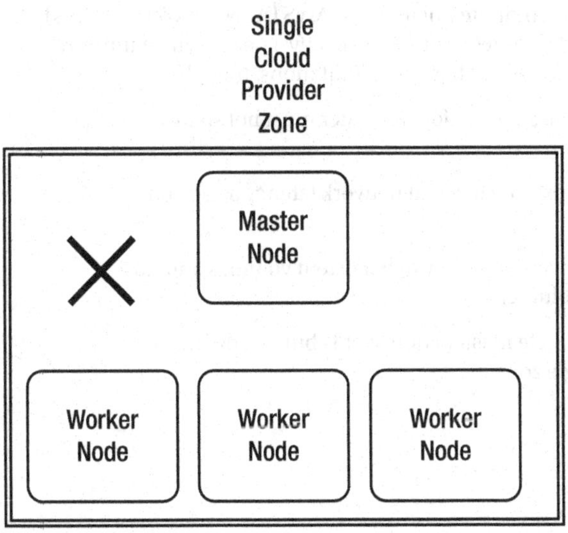

***Figure 4-1.** In a single-zone cluster no fault tolerance is provided*

D. Vohra, *Kubernetes Management Design Patterns*, DOI 10.1007/978-1-4842-2598-1_4

Solution

Starting with Kubernetes 1.2, a cluster may be provisioned across multiple cloud provider zones. The pods managed by a replication controller or service are spread across zones so that the failure of a single zone does not affect the availability of the replication controller or service in other zones, as shown in Figure 4-2.

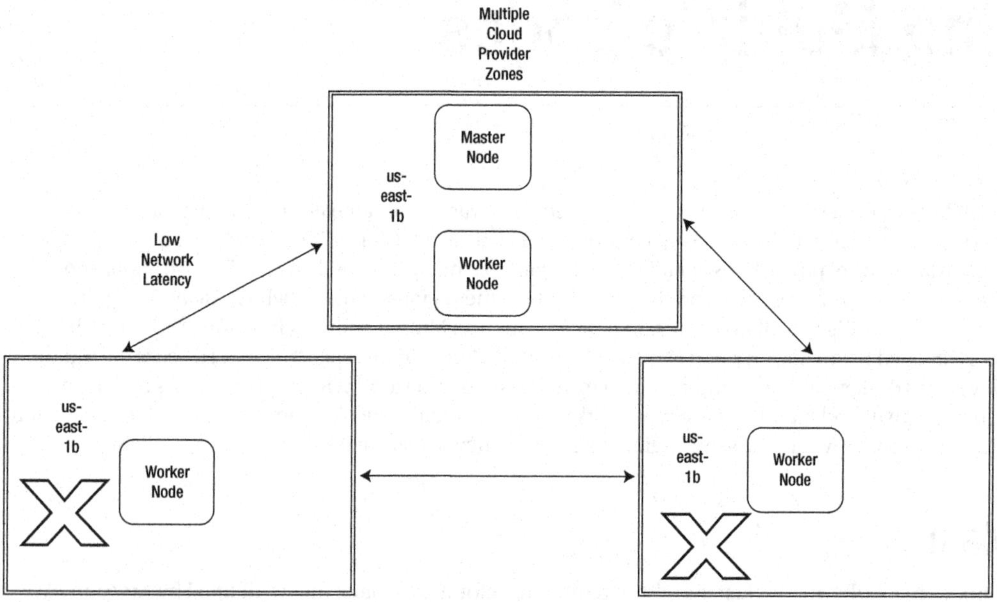

Figure 4-2. *Failure of two zones in a three-zone cluster does not cause the whole cluster to fail*

Zones are supported only with the GCE (Google Compute Engine) and AWS (Amazon Web Services) cloud providers. AWS refers to the zones as “availability zones.” Pods that specify a persistent volume are placed in the same zone as the volume. The support for zones has some limitations, though:

- The multiple zones must be located in the same region. A cluster must not span multiple cloud formations.
- The zones are assumed to be in close proximity to avoid network latency as no zone-aware routing is provided.
- Pod-volume collocation in the same zone applies only to persistent volumes and not to other types of volumes such as EBS volume.
- The nodes are in multiple zones, but a single master controller is built by default and the master controller is located in a single zone.

Overview

In this chapter we shall create a multiple-zone AWS CloudFormation on CoreOS. We shall also demonstrate volume-zone affinity for a persistent volume on a multiple-zone cluster with AWS cloud provider. The steps we'll take are as follows:

- Setting the environment
- Initializing a CloudFormation
- Configuring cluster.yaml for multiple zones
- Launching the CloudFormation
- Configuring External DNS
- Running a Kubernetes Application
- Using Multiple Zones on AWS

Setting the Environment

You'll find the details of creating a Kubernetes cluster on a CoreOS AWS CloudFormation in Chapter 2. We only need to start a single EC2 instance to launch the CloudFormation from. Create an EC2 instance using the Amazon Linux AMI, which has the AWS CLI installed by default; the AWS CLI is used to initialize and launch a CloudFormation. Obtain the Public IP address of the EC2 instance from the EC2 console. SSH log in into the EC2 instance:

```
ssh -i "docker.pem"  ec2-user@184.73.19.214
```

The Amazon Linux AMI command prompt is displayed.

Because we will be launching an AWS CloudFormation for a Kubernetes cluster, the CloudFormation stack name must be one that is not already used. If a CloudFormation stack name is already used an error similar to the following (Figure 4-3) is generated.

```
[ec2-user@ip-10-0-0-126 coreos-cluster]$ kube-aws up
Creating AWS resources. This should take around 5 minutes.
Error: Error creating cluster: AlreadyExistsException: Stack [kubernetes-coreos-
cluster] already exists
        status code: 400, request id: e1729893-4861-11e6-9731-6334ac51fa70
```

Figure 4-3. *Stack already exists error*

To find whether a CloudFormation stack name can be used, click Services ➤ CloudFormation as shown in Figure 4-4.

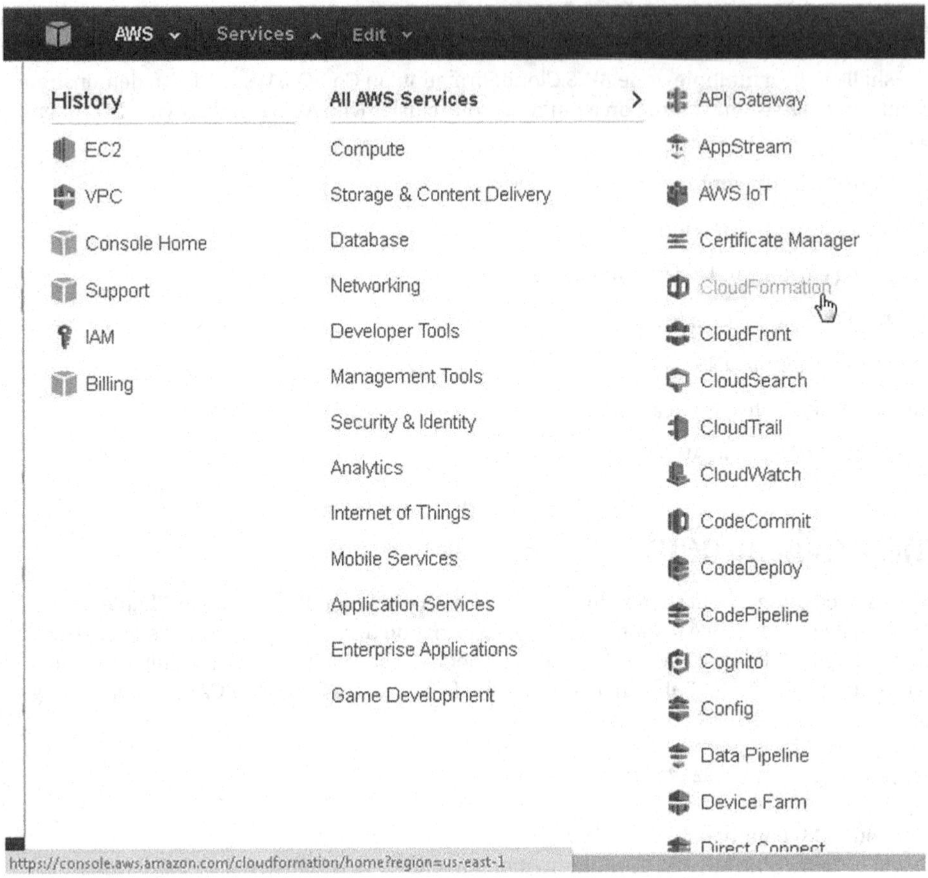

Figure 4-4. Choosing Services ➤ CloudFormation

The stacks are listed as shown in Figure 4-5. A stack name the same as one that is listed cannot be used to create a new stack.

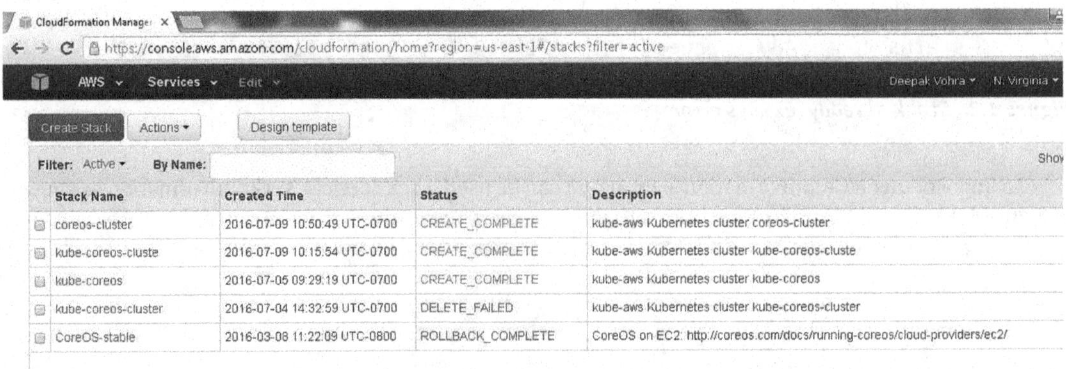

https://console.aws.amazon.com/cloudformation/home?region=us-east-1#/stacks?filter=active
AWS
Services
Edit
Deepak Vohra
N. Virginia
Create Stack
Actions
Design template
Filter: Active
By Name:
Stack Name
Created Time
Status
Description
coreos-cluster
2016-07-09 10:50:49 UTC-0700
CREATE_COMPLETE
kube-aws Kubernetes cluster coreos-cluster
kube-coreos-cluste
2016-07-09 10:15:54 UTC-0700
CREATE_COMPLETE
kube-aws Kubernetes cluster kube-coreos-cluste
kube-coreos
2016-07-05 09:29:19 UTC-0700
CREATE_COMPLETE
kube-aws Kubernetes cluster kube-coreos
kube-coreos-cluster
2016-07-04 14:32:59 UTC-0700
DELETE_FAILED
kube-aws Kubernetes cluster kube-coreos-cluster
CoreOS-stable
2016-03-08 11:22:09 UTC-0800
ROLLBACK_COMPLETE
CoreOS on EC2: http://coreos.com/docs/running-coreos/cloud-providers/ec2/

Figure 4-5. Listing the `CloudFormation` stacks

Initializing a CloudFormation

Initializing a `CloudFormation` stack is discussed in detail in Chapter 2. The procedure to create an AWS `CloudFormation` is as follows:

1. Install `Kube-aws` (required to be installed only once for the Amazon Linux instance).
2. Set up Cluster Parameters, such as creating an EC2 key pair (`kubernetes-coreos`), KMS key, and External DNS name (`oramagsearch.com`).
3. Create an Asset Directory for a cluster `CloudFormation`.
4. Initialize the cluster `CloudFormation`.
5. Render the Contents of the asset directory.

A typical command to create an EC2 key pair is as follows:

```
aws ec2 create-key-pair --key-name kubernetes-coreos --query 'KeyMaterial' --output text >
kubernetes-coreos.pem
chmod 400 kubernetes-coreos.pem
```

The command to create a KMS key is as follows:

```
aws kms --region=us-east-1 create-key --description="kube-aws assets"
```

Copy the `KeyMetadata.Arn` string and use it to initialize a `CloudFormation` stack; for example, a cluster called `kubernetes-coreos-cluster` with the asset directory `kube-coreos-cluster` is initialized as follows:

```
 mkdir kube-coreos-cluster
cd kube-coreos-cluster
kube-aws init --cluster-name=kubernetes-coreos-cluster --external-dns-name=ORAMAGSEARCH.COM
--region=us-east-1  --availability-zone=us-east-1c  --key-name=kubernetes-coreos  --kms-key-
arn="arn:aws:kms:us-east-1:xxxxxxxxxx:key/xxxxxxxxxxxxxxxxxxx"
```

The command to render the contents of an assets directory is as follows:

```
kube-aws render
```

Configuring cluster.yaml for Multiple Zones

By default a single zone is used to launch a CloudFormation. Next, we shall customize the `CloudFormation` to configure multiple zones. Open the `cluster.yaml` file in a `vi` editor:

```
sudo vi cluster.yaml
```

The region to provision the CloudFormation is set to `us-east-1` as specified in the `kube-aws init` command. The `availabilityZone` is set to `us-east-1c` also as specified in the `kube-aws init` command. For a multi-availability zone or multiple zones, comment out the `availabilityZone`. By default `workerCount`, which specifies the number of worker nodes to create, is set to 1. To demonstrate a multiple-zone cluster, the worker nodes must be set to at least the number of zones to configure. Set `workerCount` to 6 as shown in Figure 4-6.

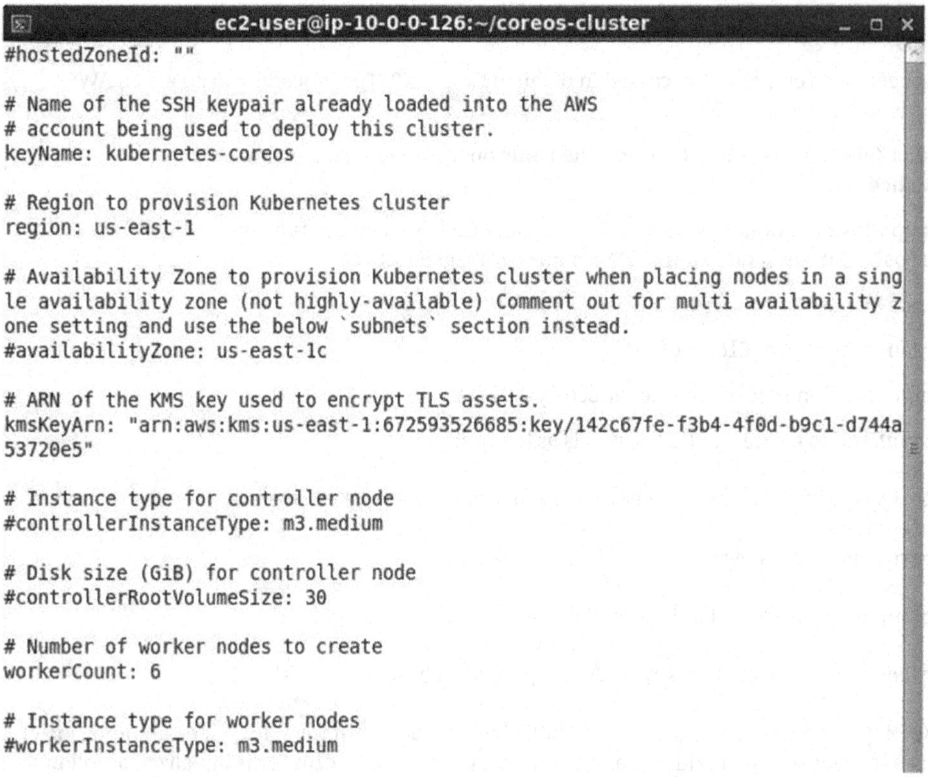

ec2-user@ip-10-0-0-126:~/coreos-cluster
#hostedZoneId: ""
Name of the SSH keypair already loaded into the AWS
account being used to deploy this cluster.
keyName: kubernetes-coreos
Region to provision Kubernetes cluster
region: us-east-1
Availability Zone to provision Kubernetes cluster when placing nodes in a sing
le availability zone (not highly-available) Comment out for multi availability z
one setting and use the below `subnets` section instead.
#availabilityZone: us-east-1c
ARN of the KMS key used to encrypt TLS assets.
kmsKeyArn: "arn:aws:kms:us-east-1:672593526685:key/142c67fe-f3b4-4f0d-b9c1-d744a
53720e5"
Instance type for controller node
#controllerInstanceType: m3.medium
Disk size (GiB) for controller node
#controllerRootVolumeSize: 30
Number of worker nodes to create
workerCount: 6
Instance type for worker nodes
#workerInstanceType: m3.medium

Figure 4-6. *Setting* `workerCount` *to 6*

`Cluster.yaml` is configured for a single availability zone by default, and the `instanceCIDR` setting specifies the CIDR for the Kubernetes subnet. For multiple availability zones the `instanceCIDR` must be commented out, as we need to configure multiple subnets in `cluster.yaml`. In setting subnets, specify the Kubernetes subnets and their CIDRs and availability zones. The objective of high availability is that failure of a single zone does not result in interruption in the service. At least two subnets must be specified for high availability of zones. Each subnet is specified as an `availabilityZone` setting and an `instanceCIDR` setting. The availability zones that could be specified must be available to create subnets. If an availability zone is not available, an error such as the one shown in Figure 4-7 is generated when the CloudFormation is launched.

```
[ec2-user@ip-10-0-0-126 coreos-cluster]$ kube-aws up
Creating AWS resources. This should take around 5 minutes.
Error: Error creating cluster: Stack creation failed: CREATE_FAILED : The follow
ing resource(s) failed to create: [Subnet1, RouteTable, IAMRoleWorker, Subnet0,
SecurityGroupController, Subnet2, SecurityGroupWorker, IAMRoleController, VPCGat
ewayAttachment].

Printing the most recent failed stack events:
CREATE_FAILED AWS::CloudFormation::Stack kubernetes-coreos-cluster The following
 resource(s) failed to create: [Subnet1, RouteTable, IAMRoleWorker, Subnet0, Sec
urityGroupController, Subnet2, SecurityGroupWorker, IAMRoleController, VPCGatewa
yAttachment].
CREATE_FAILED AWS::EC2::Subnet Subnet0 Value (us-east-1a) for parameter availabi
lityZone is invalid. Subnets can currently only be created in the following avai
lability zones: us-east-1c, us-east-1e, us-east-1b, us-east-1d.
[ec2-user@ip-10-0-0-126 coreos-cluster]$
```

Figure 4-7. *Error message when subnet could not be created because an availability zone is not valid*

Run the following command to find the availability zones.

```
ec2-availability-zones -aws-access-key <access key id> --aws-secret-key <access key>
```

The availability zones are listed as shown in Figure 4-8. As indicated, the availability zones for the us-east-1 region are `us-east-1a`, `us-east-1b`, `us-east-1c`, `us-east-1d`, and `us-east-1e`.

```
[ec2-user@ip-10-0-0-126 ~]$ ec2-describe-availability-zones --aws-access-key AKI
AJGFCP4HUFH4453FA --aws-secret-key 7BaiUETep3zPYrhrzKYpBdwkwVV16BTT+pt2/EXF
AVAILABILITYZONE        us-east-1a      available       us-east-1
AVAILABILITYZONE        us-east-1b      available       us-east-1
AVAILABILITYZONE        us-east-1c      available       us-east-1
AVAILABILITYZONE        us-east-1d      available       us-east-1
AVAILABILITYZONE        us-east-1e      available       us-east-1
[ec2-user@ip-10-0-0-126 ~]$
```

Figure 4-8. *Listing the availability zones*

The `instanceCIDR` block specifies the range of IPs to be used. Block sizes must be between a /16 netmask and a /28 netmask. Specify three subnets for three different availability zones:

```
subnets:
  -
   availabilityZone: us-east-1b
   instanceCIDR: "10.0.0.0/24"
  -
   availabilityZone: us-east-1c
   instanceCIDR: "10.0.0.0/24"
  -
   availabilityZone: us-east-1d
   instanceCIDR: "10.0.0.0/24"
```

Another setting that needs to be commented out is `controllerIP`. The `controllerIP` setting specifies the controller in a Kubernetes subnet. With two or more subnets the controller is placed in the first subnet, and `controllerIP` must be included in the `instanceCIDR` of the first subnet. If no instanceCIDRs in the configured Subnets contain the `controllerIP` and controllerIP is not commented out, the error shown in Figure 4-9 is generated.

```
[ec2-user@ip-10-0-0-126 coreos-cluster]$ kube-aws up
Error: Failed to read cluster config: file cluster.yaml: invalid cluster: No ins
tanceCIDRs in Subnets ([10.0.1.0/24 10.0.2.0/24 10.0.3.0/24]) contain controller
IP (10.0.0.50)
[ec2-user@ip-10-0-0-126 coreos-cluster]$
```

Figure 4-9. *Error message when no instanceCIDRs in the configured subnets contain the* `controllerIP`

The `subnets` must be formatted as shown in Figure 4-10.

```
ec2-user@ip-10-0-0-126:~/coreos-cluster
# ID of existing route table in existing VPC to attach subnet to. Leave blank to
 use the VPC's main route table.
# routeTableId:

# CIDR for Kubernetes VPC. If vpcId is specified, must match the CIDR of existin
g vpc.
# vpcCIDR: "10.0.0.0/16"

# CIDR for Kubernetes subnet when placing nodes in a single availability zone (n
ot highly-available) Leave commented out for multi availability zone setting and
 use the below `subnets` section instead.
# instanceCIDR: "10.0.0.0/24"

# Kubernetes subnets with their CIDRs and availability zones. Differentiating av
ailability zone for 2 or more subnets result in high-availability (failures of a
 single availability zone won't result in immediate downtimes)
subnets:
  -
     availabilityZone: us-east-1b
     instanceCIDR: "10.0.0.0/24"
  -
     availabilityZone: us-east-1c
     instanceCIDR: "10.0.1.0/24"
  -
     availabilityZone: us-east-1d
     instanceCIDR: "10.0.2.0/24"
# IP Address for the controller in Kubernetes subnet. When we have 2 or more sub
nets, the controller is placed in the first subnet and controllerIP must be incl
uded in the instanceCIDR of the first subnet. This convention will change once w
e have H/A controllers
# controllerIP: 10.0.0.50

:wq
```

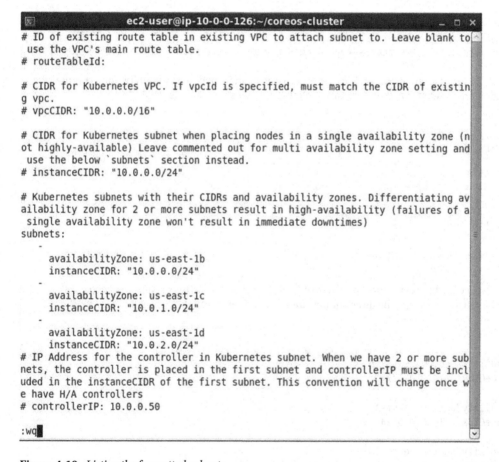

Figure 4-10. *Listing the formatted subnets*

Launching the CloudFormation

After we modify `cluster.yaml`, the CloudFormation stack must be validated. Validate the `CloudFormation` stack with the following command:

```
kube-aws validate
```

Launch the CloudFormation stack.

```
kube-aws up
```

The AWS resources, such as the EC2 instances, scaling groups, and launch configurations are created, and the CloudFormation is launched as shown in Figure 4-11.

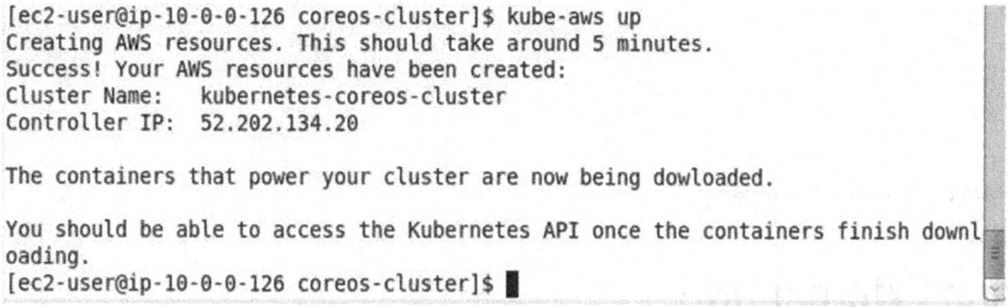

[ec2-user@ip-10-0-0-126 coreos-cluster]$ kube-aws up
Creating AWS resources. This should take around 5 minutes.
Success! Your AWS resources have been created:
Cluster Name: kubernetes-coreos-cluster
Controller IP: 52.202.134.20
The containers that power your cluster are now being dowloaded.
You should be able to access the Kubernetes API once the containers finish downl
oading.
[ec2-user@ip-10-0-0-126 coreos-cluster]$

Figure 4-11. *Launching the CloudFormation*

The status of the CloudFormation may be found with the following command:

```
kube-aws status
```

The controller IP is listed, as shown in Figure 4-12.

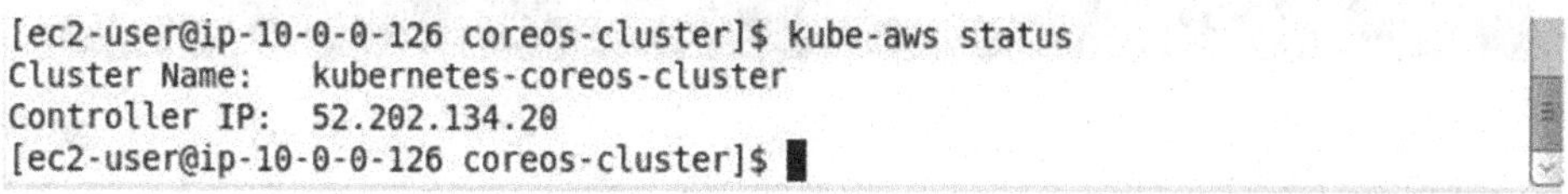

[ec2-user@ip-10-0-0-126 coreos-cluster]$ kube-aws status
Cluster Name: kubernetes-coreos-cluster
Controller IP: 52.202.134.20
[ec2-user@ip-10-0-0-126 coreos-cluster]$

Figure 4-12. *Finding the status of* `CloudFormation`

The EC2 instances launched by the CloudFormation stack are shown in Figure 4-13. As indicated in the Availability Zone column, two instances each are launched in the `us-east-1b`, `us-east-1c`, and `us-east-1d` zones. The single controller runs in zone `us-east-1b`.

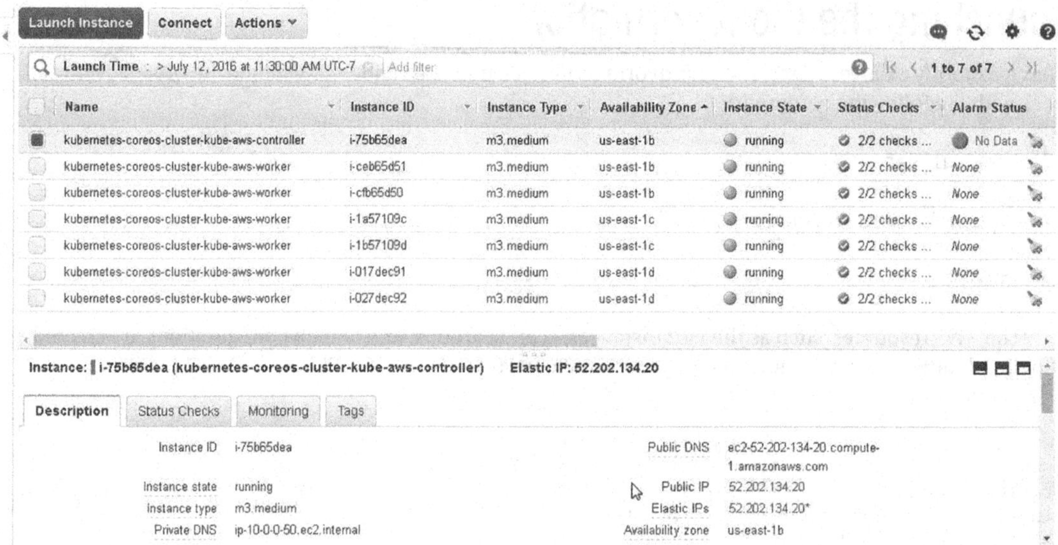

Figure 4-13. *Listing the formatted subnets*

Configuring External DNS

Configure the Public IP address of the controller instance in the Public DNS name for the `nosqlsearch.com` domain on the domain registrar. Add an A record for the Public IP of the controller instance as shown in Figure 4-14.

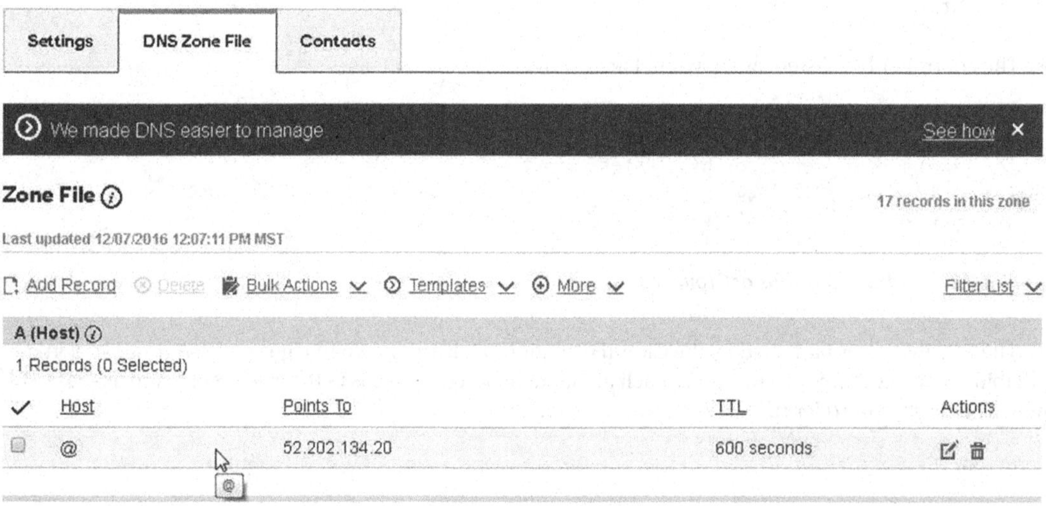

Figure 4-14. *Listing the formatted subnets*

Running a Kubernetes Application

Next, we shall test the Kubernetes cluster to confirm that pods in an application do get allocated across the nodes in the different zones. Connect to the controller instance:

```
ssh -i "kubernetes-coreos.pem" core@52.202.134.20
```

The controller instance is logged into as shown in Figure 4-15.

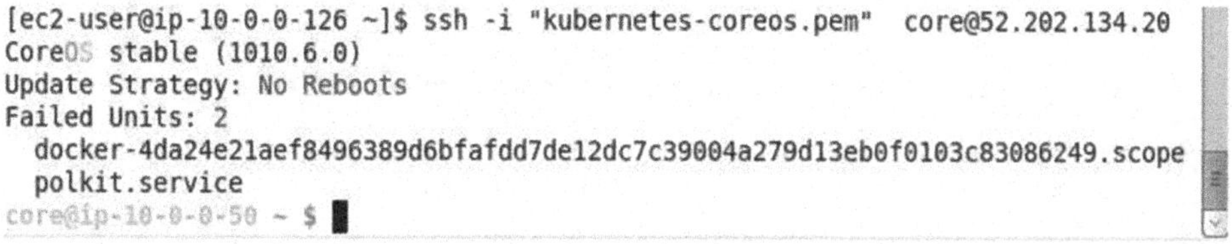

```
[ec2-user@ip-10-0-0-126 ~]$ ssh -i "kubernetes-coreos.pem"  core@52.202.134.20
CoreOS stable (1010.6.0)
Update Strategy: No Reboots
Failed Units: 2
  docker-4da24e21aef8496389d6bfafdd7de12dc7c39004a279d13eb0f0103c83086249.scope
  polkit.service
core@ip-10-0-0-50 ~ $
```

Figure 4-15. *SSH logging into the controller CoreOS instance*

Install the kubectl binaries and set permissions.

```
sudo wget https://storage.googleapis.com/kubernetes-release/release/v1.3.0/bin/linux/
amd64/./kubectl
sudo chmod +x ./kubectl
```

Kubectl binaries are installed. Move the kubectl binaries to /usr/local/bin/, which is in the path:

```
sudo mv ./kubectl /usr/local/bin/
```

List the nodes in the cluster:

```
./kubectl get nodes
```

The single master node and the six worker nodes are listed as shown in Figure 4-16.

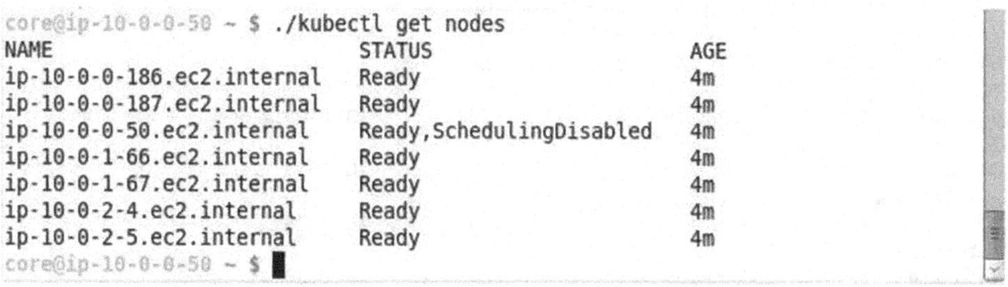

```
core@ip-10-0-0-50 ~ $ ./kubectl get nodes
NAME                         STATUS                     AGE
ip-10-0-0-186.ec2.internal   Ready                      4m
ip-10-0-0-187.ec2.internal   Ready                      4m
ip-10-0-0-50.ec2.internal    Ready,SchedulingDisabled   4m
ip-10-0-1-66.ec2.internal    Ready                      4m
ip-10-0-1-67.ec2.internal    Ready                      4m
ip-10-0-2-4.ec2.internal     Ready                      4m
ip-10-0-2-5.ec2.internal     Ready                      4m
core@ip-10-0-0-50 ~ $
```

Figure 4-16. *Listing the nodes in the Kubernetes cluster*

Run the nginx Docker image to create six pod replicas:

```
kubectl run nginx --image=nginx --replicas=6 --port=80
```

Subsequently, list the pods:

```
kubectl get pods -o wide
```

The nginx deployment is created and the pods are listed. Initially the pods may be listed as not ready, as indicated by the READY column value of 0/1 and STATUS column value of ContainerCreating in Figure 4-17.

```
core@ip-10-0-0-50 ~ $ ./kubectl run nginx --image=nginx --replicas=6 --port=80
deployment "nginx" created
core@ip-10-0-0-50 ~ $ ./kubectl get pods -o wide
NAME                     READY     STATUS              RESTARTS   AGE       IP
     NODE
nginx-198147104-1oi0n    0/1       ContainerCreating   0          13s       <none
>     ip-10-0-1-66.ec2.internal
nginx-198147104-co4o0    0/1       ContainerCreating   0          13s       <none
>     ip-10-0-0-187.ec2.internal
nginx-198147104-gd3sd    0/1       ContainerCreating   0          13s       <none
>     ip-10-0-0-186.ec2.internal
nginx-198147104-jfpp7    0/1       ContainerCreating   0          13s       <none
>     ip-10-0-2-5.ec2.internal
nginx-198147104-mtcle    0/1       ContainerCreating   0          13s       <none
>     ip-10-0-1-67.ec2.internal
nginx-198147104-pbrsh    0/1       ContainerCreating   0          13s       <none
>     ip-10-0-2-5.ec2.internal
```

Figure 4-17. *Running the Kubernetes nginx application*

Run the kubectl get pods -o wide command again after a few more seconds (up to a minute) and all the pods should be running and ready as shown in Figure 4-18. As indicated in the NODE column, each of the six pods is running on a different node, which implies that the pods are spread across the zones in the cluster. A failure of a single zone will not affect the availability of the deployment.

```
core@ip-10-0-0-50 ~ $ ./kubectl get pods -o wide
NAME                     READY     STATUS    RESTARTS   AGE       IP          NOD
E
nginx-198147104-1oi0n    1/1       Running   0          54s       10.2.86.3   ip-
10-0-1-66.ec2.internal
nginx-198147104-co4o0    1/1       Running   0          54s       10.2.65.2   ip-
10-0-0-187.ec2.internal
nginx-198147104-gd3sd    1/1       Running   0          54s       10.2.39.2   ip-
10-0-0-186.ec2.internal
nginx-198147104-jfpp7    1/1       Running   0          54s       10.2.24.3   ip-
10-0-2-5.ec2.internal
nginx-198147104-mtcle    1/1       Running   0          54s       10.2.34.2   ip-
10-0-1-67.ec2.internal
nginx-198147104-pbrsh    1/1       Running   0          54s       10.2.24.2   ip-
10-0-2-5.ec2.internal
core@ip-10-0-0-50 ~ $
```

Figure 4-18. *All pods running and ready*

Using Multiple Zones on AWS

If a Kubernetes cluster is to be started with multi-zone capability, the `MULTIZONE` parameter must be set to `true`. Setting `MULTIZONE` to `true` does not automatically start nodes running in multiple zones; it only adds the capability to manage a multi-zone cluster. If cluster nodes are to be run in multiple zones, multiple sets of nodes must be started in separate zones using the same master controller as the first zone node set. When a node set is started in a zone-aware cluster, the nodes are labeled indicating the zone in which the nodes run.

First, start a multi-zone aware cluster using the AWS Kubernetes provider by setting `MULTIZONE=true`. Setting `KUBE_AWS_ZONE` to `true` creates the master controller node and all the minion nodes in the specified zone. The `NUM_NODES` value sets the number of nodes to create. Run the following command to start a cluster in zone `us-east-1c` with three nodes:

```
curl -sS https://get.k8s.io | MULTIZONE=true KUBERNETES_PROVIDER=aws KUBE_AWS_ZONE=us-east-
1c NUM_NODES=3 bash
```

Kubernetes binaries are downloaded with the `MULTIZONE` command, as shown in Figure 4-19.

```
[ec2-user@ip-10-0-0-126 ~]$ curl -sS https://get.k8s.io | MULTIZONE=true KUBERNE
TES_PROVIDER=aws KUBE_AWS_ZONE=us-east-1c NUM_NODES=3 bash
Downloading kubernetes release v1.3.0 to /home/ec2-user/kubernetes.tar.gz
--2016-07-12 16:24:03--  https://storage.googleapis.com/kubernetes-release/relea
se/v1.3.0/kubernetes.tar.gz
Resolving storage.googleapis.com (storage.googleapis.com)... 173.194.204.128, 26
07:f8b0:400d:c00::80
Connecting to storage.googleapis.com (storage.googleapis.com)|173.194.204.128|:4
43... connected.
HTTP request sent, awaiting response... 200 OK
Length: 1486828686 (1.4G) [application/x-tar]
Saving to: 'kubernetes.tar.gz'

kubernetes.tar.gz    13%[=>                        ] 195.03M  18.0MB/s    eta 66s
```

Figure 4-19. *Starting a multi-zone aware cluster*

A multi-zone Kubernetes cluster is started as shown in Figure 4-20. What is different about the cluster is that it is aware of multiple-zones.

```
Done, listing cluster services:

Kubernetes master is running at https://52.206.28.220
Elasticsearch is running at https://52.206.28.220/api/v1/proxy/namespaces/kube-s
ystem/services/elasticsearch-logging
Heapster is running at https://52.206.28.220/api/v1/proxy/namespaces/kube-system
/services/heapster
Kibana is running at https://52.206.28.220/api/v1/proxy/namespaces/kube-system/s
ervices/kibana-logging
KubeDNS is running at https://52.206.28.220/api/v1/proxy/namespaces/kube-system/
services/kube-dns
kubernetes-dashboard is running at https://52.206.28.220/api/v1/proxy/namespaces
/kube-system/services/kubernetes-dashboard
Grafana is running at https://52.206.28.220/api/v1/proxy/namespaces/kube-system/
services/monitoring-grafana
InfluxDB is running at https://52.206.28.220/api/v1/proxy/namespaces/kube-system
/services/monitoring-influxdb

To further debug and diagnose cluster problems, use 'kubectl cluster-info dump'.

Kubernetes binaries at /home/ec2-user/kubernetes/cluster/
You may want to add this directory to your PATH in $HOME/.profile
Installation successful!
[ec2-user@ip-10-0-0-126 ~]$
```

Figure 4-20. *Starting a multi-zone aware cluster*

List the nodes with `kubectl get nodes` as shown in Figure 4-21.

```
[ec2-user@ip-10-0-0-126 ~]$ kubectl get nodes
NAME                          STATUS    AGE
ip-172-20-0-239.ec2.internal  Ready     8m
ip-172-20-0-240.ec2.internal  Ready     8m
ip-172-20-0-241.ec2.internal  Ready     8m
[ec2-user@ip-10-0-0-126 ~]$
```

Figure 4-21. *Listing the nodes*

Next, list the nodes and include the labels to be listed as shown in Figure 4-22.

```
kubectl get nodes --show-labels
```

The labels include `failure-domain.beta.kubernetes.io/region` for the region and `failure-domain.beta.kubernetes.io/zone` for the zone.

```
[ec2-user@ip-10-0-0-126 ~]$ kubectl get nodes --show-labels
NAME                          STATUS    AGE       LABELS
ip-172-20-0-239.ec2.internal  Ready     8m        beta.kubernetes.io/arch=amd64
,beta.kubernetes.io/instance-type=t2.micro,beta.kubernetes.io/os=linux,failure-d
omain.beta.kubernetes.io/region=us-east-1,failure-domain.beta.kubernetes.io/zone
=us-east-1c,kubernetes.io/hostname=ip-172-20-0-239.ec2.internal
ip-172-20-0-240.ec2.internal  Ready     8m        beta.kubernetes.io/arch=amd64
,beta.kubernetes.io/instance-type=t2.micro,beta.kubernetes.io/os=linux,failure-d
omain.beta.kubernetes.io/region=us-east-1,failure-domain.beta.kubernetes.io/zone
=us-east-1c,kubernetes.io/hostname=ip-172-20-0-240.ec2.internal
ip-172-20-0-241.ec2.internal  Ready     8m        beta.kubernetes.io/arch=amd64
,beta.kubernetes.io/instance-type=t2.micro,beta.kubernetes.io/os=linux,failure-d
omain.beta.kubernetes.io/region=us-east-1,failure-domain.beta.kubernetes.io/zone
=us-east-1c,kubernetes.io/hostname=ip-172-20-0-241.ec2.internal
[ec2-user@ip-10-0-0-126 ~]$ 
```

Figure 4-22. *Listing the nodes including the labels*

As shown in the EC2 console in Figure 4-23, all the nodes are running in the same zone, `us-east-1c`. Why the same zone even though `MULTIZONE` is set to `true`? Because the setting makes the cluster multi-zone aware and not multi-zone to start with. We shall discuss subsequently adding node sets in other zones using the same master controller.

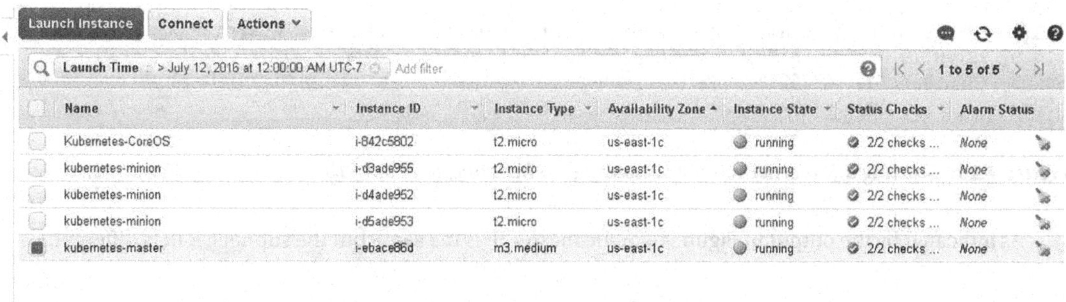

Figure 4-23. *All nodes in the same zone,* `us-east-1c`

Next, start another node set in a different zone but using the same master as the first node set. Obtain the Private IP of the master instance from the EC2 console. Run the following command in which the `MASTER_INTERNAL_IP` specifies the private IP of the master controller and `KUBE_SUBNET_CIDR` specifies the subnet CIDR. `KUBE_USE_EXISTING_MASTER` is set to `true`, implying that the existing master is to be used. The `KUBE_AWS_ZONE` is set to a different zone, `us-east-1b`.

```
KUBE_USE_EXISTING_MASTER=true MULTIZONE=true KUBERNETES_PROVIDER=aws KUBE_AWS_ZONE=us-east-
1b NUM_NODES=3 KUBE_SUBNET_CIDR=172.20.1.0/24 MASTER_INTERNAL_IP=172.20.0.9 kubernetes/
cluster/kube-up.sh
```

Another node set in a different zone, `us-east-1b`, is started as shown by the command output in Figure 4-24.

```
[ec2-user@ip-10-0-0-126 ~]$ KUBE_USE_EXISTING_MASTER=true MULTIZONE=true KUBERNE
TES_PROVIDER=aws KUBE_AWS_ZONE=us-east-1b NUM_NODES=3 KUBE_SUBNET_CIDR=172.20.1.
0/24 MASTER_INTERNAL_IP=172.20.0.9 kubernetes/cluster/kube-up.sh
Using subnet CIDR override: 172.20.1.0/24
... Starting cluster in us-east-1b using provider aws
... calling verify-prereqs
... calling kube-up
Starting cluster using os distro: jessie
Uploading to Amazon S3
+++ Staging server tars to S3 Storage: kubernetes-staging-3b2de58189ba7d2340027c
ecbbbe5060/devel
upload: ../../tmp/kubernetes.LOSThs/s3/bootstrap-script to s3://kubernetes-stagi
ng-3b2de58189ba7d2340027cecbbbe5060/devel/bootstrap-script
Uploaded server tars:
  SERVER_BINARY_TAR_URL: https://s3.amazonaws.com/kubernetes-staging-3b2de58189b
a7d2340027cecbbbe5060/devel/kubernetes-server-linux-amd64.tar.gz
  SALT_TAR_URL: https://s3.amazonaws.com/kubernetes-staging-3b2de58189ba7d234002
7cecbbbe5060/devel/kubernetes-salt.tar.gz
  BOOTSTRAP_SCRIPT_URL: https://s3.amazonaws.com/kubernetes-staging-3b2de58189ba
7d2340027cecbbbe5060/devel/bootstrap-script
INSTANCEPROFILE arn:aws:iam::672593526685:instance-profile/kubernetes-master   2
016-01-29T00:18:58Z      AIPAJR6YCBYPX27F553HI    kubernetes-master        /
ROLES    arn:aws:iam::672593526685:role/kubernetes-master         2016-01-29T00:18
:57Z     /        AROAIDG4HG76MJPGRWEEW    kubernetes-master
ASSUMEROLEPOLICYDOCUMENT        2012-10-17
STATEMENT        sts:AssumeRole  Allow
PRINCIPAL        ec2.amazonaws.com
INSTANCEPROFILE arn:aws:iam::672593526685:instance-profile/kubernetes-minion   2
016-01-29T00:19:00Z      AIPAJHMVQBPLMRBJE5MNO    kubernetes-minion        /
ROLES    arn:aws:iam::672593526685:role/kubernetes-minion         2016-01-29T00:18
:59Z     /        AROAJU44B2VYHK5GKUB3S    kubernetes-minion
```

Figure 4-24. *Starting a Kubernetes node cluster in another zone,* `us-east-1b`

As indicated by the output in Figure 4-25, the master IP is the same but the subnet CIDR is different.

```
ip-172-20-0-241.ec2.internal   Ready     40m
Validate output:
Using subnet CIDR override: 172.20.1.0/24
NAME                 STATUS    MESSAGE              ERROR
scheduler            Healthy   ok
controller-manager   Healthy   ok
etcd-1               Healthy   {"health": "true"}
etcd-0               Healthy   {"health": "true"}
Cluster validation succeeded
Done, listing cluster services:

Using subnet CIDR override: 172.20.1.0/24
Kubernetes master is running at https://52.206.28.220
Elasticsearch is running at https://52.206.28.220/api/v1/proxy/namespaces/kube-s
ystem/services/elasticsearch-logging
Heapster is running at https://52.206.28.220/api/v1/proxy/namespaces/kube-system
/services/heapster
Kibana is running at https://52.206.28.220/api/v1/proxy/namespaces/kube-system/s
ervices/kibana-logging
KubeDNS is running at https://52.206.28.220/api/v1/proxy/namespaces/kube-system/
services/kube-dns
kubernetes-dashboard is running at https://52.206.28.220/api/v1/proxy/namespaces
/kube-system/services/kubernetes-dashboard
Grafana is running at https://52.206.28.220/api/v1/proxy/namespaces/kube-system/
services/monitoring-grafana
InfluxDB is running at https://52.206.28.220/api/v1/proxy/namespaces/kube-system
/services/monitoring-influxdb

To further debug and diagnose cluster problems, use 'kubectl cluster-info dump'.

[ec2-user@ip-10-0-0-126 ~]$
```

***Figure 4-25.** The same master IP but a different subnet CIDR*

The EC2 console lists another set of nodes in a different zone, `us-east-1b` as shown in Figure 4-26. The cluster has only one master in zone `us-east-1c` but minions in different zones, `us-east-1b` and `us-east-1c`.

Launch Time : > July 12, 2016 at 12:00:00 AM UTC-7 | Add filter | 1 to 8 of 8

Name	Instance ID	Instance Type	Availability Zone	Instance State	Status Checks	Alarm Status
kubernetes-minion	i-c432da5b	t2.micro	us-east-1b	running	2/2 checks ...	None
kubernetes-minion	i-c532da5a	t2.micro	us-east-1b	running	2/2 checks ...	None
kubernetes-minion	i-c732da58	t2.micro	us-east-1b	running	2/2 checks ...	None
Kubernetes-CoreOS	i-842c5802	t2.micro	us-east-1c	running	2/2 checks ...	None
kubernetes-minion	i-d3ade955	t2.micro	us-east-1c	running	2/2 checks ...	None
kubernetes-minion	i-d4ade952	t2.micro	us-east-1c	running	2/2 checks ...	None
kubernetes-minion	i-d5ade953	t2.micro	us-east-1c	running	2/2 checks ...	None
kubernetes-master	i-ebace86d	m3.medium	us-east-1c	running	2/2 checks ...	None

***Figure 4-26.** The same master IP but a different subnet CIDR*

Listing the nodes displays six nodes, as shown in Figure 4-27.

```
[ec2-user@ip-10-0-0-126 ~]$ kubectl get nodes
NAME                          STATUS    AGE
ip-172-20-0-239.ec2.internal  Ready     56m
ip-172-20-0-240.ec2.internal  Ready     56m
ip-172-20-0-241.ec2.internal  Ready     56m
ip-172-20-1-96.ec2.internal   Ready     10m
ip-172-20-1-97.ec2.internal   Ready     10m
ip-172-20-1-98.ec2.internal   Ready     10m
[ec2-user@ip-10-0-0-126 ~]$
```

Figure 4-27. *Listing nodes in two different zones*

Listing the nodes including the labels displays six nodes, three in the `us-east-1c` zone and three in `us-east-1b`, as shown in Figure 4-28.

```
[ec2-user@ip-10-0-0-126 ~]$  kubectl get nodes --show-labels
NAME                          STATUS    AGE       LABELS
ip-172-20-0-239.ec2.internal  Ready     57m       beta.kubernetes.io/arch=amd64
,beta.kubernetes.io/instance-type=t2.micro,beta.kubernetes.io/os=linux,failure-d
omain.beta.kubernetes.io/region=us-east-1,failure-domain.beta.kubernetes.io/zone
=us-east-1c,kubernetes.io/hostname=ip-172-20-0-239.ec2.internal
ip-172-20-0-240.ec2.internal  Ready     57m       beta.kubernetes.io/arch=amd64
,beta.kubernetes.io/instance-type=t2.micro,beta.kubernetes.io/os=linux,failure-d
omain.beta.kubernetes.io/region=us-east-1,failure-domain.beta.kubernetes.io/zone
=us-east-1c,kubernetes.io/hostname=ip-172-20-0-240.ec2.internal
ip-172-20-0-241.ec2.internal  Ready     57m       beta.kubernetes.io/arch=amd64
,beta.kubernetes.io/instance-type=t2.micro,beta.kubernetes.io/os=linux,failure-d
omain.beta.kubernetes.io/region=us-east-1,failure-domain.beta.kubernetes.io/zone
=us-east-1c,kubernetes.io/hostname=ip-172-20-0-241.ec2.internal
ip-172-20-1-96.ec2.internal   Ready     11m       beta.kubernetes.io/arch=amd64
,beta.kubernetes.io/instance-type=t2.micro,beta.kubernetes.io/os=linux,failure-d
omain.beta.kubernetes.io/region=us-east-1,failure-domain.beta.kubernetes.io/zone
=us-east-1b,kubernetes.io/hostname=ip-172-20-1-96.ec2.internal
ip-172-20-1-97.ec2.internal   Ready     11m       beta.kubernetes.io/arch=amd64
,beta.kubernetes.io/instance-type=t2.micro,beta.kubernetes.io/os=linux,failure-d
omain.beta.kubernetes.io/region=us-east-1,failure-domain.beta.kubernetes.io/zone
=us-east-1b,kubernetes.io/hostname=ip-172-20-1-97.ec2.internal
ip-172-20-1-98.ec2.internal   Ready     11m       beta.kubernetes.io/arch=amd64
,beta.kubernetes.io/instance-type=t2.micro,beta.kubernetes.io/os=linux,failure-d
omain.beta.kubernetes.io/region=us-east-1,failure-domain.beta.kubernetes.io/zone
=us-east-1b,kubernetes.io/hostname=ip-172-20-1-98.ec2.internal
[ec2-user@ip-10-0-0-126 ~]$
```

Figure 4-28. *Listing nodes in two zones including labels*

Launch another node set in the `us-east-1d` zone using the same master node. Specify a different subnet CIDR for the `us-east-1d` zone.

```
KUBE_USE_EXISTING_MASTER=true MULTIZONE=true KUBERNETES_PROVIDER=aws KUBE_AWS_ZONE=us-east-
1d NUM_NODES=3 KUBE_SUBNET_CIDR=172.20.2.0/24 MASTER_INTERNAL_IP=172.20.0.9 kubernetes/
cluster/kube-up.sh
```

A node set is started in the us-east-1d zone as shown in Figure 4-29.

```
[ec2-user@ip-10-0-0-126 ~]$ KUBE_USE_EXISTING_MASTER=true MULTIZONE=true KUBERNE
TES_PROVIDER=aws KUBE_AWS_ZONE=us-east-1d NUM_NODES=3 KUBE_SUBNET_CIDR=172.20.2.
0/24 MASTER_INTERNAL_IP=172.20.0.9 kubernetes/cluster/kube-up.sh
Using subnet CIDR override: 172.20.2.0/24
... Starting cluster in us-east-1d using provider aws
... calling verify-prereqs
... calling kube-up
Starting cluster using os distro: jessie
Uploading to Amazon S3
+++ Staging server tars to S3 Storage: kubernetes-staging-3b2de58189ba7d2340027c
ecbbbe5060/devel
upload: ../../tmp/kubernetes.PiXSEQ/s3/bootstrap-script to s3://kubernetes-stagi
ng-3b2de58189ba7d2340027cecbbbe5060/devel/bootstrap-script
Uploaded server tars:
  SERVER_BINARY_TAR_URL: https://s3.amazonaws.com/kubernetes-staging-3b2de58189b
a7d2340027cecbbbe5060/devel/kubernetes-server-linux-amd64.tar.gz
  SALT_TAR_URL: https://s3.amazonaws.com/kubernetes-staging-3b2de58189ba7d234002
7cecbbbe5060/devel/kubernetes-salt.tar.gz
  BOOTSTRAP_SCRIPT_URL: https://s3.amazonaws.com/kubernetes-staging-3b2de58189ba
7d2340027cecbbbe5060/devel/bootstrap-script
INSTANCEPROFILE arn:aws:iam::672593526685:instance-profile/kubernetes-master    2
016-01-29T00:18:58Z      AIPAJR6YCBYPX27F553HI    kubernetes-master        /
ROLES    arn:aws:iam::672593526685:role/kubernetes-master         2016-01-29T00:18
:57Z     /        AROAIDG4HG76MJPGRWEEW    kubernetes-master
ASSUMEROLEPOLICYDOCUMENT          2012-10-17
STATEMENT         sts:AssumeRole  Allow
PRINCIPAL         ec2.amazonaws.com
INSTANCEPROFILE arn:aws:iam::672593526685:instance-profile/kubernetes-minion    2
016-01-29T00:19:00Z      AIPAJHMVQBPLMRBJE5MNO    kubernetes-minion        /
ROLES    arn:aws:iam::672593526685:role/kubernetes-minion         2016-01-29T00:18
:59Z     /        AROAJU44B2VYHK5GKUB3S    kubernetes-minion
```

Figure 4-29. *Launching a cluster in the us-east-1d zone*

As indicated by the cluster output in Figure 4-30, the master IP is the same but the subnet CIDR is different.

```
ip-172-20-1-98.ec2.internal    Ready     28m
Validate output:
Using subnet CIDR override: 172.20.2.0/24
NAME                 STATUS    MESSAGE              ERROR
scheduler            Healthy   ok
controller-manager   Healthy   ok
etcd-1               Healthy   {"health": "true"}
etcd-0               Healthy   {"health": "true"}
Cluster validation succeeded
Done, listing cluster services:

Using subnet CIDR override: 172.20.2.0/24
Kubernetes master is running at https://52.206.28.220
Elasticsearch is running at https://52.206.28.220/api/v1/proxy/namespaces/kube-s
ystem/services/elasticsearch-logging
Heapster is running at https://52.206.28.220/api/v1/proxy/namespaces/kube-system
/services/heapster
Kibana is running at https://52.206.28.220/api/v1/proxy/namespaces/kube-system/s
ervices/kibana-logging
KubeDNS is running at https://52.206.28.220/api/v1/proxy/namespaces/kube-system/
services/kube-dns
kubernetes-dashboard is running at https://52.206.28.220/api/v1/proxy/namespaces
/kube-system/services/kubernetes-dashboard
Grafana is running at https://52.206.28.220/api/v1/proxy/namespaces/kube-system/
services/monitoring-grafana
InfluxDB is running at https://52.206.28.220/api/v1/proxy/namespaces/kube-system
/services/monitoring-influxdb

To further debug and diagnose cluster problems, use 'kubectl cluster-info dump'.

[ec2-user@ip-10-0-0-126 ~]$
```

***Figure 4-30.** The same master IP but a different subnet CIDR*

The EC2 Console lists three minion sets, one each in the `us-east-1b`, `us-east-1c`, and `us-east-1d` zones as shown in Figure 4-31. The single master is in the `us-east-1c` zone.

Launch Instance | Connect | Actions

Launch Time : > July 12, 2016 at 12:00:00 AM UTC-7 | Add filter | 1 to 11 of 11

Name	Instance ID	Instance Type	Availability Zone	Instance State	Status Checks	Alarm Status
kubernetes-minion	i-c432da5b	t2.micro	us-east-1b	running	2/2 checks ...	None
kubernetes-minion	i-c532da5a	t2.micro	us-east-1b	running	2/2 checks ...	None
kubernetes-minion	i-c732da58	t2.micro	us-east-1b	running	2/2 checks ...	None
Kubernetes-CoreOS	i-842c5802	t2.micro	us-east-1c	running	2/2 checks ...	None
kubernetes-minion	i-d3ade955	t2.micro	us-east-1c	running	2/2 checks ...	None
kubernetes-minion	i-d4ade952	t2.micro	us-east-1c	running	2/2 checks ...	None
kubernetes-minion	i-d5ade953	t2.micro	us-east-1c	running	2/2 checks ...	None
kubernetes-master	i-ebace86d	m3.medium	us-east-1c	running	2/2 checks ...	None
kubernetes-minion	i-38b021a8	t2.micro	us-east-1d	running	2/2 checks ...	None
kubernetes-minion	i-39b021a9	t2.micro	us-east-1d	running	2/2 checks ...	None
kubernetes-minion	i-3fb021af	t2.micro	us-east-1d	running	2/2 checks ...	None

***Figure 4-31.** Listing nodes in three zones*

Listing the nodes displays 9 nodes. Some nodes may be initially in the NotReady state while the node set is started, as shown in Figure 4-32.

```
[ec2-user@ip-10-0-0-126 ~]$ kubectl get nodes
NAME                           STATUS     AGE
ip-172-20-0-239.ec2.internal   Ready      1h
ip-172-20-0-240.ec2.internal   Ready      1h
ip-172-20-0-241.ec2.internal   Ready      1h
ip-172-20-1-96.ec2.internal    Ready      34m
ip-172-20-1-97.ec2.internal    Ready      34m
ip-172-20-1-98.ec2.internal    Ready      34m
ip-172-20-2-23.ec2.internal    NotReady   30s
ip-172-20-2-24.ec2.internal    NotReady   27s
ip-172-20-2-25.ec2.internal    NotReady   26s
[ec2-user@ip-10-0-0-126 ~]$ kubectl get nodes
NAME                           STATUS    AGE
ip-172-20-0-239.ec2.internal   Ready     1h
ip-172-20-0-240.ec2.internal   Ready     1h
ip-172-20-0-241.ec2.internal   Ready     1h
ip-172-20-1-96.ec2.internal    Ready     35m
ip-172-20-1-97.ec2.internal    Ready     35m
ip-172-20-1-98.ec2.internal    Ready     35m
ip-172-20-2-23.ec2.internal    Ready     44s
ip-172-20-2-24.ec2.internal    Ready     41s
ip-172-20-2-25.ec2.internal    Ready     40s
[ec2-user@ip-10-0-0-126 ~]$
```

Figure 4-32. *Listing Kubernetes nodes*

Including the labels lists the nodes as being in three different zones, as shown in Figure 4-33.

```
[ec2-user@ip-10-0-0-126 ~]$ kubectl get node ip-172-20-1-96.ec2.internal ip-172-
20-0-241.ec2.internal ip-172-20-2-23.ec2.internal ip-172-20-2-25.ec2.internal ip
-172-20-1-98.ec2.internal ip-172-20-2-25.ec2.internal ip-172-20-1-96.ec2.interna
l ip-172-20-1-97.ec2.internal ip-172-20-0-240.ec2.internal ip-172-20-2-24.ec2.in
ternal --show-labels
NAME                          STATUS    AGE       LABELS
ip-172-20-1-96.ec2.internal   Ready     43m       beta.kubernetes.io/arch=amd64
,beta.kubernetes.io/instance-type=t2.micro,beta.kubernetes.io/os=linux,failure-d
omain.beta.kubernetes.io/region=us-east-1,failure-domain.beta.kubernetes.io/zone
=us-east-1b,kubernetes.io/hostname=ip-172-20-1-96.ec2.internal
ip-172-20-0-241.ec2.internal  Ready     1h        beta.kubernetes.io/arch=amd64
,beta.kubernetes.io/instance-type=t2.micro,beta.kubernetes.io/os=linux,failure-d
omain.beta.kubernetes.io/region=us-east-1,failure-domain.beta.kubernetes.io/zone
=us-east-1c,kubernetes.io/hostname=ip-172-20-0-241.ec2.internal
ip-172-20-2-23.ec2.internal   Ready     8m        beta.kubernetes.io/arch=amd64
,beta.kubernetes.io/instance-type=t2.micro,beta.kubernetes.io/os=linux,failure-d
omain.beta.kubernetes.io/region=us-east-1,failure-domain.beta.kubernetes.io/zone
=us-east-1d,kubernetes.io/hostname=ip-172-20-2-23.ec2.internal
ip-172-20-2-25.ec2.internal   Ready     8m        beta.kubernetes.io/arch=amd64
,beta.kubernetes.io/instance-type=t2.micro,beta.kubernetes.io/os=linux,failure-d
omain.beta.kubernetes.io/region=us-east-1,failure-domain.beta.kubernetes.io/zone
=us-east-1d,kubernetes.io/hostname=ip-172-20-2-25.ec2.internal
ip-172-20-1-98.ec2.internal   Ready     43m       beta.kubernetes.io/arch=amd64
,beta.kubernetes.io/instance-type=t2.micro,beta.kubernetes.io/os=linux,failure-d
omain.beta.kubernetes.io/region=us-east-1,failure-domain.beta.kubernetes.io/zone
=us-east-1b,kubernetes.io/hostname=ip-172-20-1-98.ec2.internal
ip-172-20-2-25.ec2.internal   Ready     8m        beta.kubernetes.io/arch=amd64
,beta.kubernetes.io/instance-type=t2.micro,beta.kubernetes.io/os=linux,failure-d
omain.beta.kubernetes.io/region=us-east-1,failure-domain.beta.kubernetes.io/zone
=us-east-1d,kubernetes.io/hostname=ip-172-20-2-25.ec2.internal
ip-172-20-1-96.ec2.internal   Ready     43m       beta.kubernetes.io/arch=amd64
,beta.kubernetes.io/instance-type=t2.micro,beta.kubernetes.io/os=linux,failure-d
omain.beta.kubernetes.io/region=us-east-1,failure-domain.beta.kubernetes.io/zone
```

Figure 4-33. *Listing nodes including labels*

A PersistentVolume (PV) is a provisioned networked storage in a cluster, and a PersistentVolumeClaim (PVC) is a request for storage by a user. A PVC consumes PV resources just as a pod consumes node resources. Next, we shall create a persistent volume claim and subsequently claim the volume in a pod specification. The objective of the application is to demonstrate that a persistent volume cannot be attached across zones. A persistent volume is labeled with the zone in which it is created, and a pod that makes use of the persistent volume is allocated in the same zone as the persistent volume. First, create a JSON specification file `claim.yaml` for a persistent volume claim:

```
sudo vi claim1.json
```

Copy the following source code into claim.json:

```
{
  "kind": "PersistentVolumeClaim",
  "apiVersion": "v1",
  "metadata": {
    "name": "claim1",
    "annotations": {
        "volume.alpha.kubernetes.io/storage-class": "foo"
    }
  },
  "spec": {
    "accessModes": [
      "ReadWriteOnce"
    ],
    "resources": {
      "requests": {
        "storage": "3Gi"
      }
    }
  }
}
```

The resulting claim1.json is shown in the vi editor in Figure 4-34.

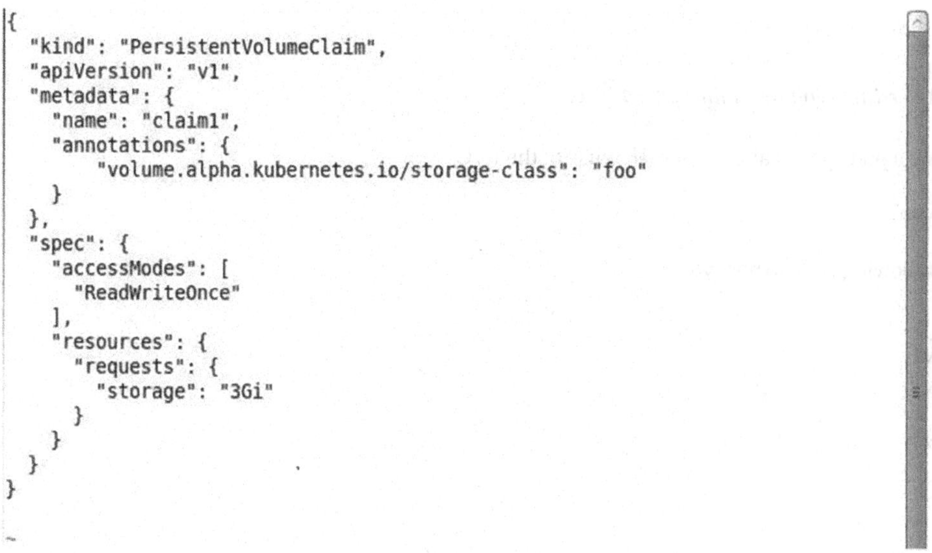
{
"kind": "PersistentVolumeClaim",
"apiVersion": "v1",
"metadata": {
"name": "claim1",
"annotations": {
"volume.alpha.kubernetes.io/storage-class": "foo"
}
},
"spec": {
"accessModes": [
"ReadWriteOnce"
],
"resources": {
"requests": {
"storage": "3Gi"
}
}
}
}

Figure 4-34. *A PersistentVolumeClaim* claim1.json

Create a PVC with the `kubectl create` command:

```
kubectl create -f claim1.json
```

List the persistent volumes, including labels:

```
kubectl get pv --show-labels
```

The persistent volume is listed as being consumed by the persistent volume claim:

```
kubectl get pvc
```

As the command's output indicates, a `persistentvolumeclaim` is created. The persistent volume is listed to be in the `us-east-1b` zone as shown in Figure 4-35.

```
[ec2-user@ip-10-0-0-126 ~]$ kubectl create -f claim1.json
persistentvolumeclaim "claim1" created
[ec2-user@ip-10-0-0-126 ~]$ kubectl get pv --show-labels
NAME                                       CAPACITY   ACCESSMODES   STATUS    CL
AIM            REASON    AGE        LABELS
pvc-f2da72bf-4856-11e6-8be4-0ab9c2d7053d   3Gi        RWO           Bound     de
fault/claim1             11s        failure-domain.beta.kubernetes.io/region=us-e
ast-1,failure-domain.beta.kubernetes.io/zone=us-east-1b
[ec2-user@ip-10-0-0-126 ~]$ kubectl get pvc
NAME      STATUS    VOLUME                                     CAPACITY   ACCESS
MODES   AGE
claim1    Bound     pvc-f2da72bf-4856-11e6-8be4-0ab9c2d7053d   0
        20s
[ec2-user@ip-10-0-0-126 ~]$ █
```

***Figure 4-35.** A PersistentVolumeClaim* `claim1.json`

Next, define a pod specification that makes use of the PVC.

```
sudo vi pod.yaml
```

Copy the following code to `pod.yaml`:

```
---
apiVersion: v1
kind: Pod
metadata:
  name: nginx
spec:
  containers:
    -
      image: nginx
      name: nginx
      volumeMounts:
        -
          mountPath: /var/www/html
          name: pv
  volumes:
    -
```

```
    name: pv
    persistentVolumeClaim:
      claimName: claim1
```

The resulting pod.yaml is shown in a vi editor in Figure 4-36.

```
---
apiVersion: v1
kind: Pod
metadata:
  name: nginx
spec:
  containers:
    -
      image: nginx
      name: nginx
      volumeMounts:
        -
          mountPath: /var/www/html
          name: pv
  volumes:
    -
      name: pv
      persistentVolumeClaim:
        claimName: claim1
```

Figure 4-36. *Using PersistentVolumeClaim* `claim1.json` *in a pod*

Create a pod from pod.yaml:

```
./kubectl create -f pod.yaml
```

A pod is created. Next, list the pods across the cluster:

```
kubectl get pods -o wide
```

The node on which the pod is running is listed, as shown in Figure 4-37.

```
[ec2-user@ip-10-0-0-126 ~]$ sudo vi pod.yaml
[ec2-user@ip-10-0-0-126 ~]$ kubectl create -f  pod.yaml
pod "nginx" created
[ec2-user@ip-10-0-0-126 ~]$ kubectl get pods -o wide
NAME      READY     STATUS              RESTARTS   AGE       IP        NODE
nginx     0/1       ContainerCreating   0          13s       <none>    ip-172-20
-1-96.ec2.internal
[ec2-user@ip-10-0-0-126 ~]$ kubectl get pods -o wide
NAME      READY     STATUS              RESTARTS   AGE       IP        NODE
nginx     0/1       ContainerCreating   0          19s       <none>    ip-172-20
-1-96.ec2.internal
[ec2-user@ip-10-0-0-126 ~]$ kubectl get pods -o wide
NAME      READY     STATUS    RESTARTS   AGE       IP           NODE
nginx     1/1       Running   0          38s       10.244.3.3   ip-172-20-1-96.e
c2.internal
[ec2-user@ip-10-0-0-126 ~]$ 
```

Figure 4-37. *Creating a pod and listing its node*

Alternatively obtain the Node IP as follows:

```
kubectl describe deployment nginx | grep Node
```

The Node IP is output as shown in Figure 4-38.

```
[ec2-user@ip-10-0-0-126 ~]$ kubectl describe pod nginx | grep Node
Node:             ip-172-20-1-96.ec2.internal/172.20.1.96
```

Figure 4-38. *A PersistentVolumeClaim claim1.json*

Next, list the node labels:

```
kubectl get node <node ip> --show-labels
```

The node is running in the zone `us-east-1b`, which is the same as the zone of the persistent volume, as shown in Figure 4-39.

```
[ec2-user@ip-10-0-0-126 ~]$ kubectl get node ip-172-20-1-96.ec2.internal --show-
labels
NAME                          STATUS    AGE       LABELS
ip-172-20-1-96.ec2.internal   Ready     23m       beta.kubernetes.io/arch=amd64,
beta.kubernetes.io/instance-type=t2.micro,beta.kubernetes.io/os=linux,failure-do
main.beta.kubernetes.io/region=us-east-1,failure-domain.beta.kubernetes.io/zone=
us-east-1b,kubernetes.io/hostname=ip-172-20-1-96.ec2.internal
[ec2-user@ip-10-0-0-126 ~]$ █
```

Figure 4-39. *A node is scheduled on the same zone as the persistent volume*

Summary

In this chapter we created a Kubernetes cluster using multiple zones on CoreOS. A multi-zone cluster is a highly available cluster. A multi-zone cluster is configured by specifying multiple Kubernetes subnets with their CIDRs and availability zones in cluster.yaml in the subnets section. We also discussed creating a multi-zone cluster on the AWS cloud provider by setting the `MULTIZONE` parameter to `true` in the `curl -sS https://get.k8s.io` command to launch a Kubernetes cluster. In the next chapter we will discuss using the Tectonic console.

CHAPTER 5

Using the Tectonic Console

Tectonic is a commercial enterprise Kubernetes platform providing enterprise-level security, scalability, and reliability. Tectonic provides an integrated platform based on Kubernetes and CoreOS Linux. The Tectonic architecture consists of Kubernetes cluster manager orchestrating rkt containers running on CoreOS. Tectonic provides Distributed Trusted Computing using cryptographic verification of the entire environment, from the hardware to the cluster. Tectonic enhances open source Kubernetes, and applications may be deployed between cloud and data center environments.

Problem

CoreOS Linux does provide a platform suitable for developing containerized applications, but a command-line interface still has to be used to run Kubernetes commands to create and manage a replication controller, deployment, pod, or service.

Solution

Tectonic Console is a graphical user interface (GUI) to manage a Kubernetes cluster from a web browser. The Console may be used to deploy new applications, create rolling upgrades for deployments, and create pods, replication controllers, and services. Some of the benefits of Tectonic Console are as follows:

- Out-of-the-box Kubernetes cluster
- Authorization framework
- Enterprise authentication
- Improved scalability
- User-friendly Dashboard
- Scheduled Updates for cluster software
- Flexible architectures
- Automatic Load Balancing and Services
- Rollbacks
- Better machine utilization
- Environment consistency across teams
- Built-in credentials storage and distribution
- Demarcation between OS and applications
- LDAP-based secure authentication

D. Vohra, *Kubernetes Management Design Patterns*, DOI 10.1007/978-1-4842-2598-1_5

Overview

The Console can be used to deploy new applications, create rolling upgrades for deployments, and create pods, replication controllers and services. We'll explore the following topics:

Setting the environment

Downloading the pull secret and the Tectonic Console manifest

Installing the pull secret and the Tectonic Console

Accessing the Tectonic Console

Using the Tectonic Console

Removing the Tectonic Console

Setting the Environment

As a prerequisite, install a Kubernetes cluster. Installing Kubernetes on CoreOS on the AWS cloud provider is discussed in Chapter 2. To reiterate briefly, first create an Amazon EC2 instance to launch an AWS CloudFormation for a Kubernetes cluster. The EC2 instance AMI should be Amazon Linux, as Amazon Client Interface (CLI) is preinstalled on an Amazon Linux AMI-based instance. Obtain the public IP address of the EC2 instance and SSH log in to the instance. Create a CloudFormation for a Kubernetes cluster consisting of one master and three worker nodes as shown in Figure 5-1.

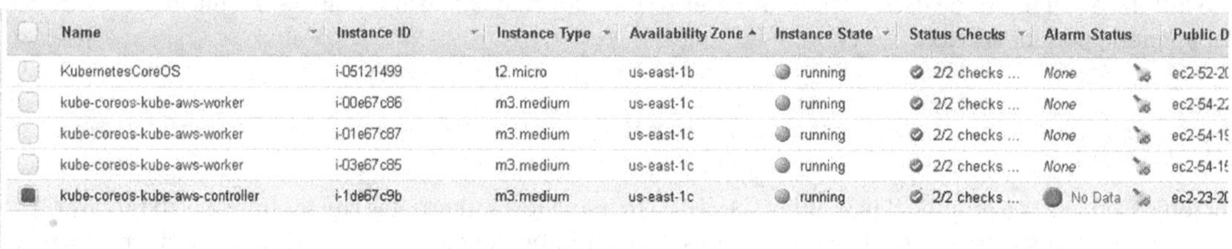

Name
Instance ID
Instance Type
Availability Zone
Instance State
Status Checks
Alarm Status
KubernetesCoreOS
i-05121499
t2.micro
us-east-1b
running
2/2 checks ...
None
kube-coreos-kube-aws-worker
i-00e67c86
m3.medium
us-east-1c
kube-coreos-kube-aws-worker
i-01e67c87
kube-coreos-kube-aws-worker
i-03e67c85
kube-coreos-kube-aws-controller
i-1de67c9b
No Data

Figure 5-1. CloudFormation EC2 instances for a Kubernetes cluster

Obtain the public IP address for the controller from the EC2 console and add an A record for the IP address to the public DNS used to initialize the CloudFormation stack as shown in Figure 5-2.

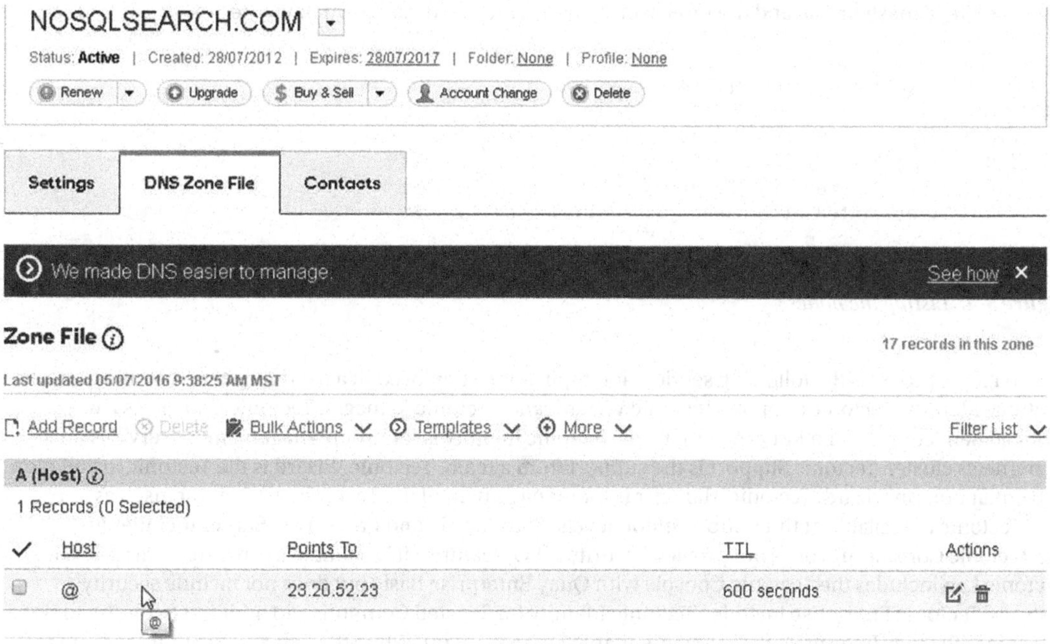

Figure 5-2. *Adding an A record for the public IP address of the controller*

SSH log in to the controller instance and install kubectl as shown in Figure 5-3.

```
[ec2-user@ip-172-30-1-188 ~]$ ssh -i "kubernetes-coreos.pem"  core@23.20.52.23
CoreOS stable (1010.6.0)
Update Strategy: No Reboots
core@ip-10-0-0-50 ~ $
```

Figure 5-3. *SSH logging into the CoreOS controller instance*

Run the following command to list the binaries.

```
kubectl get nodes
```

The single master node and the three worker nodes are listed, as shown in Figure 5-4.

```
core@ip-10-0-0-50 ~ $ ./kubectl get nodes
NAME                         STATUS                     AGE
ip-10-0-0-107.ec2.internal   Ready                      3m
ip-10-0-0-108.ec2.internal   Ready                      3m
ip-10-0-0-109.ec2.internal   Ready                      3m
ip-10-0-0-50.ec2.internal    Ready,SchedulingDisabled   3m
core@ip-10-0-0-50 ~ $
```

Figure 5-4. *Listing the nodes*

Tectonic provides the following services for applications deployed in a user's cluster: Tectonic Console, Tectonic Identity, Tectonic Support, Tectonic Wizard, and Tectonic Manager. Tectonic Console is a web management console for a Kubernetes cluster. Tectonic Identity is for user management for services on a Kubernetes cluster. Tectonic Support is the support from a team. Tectonic Wizard is the Tectonic installation and configuration wizard. Tectonic Manager is for management of the Tectonic services themselves.

Tectonic is available at three subscription levels: Starter, Lab, and Enterprise. Starter includes just the Tectonic Console and does not provide security (SSO) features; it is suitable as an initial starter level. Tectonic Lab includes the Tectonic Console with Quay Enterprise Basic but does not include security features. Tectonic Enterprise includes Tectonic Identity for Trusted Computing in addition to the Tectonic Console with Quay Enterprise Basic and is suitable for production. While the Lab and the Enterprise levels are fee-based, the Starter is free. We shall use the Tectonic Starter subscription level in this chapter. Tectonic Starter level does not authenticate users.

Next, register for the Tectonic Starter account at `https://tectonic.com/starter/`.

Downloading the Pull Secret and the Tectonic Console Manifest

Tectonic is mainly an infrastructure platform that enables enterprises to run containers with Kubernetes anywhere, securely and reliably. The Kubernetes cluster makes use of a Pull Secret to download the Tectonic Console image. The Pull Secret is a Kubernetes formatted file containing the credentials required to download the Tectonic Console image. Click on Account Assets after creating a Tectonic Starter project and click Download Kubernetes Secret for the Pull Secret file `coreos-pull-secret.yml` as shown in Figure 5-5.

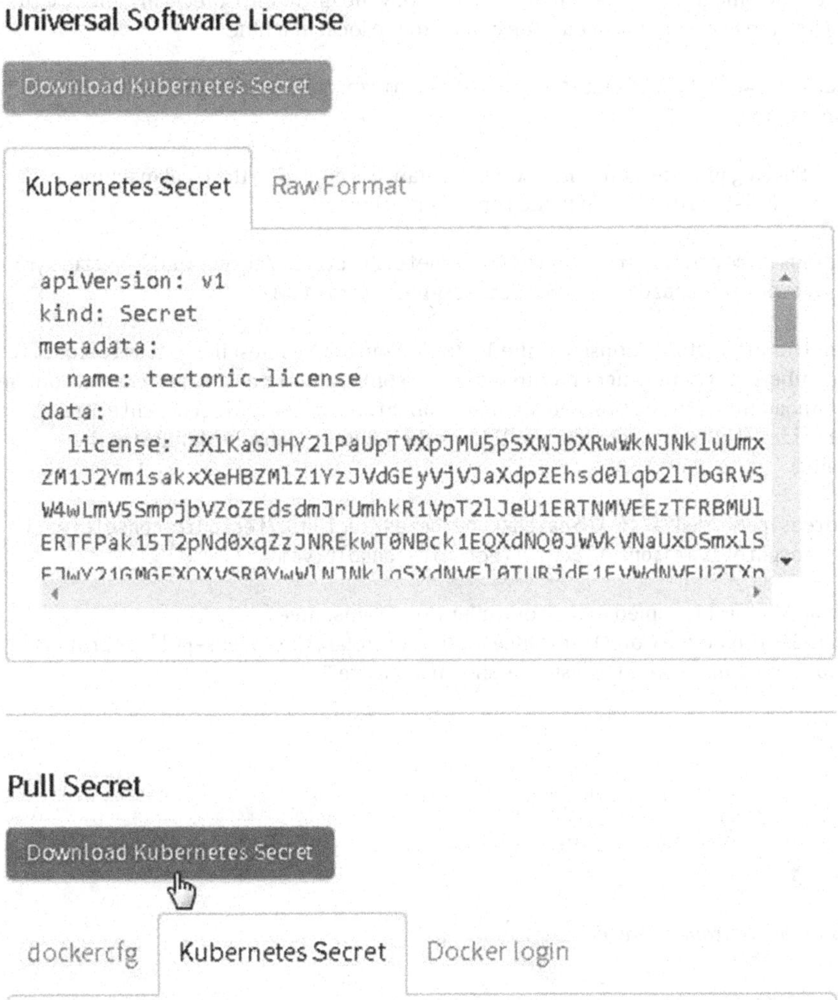

***Figure 5-5.** Downloading Kubernetes Secret*

If the Pull Secret file is downloaded to a local machine, `scp` copy the file to the CoreOS instance for the Kubernetes controller. First, the key pair may need to be copied to the local machine:

```
scp -i docker.pem ec2-user@ec2-52-201-216-175.compute-1.amazonaws.com:~/kubernetes-coreos.
pem ~/kubernetes-coreos.pem
```

The key pair used to SSH log in to the controller CoreOS instance is copied to the local machine.

Next copy the `coreos-pull-secret.yml` file to the controller instance:

```
scp -i kubernetes-coreos.pem /media/sf_VMShared/kubernetes/tectonic/coreos-pull-secret.yml
core@ec2-23-20-52-23.compute-1.amazonaws.com:~/coreos-pull-secret.yml
```

Another file required for the Tectonic Console is the Tectonic Console Manifest file `tectonic-console.yaml`, which defines the Kubernetes deployment required to run a container for the Tectonic Console on the Kubernetes cluster. Download the Tectonic Console Manifest from `https://tectonic.com/enterprise/docs/latest/deployer/files/tectonic-console.yaml`. Copy the Tectonic Console Manifest to the controller CoreOS instance.

```
scp -i kubernetes-coreos.pem /media/sf_VMShared/kubernetes/tectonic/tectonic-console.yaml
core@ec2-23-20-52-23.compute-1.amazonaws.com:~/tectonic-console.yaml
```

The Tectonic Console Manifest is copied to the controller CoreOS instance.

If the `ls -l` command is run on the CoreOS instance for the controller, the `coreos-pull-secret.yml` and the `tectonic-console.yaml` files should be listed as shown in Figure 5-6.

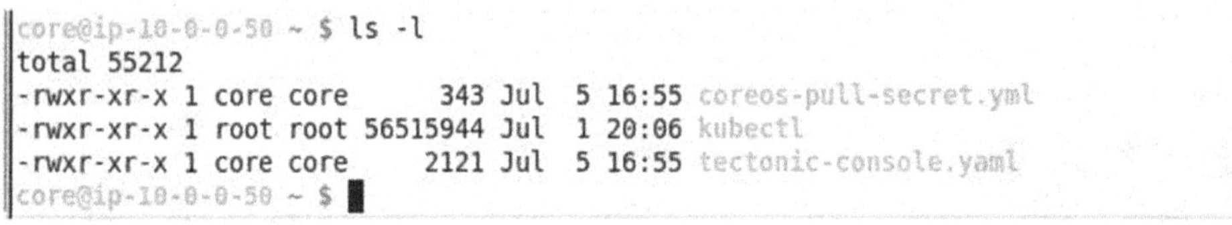

core@ip-10-0-0-50 ~ $ ls -l
total 55212
-rwxr-xr-x 1 core core   343 Jul 5 16:55 coreos-pull-secret.yml
-rwxr-xr-x 1 root root 56515944 Jul 1 20:06 kubectl
-rwxr-xr-x 1 core core   2121 Jul 5 16:55 tectonic-console.yaml
core@ip-10-0-0-50 ~ $

Figure 5-6. *Listing files in the controller CoreOS instance*

Installing the Pull Secret and the Tectonic Console Manifest

Next, install the Pull Secret on the Kubernetes cluster:

```
kubectl create -f coreos-pull-secret.yml
```

A Kubernetes Secret called `coreos-pull-secret` is created; it will be used by Kubernetes to pull and install the image for the Tectonic Console.

Next, install the Tectonic Console using the Tectonic Console Manifest, making use of the Pull Secret to pull and install the image for the `tectonic-console`. The following command creates a replication controller called `tectonic-console`.

```
kubectl create -f tectonic-console.yaml
```

List the pods, which should specify just the `tectonic-console` pod to be listed:

```
kubectl get pods -l tectonic-app=console
```

If the Tectonic Console was installed, output similar to Figure 5-7 should be generated from the preceding commands.

```
core@ip-10-0-0-50 ~ $ ./kubectl create -f coreos-pull-secret.yml
secret "coreos-pull-secret" created
core@ip-10-0-0-50 ~ $ ./kubectl create -f tectonic-console.yaml
replicationcontroller "tectonic-console-v0.1.9" created
core@ip-10-0-0-50 ~ $ ./kubectl get pods -l tectonic-app=console
NAME                            READY     STATUS    RESTARTS   AGE
tectonic-console-v0.1.9-dupbi   1/1       Running   0          7s
core@ip-10-0-0-50 ~ $ 
```

Figure 5-7. *Creating a replication controller and pod for Tectonic Console*

Accessing the Tectonic Console

Because Tectonic Starter does not authenticate users, the interface is not exposed outside the cluster, and port forwarding must be set from the controller machine to the Tectonic Console service port 9000. The following command sets up port forwarding from 127.0.0.1:9000 to port 9000 on the pod labelled `app=tectonic-console`:

```
kubectl get pods -l tectonic-app=console -o template --template="{{range.items}}{{.metadata.
name}}{{end}}" | xargs -i{} kubectl port-forward {} 9000
```

Port forwarding from the machine from which the preceding command is run, which is the controller instance, to the pod on which the container for the Tectonic Console is run, will be set up as shown in Figure 5-8.

```
core@ip-10-0-0-50 ~ $ ./kubectl get pods -l tectonic-app=console -o template --t
emplate="{{range.items}}{{.metadata.name}}{{end}}" | xargs -i{} ./kubectl port-f
orward {} 9000
Forwarding from 127.0.0.1:9000 -> 9000
Forwarding from [::1]:9000 -> 9000
```

Figure 5-8. *Setting port forwarding*

To invoke the Tectonic Console in a web browser we still need to set another port forwarding from a local machine to the controller machine, which has public IP 23.20.52.23 and public DNS `ec2-23-20-52-23.compute-1.amazonaws.com`. A port other than 9000 could be used on the local machine to forward to the Tectonic Console port. The command looks like this:

```
ssh -i kubernetes-coreos.pem -f -nNT -L 9001:127.0.0.1:9000 core@ec2-23-20-52-23.compute-1.
amazonaws.com
```

Port forwarding from the local machine on which the preceding command is run to the controller instance is set up. Access the Tectonic Console at URL `http://localhost:9001` in a browser on the local machine as shown in Figure 5-9. The port could be different if a different localhost port is forwarded.

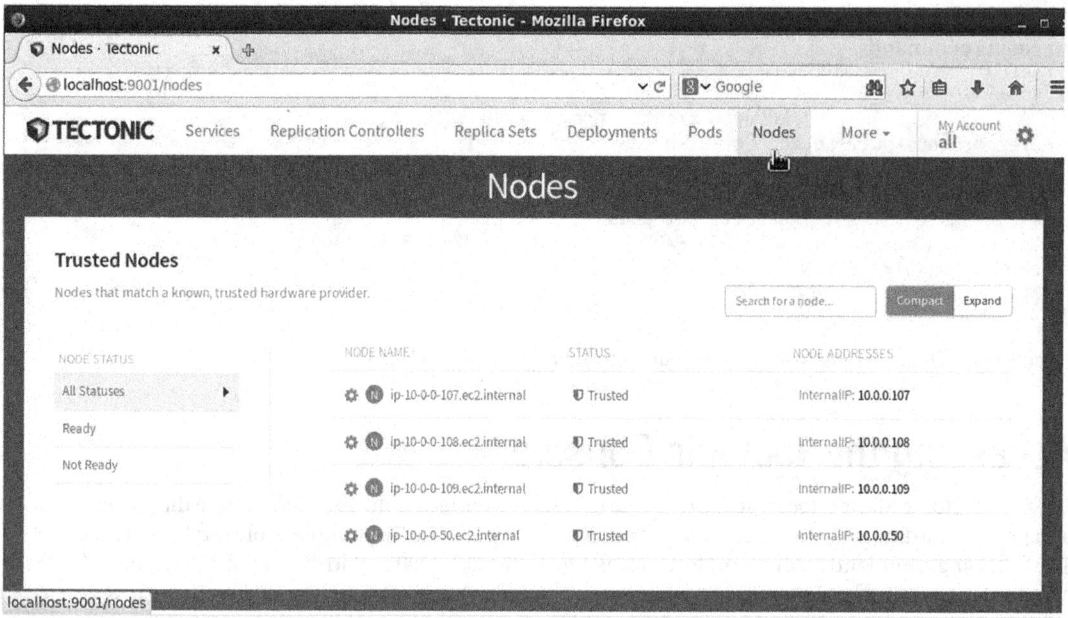

Figure 5-9. *Accessing the Tectonic Console*

Using the Tectonic Console

The Tectonic Console may be used to view the different Kubernetes objects, such as deployments, replication controllers, replica sets, pods, and services, or to create new Kubernetes objects. To display the deployments, click the Deployments tab. To create a new deployment, click the Create a New Deployment link as shown in Figure 5-10.

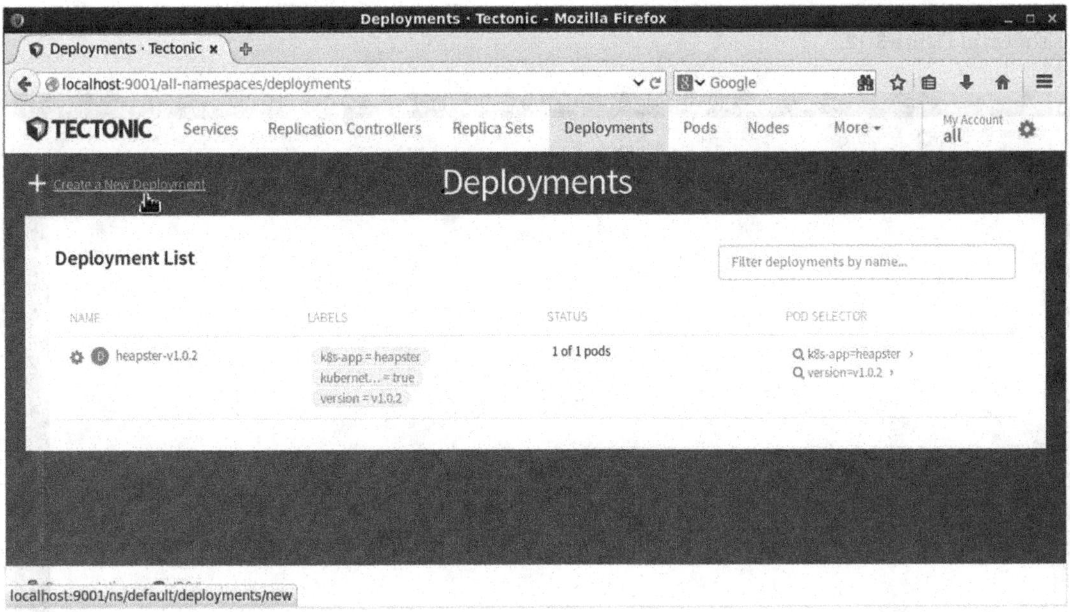

Figure 5-10. *Begin by clicking the Create a New Deployment link*

As an example, create a deployment for the `nginx` server by specifying the labels, pod selector, replicas, and pod labels as shown in Figure 5-11.

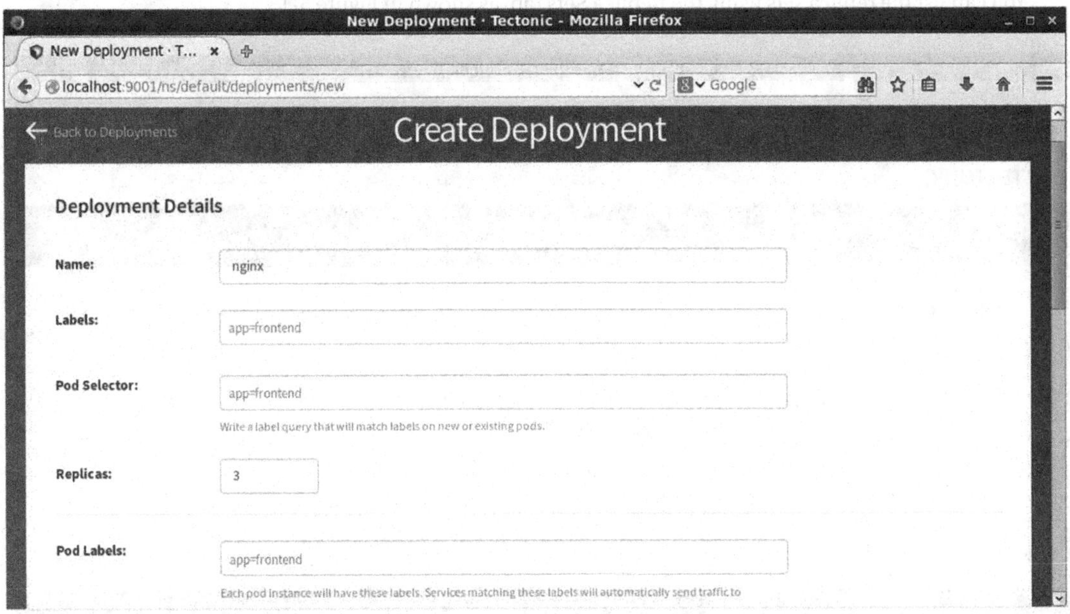

Figure 5-11. *Specifying deployment details for an `nginx` application*

Specify the container name, image, and version/tag, and click Launch Deployment as shown in Figure 5-12.

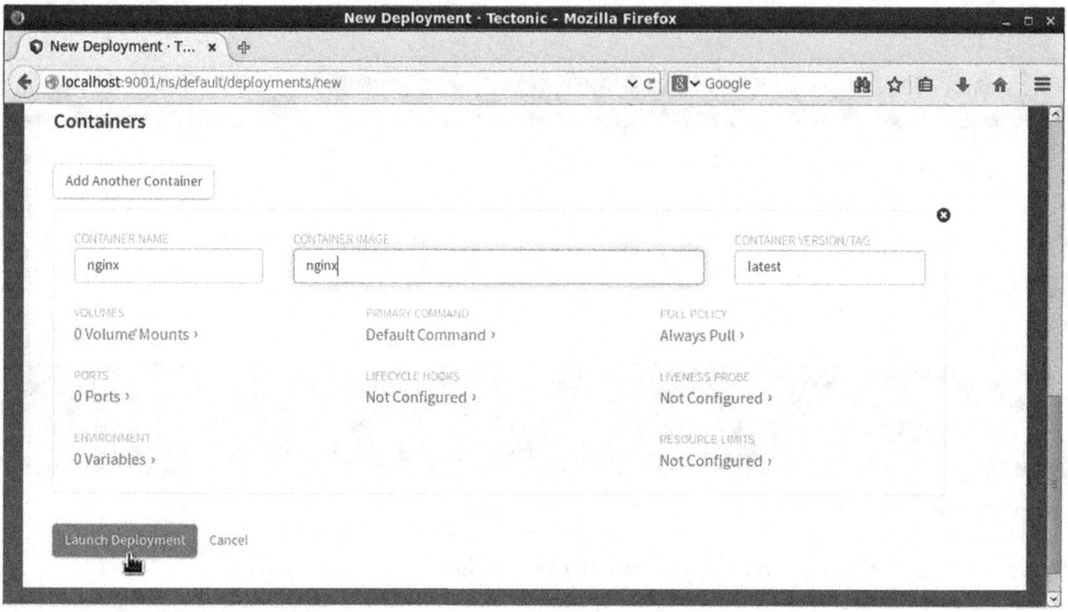

Figure 5-12. *Launching the deployment*

You can list the replica sets using the Replica Sets tab, as shown in Figure 5-13.

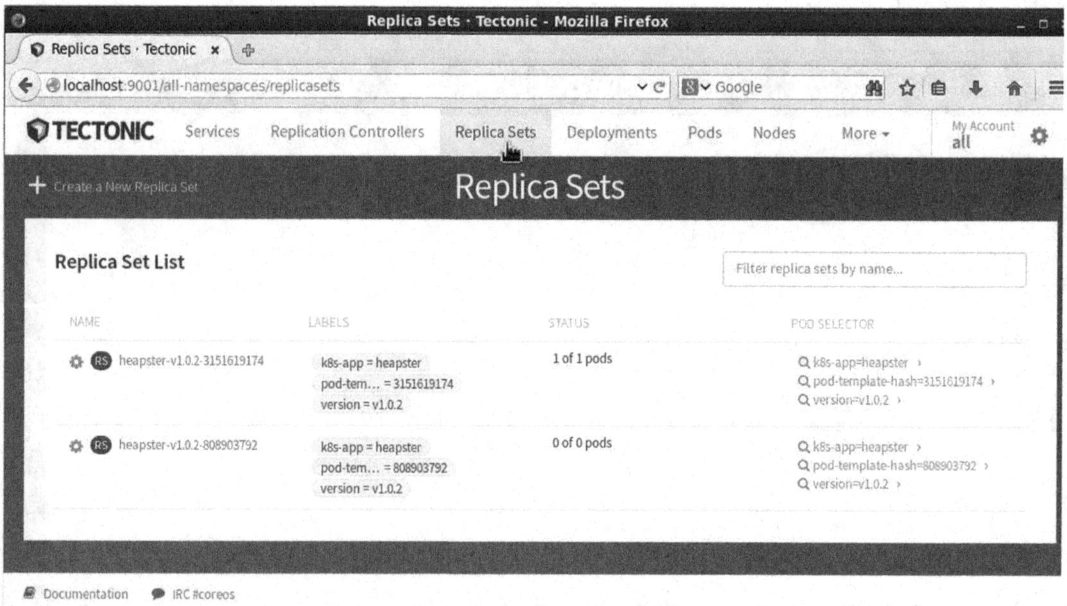

Figure 5-13. *Listing replica sets*

To list the pods, click the Pods tab. To create a new pod, click the Create a New Pod link as shown in Figure 5-14.

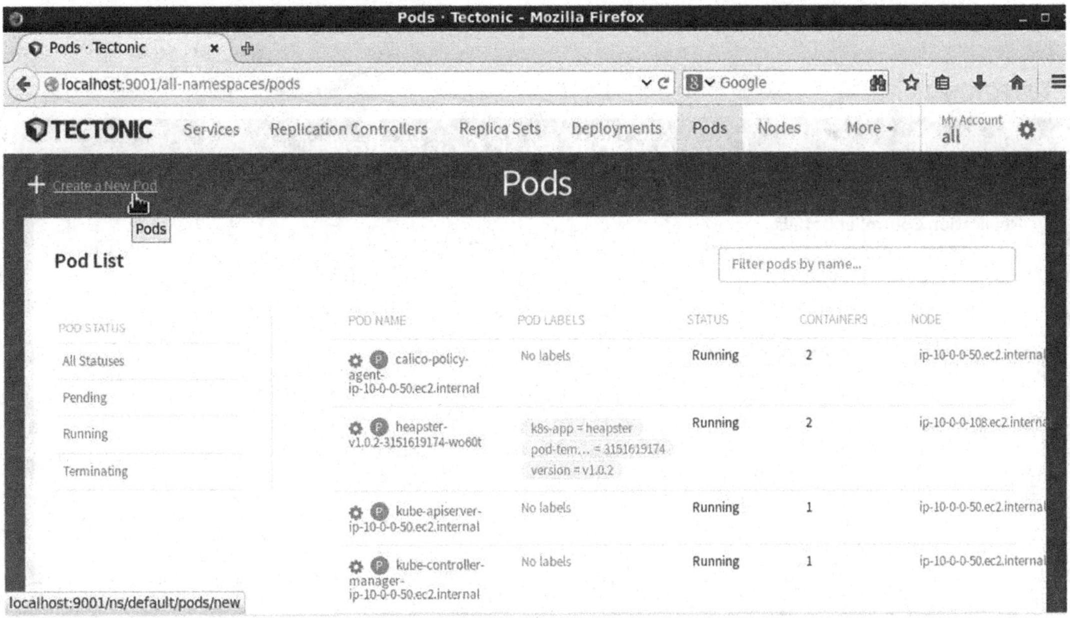

Figure 5-14. *Begin by clicking the Create a New Pod link*

To list the replication controllers, click the Replication Controllers tab. To create a new replication controller, click the Create a New Replication Controller link as shown in Figure 5-15.

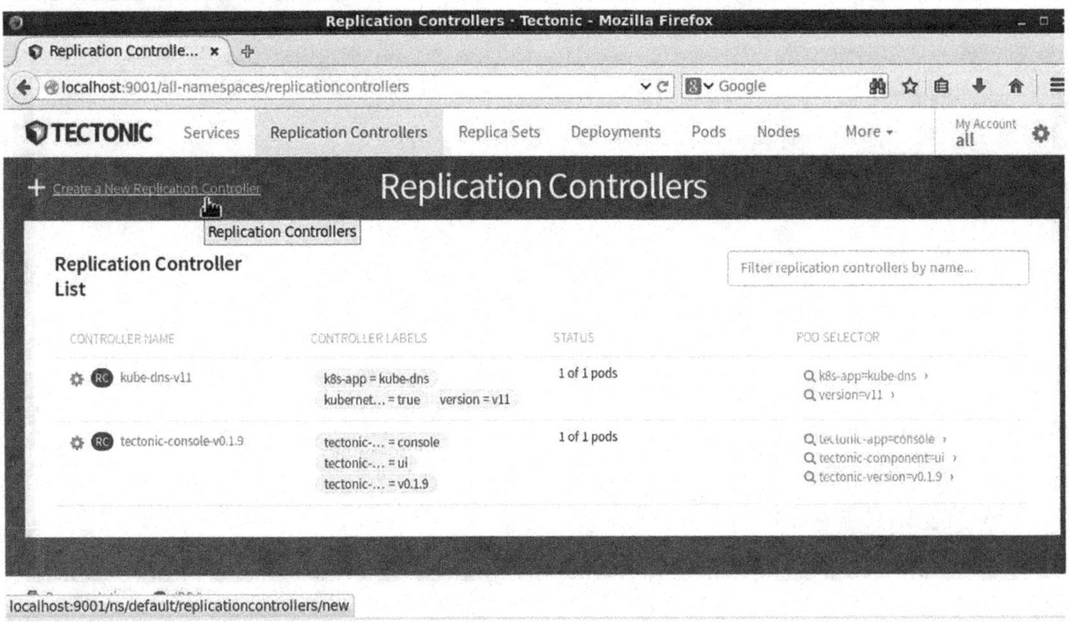

Figure 5-15. *Begin by clicking the Create a New Replication Controller link*

Specify a controller name, controller labels, pod label selector, and replicas as shown in Figure 5-16.

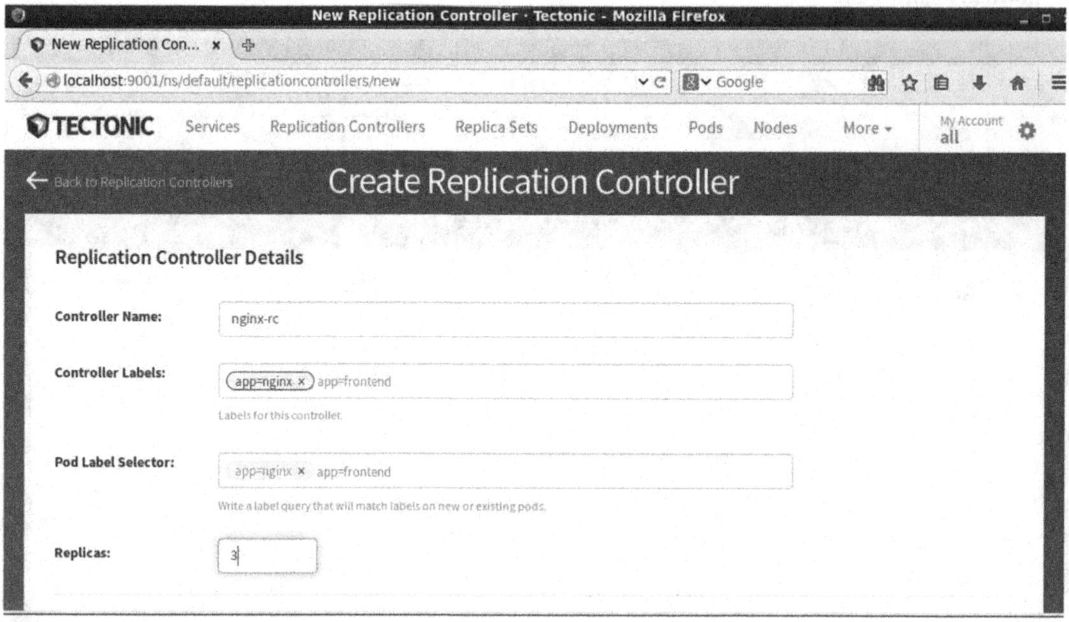

Figure 5-16. Specifying replication controller details

Specify the container name, container image, and container version/tag. Click on Launch Replication Controller as shown in Figure 5-17.

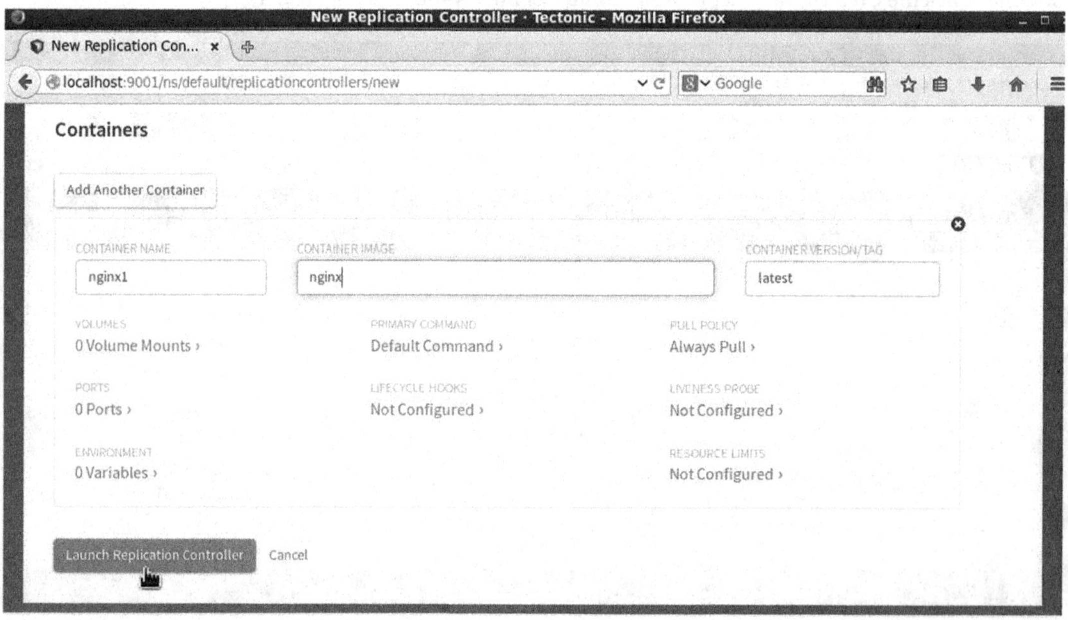

Figure 5-17. Launching Replication Controller

A new replication controller is created, as shown in Figure 5-18.

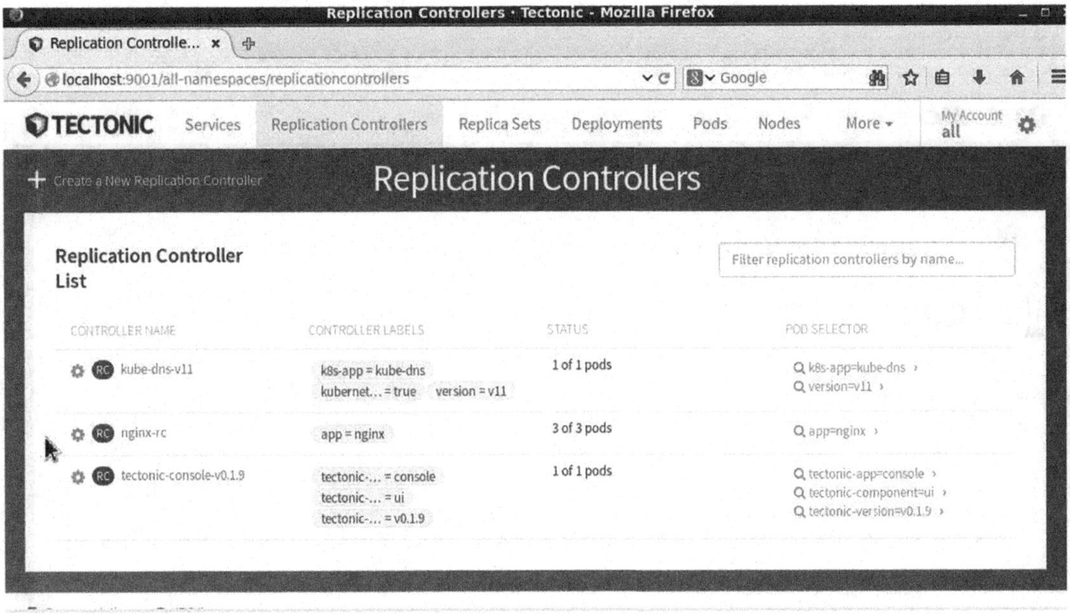

Figure 5-18. *A new replication controller*

To modify the replication controller settings, right-click the RC and select one of the options shown in Figure 5-19.

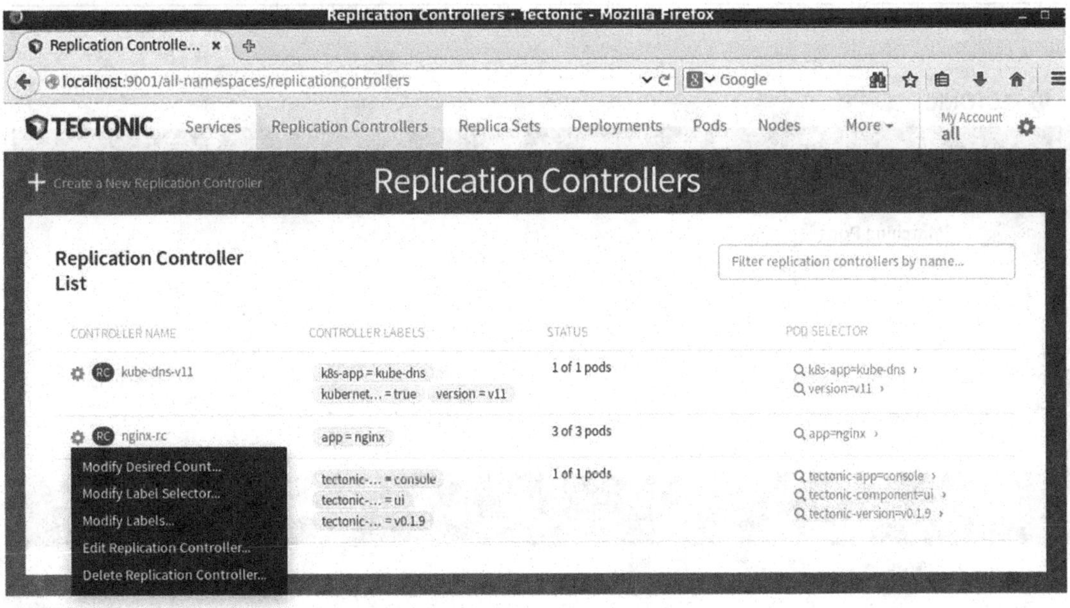

Figure 5-19. *Modifying or deleting an RC*

Click the RC to list its details. You can list the pods in the RC by using the Pods tab, as shown in Figure 5-20.

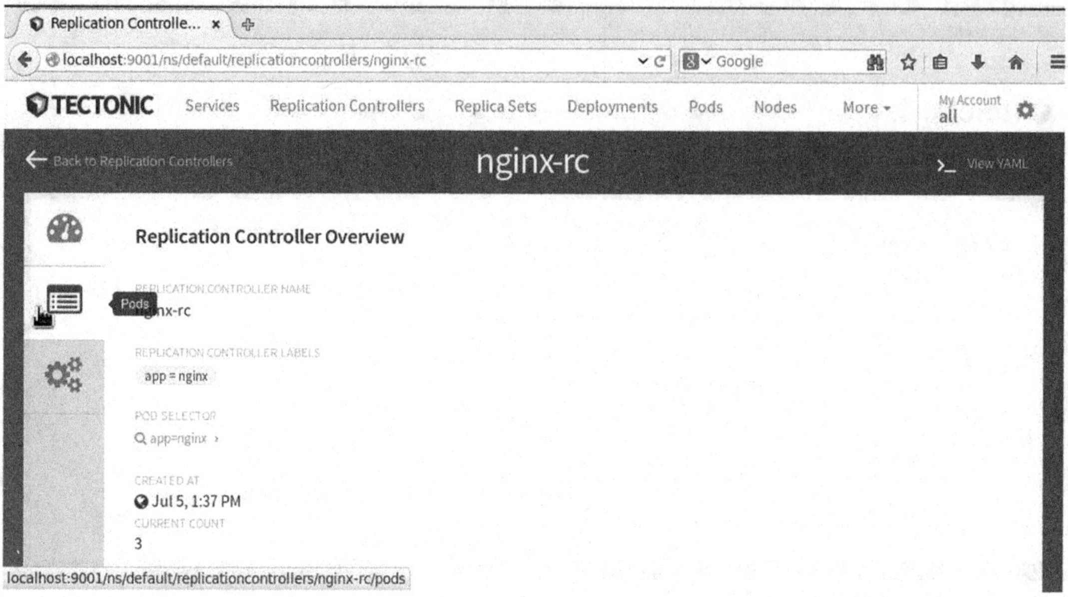

Figure 5-20. *Listing Pods in an RC*

The pods managed by the RC are listed as shown in Figure 5-21.

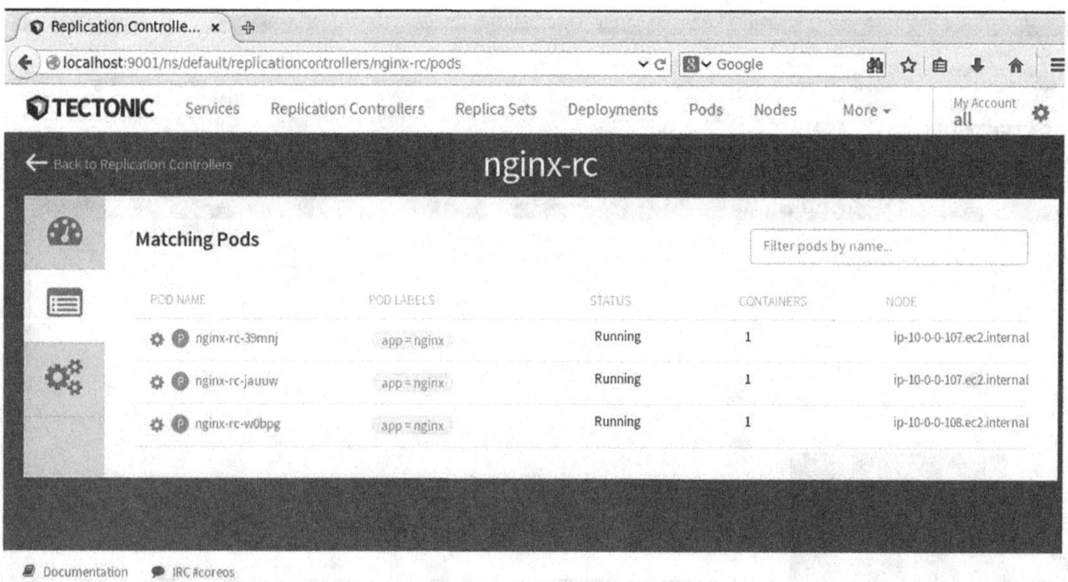

Figure 5-21. *Pods in RC* `nginx-rc`

To modify a pod's labels or delete it, right-click a pod and select one of the options shown in Figure 5-22. Click on Delete Pod to delete the pod.

***Figure 5-22.** Modifying a pod's labels or deleting a pod*

In the confirmation dialog, click Delete Pod as shown in Figure 5-23.

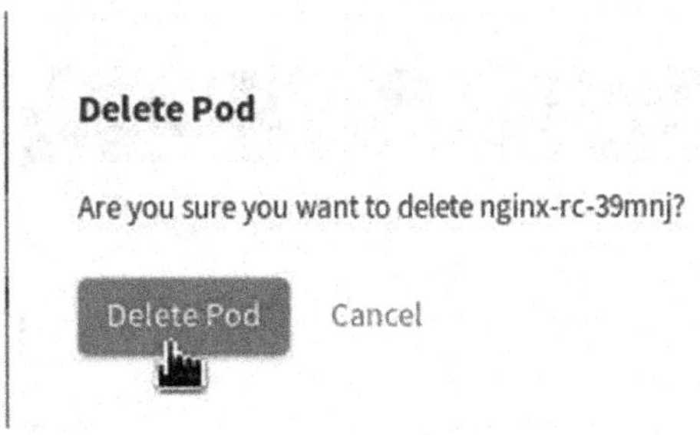

***Figure 5-23.** Deleting a pod*

If the number of pods running is not the number of replicas specified for the RC, new pods are launched for the deleted pods, and the number of pods again becomes 3, as shown in Figure 5-24.

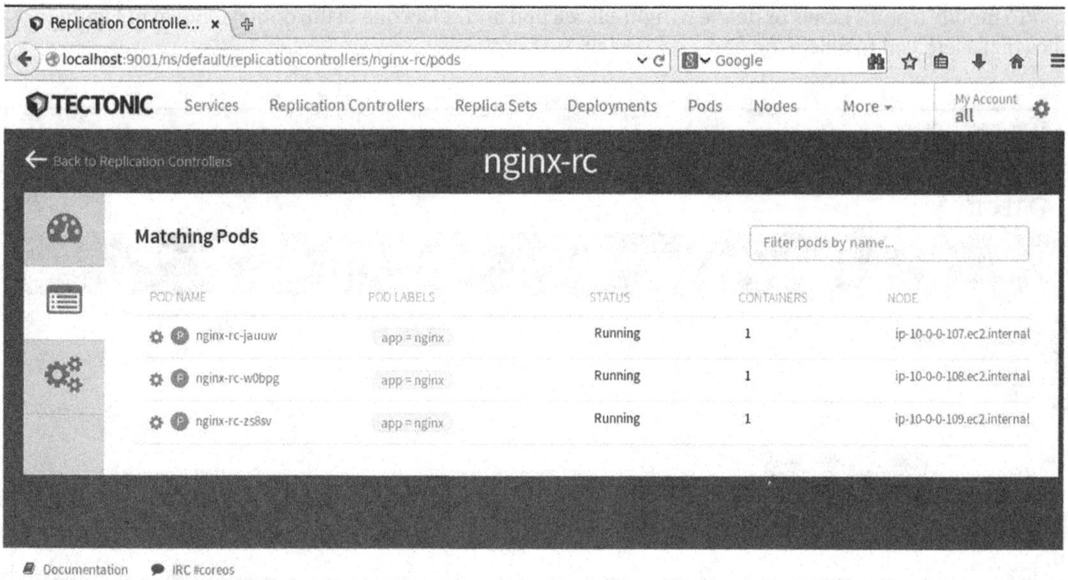

Figure 5-24. *Relaunched pod*

To list the services, click the Services tab. To create a new service click the Create a New Service link as shown in Figure 5-25.

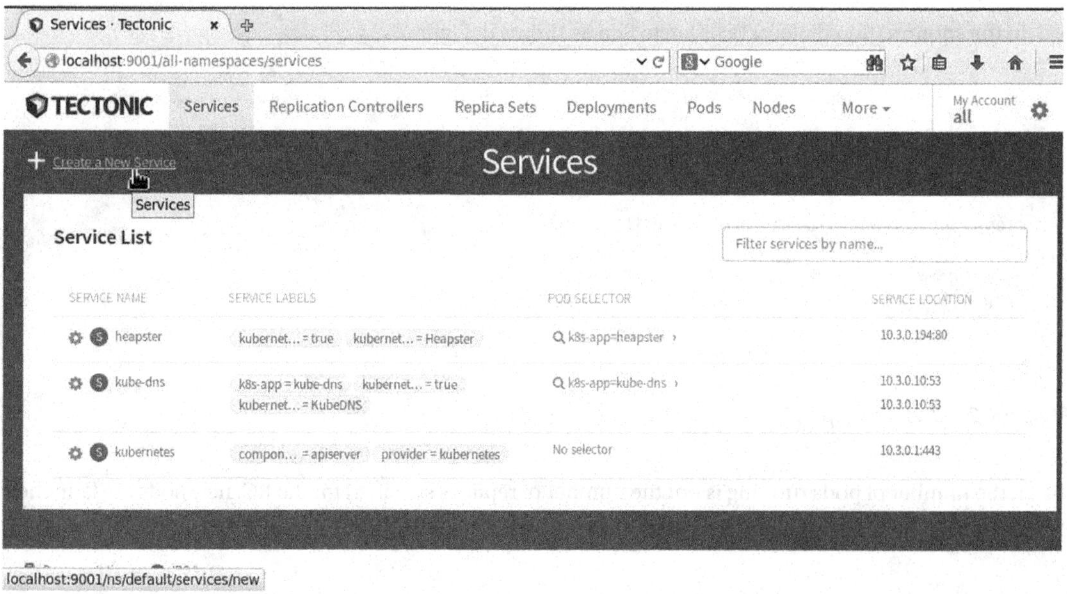

Figure 5-25. *Begin by clicking the Create a New Service link*

Specify the service details such as service name, labels, port, and routing method in the Create New Service form shown in Figure 5-26.

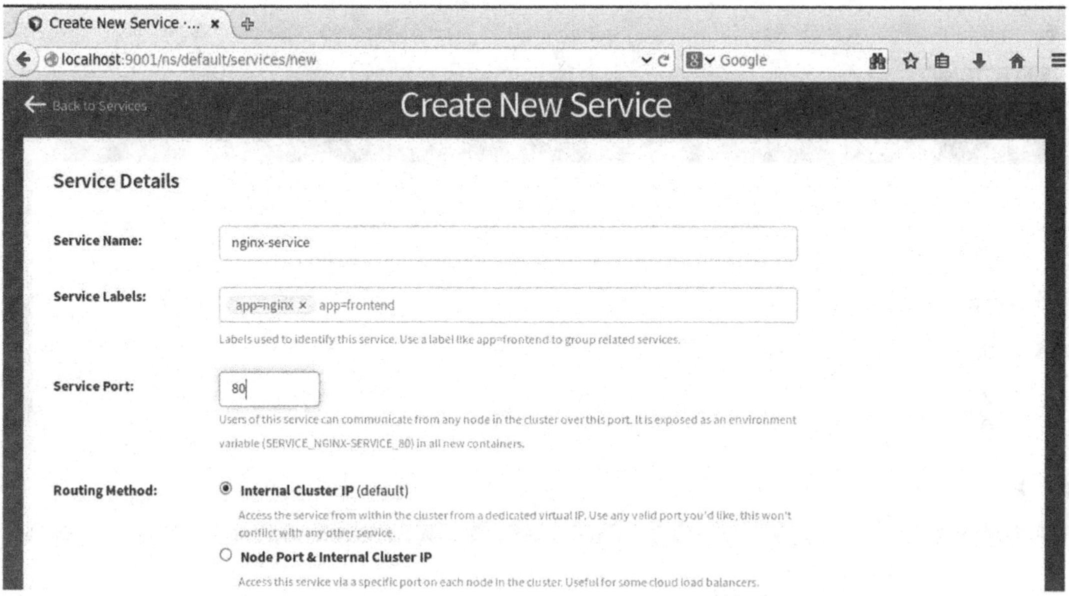

Figure 5-26. *Specifying details for the new service*

Select the Assign Any Available Port (default) to assign any port. Specify Pod Label Selector and Target Port, and click Create Service as shown in Figure 5-27.

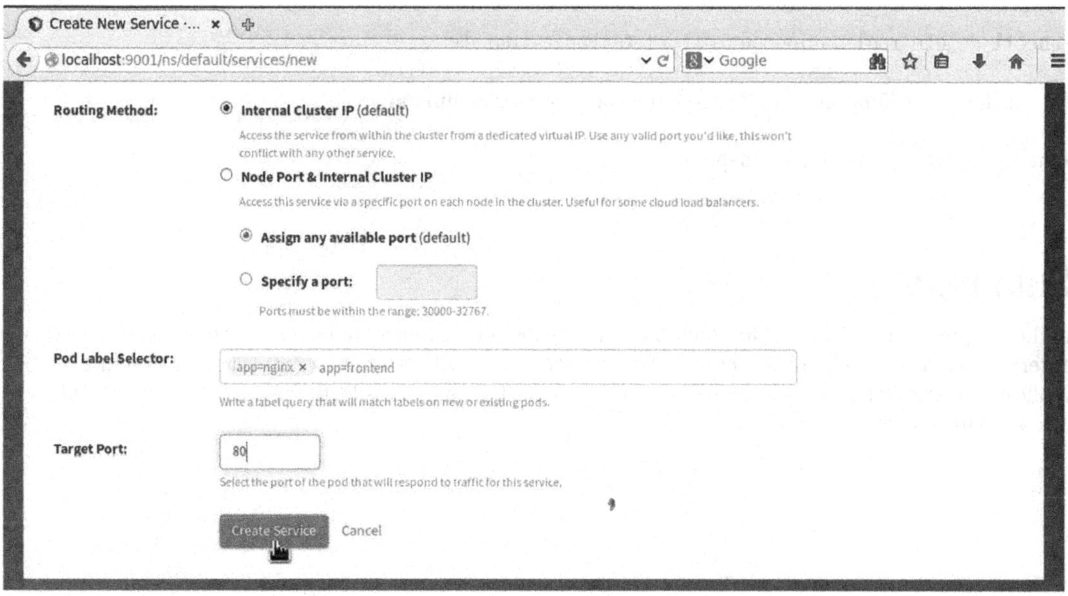

Figure 5-27. *Creating a new service*

A new Service is created, as shown in Figure 5-28.

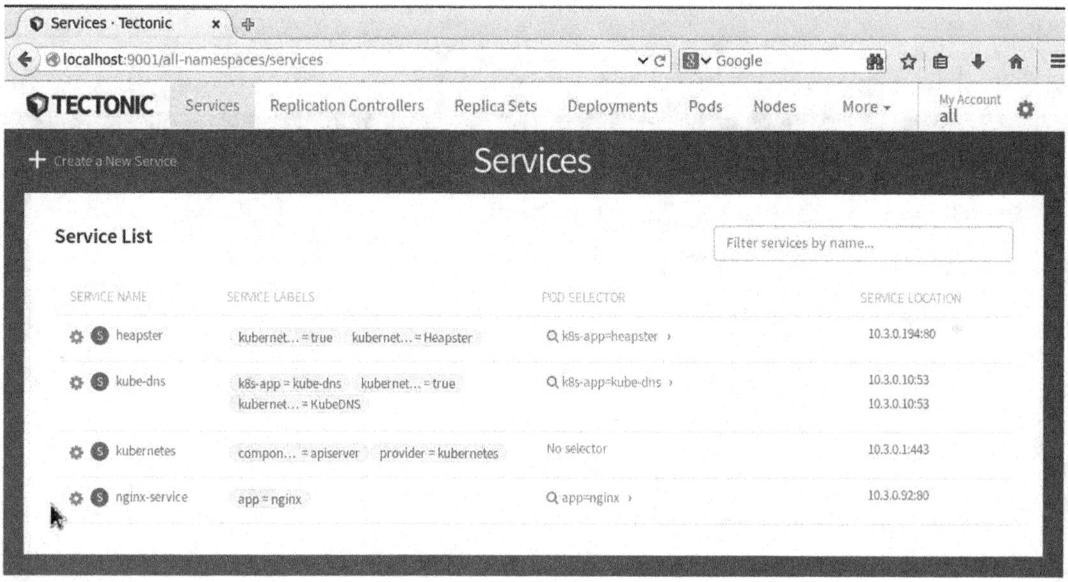

Figure 5-28. *A new service created in Tectonic Console*

Removing the Tectonic Console

To delete the Tectonic Console, run the following command:

```
kubectl delete replicationcontrollers tectonic-console
```

To delete the Kubernetes Pull Secret, run the following command:

```
kubectl delete secrets coreos-pull-secret
```

Summary

In this chapter we installed the GUI Tectonic Console, part of the free Starter version of the commercial enterprise Kubernetes platform Tectonic. We accessed the console in a browser and created a sample replication controller and service. Finally, we deleted the Tectonic Console. In the next chapter we shall discuss using Kubernetes volumes.

CHAPTER 6

Using Volumes

Kubernetes pods are invariably associated with data, and the data can either be made integral to a Docker container via its Docker image or decoupled from the Docker container.

Problem

If data (in on-disk files) is made integral to a Docker container, the following issues could result:

- The data is not persistent. The data is removed when a Docker container is restarted, which could also be due to a container crash.
- The data is container-specific and cannot be shared with other containers as such.

Solution

One of the principles of modular design is the Single Responsibility Principle (SRP). Kubernetes volumes implement the SRP by decoupling the data from a container. A volume is just a directory with or without data on some medium, which is different for different volume types. A volume is specified in a pod's spec and shared across different containers in the pod. A volume must be mounted in each container in a pod's spec independently, although it may be mounted in the different containers at the same (or different) file/directory path. A container in a pod has access to the filesystem inherited from its Docker image and the filesystem from a Kubernetes volume. A Docker image's filesystem is still at the root of the filesystem hierarchy, and a volume can only be mounted on a directory path within the root filesystem. Since volumes provide access to data outside a pod, volumes mounted in different pods are able to share the same data from the host or other external storage such as AWS EBS or a GitHub repository. Two types of volume abstractions or plugins are available: Volume and PersistentVolume. While a Volume is coupled with a pod, a PersistentVolume is provisioned on the networked cluster and is independent of a pod. Figure 6-1 shows an example of using an Amazon EBS Volume in a pod.

D. Vohra, *Kubernetes Management Design Patterns*, DOI 10.1007/978-1-4842-2598-1_6

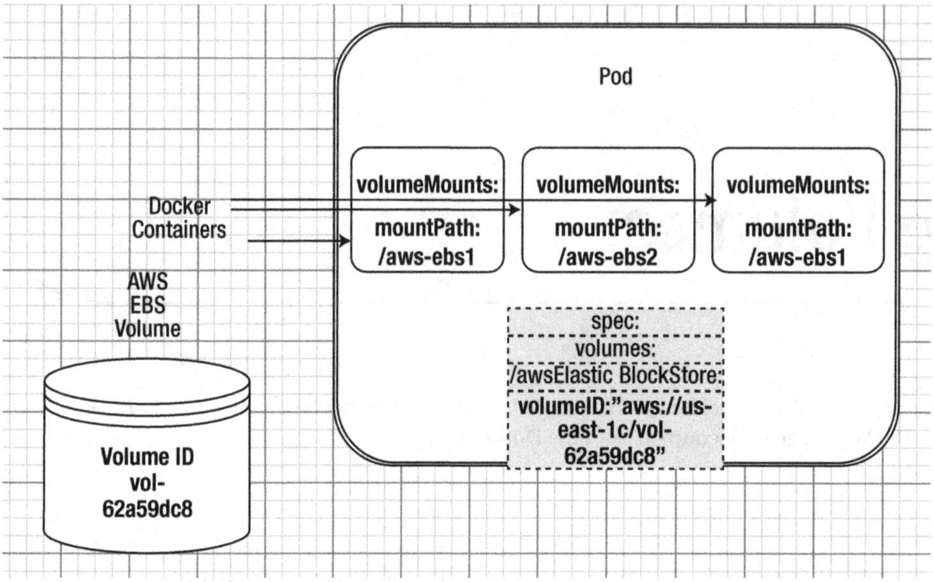

Figure 6-1. *Using a volume in a pod*

Overview

Kubernetes volumes are storage units associated with pods. A volume can be shared by pod replicas or dedicated to a single pod. Several types of volumes are supported for different types of storage, such as AWS volume, GitHub repository, or directory on the host, to list a few. The different types of volumes are described in Table 6-1.

Table 6-1. *Types of Volumes*

Volume Type	Description
`emptyDir`	A per-pod volume that is initially empty and shared by containers in a pod. Each container may mount the volume at the same or different path. By default, the volume is stored on the medium backing the machine, which could be SSD or network storage. Alternatively, the medium could be set to memory. When a pod is deleted the volume is deleted also, which means the volume is not persistent.
`hostPath`	Mounts a file or a directory form the host node's file system into the pod. Writable by root only the volume data persists even if the pod is deleted. All containers in the pod can access the volume. Designed for single node test only and supported in a multi-node cluster.
`gcePersistentDisk`	Mounts a Google Compute Engine Persistent Disk into a pod. The GCE PD's contents are not deleted if a pod is deleted and the volume is unmounted. Supported only for nodes of type GCE VMs in the same GCE project.

(*continued*)

Table 6-1. *(continued)*

Volume Type	Description
`awsElasticBlockStore`	Mounts an AWS EBS volume into a pod. The volume is persistent, as its contents are not deleted when the pod is deleted; the volume is unmounted. The node on which pods are running must be an Amazon EC2 instance in the same region and availability zone as the EBS volume. A single instance may mount an EBS volume.
`nfs`	A persistent volume; mounts a Network File System (NFS) into a pod.
`flocker`	Mounts a Flocker dataset into a pod. Flocker is an open-source clustered container data volume manager.
`gitRepo`	Clones a Git repository into an empty directory.
`persistentVolumeClaim`	Mounts a PersistentVolume into a pod.
`azureFileVolume`	Mounts a Microsoft Azure File Volume into a pod.

This chapter looks at the following topics:

- Setting the Environment
- Creating a AWS Volume
- Using a awsElasticBlockStore Volume
- Creating a Git Repo
- Using a gitRepo Volume

Setting the Environment

We will create an AWS CloudFormation on CoreOS for a Kubernetes cluster. To start, create a single EC2 instance from an Amazon Linux AMI.

SSH log in to the EC2 instance using the public IP address:

```
ssh -i "docker.pem"  ec2-user@54.173.38.246
```

Spin up a CloudFormation consisting of a single controller and three worker nodes as shown in Figure 6-2.

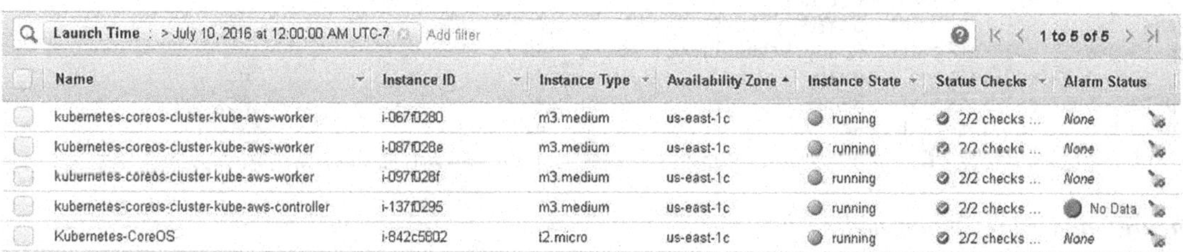

Figure 6-2. *CloudFormation EC2 instances*

Obtain the Kubernetes clusters' controller's public IP and add an A record for it to the public DNS for which the CloudFormation is created, as shown in Figure 6-3.

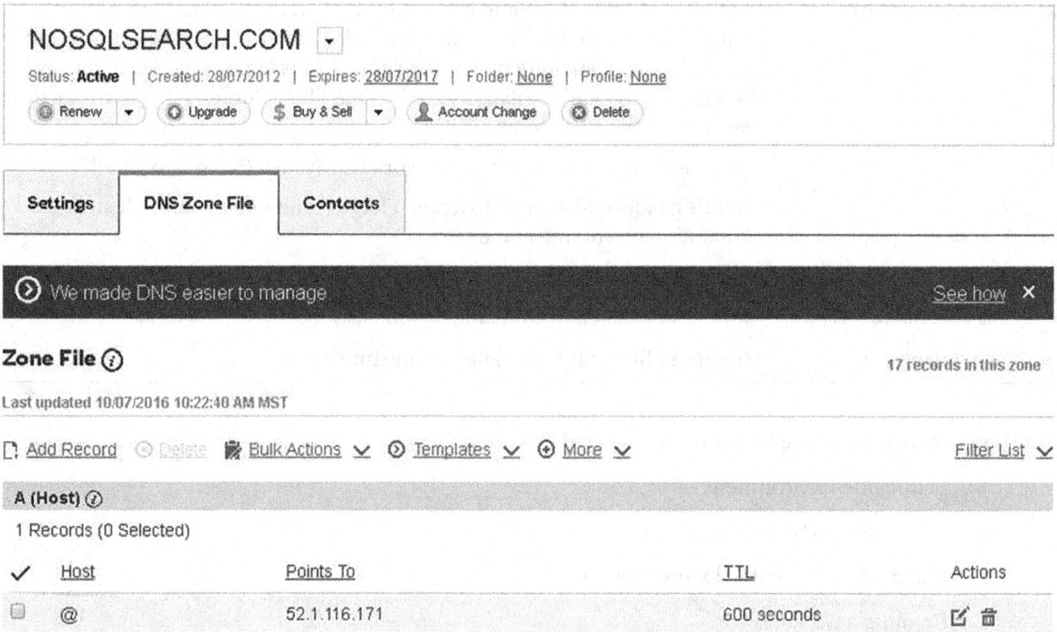

Figure 6-3. *Adding an A record for the domain*

SSH log in in to the controller instance using the public IP:

```
ssh -i "kubernetes-coreos.pem"  core@52.1.116.171
```

Install `kubectl` binaries and list the nodes in the cluster:

```
./kubectl get nodes
```

The single controller node and the three worker nodes are listed as shown in Figure 6-4.

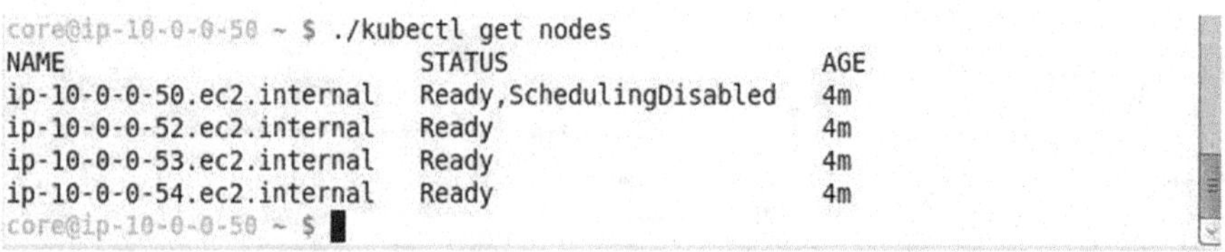

Figure 6-4. *Listing running nodes*

Creating an AWS Volume

An `awsElasticBlockStore` volume mounts an AWS EBS volume into a pod. In this section we will create an AWS EBS volume. Click on Create Volume in the EC2 Console as shown in Figure 6-5.

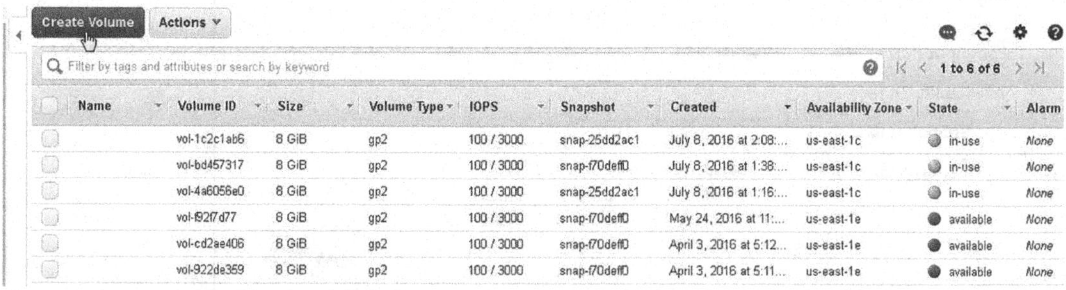

***Figure 6-5.** Begin by clicking Create Volume*

The EBS volume must be created in the same availability zone as the EC2 instance on which a pod is to mount the EBS volume. The availability zone is obtained from the EC2 console and is `us-east-1c`, as shown in Figure 6-6.

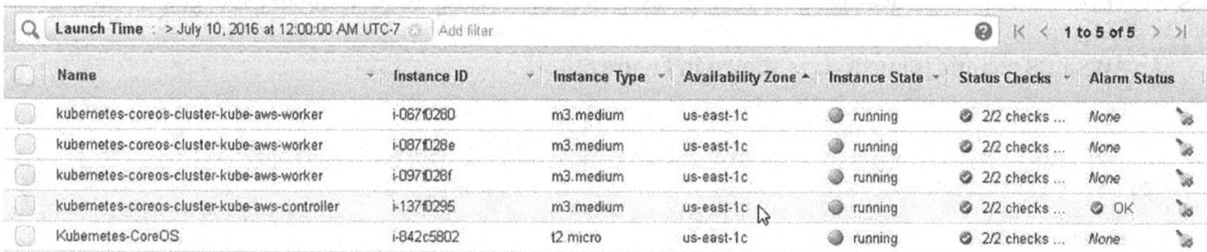

***Figure 6-6.** Obtaining the availability zone*

In the Create Volume dialog, set the Volume Type as General Purpose SSD (GP2) and the Size as 100 GiB. Set the Availability Zone as `us-east-1c` and click Create as shown in Figure 6-7.

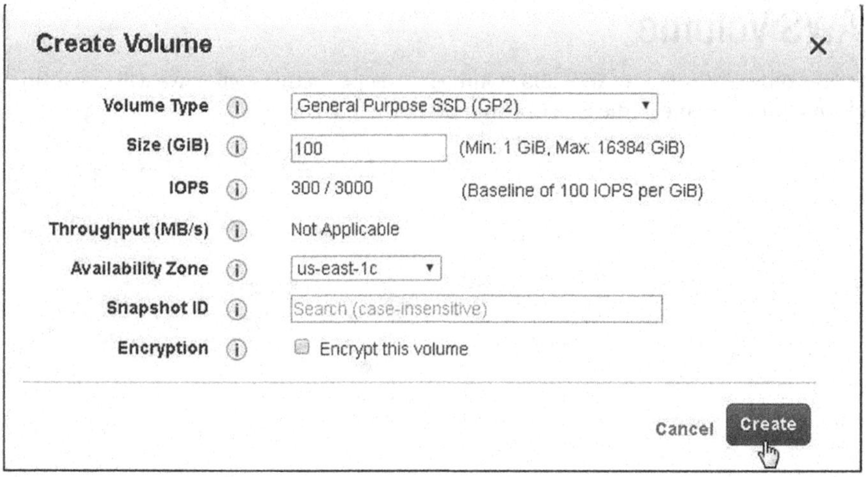

Figure 6-7. *Creating a volume*

An AWS EBS volume is created. An alternative method to create an EBS volume is with the `aws ec2 create-volume` command, as follows. The availability zone is specified with the `--availability-zone` command parameter as `us-east-1c`, the same as the EC2 instance on which the pod is running.

```
aws ec2 create-volume --availability-zone us-east-1c --size 10 --volume-type gp2
```

An AWS EBS volume is created, as shown in Figure 6-8.

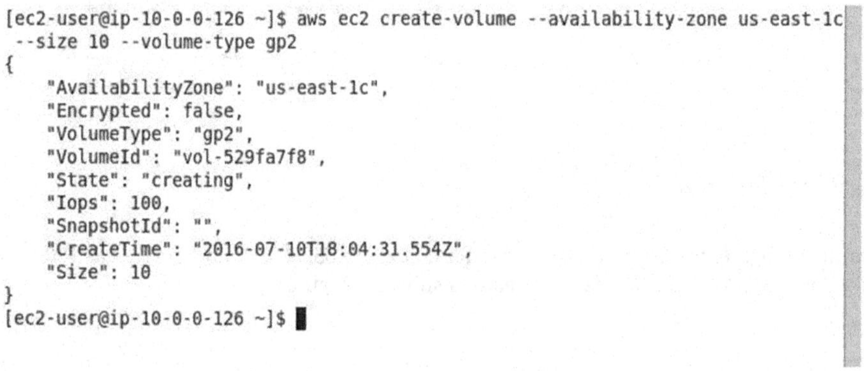

[ec2-user@ip-10-0-0-126 ~]$ aws ec2 create-volume --availability-zone us-east-1c
--size 10 --volume-type gp2
{
"AvailabilityZone": "us-east-1c",
"Encrypted": false,
"VolumeType": "gp2",
"VolumeId": "vol-529fa7f8",
"State": "creating",
"Iops": 100,
"SnapshotId": "",
"CreateTime": "2016-07-10T18:04:31.554Z",
"Size": 10
}
[ec2-user@ip-10-0-0-126 ~]$

Figure 6-8. *Creating a volume on the command line*

Using an awsElasticBlockStore Volume

Next, we will use the EBS volume in a `ReplicationController` specification file. Create a file called `pod-aws.yaml`:

```
sudo vi pod-aws.yaml
```

Specify the `awsElasticBlockStore` volume with the `volumes` key with the format of the `volumeID` set to `aws://zone/volumeid`. Obtain the `volumeID` from the EC2 console as shown in Figure 6-9.

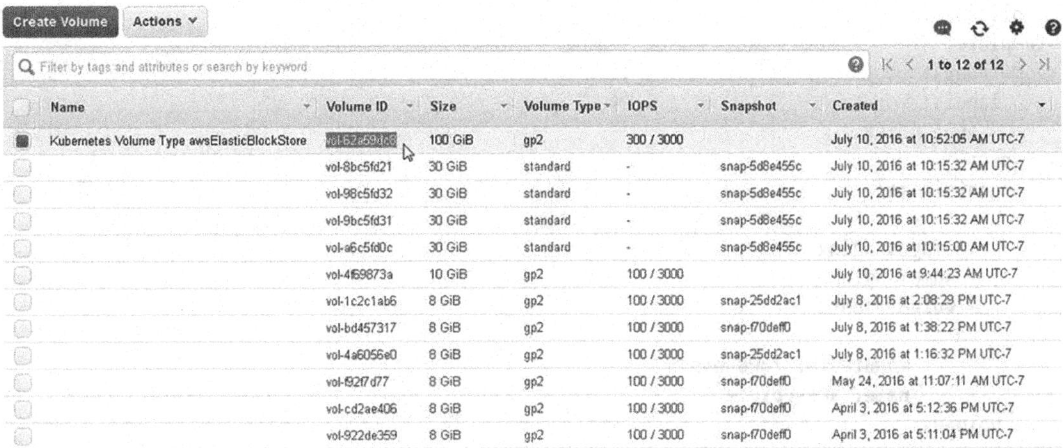

Create Volume
Actions
Filter by tags and attributes or search by keyword
1 to 12 of 12
Name
Volume ID
Size
Volume Type
IOPS
Snapshot
Created
Kubernetes Volume Type awsElasticBlockStore vol-62a59dc8 100 GiB gp2 300 / 3000 July 10, 2016 at 10:52:05 AM UTC-7
vol-8bc5fd21 30 GiB standard - snap-5d8e455c July 10, 2016 at 10:15:32 AM UTC-7
vol-98c5fd32 30 GiB standard - snap-5d8e455c July 10, 2016 at 10:15:32 AM UTC-7
vol-9bc5fd31 30 GiB standard - snap-5d8e455c July 10, 2016 at 10:15:32 AM UTC-7
vol-a6c5fd0c 30 GiB standard - snap-5d8e455c July 10, 2016 at 10:15:00 AM UTC-7
vol-4f69873a 10 GiB gp2 100 / 3000 July 10, 2016 at 9:44:23 AM UTC-7
vol-1c2c1ab6 8 GiB gp2 100 / 3000 snap-25dd2ac1 July 8, 2016 at 2:08:29 PM UTC-7
vol-bd457317 8 GiB gp2 100 / 3000 snap-f70deff0 July 8, 2016 at 1:38:22 PM UTC-7
vol-4a6056e0 8 GiB gp2 100 / 3000 snap-25dd2ac1 July 8, 2016 at 1:16:32 PM UTC-7
vol-f92f7d77 8 GiB gp2 100 / 3000 snap-f70deff0 May 24, 2016 at 11:07:11 AM UTC-7
vol-cd2ae406 8 GiB gp2 100 / 3000 snap-f70deff0 April 3, 2016 at 5:12:36 PM UTC-7
vol-922de359 8 GiB gp2 100 / 3000 snap-f70deff0 April 3, 2016 at 5:11:04 PM UTC-7

***Figure 6-9.** Obtaining the volumeID*

Specify the `fsType` as `ext4` and the volume name as `aws-volume`:

```
volumes:
  -
    awsElasticBlockStore:
      fsType: ext4
      volumeID: "aws://us-east-1c/vol-62a59dc8"
    name: aws-volume
```

The preceding volume definition is mounted with the volumeMounts key. The pod-aws.yaml file looks like this:

```
---
apiVersion: v1
kind: ReplicationController
metadata:
  labels:
    app: nginx
  name: nginx-rc
spec:
  replicas: 1
  template:
    metadata:
      labels:
        app: nginx
    spec:
      containers:
        -
          image: nginx
          name: nginx
          volumeMounts:
            -
              mountPath: /aws-ebs
              name: aws-volume
      volumes:
        -
          awsElasticBlockStore:
            fsType: ext4
            volumeID: "aws://us-east-1c/vol-62a59dc8"
          name: aws-volume
```

Save the pod-aws.yaml file with :wq as shown in Figure 6-10.

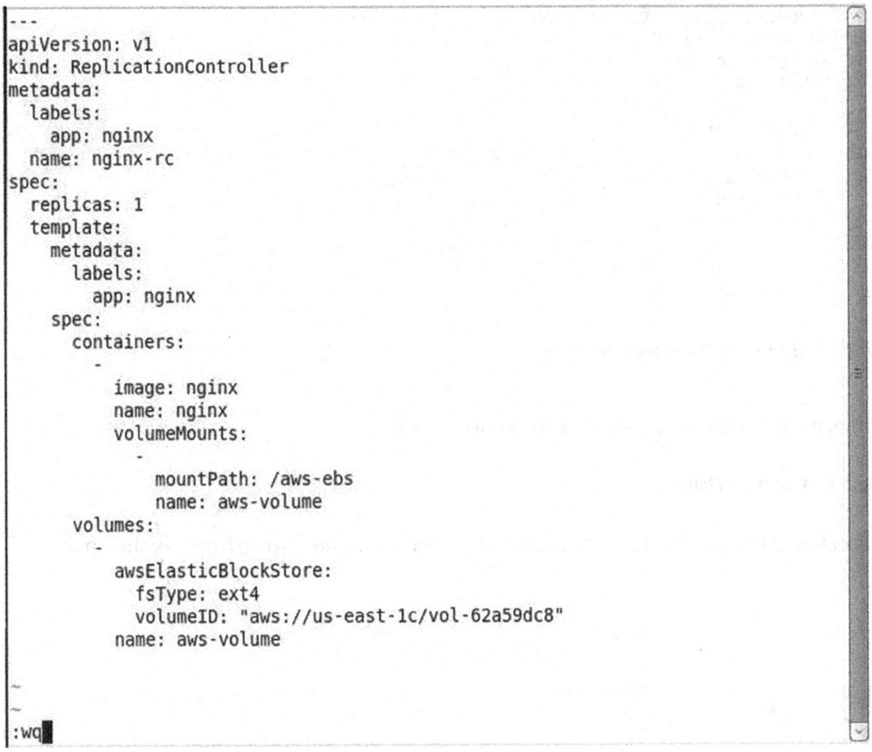

```
---
apiVersion: v1
kind: ReplicationController
metadata:
  labels:
    app: nginx
  name: nginx-rc
spec:
  replicas: 1
  template:
    metadata:
      labels:
        app: nginx
    spec:
      containers:
        -
          image: nginx
          name: nginx
          volumeMounts:
            -
              mountPath: /aws-ebs
              name: aws-volume
      volumes:
        -
          awsElasticBlockStore:
            fsType: ext4
            volumeID: "aws://us-east-1c/vol-62a59dc8"
          name: aws-volume
~
~
:wq
```

Figure 6-10. *The pod-aws.yaml*

Create a replication controller with the kubectl create command:

```
./kubectl create -f pod-aws.yaml
```

List the deployments, replication controllers, and pods:

```
./kubectl get deployments
./kubectl get rc
./kubectl get pods
```

A replication controller is created. The pod may initially be listed as not ready, as shown in Figure 6-11.

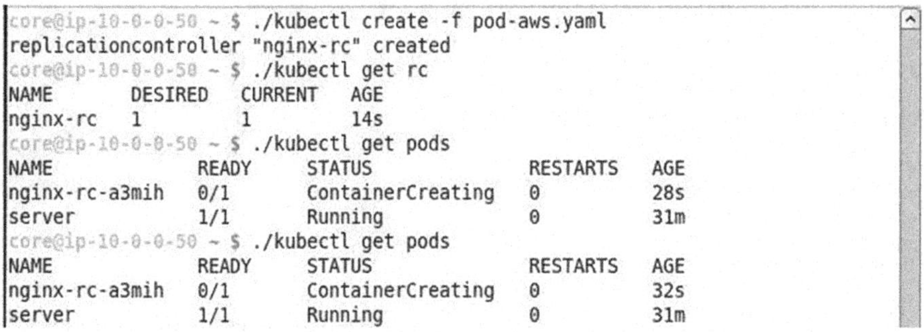

Figure 6-11. *Pod created but not yet running and ready*

Using the pod name, describe the pod with the following command:

```
kubectl describe pod nginx-rc-a3mih
```

The pod description is listed. The `AWSElasticBlockStore` volume should also be listed as shown in Figure 6-12.

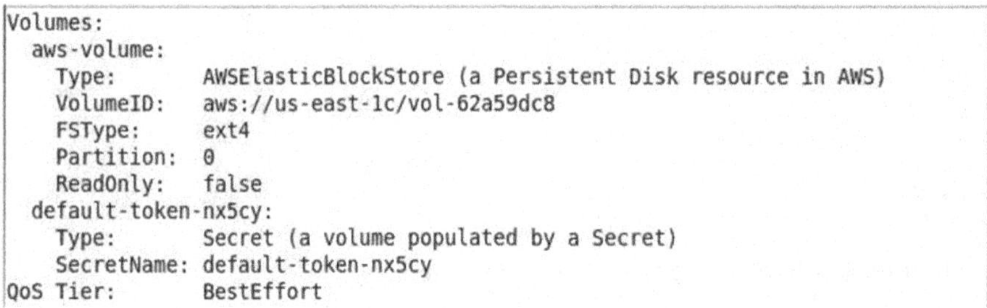

Volumes:
aws-volume:
Type: AWSElasticBlockStore (a Persistent Disk resource in AWS)
VolumeID: aws://us-east-1c/vol-62a59dc8
FSType: ext4
Partition: 0
ReadOnly: false
default-token-nx5cy:
Type: Secret (a volume populated by a Secret)
SecretName: default-token-nx5cy
QoS Tier: BestEffort

Figure 6-12. *Volume description*

List the pods again after a pause (up to a minute), and the pod should be running and ready as shown in Figure 6-13.

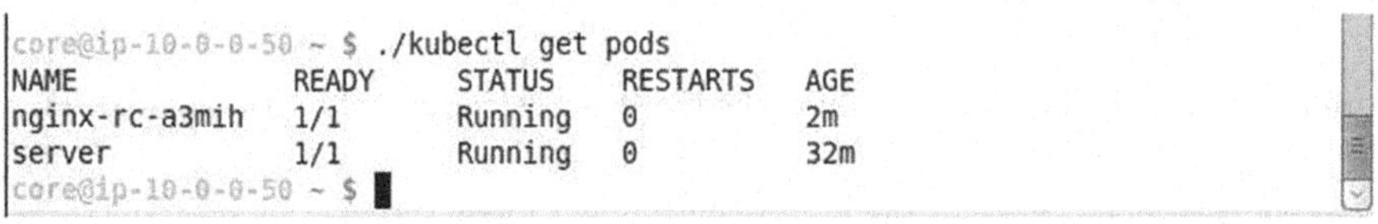

Figure 6-13. *Pod running and ready*

Using the `kubectl` exec command, start an interactive bash shell. List the files and directories with `ls -l`, and the `aws-ebs` directory should be listed; it is the mount path for the volume as shown in Figure 6-14.

```
core@ip-10-0-0-50 ~ $ ./kubectl get pods
NAME              READY     STATUS    RESTARTS   AGE
nginx-rc-a3mih    1/1       Running   0          2m
server            1/1       Running   0          32m
core@ip-10-0-0-50 ~ $
core@ip-10-0-0-50 ~ $ ./kubectl exec nginx-rc-a3mih -i -t -- bash -il
root@nginx-rc-a3mih:/# ls -l
total 132
drwxr-xr-x.  3 root root 4096 Jul 10 17:56 aws-ebs
drwxr-xr-x.  2 root root 4096 Jul 10 17:26 bin
drwxr-xr-x.  2 root root 4096 Mar 13 23:46 boot
drwxr-xr-x.  5 root root  380 Jul 10 17:56 dev
drwxr-xr-x.  1 root root 4096 Jul 10 17:56 etc
drwxr-xr-x.  2 root root 4096 Mar 13 23:46 home
drwxr-xr-x.  9 root root 4096 Jul 10 17:26 lib
drwxr-xr-x.  2 root root 4096 Jul 10 17:26 lib64
drwxr-xr-x.  2 root root 4096 May 23 17:51 media
drwxr-xr-x.  2 root root 4096 May 23 17:51 mnt
drwxr-xr-x.  2 root root 4096 May 23 17:51 opt
dr-xr-xr-x. 94 root root    0 Jul 10 17:56 proc
drwx------.  2 root root 4096 Jul 10 17:26 root
drwxr-xr-x.  1 root root 4096 Jul 10 17:56 run
drwxr-xr-x.  2 root root 4096 Jul 10 17:26 sbin
drwxr-xr-x.  2 root root 4096 May 23 17:51 srv
dr-xr-xr-x. 13 root root    0 Jul 10 17:16 sys
drwxrwxrwt.  2 root root 4096 Jun  1 18:00 tmp
drwxr-xr-x. 10 root root 4096 Jul 10 17:26 usr
drwxr-xr-x.  1 root root 4096 Jul 10 17:26 var
root@nginx-rc-a3mih:/#
```

Figure 6-14. *Starting the interactive shell and listing files*

Change directory (`cd`) to the `/aws-ebs` directory and list its contents. A default created file is listed as shown in Figure 6-15.

```
root@nginx-rc-a3mih:/# cd /aws-ebs
root@nginx-rc-a3mih:/aws-ebs# ls -l
total 16
drwx------. 2 root root 16384 Jul 10 17:56 lost+found
root@nginx-rc-a3mih:/aws-ebs#
```

Figure 6-15. *Listing the default file in the* `/aws-ebs` *directory*

Creating a Git Repo

For the `gitRepo` type of volume, we need to create a Git repository if one does not already exist. Create a GitHub account and click New Repository as shown in Figure 6-16.

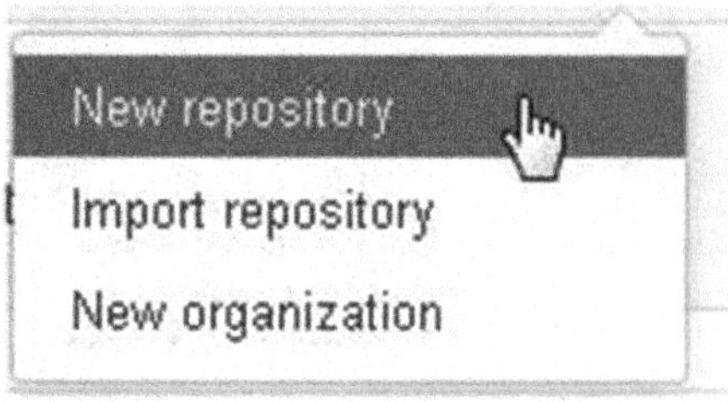

Figure 6-16. Selecting the New Repository option

In the Create a New Repository window, specify a Repository name, select the Public repository option, select Initialize This Repository with a README, and click Create Repository as shown in Figure 6-17.

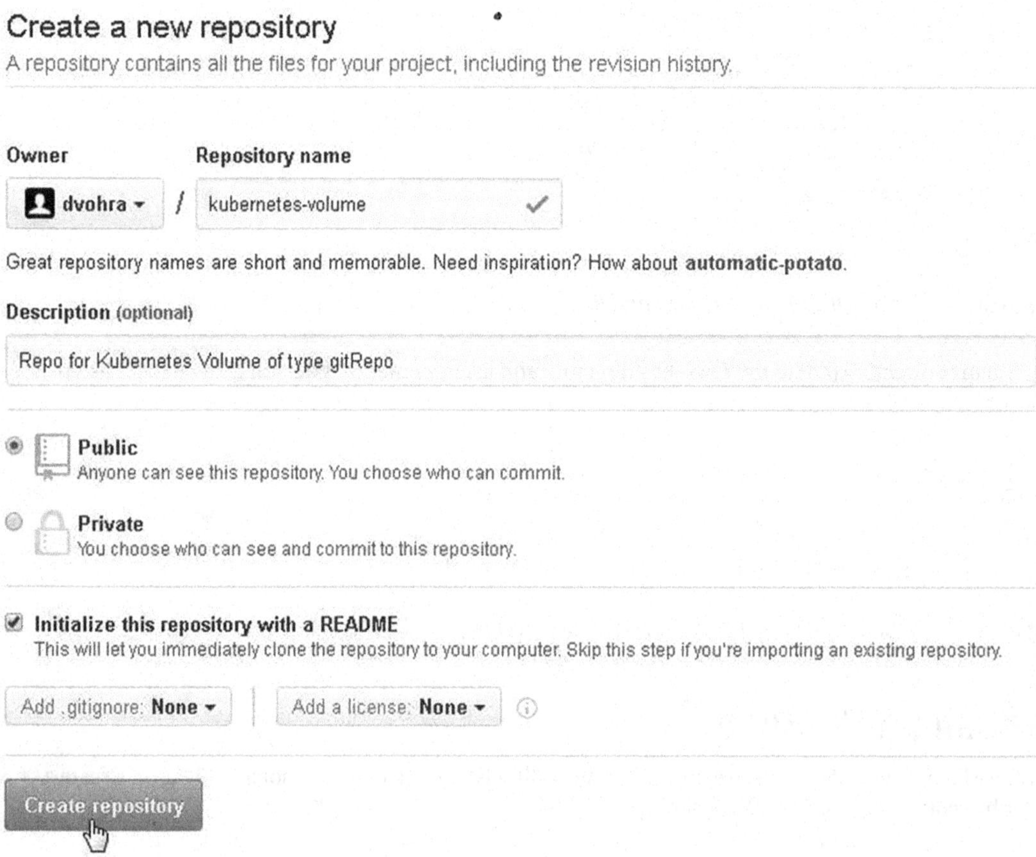

Figure 6-17. Creating a repository

A new repository is created, as shown in Figure 6-18.

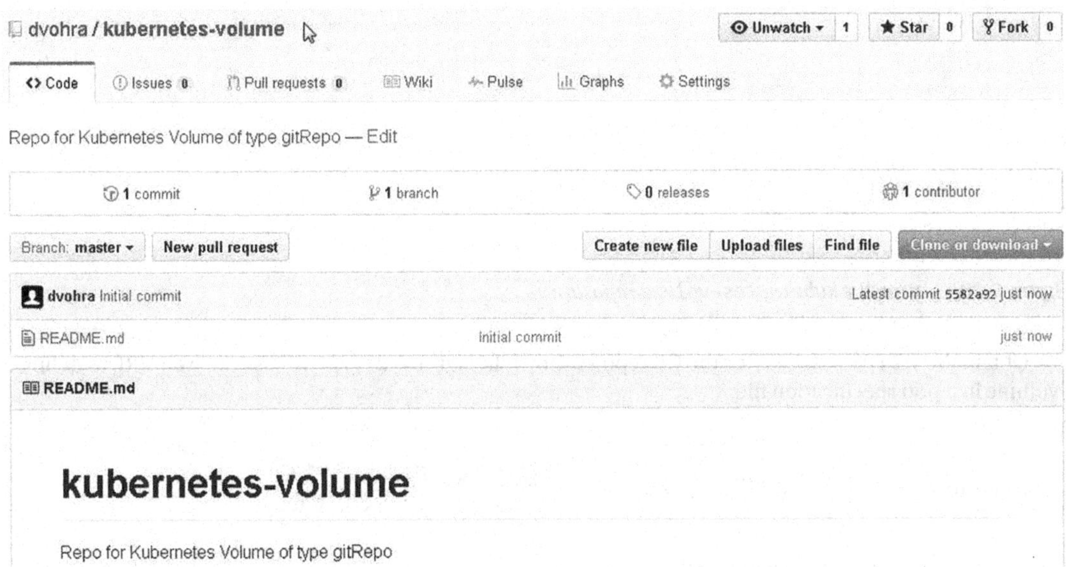

Figure 6-18. *The repository `kubernetes-volume`*

Optionally add some files (`pod.yaml`) to the repository, as shown in Figure 6-19.

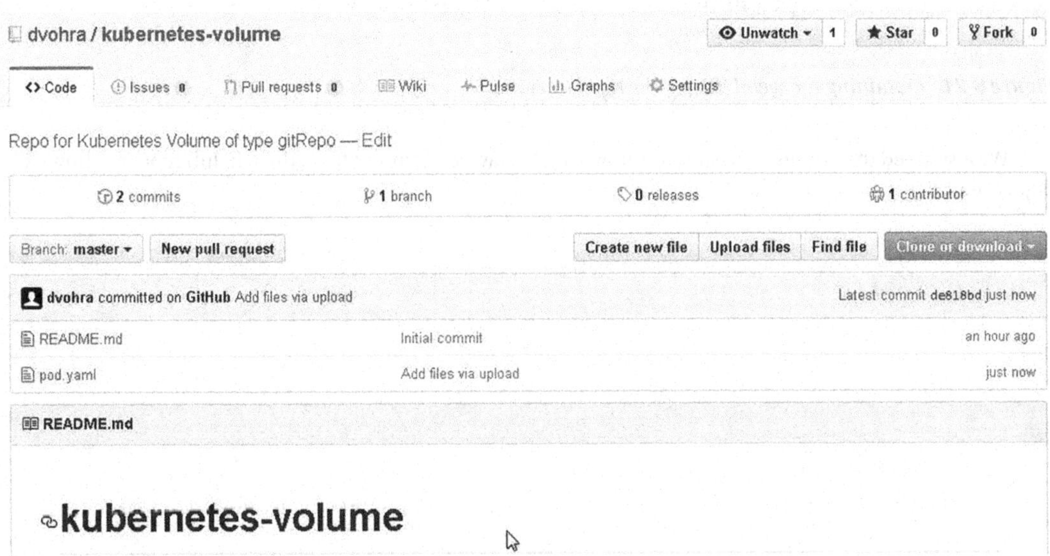

Figure 6-19. *Adding a file to the repository*

The kubernetes-volume repo should be listed in the user account, as shown in Figure 6-20.

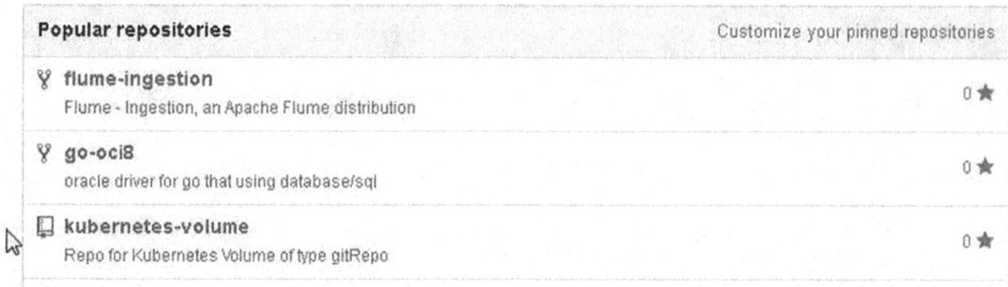

Figure 6-20. *Listing the* `kubernetes-volume` *repository*

Obtain the HTTPS web URL for the Git repo as shown in Figure 6-21. We will use the web URL to define a volume in a pod specification file.

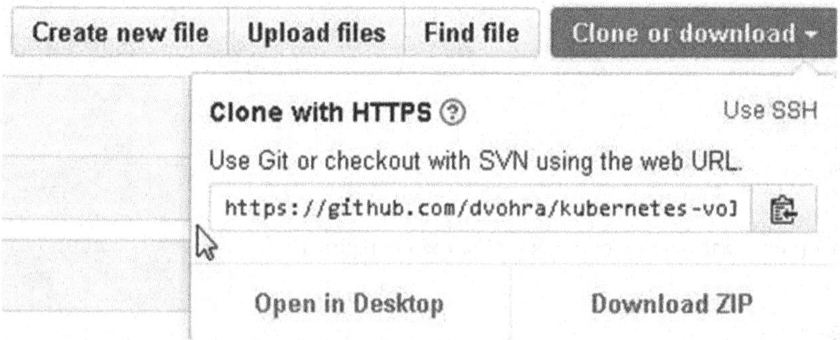

Figure 6-21. *Obtaining the web URL for the repository*

We also need the commit revision number, which may be obtained from the GitHub repo, as shown in Figure 6-22.

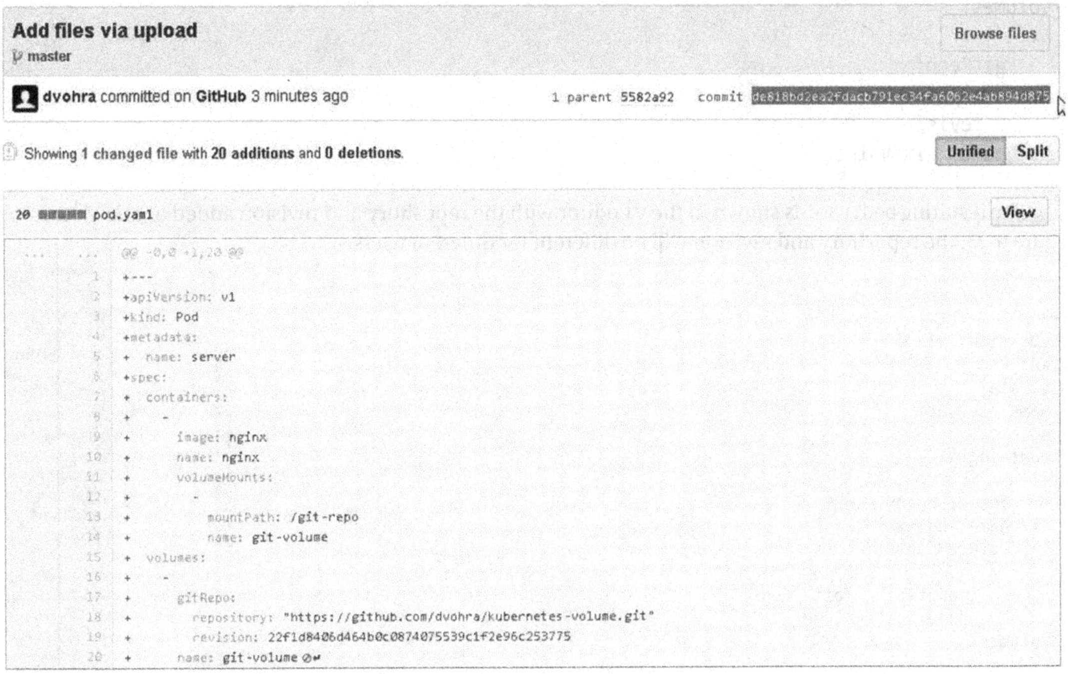

Figure 6-22. *Obtaining the commit revision number*

Using a gitRepo Volume

Create a pod specification file `pod.yaml` in which to use the `gitRepo` volume:

```
sudo vi pod.yaml
```

Copy the following listing into `pod.yaml`. The repository and revision strings are kept empty in the following listing, and values obtained from a user repository should be substituted.

```
---
apiVersion: v1
kind: Pod
metadata:
  name: server
spec:
  containers:
    -
      image: nginx
      name: nginx
      volumeMounts:
        -
          mountPath: /git-repo
          name: git-volume
```

```
  volumes:
    -
      gitRepo:
        repository: ""
        revision: ""
      name: git-volume
```

The resulting pod.yaml is shown in the vi editor with the repository and revision added as shown in Figure 6-23; the repository and revision will be different for different users.

```
---
apiVersion: v1
kind: Pod
metadata:
  name: server
spec:
  containers:
    -
      image: nginx
      name: nginx
      volumeMounts:
        -
          mountPath: /git-repo
          name: git-volume
  volumes:
    -
      gitRepo:
        repository: "https://github.com/dvohra/kubernetes-volume.git"
        revision: de818bd2ea2fdacb791ec34fa6062e4ab894d875
      name: git-volume
~
~
:wq
```

Figure 6-23. *The pod.yaml file*

Create a pod with the kubectl create command:

```
./kubectl create -f pod.yaml
```

List the replication controllers and pods:

```
./kubectl get rc
./kubectl get pods
```

As the output from the preceding commands shown in Figure 6-24 indicates, the pod "server" is created and started. Initially the pod may be listed as not running, but after a few seconds the pod should be running, as also shown in Figure 6-24.

```
core@ip-10-0-0-50 ~ $ ./kubectl create -f pod.yaml
pod "server" created
core@ip-10-0-0-50 ~ $ ./kubectl get rc
core@ip-10-0-0-50 ~ $ ./kubectl get pods
NAME      READY     STATUS              RESTARTS   AGE
server    0/1       ContainerCreating   0          22s
core@ip-10-0-0-50 ~ $ ./kubectl get pods
NAME      READY     STATUS    RESTARTS   AGE
server    1/1       Running   0          35s
core@ip-10-0-0-50 ~ $
```

Figure 6-24. *Creating a pod*

Describe the pod:

```
kubectl describe pod server
```

The `gitRepo` volume should also be listed in the description, as shown in Figure 6-25.

```
Volumes:
  git-volume:
    Type:       GitRepo (a volume that is pulled from git when the pod is create
d)
    Repository: https://github.com/dvohra/kubernetes-volume.git
    Revision:   de818bd2ea2fdacb791ec34fa6062e4ab894d875
  default-token-nx5cy:
```

Figure 6-25. *Listing the volume description*

Start an interactive shell on the "`server`" pod. List the directories and files, and you'll see the `git-repo` directory path on which the `gitRepo` volume is mounted listed as shown in Figure 6-26.

```
core@ip-10-0-0-50 ~ $ ./kubectl get pods
NAME      READY     STATUS    RESTARTS   AGE
server    1/1       Running   0          13m
core@ip-10-0-0-50 ~ $ ./kubectl exec server -i -t -- bash -il
root@server:/# ls -l
total 136
drwxr-xr-x.  2 root root 4096 Jul 10 17:26 bin
drwxr-xr-x.  2 root root 4096 Mar 13 23:46 boot
drwxr-xr-x.  5 root root  380 Jul 10 17:26 dev
drwxr-xr-x.  1 root root 4096 Jul 10 17:26 etc
drwxrwxrwx.  3 root root 4096 Jul 10 17:25 git-repo
drwxr-xr-x.  2 root root 4096 Mar 13 23:46 home
drwxr-xr-x.  9 root root 4096 Jul 10 17:26 lib
drwxr-xr-x.  2 root root 4096 Jul 10 17:26 lib64
drwxr-xr-x.  2 root root 4096 May 23 17:51 media
drwxr-xr-x.  2 root root 4096 May 23 17:51 mnt
drwxr-xr-x.  2 root root 4096 May 23 17:51 opt
dr-xr-xr-x. 85 root root    0 Jul 10 17:26 proc
drwx------.  2 root root 4096 Jul 10 17:26 root
drwxr-xr-x.  1 root root 4096 Jul 10 17:26 run
drwxr-xr-x.  2 root root 4096 Jul 10 17:26 sbin
drwxr-xr-x.  2 root root 4096 May 23 17:51 srv
dr-xr-xr-x. 13 root root    0 Jul 10 17:16 sys
drwxrwxrwt.  2 root root 4096 Jun  1 18:00 tmp
drwxr-xr-x. 10 root root 4096 Jul 10 17:26 usr
drwxr-xr-x.  1 root root 4096 Jul 10 17:26 var
root@server:/#
```

Figure 6-26. *Starting an interactive shell*

Change directory (cd) to the git-repo directory. List the directories, and the kubernetes-volume directory is listed, as shown in Figure 6-27.

```
root@server:/# cd /git-repo
root@server:/git-repo# ls -l
total 8
drwxr-xr-x. 3 root root 4096 Jul 10 17:25 kubernetes-volume
root@server:/git-repo# ▌
```

Figure 6-27. *Listing the kubernetes-volume directory*

Change directory (cd) to the kubernetes-volume directory. List the directories and the pod.yaml file on the Git repo should be listed, as shown in Figure 6-28.

```
root@server:/# cd /git-repo
root@server:/git-repo# ls -l
total 8
drwxr-xr-x. 3 root root 4096 Jul 10 17:25 kubernetes-volume
root@server:/git-repo# cd kubernetes-volume
root@server:/git-repo/kubernetes-volume# ls -l
total 16
-rw-r--r--. 1 root root  63 Jul 10 17:25 README.md
-rw-r--r--. 1 root root 417 Jul 10 17:25 pod.yaml
root@server:/git-repo/kubernetes-volume# ▌
```

Figure 6-28. *Listing files in the kubernetes-volume directory*

Summary

In this chapter we introduced the different types of Kubernetes volumes and then used two of these volumes, an awsElasticBlockStore volume and a gitRepo volume. For the awsElasticBlockStore an AWS volume had to be created, and for the gitRepo volume a Git repo had to be created. In the next chapter we will discuss using the different types of services.

CHAPTER 7

Using Services

A Kubernetes *service* is an abstraction serving a set of pods. The pods that a service defines or represents are selected using label selectors specified in the service spec. A service's label selector expression must be included in a pod's labels for the service to represent the pod. For example, if a service selector expression is `"app=hello-world"`, a pod's labels must include the label `"app=hello-world"` for the service to represent the pod. A service is accessed at one or more *endpoints* provided by the service. The number of endpoints available is equal to the number of pod replicas for a deployment/replication controller. To be able to access a service outside its cluster, the service must be exposed at an external IP address. The `ServiceType` field defines how a service is exposed. By default a `ServiceType` is `ClusterIP`, which exposes the service only within the cluster and not at an external IP. The other `ServiceTypes` are `NodePort` and `LoadBalancer`, which expose the service at an external IP.

Problem

Services are a classic example of the Single Responsibility Principle (SRP). Consider the alternative that a service is tightly coupled with a replication controller (RC) as shown in Figure 7-1. The following issues would result.

- If either the replication controller or the service is modified, the other has to be modified, too, as the two have a dependency on each other. If a replication controller is removed and replaced with another, the service would need to be replaced, too.
- For "high-functioning" DevOp teams, it is common for an application to have multiple release tracks, which could be daily or weekly. For multiple release applications it is typical to have multiple versions of replication controllers to coexist. Multiple RCs cannot coexist with a controller/service coupling.

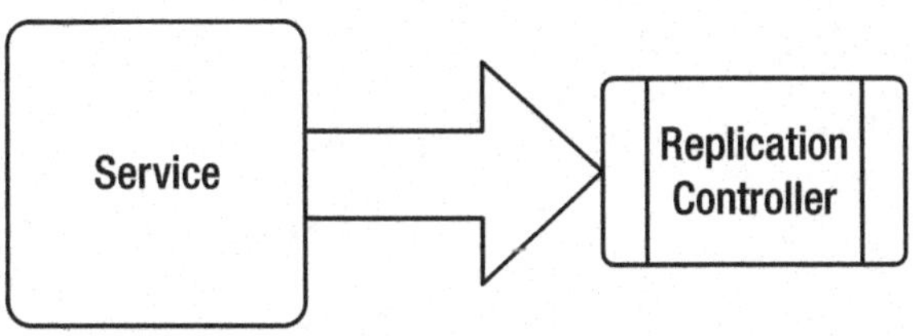

Figure 7-1. *Listing nodes in a Kubernetes cluster*

D. Vohra, *Kubernetes Management Design Patterns*, DOI 10.1007/978-1-4842-2598-1_7

Another issue associated with services is that when a new RC is created, pods do not start immediately and take a certain time (which could be a few seconds). A service representing the RC would need to know when the containers in a pod are ready so that the service can route traffic to the pod.

Solution

The service is a REST object similar to a pod and provides object-oriented benefits such as modularity or packaging, abstraction and reuse. Decoupling the service from the controller implements the SRP, and either the service or controller may be modified or deleted without having to modify or delete the other. Multiple replication controllers may be kept indefinitely, as shown in Figure 7-2, to meet the requirement of DevOps teams. A replication controller only manages the pods, and a service only exposes endpoints to access pods. Decoupling controller and service is a management design pattern.

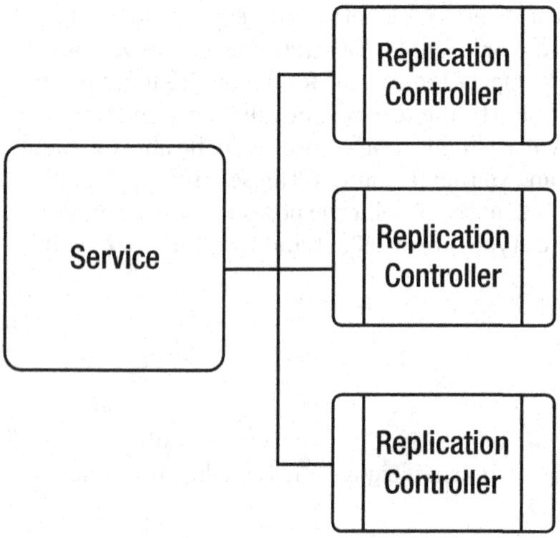

Figure 7-2. *Service associated with multiple replication controllers*

Another management pattern used in services is a readiness probe. A readiness probe is used to find whether a pod's containers are ready to receive traffic.

Overview

Table 7-1 describes the different `ServiceTypes`.

Table 7-1. *Types of Services*

ServiceType	External IP	Description
`ClusterIP`	No	The default; exposes a service from within a cluster only.
`NodePort`	Yes	In addition to exposing the service within a cluster, exposes the service at each node in the cluster at a specific port at URL `<NodeIP>:NodePort`.
`LoadBalancer`	Yes	In addition to exposing a service within the cluster and at each node in the cluster exposes the service at an external `LoadBalancer` IP.

In this chapter we shall discuss each of the `ServiceTypes` with an example. This chapter has the following sections:

Setting the Environment

Creating a ClusterIP Service

Creating a NodePort Service

Creating a LoadBalancer Service

Setting the Environment

Create an AWS EC2 instance from Amazon Linux AMI. SSH log in to the EC2 instance using the public IP address:

```
ssh -i "docker.pem"  ec2-user@107.23.131.161
```

Create a CoreOS AWS CloudFormation for a Kubernetes cluster. Add an A record for the cluster controller instance to the public DNS name for the CloudFormation and SSH log in to the controller instance:

```
ssh -i "kubernetes-coreos.pem"  core@52.203.239.87
```

Install `kubectl` binaries and list the nodes:

```
./kubectl get nodes
```

The nodes in the cluster should be listed, as shown in Figure 7-3.

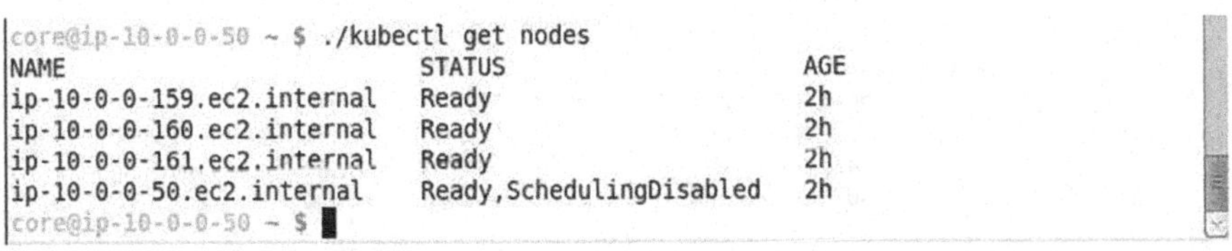
core@ip-10-0-0-50 ~ $ ./kubectl get nodes
NAME STATUS AGE
ip-10-0-0-159.ec2.internal Ready 2h
ip-10-0-0-160.ec2.internal Ready 2h
ip-10-0-0-161.ec2.internal Ready 2h
ip-10-0-0-50.ec2.internal Ready,SchedulingDisabled 2h
core@ip-10-0-0-50 ~ $

Figure 7-3. *Listing nodes in a Kubernetes cluster*

Creating a ClusterIP Service

In this section we shall create a service of type `ClusterIP`, which is the default service type. First, create a deployment using the Docker image `tutum/hello-world` with three replicas:

```
./kubectl run hello-world --image=tutum/hello-world --replicas=3 --port=80
```

Next, list the deployments:

```
./kubectl get deployments
```

A `hello-world` deployment is created and listed as shown in Figure 7-4.

```
core@ip-10-0-0-50 ~ $ ./kubectl run hello-world --image=tutum/hello-world --replicas
=3 --port=80
deployment "hello-world" created
core@ip-10-0-0-50 ~ $ ./kubectl get deployments
NAME          DESIRED   CURRENT   UP-TO-DATE   AVAILABLE   AGE
hello-world   3         3         3            3           11s
php-apache    15        15        15           12          30m
core@ip-10-0-0-50 ~ $ 
```

Figure 7-4. *Creating and listing the deployments*

List the pods:

```
./kubectl get pods
```

The three pod replicas are listed. Expose the deployment as a service of type `ClusterIP`, which is the default, but may also be specified explicitly.

```
./kubectl expose deployment hello-world --port=80 --type=ClusterIP
```

List the services:

```
./kubectl get services
```

The `hello-world` service should be listed in addition to the `kubernetes` service and any other services, as shown in Figure 7-5.

```
core@ip-10-0-0-50 ~ $ ./kubectl expose deployment hello-world --port=80 --type=Clust
erIP
service "hello-world" exposed
core@ip-10-0-0-50 ~ $ ./kubectl get services
NAME          CLUSTER-IP    EXTERNAL-IP         PORT(S)   AGE
hello-world   10.3.0.234    <none>              80/TCP    8s
kubernetes    10.3.0.1      <none>              443/TCP   1h
php-apache    10.3.0.129    a0feb07714cfd...    80/TCP    50m
core@ip-10-0-0-50 ~ $ 
```

Figure 7-5. *Creating and listing a service*

Describe the service:

```
./kubectl describe svc hello-world
```

The service description includes the service type as `ClusterIP` and three endpoints for the service, as shown in Figure 7-6.

```
core@ip-10-0-0-50 ~ $ ./kubectl describe svc hello-world
Name:                   hello-world
Namespace:              default
Labels:                 run=hello-world
Selector:               run=hello-world
Type:                   ClusterIP
IP:                     10.3.0.234
Port:                   <unset> 80/TCP
Endpoints:              10.2.12.7:80,10.2.49.7:80,10.2.83.6:80
Session Affinity:       None
No events.

core@ip-10-0-0-50 ~ $
```

***Figure 7-6.** Describing the `hello-world` service*

The service may be accessed at the `clusterIP` and each of the service endpoints. First, access the cluster IP with the command `curl cluster-ip`. The `cluster-ip` is `10.3.0.234`, so access the service at `curl 10.3.0.234`. The HTML markup for the service is output as shown in Figure 7-7.

```
core@ip-10-0-0-50 ~ $ curl 10.3.0.234
<html>
<head>
        <title>Hello world!</title>
        <link href='http://fonts.googleapis.com/css?family=Open+Sans:400,700' rel='s
tylesheet' type='text/css'>
        <style>
        body {
                background-color: white;
                text-align: center;
                padding: 50px;
                font-family: "Open Sans","Helvetica Neue",Helvetica,Arial,sans-serif
;
        }

        #logo {
                margin-bottom: 40px;
        }
        </style>
</head>
<body>
        <img id="logo" src="logo.png" />
        <h1>Hello world!</h1>
        <h3>My hostname is hello-world-3739649373-xyqhi</h3>                    <h3>
Links found</h3>
                                        <b>PHP_APACHE</b> listening in 80 available
at tcp://10.3.0.129:80<br />
                                                <b>KUBERNETES</b> listening in 443 a
vailable at tcp://10.3.0.1:443<br />
                                </body>
</html>
core@ip-10-0-0-50 ~ $
```

***Figure 7-7.** Invoking a service endpoint with `curl`*

Similarly, invoke the service at a service endpoint 10.2.12.7 as shown in Figure 7-8. The HTML markup for the service is output.

```
core@ip-10-0-0-50 ~ $ curl 10.2.12.7
<html>
<head>
        <title>Hello world!</title>
        <link href='http://fonts.googleapis.com/css?family=Open+Sans:400,700' rel='s
tylesheet' type='text/css'>
        <style>
        body {
                background-color: white;
                text-align: center;
                padding: 50px;
                font-family: "Open Sans","Helvetica Neue",Helvetica,Arial,sans-serif
;
        }

        #logo {
                margin-bottom: 40px;
        }
        </style>
</head>
<body>
        <img id="logo" src="logo.png" />
        <h1>Hello world!</h1>
        <h3>My hostname is hello-world-3739649373-ylpe3</h3>                    <h3>
Links found</h3>
                                                <b>PHP_APACHE</b> listening in 80 available
at tcp://10.3.0.129:80<br />
                                                        <b>KUBERNETES</b> listening in 443 a
vailable at tcp://10.3.0.1:443<br />
                                        </body>
</html>
core@ip-10-0-0-50 ~ $
```

Figure 7-8. *Invoking a different service endpoint*

To invoke the service in a web browser, set port forwarding from a local machine. First, copy the key-pair used to access the cluster controller instance to the local machine:

```
scp -i docker.pem ec2-user@ec2-107-23-131-161.compute-1.amazonaws.com:~/kubernetes-coreos.
pem ~/kubernetes-coreos.pem
```

Then set port forwarding from the local machine `locahost:80` to the cluster IP of the service on the controller instance:

```
ssh -i kubernetes-coreos.pem -f -nNT -L 80:10.3.0.234:80 core@ec2-52-203-239-87.compute-1.
amazonaws.com
```

Port forwarding from local machine `localhost:80` to `cluster-ip:80` is set. Invoke the service in a web browser at `http://localhost`, as shown in Figure 7-9.

Figure 7-9. *Invoking a service in a browser*

Creating a NodePort Service

In this section we shall expose the same deployment `hello-world` as a service of type `NodePort`. First, delete the service `hello-world`:

```
./kubectl delete svc hello-world
```

Then expose the deployment `hello-world` as a service of type `NodePort`:

```
./kubectl expose rc hello-world --port=80 --type=NodePort
```

A service of type `NodePort` is exposed, as shown in Figure 7-10.

```
core@ip-10-0-0-50 ~ $ ./kubectl delete svc hello-world
service "hello-world" deleted
core@ip-10-0-0-50 ~ $ ./kubectl expose deployment hello-world --port=80 --type=NodeP
ort
service "hello-world" exposed
```

Figure 7-10. *Creating a service of type NodePort*

List the services, and the `hello-world` service is displayed. In addition to a `cluster-ip`, an `external-ip <nodes>` is listed, as shown in Figure 7-11. Unlike the `cluster-ip`, the `<nodes> ip` is not a literal IP and indicates that the service is exposed at each of the nodes in the cluster.

```
core@ip-10-0-0-50 ~ $ ./kubectl get svc
NAME          CLUSTER-IP   EXTERNAL-IP   PORT(S)   AGE
hello-world   10.3.0.125   <nodes>       80/TCP    42s
kubernetes    10.3.0.1     <none>        443/TCP   2h
core@ip-10-0-0-50 ~ $
```

Figure 7-11. *Listing the `NodePort`-type service*

Access the service at the `cluster-ip` as for a service of type `ClusterIP`, and the HTML markup is displayed as shown in Figure 7-12.

```
core@ip-10-0-0-50 ~ $ curl 10.3.0.125
<html>
<head>
        <title>Hello world!</title>
        <link href='http://fonts.googleapis.com/css?family=Open+Sans:400,700' rel='s
tylesheet' type='text/css'>
        <style>
        body {
                background-color: white;
                text-align: center;
                padding: 50px;
                font-family: "Open Sans","Helvetica Neue",Helvetica,Arial,sans-serif
;
        }

        #logo {
                margin-bottom: 40px;
        }
        </style>
</head>
<body>
        <img id="logo" src="logo.png" />
        <h1>Hello world!</h1>
        <h3>My hostname is hello-world-3739649373-b8gar</h3>                    <h3>
Links found</h3>
                                                <b>PHP_APACHE</b> listening in 80 available
at tcp://10.3.0.129:80<br />
                                                        <b>KUBERNETES</b> listening in 443 a
vailable at tcp://10.3.0.1:443<br />
                                                        <b>HELLO_WORLD</b> listening in 80 a
vailable at tcp://10.3.0.234:80<br />
                                        </body>
</html>
```

Figure 7-12. *Invoking a service at `Cluster-IP`*

List the nodes, as shown in Figure 7-13.

```
core@ip-10-0-0-50 ~ $ ./kubectl get nodes
NAME                          STATUS                       AGE
ip-10-0-0-159.ec2.internal    Ready                        2h
ip-10-0-0-160.ec2.internal    Ready                        2h
ip-10-0-0-161.ec2.internal    Ready                        2h
ip-10-0-0-50.ec2.internal     Ready,SchedulingDisabled     2h
core@ip-10-0-0-50 ~ $
```

Figure 7-13. *Listing the nodes in a Kubernetes cluster*

Describe the service to list the NodePort (32624), which is the port on each of the nodes at which the service is exposed, as shown in Figure 7-14.

```
core@ip-10-0-0-50 ~ $ ./kubectl describe svc hello-world
Name:                   hello-world
Namespace:              default
Labels:                 run=hello-world
Selector:               run=hello-world
Type:                   NodePort
IP:                     10.3.0.125
Port:                   <unset> 80/TCP
NodePort:               <unset> 32624/TCP
Endpoints:              10.2.12.3:80,10.2.49.2:80,10.2.49.3:80
Session Affinity:       None
No events.

core@ip-10-0-0-50 ~ $
```

Figure 7-14. *Describing the NodePort service*

Invoke the service at a worker node with the URL Node-IP:NodePort, and the same HTML markup should be listed, as shown in Figure 7-15.

```
core@ip-10-0-0-50 ~ $ curl  http://ip-10-0-0-159.ec2.internal:32624
<html>
<head>
        <title>Hello world!</title>
        <link href='http://fonts.googleapis.com/css?family=Open+Sans:400,700' rel='s
tylesheet' type='text/css'>
        <style>
        body {
                background-color: white;
                text-align: center;
                padding: 50px;
                font-family: "Open Sans","Helvetica Neue",Helvetica,Arial,sans-serif
;
        }

        #logo {
                margin-bottom: 40px;
        }
        </style>
</head>
<body>
        <img id="logo" src="logo.png" />
        <h1>Hello world!</h1>
        <h3>My hostname is hello-world-3739649373-5ll92</h3>                    <h3>
Links found</h3>
                                        <b>PHP_APACHE</b> listening in 80 available
at tcp://10.3.0.129:80<br />
                                                <b>HELLO_WORLD</b> listening in 80 a
vailable at tcp://10.3.0.234:80<br />
                                                <b>KUBERNETES</b> listening in 443 a
```

Figure 7-15. *Invoking the service at a worker node*

Similarly, the service may be invoked at the master node using the same node port, as shown in Figure 7-16.

```
core@ip-10-0-0-50 ~ $ curl http://ip-10-0-0-50.ec2.internal:32624
<html>
<head>
        <title>Hello world!</title>
        <link href='http://fonts.googleapis.com/css?family=Open+Sans:400,700' rel='s
tylesheet' type='text/css'>
        <style>
        body {
                background-color: white;
                text-align: center;
                padding: 50px;
                font-family: "Open Sans","Helvetica Neue",Helvetica,Arial,sans-serif
;
        }

        #logo {
                margin-bottom: 40px;
        }
        </style>
</head>
<body>
        <img id="logo" src="logo.png" />
        <h1>Hello world!</h1>
        <h3>My hostname is hello-world-3739649373-5ll92</h3>                    <h3>
Links found</h3>
                                        <b>PHP_APACHE</b> listening in 80 available
at tcp://10.3.0.129:80<br />
                                                <b>HELLO_WORLD</b> listening in 80 a
vailable at tcp://10.3.0.234:80<br />
                                                <b>KUBERNETES</b> listening in 443 a
vailable at tcp://10.3.0.1:443<br />
```

Figure 7-16. *Invoking the service at the master node*

To invoke the service in a web browser, we don't need to set port forwarding. Obtain the public DNS name of the node at which to invoke the service as shown in Figure 7-17.

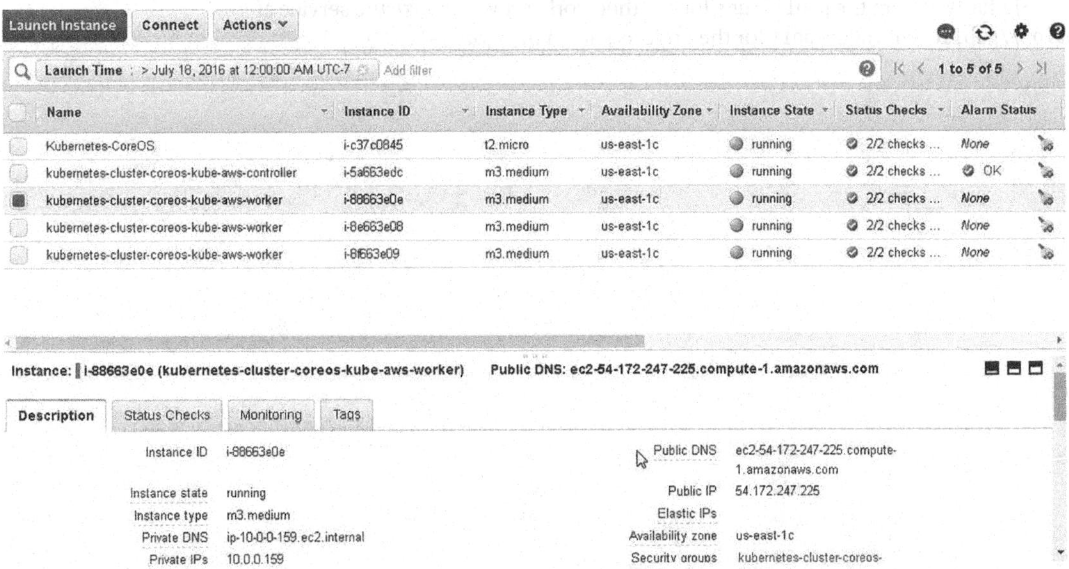

Figure 7-17. *Obtaining the public DNS*

Invoke the service in a web browser at URL `http://public-dns:32624` as shown in Figure 7-18.

Figure 7-18. *Invoking the service in a browser*

Similarly, obtain the `public-dns` for another worker node. Invoke the service at `http://public-dns:node-port` for the node as shown in Figure 7-19.

Figure 7-19. *Invoking the service at another worker node*

In addition to the `cluster-ip:80` and `node-ip:node-port`, the service may also be invoked at each of the service endpoints as shown for one of the endpoints in Figure 7-20.

```
core@ip-10-0-0-50 ~ $ curl 10.2.12.3:80
<html>
<head>
        <title>Hello world!</title>
        <link href='http://fonts.googleapis.com/css?family=Open+Sans:400,700' rel='s
tylesheet' type='text/css'>
        <style>
        body {
                background-color: white;
                text-align: center;
                padding: 50px;
                font-family: "Open Sans","Helvetica Neue",Helvetica,Arial,sans-serif
;
        }

        #logo {
                margin-bottom: 40px;
        }
        </style>
</head>
<body>
        <img id="logo" src="logo.png" />
        <h1>Hello world!</h1>
        <h3>My hostname is hello-world-3739649373-sbw5r</h3>                    <h3>
Links found</h3>
                                        <b>PHP_APACHE</b> listening in 80 available
at tcp://10.3.0.129:80<br />
                                                <b>KUBERNETES</b> listening in 443 a
vailable at tcp://10.3.0.1:443<br />
                                                <b>HELLO_WORLD</b> listening in 80 a
vailable at tcp://10.3.0.234:80<br />
```

Figure 7-20. *Invoking the service at an endpoint*

Creating a LoadBalancer Service

In this section we shall expose the same deployment as a service of type `LoadBalancer`. Delete the `hello-world` service and expose the `hello-world` deployment as a service of type `LoadBalancer`:

```
./kubectl expose deployment hello-world --port=80 --type=LoadBalancer
```

Subsequently the `hello-world` service listed should expose an external IP in addition to the `cluster-ip` as shown in Figure 7-21.

```
core@ip-10-0-0-50 ~ $ ./kubectl delete svc hello-world
service "hello-world" deleted
core@ip-10-0-0-50 ~ $ ./kubectl expose deployment hello-world --port=80 --type=LoadB
alancer
service "hello-world" exposed
core@ip-10-0-0-50 ~ $ ./kubectl get svc
NAME          CLUSTER-IP   EXTERNAL-IP        PORT(S)   AGE
hello-world   10.3.0.142   a85ad84414d08...   80/TCP    9s
kubernetes    10.3.0.1     <none>             443/TCP   2h
core@ip-10-0-0-50 ~ $ 
```

Figure 7-21. *Creating a `LoadBalancer` service*

The service is invoked at the cluster-internal `cluster-ip` for all types of Kubernetes services, as shown in Figure 7-22.

```
core@ip-10-0-0-50 ~ $ curl 10.3.0.142
<html>
<head>
        <title>Hello world!</title>
        <link href='http://fonts.googleapis.com/css?family=Open+Sans:400,700' rel='s
tylesheet' type='text/css'>
        <style>
        body {
                background-color: white;
                text-align: center;
                padding: 50px;
                font-family: "Open Sans","Helvetica Neue",Helvetica,Arial,sans-serif
;
        }

        #logo {
                margin-bottom: 40px;
        }
        </style>
</head>
<body>
        <img id="logo" src="logo.png" />
        <h1>Hello world!</h1>
        <h3>My hostname is hello-world-3739649373-5ll92</h3>                     <h3>
Links found</h3>
                                        <b>PHP_APACHE</b> listening in 80 available
at tcp://10.3.0.129:80<br />
                                                <b>HELLO_WORLD</b> listening in 80 a
vailable at tcp://10.3.0.234:80<br />
                                                <b>KUBERNETES</b> listening in 443 a
vailable at tcp://10.3.0.1:443<br />
```

Figure 7-22. *Invoking a service at* `cluster-IP`

Obtain the external IP, the `LoadBalancer` Ingress, at which the service is exposed with the following command:

```
./kubectl describe services hello-world | grep "LoadBalancer Ingress"
```

The `LoadBalancer` Ingress is listed as shown in Figure 7-23.

```
core@ip-10-0-0-50 ~ $ ./kubectl describe services hello-world | grep "LoadBalancer I
ngress"
LoadBalancer Ingress:    a85ad84414d0811e699c50a558d3101d-1977318300.us-east-1.elb.am
azonaws.com
core@ip-10-0-0-50 ~ $
```

Figure 7-23. *Obtaining the* `LoadBalancer` *Ingress*

The `LoadBalancer` Ingress may also be obtained from the service description, as shown in Figure 7-24.

```
core@ip-10-0-0-50 ~ $ ./kubectl describe svc hello-world
Name:                   hello-world
Namespace:              default
Labels:                 run=hello-world
Selector:               run=hello-world
Type:                   LoadBalancer
IP:                     10.3.0.142
LoadBalancer Ingress:   a85ad84414d0811e699c50a558d3101d-1977318300.us-east-1.elb.am
azonaws.com
Port:                   <unset> 80/TCP
NodePort:               <unset> 31653/TCP
Endpoints:              10.2.12.3:80,10.2.49.2:80,10.2.49.3:80
Session Affinity:       None
Events:
  FirstSeen     LastSeen        Count   From                    SubobjectPath   Type
Reason                  Message
  ---------     --------        -----   ----                    -------------   ----
----    ------                  -------
  5m            5m              1       {service-controller }                   Norm
al              CreatingLoadBalancer    Creating load balancer
  5m            5m              1       {service-controller }                   Norm
al              CreatedLoadBalancer     Created load balancer

core@ip-10-0-0-50 ~ $
```

Figure 7-24. *LoadBalancer Ingress also listed in the service description*

Invoke the service at the LoadBalancer Ingress IP as shown in Figure 7-25.

```
core@ip-10-0-0-50 ~ $ curl a85ad84414d0811e699c50a558d3101d-1977318300.us-east-1.elb
.amazonaws.com
<html>
<head>
        <title>Hello world!</title>
        <link href='http://fonts.googleapis.com/css?family=Open+Sans:400,700' rel='s
tylesheet' type='text/css'>
        <style>
        body {
                background-color: white;
                text-align: center;
                padding: 50px;
                font-family: "Open Sans","Helvetica Neue",Helvetica,Arial,sans-serif
;
        }

        #logo {
                margin-bottom: 40px;
        }
        </style>
</head>
<body>
        <img id="logo" src="logo.png" />
        <h1>Hello world!</h1>
        <h3>My hostname is hello-world-3739649373-5ll92</h3>                    <h3>
Links found</h3>
                                        <b>PHP_APACHE</b> listening in 80 available
at tcp://10.3.0.129:80<br />
                                                <b>HELLO_WORLD</b> listening in 80 a
vailable at tcp://10.3.0.234:80<br />
                                                <b>KUBERNETES</b> listening in 443 a
vailable at tcp://10.3.0.1:443<br />
```

Figure 7-25. *Invoking the service at the LoadBalancer Ingress*

An AWS load balancer is created for a service of type `LoadBalancer`. The `LoadBalancer Ingress` is the public DNS of the load balancer, as shown in the EC2 Console in Figure 7-26.

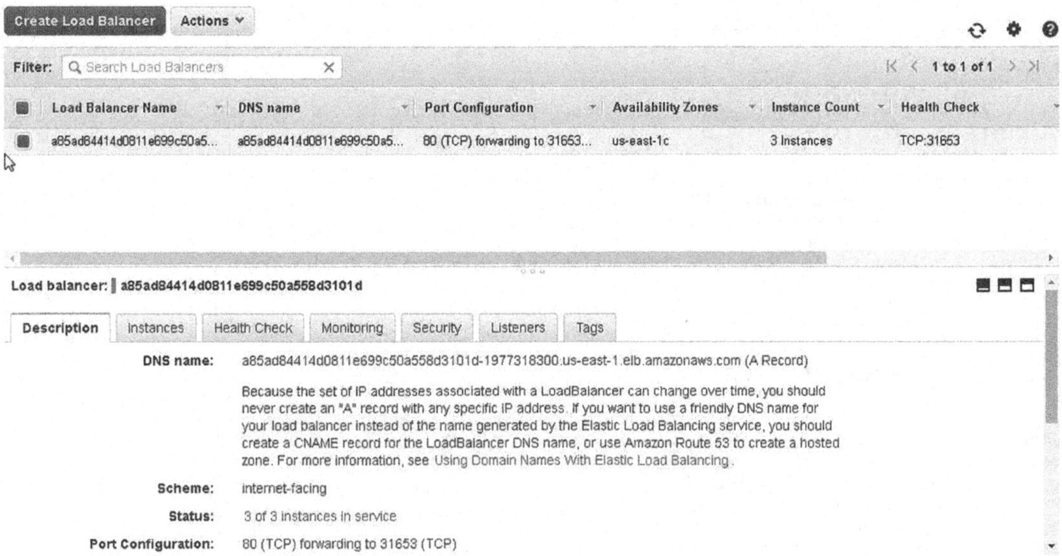

Figure 7-26. *Public DNS of the LoadBalancer*

To invoke a service of type `LoadBalancer`, access the public DNS in a browser as shown in Figure 7-27.

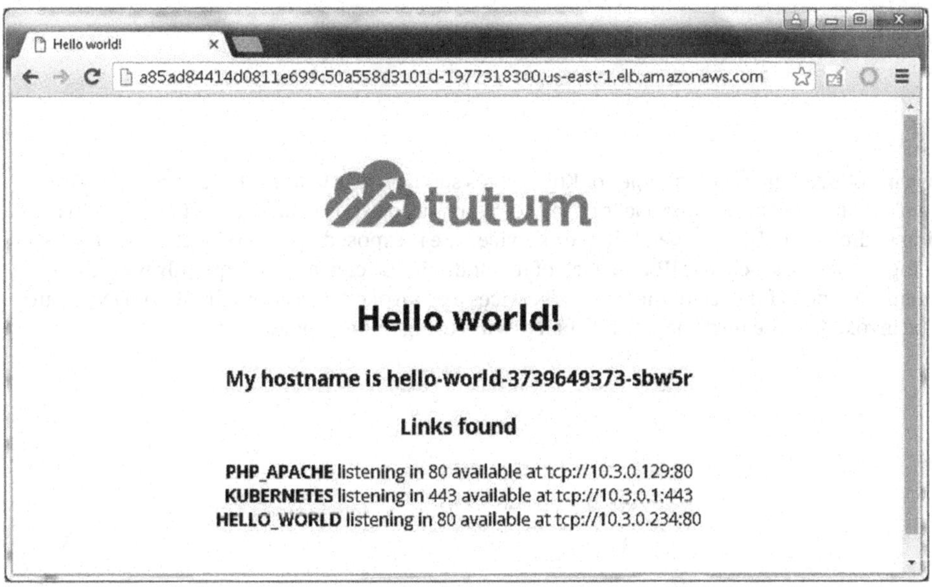

Figure 7-27. *Invoking the public DNS in a browser*

In addition to the `cluster-ip` and the load balancer public DNS, the service may also be invoked at any of the service endpoints, as shown for one of the endpoints in Figure 7-28.

```
core@ip-10-0-0-50 ~ $ curl 10.2.12.3
<html>
<head>
        <title>Hello world!</title>
        <link href='http://fonts.googleapis.com/css?family=Open+Sans:400,700' rel='s
tylesheet' type='text/css'>
        <style>
        body {
                background-color: white;
                text-align: center;
                padding: 50px;
                font-family: "Open Sans","Helvetica Neue",Helvetica,Arial,sans-serif
;
        }

        #logo {
                margin-bottom: 40px;
        }
        </style>
</head>
<body>
        <img id="logo" src="logo.png" />
        <h1>Hello world!</h1>
        <h3>My hostname is hello-world-3739649373-sbw5r</h3>                    <h3>
Links found</h3>
                                        <b>PHP_APACHE</b> listening in 80 available
at tcp://10.3.0.129:80<br />
                                                <b>KUBERNETES</b> listening in 443 a
vailable at tcp://10.3.0.1:443<br />
                                                <b>HELLO_WORLD</b> listening in 80 a
vailable at tcp://10.3.0.234:80<br />
                                </body>
```

Figure 7-28. *Invoking a service endpoint*

Summary

In this chapter we introduced the different types of Kubernetes services. The `ClusterIP` service type is the default and is invoked on a cluster IP. The `NodePort` service type is also exposed on each of the nodes in the cluster in addition to the cluster IP. The `LoadBalancer` service type is exposed on an AWS `LoadBalancer` DNS in addition to being exposed on a cluster IP, and each of the nodes in the cluster. Subsequently we created sample deployments and pods for each of the types of services and invoked them from the IPs or DNS from which they can be invoked. In the next chapter we shall discuss using rolling updates.

CHAPTER 8

Using Rolling Updates

It is common for a replication controller specification or a container image to be updated. If a replication controller is created from an earlier image or definition file, the replication controller will need to be updated.

Problem

If the Docker image or controller specification for a replication controller has been updated while the replication controller's pods are running, the replication controller will need to be deleted and a new replication controller created based on the updated Docker image or controller specification. Shutting down an application will cause the application to become unavailable. One of the DevOps and Agile software development best practices is Continuous Deployment. The objective of Continuous Deployment is to minimize the lead time between a new application release/build being developed and being used in production.

Solution

During a rolling update, pods for any earlier version replication controller are terminated and pods for the new controller started. The earlier version pods are shut down using a "graceful termination" mechanism, which provides a callback into a container a configurable amount of time before the container is terminated to allow the container to shut down gracefully, which implies that the in-memory state of the container is persisted and the open connections are closed. The "graceful termination" mechanism Kubernetes makes use of is a single-container management design pattern.

As shown in Figure 8-1, for the rolling update of a replication controller RC1 to RC2, RC1 initially has three pods and RC2 no pods. In the next phase, RC1 has two pods and RC2 one pod. In the third phase RC1 has one pod and RC2 two pods. When the rolling update is completed RC1 has no pods and RC2 three pods. The rolling update is performed one pod at a time.

D. Vohra, *Kubernetes Management Design Patterns*, DOI 10.1007/978-1-4842-2598-1_8

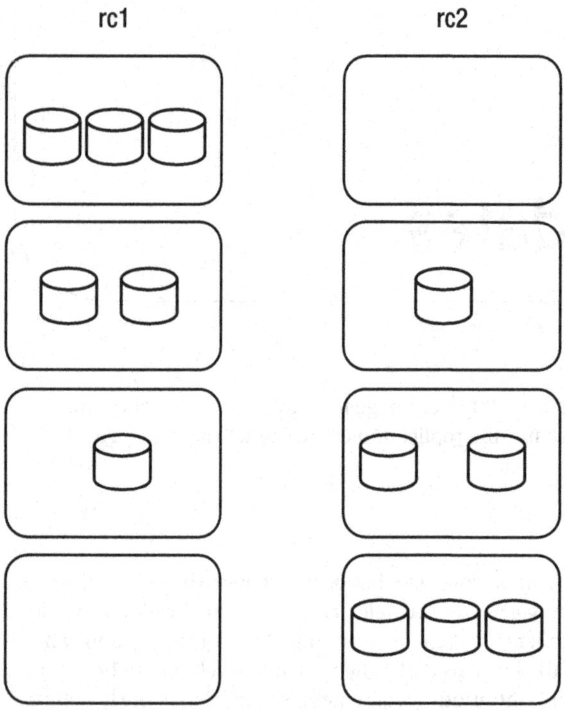

Figure 8-1. *Rolling update of RC1 to RC2*

Another management pattern used in rolling updates is the controller/service decoupling, which follows the Single Responsibility Principle. If controller and service are tightly coupled, multiple controllers cannot be associated with a single service as new replication controllers are created and earlier ones removed. One of the requirements of rolling updates is for multiple controllers to be associated with a service while an earlier version RC is deleted (a pod at a time as discussed in this chapter) and pods for a new RC are started.

Overview

Kubernetes provides a mechanism by which a running replication controller can be updated to the newer image or specification while it is running—what is called a *rolling update*. The replication controller or a service representing the replication controller does not become unavailable at any time. The RC is updated one pod at a time so that at any given time the number of pods in the RC is at the specified replication level. In this chapter we shall use a rolling update to update a replication controller and a deployment while the replication controller or deployment is running. Topics include the following:

- Setting the environment
- Rolling updates with an RC definition file
- Rolling update by updating the container image
- Rolling back an update
- Using only either a file or an image
- Rolling update on deployment with deployment file

Setting the Environment

Create an Amazon EC2 instance based on the Amazon Linux AMI. Obtain the public IP of the instance and SSH log in to the instance:

```
ssh -i "docker.pem"  ec2-user@54.87.191.230
```

Create a Kubernetes cluster using an AWS CloudFormation consisting of a single controller and three worker nodes running CoreOS, as shown in Figure 8-2.

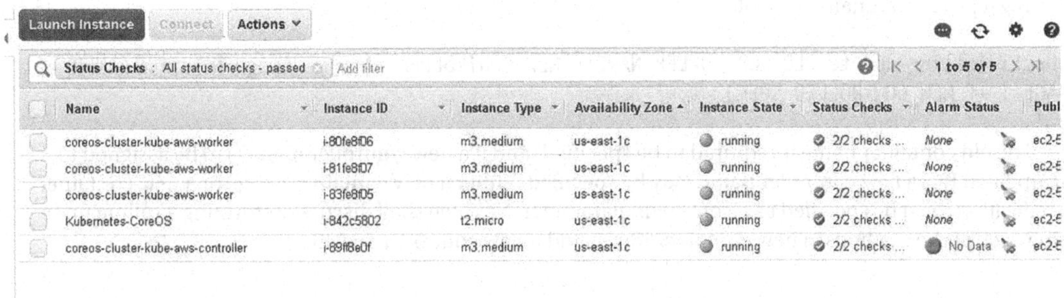

Figure 8-2. *CloudFormation EC2 instances*

After starting the cluster and setting up an A record for the controller instance IP address in the public DNS name for the CloudFormation, SSH log in to the controller instance:

```
ssh -i "kubernetes-coreos.pem"  core@52.205.169.82
```

The controller CoreOS instance is logged in as shown in Figure 8-3.

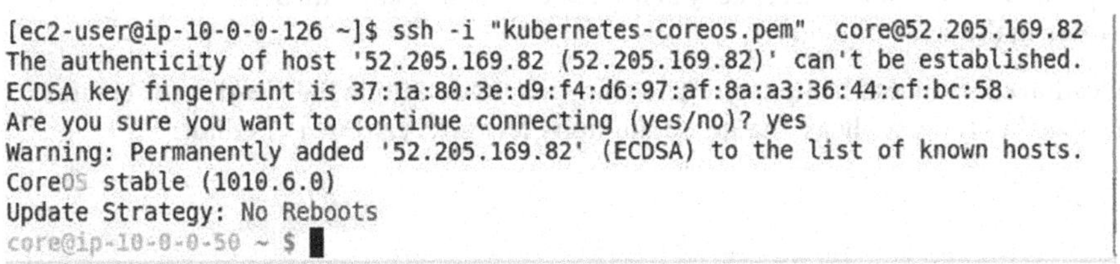

[ec2-user@ip-10-0-0-126 ~]$ ssh -i "kubernetes-coreos.pem" core@52.205.169.82
The authenticity of host '52.205.169.82 (52.205.169.82)' can't be established.
ECDSA key fingerprint is 37:1a:80:3e:d9:f4:d6:97:af:8a:a3:36:44:cf:bc:58.
Are you sure you want to continue connecting (yes/no)? yes
Warning: Permanently added '52.205.169.82' (ECDSA) to the list of known hosts.
CoreOS stable (1010.6.0)
Update Strategy: No Reboots
core@ip-10-0-0-50 ~ $

Figure 8-3. *SSH logging into the controller instance*

Install kubectl binaries and list the nodes:

```
./kubectl get nodes
```

The single controller node and the three worker nodes are listed as shown in Figure 8-4.

```
core@ip-10-0-0-50 ~ $ ./kubectl get nodes
NAME                          STATUS                     AGE
ip-10-0-0-196.ec2.internal    Ready                      14m
ip-10-0-0-197.ec2.internal    Ready                      14m
ip-10-0-0-198.ec2.internal    Ready                      14m
ip-10-0-0-50.ec2.internal     Ready,SchedulingDisabled   14m
core@ip-10-0-0-50 ~ $
```

Figure 8-4. *Listing the nodes*

The `kubectl rolling-update` command is used to perform a rolling update. The syntax for the `rolling-update` command is as follows.

```
kubectl rolling-update OLD_CONTROLLER_NAME ([NEW_CONTROLLER_NAME] --image=NEW_CONTAINER_
IMAGE | -f NEW_CONTROLLER_SPEC)
```

The old container name is required to be specified, and if a new controller name is to be assigned to the updated RC, a new controller name may be specified. Either a new container image or a new container specification must be specified as a command parameter. Next, we shall discuss performing a rolling update using each of the methods; a new container image and a new controller specification.

Rolling Update with an RC Definition File

In this section we'll discuss the rolling update of an existing replication controller by providing an RC definition file to the kubectl `rolling-update` command. The following requirements apply for rolling-updating an RC.

1. The new replication controller must be in the same namespace.
2. The new replication controller name in the definition file must not be the same as the existing replication controller being updated.
3. The new replication controller must specify at least one matching key with a nonequal value in the selector field.

First, create a replication controller to be updated. The following RC definition file `mysql.yaml` creates an RC called `mysql` and specifies three replicas. Create a definition file `mysql.yaml` in a `vi` editor:

```
sudo vi mysql.yaml
```

Copy the following source code to the definition file:

```
---
apiVersion: v1
kind: ReplicationController
metadata:
  name: mysql
  labels:
    app: mysql-app
```

```
spec:
  replicas: 3
  selector:
    app: mysql-app
    deployment: v1
  template:
    metadata:
      labels:
        app: mysql-app
        deployment: v1
    spec:
      containers:
        -
          env:
            -
              name: MYSQL_ROOT_PASSWORD
              value: mysql
          image: mysql
          name: mysql
          ports:
            -
              containerPort: 3306
```

Create a replication controller with the following command:

```
kubectl create -f mysql.yaml
```

An RC called `mysql` with three replicas should be created.

Next, modify the `mysql.yaml` file based on the requirements listed earlier. The following `mysql.yaml` specifies a different RC name and a different value for the deployment key in the selector. Optionally, the Docker image tag can be different.

```
---
apiVersion: v1
kind: ReplicationController
metadata:
  name: mysql-v1
  labels:
    app: mysql-app
spec:
  replicas: 3
  selector:
    app: mysql-app
    deployment: v2
  template:
    metadata:
      labels:
        app: mysql-app
        deployment: v2
```

```
    spec:
      containers:
        -
          env:
            -
              name: MYSQL_ROOT_PASSWORD
              value: mysql
          image: mysql:5.5
          name: mysql
          ports:
            -
              containerPort: 3306
```

Next, perform a rolling update to the RC called `mysql` using the definition file `mysql.yaml`. Optionally, specify a timeout for the rolling update. When a timeout is set, the pods updated to the new image or specification are not rolled back after the timeout has elapsed and the rolling update has terminated. The rolling update may be performed again and resumes from the previous update.

```
kubectl rolling-update mysql  -f  mysql.yaml --timeout=1m
```

The `mysql` RC is updated to `mysql-v1` as shown in Figure 8-5. Subsequently the RC mysql is deleted.

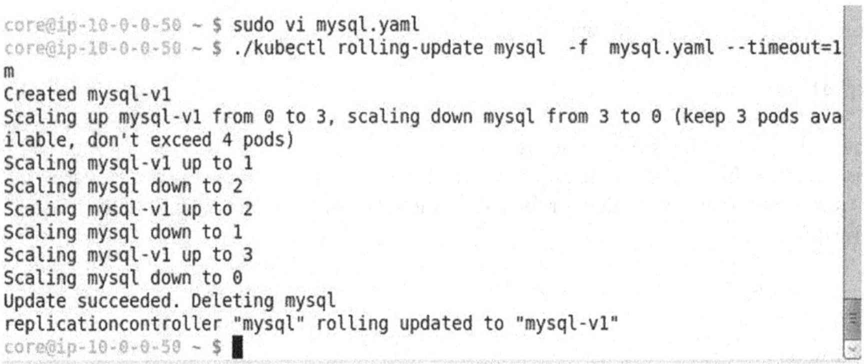

core@ip-10-0-0-50 ~ $ sudo vi mysql.yaml
core@ip-10-0-0-50 ~ $ ./kubectl rolling-update mysql -f mysql.yaml --timeout=1
m
Created mysql-v1
Scaling up mysql-v1 from 0 to 3, scaling down mysql from 3 to 0 (keep 3 pods ava
ilable, don't exceed 4 pods)
Scaling mysql-v1 up to 1
Scaling mysql down to 2
Scaling mysql-v1 up to 2
Scaling mysql down to 1
Scaling mysql-v1 up to 3
Scaling mysql down to 0
Update succeeded. Deleting mysql
replicationcontroller "mysql" rolling updated to "mysql-v1"
core@ip-10-0-0-50 ~ $

Figure 8-5. *Rolling update of a replication controller*

Delete the RC `mysql-v1`, as we shall be using the same RC name in the next section:

```
kubectl delete rc mysql-v1
```

Rolling Update by Updating the Container Image

In this section we shall update an RC by updating the Docker image. First, create an RC using the following `mysql.yaml` definition file:

```
---
apiVersion: v1
kind: ReplicationController
metadata:
  name: mysql-v1
  labels:
    app: mysql-app
spec:
  replicas: 3
  selector:
    app: mysql-app
    deployment: v1
  template:
    metadata:
      labels:
        app: mysql-app
        deployment: v1
    spec:
      containers:
        -
          env:
            -
              name: MYSQL_ROOT_PASSWORD
              value: mysql
          image: mysql:5.5
          name: mysql
          ports:
            -
              containerPort: 3306
```

Copy the preceding listing to a file `mysql.yaml` in a `vi` editor as shown in Figure 8-6.

```
---
apiVersion: v1
kind: ReplicationController
metadata:
  name: mysql-v1
  labels:
    app: mysql-app
spec:
  replicas: 3
  selector:
    app: mysql-app
    deployment: v1
  template:
    metadata:
      labels:
        app: mysql-app
        deployment: v1
    spec:
      containers:
        -
          env:
            -
              name: MYSQL_ROOT_PASSWORD
              value: mysql
          image: mysql:5.5
          name: mysql
          ports:
            -
              containerPort: 3306

~
:wq
```

Figure 8-6. *The `mysql.yaml` file in a `vi` editor*

Run the following command to create an RC:

```
kubectl create -f mysql.yaml
```

List the RC and the pods:

```
kubectl get rc
kubectl get pods
```

The `mysql-v1` RC is created and listed. The three pods also are listed as shown in Figure 8-7.

```
core@ip-10-0-0-50 ~ $ sudo vi mysql.yaml
core@ip-10-0-0-50 ~ $ ./kubectl create -f mysql.yaml
replicationcontroller "mysql-v1" created
core@ip-10-0-0-50 ~ $ ./kubectl get rc
NAME       DESIRED   CURRENT   AGE
mysql-v1   3         3         7s
core@ip-10-0-0-50 ~ $ ./kubectl get pods
NAME             READY     STATUS    RESTARTS   AGE
mysql-v1-8ekze   1/1       Running   0          14s
mysql-v1-p2udx   1/1       Running   0          14s
mysql-v1-wa9vi   1/1       Running   0          14s
core@ip-10-0-0-50 ~ $
```

Figure 8-7. *Creating an RC and listing the pods*

The following command creates a rolling update on the RC with a new image tag and new RC name. The -a option displays all labels, and the --poll-interval specifies the interval between polling the replication controller for status after update.

```
kubectl rolling-update mysql-v1   mysql --image=mysql:latest -a --poll-interval=3ms
```

The RC mysql-v1 is rolling-updated to mysql as shown in Figure 8-8. Subsequently the RC mysql-v1 is deleted.

```
core@ip-10-0-0-50 ~ $ ./kubectl rolling-update mysql-v1   mysql --image=mysql:la
test -a --poll-interval=3ms
Created mysql
Scaling up mysql from 0 to 3, scaling down mysql-v1 from 3 to 0 (keep 3 pods ava
ilable, don't exceed 4 pods)
Scaling mysql up to 1
Scaling mysql-v1 down to 2
Scaling mysql up to 2
Scaling mysql-v1 down to 1
Scaling mysql up to 3
Scaling mysql-v1 down to 0
Update succeeded. Deleting mysql-v1
replicationcontroller "mysql-v1" rolling updated to "mysql"
core@ip-10-0-0-50 ~ $
```

Figure 8-8. *Rolling update to an RC using a Docker image*

After the update, list the RC and the pods:

```
kubectl get rc
kubectl get pods
```

A different RC, mysql, and different pods are now listed, as shown in Figure 8-9.

```
core@ip-10-0-0-50 ~ $ ./kubectl get rc
NAME      DESIRED   CURRENT   AGE
mysql     3         3         3m
core@ip-10-0-0-50 ~ $ ./kubectl get pods
NAME          READY     STATUS    RESTARTS   AGE
mysql-6t00f   1/1       Running   0          2m
mysql-cg4xr   1/1       Running   0          1m
mysql-o79yj   1/1       Running   0          3m
core@ip-10-0-0-50 ~ $
```

Figure 8-9. *Listing the RC and pods*

A rolling update on an RC does not have to use a new RC name. As an example, perform a rolling update with a new image tag and same RC name.

```
kubectl rolling-update mysql   --image=mysql:5.6
```

For the purpose of updating the RC a temporary RC is created and the update is applied to the RC as shown in Figure 8-10. Subsequently the original RC mysql is deleted and the temporary RC is renamed to mysql, as a result keeping the RC name the same.

```
core@ip-10-0-0-50 ~ $ ./kubectl rolling-update mysql   --image=mysql:5.6
Created mysql-00679ccf736024b5b371245f35a7f867
Scaling up mysql-00679ccf736024b5b371245f35a7f867 from 0 to 3, scaling down mysq
l from 3 to 0 (keep 3 pods available, don't exceed 4 pods)
Scaling mysql-00679ccf736024b5b371245f35a7f867 up to 1
Scaling mysql down to 2
Scaling mysql-00679ccf736024b5b371245f35a7f867 up to 2
Scaling mysql down to 1
Scaling mysql-00679ccf736024b5b371245f35a7f867 up to 3
Scaling mysql down to 0
Update succeeded. Deleting old controller: mysql
Renaming mysql-00679ccf736024b5b371245f35a7f867 to mysql
replicationcontroller "mysql" rolling updated
core@ip-10-0-0-50 ~ $
```

Figure 8-10. *Rolling Update using the same RC name*

A rolling update does not have to be with the same Docker image. As an example, use a different image, `postgres`, to update an RC called `mysql` and based on the `mysql` image. The following command updates the `mysql` image to the `postgresql` image using `image=postgres`:

```
kubectl rolling-update mysql postgresql  --image=postgres
```

The RC `mysql` is updated to RC `postgresql` as shown in Figure 8-11.

```
core@ip-10-0-0-50 ~ $ ./kubectl rolling-update mysql postgresql  --image=postgre
s
Created postgresql
Scaling up postgresql from 0 to 3, scaling down mysql from 3 to 0 (keep 3 pods a
vailable, don't exceed 4 pods)
Scaling postgresql up to 1
Scaling mysql down to 2
Scaling postgresql up to 2
Scaling mysql down to 1
Scaling postgresql up to 3
Scaling mysql down to 0
Update succeeded. Deleting mysql
replicationcontroller "mysql" rolling updated to "postgresql"
core@ip-10-0-0-50 ~ $
```

Figure 8-11. *Rolling Update using a different Docker image*

List the RC and the pods:

```
kubectl get rc
kubectl get pods
```

A different RC and pods should be listed, as shown in Figure 8-12. Not only has the RC been updated, the pods are also running different software.

```
core@ip-10-0-0-50 ~ $ ./kubectl get rc
NAME         DESIRED   CURRENT   AGE
postgresql   3         3         4m
core@ip-10-0-0-50 ~ $ ./kubectl get pods
NAME               READY     STATUS    RESTARTS   AGE
postgresql-gh0ix   1/1       Running   0          4m
postgresql-h40u4   1/1       Running   0          2m
postgresql-vdde7   1/1       Running   0          1m
core@ip-10-0-0-50 ~ $
```

Figure 8-12. *Listing updated RC and pods*

A rolling update back to the `mysql` image-based RC may be performed by running a similar command. Then list the new RC and pods for the new RC:

```
kubectl rolling-update postgresql mysql  --image=mysql
kubectl get rc
kubectl get pods
```

The RC postgresql is updated to the `mysql` image-based RC named `mysql`, as shown in Figure 8-13. The new RC and pods are listed.

```
core@ip-10-0-0-50 ~ $ ./kubectl rolling-update postgresql mysql  --image=mysql
Created mysql
Scaling up mysql from 0 to 3, scaling down postgresql from 3 to 0 (keep 3 pods a
vailable, don't exceed 4 pods)
Scaling mysql up to 1
Scaling postgresql down to 2
Scaling mysql up to 2
Scaling postgresql down to 1
Scaling mysql up to 3
Scaling postgresql down to 0
Update succeeded. Deleting postgresql
replicationcontroller "postgresql" rolling updated to "mysql"
core@ip-10-0-0-50 ~ $ ./kubectl get rc
NAME      DESIRED   CURRENT   AGE
mysql     3         3         6m
core@ip-10-0-0-50 ~ $ ./kubectl get pods
NAME          READY     STATUS    RESTARTS   AGE
mysql-7zway   1/1       Running   0          3m
mysql-l9l4r   1/1       Running   0          6m
mysql-u92yw   1/1       Running   0          5m
core@ip-10-0-0-50 ~ $ ./kubectl describe rc mysql
Name:           mysql
Namespace:      default
Image(s):       mysql
Selector:       app=mysql-app,deployment=b96c41ab125432331f3058c0d774809f
Labels:         app=mysql-app
Replicas:       3 current / 3 desired
Pods Status:    3 Running / 0 Waiting / 0 Succeeded / 0 Failed
No volumes.
Events:
  FirstSeen     LastSeen        Count   From                            Subobjec
tPath   Type            Reason                  Message
```

Figure 8-13. *Rolling update back to an RC*

A rolling update may be terminated while in progress and resumed later. As an example, create the `ReplicationController` definition file `mysql.yaml` shown in Figure 8-14.

```
---
apiVersion: v1
kind: ReplicationController
metadata:
  name: mysql-v1
  labels:
    app: mysql-app
spec:
  replicas: 3
  selector:
    app: mysql-app
    deployment: v1
  template:
    metadata:
      labels:
        app: mysql-app
        deployment: v1
    spec:
      containers:
        -
          env:
            -
              name: MYSQL_ROOT_PASSWORD
              value: mysql
          image: mysql:5.5
          name: mysql
          ports:
            -
              containerPort: 3306
~
:wq
```

Figure 8-14. *The definition file* `mysql.yaml`

Create an RC with the following command:

```
kubectl create -f mysql.yaml
```

List the pods:

```
kubectl get pods
```

The RC `mysql-v1` is created, and the pods are listed as shown in Figure 8-15.

```
core@ip-10-0-0-50 ~ $ ./kubectl create -f mysql.yaml
replicationcontroller "mysql-v1" created
core@ip-10-0-0-50 ~ $ ./kubectl get pods
NAME             READY     STATUS    RESTARTS   AGE
mysql-v1-2blf9   1/1       Running   0          7s
mysql-v1-6zmzb   1/1       Running   0          7s
mysql-v1-zv14x   1/1       Running   0          7s
core@ip-10-0-0-50 ~ $
```

Figure 8-15. *Creating an RC and listing pods*

Perform a rolling update of the `mysql-v1` RC to a new RC called `postgresql` using a new Docker image, `postgres`:

```
kubectl rolling-update mysql-v1 postgresql  --image=postgres
```

The rolling update is started as shown in Figure 8-16.

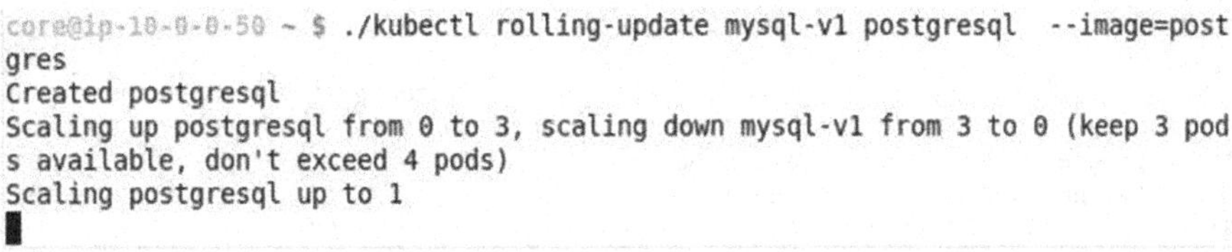
core@ip-10-0-0-50 ~ $ ./kubectl rolling-update mysql-v1 postgresql --image=post
gres
Created postgresql
Scaling up postgresql from 0 to 3, scaling down mysql-v1 from 3 to 0 (keep 3 pod
s available, don't exceed 4 pods)
Scaling postgresql up to 1

Figure 8-16. *Starting a rolling update*

While the rolling update is running, terminate the update with ^C as shown in Figure 8-17.

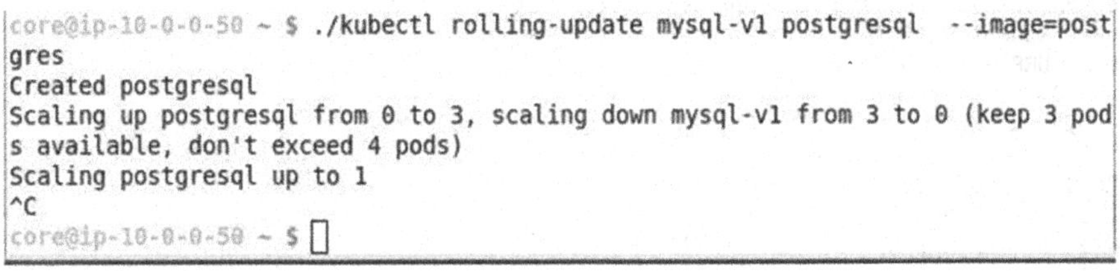
core@ip-10-0-0-50 ~ $ ./kubectl rolling-update mysql-v1 postgresql --image=post
gres
Created postgresql
Scaling up postgresql from 0 to 3, scaling down mysql-v1 from 3 to 0 (keep 3 pod
s available, don't exceed 4 pods)
Scaling postgresql up to 1
^C
core@ip-10-0-0-50 ~ $

Figure 8-17. *Terminating a rolling update*

To resume the rolling update, run the same command again:

```
kubectl rolling-update mysql-v1 postgresql  --image=postgres
```

As the output in Figure 8-18 indicates, the existing update is found and resumed.

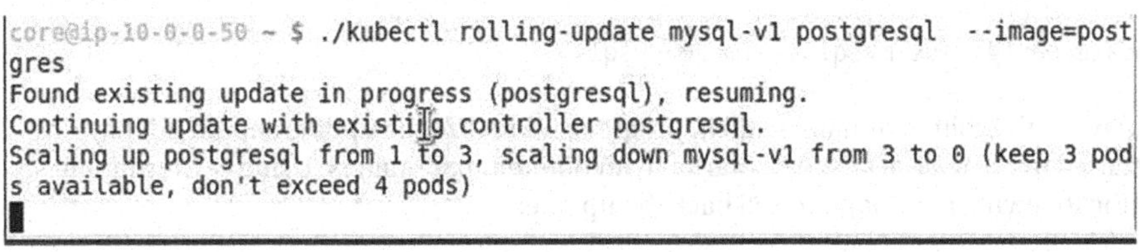
core@ip-10-0-0-50 ~ $ ./kubectl rolling-update mysql-v1 postgresql --image=post
gres
Found existing update in progress (postgresql), resuming.
Continuing update with existing controller postgresql.
Scaling up postgresql from 1 to 3, scaling down mysql-v1 from 3 to 0 (keep 3 pod
s available, don't exceed 4 pods)

Figure 8-18. *Resuming a rolling update*

The rolling update is completed using an existing update as shown in Figure 8-19. Next, list the new RC and pods.

```
core@ip-10-0-0-50 ~ $ ./kubectl rolling-update mysql-v1 postgresql  --image=post
gres
Created postgresql
Scaling up postgresql from 0 to 3, scaling down mysql-v1 from 3 to 0 (keep 3 pod
s available, don't exceed 4 pods)
Scaling postgresql up to 1
^C
core@ip-10-0-0-50 ~ $ ./kubectl rolling-update mysql-v1 postgresql  --image=post
gres
Found existing update in progress (postgresql), resuming.
Continuing update with existing controller postgresql.
Scaling up postgresql from 1 to 3, scaling down mysql-v1 from 3 to 0 (keep 3 pod
s available, don't exceed 4 pods)
Scaling mysql-v1 down to 2
Scaling postgresql up to 2
Scaling mysql-v1 down to 1
Scaling postgresql up to 3
Scaling mysql-v1 down to 0
Update succeeded. Deleting mysql-v1
replicationcontroller "mysql-v1" rolling updated to "postgresql"
core@ip-10-0-0-50 ~ $ ./kubectl get rc
NAME         DESIRED   CURRENT   AGE
mysql-v2     0         0         8m
postgresql   3         3         4m
core@ip-10-0-0-50 ~ $ ./kubectl get pods
NAME               READY     STATUS    RESTARTS   AGE
postgresql-5a0rb   1/1       Running   0          2m
postgresql-7p7a5   1/1       Running   0          1m
postgresql-g8izq   1/1       Running   0          4m
core@ip-10-0-0-50 ~ $ ▌
```

Figure 8-19. *Rolling update using existing update*

Rolling Back an Update

A rollback of a rolling update can be performed if required. As an example, a rolling update to an RC called `postgresql` is started using a new container image `mysql`:

```
kubectl rolling-update postgresql mysql  --image=mysql
```

Now suppose that while the rolling update is still in progress, we realize the update should not have been started, or was started in error, or needs to be started with different parameters. Using ^C, terminate the update. Then run the following command to roll back the update:

```
kubectl rolling-update postgresql mysql -rollback
```

When the rolling update was terminated, the `postgresql` RC had already scaled down to one pod and the `mysql` RC had already scaled up to two pods. When the rollback is performed, the existing controller `postgresql` is scaled back up from one to three pods and the `mysql` RC is scaled down from two to zero pods, as shown in Figure 8-20.

```
core@ip-10-0-0-50 ~ $ ./kubectl rolling-update postgresql mysql  --image=mysql
Created mysql
Scaling up mysql from 0 to 3, scaling down postgresql from 3 to 0 (keep 3 pods a
vailable, don't exceed 4 pods)
Scaling mysql up to 1
Scaling postgresql down to 2
Scaling mysql up to 2
Scaling postgresql down to 1
^C
core@ip-10-0-0-50 ~ $ ./kubectl rolling-update postgresql mysql --rollback
Setting "postgresql" replicas to 3
Continuing update with existing controller postgresql.
Scaling up postgresql from 1 to 3, scaling down mysql from 2 to 0 (keep 3 pods a
vailable, don't exceed 4 pods)
Scaling postgresql up to 2
```

Figure 8-20. *Rolling back a rolling update*

Next list the RC and the pods:

```
kubectl get rc
kubectl get pods
```

The `mysql` RC is not listed and instead the `postgresql` RC is listed, as shown in Figure 8-21.

```
core@ip-10-0-0-50 ~ $ ./kubectl rolling-update postgresql mysql  --image=mysql
Created mysql
Scaling up mysql from 0 to 3, scaling down postgresql from 3 to 0 (keep 3 pods a
vailable, don't exceed 4 pods)
Scaling mysql up to 1
Scaling postgresql down to 2
Scaling mysql up to 2
Scaling postgresql down to 1
^C
core@ip-10-0-0-50 ~ $ ./kubectl rolling-update postgresql mysql --rollback
Setting "postgresql" replicas to 3
Continuing update with existing controller postgresql.
Scaling up postgresql from 1 to 3, scaling down mysql from 2 to 0 (keep 3 pods a
vailable, don't exceed 4 pods)
Scaling postgresql up to 2
Scaling mysql down to 1
Scaling postgresql up to 3
Scaling mysql down to 0
Update succeeded. Deleting mysql
Error from server: replicationcontrollers "mysql" not found
core@ip-10-0-0-50 ~ $ ./kubectl get rc
NAME         DESIRED   CURRENT   AGE
mysql-v2     0         0         15m
postgresql   3         3         10m
core@ip-10-0-0-50 ~ $ ./kubectl get pods
NAME               READY     STATUS    RESTARTS   AGE
postgresql-2yq3y   1/1       Running   0          1m
postgresql-g8izq   1/1       Running   0          10m
postgresql-yg6sl   1/1       Running   0          2m
core@ip-10-0-0-50 ~ $
```

Figure 8-21. *Listing a rolled-back RC and pods*

Rollback of a deployment may be performed even after a rolling update has completed if an earlier revision is available. The rolling update of deployments is discussed in a later section.

Using Only Either File or Image

Only one of a container image or a definition file may be used, not both. To demonstrate, try specifying both image and file:

```
kubectl rolling-update mysql --image=mysql -f mysql.yaml
```

An error is generated as shown in Figure 8-22.

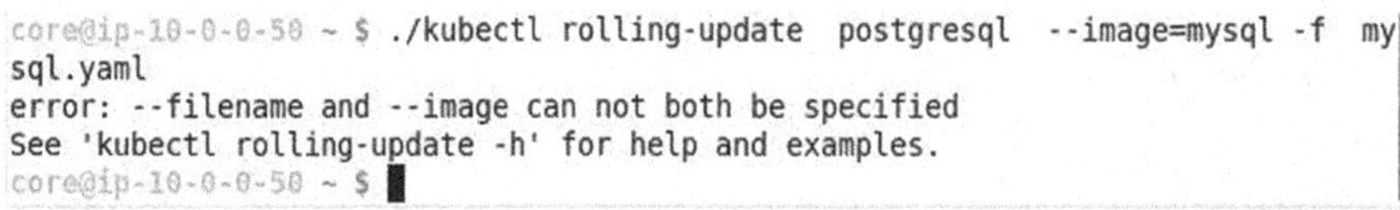

core@ip-10-0-0-50 ~ $ ./kubectl rolling-update postgresql --image=mysql -f my
sql.yaml
error: --filename and --image can not both be specified
See 'kubectl rolling-update -h' for help and examples.
core@ip-10-0-0-50 ~ $

Figure 8-22. *An error is generated if both Docker image and definition file are used*

Multiple-Container Pods

A rolling update performs an update on an RC, which consists of pod replicas, using a new container image or pod spec. If `-image` is specified in the `kubectl rolling-update` command to perform an update, the image is used to update the pods. But what if the pod is a multicontainer pod? An image can update only one of the containers in the pod, and the container must be specified using the `-container` option.

Rolling Update to a Deployment

A deployment created using a definition file has the provision to specify spec for the rolling update. The default strategy of a deployment is `rollingUpdate` and may also be specified explicitly. The other option for the strategy type is `Recreate`. The following (Table 8-1) fields may be specified for a rolling update deployment, the default.

Table 8-1. *Fields for Rolling Update to a Deployment*

Field	Description	Example
`maxUnavailable`	The maximum number of pods that may become unavailable during the update. The value may be an absolute number, such as 3, or a percentage, for example 30%. Default value is 1. The value cannot be 0 if `maxSurge` is 0.	If set to 20% the maximum number of pods that may be unavailable cannot exceed 20%, and 80% of the pods must always be available. When the update starts, the old RC is scaled down to 80% immediately and new pods started for the new RC. As new pods are started old RC pods are stopped, so that the number of pods available is always 80% of the configured replication level.
`maxSurge`	The maximum number of pods that may be running above the configured or desired level specified as a number or a percentage. Default value is 1. Cannot be 0 if maxUnavailable is 0.	If set to 10% the new RC may surge to 110% of the configured or desired number of pods immediately when the update is started, but not more than 110% of the configured replication level. As old RC pods are stopped more new RC pods are started, but at any given time the total number of pods must not exceed 110%.

The Deployment spec provides two fields (Table 8-2) for the rolling update rollback. Neither of these fields are required.

Table 8-2. *Fields for Rolling Update Rollback*

Field	Description
`rollbackTo`	The config the deployment is rolled back to in a rollback. The `RollbackConfig` provides a field `revision` to specify the revision to roll back to. If set to 0 rolls back to the last revision.
`revisionHistoryLimit`	The number of old replica sets to retain to allow a rollback.

Next, we shall demonstrate rolling update of a deployment. Create a deployment file `mysql-deployment.yaml`:

```
sudo vi mysql-deployment.yaml
```

Copy the following listing to the definition file:

```
apiVersion: extensions/v1beta1
kind: Deployment
metadata:
  name: mysql-deployment
spec:
  replicas: 5
  template:
    metadata:
      labels:
        app: mysql
```

```
    spec:
      containers:
      - name: mysql
        image: mysql:5.5
        ports:
        - containerPort: 80
  strategy:
    type: RollingUpdate
      rollingUpdate:
        maxUnavailable: 75%
        maxSurge: 30%
  rollbackTo:
    revision: 0
```

Figure 8-23 shows the definition file in a vi editor.

```
apiVersion: extensions/v1beta1
kind: Deployment
metadata:
  name: mysql-deployment
spec:
  replicas: 5
  template:
    metadata:
      labels:
        app: mysql
    spec:
      containers:
        -
          name: mysql
          image: mysql:5.5
          ports:
            -
             containerPort: 80
  strategy:
    type: RollingUpdate
    rollingUpdate:
         maxUnavailable: "75%"
         maxSurge: "30%"
  rollbackTo:
    revision: 0

~
~
~
~
~
:wq
```

***Figure 8-23.** Definition file for a deployment*

Create a deployment:

```
kubectl create -f mysql-deployment.yaml
```

Find the rollout status:

```
kubectl rollout status deployment/mysql-deployment
```

List the deployments:

```
kubectl get deployments
```

The `mysql-deployment` is created and rolled out as shown in Figure 8-24.

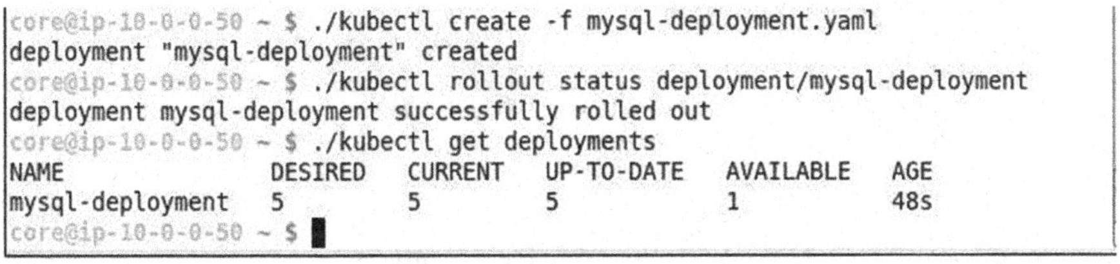

```
core@ip-10-0-0-50 ~ $ ./kubectl create -f mysql-deployment.yaml
deployment "mysql-deployment" created
core@ip-10-0-0-50 ~ $ ./kubectl rollout status deployment/mysql-deployment
deployment mysql-deployment successfully rolled out
core@ip-10-0-0-50 ~ $ ./kubectl get deployments
NAME               DESIRED   CURRENT   UP-TO-DATE   AVAILABLE   AGE
mysql-deployment   5         5         5            1           48s
core@ip-10-0-0-50 ~ $
```

Figure 8-24. *Creating and rolling out a deployment*

The Docker image specified in the definition file is `mysql:5.5`. The image may be updated using the `kubectl set image` command. As an example, update the image to the `latest` tag:

```
kubectl set image deployment/mysql-deployment mysql=mysql:latest
```

Find the deployment status, list the deployments, and describe the deployments:

```
kubectl describe deployments
```

As indicated in the output shown in Figure 8-25, the `RollingUpdateStrategy` is 75% unavailable and 30% max surge.

```
core@ip-10-0-0-50 ~ $ ./kubectl create -f mysql-deployment.yaml
deployment "mysql-deployment" created
core@ip-10-0-0-50 ~ $ ./kubectl rollout status deployment/mysql-deployment
deployment mysql-deployment successfully rolled out
core@ip-10-0-0-50 ~ $ ./kubectl get deployments
NAME               DESIRED   CURRENT   UP-TO-DATE   AVAILABLE   AGE
mysql-deployment   5         5         5            1           48s
core@ip-10-0-0-50 ~ $ ./kubectl set image deployment/mysql-deployment mysql=mysq
l:latest
deployment "mysql-deployment" image updated
core@ip-10-0-0-50 ~ $ ./kubectl rollout status deployment/mysql-deployment
deployment mysql-deployment successfully rolled out
core@ip-10-0-0-50 ~ $ ./kubectl get deployments
NAME               DESIRED   CURRENT   UP-TO-DATE   AVAILABLE   AGE
mysql-deployment   5         5         5            0           1m
core@ip-10-0-0-50 ~ $ ./kubectl describe deployment mysql-deployment
Name:                   mysql-deployment
Namespace:              default
CreationTimestamp:      Sat, 09 Jul 2016 20:22:25 +0000
Labels:                 app=mysql
Selector:               app=mysql
Replicas:               5 updated | 5 total | 0 available | 5 unavailable
StrategyType:           RollingUpdate
MinReadySeconds:        0
RollingUpdateStrategy:  75% max unavailable, 30% max surge
OldReplicaSets:         <none>
NewReplicaSet:          mysql-deployment-2839511385 (5/5 replicas created)
Events:
  FirstSeen     LastSeen        Count   From                            Subobjec
tPath   Type            Reason                                  Message
  ---------     --------        -----   ----                            --------
-----   --------        ------                                  -------
```

Figure 8-25. *Describing a deployment*

As listed in Events, one replica set is scaled down and another replica set is scaled up. Both replica sets are listed with `kubectl get rs`, but only one has pods, as shown in Figure 8-26.

```
  FirstSeen     LastSeen        Count   From                            Subobjec
tPath   Type            Reason                                  Message
  ---------     --------        -----   ----                            --------
-----   --------        ------                                  -------
  2m            2m              1       {deployment-controller }                N
ormal           ScalingReplicaSet                       Scaled up replica set my
sql-deployment-227245924 to 5
  2m            2m              2       {deployment-controller }                W
arning          DeploymentRollbackRevisionNotFound      Unable to find last revi
sion.
  59s           59s             1       {deployment-controller }                N
ormal           ScalingReplicaSet                       Scaled up replica set my
sql-deployment-2839511385 to 2
  58s           58s             1       {deployment-controller }                N
ormal           ScalingReplicaSet                       Scaled down replica set
mysql-deployment-227245924 to 2
  58s           58s             1       {deployment-controller }                N
ormal           ScalingReplicaSet                       Scaled up replica set my
sql-deployment-2839511385 to 5
  39s           39s             1       {deployment-controller }                N
ormal           ScalingReplicaSet                       Scaled down replica set
mysql-deployment-227245924 to 1
  39s           39s             1       {deployment-controller }                N
ormal           ScalingReplicaSet                       Scaled down replica set
mysql-deployment-227245924 to 0


core@ip-10-0-0-50 ~ $ ./kubectl get rs
NAME                            DESIRED   CURRENT   AGE
mysql-deployment-227245924      0         0         3m
mysql-deployment-2839511385     5         5         2m
core@ip-10-0-0-50 ~ $
```

Figure 8-26. *Scaling and listing ReplicaSets*

Alternatively, edit the deployment with `kubectl edit`:

```
kubectl edit deployment/mysql-deployment
```

As an example, the `mysql` image tag could be set to 5.5 as shown in Figure 8-27.

```
  namespace: default
  resourceVersion: "22537"
  selfLink: /apis/extensions/v1beta1/namespaces/default/deployments/mysql-deploy
ment
  uid: 0e80cfc7-4614-11e6-840e-0a975dd0e3e5
spec:
  replicas: 5
  selector:
    matchLabels:
      app: mysql
  strategy:
    rollingUpdate:
      maxSurge: 30%
      maxUnavailable: 75%
    type: RollingUpdate
  template:
    metadata:
      creationTimestamp: null
      labels:
        app: mysql
    spec:
      containers:
      - env:
        - name: MYSQL_ROOT_PASSWORD
          value: mysql
        image: mysql:5.5
        imagePullPolicy: Always
        name: mysql
        ports:
        - containerPort: 3306
          protocol: TCP
```

Figure 8-27. *Editing a deployment*

Modify the image tag to latest, the default when no tag is specified, as shown in Figure 8-28.

```
  namespace: default
  resourceVersion: "22537"
  selfLink: /apis/extensions/v1beta1/namespaces/default/deployments/mysql-deploy
ment
  uid: 0e80cfc7-4614-11e6-840e-0a975dd0e3e5
spec:
  replicas: 5
  selector:
    matchLabels:
      app: mysql
  strategy:
    rollingUpdate:
      maxSurge: 30%
      maxUnavailable: 75%
    type: RollingUpdate
  template:
    metadata:
      creationTimestamp: null
      labels:
        app: mysql
    spec:
      containers:
      - env:
        - name: MYSQL_ROOT_PASSWORD
          value: mysql
        image: mysql
        imagePullPolicy: Always
        name: mysql
        ports:
        - containerPort: 3306
          protocol: TCP
:wq
```

Figure 8-28. *Setting the image tag to* `latest`*, which is the default for the* `mysql` *Docker image*

Save the definition file with `:wq`. The message `deployment edited` indicates that the deployment has been edited as shown in Figure 8-29. List the deployments, the replica sets, and the pods. The old replica set does not have any pods, while the new replica set does.

```
core@ip-10-0-0-50 ~ $ sudo vi mysql-deployment.yaml
core@ip-10-0-0-50 ~ $ ./kubectl edit deployment/mysql-deployment
deployment "mysql-deployment" edited
core@ip-10-0-0-50 ~ $ ./kubectl rollout status deployment/mysql-deployment
deployment mysql-deployment successfully rolled out
core@ip-10-0-0-50 ~ $ ./kubectl get deployments
NAME               DESIRED   CURRENT   UP-TO-DATE   AVAILABLE   AGE
mysql-deployment   5         5         5            5           7m
core@ip-10-0-0-50 ~ $ ./kubectl get rs
NAME                          DESIRED   CURRENT   AGE
mysql-deployment-2212994012   0         0         5m
mysql-deployment-789224202    5         5         8m
core@ip-10-0-0-50 ~ $ ./kubectl get pods
NAME                               READY     STATUS    RESTARTS   AGE
mysql-deployment-789224202-5ws0p   1/1       Running   0          1m
mysql-deployment-789224202-7pib1   1/1       Running   0          1m
mysql-deployment-789224202-ferml   1/1       Running   0          1m
mysql-deployment-789224202-p69kh   1/1       Running   0          1m
mysql-deployment-789224202-ro1u3   1/1       Running   0          1m
core@ip-10-0-0-50 ~ $
```

Figure 8-29. *Deployment edited and rolled out*

Make some more rolling updates. For example, the rolling update shown in Figure 8-30 sets the image tag to 5.6.

```
core@ip-10-0-0-50 ~ $ ./kubectl set image deployment/mysql-deployment mysql=mysq
l:5.6
deployment "mysql-deployment" image updated
core@ip-10-0-0-50 ~ $ 
```

Figure 8-30. *Applying a rolling update to the* `mysql` *Docker image tag*

The `kubectl set image` command does not verify the validity of a tag. For example, suppose a `mysql` image with the invalid tag 5.5.5 is also used for a rolling update and the deployment is rolled out. Some of the pods of the old RC are stopped, but new pods are not started. Listing the pods shows that some of the pods have the Status `ImagePullBackOff`, or show another error message as illustrated in Figure 8-31.

```
core@ip-10-0-0-50 ~ $ ./kubectl set image deployment/mysql-deployment mysql=mysq
l:555
deployment "mysql-deployment" image updated
core@ip-10-0-0-50 ~ $ ./kubectl rollout status deployments mysql-deployment
deployment mysql-deployment successfully rolled out
core@ip-10-0-0-50 ~ $ ./kubectl get rs
NAME                          DESIRED   CURRENT   AGE
mysql-deployment-2212994012   0         0         9m
mysql-deployment-2296945629   2         2         2m
mysql-deployment-2801114083   5         5         22s
mysql-deployment-3585318469   0         0         2m
mysql-deployment-789224202    0         0         12m
core@ip-10-0-0-50 ~ $ ./kubectl get pods
NAME                                READY     STATUS             RESTARTS   AGE
mysql-deployment-2296945629-19o0b   1/1       Running            0          2m
mysql-deployment-2296945629-qan2a   1/1       Running            0          2m
mysql-deployment-2801114083-37h5b   0/1       ImagePullBackOff   0          45s
mysql-deployment-2801114083-k9p7v   0/1       ImagePullBackOff   0          45s
mysql-deployment-2801114083-rg12d   0/1       ErrImagePull       0          45s
mysql-deployment-2801114083-vu09g   0/1       ImagePullBackOff   0          45s
mysql-deployment-2801114083-znlrj   0/1       ImagePullBackOff   0          45s
core@ip-10-0-0-50 ~ $ 
```

Figure 8-31. *Rolling update with an invalid image tag*

As another example, rolling-update and roll out a deployment using the image `mysql:latest`. The deployment also is rolled out. But as indicated in the deployment description, only two of the pods are available, as shown in Figure 8-32.

```
core@ip-10-0-0-50 ~ $ ./kubectl describe deployment
Name:                   mysql-deployment
Namespace:              default
CreationTimestamp:      Sat, 09 Jul 2016 20:31:03 +0000
Labels:                 app=mysql
Selector:               app=mysql
Replicas:               5 updated | 5 total | 2 available | 5 unavailable
StrategyType:           RollingUpdate
MinReadySeconds:        0
RollingUpdateStrategy:  75% max unavailable, 30% max surge
OldReplicaSets:         mysql-deployment-2296945629 (2/2 replicas created)
NewReplicaSet:          mysql-deployment-2801114083 (5/5 replicas created)
Events:
  FirstSeen     LastSeen        Count   From                            Subobjec
tPath   Type            Reason                                  Message
  ---------     --------        -----   ----                            --------
-----   --------        ------                                  -------
  14m           14m             2       {deployment-controller }               W
arning          DeploymentRollbackRevisionNotFound      Unable to find last revi
sion.
  11m           11m             1       {deployment-controller }               N
ormal           ScalingReplicaSet                       Scaled up replica set my
sql-deployment-2212994012 to 2
  11m           11m             1       {deployment-controller }               N
ormal           ScalingReplicaSet                       Scaled up replica set my
sql-deployment-2212994012 to 5
  11m           11m             1       {deployment-controller }               N
ormal           ScalingReplicaSet                       Scaled down replica set
mysql-deployment-789224202 to 1
  11m           11m             1       {deployment-controller }               N
ormal           ScalingReplicaSet                       Scaled down replica set
mysql-deployment-789224202 to 0
```

Figure 8-32. *Only some of the replicas are available*

If some deployment has an error, the deployment may be rolled back to an earlier revision. List the deployment revisions.

```
kubectl rollout history deployment/mysql-deployment
```

The deployment revisions are listed as shown in Figure 8-33.

```
core@ip-10-0-0-50 ~ $ ./kubectl rollout history deployment/mysql-deployment
deployments "mysql-deployment":
REVISION        CHANGE-CAUSE
2               <none>
3               <none>
4               <none>
5               <none>
6               <none>

core@ip-10-0-0-50 ~ $
```

Figure 8-33. *Listing deployment revisions*

We need to find which deployment revision does not have an error and subsequently roll back to that revision. The details of a revision can be displayed. For example, the following command lists the detail of revision 4:

```
kubectl rollout history deployment/mysql-deployment --revision=4
```

The details of revision 4 are listed as shown in Figure 8-34.

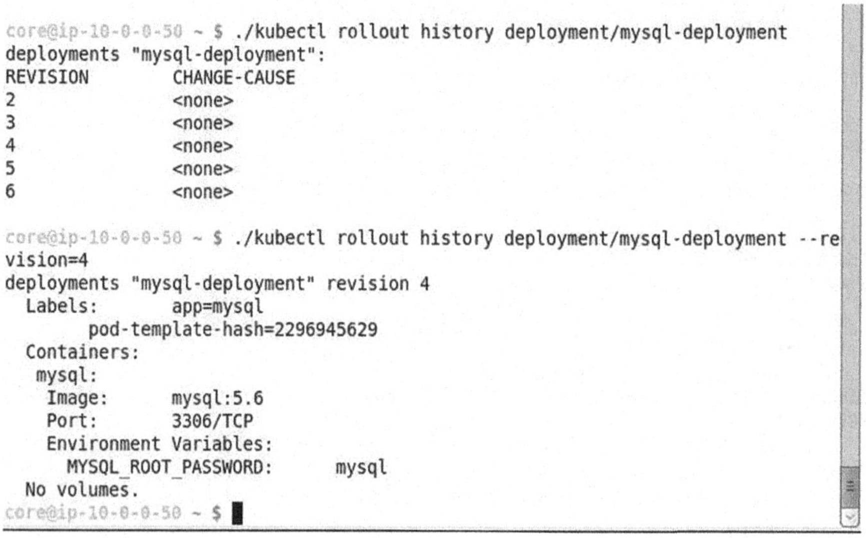
core@ip-10-0-0-50 ~ $ ./kubectl rollout history deployment/mysql-deployment
deployments "mysql-deployment":
REVISION CHANGE-CAUSE
2 <none>
3 <none>
4 <none>
5 <none>
6 <none>
core@ip-10-0-0-50 ~ $ ./kubectl rollout history deployment/mysql-deployment --revision=4
deployments "mysql-deployment" revision 4
Labels: app=mysql
pod-template-hash=2296945629
Containers:
mysql:
Image: mysql:5.6
Port: 3306/TCP
Environment Variables:
MYSQL_ROOT_PASSWORD: mysql
No volumes.
core@ip-10-0-0-50 ~ $

Figure 8-34. *Listing the details of revision 4*

To roll back to the previous version, run the following command, assuming the `rollbackTo->revision` field is set to 0 (also the default) in the deployment definition file:

```
kubectl rollout undo deployment/mysql-deployment
```

Deployment is rolled back as shown in Figure 8-35. List the pods, and you may see some of the pods still not running, which indicates that the revision rolled back to has errors.

```
core@ip-10-0-0-50 ~ $ ./kubectl rollout undo deployment/mysql-deployment
deployment "mysql-deployment" rolled back
core@ip-10-0-0-50 ~ $ ./kubectl get deployment
NAME               DESIRED   CURRENT   UP-TO-DATE   AVAILABLE   AGE
mysql-deployment   5         7         5            2           17m
core@ip-10-0-0-50 ~ $ ./kubectl get pods
NAME                                READY     STATUS             RESTARTS   AGE
mysql-deployment-2296945629-19o0b   1/1       Running            0          7m
mysql-deployment-2296945629-qan2a   1/1       Running            0          7m
mysql-deployment-3585318469-71ahh   0/1       ImagePullBackOff   0          40s
mysql-deployment-3585318469-83lam   0/1       ErrImagePull       0          40s
mysql-deployment-3585318469-nt4hs   0/1       ErrImagePull       0          40s
mysql-deployment-3585318469-vrcyw   0/1       ErrImagePull       0          40s
mysql-deployment-3585318469-y8r0z   0/1       ErrImagePull       0          40s
core@ip-10-0-0-50 ~ $
```

Figure 8-35. *Rolling back a deployment*

Either keep rolling back one revision at a time and verifying whether the revision is valid or roll back to a specific revision that is known to be valid, for example revision 4:

```
kubectl rollout undo deployment/mysql-deployment --to-revision=4
```

Now list the pods. As indicated in Figure 8-36, all pods are running.

```
core@ip-10-0-0-50 ~ $ ./kubectl rollout undo deployment/mysql-deployment
deployment "mysql-deployment" rolled back
core@ip-10-0-0-50 ~ $ ./kubectl get deployment
NAME               DESIRED   CURRENT   UP-TO-DATE   AVAILABLE   AGE
mysql-deployment   5         7         5            2           19m
core@ip-10-0-0-50 ~ $ ./kubectl get pods
NAME                                READY     STATUS             RESTARTS   AGE
mysql-deployment-2296945629-19o0b   1/1       Running            0          9m
mysql-deployment-2296945629-qan2a   1/1       Running            0          9m
mysql-deployment-3585318469-33sus   0/1       ImagePullBackOff   0          16s
mysql-deployment-3585318469-3w1e1   0/1       ErrImagePull       0          16s
mysql-deployment-3585318469-b1dxw   0/1       ErrImagePull       0          16s
mysql-deployment-3585318469-c63wa   0/1       ImagePullBackOff   0          16s
mysql-deployment-3585318469-f280y   0/1       ImagePullBackOff   0          16s
core@ip-10-0-0-50 ~ $ ./kubectl rollout undo deployment/mysql-deployment --to-re
vision=4
deployment "mysql-deployment" rolled back
core@ip-10-0-0-50 ~ $ ./kubectl get deployment
NAME               DESIRED   CURRENT   UP-TO-DATE   AVAILABLE   AGE
mysql-deployment   5         5         5            5           20m
core@ip-10-0-0-50 ~ $ ./kubectl get pods
NAME                                READY     STATUS    RESTARTS   AGE
mysql-deployment-2296945629-19o0b   1/1       Running   0          10m
mysql-deployment-2296945629-ohyu0   1/1       Running   0          19s
mysql-deployment-2296945629-q1n74   1/1       Running   0          19s
mysql-deployment-2296945629-qan2a   1/1       Running   0          10m
mysql-deployment-2296945629-rbw0p   1/1       Running   0          19s
core@ip-10-0-0-50 ~ $
```

Figure 8-36. *Rolling back to revision 4*

No further rollback is required.

Summary

In this chapter we introduced rolling updates, a feature that is useful because it lets you update a running application to a newer image or RC definition without interruption in service. We created a rolling update using an updated RC definition file and also an updated container image. We also demonstrate rolling back an update. In the next chapter we shall discuss scheduling pods on nodes.

CHAPTER 9

Scheduling Pods on Nodes

Scheduling involves finding the pods that need to be run and running (scheduling) them on nodes in a cluster.

Problem

Often containers have dependencies between them and need to be collocated on the same node to reduce the network latency between them. The pod abstraction can encapsulate multiple containers, which solves the problem of collocating containers with dependencies between them. The pattern can be extended further to dependencies between pods that need to be running on the same or a different machine (node).

Solution

In a recent publication, *Design Patterns for Container-based Distributed Systems*, by Brendan Burns and David Oppenheimer (`https://www.usenix.org/node/196347`), three types of container design patterns are discussed:

1. Single Container Management Patterns
2. Single Node, Multi-Container Application Patterns
3. Multi-Node Application Patterns

All of these design patterns require pods to be scheduled on specific nodes in a cluster. Kubernetes provides various options for scheduling pods on specific nodes within a cluster. The sequence used to schedule a pod on a node is shown in Figure 9-1.

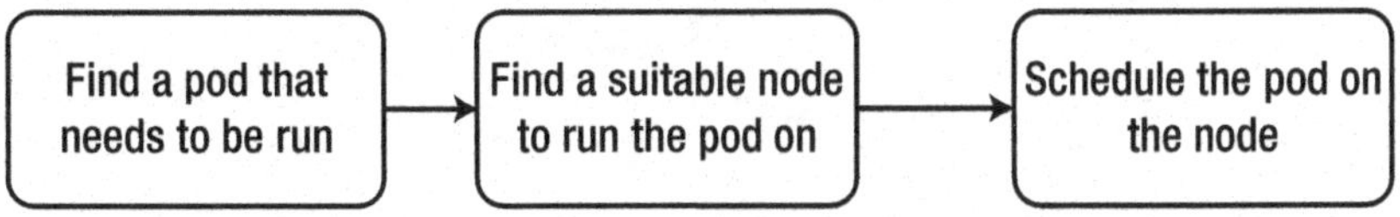

Figure 9-1. *Sequence used in scheduling a pod*

D. Vohra, *Kubernetes Management Design Patterns*, DOI 10.1007/978-1-4842-2598-1_9

Overview

Kubernetes Scheduler is a Kubernetes component or process that runs alongside the other components such as API Server. The purpose of the Scheduler is to monitor the API for pods that need to be scheduled, find a suitable node to schedule a pod, and schedule the pod, one pod at a time. This chapter looks at the following topics.

- Defining a scheduling policy
- Setting the environment
- Using the default scheduler
- Scheduling pods without a node selector
- Setting node labels
- Scheduling pods with node selector
- Setting node affinity
  - Setting requiredDuringSchedulingIgnoredDuringExecution
  - Setting preferredDuringSchedulingIgnoredDuringExecution

Defining a Scheduling Policy

Scheduling is determined by a *scheduling policy*, involving predicates and priority functions. Scheduling involves the following process, starting with all nodes being viable to schedule a pod:

1. Filter out nodes using filtering policy predicates. The objective of filtering out nodes is to exclude those nodes that do not meet certain requirements of a pod.
2. Nodes are ranked using priority functions.
3. The pod is scheduled onto the node with the highest priority. If multiple nodes have equal priority, one of the nodes is chosen at random.

Some of the salient predicates that implement filtering policy are discussed in Table 9-1.

Table 9-1. *Predicates for Filtering Policy*

Predicate	Description
`NoDiskConflict`	Evaluates whether there is any disk conflict due to the volumes requested by the pod. Supported volume types are AWS EBS, GCE PD, and Ceph RBD.
`NoVolumeZoneConflict`	Taking into consideration zone restrictions, evaluates whether the volumes a pod requests are available on the zone.
`PodFitsResources`	Verifies that the available resources (CPU and memory) on a node fit a pod's resource requirements.
`PodFitsHostPorts`	Verifies that a HostPort requested by a pod is not already taken up.
`HostName`	If the pod's spec specified a node name, filters out all the other nodes.
`MatchNodeSelector`	Filters out nodes that do not have matching labels as set in the pod's `nodeSelector` field and the `scheduler.alpha.kubernetes.io/affinity` pod annotation if specified.
`MaxEBSVolumeCount`	Verifies that the number of attached EBS Volumes does not exceed the limit of 39 available volumes (1 of the 40 available is reserved for the root volume).
`MaxGCEPDVolumeCount`	Verifies that the number of attached GCE PD Volumes does not exceed the limit of 16 available volumes.
`CheckNodeMemoryPressure`	Least priority (BestEffort) pods cannot be scheduled on nodes with memory pressure condition.
`CheckNodeDiskPressure`	Pods cannot be scheduled on nodes with a disk pressure condition.

After the unsuitable nodes have been filtered out, the remaining nodes are ranked using priority functions. Some of the salient priority functions are discussed in Table 9-2.

Table 9-2. *Priority Functions*

Priority Function	Description
`LeastRequestedPriority`	The objective of this priority function is to spread out the resource consumption across the nodes. CPU and memory are equally weighted in calculating the free resources fraction (the fraction of the node that would be free if a pod were scheduled on the node) using a formula: (capacity - sum of requests of all pods already on the node - request of pod that is being scheduled) / capacity). The node with the greatest free fraction is selected for scheduling.
`BalancedResourceAllocation`	The objective of this priority function is to balance the CPU and memory utilization rate.
`SelectorSpreadPriority`	The objective is to avoid scheduling pods in the same replication controller, replica set or service on to the same node or zone.
`CalculateAntiAffinityPriority`	The objective is to avoid scheduling pods in the same service on nodes with same label values for a particular label.

(*continued*)

Table 9-2. *(continued)*

Priority Function	Description
`ImageLocalityPriority`	The objective is to schedule on nodes that already have some or all of the image packages installed. A node with the larger size of the already installed packages is preferred.
`NodeAffinityPriority`	Evaluate node affinity using `preferredDuringSchedulingIgnoredDuringExecution` and `requiredDuringSchedulingIgnoredDuringExecution`.

The final node ranking is calculated using a weighted priority function score. Each node is given a score in the range of 1–10 for each of the applied priority functions, and the final score is calculated by assigning a weight for each priority function. For example, given three priority functions `priorityFunc1Score`, `priorityFunc2Score`, and `priorityFunc3Score`, the final score is calculated as follows:

```
RankingScoreNodeA = (weight1 * priorityFunc1Score) + (weight2 * priorityFunc2Score) +
(weight3 * priorityFunc3Score)
```

The node with the highest score is selected for scheduling a pod.

The default scheduling policy as determined by default predicates and priority functions may be customized or overridden using one of the following procedures:

1. Use a `--policy-config-file` parameter to the scheduler. The policy config file is a json file, for example `https://github.com/kubernetes/kubernetes/blob/master/examples/scheduler-policy-config.json`.
2. Modify the default predicates and/or priority functions in `plugin/pkg/scheduler/algorithm/predicates/predicates.go` and/or `plugin/pkg/scheduler/algorithm/priorities/priorities.go` respectively and register the policy in `defaultPredicates()` and/or `defaultPriorities()` in `plugin/pkg/scheduler/algorithmprovider/defaults/defaults.go`.

Setting the Environment

We shall be using a CoreOS-based AWS EC2 Cloud Formation to run a one-controller-three-worker-node Kubernetes cluster. Start an EC2 instance using Amazon Linux AMI. SSH log in to the EC2 instance:

```
ssh -i docker.pem ec2-user@54.197.206.44
```

Start a cloud configuration for a Kubernetes cluster and register the Public IP address of the controller in the Public DNS name. While configuring the cluster set the Kubernetes version to `v1.3.0_coreos.1` in the `kubernetesVersion` field in `cluster.yaml`.

Install the `kubectl` binaries. Both the Client and Server versions should be 1.3, as shown in Figure 9-2.

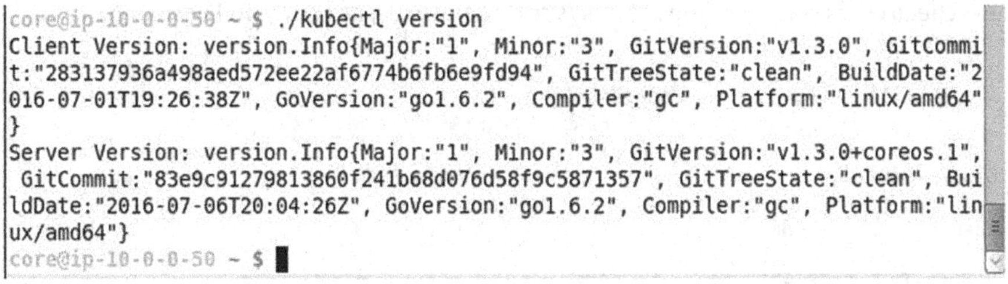

core@ip-10-0-0-50 ~ $ ./kubectl version
Client Version: version.Info{Major:"1", Minor:"3", GitVersion:"v1.3.0", GitCommit:"283137936a498aed572ee22af6774b6fb6e9fd94", GitTreeState:"clean", BuildDate:"2016-07-01T19:26:38Z", GoVersion:"go1.6.2", Compiler:"gc", Platform:"linux/amd64"}
Server Version: version.Info{Major:"1", Minor:"3", GitVersion:"v1.3.0+coreos.1", GitCommit:"83e9c91279813860f241b68d076d58f9c5871357", GitTreeState:"clean", BuildDate:"2016-07-06T20:04:26Z", GoVersion:"go1.6.2", Compiler:"gc", Platform:"linux/amd64"}
core@ip-10-0-0-50 ~ $

Figure 9-2. *Listing Kubernetes versions*

SSH log in to the controller instance:

```
ssh -i "kubernetes-coreos.pem"  core@50.19.44.241
```

List the nodes:

```
kubectl get nodes
```

The controller and three worker nodes are listed as running, but the controller node is not schedulable, as indicated by the `SchedulingDisabled` shown in Figure 9-3.

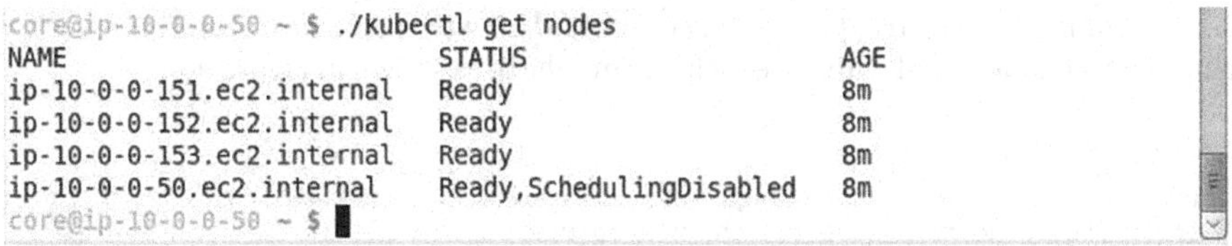

core@ip-10-0-0-50 ~ $ ./kubectl get nodes
NAME STATUS AGE
ip-10-0-0-151.ec2.internal Ready 8m
ip-10-0-0-152.ec2.internal Ready 8m
ip-10-0-0-153.ec2.internal Ready 8m
ip-10-0-0-50.ec2.internal Ready,SchedulingDisabled 8m
core@ip-10-0-0-50 ~ $

Figure 9-3. *Listing Nodes; the master node is nonschedulable*

Using the Default Scheduler

The default scheduler `kube-scheduler` is started automatically when the Kubernetes processes (components) are started. The component statuses should list the `scheduler` component, as shown in Figure 9-4.

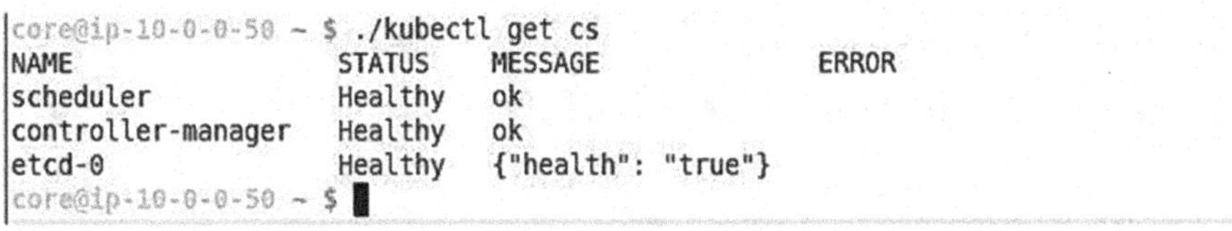

core@ip-10-0-0-50 ~ $ ./kubectl get cs
NAME STATUS MESSAGE ERROR
scheduler Healthy ok
controller-manager Healthy ok
etcd-0 Healthy {"health": "true"}
core@ip-10-0-0-50 ~ $

Figure 9-4. *Listing component status for* `scheduler`

A pod for the kube-scheduler is started in the kube-system namespace, as shown in Figure 9-5.

```
core@ip-10-0-0-50 ~ $ ./kubectl get pods --namespace=kube-system
NAME                                              READY     STATUS    RESTARTS
   AGE
heapster-v1.0.2-3151619174-3c0l2                  2/2       Running   0
   58m
kube-apiserver-ip-10-0-0-50.ec2.internal          1/1       Running   0
   58m
kube-controller-manager-ip-10-0-0-50.ec2.internal 1/1       Running   0
   59m
kube-dns-v11-uz9l4                                4/4       Running   0
   58m
kube-proxy-ip-10-0-0-213.ec2.internal             1/1       Running   0
   58m
kube-proxy-ip-10-0-0-214.ec2.internal             1/1       Running   0
   58m
kube-proxy-ip-10-0-0-215.ec2.internal             1/1       Running   0
   58m
kube-proxy-ip-10-0-0-50.ec2.internal              1/1       Running   0
   59m
kube-scheduler-ip-10-0-0-50.ec2.internal          1/1       Running   0
   59m
core@ip-10-0-0-50 ~ $
```

Figure 9-5. *listing pods in the kube-system namespace, including the kube-scheduler pod*

The kube-scheduler command can be used to start kube-scheduler with custom settings. The available command parameters can be listed with kube-scheduler -help as shown in Figure 9-6.

```
core@ip-10-0-0-50 ~ $ ./kube-scheduler -help
Usage of ./kube-scheduler:
      --address=127.0.0.1: The IP address to serve on (set to 0.0.0.0 for all in
terfaces)
      --algorithm-provider="DefaultProvider": The scheduling algorithm provider
to use, one of: DefaultProvider
      --alsologtostderr[=false]: log to standard error as well as files
      --bind-pods-burst=100: Number of bindings per second scheduler is allowed
to make during bursts
      --bind-pods-qps=50: Number of bindings per second scheduler is allowed to
continuously make
      --kubeconfig="": Path to kubeconfig file with authorization and master loc
ation information.
      --log-backtrace-at=:0: when logging hits line file:N, emit a stack trace
      --log-dir="": If non-empty, write log files in this directory
      --log-flush-frequency=5s: Maximum number of seconds between log flushes
      --logtostderr[=true]: log to standard error instead of files
      --master="": The address of the Kubernetes API server (overrides any value
 in kubeconfig)
      --policy-config-file="": File with scheduler policy configuration
      --port=10251: The port that the scheduler's http service runs on
      --profiling[=true]: Enable profiling via web interface host:port/debug/ppr
of/
      --stderrthreshold=2: logs at or above this threshold go to stderr
      --v=0: log level for V logs
      --version=false: Print version information and quit
      --vmodule=: comma-separated list of pattern=N settings for file-filtered l
ogging
core@ip-10-0-0-50 ~ $
```

Figure 9-6. *kube-scheduler command usage*

The configuration files to launch the pods for the Kubernetes components, which include the API Server, Controller Manager, Proxy, and Scheduler are in the /etc/kubernetes/manifests directory as shown in Figure 9-7; the kube-scheduler.yaml file is what we need for the scheduler.

```
core@ip-10-0-0-50 /etc/kubernetes/manifests $ ls -l
total 40
-rw-r--r--. 1 root root  748 Jul 26 16:53 calico-policy-agent.yaml
-rw-r--r--. 1 root root 1466 Jul 26 16:50 kube-apiserver.yaml
-rw-r--r--. 1 root root 1000 Jul 26 16:50 kube-controller-manager.yaml
-rw-r--r--. 1 root root  530 Jul 26 16:50 kube-proxy.yaml
-rw-r--r--. 1 root root  464 Jul 26 16:50 kube-scheduler.yaml
core@ip-10-0-0-50 /etc/kubernetes/manifests $
```

Figure 9-7. *Listing files in the /etc/kubernetes/manifests directory*

The kube-scheduler pod specification can be customized in a vi editor as shown in Figure 9-8.

```
apiVersion: v1
kind: Pod
metadata:
  name: kube-scheduler
  namespace: kube-system
spec:
  hostNetwork: true
  containers:
  - name: kube-scheduler
    image: quay.io/coreos/hyperkube:v1.2.4_coreos.1
    command:
    - /hyperkube
    - scheduler
    - --master=http://127.0.0.1:8080
    - --leader-elect=true
    livenessProbe:
      httpGet:
        host: 127.0.0.1
        path: /healthz
        port: 10251
      initialDelaySeconds: 15
      timeoutSeconds: 1
~
~
~
~
~
~
~
~
~
"kube-scheduler.yaml" 22L, 464C
```

Figure 9-8. *The kube-scheduler.yaml file in a vi editor*

The kubelet must be restarted, as shown in Figure 9-9, if the modification to the kube-scheduler pod specification is to take effect.

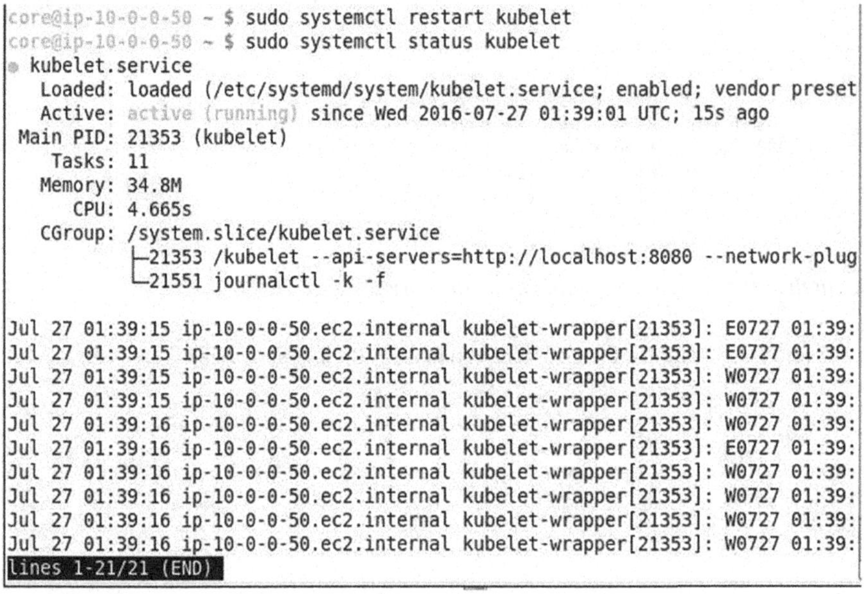

```
core@ip-10-0-0-50 ~ $ sudo systemctl restart kubelet
core@ip-10-0-0-50 ~ $ sudo systemctl status kubelet
● kubelet.service
   Loaded: loaded (/etc/systemd/system/kubelet.service; enabled; vendor preset
   Active: active (running) since Wed 2016-07-27 01:39:01 UTC; 15s ago
 Main PID: 21353 (kubelet)
    Tasks: 11
   Memory: 34.8M
      CPU: 4.665s
   CGroup: /system.slice/kubelet.service
           ├─21353 /kubelet --api-servers=http://localhost:8080 --network-plug
           └─21551 journalctl -k -f

Jul 27 01:39:15 ip-10-0-0-50.ec2.internal kubelet-wrapper[21353]: E0727 01:39:
Jul 27 01:39:15 ip-10-0-0-50.ec2.internal kubelet-wrapper[21353]: E0727 01:39:
Jul 27 01:39:15 ip-10-0-0-50.ec2.internal kubelet-wrapper[21353]: W0727 01:39:
Jul 27 01:39:15 ip-10-0-0-50.ec2.internal kubelet-wrapper[21353]: W0727 01:39:
Jul 27 01:39:16 ip-10-0-0-50.ec2.internal kubelet-wrapper[21353]: W0727 01:39:
Jul 27 01:39:16 ip-10-0-0-50.ec2.internal kubelet-wrapper[21353]: E0727 01:39:
Jul 27 01:39:16 ip-10-0-0-50.ec2.internal kubelet-wrapper[21353]: W0727 01:39:
Jul 27 01:39:16 ip-10-0-0-50.ec2.internal kubelet-wrapper[21353]: W0727 01:39:
Jul 27 01:39:16 ip-10-0-0-50.ec2.internal kubelet-wrapper[21353]: W0727 01:39:
Jul 27 01:39:16 ip-10-0-0-50.ec2.internal kubelet-wrapper[21353]: W0727 01:39:
lines 1-21/21 (END)
```

Figure 9-9. *Restarting the kubelet*

A container is started for each of the Kubernetes components, including the scheduler. The containers may be listed with the docker ps command. The k8s_kube-schduler container should be listed as shown in Figure 9-10.

```
core@ip-10-0-0-50 ~ $ sudo docker ps
CONTAINER ID        IMAGE                                   COMMAND
       CREATED             STATUS              PORTS               NAMES
d1f1f7d3f314        quay.io/calico/leader-elector:v0.1.0    "/run.sh --electi
on=c"   About an hour ago   Up About an hour                        k8s_leader-e
lector.89250a02_calico-policy-agent-ip-10-0-0-50.ec2.internal_calico-system_7d76
69564417afb929ddc4edb98cdd8f_86b65670
7d0c6d070cc0        calico/k8s-policy-agent:v0.1.4          "/dist/policy_age
nt"     About an hour ago   Up About an hour                        k8s_k8s-poli
cy-agent.45b4585_calico-policy-agent-ip-10-0-0-50.ec2.internal_calico-system_7d7
669564417afb929ddc4edb98cdd8f_b2de300a
de56581c3101        gcr.io/google_containers/pause:2.0      "/pause"
        About an hour ago   Up About an hour                        k8s_POD.6059
dfa2_calico-policy-agent-ip-10-0-0-50.ec2.internal_calico-system_7d7669564417afb
929ddc4edb98cdd8f_1848cd1b
ae4ead66828b        quay.io/coreos/hyperkube:v1.2.4_coreos.1  "/hyperkube contr
olle"   About an hour ago   Up About an hour                        k8s_kube-con
troller-manager.f40910b4_kube-controller-manager-ip-10-0-0-50.ec2.internal_kube-
system_c0c551a0956f03772329794a28e37905_1b677095
ad08375a8d01        quay.io/coreos/hyperkube:v1.2.4_coreos.1  "/hyperkube proxy
 --m"   About an hour ago   Up About an hour                        k8s_kube-pro
xy.ae2b61b3_kube-proxy-ip-10-0-0-50.ec2.internal_kube-system_7f8f464c17931de0b37
71e01a604f50c_e80e1301
ed53c1e01525        quay.io/coreos/hyperkube:v1.2.4_coreos.1  "/hyperkube sched
uler"   About an hour ago   Up About an hour                        k8s_kube-sch
eduler.ce96e6_kube-scheduler-ip-10-0-0-50.ec2.internal_kube-system_6283345906d1f
b1497bee62dac0f426a_e3ddcc3f
454be0ad24ee        quay.io/coreos/hyperkube:v1.2.4_coreos.1  "/hyperkube apise
rver"   About an hour ago   Up About an hour                        k8s_kube-api
server.ea756937_kube-apiserver-ip-10-0-0-50.ec2.internal_kube-system_e0e30a55daf
2b8f921d859015ef0c395_a6e40a04
e90f19b677fe        gcr.io/google_containers/pause:2.0      "/pause"
```

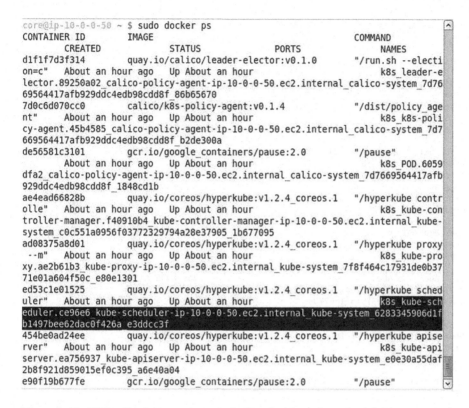

Figure 9-10. *Listing Docker containers, including the* `k8s_kube-scheduler`

The `scheduler` container cannot be terminated while the Kubernetes cluster is running. If the `scheduler` container is stopped explicitly, the container restarts as indicated in Figure 9-11 by the first container `k8s_kube-schduler` listed and started 6 seconds earlier.

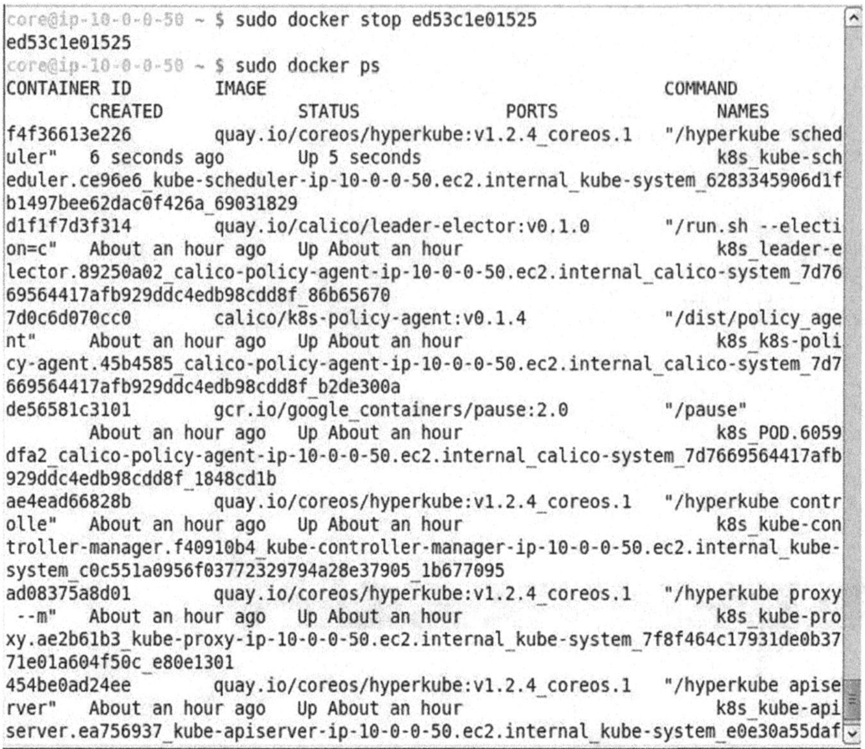

```
core@ip-10-0-0-50 ~ $ sudo docker stop ed53c1e01525
ed53c1e01525
core@ip-10-0-0-50 ~ $ sudo docker ps
CONTAINER ID        IMAGE                                        COMMAND
        CREATED             STATUS              PORTS               NAMES
f4f36613e226        quay.io/coreos/hyperkube:v1.2.4_coreos.1    "/hyperkube sched
uler"   6 seconds ago       Up 5 seconds                            k8s_kube-sch
eduler.ce96e6_kube-scheduler-ip-10-0-0-50.ec2.internal_kube-system_6283345906d1f
b1497bee62dac0f426a_69031829
d1f1f7d3f314        quay.io/calico/leader-elector:v0.1.0        "/run.sh --electi
on=c"   About an hour ago   Up About an hour                        k8s_leader-e
lector.89250a02_calico-policy-agent-ip-10-0-0-50.ec2.internal_calico-system_7d76
69564417afb929ddc4edb98cdd8f_86b65670
7d0c6d070cc0        calico/k8s-policy-agent:v0.1.4              "/dist/policy_age
nt"     About an hour ago   Up About an hour                        k8s_k8s-poli
cy-agent.45b4585_calico-policy-agent-ip-10-0-0-50.ec2.internal_calico-system_7d7
669564417afb929ddc4edb98cdd8f_b2de300a
de56581c3101        gcr.io/google_containers/pause:2.0          "/pause"
        About an hour ago   Up About an hour                        k8s_POD.6059
dfa2_calico-policy-agent-ip-10-0-0-50.ec2.internal_calico-system_7d7669564417afb
929ddc4edb98cdd8f_1848cd1b
ae4ead66828b        quay.io/coreos/hyperkube:v1.2.4_coreos.1    "/hyperkube contr
olle"   About an hour ago   Up About an hour                        k8s_kube-con
troller-manager.f40910b4_kube-controller-manager-ip-10-0-0-50.ec2.internal_kube-
system_c0c551a0956f03772329794a28e37905_1b677095
ad08375a8d01        quay.io/coreos/hyperkube:v1.2.4_coreos.1    "/hyperkube proxy
 --m"   About an hour ago   Up About an hour                        k8s_kube-pro
xy.ae2b61b3_kube-proxy-ip-10-0-0-50.ec2.internal_kube-system_7f8f464c17931de0b37
71e01a604f50c_e80e1301
454be0ad24ee        quay.io/coreos/hyperkube:v1.2.4_coreos.1    "/hyperkube apise
rver"   About an hour ago   Up About an hour                        k8s_kube-api
server.ea756937_kube-apiserver-ip-10-0-0-50.ec2.internal_kube-system_e0e30a55daf
```

Figure 9-11. *The `k8s_kube-schduler container` is restarted if stopped*

The `kube-scheduler` pod description, including the command used to start the scheduler, may be obtained with the `kubectl describe pod` command as shown in Figure 9-12.

```
core@ip-10-0-0-50 ~ $ ./kubectl describe pod kube-scheduler --namespace=kube-sy
stem
Name:           kube-scheduler
Namespace:      kube-system
Node:           ip-10-0-0-214.ec2.internal/10.0.0.214
Start Time:     Tue, 26 Jul 2016 19:46:26 +0000
Labels:         <none>
Status:         Running
IP:             10.0.0.214
Controllers:    <none>
Containers:
  second-kube-scheduler:
    Container ID:       docker://6fc7d1452c832d1fe46a8eb735f857257b5e7b3d2aa877
175f1706f23e37cf56
    Image:              quay.io/coreos/hyperkube:v1.3.2_coreos.0
    Image ID:           docker://sha256:ff57fd92809bcec1cfbdd47bf933fd6d66376f5
249dd3f7a5bac91a91a19b170
    Port:
    Command:
      /hyperkube
      scheduler
      --master=http://127.0.0.1:8080
      --leader-elect=true
    State:                      Running
      Started:                  Tue, 26 Jul 2016 19:47:36 +0000
    Ready:                      True
    Restart Count:              0
    Environment Variables:      <none>
Conditions:
  Type          Status
  Ready         True
Volumes:
```

Figure 9-12. *Listing the pod description for* `kube-scheduler`

The `scheduler` component cannot be deleted, as shown in Figure 9-13.

```
core@ip-10-0-0-50 ~ $ ./kubectl delete cs scheduler
Error from server: the server does not allow this method on the requested resource
core@ip-10-0-0-50 ~ $ █
```

Figure 9-13. *The* `scheduler` *component is not deleted*

The optional `scheduler.alpha.kubernetes.io/name` annotation on a pod can be used to specify the scheduler to use. Next, we shall demonstrate the use of the annotation. Create a pod definition file named `pod1.yaml`:

```
sudo pod1.yaml
```

In the first example, we shall not specify the `scheduler.alpha.kubernetes.io/name` annotation. Copy the following listing to the `pod1.yaml`.

```
---
apiVersion: v1
kind: Pod
metadata:
  name: pod-without-annotation
  labels:
    name: multischeduler
spec:
  containers:
    -
      image: "gcr.io/google_containers/pause:2.0"
      name: pod-without-annotation
```

The `pod1.yaml` file is shown in a `vi` editor in Figure 9-14.

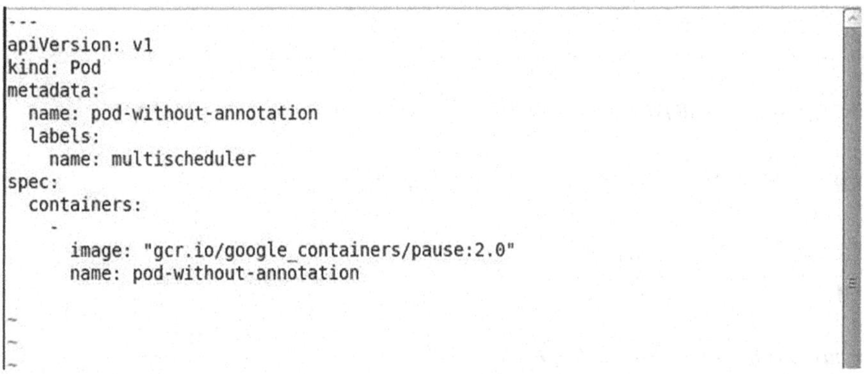

```
---
apiVersion: v1
kind: Pod
metadata:
  name: pod-without-annotation
  labels:
    name: multischeduler
spec:
  containers:
    -
      image: "gcr.io/google_containers/pause:2.0"
      name: pod-without-annotation
```

Figure 9-14. *Pod definition without scheduler annotation*

Create a pod using the definition file:

```
./kubectl create -f pod1.yaml
```

Subsequently, list the pods:

```
./kubectl get pods -o wide
```

The `pod-without-annotation` is created and listed as shown in Figure 9-15. The `default` scheduler is used to schedule the pod using the default scheduling policy.

```
core@ip-10-0-0-50 ~ $ ./kubectl create -f pod1.yaml
pod "pod-without-annotation" created
core@ip-10-0-0-50 ~ $ ./kubectl get pods -o wide
NAME                     READY     STATUS    RESTARTS   AGE       IP          NO
DE
pod-without-annotation   1/1       Running   0          18s       10.2.54.2   ip
-10-0-0-213.ec2.internal
core@ip-10-0-0-50 ~ $
```

Figure 9-15. *Pod definition without scheduler annotation*

Next, we shall use the `scheduler.alpha.kubernetes.io/name` annotation in a pod definition file. Create another pod definition file, named `pod2.yaml`, and copy the following code into it. The `scheduler.alpha.kubernetes.io/name` annotation is set to the `default-scheduler` explicitly.

```
---
apiVersion: v1
kind: Pod
metadata:
  annotations:
    scheduler.alpha.kubernetes.io/name: default-scheduler
  labels:
    name: multischeduler
  name: default-scheduler
spec:
  containers:
    -
      image: "gcr.io/google_containers/pause:2.0"
      name: pod-with-default-scheduler-annotation-container
```

The `pod2.yaml` file is shown in the `vi` editor in Figure 9-16.

```
---
apiVersion: v1
kind: Pod
metadata:
  annotations:
    scheduler.alpha.kubernetes.io/name: default-scheduler
  labels:
    name: multischeduler
  name: pod-with-default-scheduler-annotation
spec:
  containers:
    -
      image: "gcr.io/google_containers/pause:2.0"
      name: pod-with-default-scheduler-annotation-container

~
~
```

Figure 9-16. *Pod definition with scheduler annotation*

Create a pod using the pod2.yaml definition file:

```
./kubectl create -f pod2.yaml
```

The pod pod-with-default-scheduler-annotation-container is created and listed, as shown in Figure 9-17.

```
core@ip-10-0-0-50 ~ $ sudo vi pod2.yaml
core@ip-10-0-0-50 ~ $ ./kubectl create -f pod2.yaml
pod "pod-with-default-scheduler-annotation" created
core@ip-10-0-0-50 ~ $ ./kubectl get pods -o wide
NAME                                     READY     STATUS     RESTARTS   AGE
 IP           NODE
pod-with-default-scheduler-annotation   1/1       Running    0          8s
 10.2.54.3    ip-10-0-0-213.ec2.internal
pod-without-annotation                   1/1       Running    0          1m
 10.2.54.2    ip-10-0-0-213.ec2.internal
core@ip-10-0-0-50 ~ $ 
```

Figure 9-17. *Creating and listing the pod with scheduler annotation*

The default scheduler is used regardless of whether it is specified explicitly. To verify that the default-scheduler is used, list the Events. The pod named pod-with-default-scheduler-annotation-container is listed to have been scheduled using the default-scheduler, and so is the pod pod-without-annotation, as shown in Figure 9-18.

```
core@ip-10-0-0-50 ~ $ ./kubectl get events
LASTSEEN   FIRSTSEEN   COUNT     NAME                                      KIND
   SUBOBJECT                                                          TYPE
REASON       SOURCE                               MESSAGE
59s        59s         1         pod-with-default-scheduler-annotation    Pod
                                                                      Normal
Scheduled    {default-scheduler }                 Successfully assigned pod-wit
h-default-scheduler-annotation to ip-10-0-0-213.ec2.internal
58s        58s         1         pod-with-default-scheduler-annotation    Pod
   spec.containers{pod-with-default-scheduler-annotation-container}   Normal
Pulled       {kubelet ip-10-0-0-213.ec2.internal}   Container image "gcr.io/googl
e_containers/pause:2.0" already present on machine
58s        58s         1         pod-with-default-scheduler-annotation    Pod
   spec.containers{pod-with-default-scheduler-annotation-container}   Normal
Created      {kubelet ip-10-0-0-213.ec2.internal}   Created container with docker
 id 972b50807b73
57s        57s         1         pod-with-default-scheduler-annotation    Pod
   spec.containers{pod-with-default-scheduler-annotation-container}   Normal
Started      {kubelet ip-10-0-0-213.ec2.internal}   Started container with docker
 id 972b50807b73
2m         2m          1         pod-without-annotation                   Pod
                                                                      Normal
Scheduled    {default-scheduler }                 Successfully assigned pod-wit
hout-annotation to ip-10-0-0-213.ec2.internal
2m         2m          1         pod-without-annotation                   Pod
   spec.containers{pod-without-annotation}                            Normal
Pulled       {kubelet ip-10-0-0-213.ec2.internal}   Container image "gcr.io/googl
e_containers/pause:2.0" already present on machine
2m         2m          1         pod-without-annotation                   Pod
   spec.containers{pod-without-annotation}                            Normal
Created      {kubelet ip-10-0-0-213.ec2.internal}   Created container with docker
 id 5d7bb224f843
```

Figure 9-18. *The pods are scheduled using the* `default-scheduler`

Scheduling Pods without a Node Selector

The `nodeSelector` field in the pod specification may be used to select a node for the pod to be scheduled on. The `nodeSelector` field specifies a label, which should be the same as a node's label for the pod to be scheduled on the node. If a `nodeSelector` is not specified, the pod definition (`pod.yaml`) for a pod for `nginx` will be similar to the following:

```
apiVersion: v1
kind: Pod
metadata:
  name: nginx
  labels:
    env: test
spec:
  containers:
  - name: nginx
    image: nginx
    imagePullPolicy: IfNotPresent
```

Run the pod using the definition file:

```
kubectl create -f pod.yaml
```

The pod is scheduled on a suitable node using the default scheduling policy.

Setting Node Labels

Next, we shall use labels to match pods with labels. First, we need to set labels on nodes. The node names on which to set labels may be found with `kubectl get nodes`, as shown in Figure 9-3 earlier.

The syntax to label a node is as follows:

```
kubectl label nodes <node-name> <label-key>=<label-value>
```

Some built-in labels are also provided, which can also be used in the `nodeSelector` field, but only one label may be specified.

```
kubernetes.io/hostname, failure-domain.beta.kubernetes.io/zone,failure-domain.beta.
kubernetes.io/region,beta.kubernetes.io/instance-type
```

As an example, label the node `ip-10-0-0-151.ec2.internal` with the label `kubernetes.io/image-name=nginx`:

```
kubectl label nodes ip-10-0-0-151.ec2.internal kubernetes.io/image-name=nginx
Similarly, label node ip-10-0-0-152.ec2.internal.
kubectl label nodes ip-10-0-0-152.ec2.internal kubernetes.io/image-name=hello-world
```

Nodes are labeled, as shown in Figure 9-19.

```
core@ip-10-0-0-50 ~ $ ./kubectl label nodes ip-10-0-0-151.ec2.internal kubernete
s.io/image-name=nginx
node "ip-10-0-0-151.ec2.internal" labeled
core@ip-10-0-0-50 ~ $ ./kubectl label nodes ip-10-0-0-152.ec2.internal kubernete
s.io/image-name=hello-world
node "ip-10-0-0-152.ec2.internal" labeled
core@ip-10-0-0-50 ~ $
```

Figure 9-19. *Labeling nodes*

List the nodes, including the labels, using the -show-labels command argument to the kubectl get nodes command. The labels added are listed in addition to the default labels, as shown in Figure 9-20.

```
core@ip-10-0-0-50 ~ $ ./kubectl get nodes --show-labels
NAME                         STATUS                     AGE       LABELS
ip-10-0-0-151.ec2.internal   Ready                      11m       beta.kubernete
s.io/instance-type=m3.medium,failure-domain.beta.kubernetes.io/region=us-east-1,
failure-domain.beta.kubernetes.io/zone=us-east-1e,kubernetes.io/hostname=ip-10-0
-0-151.ec2.internal,kubernetes.io/image-name=nginx
ip-10-0-0-152.ec2.internal   Ready                      11m       beta.kubernete
s.io/instance-type=m3.medium,failure-domain.beta.kubernetes.io/region=us-east-1,
failure-domain.beta.kubernetes.io/zone=us-east-1e,kubernetes.io/hostname=ip-10-0
-0-152.ec2.internal,kubernetes.io/image-name=hello-world
ip-10-0-0-153.ec2.internal   Ready                      11m       beta.kubernete
s.io/instance-type=m3.medium,failure-domain.beta.kubernetes.io/region=us-east-1,
failure-domain.beta.kubernetes.io/zone=us-east-1e,kubernetes.io/hostname=ip-10-0
-0-153.ec2.internal
ip-10-0-0-50.ec2.internal    Ready,SchedulingDisabled   11m       kubernetes.io/
hostname=ip-10-0-0-50.ec2.internal
core@ip-10-0-0-50 ~ $
```

Figure 9-20. *Listing nodes including labels*

When using labels to match pods with nodes, one of the following results:

1. The pod is scheduled on the labeled node.
2. The pod is scheduled on an unlabeled node if a node affinity is specified.
3. The pod is not scheduled.

We shall discuss each of these in the following sections using the labeled and unlabeled nodes from this section.

Scheduling Pods with a Node Selector

The nodeSelector field in a pod's specification may be used to explicitly select a node for a pod. To assign a pod to a label, create a pod definition file pod-nginx.yaml. Copy the following code to the definition file:

```
apiVersion: v1
kind: Pod
metadata:
  name: nginx
  labels:
    env: test
```

```
spec:
  containers:
  - name: nginx
    image: nginx
    imagePullPolicy: IfNotPresent
  nodeSelector:
    kubernetes.io/image-name: nginx
```

The resulting `pod-nginx.yaml` is shown in a `vi` editor in Figure 9-21.

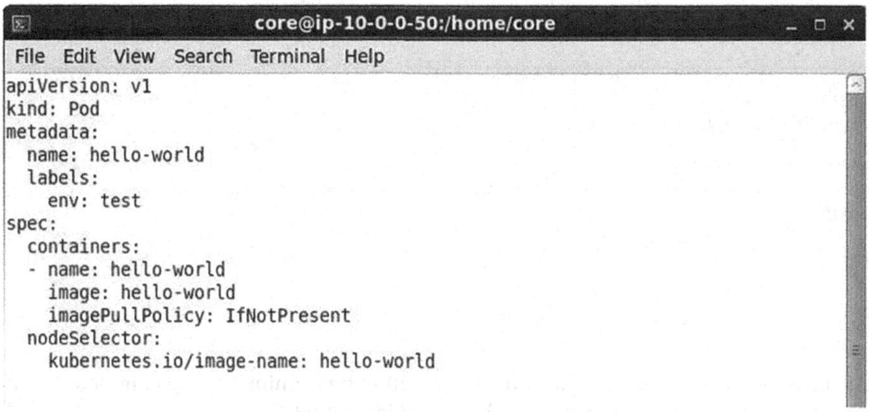

Figure 9-21. *The pod definition file* `pod-nginx.yaml`

Create a pod using the definition file:

```
kubectl create -f pod-nginx.yaml
```

Similarly, create another pod definition file `pod-helloworld.yaml`. Copy the following listing into `pod-helloworld.yaml`:

```
apiVersion: v1
kind: Pod
metadata:
  name: hello-world
  labels:
    env: test
spec:
  containers:
  - name: hello-world
    image: hello-world
    imagePullPolicy: IfNotPresent
  nodeSelector:
    kubernetes.io/image-name: hello-world
```

Create the pod using the pod definition file:

```
kubectl create -f pod-helloworld.yaml
```

List the cluster-wide pods:

```
kubectl get pods -o wide
```

As the output from the preceding commands in Figure 9-22 indicates, the two pods are created and started. Initially the pods may be not running.

```
core@ip-10-0-0-50 ~ $ ./kubectl create -f pod-nginx.yaml
pod "nginx" created
core@ip-10-0-0-50 ~ $ ./kubectl create -f pod-helloworld.yaml
pod "hello-world" created
core@ip-10-0-0-50 ~ $ ./kubectl get pods -o wide
NAME          READY     STATUS              RESTARTS   AGE       IP          NOD
E
hello-world   0/1       CrashLoopBackOff    1          9s        10.2.92.3   ip-
10-0-0-152.ec2.internal
nginx         0/1       ContainerCreating   0          18s       <none>      ip-
10-0-0-151.ec2.internal
```

Figure 9-22. *Creating pods that make use of* `nodeSelector`

List the pods again, including the nodes, and the pods should either be running or have completed. The Node column lists the node on which a pod is running, as shown in Figure 9-23.

```
core@ip-10-0-0-50 ~ $ ./kubectl get pods -o wide
NAME          READY     STATUS      RESTARTS   AGE       IP          NODE
hello-world   0/1       Completed   2          22s       10.2.92.3   ip-10-0-0-1
52.ec2.internal
nginx         1/1       Running     0          31s       10.2.17.2   ip-10-0-0-1
51.ec2.internal
```

Figure 9-23. *Listing pods including the nodes*

Using the node name, obtain the labels for each of the two nodes as shown in Figure 9-24. The labels for each of the nodes include the label specified in the `nodeSelector` for the pod scheduled on the node.

```
core@ip-10-0-0-50 ~ $ ./kubectl get nodes ip-10-0-0-152.ec2.internal --show-labe
ls
NAME                         STATUS    AGE       LABELS
ip-10-0-0-152.ec2.internal   Ready     18m       beta.kubernetes.io/instance-typ
e=m3.medium,failure-domain.beta.kubernetes.io/region=us-east-1,failure-domain.be
ta.kubernetes.io/zone=us-east-1e,kubernetes.io/hostname=ip-10-0-0-152.ec2.intern
al,kubernetes.io/image-name=hello-world
core@ip-10-0-0-50 ~ $ ./kubectl get nodes ip-10-0-0-151.ec2.internal --show-labe
ls
NAME                         STATUS    AGE       LABELS
ip-10-0-0-151.ec2.internal   Ready     19m       beta.kubernetes.io/instance-typ
e=m3.medium,failure-domain.beta.kubernetes.io/region=us-east-1,failure-domain.be
ta.kubernetes.io/zone=us-east-1e,kubernetes.io/hostname=ip-10-0-0-151.ec2.intern
al,kubernetes.io/image-name=nginx
core@ip-10-0-0-50 ~ $
```

Figure 9-24. *Listing node labels*

Next, we shall demonstrate that if multiple pods have matching labels, one of the nodes is used. Label the third node with the same label as one of the other nodes:

```
kubectl label nodes ip-10-0-0-153.ec2.internal kubernetes.io/image-name=hello-world
```

The third node is also labeled, as shown in Figure 9-25.

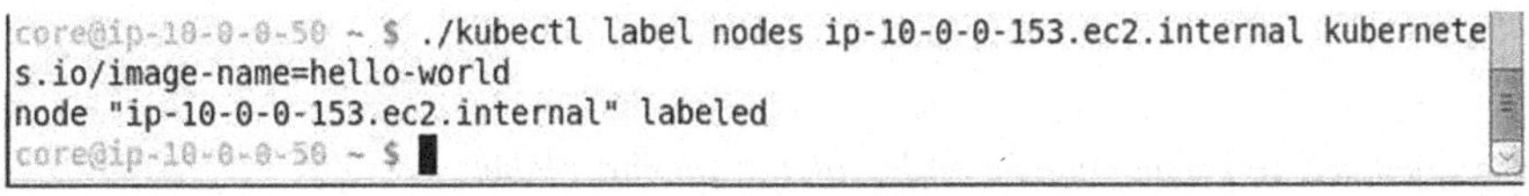

```
core@ip-10-0-0-50 ~ $ ./kubectl label nodes ip-10-0-0-153.ec2.internal kubernete
s.io/image-name=hello-world
node "ip-10-0-0-153.ec2.internal" labeled
core@ip-10-0-0-50 ~ $
```

Figure 9-25. *Labeling a third node*

Listing the node labels should display two nodes with the common label `kubernetes.io/image-name=hello-world`, as shown in Figure 9-26.

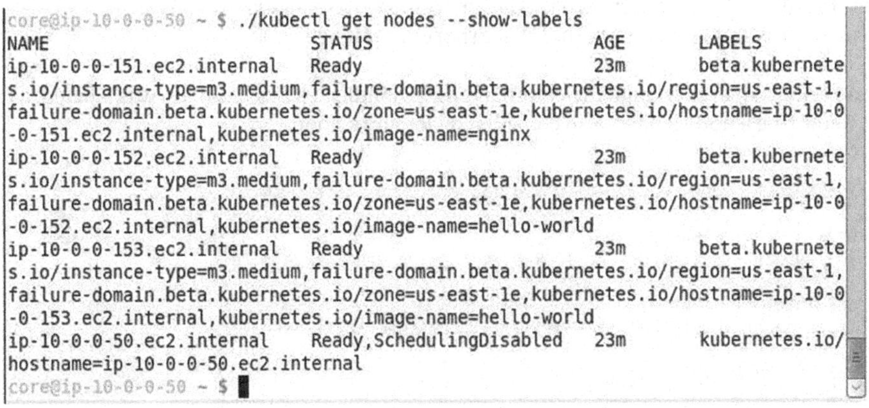

```
core@ip-10-0-0-50 ~ $ ./kubectl get nodes --show-labels
NAME                         STATUS                     AGE       LABELS
ip-10-0-0-151.ec2.internal   Ready                      23m       beta.kubernete
s.io/instance-type=m3.medium,failure-domain.beta.kubernetes.io/region=us-east-1,
failure-domain.beta.kubernetes.io/zone=us-east-1e,kubernetes.io/hostname=ip-10-0
-0-151.ec2.internal,kubernetes.io/image-name=nginx
ip-10-0-0-152.ec2.internal   Ready                      23m       beta.kubernete
s.io/instance-type=m3.medium,failure-domain.beta.kubernetes.io/region=us-east-1,
failure-domain.beta.kubernetes.io/zone=us-east-1e,kubernetes.io/hostname=ip-10-0
-0-152.ec2.internal,kubernetes.io/image-name=hello-world
ip-10-0-0-153.ec2.internal   Ready                      23m       beta.kubernete
s.io/instance-type=m3.medium,failure-domain.beta.kubernetes.io/region=us-east-1,
failure-domain.beta.kubernetes.io/zone=us-east-1e,kubernetes.io/hostname=ip-10-0
-0-153.ec2.internal,kubernetes.io/image-name=hello-world
ip-10-0-0-50.ec2.internal    Ready,SchedulingDisabled   23m       kubernetes.io/
hostname=ip-10-0-0-50.ec2.internal
core@ip-10-0-0-50 ~ $
```

Figure 9-26. *Two nodes with the same label*

Delete the pod `hello-world` with `kubectl`, as next we shall create the pod again to find which node is the pod scheduled on, given two nodes with the same label as in the `nodeSelector` field. Create the `hello-world` pod again using the same definition file. List the pod, and it should be shown on one of the two nodes that have the label `kubernetes.io/image-name=hello-world`, which are `ip-10-0-0-152.ec2.internal` and `ip-10-0-0-153.ec2.internal`. The pod is scheduled on the first node it finds with the matching label, which is `ip-10-0-0-152.ec2.internal` as shown in Figure 9-27.

```
core@ip-10-0-0-50 ~ $ ./kubectl create -f pod-helloworld.yaml
pod "hello-world" created
core@ip-10-0-0-50 ~ $ ./kubectl get pods -o wide
NAME          READY     STATUS             RESTARTS   AGE       IP          NODE
hello-world   0/1       CrashLoopBackOff   2          33s       10.2.92.3   ip-1
0-0-0-152.ec2.internal
core@ip-10-0-0-50 ~ $ ./kubectl get pods -o wide
NAME          READY     STATUS             RESTARTS   AGE       IP          NODE
hello-world   0/1       CrashLoopBackOff   3          1m        10.2.92.3   ip-1
0-0-0-152.ec2.internal
core@ip-10-0-0-50 ~ $
```

Figure 9-27. *The pod is scheduled on the first node it finds with the matching label*

Next, we shall demonstrate that if a node with a matching label is not found, the pod is not scheduled at all. We need to delete all the labels, as we shall be using the same definition files for pods and with the same `nodeSelector` field settings. Delete the label added previously to each of the nodes:

```
kubectl label nodes ip-10-0-0-151.ec2.internal kubernetes.io/image-name
kubectl label nodes ip-10-0-0-152.ec2.internal kubernetes.io/image-name
kubectl label nodes ip-10-0-0-153.ec2.internal kubernetes.io/image-name
```

The node labels are removed, even though the command output indicates that the node was labeled, as shown in Figure 9-28. Removing a node label is also considered labeling a node.

```
core@ip-10-0-0-50 ~ $ ./kubectl label nodes ip-10-0-0-153.ec2.internal kubernete
s.io/image-name-
node "ip-10-0-0-153.ec2.internal" labeled
core@ip-10-0-0-50 ~ $ ./kubectl label nodes ip-10-0-0-152.ec2.internal kubernete
s.io/image-name-
node "ip-10-0-0-152.ec2.internal" labeled
core@ip-10-0-0-50 ~ $ ./kubectl label nodes ip-10-0-0-151.ec2.internal kubernete
s.io/image-name-
node "ip-10-0-0-151.ec2.internal" labeled
core@ip-10-0-0-50 ~ $
```

Figure 9-28. *Removing node labels*

List the nodes, including labels, and the node labels should not include the labels added previously, as shown in Figure 9-29.

```
core@ip-10-0-0-50 ~ $ ./kubectl get nodes --show-labels
NAME                        STATUS                     AGE       LABELS
ip-10-0-0-151.ec2.internal  Ready                      32m       beta.kubernete
s.io/instance-type=m3.medium,failure-domain.beta.kubernetes.io/region=us-east-1,
failure-domain.beta.kubernetes.io/zone=us-east-1e,kubernetes.io/hostname=ip-10-0
-0-151.ec2.internal
ip-10-0-0-152.ec2.internal  Ready                      32m       beta.kubernete
s.io/instance-type=m3.medium,failure-domain.beta.kubernetes.io/region=us-east-1,
failure-domain.beta.kubernetes.io/zone=us-east-1e,kubernetes.io/hostname=ip-10-0
-0-152.ec2.internal
ip-10-0-0-153.ec2.internal  Ready                      32m       beta.kubernete
s.io/instance-type=m3.medium,failure-domain.beta.kubernetes.io/region=us-east-1,
failure-domain.beta.kubernetes.io/zone=us-east-1e,kubernetes.io/hostname=ip-10-0
-0-153.ec2.internal
ip-10-0-0-50.ec2.internal   Ready,SchedulingDisabled   32m       kubernetes.io/
hostname=ip-10-0-0-50.ec2.internal
core@ip-10-0-0-50 ~ $
```

Figure 9-29. *Listing node labels after removing labels*

Create the two pods again using the same pod definition files, as shown in Figure 9-30.

```
core@ip-10-0-0-50 ~ $ ./kubectl create -f pod-nginx.yaml
pod "nginx" created
core@ip-10-0-0-50 ~ $ ./kubectl create -f pod-helloworld.yaml
pod "hello-world" created
core@ip-10-0-0-50 ~ $
core@ip-10-0-0-50 ~ $
```

Figure 9-30. *Creating pods using definition files used earlier*

List the pods cluster-wide. The pods are listed with the STATUS column value as Pending, as shown in Figure 9-31, because none of the nodes have labels that are the same as specified in the `nodeSelector` field.

```
core@ip-10-0-0-50 ~ $ ./kubectl get pods -o wide
NAME          READY     STATUS    RESTARTS   AGE       IP         NODE
hello-world   0/1       Pending   0          56s       <none>
nginx         0/1       Pending   0          1m        <none>
core@ip-10-0-0-50 ~ $
```

Figure 9-31. *Pods with "pending" status*

Add labels to the nodes to match the `nodeSelector` field settings in the pod definitions, as shown in Figure 9-32.

```
core@ip-10-0-0-50 ~ $ ./kubectl label nodes ip-10-0-0-151.ec2.internal kubernete
s.io/image-name=nginx
node "ip-10-0-0-151.ec2.internal" labeled
core@ip-10-0-0-50 ~ $ ./kubectl label nodes ip-10-0-0-152.ec2.internal kubernete
s.io/image-name=hello-world
node "ip-10-0-0-152.ec2.internal" labeled
core@ip-10-0-0-50 ~ $
```

Figure 9-32. *Labeling nodes to match `nodeSelector` labels*

Then list the pods; the pods should not be in Pending status, having completed or running as shown in Figure 9-33. The pods are scheduled when suitable nodes are found.

```
core@ip-10-0-0-50 ~ $ ./kubectl get pods -o wide
NAME          READY     STATUS             RESTARTS   AGE       IP           NODE
hello-world   0/1       CrashLoopBackOff   2          2m        10.2.92.3    ip-1
0-0-0-152.ec2.internal
nginx         1/1       Running            0          2m        10.2.17.2    ip-1
0-0-0-151.ec2.internal
core@ip-10-0-0-50 ~ $
```

Figure 9-33. *Previously Pendingpods are scheduled when nodes with matching labels are found*

If node labels are modified at runtime, for example if a label from a node is removed, a Running pod does not have its status changed to Pending and continues to run if running even though the node on which the pod is running does not have a matching label. As an example, remove the labels from the node on which the `nginx` pod is running, and the pod continues to run as shown in Figure 9-34.

```
core@ip-10-0-0-50 ~ $ ./kubectl label nodes ip-10-0-0-151.ec2.internal kubernete
s.io/image-name-
node "ip-10-0-0-151.ec2.internal" labeled
core@ip-10-0-0-50 ~ $ ./kubectl get pods -o wide
NAME          READY     STATUS             RESTARTS   AGE       IP           NODE
hello-world   0/1       CrashLoopBackOff   4          4m        10.2.92.3    ip-1
0-0-0-152.ec2.internal
nginx         1/1       Running            0          4m        10.2.17.2    ip-1
0-0-0-151.ec2.internal
core@ip-10-0-0-50 ~ $
```

Figure 9-34. *A running pod continues to run on a node even though matching labels from node are removed*

Setting Node Affinity

Starting with version 1.2, Kubernetes offers an alpha version of a new mechanism for selecting nodes, called *node affinity*. The alpha version of node affinity is based on labels, but support for other types of node affinity is planned to be added, such as scheduling pods on a node based on which other pods are running on the node. Currently, two types of node affinity are supported as discussed in Table 9-3.

Table 9-3. *Types of Node Affinity*

Node Affinity	Description
`requiredDuringScheduling IgnoredDuringExecution`	Specifies a node affinity condition that must be met. Similar to `nodeSelector` but declarative. `IgnoredDuringExecution` implies that the node affinity requirement is ignored once a pod is running. For example, if a label on a node is changed to make a running pod non schedulable on the node, the pod continues to run on the node. If both `nodeSelector` and `nodeAffinity` are set and `nodeAffinity` is `requiredDuringSchedulingIgnoredDuringExecution`, both must be met for a pod to be scheduled on a node.
`preferredDuringScheduling IgnoredDuringExecution`	A node affinity a scheduler tries to implement but does not guarantee. A pod can be scheduled on a specified labeled node or not based on matching labels. A pod can even be scheduled on an unlabeled node. If `nodeAffinity` is set to `preferredDuringSchedulingIgnoredDuringExecution` and none of the nodes meet the settings, another node is scheduled on. If both `nodeSelector` and `nodeAffinity` are set and `nodeAffinity` is `preferredDuringSchedulingIgnoredDuringExecution`, only the `nodeSelector` must be met, as the other is only a hint for a preference.

Node affinity in the alpha version is specified using annotations, but these will be replaced with fields. An example `nodeAffinity requiredDuringSchedulingIgnoredDuringExecution` setting using annotations is as follows:

```
annotations:
    scheduler.alpha.kubernetes.io/affinity: >
      {
        "nodeAffinity": {
          "requiredDuringSchedulingIgnoredDuringExecution": {
            "nodeSelectorTerms": [
              {
                "matchExpressions": [
                  {
                    "key": " kubernetes.io/image-name",
                    "operator": "In",
                    "values": ["image1", "image2"]
                  }
                ]
              }
            ]
          }
        }
      }
    another-annotation-key: another-annotation-value
```

The another-annotation-key: another-annotation-value setting implies that from the nodes found suitable with the nodeAffinity condition, the node with the another-annotation-key: another-annotation-value label should be preferred, which again is a hint for a preference that may or may not be implemented. The another-annotation-key: another-annotation-value is found to be implemented with requiredDuringSchedulingIgnoredDuringExecution and not with preferredDuringSchedulingIgnoredDuringExecution. In addition to the In operator, the other supported operators are NotIn, Exists, DoesNotExist, Gt and Lt.

Next, we shall discuss each of the node affinities with an example.

Setting requiredDuringSchedulingIgnoredDuringExecution

Create a pod definition file pod-node-affinity.yaml for a pod named with-labels and set the nodeAffinity to requiredDuringSchedulingIgnoredDuringExecution with matching expressions for nodeSelectorTerms to be a label kubernetes.io/image-name with value as one of nginx2 or hello-world2. The another-annotation-key: another-annotation-value is kubernetes.io/image-name: nginx. The container image is nginx.

```
apiVersion: v1
kind: Pod
metadata:
  name: with-labels
  annotations:
    scheduler.alpha.kubernetes.io/affinity: >
      {
        "nodeAffinity": {
          "requiredDuringSchedulingIgnoredDuringExecution": {
            "nodeSelectorTerms": [
              {
                "matchExpressions": [
                  {
                    "key": "kubernetes.io/image-name",
                    "operator": "In",
                    "values": ["nginx2", "hello-world2"]
                  }
                ]
              }
            ]
          }
        }
      }
    kubernetes.io/image-name: nginx
spec:
  containers:
  - name: with-labels
    image: nginx
```

List the nodes, including labels. The resulting labels on nodes should not include the required labels nginx2 or hello-world2, as shown in Figure 9-35.

```
core@ip-10-0-0-50 ~ $ ./kubectl get nodes --show-labels
NAME                          STATUS                     AGE       LABELS
ip-10-0-0-151.ec2.internal    Ready                      53m       beta.kubernete
s.io/instance-type=m3.medium,failure-domain.beta.kubernetes.io/region=us-east-1,
failure-domain.beta.kubernetes.io/zone=us-east-1e,kubernetes.io/hostname=ip-10-0
-0-151.ec2.internal,kubernetes.io/image-name=nginx
ip-10-0-0-152.ec2.internal    Ready                      53m       beta.kubernete
s.io/instance-type=m3.medium,failure-domain.beta.kubernetes.io/region=us-east-1,
failure-domain.beta.kubernetes.io/zone=us-east-1e,kubernetes.io/hostname=ip-10-0
-0-152.ec2.internal,kubernetes.io/image-name=hello-world
ip-10-0-0-153.ec2.internal    Ready                      53m       beta.kubernete
s.io/instance-type=m3.medium,failure-domain.beta.kubernetes.io/region=us-east-1,
failure-domain.beta.kubernetes.io/zone=us-east-1e,kubernetes.io/hostname=ip-10-0
-0-153.ec2.internal
ip-10-0-0-50.ec2.internal     Ready,SchedulingDisabled   53m       kubernetes.io/
hostname=ip-10-0-0-50.ec2.internal
core@ip-10-0-0-50 ~ $
```

Figure 9-35. *None of the nodes have matching labels*

The pod-node-affinity.yaml file is shown in a vi editor in Figure 9-36.

```
apiVersion: v1
kind: Pod
metadata:
  name: with-labels
  annotations:
    scheduler.alpha.kubernetes.io/affinity: >
      {
        "nodeAffinity": {
          "requiredDuringSchedulingIgnoredDuringExecution": {
            "nodeSelectorTerms": [
              {
                "matchExpressions": [
                  {
                    "key": "kubernetes.io/image-name",
                    "operator": "In",
                    "values": ["nginx2", "hello-world2"]
                  }
                ]
              }
            ]
          }
        }
      }
#     kubernetes.io/image-name: nginx
spec:
  containers:
  - name: with-labels
    image: nginx

~
```

Figure 9-36. *The pod-node-affinity.yaml definition file*

Create the pod from the definition file:

```
kubectl create -f pod-node-affinity.yaml
```

The pod with-labels is created as shown in Figure 9-37.

```
core@ip-10-0-0-50 ~ $ sudo vi pod-node-affinity.yaml
core@ip-10-0-0-50 ~ $ ./kubectl create -f pod-node-affinity.yaml
pod "with-labels" created
```

Figure 9-37. *Creating the pod with-labels*

List the pods across the cluster. The pod STATUS is Pending because none of the nodes have the label nginx2 or hello-world2, as shown in Figure 9-38.

```
core@ip-10-0-0-50 ~ $ ./kubectl get pods -o wide
NAME          READY     STATUS    RESTARTS   AGE       IP        NODE
with-labels   0/1       Pending   0          27s       <none>
core@ip-10-0-0-50 ~ $
```

Figure 9-38. *Listing pods with Pending status*

Subsequently, add one of the required labels to one of the nodes, for example the hello-world2 label to the ip-10-0-0-153.ec2.internal node. The STATUS of the with-labels pod changes from Pending to Running, as shown in Figure 9-39.

```
core@ip-10-0-0-50 ~ $ ./kubectl label nodes ip-10-0-0-153.ec2.internal kubernete
s.io/image-name=hello-world2
node "ip-10-0-0-153.ec2.internal" labeled
core@ip-10-0-0-50 ~ $ ./kubectl get pods -o wide
NAME          READY     STATUS    RESTARTS   AGE       IP        NODE
with-labels   0/1       Pending   0          1m        <none>
core@ip-10-0-0-50 ~ $ ./kubectl get pods -o wide
NAME          READY     STATUS              RESTARTS   AGE       IP        NODE
with-labels   0/1       ContainerCreating   0          1m        <none>    ip-10
-0-0-153.ec2.internal
core@ip-10-0-0-50 ~ $ ./kubectl get pods -o wide
NAME          READY     STATUS              RESTARTS   AGE       IP        NODE
with-labels   0/1       ContainerCreating   0          1m        <none>    ip-10
-0-0-153.ec2.internal
core@ip-10-0-0-50 ~ $ ./kubectl get pods -o wide
NAME          READY     STATUS              RESTARTS   AGE       IP        NODE
with-labels   0/1       ContainerCreating   0          1m        <none>    ip-10
-0-0-153.ec2.internal
core@ip-10-0-0-50 ~ $ ./kubectl get pods -o wide
NAME          READY     STATUS    RESTARTS   AGE       IP          NODE
with-labels   1/1       Running   0          1m        10.2.94.3   ip-10-0-0-153
.ec2.internal
core@ip-10-0-0-50 ~ $
```

Figure 9-39. *The pod Status changes from Pending to Running*

Next, we shall demonstrate that if both nodeAffinity and nodeSelector are specified with nodeAffinity set to requiredDuringSchedulingIgnoredDuringExecution, both conditions must be met. Add a nodeSelector label to pod-node-affinity.yaml:

```
nodeSelector:
    kubernetes.io/image-name: nginx
```

The modified pod-node-affinity.yaml is shown in a vi editor in Figure 9-40.

```
kind: Pod
metadata:
  name: with-labels
  annotations:
    scheduler.alpha.kubernetes.io/affinity: >
      {
        "nodeAffinity": {
          "requiredDuringSchedulingIgnoredDuringExecution": {
            "nodeSelectorTerms": [
              {
                "matchExpressions": [
                  {
                    "key": "kubernetes.io/image-name",
                    "operator": "In",
                    "values": ["nginx2", "hello-world2"]
                  }
                ]
              }
            ]
          }
        }
      }
#     kubernetes.io/image-name: nginx
spec:
  containers:
  - name: with-labels
    image: nginx
  nodeSelector:
    kubernetes.io/image-name: nginx
:wq
```

Figure 9-40. *Adding nodeSelector in addition to nodeAffinity set to requiredDuringSchedulingIgnoredDuringExecution*

We had added a node label kubernetes.io/image-name with the value hello-world2, but none of the nodes has the label kubernetes.io/image-name: nginx. When the pod is created, it is created but is not scheduled, as indicated by the Pending status in Figure 9-41.

```
core@ip-10-0-0-50 ~ $ sudo vi pod-node-affinity.yaml
core@ip-10-0-0-50 ~ $ ./kubectl create -f pod-node-affinity.yaml
pod "with-labels" created
core@ip-10-0-0-50 ~ $ ./kubectl get pods -o wide
NAME          READY     STATUS    RESTARTS   AGE       IP        NODE
with-labels   0/1       Pending   0          9s        <none>
core@ip-10-0-0-50 ~ $
```

Figure 9-41. *The pod is created but not scheduled*

Modify the nodeSelector field to specify a label that exists in addition to the required label from the node affinity. Add the label kubernetes.io/host-name: ip-10-0-0-151.ec2.internal as shown in the vi editor in Figure 9-42.

```
kind: Pod
metadata:
  name: with-labels
  annotations:
    scheduler.alpha.kubernetes.io/affinity: >
      {
        "nodeAffinity": {
          "requiredDuringSchedulingIgnoredDuringExecution": {
            "nodeSelectorTerms": [
              {
                "matchExpressions": [
                  {
                    "key": "kubernetes.io/image-name",
                    "operator": "In",
                    "values": ["nginx2", "hello-world2"]
                  }
                ]
              }
            ]
          }
        }
      }
#     kubernetes.io/image-name: nginx
spec:
  containers:
  - name: with-labels
    image: nginx
  nodeSelector:
    kubernetes.io/hostname: ip-10-0-0-153.ec2.internal
:wq
```

Figure 9-42. *Specifying a* `nodeSelector` *label that exists*

Delete the `with-labels` pod. Create the pod with the updated pod definition file. You'll see that the pod is scheduled and is running on the scheduled host as shown in Figure 9-43 with both the `nodeSelector` and node affinity conditions met.

```
core@ip-10-0-0-50 ~ $ sudo vi pod-node-affinity.yaml
core@ip-10-0-0-50 ~ $ ./kubectl create -f pod-node-affinity.yaml
pod "with-labels" created
core@ip-10-0-0-50 ~ $ ./kubectl get pods -o wide
NAME          READY     STATUS    RESTARTS   AGE       IP          NODE
with-labels   1/1       Running   0          12s       10.2.94.3   ip-10-0-0-153
.ec2.internal
core@ip-10-0-0-50 ~ $ 
```

Figure 9-43. *Both the* `nodeSelector` *and node affinity conditions are met*

Next, we shall demonstrate that if multiple label values as specified in the `matchExpressions` field match, the first node with the matching expression is used. Add or overwrite labels to add `kubernetes.io/image-name: nginx` to one of the nodes and `kubernetes.io/image-name: hello-world` to two of the three nodes, as shown in Figure 9-44.

```
core@ip-10-0-0-50 ~ $ ./kubectl label nodes --overwrite ip-10-0-0-151.ec2.intern
al kubernetes.io/image-name=nginx
node "ip-10-0-0-151.ec2.internal" labeled
core@ip-10-0-0-50 ~ $ ./kubectl label nodes --overwrite ip-10-0-0-153.ec2.intern
al kubernetes.io/image-name=hello-world
node "ip-10-0-0-153.ec2.internal" labeled
core@ip-10-0-0-50 ~ $ ./kubectl get nodes --show-labels
NAME                         STATUS                     AGE       LABELS
ip-10-0-0-151.ec2.internal   Ready                      1h        beta.kubernete
s.io/instance-type=m3.medium,failure-domain.beta.kubernetes.io/region=us-east-1,
failure-domain.beta.kubernetes.io/zone=us-east-1e,kubernetes.io/hostname=ip-10-0
-0-151.ec2.internal,kubernetes.io/image-name=nginx
ip-10-0-0-152.ec2.internal   Ready                      1h        beta.kubernete
s.io/instance-type=m3.medium,failure-domain.beta.kubernetes.io/region=us-east-1,
failure-domain.beta.kubernetes.io/zone=us-east-1e,kubernetes.io/hostname=ip-10-0
-0-152.ec2.internal,kubernetes.io/image-name=hello-world
ip-10-0-0-153.ec2.internal   Ready                      1h        beta.kubernete
s.io/instance-type=m3.medium,failure-domain.beta.kubernetes.io/region=us-east-1,
failure-domain.beta.kubernetes.io/zone=us-east-1e,kubernetes.io/hostname=ip-10-0
-0-153.ec2.internal,kubernetes.io/image-name=hello-world
ip-10-0-0-50.ec2.internal    Ready,SchedulingDisabled   1h        kubernetes.io/
hostname=ip-10-0-0-50.ec2.internal
core@ip-10-0-0-50 ~ $
```

Figure 9-44. *Adding labels to nodes*

Modify the pod-node-affinity.yaml to add both the nginx and hello-world for expressions to match as shown in Figure 9-45.

```
apiVersion: v1
kind: Pod
metadata:
  name: with-labels
  annotations:
    scheduler.alpha.kubernetes.io/affinity: >
      {
        "nodeAffinity": {
          "requiredDuringSchedulingIgnoredDuringExecution": {
            "nodeSelectorTerms": [
              {
                "matchExpressions": [
                  {
                    "key": "kubernetes.io/image-name",
                    "operator": "In",
                    "values": ["nginx", "hello-world"]
                  }
                ]
              }
            ]
          }
        }
      }
#     kubernetes.io/image-name: nginx2
spec:
  containers:
  - name: with-labels
    image: nginx
#  nodeSelector:
#    kubernetes.io/hostname: ip-10-0-0-153.ec2.internal
~
:wq
```

Figure 9-45. *Setting* `matchExpressions` *label values*

Delete the pod with-labels and create the pod again as shown in Figure 9-46. The pod is scheduled on the node with the label kubernetes.io/image-name: nginx.

```
core@ip-10-0-0-50 ~ $ ./kubectl create -f pod-node-affinity.yaml
pod "with-labels" created
core@ip-10-0-0-50 ~ $ ./kubectl get pods -o wide
NAME          READY     STATUS    RESTARTS   AGE       IP          NODE
with-labels   1/1       Running   0          16s       10.2.17.2   ip-10-0-0-151
.ec2.internal
core@ip-10-0-0-50 ~ $ ▌
```

Figure 9-46. *Scheduling a pod on the first matching node*

Next, we shall demonstrate that the node labeled another-annotation-key with value another-annotation-value is preferred if node affinity is requiredDuringSchedulingIgnoredDuringExecution. Add or overwrite node labels so that a node exists with each of the label values nginx2 and hello-world2 for key kubernetes.io/image-name as shown in Figure 9-47.

```
core@ip-10-0-0-50 ~ $ ./kubectl label nodes --overwrite ip-10-0-0-153.ec2.intern
al kubernetes.io/image-name=hello-world2
node "ip-10-0-0-153.ec2.internal" labeled
core@ip-10-0-0-50 ~ $ kubectl label nodes --overwrite ip-10-0-0-151.ec2.internal
 kubernetes.io/image-name=nginx2
-bash: kubectl: command not found
core@ip-10-0-0-50 ~ $ ./kubectl label nodes --overwrite ip-10-0-0-151.ec2.intern
al kubernetes.io/image-name=nginx2
node "ip-10-0-0-151.ec2.internal" labeled
core@ip-10-0-0-50 ~ $ ./kubectl get nodes --show-labels
NAME                         STATUS                     AGE       LABELS
ip-10-0-0-151.ec2.internal   Ready                      1h        beta.kubernete
s.io/instance-type=m3.medium,failure-domain.beta.kubernetes.io/region=us-east-1,
failure-domain.beta.kubernetes.io/zone=us-east-1e,kubernetes.io/hostname=ip-10-0
-0-151.ec2.internal,kubernetes.io/image-name=nginx2
ip-10-0-0-152.ec2.internal   Ready                      1h        beta.kubernete
s.io/instance-type=m3.medium,failure-domain.beta.kubernetes.io/region=us-east-1,
failure-domain.beta.kubernetes.io/zone=us-east-1e,kubernetes.io/hostname=ip-10-0
-0-152.ec2.internal,kubernetes.io/image-name=hello-world
ip-10-0-0-153.ec2.internal   Ready                      1h        beta.kubernete
s.io/instance-type=m3.medium,failure-domain.beta.kubernetes.io/region=us-east-1,
failure-domain.beta.kubernetes.io/zone=us-east-1e,kubernetes.io/hostname=ip-10-0
-0-153.ec2.internal,kubernetes.io/image-name=hello-world2
ip-10-0-0-50.ec2.internal    Ready,SchedulingDisabled   1h        kubernetes.io/
hostname=ip-10-0-0-50.ec2.internal
core@ip-10-0-0-50 ~ $ ▌
```

Figure 9-47. *Adding the label values nginx2 and hello-world2 for key kubernetes.io/image-name*

In the pod-node-affinity.yaml file, set another-annotation-key kubernetes.io/image-name to nginx2 and comment out the nodeSelector field as shown in Figure 9-48.

```
apiVersion: v1
kind: Pod
metadata:
  name: with-labels
  annotations:
    scheduler.alpha.kubernetes.io/affinity: >
      {
        "nodeAffinity": {
          "requiredDuringSchedulingIgnoredDuringExecution": {
            "nodeSelectorTerms": [
              {
                "matchExpressions": [
                  {
                    "key": "kubernetes.io/image-name",
                    "operator": "In",
                    "values": ["nginx2", "hello-world2"]
                  }
                ]
              }
            ]
          }
        }
      }
    kubernetes.io/image-name: nginx2
spec:
  containers:
  - name: with-labels
    image: nginx
#  nodeSelector:
#    kubernetes.io/hostname: ip-10-0-0-153.ec2.internal
~
:wq
```

Figure 9-48. *Setting* `another-annotation-key` *and removing* `nodeSelector`

Delete the pod `with-labels` and create the pod again. The pod is scheduled on the node with the label `kubernetes.io/image-name: nginx2`, as indicated by the NODE in the pod listing in Figure 9-49.

```
core@ip-10-0-0-50 ~ $ ./kubectl delete pod with-labels
pod "with-labels" deleted
core@ip-10-0-0-50 ~ $ sudo vi pod-node-affinity.yaml
core@ip-10-0-0-50 ~ $ ./kubectl create -f pod-node-affinity.yaml
pod "with-labels" created
core@ip-10-0-0-50 ~ $ ./kubectl get pods -o wide
NAME          READY     STATUS    RESTARTS   AGE       IP            NODE
with-labels   1/1       Running   0          7s        10.2.17.2     ip-10-0-0-151
.ec2.internal
core@ip-10-0-0-50 ~ $
```

Figure 9-49. *The pod is scheduled on another-annotation-key valued node*

Setting preferredDuringSchedulingIgnoredDuringExecution

In this section we will use the node affinity `preferredDuringSchedulingIgnoredDuringExecution`, which is only a hint to the scheduler and not guaranteed. A slightly different set of node values is used for the example, as shown in Figure 9-50.

```
core@ip-10-0-0-50 ~ $ ./kubectl get nodes
NAME                          STATUS                     AGE
ip-10-0-0-222.ec2.internal    Ready                      22m
ip-10-0-0-223.ec2.internal    Ready                      22m
ip-10-0-0-224.ec2.internal    Ready                      22m
ip-10-0-0-50.ec2.internal     Ready,SchedulingDisabled   22m
core@ip-10-0-0-50 ~ $
```

Figure 9-50. *Listing nodes used for node affinity* `preferredDuringSchedulingIgnoredDuringExecution` *example*

Set the label key `kubernetes.io/image-name` to `nginx` on one of the nodes and `hello-world` on another node as shown in Figure 9-51. The third node is kept unlabeled.

```
core@ip-10-0-0-50 ~ $ ./kubectl label nodes --overwrite ip-10-0-0-222.ec2.intern
al kubernetes.io/image-name=hello-world
node "ip-10-0-0-222.ec2.internal" labeled
core@ip-10-0-0-50 ~ $ ./kubectl label nodes ip-10-0-0-223.ec2.internal kubernete
s.io/image-name=nginx
node "ip-10-0-0-223.ec2.internal" labeled
core@ip-10-0-0-50 ~ $
```

Figure 9-51. *Setting node labels*

List the labels for each node as shown in Figure 9-52.

```
core@ip-10-0-0-50 ~ $ ./kubectl get nodes --show-labels
NAME                          STATUS                     AGE       LABELS
ip-10-0-0-222.ec2.internal    Ready                      32m       beta.kubernete
s.io/arch=amd64,beta.kubernetes.io/instance-type=m3.medium,beta.kubernetes.io/os
=linux,failure-domain.beta.kubernetes.io/region=us-east-1,failure-domain.beta.ku
bernetes.io/zone=us-east-1e,kubernetes.io/hostname=ip-10-0-0-222.ec2.internal,ku
bernetes.io/image-name=hello-world
ip-10-0-0-223.ec2.internal    Ready                      32m       beta.kubernete
s.io/arch=amd64,beta.kubernetes.io/instance-type=m3.medium,beta.kubernetes.io/os
=linux,failure-domain.beta.kubernetes.io/region=us-east-1,failure-domain.beta.ku
bernetes.io/zone=us-east-1e,kubernetes.io/hostname=ip-10-0-0-223.ec2.internal,ku
bernetes.io/image-name=nginx
ip-10-0-0-224.ec2.internal    Ready                      32m       beta.kubernete
s.io/arch=amd64,beta.kubernetes.io/instance-type=m3.medium,beta.kubernetes.io/os
=linux,failure-domain.beta.kubernetes.io/region=us-east-1,failure-domain.beta.ku
bernetes.io/zone=us-east-1e,kubernetes.io/hostname=ip-10-0-0-224.ec2.internal
ip-10-0-0-50.ec2.internal     Ready,SchedulingDisabled   32m       beta.kubernete
s.io/arch=amd64,beta.kubernetes.io/os=linux,kubernetes.io/hostname=ip-10-0-0-50.
ec2.internal
core@ip-10-0-0-50 ~ $
```

Figure 9-52. *Listing node labels*

As discussed earlier, NodeAffinity is a priority function; and priority functions have weight allocated to them in ranking nodes. Create a pod definition file podNodeAffinity.yaml and allocate a weight of 75 for a pod using node affinity preferredDuringSchedulingIgnoredDuringExecution. Set the expressions to match to the label key kubernetes.io/image-name to be either nginx or hello-world.

```
apiVersion: v1
kind: Pod
metadata:
  name: with-labels
  annotations:
    scheduler.alpha.kubernetes.io/affinity: >
      {
        "nodeAffinity": {
          "preferredDuringSchedulingIgnoredDuringExecution": [
            {
              "weight": 75,
              "preference":
              {
                "matchExpressions": [
                  {
                    "key": "kubernetes.io/image-name",
                    "operator": "In",
                    "values": ["nginx", "hello-world"]
                  }
                ]
              }
            }
          ]
        }
      }
    kubernetes.io/image-name: hello-world
spec:
  containers:
  - name: with-labels
    image: nginx
```

The pod definition file podNodeAffinity.yaml is shown in a vi editor in Figure 9-53.

```
apiVersion: v1
kind: Pod
metadata:
  name: with-labels
  annotations:
    scheduler.alpha.kubernetes.io/affinity: >
      {
        "nodeAffinity": {
          "preferredDuringSchedulingIgnoredDuringExecution": [
            {
              "weight": 75,
              "preference":
              {
                "matchExpressions": [
                  {
                    "key": "kubernetes.io/image-name",
                    "operator": "In",
                    "values": ["nginx", "hello-world"]
                  }
                ]
              }
            }
          ]
        }
      }
#     kubernetes.io/image-name: hello-world
spec:
  containers:
  - name: with-labels
    image: nginx

:wq
```

Figure 9-53. *Pod definition file podNodeAffinity.yaml*

Create the with-labels pod using the pod definition file. List the cluster-wide pods. The with-labels pod is scheduled on the node with the label kubernetes.io/image-name: nginx, as shown in Figure 9-54. The scheduling policy does not just constitute the priority functions, and the node affinity is not the only priority function; and with node affinity being soft, the pod could have been allocated to a random node or the allocation could be based on the result of the priority function's score calculation.

```
core@ip-10-0-0-50 ~ $ sudo vi podNodeAffinity.yaml
core@ip-10-0-0-50 ~ $ ./kubectl create -f podNodeAffinity.yaml
pod "with-labels" created
core@ip-10-0-0-50 ~ $ ./kubectl get pods -o wide
NAME          READY     STATUS    RESTARTS   AGE       IP          NODE
with-labels   1/1       Running   0          26s       10.2.45.2   ip-10-0-0-223
.ec2.internal
core@ip-10-0-0-50 ~ $
```

Figure 9-54. *Scheduing pod using node affinity preferredDuringSchedulingIgnoredDuringExecution*

Add the another-annotation-key: another-annotation-value as kubernetes.io/image-name: hello-world as shown in Figure 9-55.

```
apiVersion: v1
kind: Pod
metadata:
  name: with-labels
  annotations:
    scheduler.alpha.kubernetes.io/affinity: >
      {
        "nodeAffinity": {
          "preferredDuringSchedulingIgnoredDuringExecution": [
            {
              "weight": 75,
              "preference":
              {
                "matchExpressions": [
                  {
                    "key": "kubernetes.io/image-name",
                    "operator": "In",
                    "values": ["nginx", "hello-world"]
                  }
                ]
              }
            }
          ]
        }
      }
    kubernetes.io/image-name: hello-world
spec:
  containers:
  - name: with-labels
    image: nginx

:wq
```

Figure 9-55. *Adding another-annotation-key: another-annotation-value*

Delete the `with-label` pod and create the pod again as shown in Figure 9-56. The pod is again scheduled on the node with the label `kubernetes.io/image-name: nginx`.

```
core@ip-10-0-0-50 ~ $ ./kubectl create -f podNodeAffinity.yaml
pod "with-labels" created
core@ip-10-0-0-50 ~ $ ./kubectl get pods -o wide
NAME          READY     STATUS    RESTARTS   AGE       IP          NODE
with-labels   1/1       Running   0          8s        10.2.45.2   ip-10-0-0-223
.ec2.internal
core@ip-10-0-0-50 ~ $
```

Figure 9-56. *Scheduling a pod with node affinity*

The node affinity `preferredDuringSchedulingIgnoredDuringExecution` is only a hint. To demonstrate that, set all the options for the `kubernetes.io/image-name` label key to `hello-world`, both in the `In` expression and in the `another` annotation as shown in Figure 9-57.

```
apiVersion: v1
kind: Pod
metadata:
  name: with-labels
  annotations:
    scheduler.alpha.kubernetes.io/affinity: >
      {
        "nodeAffinity": {
          "preferredDuringSchedulingIgnoredDuringExecution": [
            {
              "weight": 75,
              "preference":
              {
                "matchExpressions": [
                  {
                    "key": "kubernetes.io/image-name",
                    "operator": "In",
                    "values": ["hello-world", "hello-world"]
                  }
                ]
              }
            }
          ]
        }
      }
    kubernetes.io/image-name: hello-world
spec:
  containers:
  - name: with-labels
    image: nginx

:wq
```

Figure 9-57. *Setting all label values to* `nginx`

Delete and create the pod again. The pod is scheduled on the node with `kubernetes.io/image-name` label key set to `hello-world`, as shown in Figure 9-58. Again the scheduler does not guarantee pod allocation to a node with the specified labels when the node affinity is `preferredDuringSchedulingIgnoredDuringExecution`. With the same settings, the pod could just as well have been allocated to a different node.

```
core@ip-10-0-0-50 ~ $ ./kubectl create -f podNodeAffinity.yaml
pod "with-labels" created
core@ip-10-0-0-50 ~ $ ./kubectl get pods -o wide
NAME          READY     STATUS              RESTARTS   AGE       IP         NODE
with-labels   0/1       ContainerCreating   0          8s        <none>     ip-10
-0-0-222.ec2.internal
core@ip-10-0-0-50 ~ $ ./kubectl get pods -o wide
NAME          READY     STATUS    RESTARTS   AGE       IP           NODE
with-labels   1/1       Running   0          24s       10.2.100.3   ip-10-0-0-22
2.ec2.internal
core@ip-10-0-0-50 ~ $
```

Figure 9-58. *Scheduling a pod with node affinity* `preferredDuringSchedulingIgnoredDuringExecution` *does not guarantee pod schedulement on a particular node*

As another example, specify all the `kubernetes.io/image-name` key values to those not used in node labels, as shown in Figure 9-59.

```
apiVersion: v1
kind: Pod
metadata:
  name: with-labels
  annotations:
    scheduler.alpha.kubernetes.io/affinity: >
      {
        "nodeAffinity": {
          "preferredDuringSchedulingIgnoredDuringExecution": [
            {
              "weight": 75,
              "preference":
              {
                "matchExpressions": [
                  {
                    "key": "kubernetes.io/image-name",
                    "operator": "In",
                    "values": ["helloworld", "nginx2"]
                  }
                ]
              }
            }
          ]
        }
      }
    kubernetes.io/image-name: helloworld
spec:
  containers:
  - name: with-labels
    image: nginx

:wq
```

Figure 9-59. *Setting all the* `kubernetes.io/image-name` *key values to non existing values*

Delete the pod `with-labels` and create the pod again. The pod is still scheduled even though none of the nodes have matching labels, as shown in Figure 9-60. By comparison, when we used the node affinity `requiredDuringSchedulingIgnoredDuringExecution` with none of the nodes having matching labels, the pods were placed in Pending status until a matching label was added. Now the pod is scheduled because the `preferredDuringSchedulingIgnoredDuringExecution` setting is not binding and is only a hint.

```
core@ip-10-0-0-50 ~ $ ./kubectl create -f podNodeAffinity.yaml
pod "with-labels" created
core@ip-10-0-0-50 ~ $ ./kubectl get pods -o wide
NAME          READY     STATUS    RESTARTS   AGE       IP          NODE
with-labels   1/1       Running   0          6s        10.2.45.2   ip-10-0-0-223
.ec2.internal
core@ip-10-0-0-50 ~ $
```

Figure 9-60. *Pods are scheduled even though no nodes with matching labels are found*

The `nodeSelector` field if specified with node affinity `preferredDuringSchedulingIgnoredDuringExecution` is still guaranteed. Add the `nodeSelector` field with the label `kubernetes.io/image-name: nginx` as shown in Figure 9-61. All the other matching expressions are set to `kubernetes.io/image-name: hello-world`.

```
metadata:
  name: with-labels
  annotations:
    scheduler.alpha.kubernetes.io/affinity: >
      {
        "nodeAffinity": {
          "preferredDuringSchedulingIgnoredDuringExecution": [
            {
              "weight": 75,
              "preference":
              {
                "matchExpressions": [
                  {
                    "key": "kubernetes.io/image-name",
                    "operator": "In",
                    "values": ["hello-world", "hello-world"]
                  }
                ]
              }
            }
          ]
        }
      }
    kubernetes.io/image-name: hello-world
spec:
  containers:
  - name: with-labels
    image: nginx
  nodeSelector:
    kubernetes.io/image-name: nginx

:wq
```

Figure 9-61. *Setting* `nodeSelector` *in addiiton to node affinity* *`preferredDuringSchedulingIgnoredDuringExecution`*

Delete and create the `with-labels` pod again. The pod is scheduled on the node with `kubernetes.io/image-name: nginx` label because the `nodeSelector` expression is `kubernetes.io/image-name: nginx` as shown in Figure 9-62.

```
core@ip-10-0-0-50 ~ $ sudo vi podNodeAffinity.yaml
core@ip-10-0-0-50 ~ $ ./kubectl create -f podNodeAffinity.yaml
pod "with-labels" created
core@ip-10-0-0-50 ~ $ ./kubectl get pods -o wide
NAME          READY     STATUS    RESTARTS   AGE       IP           NODE
with-labels   1/1       Running   0          21s       10.2.45.2    ip-10-0-0-223
.ec2.internal
core@ip-10-0-0-50 ~ $
```

Figure 9-62. *The pod is scheduled on the node with label matching the* `nodeSelector` *expression*

Summary

In this chapter we first discussed the default scheduling policy used by Kubernetes. Then we used the default scheduler and also the node selector to schedule pods on nodes. We also discussed scheduling pods using node affinity. In the next chapter we shall discuss configuring compute resources.

CHAPTER 10

Configuring Compute Resources

Kubernetes's resource model is simple, regular, extensible and precise. The Kubernetes container cluster manager provides two types of resources: compute resources and API resources. Supported compute resources (simply called "resources" in this chapter) are CPU and RAM (or memory). Support for other compute resources, such as network bandwidth, network operations, storage space, storage operations, and storage time may be added later.

Problem

A Kubernetes node capacity in terms of allocable resources (CPU and memory) is fixed and has to be apportioned among the different pods running on the node. A pod also has some fixed requirements for resources (CPU and memory) with some flexibility in resource consumption. The problem in resource usage is how to allocate resources to the different pods and also add some flexibility for a pod to be able to use more than the minimum requested resources if available.

Solution

Kubernetes provides a flexible resource usage design pattern based on *requests* and *limits* as shown in Figure 10-1. A *request* is the minimum resource (CPU and memory) a container in a pod requests so it can be scheduled and run on a node. A *limit* is the maximum resource (CPU and memory) that can be allocated to a container.

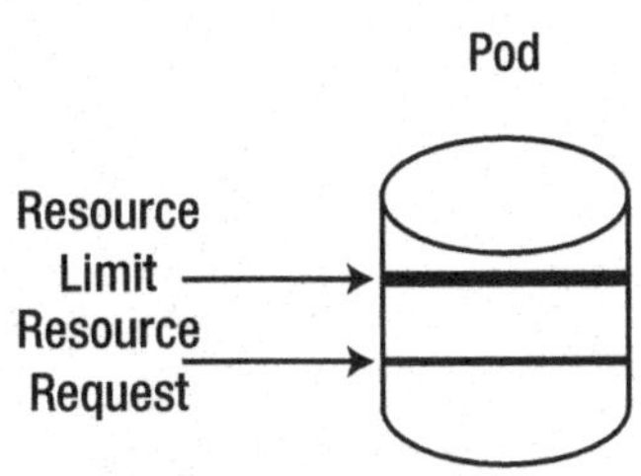

Figure 10-1. *Kubernetes resource request and limit*

D. Vohra, *Kubernetes Management Design Patterns*, DOI 10.1007/978-1-4842-2598-1_10

Overview

The two types of resources, compute resources and API resources, are shown in Figure 10-2. Compute resources are measurable quantities that can be requested by containers in a pod, allocated to containers and consumed by containers. API resources are Kubernetes objects such as pods and services, which are written to and retrieved from the API server.

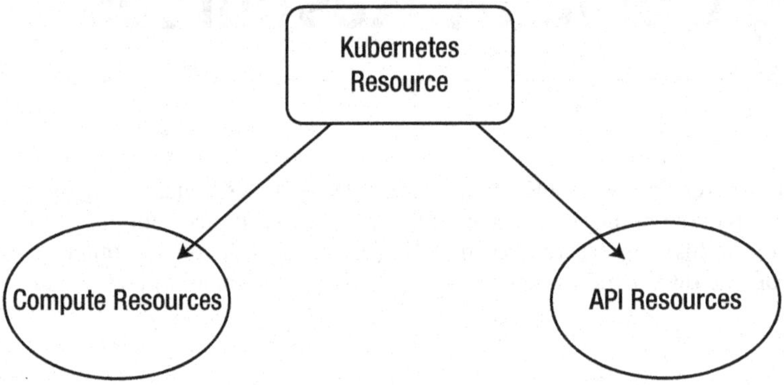

Figure 10-2. *Kubernetes resource types*

We will only be discussing compute resources in this chapter. By default, compute resources available to a container or a pod are limited only by the node capacity. While resources are consumed by containers in a pod (a pod can have one or more container), resources are also implied to be consumed by pods. The resources requested, allocated, and consumed by a pod are the total of the resources requested, allocated, and consumed by the containers in the pod. Node capacity comprises the resources available to a node in terms of CPUs, memory, and the maximum number of pods that can be scheduled on the node. The total of all allocated resources for each resource (CPUs, memory) to containers running on a node cannot exceed the node capacity for the resource. Kubernetes Scheduler ensures that sufficient resources are available on a node before it schedules a pod on the node. Even after scheduling a node, the Scheduler ensures that the total of allocated resources on a node does not exceed the node capacity, which it cannot by virtue of the node capacity. The Scheduler only monitors the containers started by the kubelet and not containers started by the Docker engine. This chapter looks at the following topics:

- Types of compute resources
- Resource requests and limits
- Quality of service
- Setting the environment
- Finding node capacity
- Creating a pod with resources specified
- Overcommitting resource limits
- Reserving node resources

Types of Compute Resources

Kubernetes provides two types of compute resources, CPUs and memory, as shown in Figure 10-3.

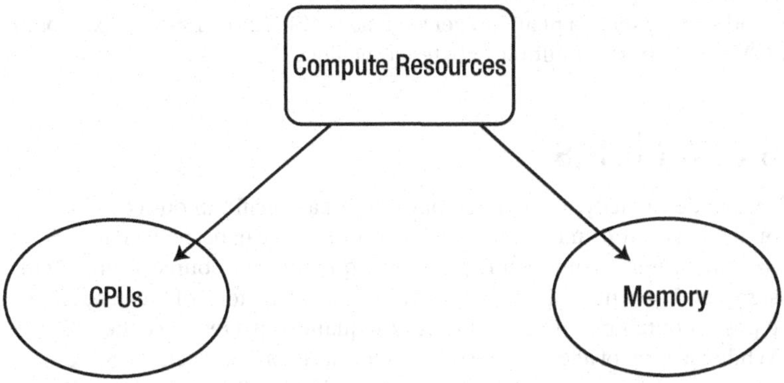

Figure 10-3. *Types of compute resources*

A compute resource is also referred to simply as a "resource," and each resource type is a distinctly measurable quantity at the container level. By default a pod's compute resources are unbounded, only limited by the node capacity. A pod's container could optionally specify resource request and limit levels for each type of resource, as discussed in the next section. Specifying explicit values for resource request and limit is recommended for the following reasons:

Doing so makes it easier for the Scheduler to assign pods on a node.

It makes it easier for a Scheduler to handle excess resources and contention of resources.

Available node capacity could make some pods non-schedulable on the node if the pod's containers require more capacity than the node capacity. Specifying resource requests and limits makes feasible a better design of the pod scheduling.

Separate namespaces could be created for development and production workloads with separate resource requests and limits, the resource consumption being different for different types of workloads.

More efficient utilization of a cluster's resources is made feasible by specifying explicit requests and limits for resources. While exceeding a node's capacity is one issue, a node could be underutilized if a pod that consumes only a fraction of the node's capacity is scheduled on the node, with the remaining node capacity neither suitable for scheduling another pod nor used by the pod scheduled.

CPUs are the processor cycles and measured in units of CPU cores (or just "CPUs"); one CPU core could be one AWS vCPU, one GCP core, one Azure vCore, or one hyperthread on a bare-metal Intel processor with hyperthreading. A value of 1 in the cpu field is 1000 millicpu. The value can be multiples of 1 such as 2, 3, or 4. Fractional CPU values can also be specified and translate to x1000 millicpu. For example, a value of .001 is 1 millicpu, which is the lowest value that can be specified; a finer precision is not feasible.

The `memory` field unit is bytes and may be set as a plain integer such as 134217728 or 135e6, a fixed-point integer with an SI suffix such as 135M, or the binary multiple of bytes equivalent 128Mi.

Resource Requests and Limits

In addition to the limits imposed by a node capacity, a container may request a specific amount of a resource and also impose a limit on the maximum amount of resource a container can be allowed to use. These are called the container *request* and *limit*. A container *request* is the quantity of resource a container is guaranteed; a scheduler won't assign a pod on a node if the node cannot provide the total of the containers' requests for each of the resource types. A container limit is the maximum quantity of a resource the system allows a container to use. While the total of allocated resource requests cannot exceed the node capacity limit for the resource, the total of resource limits may exceed the node capacity limit—assuming that each of the containers on a node won't be using the maximum resource limit concurrently. When the total of resource limits of all pods running on a node exceeds the node capacity, the node is said to be *overcommitted*. Each container may exceed the guaranteed resource allocated to it via the resource request, up to the resource limit as long as the total resource consumption on a node does not exceed the node capacity. But if due to contention of resources the total of resource consumption by containers on a node exceeds the node capacity, or tends to exceed the node capacity, some pods may have to be terminated; and if the `restartPolicy` is set to Always the pod may be restarted.

Resource guarantees are either *compressible* or *incompressible*. CPU resource guarantees are compressible and memory resource guarantees are incompressible. A compressible CPU resource guarantee implies that pods or more specifically containers are throttled if they exceed their CPU limit. A container could be throttled back to its guaranteed CPU level if the excess memory allocated to it is requested by another process such as a newly started pod or a system task or daemon. If extra CPU is available after all the pods on the node have been allocated, the minimum requested (guaranteed) CPU and the system tasks and daemons are getting the CPU they need, the extra CPU is distributed among the pods in the proportion of their minimum CPU requests (the guaranteed CPU). For example, if a node has three pods with one allocated a guaranteed CPU of 150m, the second a guaranteed CPU of 300m, and the third a guaranteed CPU of 450m, the extra CPU is distributed in the same proportion 1:2:3 up to the limit of each container. CPU resource is an elastic resource allocated within the range of the minimum request guarantee and the resource limit. Memory resource guarantee is elastic in one direction only; a container or pod can use more memory than the minimum requested (guaranteed) up to the limit, but if a container consumes more than the request level memory, the pod could be terminated if another pod that was consuming less than the minimum guaranteed level starts to consume more memory or if a system task or daemon requests more memory. A container consuming less than and up to the request level guaranteed memory is never terminated unless some system task or daemon has requested more memory. And a container consuming more memory than the limit is terminated regardless of excess memory availability.

When referring to node capacity, what is implied is *node allocable*, as some resources must be reserved for system components and Kubernetes components. The resource request and limit define a range 0 <= request <=Node Allocatable and request <= limit.

Pod specification provides the fields shown in Table 10-1 for resource requests and limits.

Table 10-1. *Pod Specification Fields for Compute Resources*

Pod Spec Field	Description
spec.container[].resources.requests.cpu	CPU resource requested by a container. The container is guaranteed the specified requested CPU. The Scheduler schedules a pod based on the requested CPU and the available CPU on a node. Defaults to spec.container[].resources.limits.cpu if not specified.
spec.container[].resources.requests.memory	Memory resource requested by a container. The container is guaranteed the specified requested memory. The Scheduler schedules a pod based on the requested memory and the available memory on a node. Defaults to spec.container[].resources.limits.memory if not specified.
spec.container[].resources.limits.cpu	The upper limit on the CPU a container can use. The Scheduler does not take into consideration the CPU limit. The spec.container[].resources.limits.cpu value must be greater than or equal to spec.container[].resources.requests.cpu. Defaults to the allocable node capacity.
spec.container[].resources.limits.memory	The upper limit on the memory a container can use. The Scheduler does not take into consideration the memory limit. The spec.container[].resources.limits.memory value must be greater than or equal to spec.container[].resources.requests.memory. Defaults to the allocable node capacity.

Specifying the resource fields is optional; if it is unset the values could be set to 0 or default values and the implementation varies with cluster configuration. The following are some examples of the field settings for cpu and memory:

```
containers:
  - name: db
    image: mysql
    resources:
      requests:
        memory: "64Mi"
        cpu: ".1"
      limits:
        memory: "128Mi"
        cpu: ".5"

containers:
  - name: db
    image: mysql
    resources:
```

```
      requests:
        memory: "64Mi"
        cpu: "100m"
      limits:
        memory: "64Mi"
        cpu: "500m"

containers:
  - name: db
    image: mysql
    resources:
      requests:
        memory: "1Gi"
        cpu: "250m"
      limits:
        memory: "2Gi"
        cpu: "250m"
```

The requests and limits are applied to the Docker `run` command when starting a container as shown in Table 10-2.

Table 10-2. *The Docker* `run` *Command Option Equivalents for Pod Spec Fields*

Spec Field	Docker run Command Option	Description
`spec.container[].resources.requests.cpu`	`--cpu-shares`	CPU shares
`spec.container[].resources.limits.cpu`	`--cpu-quota`	Sets the CPU CFS (Completely Fair Scheduler) quota
`spec.container[].resources.limits.memory`	`--memory flag`	Memory limit

Quality of Service

Kubernetes's Quality of Service (QoS) is a level for the resource availability. Pods or containers within a pod that need a minimum level of resources can request guaranteed resources with the `spec.container[].resources.requests.cpu` and `spec.container[].resources.requests.memory` fields. Pods that do not need guaranteed resources can omit specifying the request levels. Three QoS classes are provided for containers for each of the resource types. The QoS classes are based on requests and limits and are as shown in Table 10-3 in decreasing order of priority.

Table 10-3. *QoS Classes*

QoS Class	Description
Guaranteed	Limits and optionally requests (not equal to 0) are set for all the resources across all the containers and they are all equal. Requests default to limits if not set. These are the highest-priority pods and not terminated (due to memory) or throttled (due to CPU) unless a system task or daemon requests a resource and a lower priority pod is not available.
Burstable	Requests and optionally limits (not equal to 0) are set for one or more resources across one or more containers and they are not equal. These pods have intermediate priority and have some level of resource guarantee. If CPU is required by a higher priority pod or system and no Best-Effort pod is running, the pod's CPU could be throttled. Similarly, if memory is required by a higher priority pod or system and no Best-Effort pod is running the pod could be terminated.
Best-Effort	Requests and limits are not set for any of the resources for any of the containers. These are the lowest priority pods and could be terminated if memory resource is required by another pod at a higher priority or a system task or daemon needs memory. The CPU could be throttled if required by other pods and system.

The QoS policy assumes that swap is disabled.

Setting the Environment

Create a Kubernetes cluster as an AWS CloudFormation with CoreOS Linux. First, create an AWS EC2 instance from Amazon Linux AMI. SSH log in to the EC2 instance.

```
ssh -i "docker.pem"  ec2-user@174.129.50.31
```

Launch a CloudFormation for a Kubernetes cluster with one controller node and three worker nodes. Install the kubectl binaries and list the nodes:

```
./kubectl get nodes
```

The nodes in the Kubernetes cluster are listed, as shown in Figure 10-4.

```
core@ip-10-0-0-50 ~ $ ./kubectl get nodes
NAME                        STATUS                     AGE
ip-10-0-0-50.ec2.internal   Ready,SchedulingDisabled   2m
ip-10-0-0-63.ec2.internal   Ready                      2m
ip-10-0-0-64.ec2.internal   Ready                      2m
ip-10-0-0-65.ec2.internal   Ready                      2m
core@ip-10-0-0-50 ~ $
```

Figure 10-4. *Kubernetes node cluster*

Finding Node Capacity

A node's capacity may be found by describing the node. For example:

```
kubectl describe node ip-10-0-0-50.ec2.internal
```

The Capacity field lists the node capacity in terms of CPU, memory, and number of pods. The Allocatable field lists the allocable CPU, memory, and number of pods as shown in Figure 10-5.

```
Addresses:       10.0.0.64,10.0.0.64,54.243.23.193
Capacity:
 cpu:            1
 memory:         3857824Ki
 pods:           110
Allocatable:
 cpu:            1
 memory:         3857824Ki
 pods:           110
```

Figure 10-5. *Node capacity, total and allocatable*

The CPU and Memory Requests and Limits including allocated resources are also listed but should initially all be 0 if no pod is running on the node, as shown in Figure 10-6.

```
Non-terminated Pods:            (5 in total)
  Namespace                     Name                                          C
PU Requests     CPU Limits      Memory Requests Memory Limits
  ---------                     ----                                          -
-----------     ----------      --------------- -------------
  calico-system                 calico-policy-agent-ip-10-0-0-50.ec2.internal 0
 (0%)           0 (0%)          0 (0%)          0 (0%)
  kube-system                   kube-apiserver-ip-10-0-0-50.ec2.internal      0
 (0%)           0 (0%)          0 (0%)          0 (0%)
  kube-system                   kube-controller-manager-ip-10-0-0-50.ec2.intern
al              0 (0%)          0 (0%)          0 (0%)          0 (0%)
  kube-system                   kube-proxy-ip-10-0-0-50.ec2.internal          0
 (0%)           0 (0%)          0 (0%)          0 (0%)
  kube-system                   kube-scheduler-ip-10-0-0-50.ec2.internal      0
 (0%)           0 (0%)          0 (0%)          0 (0%)
Allocated resources:
  (Total limits may be over 100 percent, i.e., overcommitted. More info: http:/
/releases.k8s.io/HEAD/docs/user-guide/compute-resources.md)
  CPU Requests  CPU Limits      Memory Requests Memory Limits
  ------------  ----------      --------------- -------------
  0 (0%)        0 (0%)          0 (0%)          0 (0%)
No events.

core@ip-10-0-0-50 ~ $
```

Figure 10-6. *CPU and memory requests and limits*

For the controller node, the node description should always list the allocated resources as 0 because the node is not schedulable, as indicated by the `NodeNotSchedulable` in the Type column in Figure 10-7.

```
Allocated resources:
  (Total limits may be over 100 percent, i.e., overcommitted. More info: http://
releases.k8s.io/HEAD/docs/user-guide/compute-resources.md)
  CPU Requests  CPU Limits      Memory Requests Memory Limits
  ------------  ----------      --------------- -------------
  0 (0%)        0 (0%)          0 (0%)          0 (0%)
Events:
  FirstSeen     LastSeen        Count   From                                   S
ubobjectPath    Type            Reason                  Message
  ---------     --------        -----   ----                                   -
-----------     --------        ------                  -------
  11m           11m             1       {kubelet ip-10-0-0-50.ec2.internal}    N
ormal           Starting                Starting kubelet.
  11m           11m             1       {kubelet ip-10-0-0-50.ec2.internal}    N
ormal           NodeNotSchedulable      Node ip-10-0-0-50.ec2.internal status is
 now: NodeNotSchedulable
  10m           10m             1       {kube-proxy ip-10-0-0-50.ec2.internal} N
ormal           Starting                Starting kube-proxy.
```

Figure 10-7. *The controller node is not schedulable*

Creating a Pod with Resources Specified

In this section we will create an example pod with a resource request and limit specified for the container. Create a definition file `mysql.yaml` using the Docker image `mysql` for a replication controller. Specify container resource request and limit. The same resource type may be specified only once in a list.

```
---
apiVersion: v1
kind: ReplicationController
metadata:
  name: mysql-v1
  labels:
    app: mysql-app
spec:
  replicas: 3
  selector:
    app: mysql-app
    deployment: v1
  template:
    metadata:
      labels:
        app: mysql-app
        deployment: v1
    spec:
      containers:
        -
          env:
            -
              name: MYSQL_ROOT_PASSWORD
              value: mysql
          image: mysql
          name: mysql
```

```
          ports:
            -
              containerPort: 3306
          resources:
            requests:
              memory: "64Mi"
              cpu: "250m"
            limits:
              memory: "128Mi"
              cpu: "500m"
```

The definition file `mysql.yaml` is shown in the `vi` editor in Figure 10-8.

```
  labels:
    app: mysql-app
spec:
  replicas: 3
  selector:
    app: mysql-app
    deployment: v1
  template:
    metadata:
      labels:
        app: mysql-app
        deployment: v1
    spec:
      containers:
        -
          env:
            -
              name: MYSQL_ROOT_PASSWORD
              value: mysql
          image: mysql
          name: mysql
          ports:
            -
              containerPort: 3306
          resources:
            requests:
              memory: "64Mi"
              cpu: "250m"
            limits:
              memory: "128Mi"
              cpu: "500m"
:wq
```

Figure 10-8. *Replication controller definition file* `mysql.yaml`

Create a replication controller using the definition file:

```
./kubectl create -f mysql.yaml
```

List the cluster-wide pods:

```
./kubectl get pods
```

Initially the pods may be not running or Ready. List the pods after a minute, and all the pods should be running. Each pod is scheduled on a different node, as shown in Figure 10-9.

```
core@ip-10-0-0-50 ~ $ ./kubectl create -f mysql.yaml
replicationcontroller "mysql-v1" created
core@ip-10-0-0-50 ~ $ ./kubectl get pods -o wide
NAME             READY     STATUS    RESTARTS   AGE       IP           NODE
mysql-v1-80tj3   1/1       Running   0          13s       10.2.56.3    ip-10-0-0
-63.ec2.internal
mysql-v1-kn53w   1/1       Running   0          13s       10.2.83.2    ip-10-0-0
-64.ec2.internal
mysql-v1-pfd3r   1/1       Running   0          13s       10.2.39.3    ip-10-0-0
-65.ec2.internal
core@ip-10-0-0-50 ~ $
```

Figure 10-9. *Each pod is scheduled on a different node*

Describe a node to find the resource consumption on the node, as shown in Figure 10-10. Only one pod is running on the node. The CPU and Memory Requests and Limits for each pod in the default namespace are listed. The MySQL pod CPU request of 250m and CPU Limit of 500m and Memory Request of 64Mi and Memory Limit of 128 Mi are listed. The allocated CPU and Memory Requests and Limits are also listed. Allocated CPU and Memory requests are less than the limits, which is the desired level.

```
Non-terminated Pods:            (3 in total)
  Namespace                     Name                                            C
PU Requests     CPU Limits      Memory Requests Memory Limits
  ---------                     ----                                            -
-----------     ----------      --------------- -------------
  default                       mysql-v1-80tj3                                  2
50m (25%)       500m (50%)      64Mi (1%)       128Mi (3%)
  kube-system                   kube-dns-v11-uzc57                              3
10m (31%)       310m (31%)      170Mi (4%)      920Mi (24%)
  kube-system                   kube-proxy-ip-10-0-0-63.ec2.internal            0
 (0%)           0 (0%)          0 (0%)          0 (0%)
Allocated resources:
  (Total limits may be over 100 percent, i.e., overcommitted. More info: http:/
/releases.k8s.io/HEAD/docs/user-guide/compute-resources.md)
  CPU Requests  CPU Limits      Memory Requests Memory Limits
  ------------  ----------      --------------- -------------
  560m (56%)    810m (81%)      234Mi (6%)      1048Mi (27%)
No events.

core@ip-10-0-0-50 ~ $ ./kubectl get pods
NAME             READY     STATUS    RESTARTS   AGE
mysql-v1-80tj3   1/1       Running   2          1m
mysql-v1-kn53w   1/1       Running   2          1m
mysql-v1-pfd3r   1/1       Running   2          1m
core@ip-10-0-0-50 ~ $
```

Figure 10-10. *CPU and memory requests and limits on a schedulable node*

Describe a pod started with the previously discussed settings, and the Limits and Requests for the resource types should be listed as shown in Figure 10-11 (the pod name can be from a different run with the same settings).

```
core@ip-10-0-0-50 ~ $ ./kubectl describe pod mysql-v1-f3j7k
Name:           mysql-v1-f3j7k
Namespace:      default
Node:           ip-10-0-0-63.ec2.internal/10.0.0.63
Start Time:     Mon, 11 Jul 2016 16:35:02 +0000
Labels:         app=mysql-app
                deployment=v1
Status:         Running
IP:             10.2.56.3
Controllers:    ReplicationController/mysql-v1
Containers:
  mysql:
    Container ID:       docker://5c5df522ab85de6eb02ddb1d153d7743878a21444065915
3e16136eff9ce3240
    Image:              mysql
    Image ID:           docker://sha256:1195b21c3a45d9bf93aae497f2538f89a09aaded
18d6648753aa3ce76670f41d
    Port:               3306/TCP
    Limits:
      cpu:      500m
      memory:   128Mi
    Requests:
      cpu:              250m
      memory:           64Mi
    State:              Running
```

Figure 10-11. *Pod CPU and memory requests and limits*

The resource limits must be set higher than the requests. As an example, set the limits to be lower than the requests, as shown in Figure 10-12.

```
spec:
  replicas: 3
  selector:
    app: mysql-app
    deployment: v1
  template:
    metadata:
      labels:
        app: mysql-app
        deployment: v1
    spec:
      containers:
        -
          env:
            -
              name: MYSQL_ROOT_PASSWORD
              value: mysql
          image: mysql
          name: mysql
          ports:
            -
              containerPort: 3306
          resources:
            requests:
              memory: "64Mi"
              cpu: "250m"
            limits:
              memory: "60Mi"
              cpu: "200m"

~
:wq
```

Figure 10-12. *Pod CPU and memory requests set higher than the limits*

When the pod is created an error is generated, indicating that the CPU and memory limits must be higher than the requests, as shown in Figure 10-13.

```
core@ip-10-0-0-50 ~ $ ./kubectl delete rc mysql-v1
replicationcontroller "mysql-v1" deleted
core@ip-10-0-0-50 ~ $ sudo vi mysql.yaml
core@ip-10-0-0-50 ~ $ ./kubectl create -f mysql.yaml
The ReplicationController "mysql-v1" is invalid.

* spec.template.spec.containers[0].resources.limits[cpu]: Invalid value: "200m":
 must be greater than or equal to request
* spec.template.spec.containers[0].resources.limits[memory]: Invalid value: "60M
i": must be greater than or equal to request
core@ip-10-0-0-50 ~ $
```

Figure 10-13. *Error indicating an invalid value for resource limits*

The cpu may be specified as fractions (for example 0.3) instead of absolute value, as shown in Figure 10-14. A cpu value of 0.3 is 300m. The requests are equal to the limits in the example.

```
    app: mysql-app
spec:
  replicas: 3
  selector:
    app: mysql-app
    deployment: v1
  template:
    metadata:
      labels:
        app: mysql-app
        deployment: v1
    spec:
      containers:
        -
          env:
            -
              name: MYSQL_ROOT_PASSWORD
              value: mysql
          image: mysql
          name: mysql
          ports:
            -
              containerPort: 3306
          resources:
            requests:
              memory: "385782Ki"
              cpu: "0.3"
            limits:
              memory: "3857824Ki"
              cpu: "0.3"

:wq
```

Figure 10-14. *CPU specified as a fraction*

Create the replication controller and list the pods. The three replicas are scheduled on three different nodes. Scale the RC to six pods. The six pods are scheduled on the three nodes with two pods on each node, as shown in Figure 10-15.

```
core@ip-10-0-0-50 ~ $ ./kubectl scale --replicas=6 rc/mysql-v1
replicationcontroller "mysql-v1" scaled
core@ip-10-0-0-50 ~ $ ./kubectl get pods -o wide
NAME             READY     STATUS    RESTARTS   AGE       IP          NODE
mysql-v1-c8aed   1/1       Running   0          23m       10.2.56.3   ip-10-0-0
-63.ec2.internal
mysql-v1-ckywi   1/1       Running   0          7m        10.2.56.4   ip-10-0-0
-63.ec2.internal
mysql-v1-gl2r4   1/1       Running   0          23m       10.2.39.3   ip-10-0-0
-65.ec2.internal
mysql-v1-kgp2t   1/1       Running   0          7m        10.2.83.2   ip-10-0-0
-64.ec2.internal
mysql-v1-q9nep   1/1       Running   0          2m        10.2.39.4   ip-10-0-0
-65.ec2.internal
mysql-v1-qins5   1/1       Running   0          23m       10.2.83.3   ip-10-0-0
-64.ec2.internal
core@ip-10-0-0-50 ~ $
```

Figure 10-15. *Two pods are scheduled on each node*

The number of pod replicas has a limit, as the per-node resource capacity could start to be approached with more replicas. With the previous settings seven replicas are scheduled, as shown in Figure 10-16. One of the nodes has three pods.

```
core@ip-10-0-0-50 ~ $ ./kubectl scale --replicas=7 rc/mysql-v1
replicationcontroller "mysql-v1" scaled
core@ip-10-0-0-50 ~ $ ./kubectl get pods -o wide
NAME             READY     STATUS    RESTARTS   AGE       IP          NODE
mysql-v1-b3ucj   1/1       Running   0          55s       10.2.83.4   ip-10-0-0
-64.ec2.internal
mysql-v1-c8aed   1/1       Running   0          26m       10.2.56.3   ip-10-0-0
-63.ec2.internal
mysql-v1-ckywi   1/1       Running   0          10m       10.2.56.4   ip-10-0-0
-63.ec2.internal
mysql-v1-gl2r4   1/1       Running   0          26m       10.2.39.3   ip-10-0-0
-65.ec2.internal
mysql-v1-kgp2t   1/1       Running   0          10m       10.2.83.2   ip-10-0-0
-64.ec2.internal
mysql-v1-q9nep   1/1       Running   0          5m        10.2.39.4   ip-10-0-0
-65.ec2.internal
mysql-v1-qins5   1/1       Running   0          26m       10.2.83.3   ip-10-0-0
-64.ec2.internal
core@ip-10-0-0-50 ~ $
```

Figure 10-16. *Kubernetes cluster capacity has a limit, allowing seven pods to be scheduled on three nodes in this example*

Describe the node with the three pods, and you'll see that resource consumption is at 90% for both CPU and memory, as shown in Figure 10-17. No more pods can be scheduled on the pod.

```
Non-terminated Pods:            (4 in total)
  Namespace                     Name                                            C
PU Requests     CPU Limits      Memory Requests Memory Limits
  ---------                     ----                                            -
------------    ----------      --------------- -------------
  default                       mysql-v1-b3ucj                                  3
00m (30%)       300m (30%)      385782Ki (9%)   3857824Ki (100%)
  default                       mysql-v1-kgp2t                                  3
00m (30%)       300m (30%)      385782Ki (9%)   3857824Ki (100%)
  default                       mysql-v1-qins5                                  3
00m (30%)       300m (30%)      385782Ki (9%)   3857824Ki (100%)
  kube-system                   kube-proxy-ip-10-0-0-64.ec2.internal            0
 (0%)           0 (0%)          0 (0%)          0 (0%)
Allocated resources:
  (Total limits may be over 100 percent, i.e., overcommitted. More info: http:/
/releases.k8s.io/HEAD/docs/user-guide/compute-resources.md)
  CPU Requests  CPU Limits      Memory Requests Memory Limits
  ------------  ----------      --------------- -------------
  900m (90%)    900m (90%)      1157346Ki (29%) 11573472Ki (300%)
No events.

core@ip-10-0-0-50 ~ $
```

Figure 10-17. *Resource consumption is at 90%*

The minimum memory limit allowed is 4 MB.

Limit on Number of Pods

The number of pods that can be scheduled on a node is limited by the allocable node capacity, which includes the limit of 110 on the number of pods. To demonstrate, scale the RC to 400 pods. The RC is scaled to 400 replicas and no error is generated, as shown in Figure 10-18.

```
core@ip-10-0-0-50 ~ $ ./kubectl scale --replicas=400 rc/mysql-v1
replicationcontroller "mysql-v1" scaled
core@ip-10-0-0-50 ~ $ 
```

Figure 10-18. *Scaling to 400 nodes*

But 400 pods cannot run on three nodes; this is limited not only by the limit on the number of pods per node but also by the allocable CPU and memory. The pods that cannot run are put in Pending status and no node is allocated to them, as shown in Figure 10-19.

```
core@ip-10-0-0-50 ~ $ ./kubectl get pods -o wide
NAME             READY     STATUS    RESTARTS   AGE       IP         NODE
mysql-v1-02ptf   0/1       Pending   0          30s       <none>
mysql-v1-076yo   0/1       Pending   0          35s       <none>
mysql-v1-087wk   0/1       Pending   0          40s       <none>
mysql-v1-08dwx   0/1       Pending   0          30s       <none>
mysql-v1-0a5s5   0/1       Pending   0          37s       <none>
mysql-v1-0dngp   0/1       Pending   0          46s       <none>
mysql-v1-0ilqr   0/1       Pending   0          33s       <none>
mysql-v1-0l0w4   0/1       Pending   0          32s       <none>
mysql-v1-0rbl5   0/1       Pending   0          44s       <none>
mysql-v1-0rgui   0/1       Pending   0          33s       <none>
mysql-v1-0w8ht   0/1       Pending   0          36s       <none>
mysql-v1-16sf9   0/1       Pending   0          44s       <none>
mysql-v1-183yv   0/1       Pending   0          34s       <none>
mysql-v1-1dfzl   0/1       Pending   0          30s       <none>
mysql-v1-1elp2   0/1       Pending   0          44s       <none>
mysql-v1-1ffkn   0/1       Pending   0          30s       <none>
mysql-v1-1mh9d   0/1       Pending   0          38s       <none>
mysql-v1-1ofg5   0/1       Pending   0          47s       <none>
mysql-v1-1ojz6   0/1       Pending   0          31s       <none>
mysql-v1-1pl9f   0/1       Pending   0          34s       <none>
mysql-v1-1pswb   0/1       Pending   0          34s       <none>
mysql-v1-1uqyb   0/1       Pending   0          47s       <none>
mysql-v1-1x88g   0/1       Pending   0          45s       <none>
mysql-v1-22gkg   0/1       Pending   0          39s       <none>
mysql-v1-23gx5   0/1       Pending   0          34s       <none>
mysql-v1-27ol8   0/1       Pending   0          34s       <none>
mysql-v1-2839x   0/1       Pending   0          34s       <none>
mysql-v1-2acfx   0/1       Pending   0          38s       <none>
mysql-v1-2i4cl   0/1       Pending   0          41s       <none>
mysql-v1-2ixqd   0/1       Pending   0          32s       <none>
```

Figure 10-19. *Pods put in Pending status*

Scale the RC back to five replicas. The Pending pods are not immediately removed. But five running pods are listed, as shown in Figure 10-20.

```
core@ip-10-0-0-50 ~ $ ./kubectl scale --replicas=5 rc/mysql-v1
replicationcontroller "mysql-v1" scaled
core@ip-10-0-0-50 ~ $ ./kubectl get pods -o wide
NAME             READY     STATUS      RESTARTS   AGE        IP          NODE
mysql-v1-087wk   0/1       Pending     0          3m         <none>
mysql-v1-2i4cl   0/1       Pending     0          3m         <none>
mysql-v1-2n792   0/1       Pending     0          3m         <none>
mysql-v1-2s3rd   0/1       Pending     0          3m         <none>
mysql-v1-2tnkn   0/1       Pending     0          3m         <none>
mysql-v1-38f0p   0/1       Pending     0          3m         <none>
mysql-v1-3aiy6   0/1       Pending     0          3m         <none>
mysql-v1-3lxxb   0/1       Pending     0          3m         <none>
mysql-v1-5ldcn   0/1       Pending     0          3m         <none>
mysql-v1-60nlf   0/1       Pending     0          3m         <none>
mysql-v1-630i9   0/1       Pending     0          3m         <none>
mysql-v1-72psi   0/1       Pending     0          3m         <none>
mysql-v1-7hgki   0/1       Pending     0          3m         <none>
mysql-v1-8go2u   0/1       Pending     0          3m         <none>
mysql-v1-8k0o2   0/1       Pending     0          3m         <none>
mysql-v1-8umyf   0/1       Pending     0          3m         <none>
mysql-v1-bb5fs   0/1       Pending     0          3m         <none>
mysql-v1-bz5s7   0/1       Pending     0          3m         <none>
mysql-v1-c8aed   1/1       Running     0          19m        10.2.56.3   ip-10
-0-0-63.ec2.internal
mysql-v1-cad66   0/1       Pending     0          3m         <none>
mysql-v1-cc5aw   0/1       Pending     0          3m         <none>
mysql-v1-cfszj   0/1       Pending     0          3m         <none>
mysql-v1-ckywi   1/1       Running     0          3m         10.2.56.4   ip-10
-0-0-63.ec2.internal
mysql-v1-cqcf5   0/1       Pending     0          3m         <none>
```

Figure 10-20. *Pods put in pending status*

Scale the RC to 10 replicas. Only seven pods are Running and the others are Pending, as shown in Figure 10-21.

```
core@ip-10-0-0-50 ~ $ ./kubectl scale --replicas=10 rc/mysql-v1
replicationcontroller "mysql-v1" scaled
core@ip-10-0-0-50 ~ $ ./kubectl get pods -o wide
NAME             READY     STATUS    RESTARTS   AGE       IP          NODE
mysql-v1-3n0tv   0/1       Pending   0          10s       <none>
mysql-v1-c8aed   1/1       Running   0          21m       10.2.56.3   ip-10-0-0
-63.ec2.internal
mysql-v1-ckywi   1/1       Running   0          5m        10.2.56.4   ip-10-0-0
-63.ec2.internal
mysql-v1-cmkod   0/1       Pending   0          10s       <none>
mysql-v1-gl2r4   1/1       Running   0          21m       10.2.39.3   ip-10-0-0
-65.ec2.internal
mysql-v1-kgp2t   1/1       Running   0          5m        10.2.83.2   ip-10-0-0
-64.ec2.internal
mysql-v1-q9nep   1/1       Running   0          10s       10.2.39.4   ip-10-0-0
-65.ec2.internal
mysql-v1-qins5   1/1       Running   0          21m       10.2.83.3   ip-10-0-0
-64.ec2.internal
mysql-v1-u51zs   1/1       Running   0          10s       10.2.83.4   ip-10-0-0
-64.ec2.internal
mysql-v1-wek22   0/1       Pending   0          10s       <none>
core@ip-10-0-0-50 ~ $
```

Figure 10-21. *Scaling to 10 replicas has only seven of the 10 pods Running*

Overcommitting Resource Limits

As shown in an earlier example, a maximum of three pods can be scheduled on a node with the allocated requests consuming 90% of allocable CPU. The memory limits are at 300%, which makes the limits overcommitted. If all the pods were to request their maximum allocable memory concurrently, the resource consumption would exceed 100% and some pods would terminate. Even with a single pod on a node the memory limits are overcommitted at 109%, though not by much, as shown in Figure 10-22.

```
Non-terminated Pods:            (3 in total)
  Namespace                     Name                                    C
PU Requests     CPU Limits      Memory Requests Memory Limits
  ---------                     ----                                    -
-----------     ----------      --------------- -------------
  default                       mysql-v1-gl2r4                          3
00m (30%)       300m (30%)      385782Ki (9%)   3857824Ki (100%)
  kube-system                   heapster-v1.0.2-3151619174-5dqrl        1
50m (15%)       150m (15%)      366Mi (9%)      366Mi (9%)
  kube-system                   kube-proxy-ip-10-0-0-65.ec2.internal    0
 (0%)           0 (0%)          0 (0%)          0 (0%)
Allocated resources:
  (Total limits may be over 100 percent, i.e., overcommitted. More info: http:/
/releases.k8s.io/HEAD/docs/user-guide/compute-resources.md)
  CPU Requests  CPU Limits      Memory Requests Memory Limits
  ------------  ----------      --------------- -------------
  450m (45%)    450m (45%)      760566Ki (19%)  4232608Ki (109%)
```

Figure 10-22. *Overcommitted memory limits*

Reserving Node Resources

Pods are not the only objects or processes consuming resources on a node. It may be suitable to reserve some resources for non-pod processes such as system processes. Resources may be reserved by running a placeholder pod. Create a pod definition file `pod-reserve-resource.yaml`. Run the Docker image `gcr.io/google_containers/pause` and specify resource limits for resources to be reserved such as 200m for cpu and 200Mi for `memory`.

```
apiVersion: v1
kind: Pod
metadata:
  name: reserve-resource
spec:
  containers:
  - name: reserve-resource
    image: gcr.io/google_containers/pause:0.8.0
    resources:
      limits:
        cpu: "0.1"
        memory: 200Mi
```

The pod definition file is shown in a vi editor in Figure 10-23.

```
apiVersion: v1
kind: Pod
metadata:
  name: reserve-resource
spec:
  containers:
  - name: reserve-resource
    image: gcr.io/google_containers/pause:0.8.0
    resources:
      limits:
        cpu: ".1"
        memory: "200Mi"
~
~
~
```

Figure 10-23. *Pod definition to reserve some resources*

First, create the placeholder pod as shown in Figure 10-24. Then create the MySQL RC.

```
core@ip-10-0-0-50 ~ $ ./kubectl delete rc mysql-v1
replicationcontroller "mysql-v1" deleted
core@ip-10-0-0-50 ~ $ ls -l
total 55212
-rwxr-xr-x 1 root root 56515944 Jul  1 20:06 kubectl
-rw-r--r-- 1 root root      685 Jul 11 18:13 mysql.yaml
-rw-r--r-- 1 root root      226 Jul 11 18:18 pod-reserve-resource.yaml
core@ip-10-0-0-50 ~ $ ./kubectl create -f pod-reserve-resource.yaml
pod "reserve-resource" created
core@ip-10-0-0-50 ~ $ ./kubectl get pods
NAME               READY     STATUS    RESTARTS   AGE
reserve-resource   1/1       Running   0          10s
core@ip-10-0-0-50 ~ $ ./kubectl create -f mysql.yaml
replicationcontroller "mysql-v1" created
core@ip-10-0-0-50 ~ $ ./kubectl get pods
NAME               READY     STATUS    RESTARTS   AGE
mysql-v1-c8aed     1/1       Running   0          7s
mysql-v1-gl2r4     1/1       Running   0          7s
mysql-v1-qins5     1/1       Running   0          7s
reserve-resource   1/1       Running   0          39s
core@ip-10-0-0-50 ~ $
```

Figure 10-24. *Creating the resource reserving pod and RC for MySQL*

Describe the reserve-resource pod, and you'll see that it is reserving the specified resources as shown in Figure 10-25.

```
core@ip-10-0-0-50 ~ $ ./kubectl describe pod reserve-resource
Name:           reserve-resource
Namespace:      default
Node:           ip-10-0-0-64.ec2.internal/10.0.0.64
Start Time:     Mon, 11 Jul 2016 18:22:09 +0000
Labels:         <none>
Status:         Running
IP:             10.2.83.2
Controllers:    <none>
Containers:
  reserve-resource:
    Container ID:       docker://4bb88ca8468d834db1a97fe9b94ee3341ca95967553abb
4a06406178f6cbb93d
    Image:              gcr.io/google_containers/pause:0.8.0
    Image ID:           docker://sha256:bf595365a5588ec1bae3e9dc9efde13672f7b75
61b6cc4514a82f07be9d01ca6
    Port:
    Limits:
      cpu:      100m
      memory:   200Mi
    Requests:
      cpu:                      100m
      memory:                   200Mi
    State:                      Running
      Started:                  Mon, 11 Jul 2016 18:22:10 +0000
    Ready:                      True
    Restart Count:              0
    Environment Variables:      <none>
Conditions:
  Type          Status
  Ready         True
Volumes:
```

Figure 10-25. *Pod description for the resource-reserving pod*

Summary

In this chapter we discussed the configuration and use of compute resources. The two compute resources that are configurable are CPU and memory. Two configuration values may be specified for each of these resources, the requested value and the limiting value. Then we created a pod with compute resource request and limit configured. We also discussed overcommitting resources and reserving resources on a node. In the next chapter we shall discuss using configmaps.

CHAPTER 11

Using ConfigMaps

In Chapter 10 and some earlier chapters, we used the `spec: containers: env:` field to specify an environment variable for the Docker image `mysql` for the MySQL database.

Problem

Consider the use case that some environment variables such as username and password for a database are to be used in multiple replication controller or pod definition files. The username and password value would need to be specified in each of the definition files. And if the username and password were to change, all the definition files would need to be updated as well, which could be very tedious. Alternatively, variable values could be supplied to `kubectl` when a command is run, which involves specifying command-line flags each time the command is run.

Solution

The ConfigMap management pattern is a map of configuration properties that can be used in definition files for pods, replication controllers, and other Kubernetes objects to configure environment variables, command arguments, and configuration files such as key-value pairs in volumes, to list a few example uses. A single ConfigMap may package multiple configuration properties as key/value pairs. By creating ConfigMaps, you specify the configuration properties in a single configuration map, which can be updated as required without having to update each of the definition files in which the ConfigMap is used. Decoupling the containers from the configuration data provides portability of the applications running in the containers.

Overview

A ConfigMap definition file schema provides for the following (Table 11-1) fields.

Table 11-1. *ConfigMap Fields*

Field	Description
`kind`	The resource type. Must be set to `ConfigMap`.
`apiVersion`	Version of the schema.
`metadata`	Metadata such as name, labels, namespace and annotations.
`data`	Configuration data as key/value pairs.

D. Vohra, *Kubernetes Management Design Patterns*, DOI 10.1007/978-1-4842-2598-1_11

In this chapter we shall discuss ConfigMaps and some common uses of them. This chapter covers the following topics:

- The kubectl `create configmap` command
- Setting the environment
- Creating ConfigMaps from directories
- Creating ConfigMaps from files
- Creating ConfigMaps from literal values
- Consuming a ConfigMap in a volume

Kubectl create configmap Command

The `kubectl create configmap` command is used to create a ConfigMap from a file, directory, or literal values and has the following syntax:

```
kubectl create configmap NAME [--from-file=[key=]source] [--from-literal=key1=value1]
[--dry-run]
```

When creating a ConfigMap from a file, the file name forms the key in the ConfigMap and the content of the file forms the value. When creating a ConfigMap from a directory, a ConfigMap key/value pair is created from each of the files in the directory with the file name being the key and the file content being the value. Only regular files in a directory are used to create ConfigMap entries, and other directory contents such as subdirectories and symlinks are omitted. The command argument for creating a ConfigMap from a directory or file is the same, `--from-file`.

In the following sections we will set the environment and create ConfigMaps from a directory, files, and literal values and also consume the ConfigMaps in a pod as environment variables, command arguments, or config files in a volume.

Setting the Environment

Create a Kubernetes cluster using an AWS CloudFormation. SSH log in to the controller instance, install the `kubectl` binaries, and list the nodes, as discussed in Chapter 2. The number of nodes in the cluster is a variable, the default being one schedulable worker node and one controller node. The `kubectl get nodes` command lists six worker nodes and one controller node.

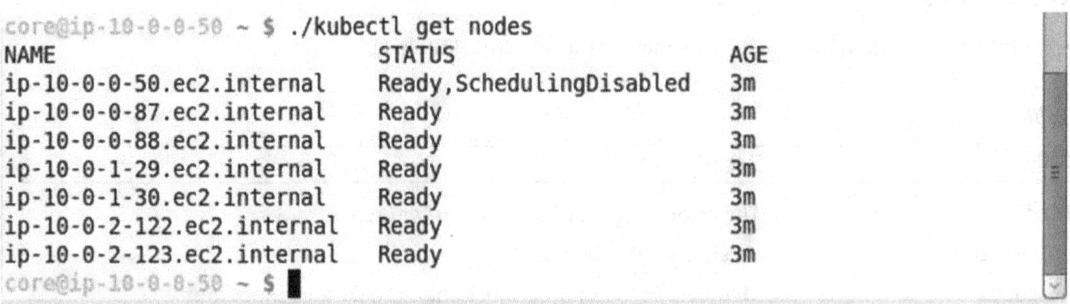

core@ip-10-0-0-50 ~ $ ./kubectl get nodes
NAME STATUS AGE
ip-10-0-0-50.ec2.internal Ready,SchedulingDisabled 3m
ip-10-0-0-87.ec2.internal Ready 3m
ip-10-0-0-88.ec2.internal Ready 3m
ip-10-0-1-29.ec2.internal Ready 3m
ip-10-0-1-30.ec2.internal Ready 3m
ip-10-0-2-122.ec2.internal Ready 3m
ip-10-0-2-123.ec2.internal Ready 3m
core@ip-10-0-0-50 ~ $

Figure 11-1. *Kubernetes cluster nodes*

Creating ConfigMaps from Directories

In this section we shall create a ConfigMap from files in a directory. First, create a directory `/mysql/env` and set the directory's permissions to global (777):

```
sudo  mkdir /mysql/env
sudo chmod -R 777 /mysql/env
```

The `/mysql/env` directory is created as shown in Figure 11-2. CD (change directory) to the `/mysql/env` directory.

core@ip-10-0-0-50 ~ $ sudo mkdir -p /mysql/env
core@ip-10-0-0-50 ~ $ sudo chmod -R 777 /mysql/env
core@ip-10-0-0-50 ~ $ cd /mysql/env
core@ip-10-0-0-50 /mysql/env $

Figure 11-2. *Creating the `/mysql/env` directory*

Create five files, each with a file name that would form the key for a configuration property in the ConfigMap as listed in Table 11-2.

Table 11-2. *ConfigMap Fields*

File name	File content
`mysql.root.password`	mysql
`mysql.user`	mysql
`mysql.password`	mysql
`mysql.allow.empty.password`	no
`mysql.database`	mysql

Use the `vi` editor to create each of the files; for example:

```
sudo vi mysql.root.password
```

Specify the value that is to be used as the root password and save the file with `:wq` as shown in Figure 11-3.

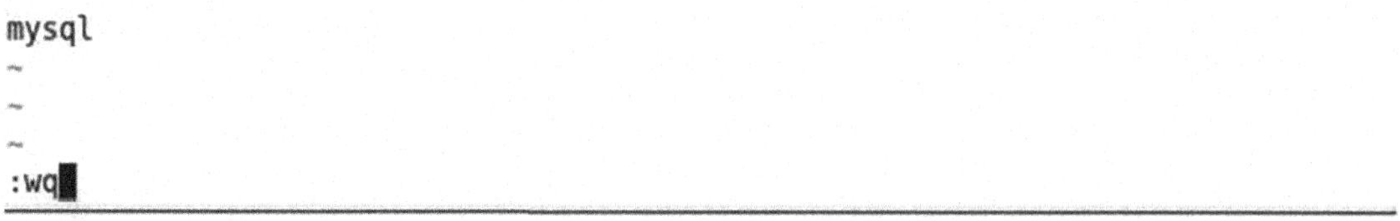

Figure 11-3. *File `mysql.root.password`*

Similarly, the value stored in the `mysql.allow.empty.password` would be `no` as shown in Figure 11-4.

```
no

~
~
:wq
```

Figure 11-4. *File `mysql.allow.empty.password`*

The files are to be created in the directory `/mysql/env`, as shown in Figure 11-5.

```
core@ip-10-0-0-50 /mysql/env $ ls -l
total 32
-rw-r--r--. 1 root root 4 Jul 16 18:52 mysql.allow.empty.password
-rw-r--r--. 1 root root 6 Jul 16 18:51 mysql.password
-rw-r--r--. 1 root root 6 Jul 16 18:50 mysql.root.password
-rw-r--r--. 1 root root 6 Jul 16 18:51 mysql.user
core@ip-10-0-0-50 /mysql/env $
```

Figure 11-5. *Files for generating ConfigMaps*

Create a ConfigMap called `mysql-config` from the directory `/mysql/env`.

```
./kubectl create configmap mysql-config --from-file=/mysql/env
```

The ConfigMap `mysql-config` is created as shown in Figure 11-6.
Describe the ConfigMap:

```
./kubectl describe configmaps mysql-config
```

The configuration data stored in the ConfigMap, which essentially consists of key/value pairs created from the files in the directory, is listed as shown in Figure 11-6.

```
core@ip-10-0-0-50 ~ $  ./kubectl create configmap mysql-config --from-file=/mysq
l/env
configmap "mysql-config" created
core@ip-10-0-0-50 ~ $ ./kubectl describe configmaps mysql-config
Name:           mysql-config
Namespace:      default
Labels:         <none>
Annotations:    <none>

Data
====
mysql.allow.empty.password:     4 bytes
mysql.database:                 6 bytes
mysql.password:                 6 bytes
mysql.root.password:            6 bytes
mysql.user:                     6 bytes


core@ip-10-0-0-50 ~ $
```

Figure 11-6. *Creating a ConfigMap from a directory*

You can list the ConfigMap YAML definition with the following command:

```
./kubectl get configmaps mysql-config -o yaml
```

The `mysql-config` definition file is listed as shown in Figure 11-7.

```
core@ip-10-0-0-50 ~ $ ./kubectl get configmaps mysql-config -o yaml
apiVersion: v1
data:
  mysql.allow.empty.password: |
    no
  mysql.database: |
    mysql
  mysql.password: |
    mysql
  mysql.root.password: |
    mysql
  mysql.user: |
    mysql
kind: ConfigMap
metadata:
  creationTimestamp: 2016-07-16T18:59:18Z
  name: mysql-config
  namespace: default
  resourceVersion: "12088"
  selfLink: /api/v1/namespaces/default/configmaps/mysql-config
  uid: 66015cea-4b87-11e6-ac0d-1241999f191f
core@ip-10-0-0-50 ~ $
```

Figure 11-7. *ConfigMap definition file*

Next, consume the ConfigMap in a replication controller; to do that, create a definition file `mysql.yaml`:

```
sudo vi mysql.yaml
```

Use the config map `mysql-config` to obtain environment variable values for the MySQL database Docker image `mysql`.

```
---
apiVersion: v1
kind: ReplicationController
metadata:
  labels:
    app: mysql-app
  name: mysql
spec:
  replicas: 3
  selector:
    app: mysql-app
  template:
    metadata:
      labels:
        app: mysql-app
    spec:
      containers:
        -
          env:
            -
              name: MYSQL_ROOT_PASSWORD
              valueFrom:
                configMapKeyRef:
                  key: mysql.root.password
                  name: mysql-config
            -
              name: MYSQL_DATABASE
              valueFrom:
                configMapKeyRef:
                  key: mysql.database
                  name: mysql-config
            -
              name: MYSQL_USER
              valueFrom:
                configMapKeyRef:
                  key: mysql.user
                  name: mysql-config
            -
              name: MYSQL_PASSWORD
              valueFrom:
                configMapKeyRef:
                  key: mysql.user
                  name: mysql-config
            -
```

```
        name: MYSQL_ALLOW_EMPTY_PASSWORD
        valueFrom:
          configMapKeyRef:
            key: mysql.allow.empty.password
            name: mysql-config
    image: mysql
    name: mysql
    ports:
      -
        containerPort: 3306
```

The mysql.yaml is shown in the vi editor in Figure 11-8.

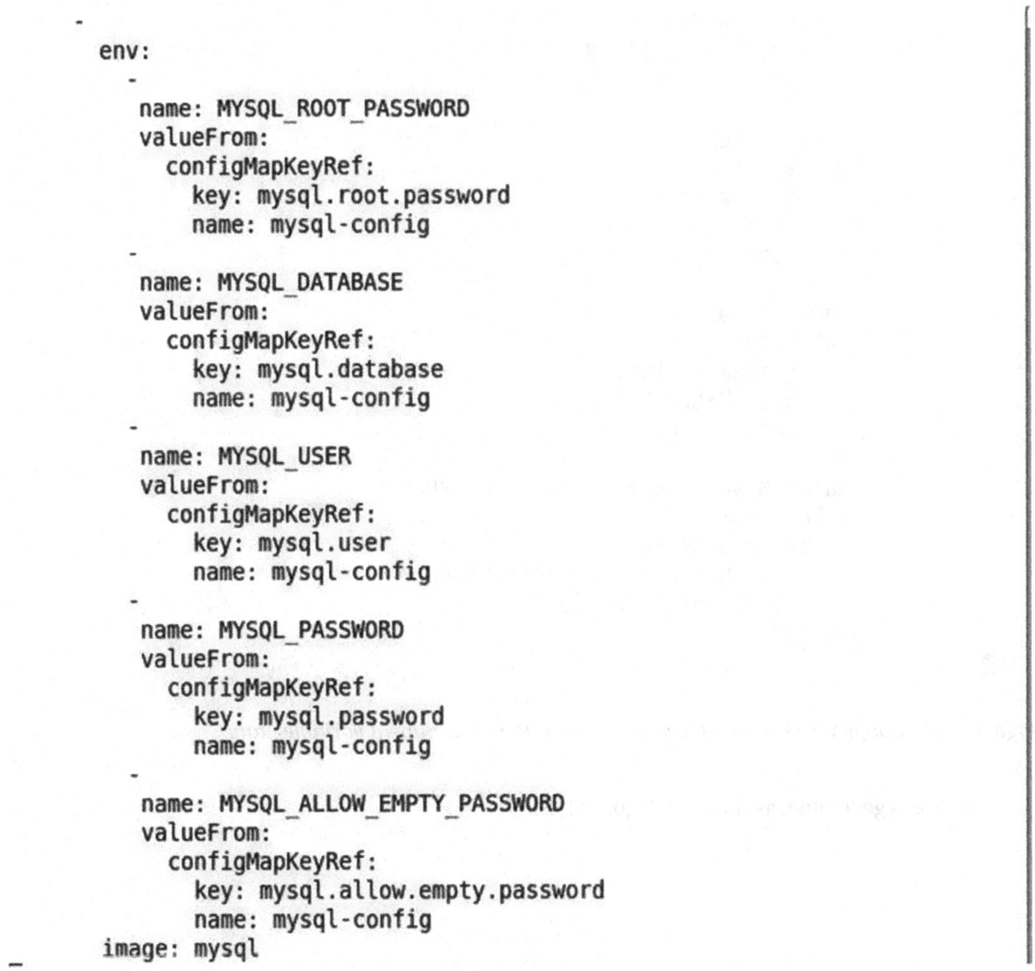

```
-
  env:
    -
      name: MYSQL_ROOT_PASSWORD
      valueFrom:
        configMapKeyRef:
          key: mysql.root.password
          name: mysql-config
    -
      name: MYSQL_DATABASE
      valueFrom:
        configMapKeyRef:
          key: mysql.database
          name: mysql-config
    -
      name: MYSQL_USER
      valueFrom:
        configMapKeyRef:
          key: mysql.user
          name: mysql-config
    -
      name: MYSQL_PASSWORD
      valueFrom:
        configMapKeyRef:
          key: mysql.password
          name: mysql-config
    -
      name: MYSQL_ALLOW_EMPTY_PASSWORD
      valueFrom:
        configMapKeyRef:
          key: mysql.allow.empty.password
          name: mysql-config
  image: mysql
```

Figure 11-8. *Using ConfigMap key reference in an RC definition file*

The key for a ConfigMap may not be any arbitrary name but must follow a specific regexp. To demonstrate, use the key the same as the environment variable name as shown in Figure 11-9.

```
          env:
            -
              name: MYSQL_ROOT_PASSWORD
              valueFrom:
                configMapKeyRef:
                  key: MYSQL_ROOT_PASSWORD
                  name: mysql-config
            -
              name: MYSQL_DATABASE
              valueFrom:
                configMapKeyRef:
                  key: MYSQL_DATABASE
                  name: mysql-config
            -
              name: MYSQL_USER
              valueFrom:
                configMapKeyRef:
                  key: MYSQL_USER
                  name: mysql-config
            -
              name: MYSQL_PASSWORD
              valueFrom:
                configMapKeyRef:
                  key: MYSQL_PASSWORD
                  name: mysql-config
            -
              name: MYSQL_ALLOW_EMPTY_PASSWORD
              valueFrom:
                configMapKeyRef:
                  key: MYSQL_ALLOW_EMPTY_PASSWORD
                  name: mysql-config
          image: mysql
:wq
```

Figure 11-9. *ConfigMap key ref set to same value as the environment variable name*

An error is generated, as shown in Figure 11-10.

```
core@ip-10-0-0-50 ~ $ ./kubectl create -f mysql.yaml
The ReplicationController "mysql" is invalid.

* spec.template.spec.containers[0].env[0].valueFrom.configMapKeyRef.key: Invalid
 value: "MYSQL_ROOT_PASSWORD": must have at most 253 characters and match regex
\.?[a-z0-9]([-a-z0-9]*[a-z0-9])?(\.[a-z0-9]([-a-z0-9]*[a-z0-9])?)*
* spec.template.spec.containers[0].env[1].valueFrom.configMapKeyRef.key: Invalid
 value: "MYSQL_DATABASE": must have at most 253 characters and match regex \.?[a
-z0-9]([-a-z0-9]*[a-z0-9])?(\.[a-z0-9]([-a-z0-9]*[a-z0-9])?)*
* spec.template.spec.containers[0].env[2].valueFrom.configMapKeyRef.key: Invalid
 value: "MYSQL_USER": must have at most 253 characters and match regex \.?[a-z0-
9]([-a-z0-9]*[a-z0-9])?(\.[a-z0-9]([-a-z0-9]*[a-z0-9])?)*
* spec.template.spec.containers[0].env[3].valueFrom.configMapKeyRef.key: Invalid
 value: "MYSQL_PASSWORD": must have at most 253 characters and match regex \.?[a
-z0-9]([-a-z0-9]*[a-z0-9])?(\.[a-z0-9]([-a-z0-9]*[a-z0-9])?)*
* spec.template.spec.containers[0].env[4].valueFrom.configMapKeyRef.key: Invalid
 value: "MYSQL_ALLOW_EMPTY_PASSWORD": must have at most 253 characters and match
 regex \.?[a-z0-9]([-a-z0-9]*[a-z0-9])?(\.[a-z0-9]([-a-z0-9]*[a-z0-9])?)*
core@ip-10-0-0-50 ~ $
```

Figure 11-10. *Error indicating invalid value for ConfigMap key ref*

Delete the `mysql` RC if it already exists and create a replication controller from the definition file with a valid `ConfigMapKeyRef` as in Figure 11-8.

```
./kubectl create -f mysql.yaml
```

List the RC and the pods:

```
./kubectl get rc
./kubectl get pods
```

The RC and pods are created as shown in Figure 11-11.

```
core@ip-10-0-0-50 ~ $ ./kubectl delete rc mysql
replicationcontroller "mysql" deleted
core@ip-10-0-0-50 ~ $ sudo vi mysql.yaml
core@ip-10-0-0-50 ~ $ ./kubectl create -f mysql.yaml
replicationcontroller "mysql" created
core@ip-10-0-0-50 ~ $ ./kubectl get rc
NAME      DESIRED   CURRENT   AGE
mysql     3         3         8s
core@ip-10-0-0-50 ~ $ ./kubectl get pods
NAME          READY     STATUS    RESTARTS   AGE
mysql-1cwns   1/1       Running   0          8s
mysql-5eegy   1/1       Running   0          8s
mysql-unuye   1/1       Running   0          8s
core@ip-10-0-0-50 ~ $
```

Figure 11-11. *Creating a replication controller with a valid definition file*

Creating ConfigMaps from Files

Next, we shall create a ConfigMap using only some of the files in the `/mysql/env` directory. Only the `MYSQL_ROOT_PASSWORD` environment variable is mandatory. As an example, create a ConfigMap called `mysql-config-2` from the `mysql.allow.empty.password` and `mysql.root.password` files.

```
/kubectl create configmap mysql-config-2 --from-file=/mysql/env/mysql.root.password --from-
file=/mysql/env/mysql.allow.empty.password
```

The `mysql-config-2` ConfigMap is created as shown in Figure 11-12. Next, describe the ConfigMap. The two key/value pairs are listed. The ConfigMap may also be listed as a YAML.

```
core@ip-10-0-0-50 ~ $ ./kubectl create configmap mysql-config-2 --from-file=/my
sql/env/mysql.root.password --from-file=/mysql/env/mysql.allow.empty.password
configmap "mysql-config-2" created
core@ip-10-0-0-50 ~ $ ./kubectl describe configmaps mysql-config-2
Name:           mysql-config-2
Namespace:      default
Labels:         <none>
Annotations:    <none>

Data
====
mysql.allow.empty.password:     3 bytes
mysql.root.password:            6 bytes


core@ip-10-0-0-50 ~ $ ./kubectl get configmaps mysql-config-2 -o yaml
apiVersion: v1
data:
  mysql.allow.empty.password: |
    no
  mysql.root.password: |
    mysql
kind: ConfigMap
metadata:
  creationTimestamp: 2016-07-16T19:22:39Z
  name: mysql-config-2
  namespace: default
  resourceVersion: "16040"
  selfLink: /api/v1/namespaces/default/configmaps/mysql-config-2
  uid: a9245c47-4b8a-11e6-ac0d-1241999f191f
core@ip-10-0-0-50 ~ $
```

Figure 11-12. *Creating ConfigMap from files*

Next, consume the ConfigMap in a replication controller definition file `mysql.yaml`.

```
  ---
apiVersion: v1
kind: ReplicationController
metadata:
  labels:
    app: mysql-app
  name: mysql
spec:
  replicas: 3
  selector:
    app: mysql-app
  template:
    metadata:
      labels:
        app: mysql-app
    spec:
      containers:
        -
          env:
            -
              name: MYSQL_ROOT_PASSWORD
              valueFrom:
                configMapKeyRef:
                  key: mysql.root.password
                  name: mysql-config-2

            -
              name: MYSQL_ALLOW_EMPTY_PASSWORD
              valueFrom:
                configMapKeyRef:
                  key: mysql.allow.empty.password
                  name: mysql-config-2
          image: mysql
          name: mysql
          ports:
            -
              containerPort: 3306
```

The `mysql.yaml` definition file is shown in the vi editor in Figure 11-13.

```
---
apiVersion: v1
kind: ReplicationController
metadata:
  labels:
    app: mysql-app
  name: mysql
spec:
  replicas: 3
  selector:
    app: mysql-app
  template:
    metadata:
      labels:
        app: mysql-app
    spec:
      containers:
        -
          env:
            -
              name: MYSQL_ROOT_PASSWORD
              valueFrom:
                configMapKeyRef:
                  key: mysql.root.password
                  name: mysql-config-2
            -
              name: MYSQL_ALLOW_EMPTY_PASSWORD
              valueFrom:
                configMapKeyRef:
                  key: mysql.allow.empty.password
                  name: mysql-config-2
          image: mysql
:wq
```

Figure 11-13. *Consuming ConfigMaps*

Create a replication controller from the definition file:

```
./kubectl create -f mysql.yaml
```

List the RC and the pods:

```
./kubectl get rc
./kubectl get pods
```

The RC and pods are created and listed as shown in Figure 11-14.

```
core@ip-10-0-0-50 ~ $ ./kubectl create -f mysql.yaml
replicationcontroller "mysql" created
core@ip-10-0-0-50 ~ $ ./kubectl get rc
NAME      DESIRED   CURRENT   AGE
mysql     3         3         7s
core@ip-10-0-0-50 ~ $ ./kubectl get pods
NAME          READY     STATUS    RESTARTS   AGE
mysql-96a3s   1/1       Running   0          7s
mysql-b19pk   1/1       Running   0          7s
mysql-mveyp   1/1       Running   0          7s
core@ip-10-0-0-50 ~ $
```

***Figure 11-14.** Creating replication controller and listing pods*

Describe a pod, and the ConfigMap `mysql-config-2` with the data should be listed as shown in Figure 11-15.

```
core@ip-10-0-0-50 ~ $ ./kubectl describe pod mysql-96a3s
Name:           mysql-96a3s
Namespace:      default
Node:           ip-10-0-0-88.ec2.internal/10.0.0.88
Start Time:     Sat, 16 Jul 2016 19:33:38 +0000
Labels:         app=mysql-app
Status:         Running
IP:             10.2.40.2
Controllers:    ReplicationController/mysql
Containers:
  mysql:
    Container ID:       docker://7084958b889c213ad55c58afc5013e290cee5933215e10
6deae90573789f1979
    Image:              mysql
    Image ID:           docker://sha256:1195b21c3a45d9bf93aae497f2538f89a09aade
d18d6648753aa3ce76670f41d
    Port:               3306/TCP
    State:              Running
      Started:          Sat, 16 Jul 2016 19:33:39 +0000
    Ready:              True
    Restart Count:      0
    Environment Variables:
      MYSQL_ROOT_PASSWORD:              <set to the key 'mysql.root.password' o
f config map 'mysql-config-2'>
      MYSQL_ALLOW_EMPTY_PASSWORD:       <set to the key 'mysql.allow.empty.pass
word' of config map 'mysql-config-2'>
Conditions:
  Type          Status
  Ready         True
Volumes:
  default-token-ni84s:
    Type:       Secret (a volume populated by a Secret)
    SecretName: default-token-ni84s
```

***Figure 11-15.** Pod description includes environment variables' values consuming ConfigMaps*

Creating ConfigMaps from Literal Values

In this section we shall create and consume a ConfigMap using literal key/value pairs specified on the command line with the `--from-literal` option. As an example, create a ConfigMap called `hello-config` with two key/value pairs, `message1=hello` and `message2=kubernetes`.

```
kubectl create configmap hello-config --from-literal=message1=hello --from-
literal=message2=kubernetes
```

A ConfigMap `hello-config` with two key/value pairs is created as shown in Figure 11-16. Describe the `configmap` to list the key/values.

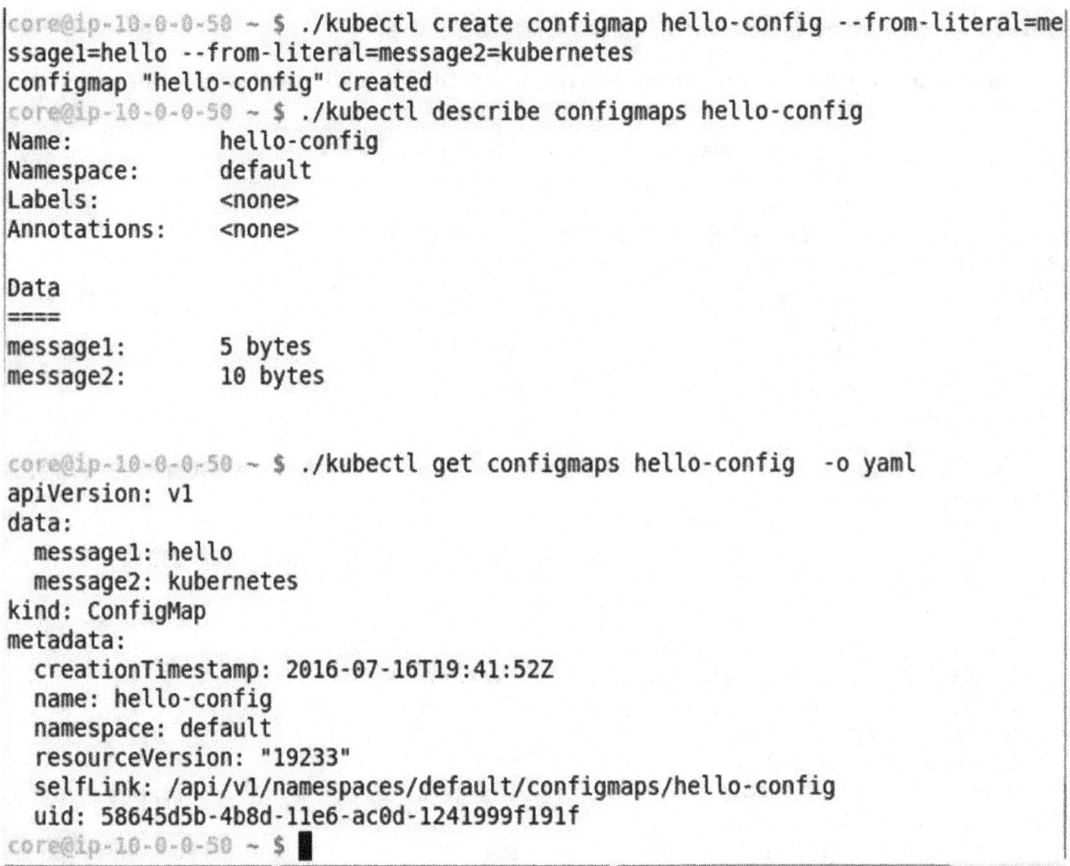

```
core@ip-10-0-0-50 ~ $ ./kubectl create configmap hello-config --from-literal=me
ssage1=hello --from-literal=message2=kubernetes
configmap "hello-config" created
core@ip-10-0-0-50 ~ $ ./kubectl describe configmaps hello-config
Name:           hello-config
Namespace:      default
Labels:         <none>
Annotations:    <none>

Data
====
message1:       5 bytes
message2:       10 bytes


core@ip-10-0-0-50 ~ $ ./kubectl get configmaps hello-config  -o yaml
apiVersion: v1
data:
  message1: hello
  message2: kubernetes
kind: ConfigMap
metadata:
  creationTimestamp: 2016-07-16T19:41:52Z
  name: hello-config
  namespace: default
  resourceVersion: "19233"
  selfLink: /api/v1/namespaces/default/configmaps/hello-config
  uid: 58645d5b-4b8d-11e6-ac0d-1241999f191f
core@ip-10-0-0-50 ~ $ 
```

***Figure 11-16.** Creating ConfigMaps from literal values*

Create a pod definition file `hello-world.yaml` to consume the ConfigMap `hello-world`. The pod is based on the Ubuntu Docker image and runs a `/bin/echo` command with the two configuration properties in the ConfigMap as arguments.

```
---
apiVersion: v1
kind: Pod
metadata:
  labels:
    app: helloApp
  name: hello-world
spec:
  containers:
    -
      args:
        - " $(MESSAGE1)"
        - " $(MESSAGE2)"
      command:
        - /bin/echo
      env:
        -
          name: MESSAGE1
          valueFrom:
            configMapKeyRef:
              key: message1
              name: hello-config
        -
          name: MESSAGE2
          valueFrom:
            configMapKeyRef:
              key: message2
              name: hello-config
      image: ubuntu
      name: hello
```

The pod definition file `hello.yaml` is shown in the `vi` editor in Figure 11-17.

```
metadata:
  labels:
    app: helloApp
  name: hello-world
spec:
  containers:
    -
      args:
        - " $(MESSAGE1)"
        - " $(MESSAGE2)"
      command:
        - /bin/echo
      env:
        -
          name: MESSAGE1
          valueFrom:
            configMapKeyRef:
              key: message1
              name: hello-config
        -
          name: MESSAGE2
          valueFrom:
            configMapKeyRef:
              key: message2
              name: hello-config
      image: ubuntu
      name: hello

:wq
```

Figure 11-17. *Pod definition file consuming ConfigMaps*

List the ConfigMap `hello-world`. The ConfigMap has two data key/value pairs.

Create a pod from the definition file:

```
./kubectl create -f hello-world.yaml
```

List the pods:

```
./kubectl get pods
```

The `hello-world` pod is listed as `Completed` as shown in Figure 11-18.

```
core@ip-10-0-0-50 ~ $ ./kubectl get configmaps hello-config  -o yaml
apiVersion: v1
data:
  message1: hello
  message2: kubernetes
kind: ConfigMap
metadata:
  creationTimestamp: 2016-07-16T19:41:52Z
  name: hello-config
  namespace: default
  resourceVersion: "19233"
  selfLink: /api/v1/namespaces/default/configmaps/hello-config
  uid: 58645d5b-4b8d-11e6-ac0d-1241999f191f
core@ip-10-0-0-50 ~ $ sudo vi hello-world.yaml
core@ip-10-0-0-50 ~ $  ./kubectl create -f hello-world.yaml
pod "hello-world" created
core@ip-10-0-0-50 ~ $ ./kubectl get pods
NAME           READY     STATUS              RESTARTS   AGE
hello-world    0/1       ContainerCreating   0          9s
mysql-t316q    1/1       Running             0          6m
mysql-wwei3    1/1       Running             0          6m
mysql-xsnjt    1/1       Running             0          6m
core@ip-10-0-0-50 ~ $ ./kubectl get pods
NAME           READY     STATUS      RESTARTS   AGE
hello-world    0/1       Completed   0          18s
mysql-t316q    1/1       Running     0          6m
mysql-wwei3    1/1       Running     0          6m
mysql-xsnjt    1/1       Running     0          6m
core@ip-10-0-0-50 ~ $
```

Figure 11-18. *Creating pod-consuming ConfigMaps*

List the logs generated from the pod:

```
./kubectl logs hello-world
```

The message generated from the two key/value pairs should be output as shown in Figure 11-19.

```
core@ip-10-0-0-50 ~ $ ./kubectl get pods
NAME           READY     STATUS      RESTARTS   AGE
hello-world    0/1       Completed   0          18s
mysql-t316q    1/1       Running     0          6m
mysql-wwei3    1/1       Running     0          6m
mysql-xsnjt    1/1       Running     0          6m
core@ip-10-0-0-50 ~ $ ./kubectl logs hello-world
 hello  kubernetes
core@ip-10-0-0-50 ~ $
```

Figure 11-19. *Pod logs include the message generated using ConfigMaps*

Consuming a ConfigMap in a Volume

In this section we shall create a ConfigMap to store a certificate key-value pair and consume the ConfigMap in a volume. Create a definition file `cert.yaml` for a ConfigMap in which to specify the certificate.

```
apiVersion: v1
kind: ConfigMap
metadata:
  name: nginx-cert
data:
  cert.pem: |-
    -----BEGIN CERTIFICATE-----
    abc
    -----END CERTIFICATE-----
  privkey.pem: |-
    -----BEGIN PRIVATE KEY-----
    abc
    -----END PRIVATE KEY-----
```

The ConfigMap definition file is shown in the vi editor in Figure 11-20.

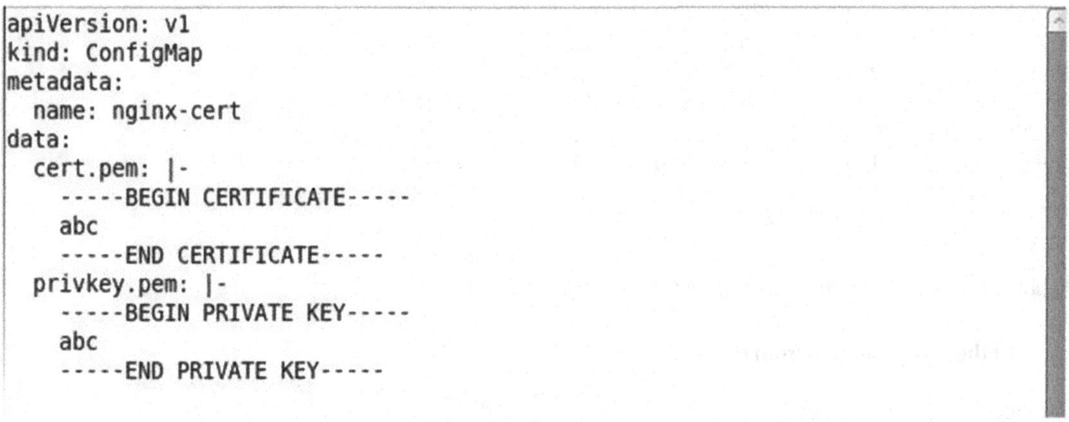

```
apiVersion: v1
kind: ConfigMap
metadata:
  name: nginx-cert
data:
  cert.pem: |-
    -----BEGIN CERTIFICATE-----
    abc
    -----END CERTIFICATE-----
  privkey.pem: |-
    -----BEGIN PRIVATE KEY-----
    abc
    -----END PRIVATE KEY-----
```

***Figure 11-20.** ConfigMap to store a certificate key-value pair*

Create a ConfigMap from the definition file as shown in Figure 11-21.

```
./kubectl create -f cert.yaml
```

Describe the ConfigMap to list the two key/value pairs as shown in Figure 11-21.

```
core@ip-10-0-0-50 ~ $ sudo vi cert.yaml
core@ip-10-0-0-50 ~ $ ./kubectl create -f cert.yaml
configmap "nginx-cert" created
core@ip-10-0-0-50 ~ $ ./kubectl get configmaps nginx-cert -o yaml
apiVersion: v1
data:
  cert.pem: |-
    -----BEGIN CERTIFICATE-----
    abc
    -----END CERTIFICATE-----
  privkey.pem: |-
    -----BEGIN PRIVATE KEY-----
    abc
    -----END PRIVATE KEY-----
kind: ConfigMap
metadata:
  creationTimestamp: 2016-07-16T20:52:47Z
  name: nginx-cert
  namespace: default
  resourceVersion: "30843"
  selfLink: /api/v1/namespaces/default/configmaps/nginx-cert
  uid: 408e0916-4b97-11e6-ac0d-1241999f191f
core@ip-10-0-0-50 ~ $ ./kubectl describe configmaps nginx-cert
Name:           nginx-cert
Namespace:      default
Labels:         <none>
Annotations:    <none>

Data
====
privkey.pem:    57 bytes
cert.pem:       57 bytes
```

Figure 11-21. *Creating and listing a ConfigMap storing key/value pairs*

Next, consume the ConfigMap in a pod. Create a volume of type ConfigMap from the `nginx-cert` ConfigMap. Mount the volume in the pod at some directory `cert` from which the certificate can be retrieved, such as `/etc/config/`.

```
---
apiVersion: v1
kind: Pod
metadata:
  name: configmap-volume
spec:
  containers:
    -
      image: nginx
      name: nginx
      volumeMounts:
        -
```

```
        mountPath: /etc/config/cert
        name: config-volume
        readOnly: true
    volumes:
      -
        configMap:
          name: nginx-cert
        name: config-volume
```

The pod definition file is shown in the vi editor in Figure 11-22.

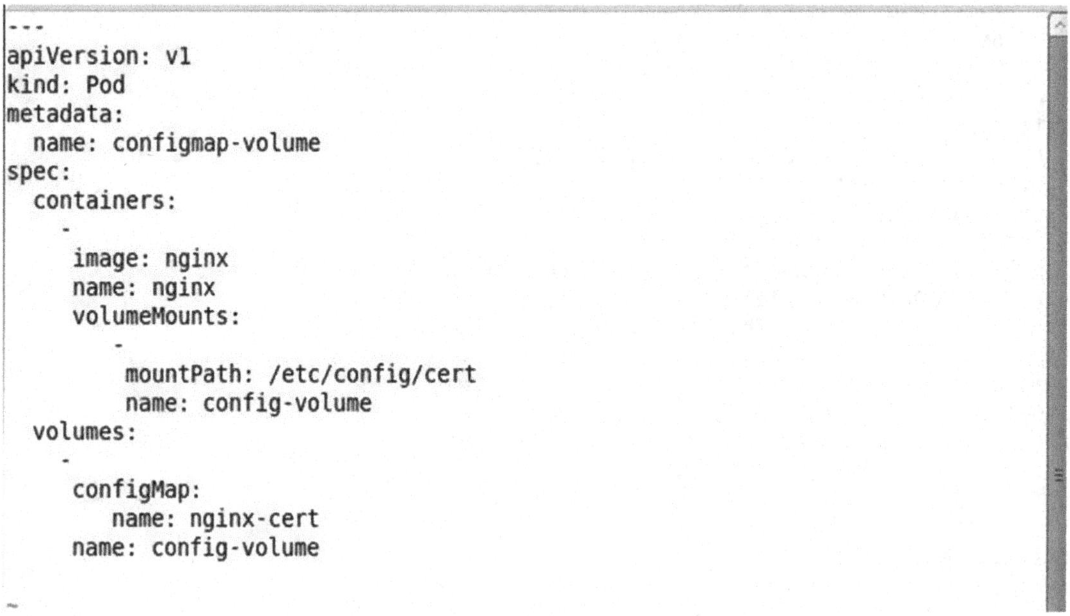

```
---
apiVersion: v1
kind: Pod
metadata:
  name: configmap-volume
spec:
  containers:
    -
      image: nginx
      name: nginx
      volumeMounts:
        -
          mountPath: /etc/config/cert
          name: config-volume
  volumes:
    -
      configMap:
        name: nginx-cert
      name: config-volume
~
```

Figure 11-22. *Pod consuming a ConfigMap in a volume mount*

Create a pod from the definition file and list the pods as shown in Figure 11-23.

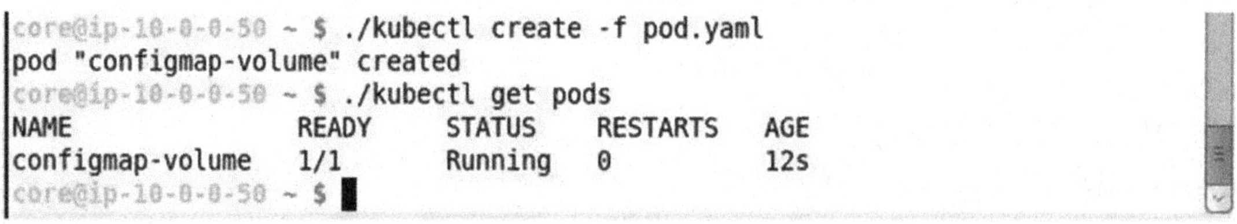

```
core@ip-10-0-0-50 ~ $ ./kubectl create -f pod.yaml
pod "configmap-volume" created
core@ip-10-0-0-50 ~ $ ./kubectl get pods
NAME               READY     STATUS    RESTARTS   AGE
configmap-volume   1/1       Running   0          12s
core@ip-10-0-0-50 ~ $
```

Figure 11-23. *Creating and listing a pod*

Describe the pod to list the volume of type ConfigMap as shown in Figure 11-24.

```
core@ip-10-0-0-50 ~ $ ./kubectl get pods
NAME               READY     STATUS    RESTARTS   AGE
configmap-volume   1/1       Running   0          12s
core@ip-10-0-0-50 ~ $ ./kubectl describe pod configmap-volume
Name:           configmap-volume
Namespace:      default
Node:           ip-10-0-0-88.ec2.internal/10.0.0.88
Start Time:     Sat, 16 Jul 2016 20:56:47 +0000
Labels:         <none>
Status:         Running
IP:             10.2.40.2
Controllers:    <none>
Containers:
  nginx:
    Container ID:               docker://aa7d39f31c6d8946837cb546bd05772d0b5a63
019afb8e65b8eb719fe5b5dc70
    Image:                      nginx
    Image ID:                   docker://sha256:0d409d33b27e47423b049f7f863faa0
8655a8c901749c2b25b93ca67d01a470d
    Port:
    State:                      Running
      Started:                  Sat, 16 Jul 2016 20:56:48 +0000
    Ready:                      True
    Restart Count:              0
    Environment Variables:      <none>
Conditions:
  Type          Status
  Ready         True
Volumes:
  config-volume:
    Type:       ConfigMap (a volume populated by a ConfigMap)
    Name:       nginx-cert
```

Figure 11-24. *Pod description lists volume of type ConfigMap*

Summary

In this chapter we introduced ConfigMaps, which are maps of configuration properties that may be used in Kubernetes object definitions such as pods, replication controllers, and also to set environment variables and command arguments. Subsequently we discussed creating ConfigMaps from directories, files, and literal values, and finally consuming the ConfigMaps. In the next chapter we shall discuss setting resource quotas.

CHAPTER 12

Using Resource Quotas

In Chapter 10 we introduced a resource consumption model based on *requests* and *limits,* using which resources (CPU and memory) are allocated to a pod's containers.

Problem

Although we discussed allocating resources to a pod's containers, we did not take some other factors into consideration. The resource requirements vary from one development team to another. If one development team were to use all or most of the resources on a node, another team would not be able to run any application on the same node. Second, the resource requirements vary across the different phases of application development. Application development would have different resource usage than application testing and application in-production work. The resource allocation pattern discussed in Chapter 10 does not provide a solution for any of these factors.

Solution

Kubernetes provides a management design pattern for elastic quotas. Elastic quotas are not completely elastic, and a fixed upper limit that is flexible to some extent based on the scope (discussed later in this chapter) is imposed. Resource quotas are a specification for limiting the use of certain resources in a particular namespace. The quota is not on a particular object, such as a pod or a replication controller, but on the aggregate use within a namespace. The objective is to provide a fair share of resources to different teams, with each team assigned a namespace with quotas. Another application of quotas is creating different namespaces for production, development, and testing; different phases of application development have different resource requirements. Creating or updating a resource should not exceed the quota restraint, failing which the resource is not created or updated, and an error message is generated. Quotas could be set on compute resources (CPU and memory), which were discussed in chapter 10, and object counts (such as pods, replication controllers, services, load balancers, and ConfigMaps, to list a few). When a quota is set for compute resources, requests or limits must be specified for those resources. Quotas are enabled by default. The total cluster capacity, which could vary if nodes are added or removed, is not a limiting factor when setting quotas. The total of the quotas of namespaces could exceed the cluster capacity, and resource contention will be resolved on a first-come-first-served basis. Resource contention is resolved before a resource is created and does not affect resources already created. Once a resource has been created, any changes to the quota setting do not affect the resource.

D. Vohra, *Kubernetes Management Design Patterns*, DOI 10.1007/978-1-4842-2598-1_12

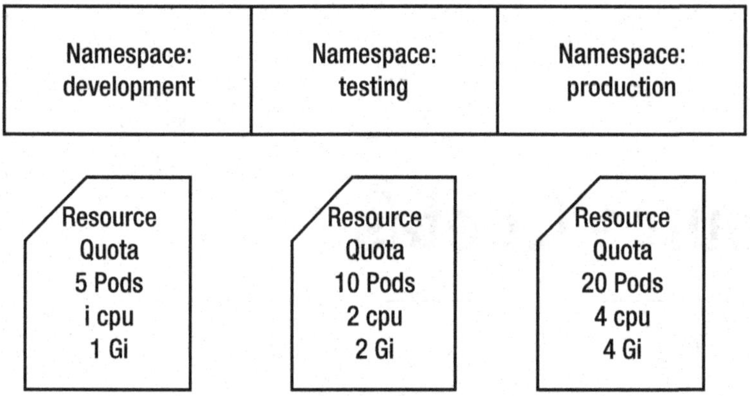

Figure 12-1. *Different resource quotas for different namespaces*

A quota could optionally be associated with a scope, which further limits the types of resources a quota would be applied to. The available scopes are `Terminating`, `NotTerminating`, `BestEffort`, and `NotBestEffort`. `Terminating` scope is for pods that terminate, and `NotTerminating` scope is for pods that do not terminate. `BestEffort` scope is for pods that have best-effort quality of service, and `NotBestEffort` scope is for pods that do not have a best-effort quality of service. The resource quota spec fields are discussed in Table 12-1.

Table 12-1. *Resource Quota Spec Fields*

Field	Description
`kind`	Should be set to `ResourceQuota`.
`apiVersion`	Schema version.
`metadata`	Metadata such as name, labels, and annotations.
`spec`	The `ResourceQuota` spec provides two fields: `hard`, which specifies the hard limits for each defined resource, and `scopes`, which sets the scopes. A quota measures the usage of a resource only if it matches the intersection of the scopes. The spec defines the desired settings for `hard` limits.
`status`	The `status` is the actual use of resources and is set with `hard` and `used`. The `hard` status is the enforced hard limits, and `used` is the actual total usage of a resource in a namespace. The `status` values are those actually implemented in contrast to the desired settings in the spec.

Overview

In this chapter we will discuss using resource quotas with Kubernetes applications. This chapter covers the following topics.

Setting the environment

Defining compute resource quotas

Exceeding compute resource quotas

Defining object quotas

Exceeding object resource quotas

Defining best-effort quotas

Using quotas

Exceeding object quotas

Exceeding the ConfigMaps quota

Setting the Environment

Create a Kubernetes cluster with an AWS CloudFormation with one controller node and three worker nodes as shown in Figure 12-2.

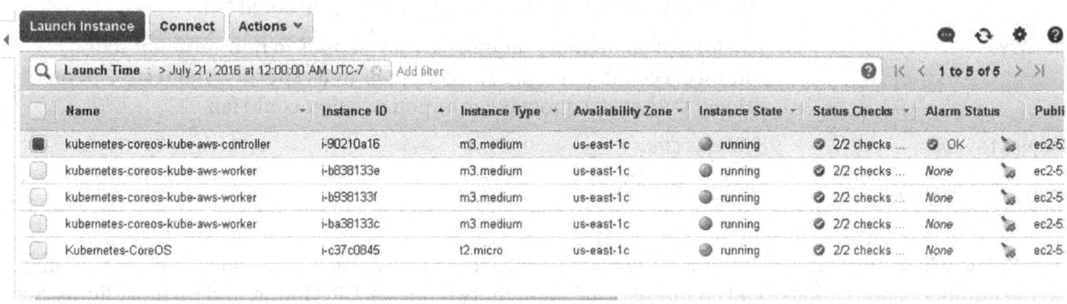

Figure 12-2. *CloudFormation for a Kubernetes cluster on CoreOS*

SSH log in to the controller instance, install `kubectl` binaries, and list the nodes:

```
./kubectl get nodes
```

The controller instance and the worker nodes should be listed as shown in Figure 12-3.

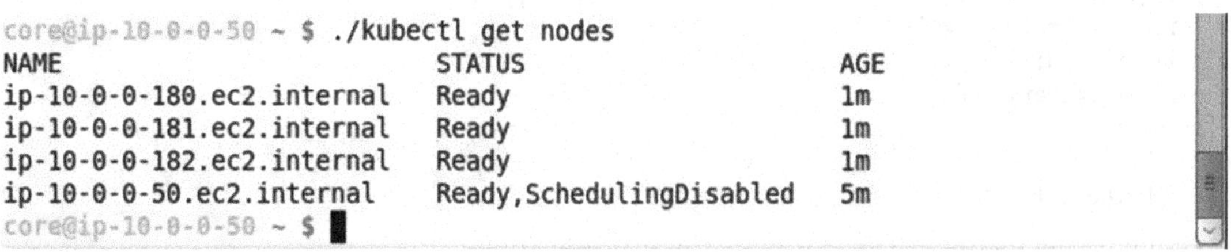

core@ip-10-0-0-50 ~ $ ./kubectl get nodes
NAME STATUS AGE
ip-10-0-0-180.ec2.internal Ready 1m
ip-10-0-0-181.ec2.internal Ready 1m
ip-10-0-0-182.ec2.internal Ready 1m
ip-10-0-0-50.ec2.internal Ready,SchedulingDisabled 5m
core@ip-10-0-0-50 ~ $

Figure 12-3. *Listing the Kubernetes cluster nodes*

Defining Compute Resource Quotas

The compute resource quotas limit the total compute resources used by pods in a namespace. Table 12-2 lists the compute resources supported.

Table 12-2. *Supported Compute Resources*

Compute Resource	Description
`cpu`	The total of all `cpu` requests across all pods in non-terminal state cannot exceed this setting. The container must specify a requests->CPU value if the `cpu` quota is set, or pod creation could fail.
`limits.cpu`	The total of all CPU limits across all pods in non-terminal state cannot exceed this setting. The container must specify a limits->CPU value if the `limits.cpu` quota is set, or pod creation could fail.
`limits.memory`	The total of all memory limits across all pods in non-terminal state cannot exceed this setting. The container must specify a limits->memory value if the `limits.memory` quota is set, or pod creation could fail.
`memory`	The total of all memory requests across all pods in non-terminal state cannot exceed this setting. The container must specify a requests->memory value if the `memory` quota is set. or pod creation could fail.
`requests.cpu`	Same as `cpu`.
`requests.memory`	Same as `memory`.

Create a ResourceQuota definition file `compute-resource-quotas.yaml`. In the spec field set hard limits on the number of pods, total of CPU requests, total of memory requests, CPU limits, and memory limits. Set `NotBestEffort` as a scope in the `scopes` list.

```
apiVersion: v1
kind: ResourceQuota
metadata:
  name: compute-resource-quotas
spec:
  hard:
    pods: "10"
    requests.cpu: "1"
    requests.memory: 2Gi
    limits.cpu: "2"
    limits.memory: 4Gi
  scopes:
    -
      NotBestEffort
```

The definition file is shown in the `vi` editor in Figure 12-4.

```
apiVersion: v1
kind: ResourceQuota
metadata:
  name: compute-resource-quotas
spec:
  hard:
    pods: "10"
    requests.cpu: "1"
    requests.memory: 2Gi
    limits.cpu: "2"
    limits.memory: 4Gi
  scopes:
     -
      NotBestEffort

~
```

Figure 12-4. *ResourceQuota definition file*

Create the ResourceQuota in the default namespace:

```
./kubectl create -f compute-resource-quotas.yaml --namespace=default
```

The ResourceQuota is created as shown in Figure 12-5.

```
core@ip-10-0-0-50 ~ $ sudo vi compute-resource-quotas.yaml
core@ip-10-0-0-50 ~ $ ./kubectl create -f compute-resource-quotas.yaml --namespa
ce=default
resourcequota "compute-resource-quotas" created
core@ip-10-0-0-50 ~ $
```

Figure 12-5. *Creating a ResourceQuota*

List the quotas:

```
./kubectl get quota --namespace=default
```

The `compute-resource-quotas` quota should be listed as shown in Figure 12-6.

```
core@ip-10-0-0-50 ~ $ ./kubectl get quota --namespace=default
NAME                      AGE
compute-resource-quotas   24s
core@ip-10-0-0-50 ~ $
```

Figure 12-6. *Listing the quotas in the default namespace*

Describe the quota compute-resource-quotas:

```
./kubectl describe quota compute-resource-quotas --namespace=default
```

The quota description includes the used resources and hard limits. Because we have not yet created any resource, the Used column values are all 0, as shown in Figure 12-7.

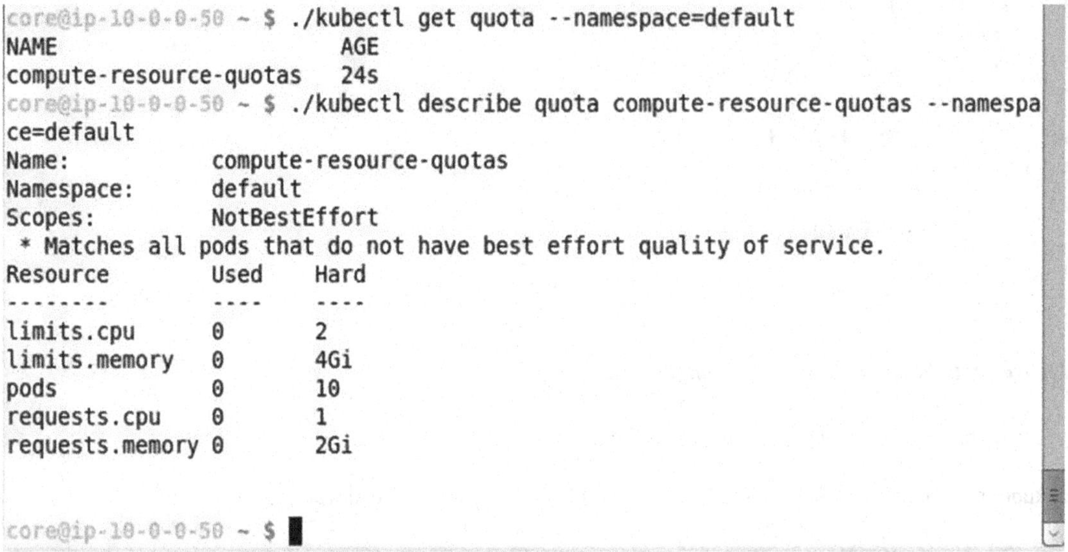
core@ip-10-0-0-50 ~ $ ./kubectl get quota --namespace=default
NAME AGE
compute-resource-quotas 24s
core@ip-10-0-0-50 ~ $ ./kubectl describe quota compute-resource-quotas --namespace=default
Name: compute-resource-quotas
Namespace: default
Scopes: NotBestEffort
* Matches all pods that do not have best effort quality of service.
Resource Used Hard
-------- ---- ----
limits.cpu 0 2
limits.memory 0 4Gi
pods 0 10
requests.cpu 0 1
requests.memory 0 2Gi
core@ip-10-0-0-50 ~ $

Figure 12-7. *Describing compute-resource-quotas*

Exceeding Compute Resource Quotas

Next, we shall use the resource quotas to limit the use of compute resources in the default namespace. Create an RC definition file mysql.yaml:

```
---
apiVersion: v1
kind: ReplicationController
metadata:
  name: mysql-rc
  labels:
    app: mysql-app
spec:
  replicas: 3
  selector:
    app: mysql-app
    deployment: v1
  template:
    metadata:
      labels:
        app: mysql-app
```

```
        deployment: v1
    spec:
      containers:
        -
          env:
            -
              name: MYSQL_ROOT_PASSWORD
              value: mysql
          image: mysql
          name: mysql
          ports:
            -
              containerPort: 3306
          resources:
            requests:
              memory: "640Mi"
              cpu: "500m"
            limits:
              memory: "1280Mi"
              cpu: "2"
```

Create a replication controller with 10 replicas:

```
./kubectl scale rc mysql-rc --replicas=10
```

Next, describe the compute-resource-quotas. The Used column lists the actual used resources. None of the used resources exceed the hard limits, as shown in Figure 12-8.

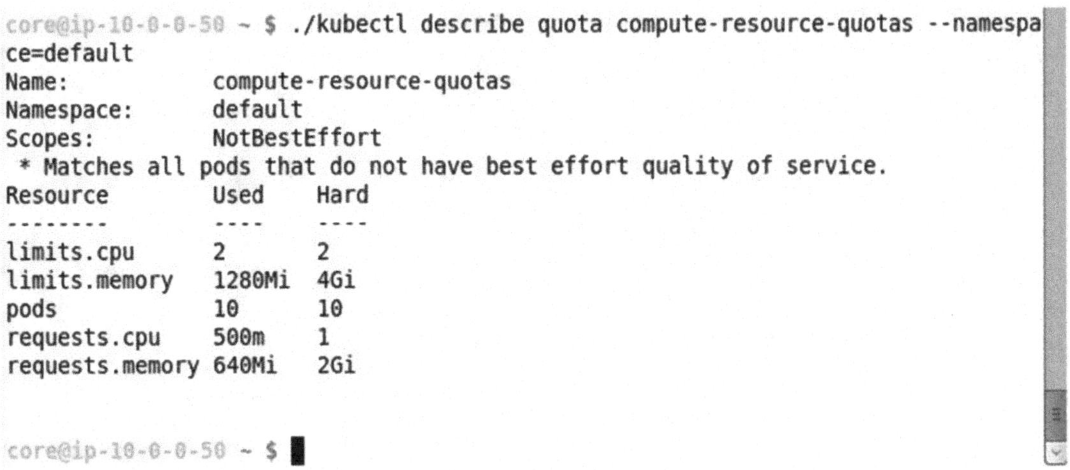

```
core@ip-10-0-0-50 ~ $ ./kubectl describe quota compute-resource-quotas --namespa
ce=default
Name:           compute-resource-quotas
Namespace:      default
Scopes:         NotBestEffort
 * Matches all pods that do not have best effort quality of service.
Resource        Used    Hard
--------        ----    ----
limits.cpu      2       2
limits.memory   1280Mi  4Gi
pods            10      10
requests.cpu    500m    1
requests.memory 640Mi   2Gi


core@ip-10-0-0-50 ~ $
```

Figure 12-8. *Used resources do not exceed the hard limits*

To demonstrate that hard limits cannot be exceeded, scale the RC to 20 replicas:

```
./kubectl scale rc mysql-rc --replicas=20
```

Now describe the `compute-resources-quota`. The Used column still has 10 in the pods row, as shown in Figure 12-9.

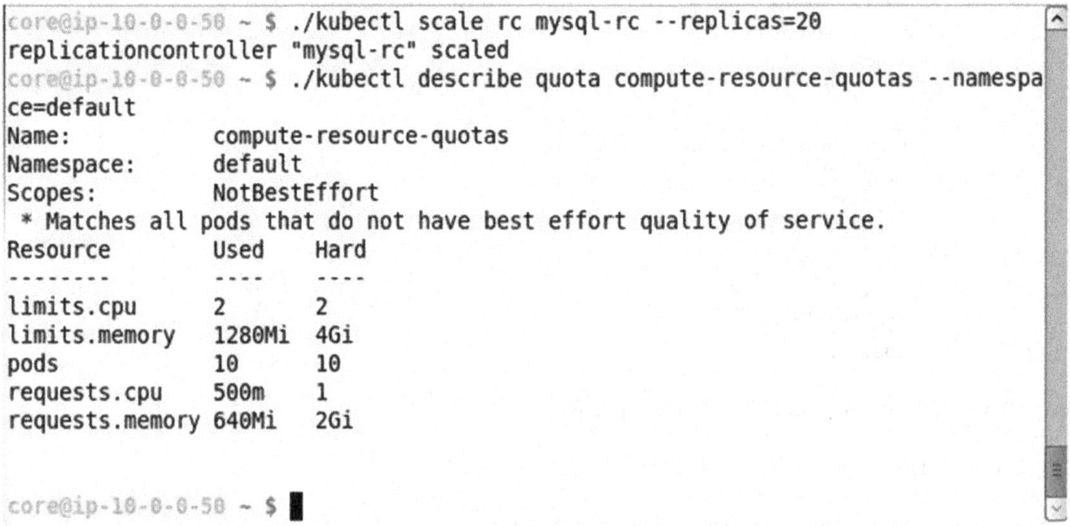

```
core@ip-10-0-0-50 ~ $ ./kubectl scale rc mysql-rc --replicas=20
replicationcontroller "mysql-rc" scaled
core@ip-10-0-0-50 ~ $ ./kubectl describe quota compute-resource-quotas --namespa
ce=default
Name:            compute-resource-quotas
Namespace:       default
Scopes:          NotBestEffort
 * Matches all pods that do not have best effort quality of service.
Resource         Used    Hard
--------         ----    ----
limits.cpu       2       2
limits.memory    1280Mi  4Gi
pods             10      10
requests.cpu     500m    1
requests.memory  640Mi   2Gi


core@ip-10-0-0-50 ~ $
```

Figure 12-9. *Pods not exceeding the hard limit even though scaled to do so*

Describe the RC, and you'll see that Replicas are listed as 10 current / 20 desired, as shown in Figure 12-10.

```
core@ip-10-0-0-50 ~ $ ./kubectl scale rc mysql-rc --replicas=20
replicationcontroller "mysql-rc" scaled
core@ip-10-0-0-50 ~ $ ./kubectl describe rc mysql-rc
Name:           mysql-rc
Namespace:      default
Image(s):       mysql
Selector:       app=mysql-app,deployment=v1
Labels:         app=mysql-app
Replicas:       10 current / 20 desired
Pods Status:    10 Running / 0 Waiting / 0 Succeeded / 0 Failed
No volumes.
Events:
  FirstSeen     LastSeen        Count   From                            Subobjec
tPath   Type            Reason                  Message
  ---------     --------        -----   ----                            --------
-----   --------        ------                  -------
  23m           23m             1       {replication-controller }              N
ormal           SuccessfulCreate        Created pod: mysql-rc-1nyks
  23m           23m             1       {replication-controller }              N
ormal           SuccessfulCreate        Created pod: mysql-rc-h2q9h
  23m           23m             1       {replication-controller }              N
ormal           SuccessfulCreate        Created pod: mysql-rc-rgxzs
  22m           22m             1       {replication-controller }              N
ormal           SuccessfulCreate        Created pod: mysql-rc-y6cvy
  22m           22m             1       {replication-controller }              N
ormal           SuccessfulCreate        Created pod: mysql-rc-5j4gp
  22m           22m             1       {replication-controller }              N
ormal           SuccessfulCreate        Created pod: mysql-rc-xhf84
  22m           22m             1       {replication-controller }              N
```

Figure 12-10. *Describing the replication controller: 10 current replicas instead of the 20 desired*

List the pods cluster-wide, and you may see some of the pods being terminated or restarted if some other compute resource is exceeded, as shown in Figure 12-11.

```
core@ip-10-0-0-50 ~ $ ./kubectl get pods -o wide
NAME             READY     STATUS             RESTARTS   AGE       IP            N
ODE
mysql-rc-1nyks   1/1       Running            4          5m        10.2.26.2     i
p-10-0-0-180.ec2.internal
mysql-rc-5911t   0/1       CrashLoopBackOff   3          4m        10.2.47.4     i
p-10-0-0-182.ec2.internal
mysql-rc-5j4gp   0/1       CrashLoopBackOff   3          4m        10.2.47.3     i
p-10-0-0-182.ec2.internal
mysql-rc-h2q9h   0/1       CrashLoopBackOff   4          5m        10.2.98.3     i
p-10-0-0-181.ec2.internal
mysql-rc-k07te   1/1       Running            3          4m        10.2.26.6     i
p-10-0-0-180.ec2.internal
mysql-rc-rgxzs   1/1       Running            4          5m        10.2.26.3     i
p-10-0-0-180.ec2.internal
mysql-rc-uf3za   1/1       Running            3          4m        10.2.26.5     i
p-10-0-0-180.ec2.internal
mysql-rc-xhf84   1/1       Running            3          4m        10.2.26.4     i
p-10-0-0-180.ec2.internal
mysql-rc-xj2oj   1/1       Running            4          4m        10.2.98.5     i
p-10-0-0-181.ec2.internal
mysql-rc-y6cvy   1/1       Running            4          4m        10.2.98.4     i
p-10-0-0-181.ec2.internal
core@ip-10-0-0-50 ~ $
```

Figure 12-11. *Pods terminated or restarted if some resource is exceeded*

Defining Object Quotas

In this section we will set object quotas and demonstrate what happens when the object quotas are exceeded: the resource object is not created. Create a ResourceQuota definition file `object-quotas.yaml`. Specify hard limits for the number of ConfigMaps, replication controllers, and services:

```
apiVersion: v1
kind: ResourceQuota
metadata:
  name: object-quotas
spec:
  hard:
    configmaps: "5"
    replicationcontrollers: "1"
    services: "2"
```

The definition file is shown in the `vi` editor in Figure 12-12.

```
apiVersion: v1
kind: ResourceQuota
metadata:
  name: object-quotas
spec:
  hard:
    configmaps: "5"
    replicationcontrollers: "1"
    services: "2"
```

Figure 12-12. *ResourceQuota definition file for object quotas*

Create the ResourceQuota from the definition file in the default namespace as shown in Figure 12-13.

```
./kubectl create -f  object-quotas.yaml --namespace=default
```

Then list and describe the quota:

```
./kubectl get quota --namespace=default
./kubectl describe quota object-quotas --namespace=default
```

The resource quota is created and listed as shown in Figure 12-13. The quota description includes the Used resources and Hard limits.

```
core@ip-10-0-0-50 ~ $ ./kubectl create -f  object-quotas.yaml --namespace=defaul
t
resourcequota "object-quotas" created
core@ip-10-0-0-50 ~ $ ./kubectl get quota --namespace=default
NAME                      AGE
compute-resource-quotas   10m
object-quotas             12s
core@ip-10-0-0-50 ~ $ ./kubectl describe quota object-quotas --namespace=default
Name:                   object-quotas
Namespace:              default
Resource                Used    Hard
--------                ----    ----
configmaps              0       5
replicationcontrollers  0       1
services                1       2


core@ip-10-0-0-50 ~ $
```

Figure 12-13. *Creating, listing, and describing the resource quota for object quotas*

Exceeding Object Quotas

In this section we will demonstrate that object quotas cannot be exceeded; instead, the resource object that would exceed the hard limit is not created. First, create an RC definition file `mysql-rc.yaml`.

```
---
apiVersion: v1
kind: ReplicationController
metadata:
  name: mysql-rc
  labels:
    app: mysql-app
spec:
  replicas: 3
  selector:
    app: mysql-app
    deployment: v1
  template:
    metadata:
      labels:
        app: mysql-app
        deployment: v1
    spec:
      containers:
        -
          env:
            -
              name: MYSQL_ROOT_PASSWORD
              value: mysql
          image: mysql
          name: mysql
          ports:
            -
              containerPort: 3306
          resources:
            requests:
              memory: "64Mi"
              cpu: "0.1"
            limits:
              memory: "128Mi"
              cpu: "0.2"
```

The definition file is shown in the vi editor in Figure 12-14.

```
    app: mysql-app
spec:
  replicas: 3
  selector:
    app: mysql-app
    deployment: v1
  template:
    metadata:
      labels:
        app: mysql-app
        deployment: v1
    spec:
      containers:
        -
          env:
            -
              name: MYSQL_ROOT_PASSWORD
              value: mysql
          image: mysql
          name: mysql
          ports:
            -
              containerPort: 3306
          resources:
             requests:
               memory: "64Mi"
               cpu: ".1"
             limits:
               memory: "128Mi"
               cpu: ".2"

:wq
```

Figure 12-14. *ReplicationController definition file*

Create the RC and list the RC and pods as shown in Figure 12-15.

```
core@ip-10-0-0-50 ~ $ ./kubectl get pods -o wide
NAME              READY     STATUS     RESTARTS    AGE         IP            NODE
mysql-rc-b6j4o    1/1       Running    0           29s         10.2.26.2     ip-10-0-0-
180.ec2.internal
mysql-rc-t09up    1/1       Running    0           28s         10.2.47.3     ip-10-0-0-
182.ec2.internal
mysql-rc-zxdun    1/1       Running    0           29s         10.2.98.3     ip-10-0-0-
181.ec2.internal
core@ip-10-0-0-50 ~ $
```

Figure 12-15. *Creating and listing an RC*

Listing the pods cluster-wide indicates that each of the pods was scheduled on a different node, as shown in Figure 12-16.

```
core@ip-10-0-0-50 ~ $ ./kubectl get pods -o wide
NAME              READY     STATUS    RESTARTS   AGE       IP           NODE
mysql-rc-b6j4o    1/1       Running   0          29s       10.2.26.2    ip-10-0-0-
180.ec2.internal
mysql-rc-t09up    1/1       Running   0          28s       10.2.47.3    ip-10-0-0-
182.ec2.internal
mysql-rc-zxdun    1/1       Running   0          29s       10.2.98.3    ip-10-0-0-
181.ec2.internal
core@ip-10-0-0-50 ~ $
```

Figure 12-16. *Each of the three pods is scheduled on a different node, keeping in consideration the resource consumption*

Next, create another replication controller from another RC definition file, similar to the first. The second RC is not created, and the error message indicates that the `object-quotas` quota is exceeded, as shown in Figure 12-17.

```
core@ip-10-0-0-50 ~ $ sudo vi mysql2.yaml
core@ip-10-0-0-50 ~ $ ./kubectl create -f mysql2.yaml
Error from server: error when creating "mysql2.yaml": replicationcontrollers "my
sql-rc2" is forbidden: Exceeded quota: object-quotas, requested: replicationcont
rollers=1, used: replicationcontrollers=1, limited: replicationcontrollers=1
core@ip-10-0-0-50 ~ $
```

Figure 12-17. *Error message indicates that the `object-quotas` quota is exceeded for `replicationcontrollers`*

The hard limit on the number of services is 2. Create one service and create another with a different name than the default. The second service is not created, and the error message indicates that the `object-quota` quota is being exceeded, as shown in Figure 12-18.

```
core@ip-10-0-0-50 ~ $ ./kubectl expose rc mysql-rc --port=3306 --type=LoadBalanc
er
service "mysql-rc" exposed
core@ip-10-0-0-50 ~ $ ./kubectl expose rc mysql-rc --name="mysql-svc" --port=330
6 --type=LoadBalancer
Error from server: services "mysql-svc" is forbidden: Exceeded quota: object-quo
tas, requested: services=1, used: services=2, limited: services=2
core@ip-10-0-0-50 ~ $
```

Figure 12-18. *Error message indicates that the `object-quotas` quota is exceeded for services*

Next, we shall demonstrate exceeding a ConfigMaps quota. Chapter 11 showed how to create ConfigMaps, but I'll briefly repeat the procedure here. We shall create some ConfigMaps from files in a directory. The file names must be the same as the ConfigMap key, and the value is the content of the file. Create a directory and set its permissions:

```
sudo mkdir /mysql/env
sudo chmod -R 777 /mysql/env
cd  /mysql/env
```

Add the five files listed in Table 12-3 to the directory.

Table 12-3. *Files from Which to Create ConfigMaps*

File	Content
`mysql.root.password`	mysql
`mysql.database`	mysqldb
`mysql.user`	mysql
`mysql.password`	mysql
`mysql.allow.empty.password`	no

Create five ConfigMaps from the five files.

```
./kubectl create configmap mysql-config --from-file=/mysql/env/mysql.root.password
./kubectl create configmap mysql-config2 --from-file=/mysql/env/mysql.database
./kubectl create configmap mysql-config3 --from-file=/mysql/env/mysql.user
./kubectl create configmap mysql-config4 --from-file=/mysql/env/mysql.password
./kubectl create configmap mysql-config5 --from-file=/mysql/env/allow.empty.password
```

The five ConfigMaps are created as shown in Figure 12-19.

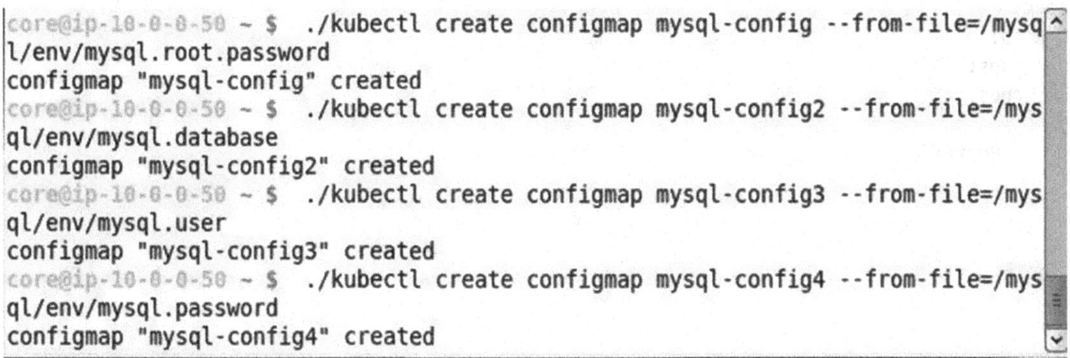
core@ip-10-0-0-50 ~ $ ./kubectl create configmap mysql-config --from-file=/mysql/env/mysql.root.password
configmap "mysql-config" created
core@ip-10-0-0-50 ~ $ ./kubectl create configmap mysql-config2 --from-file=/mysql/env/mysql.database
configmap "mysql-config2" created
core@ip-10-0-0-50 ~ $ ./kubectl create configmap mysql-config3 --from-file=/mysql/env/mysql.user
configmap "mysql-config3" created
core@ip-10-0-0-50 ~ $ ./kubectl create configmap mysql-config4 --from-file=/mysql/env/mysql.password
configmap "mysql-config4" created

Figure 12-19. *Creating ConfigMaps*

The hard limit on the number of ConfigMaps is 5. Create another file, named `mysql.config`, and set its content to mysql. Create, or try to create, the sixth ConfigMap:

```
./kubectl create configmap mysql-config6 --from-file=/mysql/env/mysql.config
```

An error message indicates that the number of ConfigMaps is being exceeded, as shown in Figure 12-20.

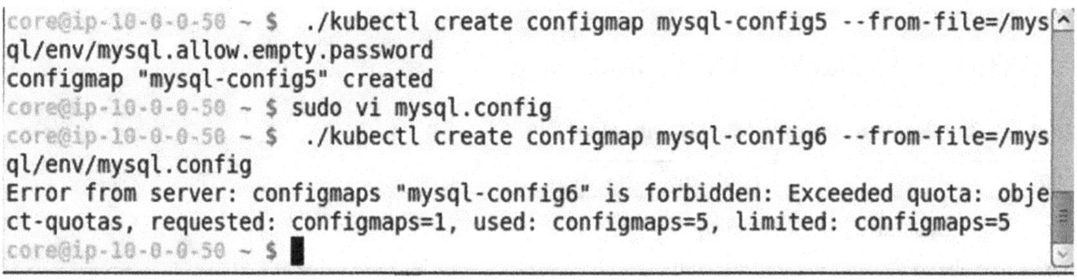
core@ip-10-0-0-50 ~ $ ./kubectl create configmap mysql-config5 --from-file=/mysql/env/mysql.allow.empty.password
configmap "mysql-config5" created
core@ip-10-0-0-50 ~ $ sudo vi mysql.config
core@ip-10-0-0-50 ~ $ ./kubectl create configmap mysql-config6 --from-file=/mysql/env/mysql.config
Error from server: configmaps "mysql-config6" is forbidden: Exceeded quota: object-quotas, requested: configmaps=1, used: configmaps=5, limited: configmaps=5
core@ip-10-0-0-50 ~ $

Figure 12-20. *Error message indicates that the `object-quotas` quota is exceeded for ConfigMaps*

Defining Best-Effort Scope Quotas

The `BestEffort` scope quota is used only for tracking pods. And if excess resources are available, pods in excess of the hard limit could be scheduled, although the pods (exceeding the hard limit) would be the first to be terminated if resources are required for another object. To demonstrate, create a ResourceQuota definition file `best-effort-quotas.yaml`. Set the hard limit on the number of pods to 5. Set `scopes` to `BestEffort`.

```
apiVersion: v1
kind: ResourceQuota
metadata:
  name: best-effort-quotas
spec:
  hard:
    pods: "5"
  scopes:
      -
      BestEffort
```

The definition file is shown in the vi editor in Figure 12-21.

```
apiVersion: v1
kind: ResourceQuota
metadata:
  name: best-effort-quotas
spec:
  hard:
    pods: "5"
  scopes:
      -
      BestEffort
```

Figure 12-21. *ResourceQuota definition file with scope* `BestEffort`

We shall use the quota in a separate namespace. Create a namespace called *best-effort*.

```
./kubectl create namespace best-effort
```

Create the ResourceQuota from the definition file as shown in Figure 12-22.

```
./kubectl create -f  best-effort-quotas.yaml --namespace=best-effort
```

List the quota and describe it:

```
./kubectl get quota --namespace=best-effort
./kubectl describe quota best-effort-quotas --namespace=best-effort
```

The `BestEffort` scope quota is created, listed, and described as shown in Figure 12-22.

```
core@ip-10-0-0-50 ~ $ ./kubectl create namespace best-effort
namespace "best-effort" created
core@ip-10-0-0-50 ~ $ ./kubectl create -f  best-effort-quotas.yaml --namespace=b
est-effort
resourcequota "best-effort-quotas" created
core@ip-10-0-0-50 ~ $ ./kubectl get quota --namespace=best-effort
NAME                 AGE
best-effort-quotas   13s
core@ip-10-0-0-50 ~ $ ./kubectl describe quota best-effort-quotas --namespace=be
st-effort
Name:           best-effort-quotas
Namespace:      best-effort
Scopes:         BestEffort
 * Matches all pods that have best effort quality of service.
Resource        Used    Hard
--------        ----    ----
pods            0       5


core@ip-10-0-0-50 ~ $
```

Figure 12-22. *Creating and describing a ResourceQuota with scope `BestEffort` in namespace `best-effort`*

Using the same RC definition file `mysql.yaml`, create an RC and list the three pods as shown in Figure 12-23.

```
core@ip-10-0-0-50 ~ $ ./kubectl create -f mysql.yaml --namespace=best-effort
replicationcontroller "mysql-rc" created
core@ip-10-0-0-50 ~ $ ./kubectl get pods -o wide --namespace=best-effort
NAME             READY     STATUS    RESTARTS   AGE       IP            NODE
mysql-rc-fcrcq   1/1       Running   0          16s       10.2.98.7     ip-10-0-0-
181.ec2.internal
mysql-rc-i9ynz   1/1       Running   0          16s       10.2.47.6     ip-10-0-0-
182.ec2.internal
mysql-rc-s55kd   1/1       Running   0          16s       10.2.26.8     ip-10-0-0-
180.ec2.internal
core@ip-10-0-0-50 ~ $
core@ip-10-0-0-50 ~ $
```

Figure 12-23. *Creating an RC and listing the pods*

Scale the RC to five pods, which is also the hard limit. The RC is scaled as shown in Figure 12-24.

```
core@ip-10-0-0-50 ~ $ ./kubectl scale rc mysql-rc --replicas=5
replicationcontroller "mysql-rc" scaled
core@ip-10-0-0-50 ~ $ ./kubectl scale rc mysql-rc --replicas=5 --namespace=best-
effort
replicationcontroller "mysql-rc" scaled
```

Figure 12-24. *Scaling the replicas to the hard limit of 5*

Scale the RC to six pods, which would exceed the hard limit. The RC is scaled as shown in Figure 12-25.

```
core@ip-10-0-0-50 ~ $ ./kubectl scale rc mysql-rc --replicas=6 --namespace=best-
effort
replicationcontroller "mysql-rc" scaled
```

Figure 12-25. *Scaling the replicas to exceed the hard limit of 5*

Describe the RC, and the Replicas value is listed as 6 current / 6 desired, as shown in Figure 12-26. Even though the hard limit on the number of pods is exceeded, an extra pod is scheduled because the scope is set to `BestEffort`.

```
core@ip-10-0-0-50 ~ $ ./kubectl describe rc --namespace=best-effort
Name:           mysql-rc
Namespace:      best-effort
Image(s):       mysql
Selector:       app=mysql-app,deployment=v1
Labels:         app=mysql-app
Replicas:       6 current / 6 desired
Pods Status:    6 Running / 0 Waiting / 0 Succeeded / 0 Failed
No volumes.
Events:
  FirstSeen     LastSeen        Count   From                            Subobjec
tPath   Type            Reason                  Message
  ---------     --------        -----   ----                            --------
-----   --------        ------                  -------
  7m            7m              1       {replication-controller }              N
ormal           SuccessfulCreate        Created pod: mysql-rc-s55kd
  7m            7m              1       {replication-controller }              N
ormal           SuccessfulCreate        Created pod: mysql-rc-fcrcq
  7m            7m              1       {replication-controller }              N
ormal           SuccessfulCreate        Created pod: mysql-rc-i9ynz
  5m            5m              1       {replication-controller }              N
ormal           SuccessfulCreate        Created pod: mysql-rc-5cnmg
  5m            5m              1       {replication-controller }              N
ormal           SuccessfulCreate        Created pod: mysql-rc-dnkuf
  1m            1m              1       {replication-controller }              N
ormal           SuccessfulCreate        Created pod: mysql-rc-739se

core@ip-10-0-0-50 ~ $
```

Figure 12-26. *The replicas exceed the hard limit because the scope is* `BestEffort`

Summary

In this chapter we introduced resource quotas, a specification for limiting the allocation of certain resources to a particular namespace with the objective of distributing the resources in a fair, shared manner. The quotas may be set on compute resources and objects. In the next chapter we will discuss autoscaling.

CHAPTER 13

Using Autoscaling

Starting new pods may sometimes be required in a Kubernetes cluster, for example, to meet the requirements of an increased load. The replication controller has the ability to restart a container, which is actually starting a replacement container, if a container in a pod were to fail.

Problem

Cluster load is a variable, and depending on application use requirements, cluster load can increase or decrease. One of the benefits of the Kubernetes cluster manager is the ability to scale a cluster of containers (pods) as required. If more load is expected, a user may scale up (increase the number of pods) and if less load is expected, a user may scale down (decrease the number of pods). But a user-intervened scaling model is suitable only for development and a small-scale cluster. For a production-level cluster in which the load is not predictable and high availability is a requirement, user-initiated scaling may not be timely or proportional to the load requirements.

Solution

For production-level clusters Kubernetes provides the autoscaling management design pattern. Autoscaling is based on the volatile configuration pattern. A horizontal pod autoscaler (HPA) can be created with a preconfigured minimum and maximum number of pods within which to scale a cluster. When load is increased on a running cluster, the HPA automatically increases the number of pods in proportion to the load requirements up to the configured maximum number of pods, as shown in Figure 13-1, and when the load decreases the HPA decreases the number of pods proportionally without user intervention.

D. Vohra, *Kubernetes Management Design Patterns*, DOI 10.1007/978-1-4842-2598-1_13

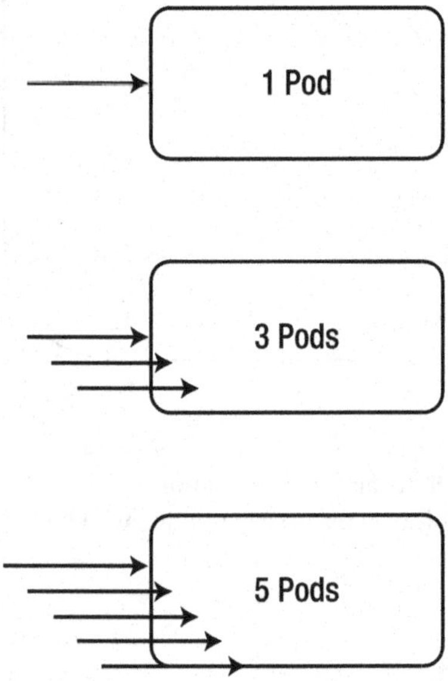

Figure 13-1. *Increasing the load increases the number of pods*

An HPA has two main benefits over user-intervened scaling: the scaling is automatic, and extra pods are not kept running consuming resources that could be used for some other application. An autoscaler may be created for a replication controller, replica set, or deployment. An autoscaler uses `heapster` to collect CPU utilization of a resource, based on which it determines whether more or fewer pods should be run. Autoscaling is based on a target CPU utilization, implying that the CPU utilization of a resource such as a deployment should be x%.

Overview

In this chapter we shall demonstrate the use of autoscaling. This chapter discusses the following topics.

- Setting the environment
- Running PHP Apache Server deployment
- Creating a service
- Creating a horizontal pod autoscaler
- Increasing load

Setting the Environment

Create a Kubernetes cluster running as a CoreOS AWS CloudFormation consisting of one controller node and three worker nodes. List the nodes:

```
./kubectl get nodes
```

The single controller node and the worker nodes should be listed as shown in Figure 13-2.

```
core@ip-10-0-0-50 ~ $ ./kubectl get nodes
NAME                         STATUS                     AGE
ip-10-0-0-109.ec2.internal   Ready                      2m
ip-10-0-0-110.ec2.internal   Ready                      2m
ip-10-0-0-111.ec2.internal   Ready                      2m
ip-10-0-0-50.ec2.internal    Ready,SchedulingDisabled   2m
core@ip-10-0-0-50 ~ $
```

***Figure 13-2.** Listing Kubernetes nodes*

List the services across all namespaces as shown in Figure 13-3. The heapster service, which monitors the CPU utilization, should be listed in the kube-system namespace.

```
core@ip-10-0-0-50 ~ $ ./kubectl get svc --all-namespaces
NAMESPACE     NAME         CLUSTER-IP   EXTERNAL-IP   PORT(S)         AGE
default       kubernetes   10.3.0.1     <none>        443/TCP         35m
kube-system   heapster     10.3.0.52    <none>        80/TCP          35m
kube-system   kube-dns     10.3.0.10    <none>        53/UDP,53/TCP   35m
core@ip-10-0-0-50 ~ $
```

***Figure 13-3.** Listing services across all namespaces*

List pods across all the namespaces, and the heapster pod should be listed as shown in Figure 13-4.

```
core@ip-10-0-0-50 ~ $ ./kubectl get pods --namespace=kube-system
NAME                                                  READY     STATUS    RESTARTS
   AGE
heapster-v1.0.2-3151619174-v7r2x                      2/2       Running   0
   56m
kube-apiserver-ip-10-0-0-50.ec2.internal              1/1       Running   0
   56m
kube-controller-manager-ip-10-0-0-50.ec2.internal     1/1       Running   0
   56m
kube-dns-v11-1xc5y                                    4/4       Running   0
   55m
kube-proxy-ip-10-0-0-109.ec2.internal                 1/1       Running   0
   55m
kube-proxy-ip-10-0-0-110.ec2.internal                 1/1       Running   0
   55m
kube-proxy-ip-10-0-0-111.ec2.internal                 1/1       Running   0
   56m
kube-proxy-ip-10-0-0-50.ec2.internal                  1/1       Running   0
   56m
kube-scheduler-ip-10-0-0-50.ec2.internal              1/1       Running   0
   56m
mysql-rc-utaqt                                        1/1       Running   0
   4m
core@ip-10-0-0-50 ~ $
```

***Figure 13-4.** Listing pods across all namespaces*

Running a PHP Apache Server Deployment

First, we need to create a resource to scale. Create a deployment resource using the Docker image `gcr.io/google_containers/hpa-example`. Set CPU requests to 200m.

```
./kubectl run php-apache --image=gcr.io/google_containers/hpa-example --requests=cpu=200m
```

A deployment called `php-apache` is created as shown in Figure 13-5.

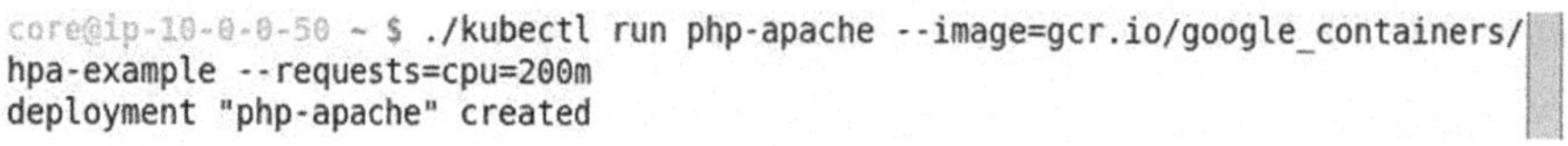

Figure 13-5. *Creating a deployment for PHP and Apache*

List the deployments:

```
./kubectl get deployment
```

The `php-apache` deployment should be listed as shown in Figure 13-6.

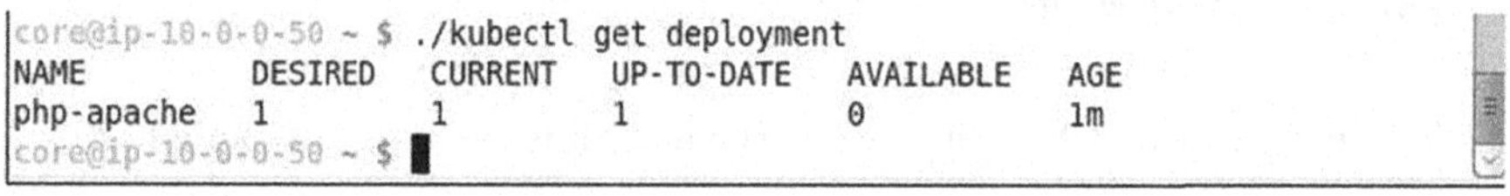

Figure 13-6. *Listing the deployments*

Creating a Service

Create a service of type `LoadBalancer` by exposing the deployment on port 80.

```
./kubectl expose  deployment php-apache --port=80 --type=LoadBalancer
```

A service is created and then listed as shown in Figure 13-7.

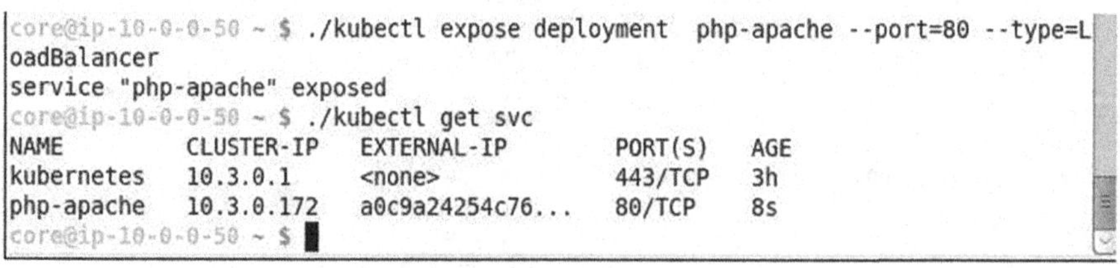

core@ip-10-0-0-50 ~ $ ./kubectl expose deployment php-apache --port=80 --type=L
oadBalancer
service "php-apache" exposed
core@ip-10-0-0-50 ~ $ ./kubectl get svc
NAME CLUSTER-IP EXTERNAL-IP PORT(S) AGE
kubernetes 10.3.0.1 <none> 443/TCP 3h
php-apache 10.3.0.172 a0c9a24254c76... 80/TCP 8s
core@ip-10-0-0-50 ~ $

Figure 13-7. *Creating a service*

List the pods, and a single pod is listed as shown in Figure 13-8.

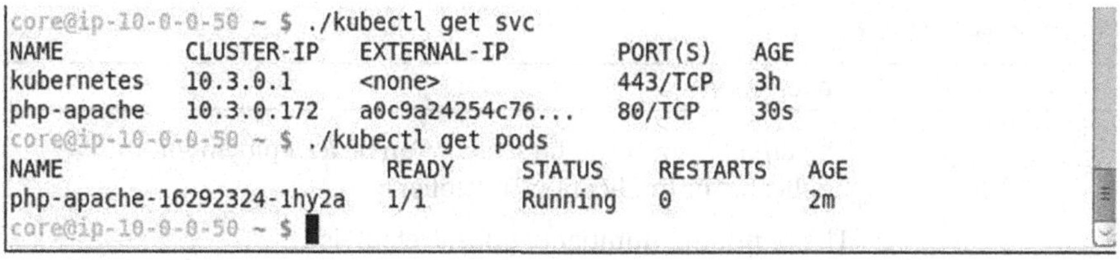

Figure 13-8. *Listing the pods*

We shall invoke the service, which provides an external IP, to put load on the deployment and test whether varying loads make the autoscaler alter the number of pods proportionately. Obtain the `LoadBalancer Ingress` for the service:

```
./kubectl describe services php-apache | grep "LoadBalancer Ingress"
```

The public DNS at which the service may be invoked is listed, as shown in Figure 13-9.

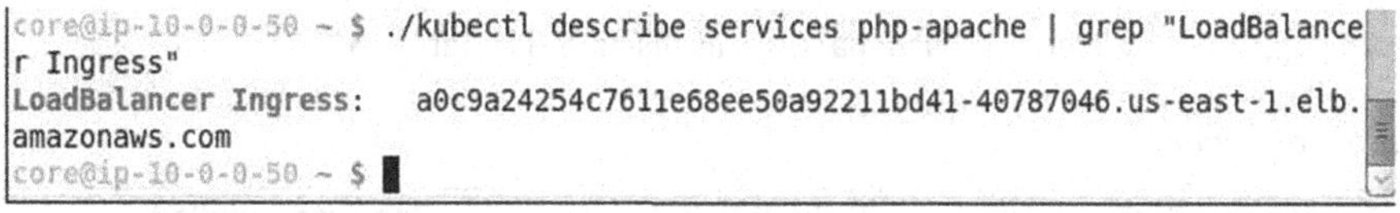

core@ip-10-0-0-50 ~ $ ./kubectl describe services php-apache | grep "LoadBalance
r Ingress"
LoadBalancer Ingress: a0c9a24254c7611e68ee50a92211bd41-40787046.us-east-1.elb.
amazonaws.com
core@ip-10-0-0-50 ~ $

Figure 13-9. *Obtaining the `LoadBalancer Ingress`*

Invoke the service using the `Load Balancer Ingress`. An output such as "OK!" is generated as shown in Figure 13-10; the `php-apache` deployment is designed only for testing and more elaborate output is not generated.

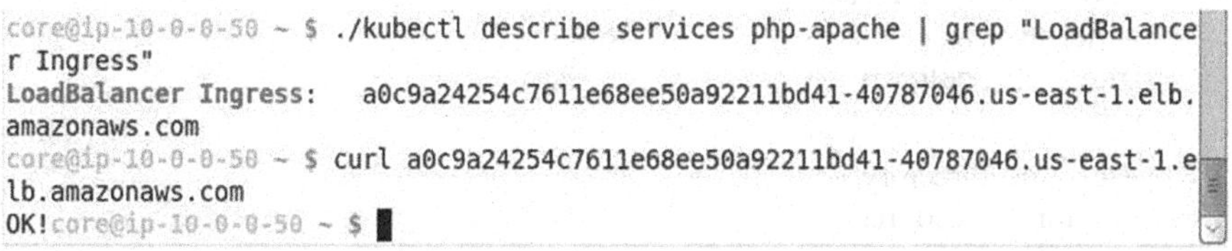

core@ip-10-0-0-50 ~ $ ./kubectl describe services php-apache | grep "LoadBalance
r Ingress"
LoadBalancer Ingress: a0c9a24254c7611e68ee50a92211bd41-40787046.us-east-1.elb.
amazonaws.com
core@ip-10-0-0-50 ~ $ curl a0c9a24254c7611e68ee50a92211bd41-40787046.us-east-1.e
lb.amazonaws.com
OK!core@ip-10-0-0-50 ~ $

Figure 13-10. *Invoking the `LoadBalancer Ingress`*

Creating a Horizontal Pod Autoscaler

Next, we shall create a horizontal pod autoscaler for the deployment. An HPA can be created using one of two available methods:

- A HorizontalPodAutoscaler object
- The `kubectl autoscale` command

The HorizontalPodAutoscaler specification provides the fields shown in Table 13-1.

Table 13-1. *HorizontalPodAutoscaler Spec Fields*

Field	Description
`scaleTargetRef`	The target resource to be scaled. Can be a Deployment, ReplicaSet or ReplicationController.
`minReplicas`	The minimum number of pods. Default is 1.
`maxReplicas`	The maximum number of pods. Cannot be less than `minReplicas`.
`targetCPUUtilizationPercentage`	The target average CPU utilization. If not specified, a default autoscaler policy is used,

The `kubectl autoscale` command has the following syntax, which essentially provides the same settings as the specification.

```
kubectl autoscale (-f FILENAME | TYPE NAME | TYPE/NAME) [--min=MINPODS] --max=MAXPODS
[--cpu-percent=CPU] [flags]
```

Some of the options supported by `kubectl autoscale` are as discussed in Table 13-2.

Table 13-2. *kubectl autoscale Options*

Option	Description	Default Value	Required (explicit or default)
`--cpu-percent`	The target average CPU utilization over all the pods in the resource represented as a percentage of the CPU requests. If not set or negative, a default autoscaling policy is used.	-1	Yes
`-f, --filename`	File name, directory, or URL for the resource to autoscale.	[]	Yes
`--max`	Upper limit for the number of pods.	-1	Yes
`--min`	Lower limit for the number of pods. If not specified or -ve a default value is used.	-1	Yes
`--name`	The name of the newly created object.	""	No

Using the `kubectl autoscale` command, create a horizontal pod autoscaler. Set target CPU utilization to 100% and set minimum number of pods to 3 and maximum number of pods to 10.

```
./kubectl autoscale rc php-apache --cpu-percent=100 --min=3 --max=10
```

The deployment is autoscaled and an HPA is created, as shown in Figure 13-11.

```
core@ip-10-0-0-50 ~ $ ./kubectl autoscale deployment php-apache --cpu-percent=10
0 --min=3 --max=10
deployment "php-apache" autoscaled
core@ip-10-0-0-50 ~ $ ▌
```

Figure 13-11. *Creating a horizontal pod autoscaler*

List the HPA:

```
./kubectl get hpa
```

The single HPA should be listed as shown in Figure 13-12. The TARGET column lists the target CPU utilization, the CURRENT column lists the current CPU utilization, the MINPODS column lists the minimum number of pods, and the MAXPODS lists the maximum number of pods. Because the CPU utilization takes a while to be monitored by `heapster`, the CURRENT column is indicating a value of `<waiting>`.

```
core@ip-10-0-0-50 ~ $ ./kubectl autoscale deployment php-apache --cpu-percent=10
0 --min=3 --max=10
deployment "php-apache" autoscaled
core@ip-10-0-0-50 ~ $ ./kubectl get hpa
NAME         REFERENCE                 TARGET     CURRENT      MINPODS    MAXPODS    A
GE
php-apache   Deployment/php-apache     100%       <waiting>    3          10         1
9s
core@ip-10-0-0-50 ~ $ ▌
```

Figure 13-12. *Listing the horizontal pod autoscaler*

List the pods. The number of pods has increased from 1 in the initial deployment to 3 (the minimum number of pods in the HPA) as shown in Figure 13-13.

```
core@ip-10-0-0-50 ~ $ ./kubectl get pods
NAME                          READY     STATUS     RESTARTS    AGE
php-apache-16292324-1hy2a     1/1       Running    0           10m
php-apache-16292324-hpwqo     1/1       Running    0           3m
php-apache-16292324-wmg6k     1/1       Running    0           3m
core@ip-10-0-0-50 ~ $ ▌
```

Figure 13-13. *Number of pods scaled to the minimum number of pods in the horizontal pod autoscaler*

List the HPA again, and the CURRENT CPU utilization is at 0% as no load is being put on the deployment as shown in Figure 13-14.

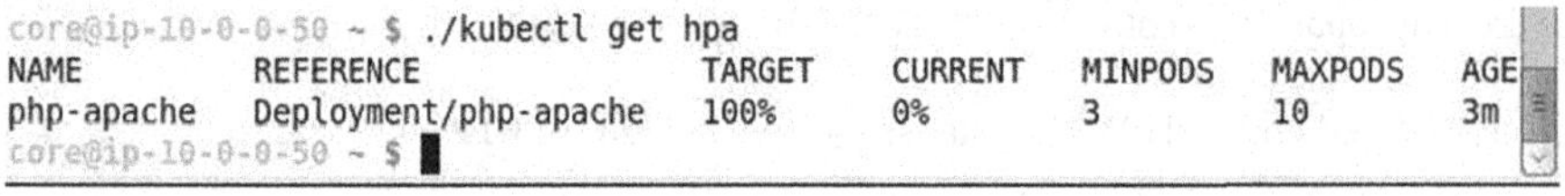

Figure 13-14. *CPU Utilization is at 0%*

Increasing Load

Next, we shall demonstrate what increasing load on the deployment does to the number of pods and CPU utilization. Run the following command by substituting the LoadBalancer `Ingress` to put some load on the deployment:

```
curl <LoadBalancer Ingress>
```

In another terminal, get the HPA. The number of pods is listed as 3 because the CPU utilization at 22% is below the target CPU Utilization of 100%, as shown in Figure 13-15.

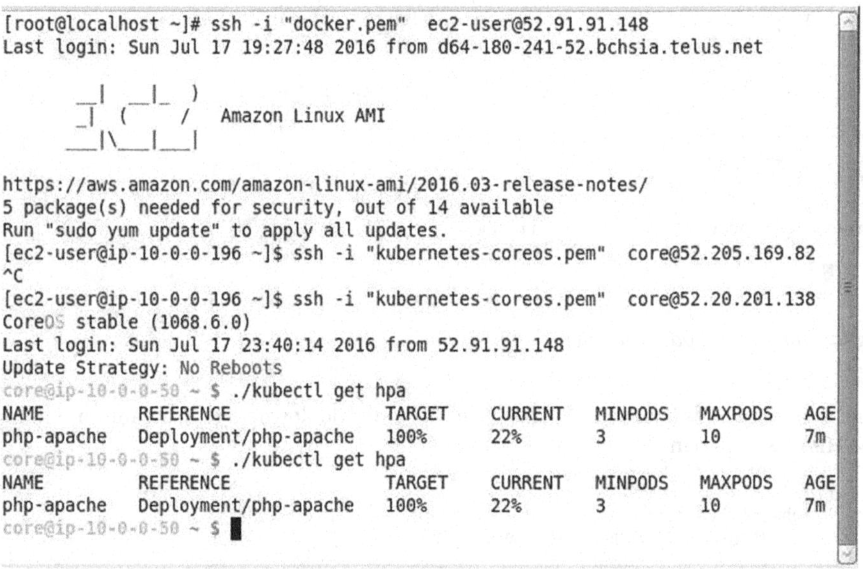

[root@localhost ~]# ssh -i "docker.pem" ec2-user@52.91.91.148
Last login: Sun Jul 17 19:27:48 2016 from d64-180-241-52.bchsia.telus.net
Amazon Linux AMI
https://aws.amazon.com/amazon-linux-ami/2016.03-release-notes/
5 package(s) needed for security, out of 14 available
Run "sudo yum update" to apply all updates.
[ec2-user@ip-10-0-0-196 ~]$ ssh -i "kubernetes-coreos.pem" core@52.205.169.82
^C
[ec2-user@ip-10-0-0-196 ~]$ ssh -i "kubernetes-coreos.pem" core@52.20.201.138
CoreOS stable (1068.6.0)
Last login: Sun Jul 17 23:40:14 2016 from 52.91.91.148
Update Strategy: No Reboots
core@ip-10-0-0-50 ~ $ ./kubectl get hpa
NAME REFERENCE TARGET CURRENT MINPODS MAXPODS AGE
php-apache Deployment/php-apache 100% 22% 3 10 7m
core@ip-10-0-0-50 ~ $ ./kubectl get hpa
NAME REFERENCE TARGET CURRENT MINPODS MAXPODS AGE
php-apache Deployment/php-apache 100% 22% 3 10 7m
core@ip-10-0-0-50 ~ $

Figure 13-15. *CPU utilization increases to 22%*

Run the following command loop by substituting the `LoadBalancer Ingress` to put more load on the deployment:

```
while true; do curl <loadbalancer ingress>; done
```

Invoking the service in a loop outputs the same message repeatedly, as shown in Figure 13-16.

```
core@ip-10-0-0-50 ~ $ ./kubectl describe services php-apache | grep "LoadBalance
r Ingress"
LoadBalancer Ingress:    a0c9a24254c7611e68ee50a92211bd41-40787046.us-east-1.elb.
amazonaws.com
core@ip-10-0-0-50 ~ $ curl a0c9a24254c7611e68ee50a92211bd41-40787046.us-east-1.e
lb.amazonaws.com
OK!core@ip-10-0-0-50 ~ $ while true;
> do curl a0c9a24254c7611e68ee50a92211bd41-40787046.us-east-1.elb.amazonaws.com;
done
OK!OK!OK!OK!OK!OK!OK!OK!OK!OK!OK!OK!OK!OK!OK!OK!OK!OK!OK!OK!OK!OK!OK!OK!OK!OK!OK
!OK!OK!OK!OK!OK!OK!OK!OK!OK!OK!OK!OK!OK!OK!OK!OK!OK!OK!OK!OK!OK!OK!OK!OK!OK!OK!O
K!OK!OK!OK!OK!OK!OK!OK!OK!OK!OK!OK!OK!OK!OK!OK!OK!OK!OK!OK!OK!OK!OK!OK!OK!OK!OK!
OK!OK!OK!OK!OK!OK!OK!OK!OK!OK!OK!OK!OK!OK!OK!OK!OK!OK!OK!OK!OK!OK!OK!OK!OK!OK!OK
!OK!OK!OK!OK!OK!OK!OK!OK!OK!OK!OK!OK!OK!OK!OK!OK!OK!OK!OK!OK!OK!OK!OK!OK!OK!OK!O
K!OK!OK!OK!OK!OK!OK!OK!OK!OK!OK!OK!OK!OK!OK!OK!OK!OK!OK!OK!OK!OK!OK!OK!OK!OK!OK!
OK!OK!OK!OK!OK!OK!OK!OK!OK!OK!OK!OK!OK!OK!OK!OK!OK!OK!OK!OK!OK!OK!OK!OK!OK!OK!OK
!OK!OK!OK!OK!OK!OK!OK!OK!OK!OK!OK!OK!OK!OK!OK!OK!OK!OK!OK!OK!OK!OK!OK!OK!OK!OK!O
K!OK!OK!OK!OK!OK!OK!OK!OK!OK!OK!OK!OK!OK!OK!OK!OK!OK!OK!OK!OK!OK!OK!OK!OK!OK!OK!
OK!OK!OK!OK!OK!OK!OK!OK!OK!OK!OK!OK!OK!OK!OK!OK!OK!OK!OK!OK!OK!OK!OK!OK!OK!OK!OK
!OK!OK!OK!OK!OK!OK!OK!OK!OK!OK!OK!OK!OK!OK!OK!OK!OK!OK!OK!OK!OK!OK!OK!OK!OK!OK!O
K!OK!OK!OK!OK!OK!OK!OK!OK!OK!OK!OK!OK!OK!OK!OK!OK!OK!OK!OK!OK!OK!OK!OK!OK!OK!OK!
OK!OK!OK!OK!OK!OK!OK!OK!OK!OK!OK!OK!OK!OK!OK!OK!OK!OK!OK!OK!OK!OK!OK!OK!OK!OK!OK
!OK!OK!OK!OK!OK!OK!OK!OK!OK!OK!OK!OK!OK!OK!OK!OK!OK!OK!OK!OK!OK!OK!OK!OK!OK!OK!O
K!OK!OK!OK!OK!OK!OK!OK!OK!OK!OK!OK!OK!OK!OK!OK!OK!OK!OK!OK!OK!OK!OK!OK!OK!OK!OK!
OK!OK!OK!OK!OK!OK!OK!OK!OK!OK!OK!OK!OK!OK!OK!OK!OK!OK!OK!OK!OK!OK!OK!OK!OK!OK!OK
!OK!OK!OK!OK!OK!OK!OK!OK!OK!OK!OK!
```

Figure 13-16. *Invoking a service in a loop*

List the horizontal pod autoscaler:

```
./kubectl get hpa
```

The CURRENT column value has become 224%, which indicates an increased load on the deployment, as shown in Figure 13-17. The CPU utilization is above the target CPU utilization.

```
core@ip-10-0-0-50 ~ $ ./kubectl get hpa
NAME         REFERENCE                 TARGET     CURRENT    MINPODS    MAXPODS    AGE
php-apache   Deployment/php-apache     100%       224%       3          10         12m
core@ip-10-0-0-50 ~ $
```

Figure 13-17. *Current CPU utilization above the target*

The number of pods is still 3 because it takes a while for the number of pods to increase and the cluster to stabilize, as shown in Figure 13-18.

```
core@ip-10-0-0-50 ~ $ ./kubectl get deployment
NAME         DESIRED   CURRENT   UP-TO-DATE   AVAILABLE   AGE
php-apache   3         3         3            3           15m
```

Figure 13-18. *The number of pods is still 3 as it takes a while for the cluster to stabilize when load is increased*

List the deployment after a few more seconds, and the number of pods has increased to 5 as shown in Figure 13-19. The autoscaler has scaled up the cluster by increasing the number of pods.

```
core@ip-10-0-0-50 ~ $ ./kubectl get hpa
NAME         REFERENCE              TARGET    CURRENT   MINPODS   MAXPODS   AGE
php-apache   Deployment/php-apache  100%      224%      3         10        12m
core@ip-10-0-0-50 ~ $ ./kubectl get deployment
NAME         DESIRED   CURRENT   UP-TO-DATE   AVAILABLE   AGE
php-apache   5         5         5            5           19m
core@ip-10-0-0-50 ~ $
```

Figure 13-19. *The number of pods increases to 5 when load is increased*

Summary

This chapter introduced autoscaling. To demonstrate autoscaling we create a PHP Apache Server deployment and created a service for the deployment. Subsequently we created a horizontal pod autoscaler and tested autoscaling by increasing load on the Apache server. In the next chapter we shall discuss configuring logging.

CHAPTER 14

Configuring Logging

Logging is the process of collecting and storing log messages generated by different components of a system (which would be a Kubernetes cluster) and by applications running on the cluster.

Problem

One of the problems associated with logging is demarcating the components and applications generating logging messages. Another problem is decoupling the logging from the component/application. The component generating logs in a Kubernetes application would be a container in a pod.

Solution

A container runs in isolation on the Docker Engine and is an object from which the single-container management pattern of tracking an application running within a container, including application-specific logging, can be used. Similarly, a pod is an object generating its own logging messages, and so is a replication controller and a service.

A design pattern introduced in the recent publication *Design Patterns for Container-based Distributed Systems*, by Brendan Burns and David Oppenheimer (`https://www.usenix.org/node/196347`) is a single-node multi-container application pattern called the *Sidecar Pattern,* using which a main container (for example a container generating web server logs) could be paired with a "logsaver" sidecar container, as shown in Figure 14-1, to collect the web server's logs from the local disk filesystem and stream them to a cluster storage system. Sidecar containers are made feasible by containers on the same machine being able to share a local disk volume.

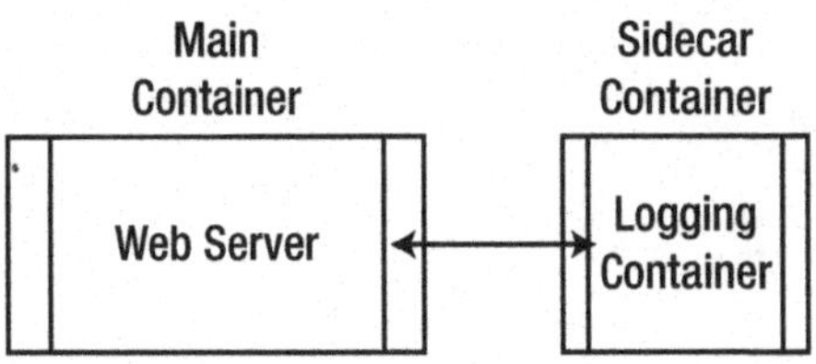

Figure 14-1. *Sidecar container for logging*

D. Vohra, *Kubernetes Management Design Patterns*, DOI 10.1007/978-1-4842-2598-1_14

Another single-node, multiple-container application pattern, called the *Adapter Pattern,* could be used to create an Adapter container (Figure 14-2) to provide a unified interface for aggregating logs from multiple containers (or pods) on a node running the same or a different application.

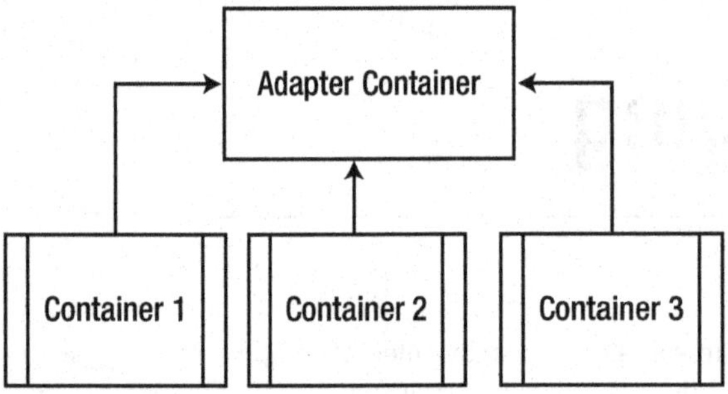

Figure 14-2. *Listing Kubernetes nodes*

Using a logging-specific container provides separation of concerns, a modular design principle.

Overview

By default, Kubernetes components such as apiserver and kubelet use the "glog" logging library. For cluster-level logging various options are available, two of which are as follows:

Logging to Google Cloud Logging

Logging to Elasticsearch and Kibana

In this chapter we shall discuss getting the single pod/container logs and also cluster-level logging with Elasticsearch and Kibana. The procedure to use cluster-level logging with Elasticsearch and Kibana is as follows.

1. Start Elasticsearch.
2. Start a Replication Controller from which logs are to be collected.
3. Start Fluentd and Elasticsearch to collect logs.
4. Start Kibana to view the logs.

This chapter covers the following topics:

- Setting the environment
- Getting the logs generated by the default logger
- Docker log files
- Cluster-level logging with Elasticsearch and Kibana
- Starting Elastic Search

- Starting a replication controller
- Starting Fluentd and Elasticsearch to collect logs
- Starting Kibana

Setting the Environment

Create a Kubernetes cluster using a CoreOS-based AWS CloudFormation. List the nodes with `kubectl get nodes`. The controller and worker nodes should be listed; we have used a single-controller, three-worker node cluster as shown in Figure 14-3.

```
core@ip-10-0-0-50 ~ $ ./kubectl get nodes
NAME                          STATUS                     AGE
ip-10-0-0-206.ec2.internal    Ready                      28s
ip-10-0-0-207.ec2.internal    Ready                      28s
ip-10-0-0-208.ec2.internal    Ready                      28s
ip-10-0-0-50.ec2.internal     Ready,SchedulingDisabled   28s
core@ip-10-0-0-50 ~ $
```

Figure 14-3. *Listing Kubernetes nodes*

Getting the Logs Generated by Default Logger

The logs generated by a running pod may be obtained with the `kubectl logs` *<POD>* command. If a pod has more than one container, the logs for a particular container may be obtained with the command `kubectl logs` *<POD> <container>*. Kubernetes performs log rotation, and only the latest logs are available to kubectl logs.

First, create a sample pod from which to get the logs. Use the following listing to create a pod definition file `counter-pod.yaml`; the pod generates a message using a counter.

```
---
apiVersion: v1
kind: Pod
metadata:
  name: counter
spec:
  containers:
    -
      args:
        - bash
        - "-c"
        - "for ((i = 0; ; i++)); do echo \"$i: $(date)\"; sleep 1; done"
      image: "ubuntu:14.04"
      name: count
```

The pod definition file is shown in the `vi` editor in Figure 14-4.

```
---
apiVersion: v1
kind: Pod
metadata:
  name: counter
spec:
  containers:
    -
      args:
        - bash
        - "-c"
        - "for ((i = 0; ; i++)); do echo \"$i: $(date)\"; sleep 1; done"
      image: "ubuntu:14.04"
      name: count

~
```

Figure 14-4. *Counter pod definition file*

Create a pod from the pod definition file:

```
./kubectl create -f  counter-pod.yaml
```

The `counter` pod is generated. List the pods. Get the logs for the pod `counter`:

```
./kubectl logs counter
```

The logs are listed as shown in Figure 14-5.

```
core@ip-10-0-0-50 ~ $ sudo vi counter-pod.yaml
core@ip-10-0-0-50 ~ $ ./kubectl create -f  counter-pod.yaml
pod "counter" created
core@ip-10-0-0-50 ~ $ ./kubectl get pods
NAME      READY     STATUS              RESTARTS   AGE
counter   0/1       ContainerCreating   0          10s
core@ip-10-0-0-50 ~ $ ./kubectl get pods
NAME      READY     STATUS              RESTARTS   AGE
counter   0/1       ContainerCreating   0          23s
core@ip-10-0-0-50 ~ $ ./kubectl logs counter
0: Wed Jul 27 19:21:05 UTC 2016
1: Wed Jul 27 19:21:06 UTC 2016
2: Wed Jul 27 19:21:07 UTC 2016
3: Wed Jul 27 19:21:08 UTC 2016
4: Wed Jul 27 19:21:09 UTC 2016
5: Wed Jul 27 19:21:10 UTC 2016
6: Wed Jul 27 19:21:11 UTC 2016
7: Wed Jul 27 19:21:12 UTC 2016
8: Wed Jul 27 19:21:13 UTC 2016
9: Wed Jul 27 19:21:14 UTC 2016
10: Wed Jul 27 19:21:15 UTC 2016
11: Wed Jul 27 19:21:16 UTC 2016
core@ip-10-0-0-50 ~ $
```

Figure 14-5. *Creating the counter pod and getting pod logs*

Docker Log Files

By default the Docker containers log file directories are in the /var/lib/docker/containers directory. CD (change directory) to the /var/lib/docker/containers directory and list the files and directories. A log directory exists for each of the Docker containers, as shown in Figure 14-6.

```
core@ip-10-0-0-50 /var/lib/docker/containers $ sudo ls -l
total 88
drwx------. 2 root root 4096 Jul 27 18:58 041501f4cecbfa26c89c8369282fe13a7e01c8
1c28152d248e6575a22d20de24
drwx------. 3 root root 4096 Jul 27 18:57 1f58566a7617c7327808297e280ec803dae2bf
dbf1b23d29da52c2095dbe4e76
drwx------. 3 root root 4096 Jul 27 18:57 33fb20dfb63881369d02566eb2eb8a3ba5cc1b
e07daf0e70381aa13ffaed6e57
drwx------. 3 root root 4096 Jul 27 18:57 365da624bcd5590fea6f9fb5d7e1b4712cdc79
a3c3c62724a422ab0d064e6f6a
drwx------. 3 root root 4096 Jul 27 18:58 68bcd06c7c718a04d97a94bc58309f4832fef5
f7cf38bd54cb90b6a1dafbe64f
drwx------. 2 root root 4096 Jul 27 18:58 6ef0f0bdaac8ac53dfa9dfb6af853978365774
2932e25349c7f4f5277eaaf276
drwx------. 3 root root 4096 Jul 27 18:57 9479ac4a8bd76f560fa5ba6156f060264081ee
70d37ebc7c4b42c73370f5a313
drwx------. 2 root root 4096 Jul 27 18:59 d4dbad8595cf3f16c6e6b64b4f747c66cb2f27
92fcf31611ff3a3a2ab7379019
drwx------. 2 root root 4096 Jul 27 18:58 dda5e849d5063a2f9fa9c72aa51d76174bf2ed
```

Figure 14-6. *Docker container log directories*

To access a container directory we need to set permissions with chmod +x as shown in Figure 14-7. Then CD to the container directory.

```
core@ip-10-0-0-50 /var/lib/docker/containers $ sudo chmod +x 041501f4cecbfa26c89
c8369282fe13a7e01c81c28152d248e6575a22d20de24
core@ip-10-0-0-50 /var/lib/docker/containers $ cd 041501f4cecbfa26c89c8369282fe1
3a7e01c81c28152d248e6575a22d20de24
```

Figure 14-7. *Setting Permissions on a Docker container log directory*

List the files in the container directory as shown in Figure 14-8. The containerid-json.log file is the log file generated by the container.

```
core@ip-10-0-0-50 /var/lib/docker/containers/041501f4cecbfa26c89c8369282fe13a7e0
1c81c28152d248e6575a22d20de24 $ sudo ls -l
total 24
-rw-r-----. 1 root root 1030 Jul 27 18:58 041501f4cecbfa26c89c8369282fe13a7e01c8
1c28152d248e6575a22d20de24-json.log
-rw-r--r--. 1 root root 3135 Jul 27 18:58 config.v2.json
-rw-r--r--. 1 root root 1229 Jul 27 18:58 hostconfig.json
core@ip-10-0-0-50 /var/lib/docker/containers/041501f4cecbfa26c89c8369282fe13a7e0
1c81c28152d248e6575a22d20de24 $
```

Figure 14-8. *Listing log files for a Docker container*

Open the `-json.log` file in a vi editor. The JSON logs should be displayed as shown in Figure 14-9.

```
core@ip-10-0-0-50:/var/lib/docker/containers/041501f4cecbfa26c89c83692
File Edit View Search Terminal Help
{"log":"I0727 18:58:24.249275       1 server.go:200] Using iptables Proxier.\n",
"stream":"stderr","time":"2016-07-27T18:58:24.264395246Z"}
{"log":"I0727 18:58:24.249401       1 server.go:213] Tearing down userspace rule
s.\n","stream":"stderr","time":"2016-07-27T18:58:24.264432779Z"}
{"log":"I0727 18:58:24.331715       1 conntrack.go:36] Setting nf_conntrack_max
to 262144\n","stream":"stderr","time":"2016-07-27T18:58:24.353325373Z"}
{"log":"I0727 18:58:24.331784       1 conntrack.go:41] Setting conntrack hashsiz
e to 65536\n","stream":"stderr","time":"2016-07-27T18:58:24.353351574Z"}
{"log":"I0727 18:58:24.332047       1 conntrack.go:46] Setting nf_conntrack_tcp_
timeout_established to 86400\n","stream":"stderr","time":"2016-07-27T18:58:24.35
3358813Z"}
{"log":"E0727 18:58:24.332656       1 event.go:202] Unable to write event: 'Post
 http://127.0.0.1:8080/api/v1/namespaces/default/events: dial tcp 127.0.0.1:8080
: connection refused' (may retry after sleeping)\n","stream":"stderr","time":"20
16-07-27T18:58:24.35336476Z"}
~
~
~
~
~
~
~
<f4cecbfa26c89c8369282fe13a7e01c81c28152d248e6575a22d20de24-json.log" 6L, 1030C
```

Figure 14-9. *Docker container logs in JSON format*

Logs of the system components are in the `/var/log` directory as shown in Figure 14-10.

```
core@ip-10-0-0-50 ~ $ cd /var/log
core@ip-10-0-0-50 /var/log $ ls -l
total 48
-rw-------. 1 root utmp                0 Jul 27 18:52 btmp
-rw-r--r--. 1 root root                0 Jul 27 18:52 faillog
drwxr-sr-x. 4 root systemd-journal  4096 Jul 27 18:51 journal
-rw-r--r--. 1 root root           146292 Jul 27 19:11 lastlog
drwx------. 2 root root             4096 Jul 18 06:27 sssd
-rw-------. 1 root root            32064 Jul 27 19:11 tallylog
-rw-rw-r--. 1 root utmp             2688 Jul 27 19:11 wtmp
core@ip-10-0-0-50 /var/log $
```

Figure 14-10. *System component logs*

Cluster-Level Logging with Elasticsearch and Kibana

Cluster-level logging collects the standard output and standard error logs of applications running in containers. For aggregating log files of applications running within containers, the Fluentd aggregator can be used. In this section we shall configure and use cluster-level logging with Fluentd, Elasticsearch, and Kibana. Fluentd is an open source data collector for a unified logging layer. Unified logging implies that Fluentd decouples data sources from backend systems. The data source for the example would be logs generated in a Kubernetes cluster, and the backend would be Elasticsearch. Elasticsearch is an open source distributed, highly available, document-oriented, RESTful search engine designed for the cloud environment and built on top of Lucene. Kibana is an open source analytics and search dashboard for Elasticsearch and is accessed from a web browser. The three components of the cluster-level logging are shown in Figure 14-11.

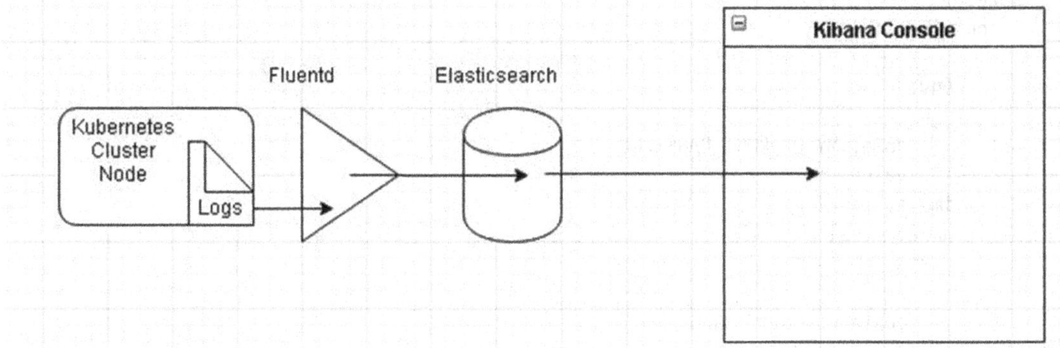

Figure 14-11. *Cluster-level logging components*

To configure logging, use the following procedure:

1. Start the MySQL replication controller and pods.
2. Start the Elasticsearch service.
3. Start Fluentd.
4. Start Kibana.
5. Access the logs in KIbana.

The following sections discuss each of the preceding steps in detail.

Starting a Replication Controller

To generate some application logs in pods we shall start a sample replication controller. Create an RC definition file for a `mysql` Docker image-based container. The RC is created in the `kube-system` namespace.

```
---
apiVersion: v1
kind: ReplicationController
metadata:
  labels:
    app: mysqlapp
  name: mysql-rc
namespace: kube-system
spec:
  replicas: 3
  selector:
    app: mysqlapp
  template:
    metadata:
      labels:
        app: mysqlapp
```

```
spec:
  containers:
    -
      env:
        -
          name: MYSQL_ROOT_PASSWORD
          value: mysql
      image: mysql
      name: mysql
      ports:
        -
          containerPort: 3306
```

The RC definition file is shown in a vi editor in Figure 14-12.

```
---
apiVersion: v1
kind: ReplicationController
metadata:
  labels:
    app: mysqlapp
  name: mysql-rc
  namespace: kube-system
spec:
  replicas: 3
  selector:
    app: mysqlapp
  template:
    metadata:
      labels:
        app: mysqlapp
    spec:
      containers:
        -
          env:
            -
              name: MYSQL_ROOT_PASSWORD
              value: mysql
          image: mysql
          name: mysql
          ports:
            -
              containerPort: 3306

~
:wq
```

Figure 14-12. *Replication controller definition file*

Create an RC with `kubectl create` using the definition file:

```
./kubectl create -f  mysql-rc.yaml
```

List the RC:

```
./kubectl get rc -namespace=kube-system
```

The `mysql-rc` RC should be listed as shown in Figure 14-13.

```
core@ip-10-0-0-50 ~ $ sudo vi mysql-rc.yaml
core@ip-10-0-0-50 ~ $ ./kubectl create -f mysql-rc.yaml
replicationcontroller "mysql-rc" created
core@ip-10-0-0-50 ~ $ ./kubectl get rc --namespace=kube-system
NAME                       DESIRED   CURRENT   AGE
elasticsearch-logging-v1   2         2         21m
kibana-logging-v1          1         1         9m
kube-dns-v11               1         1         26m
mysql-rc                   3         3         11s
```

Figure 14-13. *Creating and listing a replication controller in the `kube-system` namespace*

List the pods in the `kube-system` namespace, and the `mysql` pods should be listed as shown in Figure 14-14.

```
core@ip-10-0-0-50 ~ $ ./kubectl get pods --namespace=kube-system
NAME                                                READY     STATUS
  RESTARTS   AGE
elasticsearch-logging-v1-3eqmk                      1/1       Running
  0          22m
elasticsearch-logging-v1-mnjy8                      1/1       Running
  0          22m
fluentd-elasticsearch                               1/1       Running
  0          13m
heapster-v1.0.2-3151619174-kl0ek                    2/2       Running
  0          25m
kibana-logging-v1-sdb3m                             1/1       Running
  0          9m
kube-apiserver-ip-10-0-0-50.ec2.internal            1/1       Running
  0          26m
kube-controller-manager-ip-10-0-0-50.ec2.internal   1/1       Running
  0          26m
kube-dns-v11-or90k                                  4/4       Running
  0          25m
kube-proxy-ip-10-0-0-206.ec2.internal               1/1       Running
  0          25m
kube-proxy-ip-10-0-0-207.ec2.internal               1/1       Running
```

Figure 14-14. *Listing pods in the `kube-system` namespace*

Starting Elastic Search

In this section we shall create a replication controller and service for Elasticsearch using the Docker image `gcr.io/google_containers/elasticsearch:1.9`. Create an RC definition file `es-controller.yaml` and copy the following listing into it.

```
---
apiVersion: v1
kind: ReplicationController
metadata:
  labels:
    k8s-app: elasticsearch-logging
    kubernetes.io/cluster-service: "true"
    version: v1
  name: elasticsearch-logging-v1
  namespace: kube-system
spec:
  replicas: 2
  selector:
    k8s-app: elasticsearch-logging
    version: v1
  template:
    metadata:
      labels:
        k8s-app: elasticsearch-logging
        kubernetes.io/cluster-service: "true"
        version: v1
    spec:
      containers:
        -
          image: "gcr.io/google_containers/elasticsearch:1.9"
          name: elasticsearch-logging
          ports:
            -
              containerPort: 9200
              name: db
              protocol: TCP
            -
              containerPort: 9300
              name: transport
              protocol: TCP
          resources:
            limits:
              cpu: "0.1"
            requests:
              cpu: "0.1"
          volumeMounts:
            -
              mountPath: /data
              name: es-persistent-storage
```

```
    volumes:
      -
        emptyDir: {}
        name: es-persistent-storage
```

Create an RC using the definition file:

```
./kubectl create -f  es-controller.yaml
```

Create a service definition file `es-service.yaml` for the Elasticsearch RC. Expose the service at port 9200. The selector labels should match labels in the pod.

```
---
apiVersion: v1
kind: Service
metadata:
  labels:
    k8s-app: elasticsearch-logging
    kubernetes.io/cluster-service: "true"
    kubernetes.io/name: Elasticsearch
  name: elasticsearch-logging
  namespace: kube-system
spec:
  ports:
    -
      port: 9200
      protocol: TCP
      targetPort: db
  selector:
    k8s-app: elasticsearch-logging
```

Create a service from the definition file:

```
./kubectl create -f  es-service.yaml
```

The RC, pods, and service for Elasticsearch are created in the `kube-system` namespace and may be listed and described as shown in Figure 14-15.

```
core@ip-10-0-0-50 ~ $ sudo vi es-service.yaml
core@ip-10-0-0-50 ~ $ sudo vi es-controller.yaml
core@ip-10-0-0-50 ~ $ ./kubectl create -f  es-controller.yaml
replicationcontroller "elasticsearch-logging-v1" created
core@ip-10-0-0-50 ~ $ ./kubectl create -f  es-service.yaml
service "elasticsearch-logging" created
core@ip-10-0-0-50 ~ $ ./kubectl get rc --namespace=kube-system
NAME                       DESIRED   CURRENT   AGE
elasticsearch-logging-v1   2         2         32s
kube-dns-v11               1         1         4m
core@ip-10-0-0-50 ~ $ ./kubectl get svc --namespace=kube-system
NAME                    CLUSTER-IP    EXTERNAL-IP   PORT(S)         AGE
elasticsearch-logging   10.3.0.79     <none>        9200/TCP        34s
heapster                10.3.0.18     <none>        80/TCP          5m
kube-dns                10.3.0.10     <none>        53/UDP,53/TCP   5m
core@ip-10-0-0-50 ~ $ ./kubectl get pods --namespace=kube-system
NAME                                             READY     STATUS
  RESTARTS   AGE
elasticsearch-logging-v1-3eqmk                   0/1       ContainerCreating
  0          1m
elasticsearch-logging-v1-mnjy8                   0/1       ContainerCreating
  0          1m
heapster-v1.0.2-3151619174-kl0ek                 2/2       Running
  0          4m
```

Figure 14-15. *Creating an RC and service for Elasticsearch*

Describe the Elasticsearch service to list the service endpoints as shown in Figure 14-16.

```
core@ip-10-0-0-50 ~ $ ./kubectl describe svc elasticsearch-logging --namespace=k
ube-system
Name:                   elasticsearch-logging
Namespace:              kube-system
Labels:                 k8s-app=elasticsearch-logging
                        kubernetes.io/cluster-service=true
                        kubernetes.io/name=Elasticsearch
Selector:               k8s-app=elasticsearch-logging
Type:                   ClusterIP
IP:                     10.3.0.79
Port:                   <unset> 9200/TCP
Endpoints:              10.2.15.2:9200,10.2.69.3:9200
Session Affinity:       None
No events.

core@ip-10-0-0-50 ~ $
```

Figure 14-16. *Describing the Elasticsearch service*

Invoke the service endpoints to invoke the Elasticsearch service, as shown in Figure 14-17.

```
core@ip-10-0-0-50 ~ $ curl 10.2.15.2:9200
{
  "status" : 200,
  "name" : "Jason",
  "cluster_name" : "kubernetes-logging",
  "version" : {
    "number" : "1.5.2",
    "build_hash" : "62ff9868b4c8a0c45860bebb259e21980778ab1c",
    "build_timestamp" : "2015-04-27T09:21:06Z",
    "build_snapshot" : false,
    "lucene_version" : "4.10.4"
  },
  "tagline" : "You Know, for Search"
}
core@ip-10-0-0-50 ~ $ curl 10.2.69.3:9200
{
  "status" : 200,
  "name" : "Maestro",
  "cluster_name" : "kubernetes-logging",
  "version" : {
    "number" : "1.5.2",
    "build_hash" : "62ff9868b4c8a0c45860bebb259e21980778ab1c",
    "build_timestamp" : "2015-04-27T09:21:06Z",
    "build_snapshot" : false,
    "lucene_version" : "4.10.4"
  },
  "tagline" : "You Know, for Search"
}
core@ip-10-0-0-50 ~ $
```

***Figure 14-17.** Invoke testing for the Elasticsearch service*

The kubectl cluster info should list the Elasticsearch as running, as shown in Figure 14-18.

```
core@ip-10-0-0-50 ~ $ ./kubectl cluster-info
Kubernetes master is running at http://localhost:8080
Elasticsearch is running at http://localhost:8080/api/v1/proxy/namespaces/kube-s
ystem/services/elasticsearch-logging
Heapster is running at http://localhost:8080/api/v1/proxy/namespaces/kube-system
/services/heapster
KubeDNS is running at http://localhost:8080/api/v1/proxy/namespaces/kube-system/
services/kube-dns

To further debug and diagnose cluster problems, use 'kubectl cluster-info dump'.
core@ip-10-0-0-50 ~ $
```

***Figure 14-18.** Elasticsearch service listed as Running in Kubernetes Cluster Info*

Starting Fluentd to Collect Logs

Having started the data source (the Kuebrnetes cluster application) and the backend database (Elasticsearch), next we shall start the unifying layer between the two, Fluentd. Create a pod definition file `fluentd-es.yaml` for Fluentd and copy the following listing to the definition file. The Docker image `fabric8/fluentd-kubernetes:v1.9` is used in the pod's container. The Elasticsearch endpoint URL and port to interface with are also specified. The pod mounts the system log directory `/var/log` and the Docker containers directory `/var/lib/docker/containers` from the host path. Volumes of type `hostPath` are used. A different log directory could also be mounted.

```
---
apiVersion: v1
kind: Pod
metadata:
  name: fluentd-elasticsearch
spec:
  containers:
    -
      env:
        -
          name: ELASTICSEARCH_HOST
          value: "10.2.15.2"
        -
          name: ELASTICSEARCH_PORT
          value: "9200"
      image: "fabric8/fluentd-kubernetes:v1.9"
      name: fluentd-elasticsearch
      resources:
        limits:
          cpu: "0.1"
      securityContext:
        privileged: true
      volumeMounts:
        -
          mountPath: /var/log
          name: varlog
        -
          mountPath: /var/lib/docker/containers
          name: varlibdockercontainers
          readOnly: true
  volumes:
    -
      hostPath:
        path: /var/log
      name: varlog
    -
      hostPath:
        path: /var/lib/docker/containers
      name: varlibdockercontainers
```

The pod definition file is shown in the vi editor in Figure 14-19.

```
---
apiVersion: v1
kind: Pod
metadata:
  name: fluentd-elasticsearch
spec:
  containers:
    -
      env:
        -
          name: ELASTICSEARCH_HOST
          value: "10.2.15.2"
        -
          name: ELASTICSEARCH_PORT
          value: "9200"
      image: "fabric8/fluentd-kubernetes:v1.9"
      name: fluentd-elasticsearch
      resources:
        limits:
          cpu: "0.1"
      securityContext:
        privileged: true
      volumeMounts:
        -
          mountPath: /var/log
          name: varlog
        -
          mountPath: /var/lib/docker/containers
:wq
```

Figure 14-19. *Pod definition file for `fluentd`*

Create the pod for Fluentd:

```
./kubectl create -f  fluentd-es.yaml
```

The pod is created in the `kube-system` namespace as shown in Figure 14-20.

```
core@ip-10-0-0-50 ~ $ sudo vi fluentd-es.yaml
core@ip-10-0-0-50 ~ $ ./kubectl create -f  fluentd-es.yaml
pod "fluentd-elasticsearch" created
core@ip-10-0-0-50 ~ $ ./kubectl get pods --namespace=kube-system
NAME                                                 READY     STATUS    RESTARTS
   AGE
elasticsearch-logging-v1-3eqmk                       1/1       Running   0
   8m
elasticsearch-logging-v1-mnjy8                       1/1       Running   0
   8m
fluentd-elasticsearch                                1/1       Running   0
   21s
heapster-v1.0.2-3151619174-kl0ek                     2/2       Running   0
   12m
kube-apiserver-ip-10-0-0-50.ec2.internal             1/1       Running   0
   12m
kube-controller-manager-ip-10-0-0-50.ec2.internal    1/1       Running   0
   12m
kube-dns-v11-or90k                                   4/4       Running   0
   12m
kube-proxy-ip-10-0-0-206.ec2.internal                1/1       Running   0
   12m
kube-proxy-ip-10-0-0-207.ec2.internal                1/1       Running   0
   12m
kube-proxy-ip-10-0-0-208.ec2.internal                1/1       Running   0
   12m
kube-proxy-ip-10-0-0-50.ec2.internal                 1/1       Running   0
   12m
kube-scheduler-ip-10-0-0-50.ec2.internal             1/1       Running   0
   12m
core@ip-10-0-0-50 ~ $ 
```

Figure 14-20. *Creating and listing pod for fluentd*

Starting Kibana

Next, we shall start Kibana to view the logs. Create an RC definition file `kibana-rc.yaml` and copy the following listing to the file. The container image for Kibana is `gcr.io/google_containers/kibana:1.3`. The URL for Elasticsearch also needs to be specified.

```
---
apiVersion: v1
kind: ReplicationController
metadata:
  labels:
    k8s-app: kibana-logging
    kubernetes.io/cluster-service: "true"
    version: v1
  name: kibana-logging-v1
  namespace: kube-system
spec:
  replicas: 1
  selector:
    k8s-app: kibana-logging
    version: v1
```

```
template:
  metadata:
    labels:
      k8s-app: kibana-logging
      kubernetes.io/cluster-service: "true"
      version: v1
  spec:
    containers:
      -
        env:
          -
            name: ELASTICSEARCH_URL
            value: "http://10.2.15.2:9200"
        image: "gcr.io/google_containers/kibana:1.3"
        name: kibana-logging
        ports:
          -
            containerPort: 5601
            name: ui
            protocol: TCP
        resources:
          limits:
            cpu: "0.1"
          requests:
            cpu: "0.1"
```

The RC definition file is shown in the vi editor in Figure 14-21.

```
  replicas: 1
  selector:
    k8s-app: kibana-logging
    version: v1
  template:
    metadata:
      labels:
        k8s-app: kibana-logging
        kubernetes.io/cluster-service: "true"
        version: v1
    spec:
      containers:
        -
          env:
            -
              name: ELASTICSEARCH_URL
              value: "http://10.2.15.2:9200"
          image: "gcr.io/google_containers/kibana:1.3"
          name: kibana-logging
          ports:
            -
              containerPort: 5601
              name: ui
              protocol: TCP
          resources:
            limits:
              cpu: "0.1"
            requests:
              cpu: "0.1"

:wq
```

Figure 14-21. *Replication controller definition file for Kibana*

Create a service definition file `kibana-service.yaml` for the RC and copy the following listing to the file. The Kibana service is exposed at port 5601.

```
---
apiVersion: v1
kind: Service
metadata:
  labels:
    k8s-app: elasticsearch-logging
    kubernetes.io/cluster-service: "true"
    kubernetes.io/name: Kibana
  name: kibana-logging
  namespace: kube-system
spec:
  ports:
    -
      port: 5601
      protocol: TCP
  selector:
    k8s-app: kibana-logging
```

The service definition file in the vi editor is shown in Figure 14-22.

```
---
apiVersion: v1
kind: Service
metadata:
  labels:
    k8s-app: elasticsearch-logging
    kubernetes.io/cluster-service: "true"
    kubernetes.io/name: Kibana
  name: kibana-logging
  namespace: kube-system
spec:
  ports:
    -
      port: 5601
      protocol: TCP
  selector:
    k8s-app: kibana-logging

~
```

Figure 14-22. *Service definition file for Kibana*

Create an RC for Kibana:

```
./kubectl create -f  kibana-rc.yaml
```

Also, create the Kibana service:

```
./kubectl create -f  kibana-service.yaml
```

Kibana RC and service are created as shown in Figure 14-23. List the RC and service, which are in the `kube-system` namespace.

```
core@ip-10-0-0-50 ~ $ sudo vi kibana-rc.yaml
core@ip-10-0-0-50 ~ $ sudo vi kibana-service.yaml
core@ip-10-0-0-50 ~ $ ./kubectl create -f kibana-rc.yaml
replicationcontroller "kibana-logging-v1" created
core@ip-10-0-0-50 ~ $ ./kubectl create -f kibana-service.yaml
service "kibana-logging" created
core@ip-10-0-0-50 ~ $ ./kubectl get rc --namespace=kube-system
NAME                       DESIRED   CURRENT   AGE
elasticsearch-logging-v1   2         2         13m
kibana-logging-v1          1         1         50s
kube-dns-v11               1         1         17m
core@ip-10-0-0-50 ~ $ ./kubectl get svc --namespace=kube-system
NAME                    CLUSTER-IP    EXTERNAL-IP   PORT(S)         AGE
elasticsearch-logging   10.3.0.79     <none>        9200/TCP        13m
heapster                10.3.0.18     <none>        80/TCP          18m
kibana-logging          10.3.0.213    <none>        5601/TCP        1m
kube-dns                10.3.0.10     <none>        53/UDP,53/TCP   18m
core@ip-10-0-0-50 ~ $
```

Figure 14-23. *Creating and listing RC and service for Kibana*

Describe the service to obtain the service endpoint, which is 10.2.15.4:5601, as shown in Figure 14-24.

```
core@ip-10-0-0-50 ~ $ ./kubectl describe svc kibana-logging --namespace=kube-sys
tem
Name:                   kibana-logging
Namespace:              kube-system
Labels:                 k8s-app=elasticsearch-logging
                        kubernetes.io/cluster-service=true
                        kubernetes.io/name=Kibana
Selector:               k8s-app=kibana-logging
Type:                   ClusterIP
IP:                     10.3.0.213
Port:                   <unset> 5601/TCP
Endpoints:              10.2.15.4:5601
Session Affinity:       None
No events.

core@ip-10-0-0-50 ~ $ ▌
```

Figure 14-24. *Describing the Kibana logging service*

To access Kibana Dashboard from a web browser set port forwarding from a local machine. First, we need to copy the key-pair for the CoreOS Kubernetes controller instance to be able to SSH into the controller instance to set port forwarding:

```
scp -i docker.pem ec2-user@ec2-54-208-177-36.compute-1.amazonaws.com:~/kubernetes-coreos.pem
~/kubernetes-coreos.pem
ssh -i kubernetes-coreos.pem -f -nNT -L  5601:10.2.15.4:5601:5601 core@ec2-52-207-33-106.
compute-1.amazonaws.com
```

Port forwarding is set.

Access the Kibana Dashboard from a browser on the local machine with the URL `http://localhost:5601`. The Kibana Dashboard is started, as shown in Figure 14-25.

Figure 14-25. *Kibana Dashboard*

For using Kibana, refer the Kibana documentation. An index pattern may be configured for search as shown in Figure 14-26.

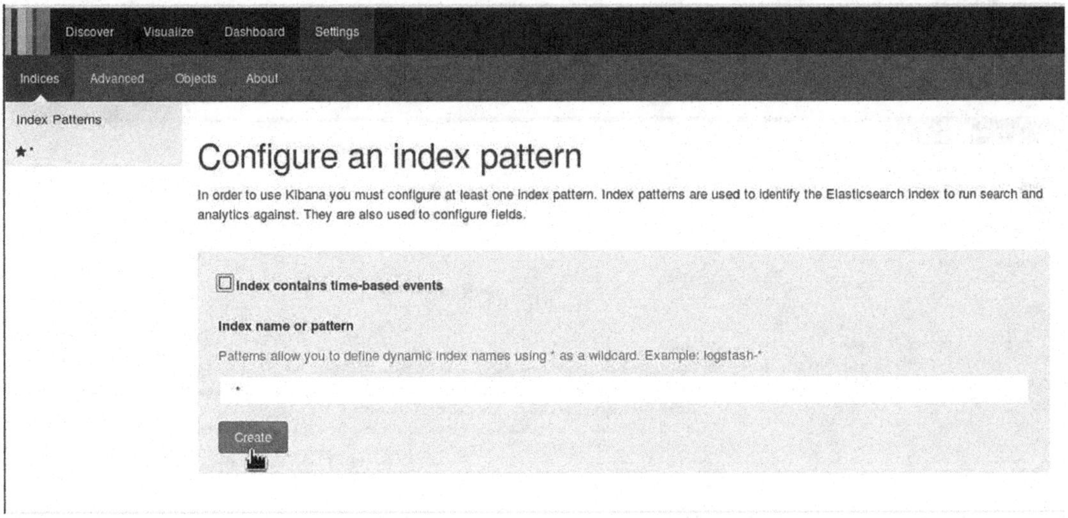

***Figure 14-26.** Configuring an index pattern*

The logs collected from the Kubernetes cluster by Fluentd and the log messages generated by Fluentd itself are displayed as shown in Figure 14-27.

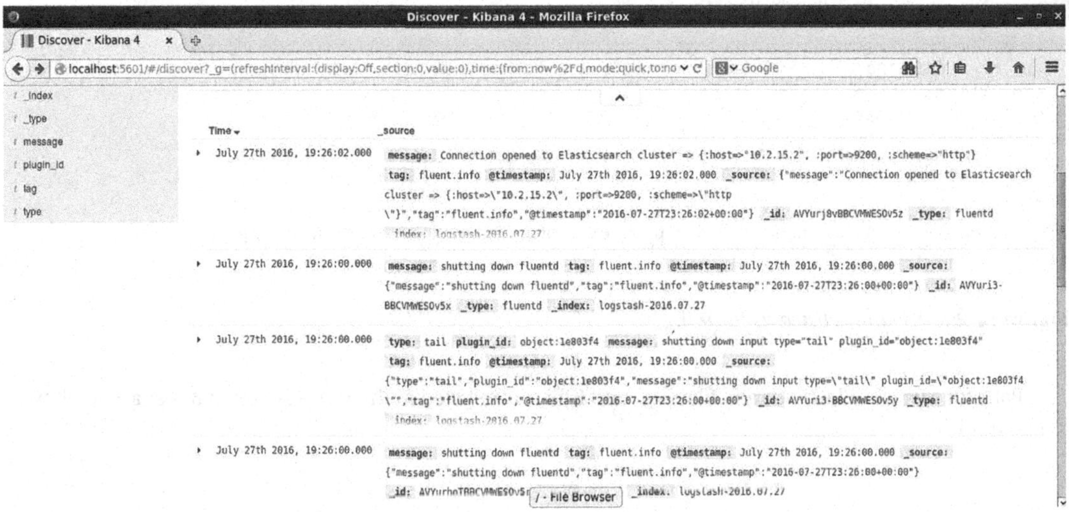

***Figure 14-27.** Displaying log messages in Kibana*

The fields may be navigated from the Popular Fields list as shown in Figure 14-28.

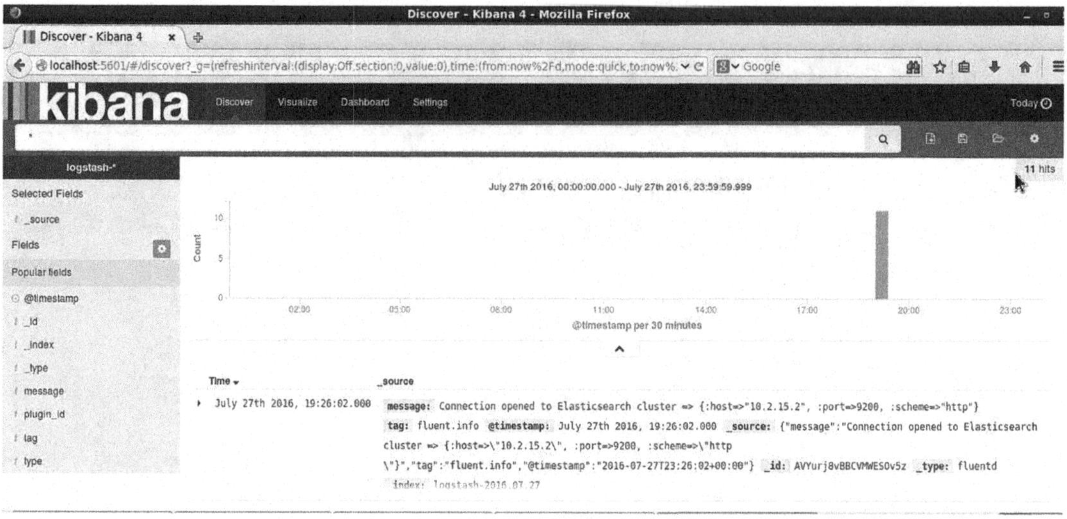

Figure 14-28. *Popular fields in the index*

The Kubernetes cluster info should also list Kibana in addition to the Elasticsearch service as shown in Figure 14-29.

```
core@ip-10-0-0-50 ~ $ ./kubectl cluster-info
Kubernetes master is running at http://localhost:8080
Elasticsearch is running at http://localhost:8080/api/v1/proxy/namespaces/kube-s
ystem/services/elasticsearch-logging
Heapster is running at http://localhost:8080/api/v1/proxy/namespaces/kube-system
/services/heapster
Kibana is running at http://localhost:8080/api/v1/proxy/namespaces/kube-system/s
ervices/kibana-logging
KubeDNS is running at http://localhost:8080/api/v1/proxy/namespaces/kube-system/
services/kube-dns

To further debug and diagnose cluster problems, use 'kubectl cluster-info dump'.
core@ip-10-0-0-50 ~ $
```

Figure 14-29. *Kibana is listed as Running*

Pods for MySQL, Elasticsearch, Fluentd, and Kibana are listed in the `kube-system` namespace as shown in Figure 14-30.

```
core@ip-10-0-0-50 ~ $ ./kubectl get pods --namespace=kube-system
NAME                                                READY     STATUS    RESTARTS
   AGE
elasticsearch-logging-v1-3eqmk                      1/1       Running   0
   22m
elasticsearch-logging-v1-mnjy8                      1/1       Running   0
   22m
fluentd-elasticsearch                               1/1       Running   0
   14m
heapster-v1.0.2-3151619174-kl0ek                    2/2       Running   0
   26m
kibana-logging-v1-sdb3m                             1/1       Running   0
   9m
kube-apiserver-ip-10-0-0-50.ec2.internal            1/1       Running   0
   27m
kube-controller-manager-ip-10-0-0-50.ec2.internal   1/1       Running   0
   27m
kube-dns-v11-or90k                                  4/4       Running   0
   26m
kube-proxy-ip-10-0-0-206.ec2.internal               1/1       Running   0
   26m
kube-proxy-ip-10-0-0-207.ec2.internal               1/1       Running   0
   26m
kube-proxy-ip-10-0-0-208.ec2.internal               1/1       Running   0
   26m
kube-proxy-ip-10-0-0-50.ec2.internal                1/1       Running   0
   27m
kube-scheduler-ip-10-0-0-50.ec2.internal            1/1       Running   0
   27m
mysql-rc-5jfdy                                      1/1       Running   0
   59s
mysql-rc-nnhmt                                      1/1       Running   0
```

Figure 14-30. *Pods for MySQL, Elasticsearch, Fluentd, and Kibana*

Summary

In this chapter we introduced logging, including the default logger and the Docker log files. Subsequently we demonstrate using cluster-level logging to collect and monitor logs with Elasticsearch, Fluentd, and Kibana. In the next chapter we shall discuss using a high-availability master with OpenShift.

PART III

High Availability

CHAPTER 15

Using an HA Master with OpenShift

A Platform as a Service (PaaS) is a cloud platform on which applications may be developed, run, and managed with almost no configuration as the platform provides the application infrastructure including networking, storage, OS, runtime middleware, databases, and other dependency services. Kubernetes is the most commonly used container cluster manager and can be used as the foundation for developing a PaaS. OpenShift is an example of a PaaS.

OpenShift Origin is an open source container application platform providing full application life-cycle management. OpenShift Origin provides standardization through containerization. OpenShift includes an embedded Kubernetes cluster manager to orchestrate Docker containers.

Problem

A single master in a Kubernetes cluster is a single point of failure (SPOF). Failure of the node on which the master controller is running causes the Kubernetes cluster to fail and become inaccessible. At the time of developing this book, CoreOS does not support a high-availability (HA) controller out-of-the-box. CoreOS does provision an Auto Scaling Group and a Launch Configuration so that if a worker node is stopped or fails, another worker node is started.

Solution

Using a high availability (HA) master, which consists of more than one Kubernetes master with failover configured, provides high availability to the cluster, and failure of a single master does not cause the cluster to fail. An alternative to the CoreOS Linux-based cluster is to use the OpenShift platform, which can configure multiple master nodes. Amazon Elastic Load Balancers may be used to provide failover from a controller node running in one zone to a controller node running in another zone with an Inter-AWS Zone High-availability Architecture. AWS does not support Inter-AWS Region High-Availability Architecture for Elastic Load Balancers. HA master is a Kubernetes design pattern that is implemented by only some of the tools, such as the Kubernetes-based PaaS OpenShift. The OpenShift HA Master is based on the Active-Active architectural pattern, in which both master nodes are active and provide redundancy. An Elastic Load Balancer is used to distribute the load across the two master nodes. The HA master controller API server is exposed on the Load Balancer, as shown in Figure 15-1, and not directly on the master nodes.

D. Vohra, *Kubernetes Management Design Patterns*, DOI 10.1007/978-1-4842-2598-1_15

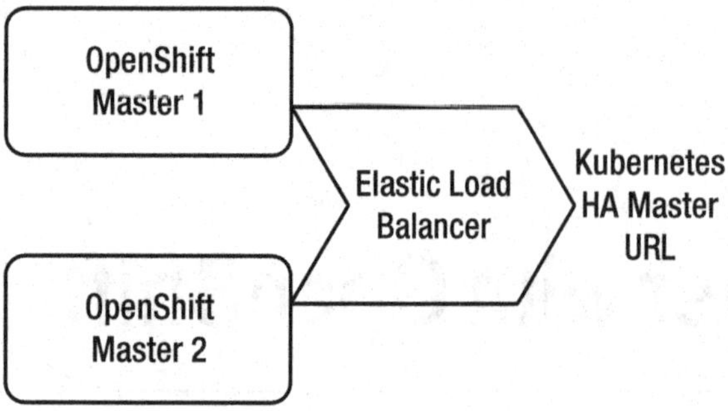

Figure 15-1. *OpenShift HA master*

Overview

A typical production level OpenShift Origin cluster would consist of a high-availability master. In this chapter we shall discuss such a high-availability master OpenShift Origin cluster. The stages are as follows:

- Setting the environment
- Installing the credentials
- Installing the network manager
- Installing OpenShift Ansible
- Configuring Ansible
- Running Ansible Playbook
- Testing the cluster
- Testing the HA

Setting the Environment

The OpenShift cluster we shall create consists of the following EC2 instances.

- 1 Ubuntu instance for OpenShift Ansible
- 2 CentOS 7 for OpenShift Masters
- 1 CentOS 7 for HAProxy
- 1 CentOS 7 for OpenShift Worker
- 1 Centos 7 for etcd

CentOS 7 instances may be launched from `https://aws.amazon.com/marketplace/pp/B00O7WM7QW`. Select a Region and click Continue. In the Launch on EC2:CentOS 7 (x86_64) - with Updates HVM dialog that appears, select an m3.large or larger EC2 Instance Type. For VPC select EC2 Classic. For Key Pair select a pre-existing key pair (`docker.pem` in the example). Click the button Launch With 1-Click. The CentOS instances are shown in Figure 15-2.

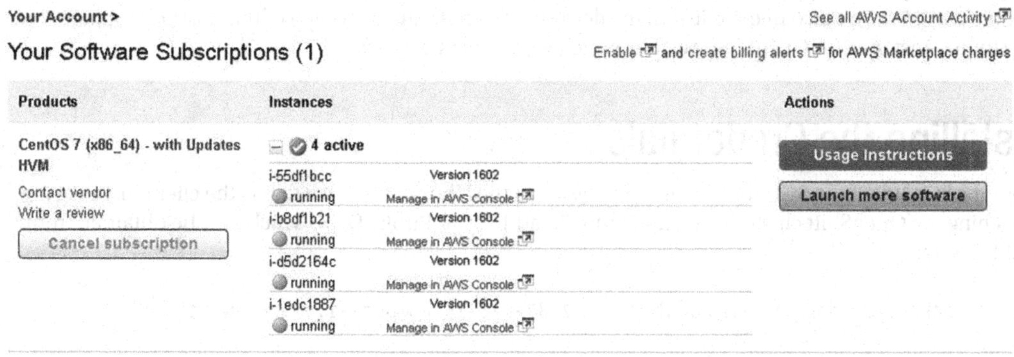

Figure 15-2. *Launching CentoOS instances*

Launch one EC2 instance based on the Ubuntu AMI. The required instances for the OpenShift cluster are shown in Figure 15-3. Additional master, worker and Etcd instances may be added, but we have used the minimum number of instances to define a HA master cluster.

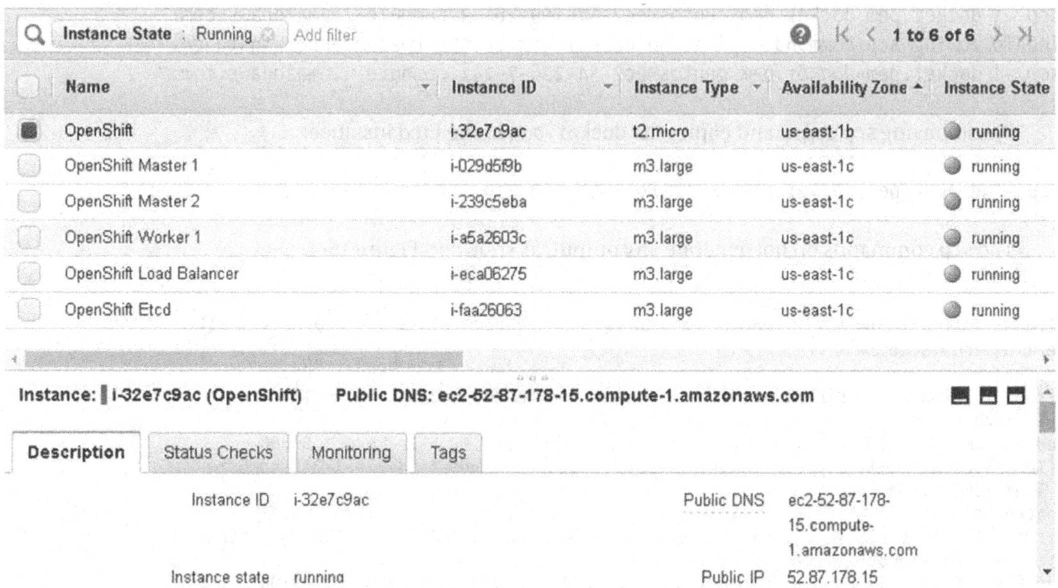

Figure 15-3. *CentoOS instances for OpenShift cluster*

The following software needs to be installed:

- Docker on each CoreOS instance
- Etcd on the etcd instances
- HAProxy on the LoadBalancer instance
- Network Manager on each CentOS instance

All of the preceding software except the Network Manager is installed automatically when we run the Ansible playbook. We also need to install the `docker.pem` credentials on each of the CoreOS instances and the Ubuntu instance for OpenShift Ansible, which we shall install next.

Installing the Credentials

From the local machine SCP copy the `docker.pem` into the Ubuntu instance that is the client instance for launching the OpenShift cluster using the Public IP address or Public DNS, which may be obtained from the EC2 Console:

```
scp -i docker.pem docker.pem ubuntu@ec2-52-87-178-15.compute-1.amazonaws.com:~
```

Similarly, obtain the Public DNS for each of the CentOS instances, the ones for the masters, worker, Etcd, and LoadBalancer. SCP copy the `docker.pem` file to each of the CentOS instances. The following `scp` commands copy the `docker.pem` file to the master instances:

```
scp -i docker.pem docker.pem centos@ec2-54-90-107-98.compute-1.amazonaws.com:~
scp -i docker.pem docker.pem centos@ec2-54-221-182-68.compute-1.amazonaws.com:~
The following scp command copies the docker.pem to the Worker instance.
scp -i docker.pem docker.pem centos@ec2-54-159-26-13.compute-1.amazonaws.com:~
The following scp command copies the docker.pem to the LoadBalancer instance.
scp -i docker.pem docker.pem centos@ec2-54-226-7-241.compute-1.amazonaws.com:~
```

The following `scp` command copies the `docker.pem` to the Etcd instance:

```
scp -i docker.pem docker.pem centos@ec2-54-160-210-253.compute-1.amazonaws.com:~
```

The `scp` commands do not generate any output, as shown in Figure 15-4.

```
[root@localhost ~]# scp -i docker.pem docker.pem centos@ec2-54-221-182-68.comput
e-1.amazonaws.com:~
docker.pem                                    100% 1696     1.7KB/s   00:00
[root@localhost ~]# scp -i docker.pem docker.pem centos@ec2-54-159-26-13.compute
-1.amazonaws.com:~
docker.pem                                    100% 1696     1.7KB/s   00:00
[root@localhost ~]# scp -i docker.pem docker.pem centos@ec2-54-226-7-241.compute
-1.amazonaws.com:~
docker.pem                                    100% 1696     1.7KB/s   00:00
[root@localhost ~]# scp -i docker.pem docker.pem centos@ec2-54-160-210-253.compu
te-1.amazonaws.com:~
docker.pem                                    100% 1696     1.7KB/s   00:00
```

Figure 15-4. *Copying `docker.pem` to each of the CoreOS instances*

Installing the Network Manager

For network connectivity the OpenShift cluster makes use of Network Manager, which we need to install on each of the CentOS instances. SSH log in into each of the CentOS instances:

```
ssh -i docker.pem centos@ec2-54-90-107-98.compute-1.amazonaws.com
ssh -i docker.pem centos@ec2-54-221-182-68.compute-1.amazonaws.com
ssh -i docker.pem centos@ec2-54-159-26-13.compute-1.amazonaws.com
ssh -i docker.pem centos@ec2-54-226-7-241.compute-1.amazonaws.com
ssh -i docker.pem centos@ec2-54-160-210-253.compute-1.amazonaws.com
```

Run the following commands on each of the CentOS instances to install, start, and enable the Network Manager and find its status:

```
sudo yum install NetworkManager
sudo systemctl start NetworkManager
sudo systemctl enable NetworkManager
sudo systemctl status NetworkManager
```

Installing OpenShift via Ansible on the Client Machine

We shall use the Ansible software automation platform to install the OpenShift software remotely from the Ubuntu instance. We do not need to log into each of the OpenShift cluster instances to launch any software other than the Network Manager, which we already have installed. SSH log into the Ubuntu instance:

```
ssh -i "docker.pem" ubuntu@ec2-52-87-178-15.compute-1.amazonaws.com
```

Ubuntu builds for Ansible are available in the Ubuntu Personal Package Archive (PPA). To configure PPA and install Ansible, first run the following commands:

```
 sudo apt-get install software-properties-common
sudo apt-add-repository ppa:ansible/ansible
```

The Ansible PPA is added to the repository as shown in Figure 15-5.

```
ubuntu@ip-10-0-0-120:~$  sudo apt-get install software-properties-common
Reading package lists... Done
Building dependency tree
Reading state information... Done
software-properties-common is already the newest version.
0 upgraded, 0 newly installed, 0 to remove and 0 not upgraded.
ubuntu@ip-10-0-0-120:~$  sudo apt-add-repository ppa:ansible/ansible
 Ansible is a radically simple IT automation platform that makes your applicatio
ns and systems easier to deploy. Avoid writing scripts or custom code to deploy
and update your applications— automate in a language that approaches plain Engli
sh, using SSH, with no agents to install on remote systems.

http://ansible.com/
 More info: https://launchpad.net/~ansible/+archive/ubuntu/ansible
Press [ENTER] to continue or ctrl-c to cancel adding it

gpg: keyring `/tmp/tmpiz0jc4ly/secring.gpg' created
gpg: keyring `/tmp/tmpiz0jc4ly/pubring.gpg' created
gpg: requesting key 7BB9C367 from hkp server keyserver.ubuntu.com
gpg: /tmp/tmpiz0jc4ly/trustdb.gpg: trustdb created
gpg: key 7BB9C367: public key "Launchpad PPA for Ansible, Inc." imported
gpg: Total number processed: 1
gpg:               imported: 1  (RSA: 1)
OK
ubuntu@ip-10-0-0-120:~$ ▌
```

Figure 15-5. *Installing Ansible PPA*

Update the repository and install Ansible:

```
sudo apt-get update
sudo apt-get install ansible
```

Ansible is installed on the Ubuntu instance.

Download the openshift-ansible git repository. CD (change directory) to the openshift-ansible directory:

```
git clone https://github.com/openshift/openshift-ansible.git
cd openshift-ansible
```

To list the default settings for the IP addresses and host names run the following command:

```
ansible-playbook playbooks/byo/openshift_facts.yml
```

The command output is shown in Figure 15-6.

```
ubuntu@ip-10-0-0-120:~/openshift-ansible$ ansible-playbook playbooks/byo/openshi
ft_facts.yml
 [WARNING]: provided hosts list is empty, only localhost is available


PLAY [localhost] ***************************************************************

TASK [Verify Ansible version is greater than or equal to 2.1.0.0] **************
skipping: [localhost]

PLAY [localhost] ***************************************************************

TASK [include_vars] ************************************************************
ok: [localhost]

TASK [add_host] ****************************************************************
[DEPRECATION WARNING]: Using bare variables is deprecated. Update your playbooks
 so that the environment value uses the full variable syntax
('{{g_all_hosts}}').
This feature will be removed in a future release.
Deprecation warnings can be disabled by setting deprecation_warnings=False in
ansible.cfg.

PLAY [l_oo_all_hosts] **********************************************************
skipping: no hosts matched
```

Figure 15-6. *Listing the default settings for the IP addresses and hostnames*

The default IP address/hostname settings are output as shown in Figure 15-7.

```
TASK [Evaluate oo_etcd_to_config] **********************************************

TASK [Evaluate oo_masters_to_config] *******************************************

TASK [Evaluate oo_nodes_to_config] *********************************************

TASK [Evaluate oo_nodes_to_config] *********************************************

TASK [Evaluate oo_first_etcd] **************************************************
skipping: [localhost]

TASK [Evaluate oo_first_master] ************************************************
skipping: [localhost]

TASK [Evaluate oo_lb_to_config] ************************************************

TASK [Evaluate oo_nfs_to_config] ***********************************************

PLAY [Gather Cluster facts] ****************************************************
skipping: no hosts matched

PLAY RECAP *********************************************************************
localhost                  : ok=1    changed=0    unreachable=0    failed=0

ubuntu@ip-10-0-0-120:~/openshift-ansible$ ▌
```

Figure 15-7. *Default IP address/hostname settings*

Configuring Ansible

Some of the Ansible configuration settings may be modified in the /etc/ansible/ansible.cfg configuration file. We need to modify some of these settings for OpenShift Ansible. Open the /etc/ansible/ansible.cfg file in a vi editor.

```
sudo vi /etc/ansible/ansible.cfg
```

Add/modify the following settings in the [defaults] header.

```
sudo= yes
ask_sudo_pass=False
ask_pass=False
remote_user = centos
host_key_checking = False
timeout=0
private_key_file= ~/docker.pem
```

Some of the settings are shown in ansible.cfg in Figure 15-8.

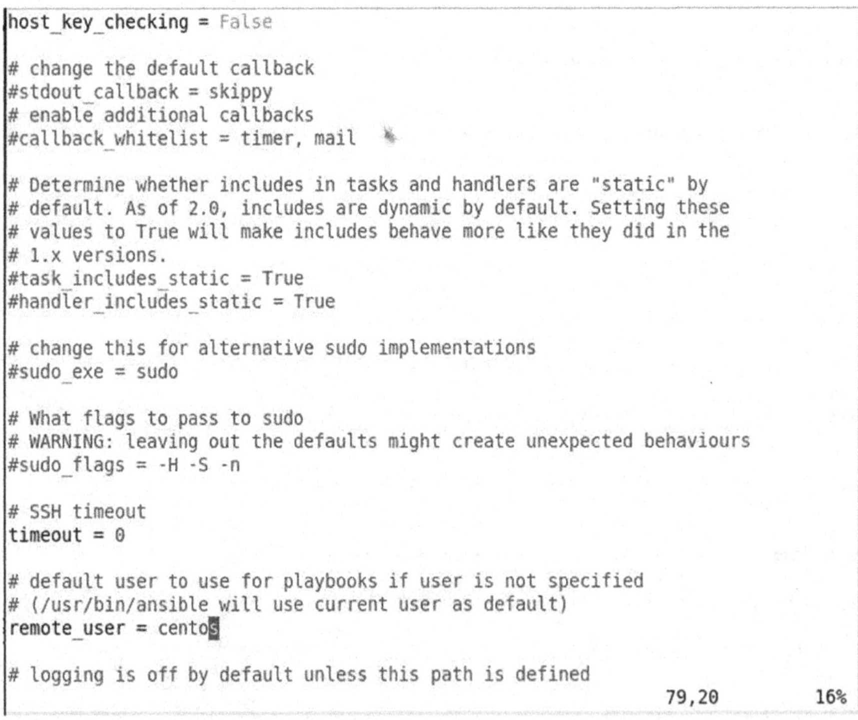

host_key_checking = False

change the default callback
#stdout_callback = skippy
enable additional callbacks
#callback_whitelist = timer, mail

Determine whether includes in tasks and handlers are "static" by
default. As of 2.0, includes are dynamic by default. Setting these
values to True will make includes behave more like they did in the
1.x versions.
#task_includes_static = True
#handler_includes_static = True

change this for alternative sudo implementations
#sudo_exe = sudo

What flags to pass to sudo
WARNING: leaving out the defaults might create unexpected behaviours
#sudo_flags = -H -S -n

# SSH timeout
timeout = 0

# default user to use for playbooks if user is not specified
# (/usr/bin/ansible will use current user as default)
remote_user = centos

logging is off by default unless this path is defined
79,20 16%

Figure 15-8. *Configuring ansible.cfg*

These properties are spread out throughout the file and are not collocated, as shown in Figure 15-9.

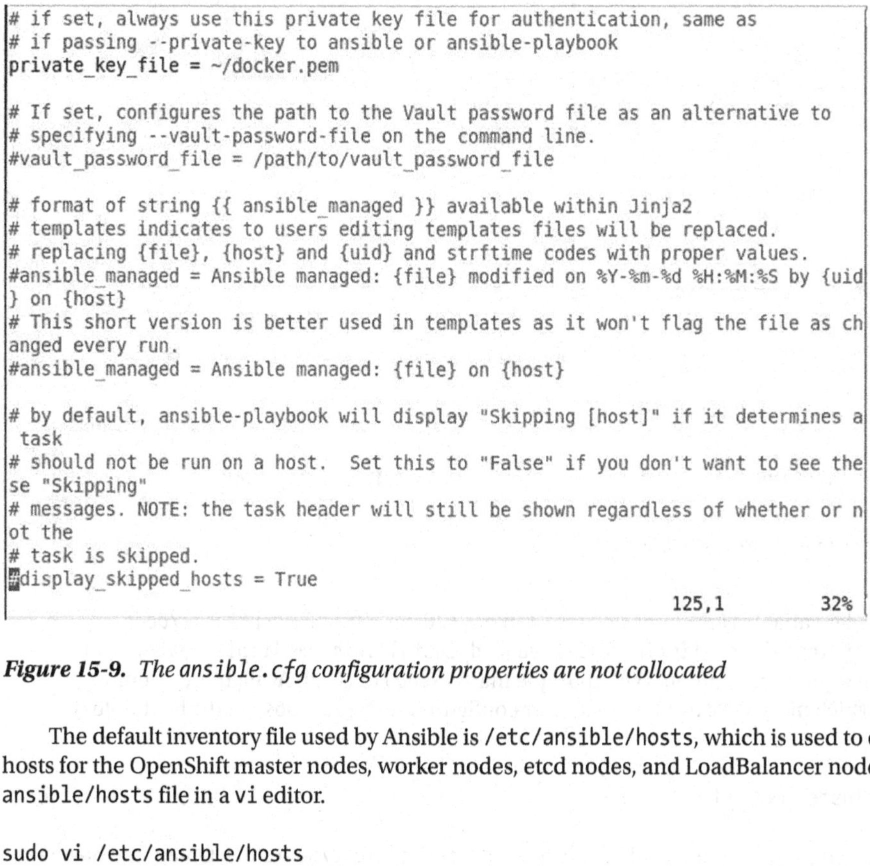

```
# if set, always use this private key file for authentication, same as
# if passing --private-key to ansible or ansible-playbook
private_key_file = ~/docker.pem

# If set, configures the path to the Vault password file as an alternative to
# specifying --vault-password-file on the command line.
#vault_password_file = /path/to/vault_password_file

# format of string {{ ansible_managed }} available within Jinja2
# templates indicates to users editing templates files will be replaced.
# replacing {file}, {host} and {uid} and strftime codes with proper values.
#ansible_managed = Ansible managed: {file} modified on %Y-%m-%d %H:%M:%S by {uid
} on {host}
# This short version is better used in templates as it won't flag the file as ch
anged every run.
#ansible_managed = Ansible managed: {file} on {host}

# by default, ansible-playbook will display "Skipping [host]" if it determines a
 task
# should not be run on a host.  Set this to "False" if you don't want to see the
se "Skipping"
# messages. NOTE: the task header will still be shown regardless of whether or n
ot the
# task is skipped.
#display_skipped_hosts = True
                                                          125,1          32%
```

Figure 15-9. *The `ansible.cfg` configuration properties are not collocated*

The default inventory file used by Ansible is `/etc/ansible/hosts`, which is used to configure the hosts for the OpenShift master nodes, worker nodes, etcd nodes, and LoadBalancer node. Open the `/etc/ansible/hosts` file in a `vi` editor.

```
sudo vi /etc/ansible/hosts
```

At the top of the file configure the following:

```
[OSEv3:children]
masters
etcd
lb
nodes
```

Next, specify some variables:

```
 [OSEv3:vars]
ansible_user=centos
ansible_sudo=true
deployment_type=origin
ansible_ssh_private_key_file=~/docker.pem
```

The top section of the `/etc/ansible/hosts` file is shown in Figure 15-10.

```
# This is the default ansible 'hosts' file.
#
# It should live in /etc/ansible/hosts
#
#   - Comments begin with the '#' character
#   - Blank lines are ignored
#   - Groups of hosts are delimited by [header] elements
#   - You can enter hostnames or ip addresses
#   - A hostname/ip can be a member of multiple groups
[OSEv3:children]
masters
etcd
lb
nodes

# Ex 1: Ungrouped hosts, specify before any group headers.
[OSEv3:vars]
ansible_user=centos
ansible_sudo=true
deployment_type=origin
ansible_ssh_private_key_file=~/docker.pem

"/etc/ansible/hosts" 77L, 3193C                          1,1           Top
```

Figure 15-10. *The /etc/ansible/hosts file*

Several other cluster variables are supported (see Table 2. Cluster Variables at https://docs.openshift.org/latest/install_config/install/advanced_install.html#multiple-masters), but we have used only the minimum required. With multiple masters the HA (High Availability) method native is supported, which makes use of a LoadBalancer configured with [lb] host in the hosts file or preconfigured.

```
openshift_master_cluster_method=native
```

We shall be specifying a host for the load balancer in the /etc/ansible/hosts file. Obtain the hostname or the Public DNS or the Public IP for the load balancer instance from the EC2 Console and specify the same in the following settings in the /etc/ansible/hosts file:

```
openshift_master_cluster_hostname=ec2-54-226-7-241.compute-1.amazonaws.com
openshift_master_cluster_public_hostname=ec2-54-226-7-241.compute-1.amazonaws.com
```

Next, specify the masters in the /etc/ansible/hosts file.

Several host variables (see Table 1. Host Variables at the URL shown above) are supported, but we have used only the host variables shown in Table 15-1 for the master, worker, etcd and lb.

Table 15-1. *Host Variables*

Host Variable	Description	ExampleValue
openshift_ip	Private IP which may be obtained from the EC2 Console	10.156.14.183
openshift_public_ip	Public IP which may be obtained from the EC2 Console	54.90.107.98
openshift_hostname	The hostname for the host which may be obtained from the Private DNS in the EC2 Console	ip-10-156-14-183.ec2.internal
openshift_public_hostname	The public hostname for the host which may be obtained from the Public DNS in the EC2 Console	ec2-54-90-107-98.compute-1.amazonaws.com

Similarly configure the [etcd], [lb] and [nodes] sections. The masters are also listed in the [nodes] but made non-schedulable with openshift_schedulable set to false and have the labels added with openshift_node_labels. The hosts settings should be similar to the following; the hostnames and IP address would be different for different users.

```
[masters]
ec2-54-90-107-98.compute-1.amazonaws.com openshift_ip=10.156.14.183 openshift_public_
ip=54.90.107.98 openshift_hostname=ip-10-156-14-183.ec2.internal openshift_public_
hostname=ec2-54-90-107-98.compute-1.amazonaws.com
ec2-54-221-182-68.compute-1.amazonaws.com openshift_ip=10.154.46.153 openshift_public_
ip=54.221.182.68 openshift_hostname=ip-10-154-46-153.ec2.internal openshift_public_
hostname=ec2-54-221-182-68.compute-1.amazonaws.com

[etcd]
ec2-54-160-210-253.compute-1.amazonaws.com openshift_ip=10.153.195.121 openshift_public_
ip=54.160.210.253 openshift_hostname=ip-10-153-195-121.ec2.internal openshift_public_
hostname=ec2-54-160-210-253.compute-1.amazonaws.com

[lb]
ec2-54-226-7-241.compute-1.amazonaws.com openshift_ip=10.154.38.224 openshift_public_
ip=54.226.7.241 openshift_hostname=ip-10-154-38-224.ec2.internal openshift_public_
hostname=ec2-54-226-7-241.compute-1.amazonaws.com

[nodes]
ec2-54-90-107-98.compute-1.amazonaws.com openshift_ip=10.156.14.183 openshift_public_
ip=54.90.107.98 openshift_hostname=ip-10-156-14-183.ec2.internal openshift_public_
hostname=ec2-54-90-107-98.compute-1.amazonaws.com openshift_node_labels="{'region':
'primary', 'zone': 'east'}" openshift_schedulable=false
ec2-54-221-182-68.compute-1.amazonaws.com openshift_ip=10.154.46.153 openshift_public_
ip=54.221.182.68 openshift_hostname=ip-10-154-46-153.ec2.internal openshift_public_
hostname=ec2-54-221-182-68.compute-1.amazonaws.com openshift_node_labels="{'region':
'primary', 'zone': 'east'}" openshift_schedulable=false
ec2-54-159-26-13.compute-1.amazonaws.com  openshift_ip=10.113.176.99 openshift_public_
ip=54.159.26.13 openshift_hostname=ip-10-113-176-99.ec2.internal openshift_public_
hostname=ec2-54-159-26-13.compute-1.amazonaws.com openshift_node_labels="{'region':
'primary', 'zone': 'east'}"
```

Running the Ansible Playbook

The default inventory file is `/etc/ansible/hosts` but another file may be configured with the inventory setting in the `ansible.cfg`, for example:

```
inventory = /etc/ansible/inventory/hosts
```

We have configured the default inventory file `/etc/ansible/hosts`. Start the OpenShift cluster by running the Ansible playbook:

```
ansible-playbook ~/openshift-ansible/playbooks/byo/config.yml
```

The OpenShift software such as Docker, HAProxy, and so on are installed and started on the configured hosts, as shown in Figure 15-11.

```
TASK [openshift_hosted : set_fact] *********************************************
skipping: [ec2-54-90-107-98.compute-1.amazonaws.com]

TASK [openshift_hosted : Determine if volume is already attached to dc/docker-re
gistry] ***
skipping: [ec2-54-90-107-98.compute-1.amazonaws.com]

TASK [openshift_hosted : set_fact] *********************************************
skipping: [ec2-54-90-107-98.compute-1.amazonaws.com]

TASK [openshift_hosted : Add volume to dc/docker-registry] *********************
skipping: [ec2-54-90-107-98.compute-1.amazonaws.com]

TASK [openshift_hosted : Delete temp directory] ********************************
ok: [ec2-54-90-107-98.compute-1.amazonaws.com]

PLAY RECAP *********************************************************************
ec2-54-159-26-13.compute-1.amazonaws.com : ok=143  changed=42   unreachable=0
 failed=0
ec2-54-160-210-253.compute-1.amazonaws.com : ok=97   changed=34   unreachable=0
   failed=0
ec2-54-221-182-68.compute-1.amazonaws.com : ok=274  changed=91   unreachable=0
  failed=0
ec2-54-226-7-241.compute-1.amazonaws.com : ok=71   changed=17   unreachable=0
 failed=0
ec2-54-90-107-98.compute-1.amazonaws.com : ok=411  changed=106  unreachable=0
 failed=0
localhost                  : ok=15   changed=9    unreachable=0    failed=0

ubuntu@ip-10-0-0-128:~/openshift-ansible$
```

Figure 15-11. *Running the Ansible Playbook*

SSH log in to one of the master instances and list the nodes in the OpenShift cluster:

```
oc get nodes
```

The three nodes, two of them non-schedulable, are listed as shown in Figure 15-12.

```
[root@localhost ~]# ssh -i docker.pem centos@ec2-54-90-107-98.compute-1.amazonaw
s.com
Last login: Tue Aug  9 01:17:23 2016 from ec2-52-87-178-15.compute-1.amazonaws.c
om
[centos@ip-10-156-14-183 ~]$ sudo oc get nodes
NAME                            STATUS                        AGE
ip-10-113-176-99.ec2.internal   Ready                         33m
ip-10-154-46-153.ec2.internal   Ready,SchedulingDisabled      33m
ip-10-156-14-183.ec2.internal   Ready,SchedulingDisabled      33m
[centos@ip-10-156-14-183 ~]$ █
```

Figure 15-12. *The nodes in the OpenShift cluster*

Testing the Cluster

To test the OpenShift cluster, log in to the cluster.

```
oc login
```

Specify Username as system and Password as admin. The OpenShift cluster is logged in. Initially no projects are created, as shown in Figure 15-13.

```
[centos@ip-10-156-14-183 ~]$ oc login
Authentication required for https://ec2-54-226-7-241.compute-1.amazonaws.com:844
3 (openshift)
Username: system
Password:
Login successful.

You don't have any projects. You can try to create a new project, by running

    $ oc new-project <projectname>

[centos@ip-10-156-14-183 ~]$ █
```

Figure 15-13. *Logging into the OpenShift cluster*

Create a new project, for example `hello-openshift` with the oc `new-project` command:

```
oc new-project hello-openshift
```

The `hello-openshift` project is created as shown in Figure 15-14.

```
[centos@ip-10-156-14-183 ~]$ oc new-project hello-openshift
Now using project "hello-openshift" on server "https://ec2-54-226-7-241.compute-
1.amazonaws.com:8443".

You can add applications to this project with the 'new-app' command. For example
, try:

    $ oc new-app centos/ruby-22-centos7~https://github.com/openshift/ruby-hello-
world.git

to build a new hello-world application in Ruby.
[centos@ip-10-156-14-183 ~]$ █
```

Figure 15-14. *Creating the `hello-openshift` project*

Find the project status:

```
oc status
```

Create a new OpenShift application with the `oc new-app` command.

```
oc new-app openshift/ruby-20-centos7~https://github.com/openshift/ruby-hello-world.git
```

A new OpenShift application is created.

To delete all the objects for an application run the following command:

```
oc delete all -l app=appName
```

For example, to delete all the objects for the `hello-world` application, run the following command:

```
oc delete all -l app=hello-world
```

Create some other application with the `oc new-app` command. The image tag may be specified, for example for the `openshift/deployment-example` Docker image.

```
oc new-app openshift/deployment-example:v1
```

An OpenShift application is created. Initially the `oc get pods` command may list the pods as not running, but with Status ContainerCreating as shown in Figure 15-15.

```
[centos@ip-10-156-14-183 ~]$ oc get pods
NAME                         READY     STATUS              RESTARTS   AGE
deployment-example-1-deploy  0/1       ContainerCreating   0          17s
[centos@ip-10-156-14-183 ~]$ oc get pods
NAME                         READY     STATUS              RESTARTS   AGE
deployment-example-1-deploy  0/1       ContainerCreating   0          22s
```

Figure 15-15. *Listing the pods*

Multiple applications from the same Docker image may be started concurrently; for example, run the same command again:

```
oc new-app openshift/deployment-example:v1
```

When both the applications have started, two pods are listed, as shown in Figure 15-16.

```
[centos@ip-10-156-14-183 ~]$ oc get pods
NAME                         READY     STATUS    RESTARTS   AGE
deployment-example-1-awoib   1/1       Running   0          4s
deployment-example-1-deploy  1/1       Running   0          38s
[centos@ip-10-156-14-183 ~]$ 
```

Figure 15-16. *Running multiple applications concurrently*

The node on which a pod is running may be listed with the following command:

```
oc get -o wide pods
```

The node for the pod also is listed as shown in Figure 15-17.

```
[centos@ip-10-156-14-183 ~]$ oc get -o wide pods
NAME                         READY     STATUS     RESTARTS    AGE       NODE
deployment-example-1-awoib   1/1       Running    0           1m        ip-10-113-
176-99.ec2.internal
[centos@ip-10-156-14-183 ~]$ ▌
```

Figure 15-17. *Listing pods including the nodes*

The `oc describe` command is used to describe a deployment:

```
oc describe dc/deployment-example
```

The services are listed with the following command:

```
oc get services
```

List all OpenShift objects with the following command:

```
oc get all
```

Testing the High Availability

With multiple masters and High availability configured with the native method, the load balancer distributes the master load across the masters. The master API server is exposed on the IP Address of the load balancer, but actually one API server is running on each of the masters. The two master instances and the single worker instance are shown in Figure 15-18.

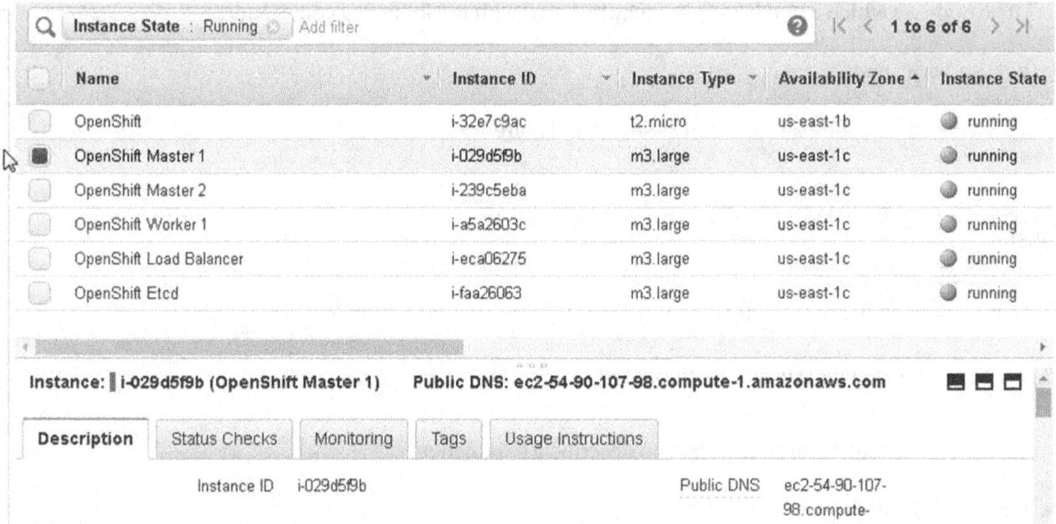

Figure 15-18. *EC2 instances running OpenShift masters and worker*

To demonstrate the high availability of the cluster, shut down one of the masters. Select the master instance in the EC2 Console and in Actions select Instance State ➤ Stop as shown in Figure 15-19.

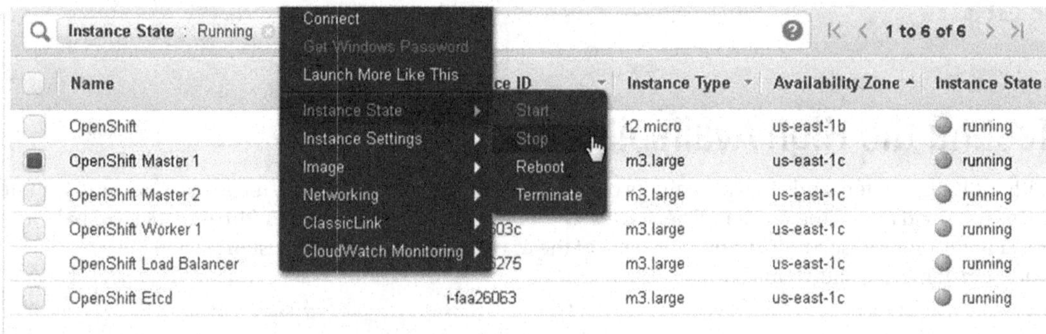

Figure 15-19. *Stopping an OpenShift master*

In the Stop Instances dialog click on Yes, Stop as shown in Figure 15-20.

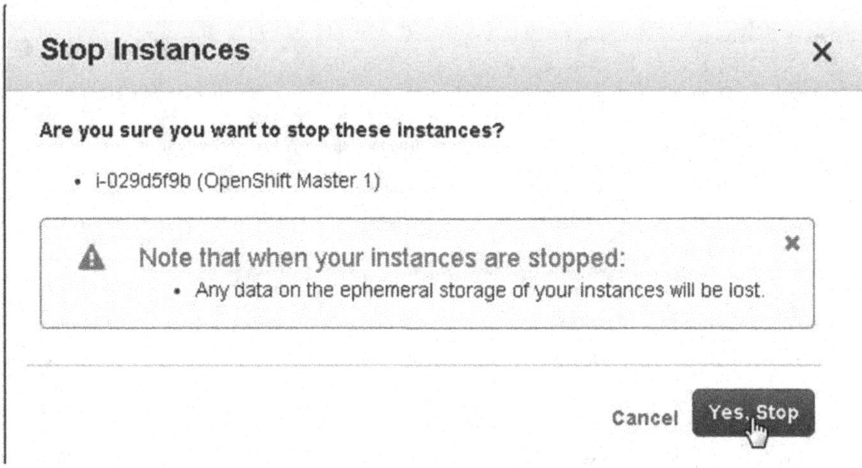

Figure 15-20. *The Stop Instances dialog*

One of the masters starts to shut down, as shown in Figure 15-21.

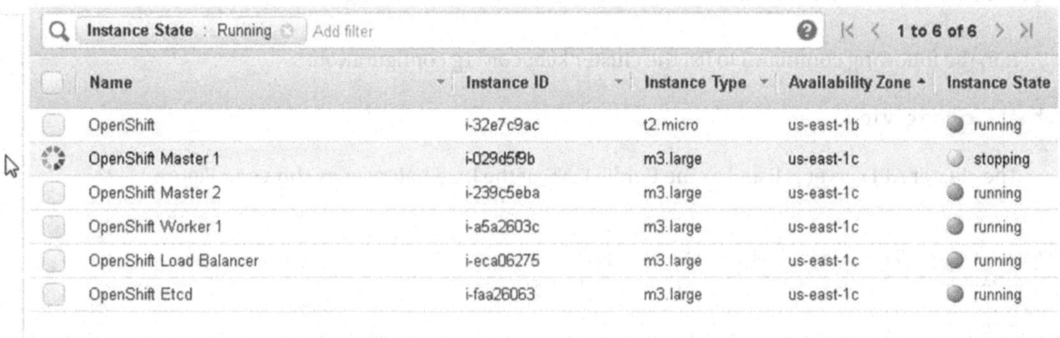

Figure 15-21. *One of the OpenShift masters stopping*

After the master shuts down, the load balancer and the other masters should still be running as shown in Figure 15-22.

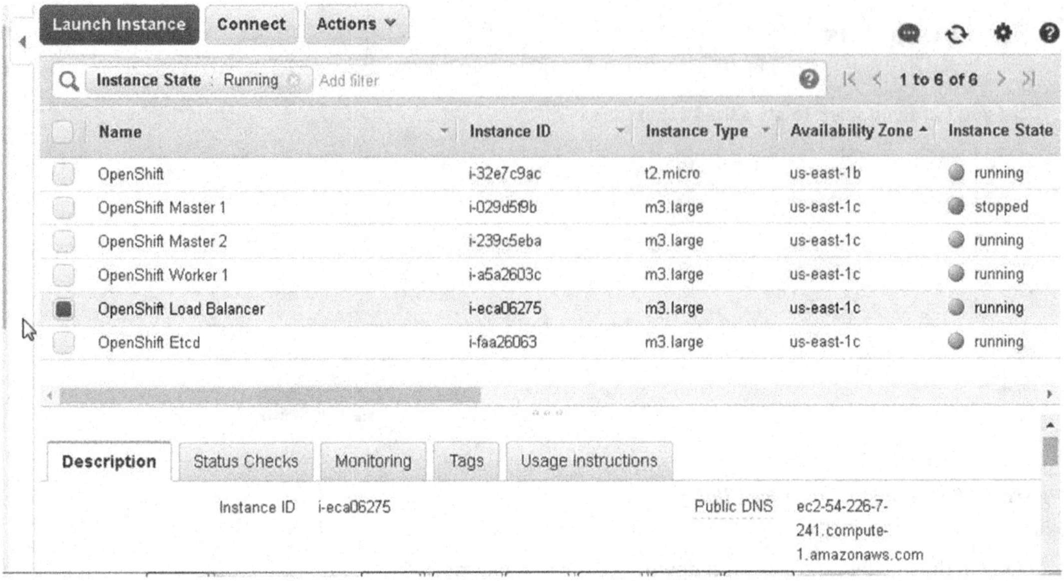

***Figure 15-22.** OpenShift Load Balancer and the other master still running*

Run the following command to list the cluster kubeconfig configuration.

```
kubectl config view
```

The cluster API server is listed as the Public DNS of the load balancer as shown in Figure 15-23.

```
[centos@ip-10-154-46-153 ~]$ kubectl config view
apiVersion: v1
clusters:
- cluster:
    certificate-authority-data: REDACTED
    server: https://ec2-54-226-7-241.compute-1.amazonaws.com:8443
  name: ec2-54-226-7-241-compute-1-amazonaws-com:8443
contexts:
- context:
    cluster: ec2-54-226-7-241-compute-1-amazonaws-com:8443
    namespace: default
    user: system:admin/ec2-54-226-7-241-compute-1-amazonaws-com:8443
  name: default/ec2-54-226-7-241-compute-1-amazonaws-com:8443/system:admin
current-context: default/ec2-54-226-7-241-compute-1-amazonaws-com:8443/system:ad
min
kind: Config
preferences: {}
users:
- name: system:admin/ec2-54-226-7-241-compute-1-amazonaws-com:8443
  user:
    client-certificate-data: REDACTED
    client-key-data: REDACTED
[centos@ip-10-154-46-153 ~]$
```

***Figure 15-23.** Listing the cluster kubeconfig configuration*

Alternatively, run the following command to list the cluster info.

```
kubectl cluster-info
```

The Kubernetes master URL listed is constructed from the Public DNS of the load balancer as shown in Figure 15-24.

```
[centos@ip-10-154-46-153 ~]$ kubectl cluster-info
Kubernetes master is running at https://ec2-54-226-7-241.compute-1.amazonaws.com
:8443
[centos@ip-10-154-46-153 ~]$ ▌
```

Figure 15-24. *Listing the cluster info*

SSH log in to the other master instance and list the nodes with `oc get nodes`. One of the master nodes is listed as NotReady, while the other master node is Ready, as shown in Figure 15-25. If the stopped master is restarted, it is again listed as Ready.

```
[centos@ip-10-154-46-153 ~]$ oc get nodes
NAME                          STATUS                        AGE
ip-10-113-176-99.ec2.internal   Ready                         1h
ip-10-154-46-153.ec2.internal   Ready,SchedulingDisabled      1h
ip-10-156-14-183.ec2.internal   NotReady,SchedulingDisabled   1h
[centos@ip-10-154-46-153 ~]$ oc get nodes
NAME                          STATUS                     AGE
ip-10-113-176-99.ec2.internal   Ready                      1h
ip-10-154-46-153.ec2.internal   Ready,SchedulingDisabled   1h
ip-10-156-14-183.ec2.internal   Ready,SchedulingDisabled   1h
[centos@ip-10-154-46-153 ~]$ ▌
```

Figure 15-25. *Listing nodes, schedulable and non-schedulable*

Summary

In this chapter we introduced another platform, called OpenShift, which is a PaaS platform with embedded Kubernetes. A single master is a single point of failure (SPOF). We discussed creating a high-availability master with OpenShift. In the next chapter we shall discuss creating a high-availability web site.

CHAPTER 16

Developing a Highly Available Website

In Chapter 4 we used multiple AWS availability zones to provide fault tolerance for failure of a zone. But a high-availability master was not used, and the single master is a single point of failure. In Chapter 15 we did use a high-availability master with OpenShift and Ansible, but the single elastic load balancer remains a single point of failure.

Problem

For a high-availability website, multiple public DNSes need to be configured. Another problem is that Amazon Elastic Load Balancers do not support Inter-AWS Region High-availability Architecture, in which the multiple master controllers in an HA master can be located in different AWS Regions. Amazon Elastic Load Balancers only support Inter-AWS Zone High-availability Architecture within the same region. While AWS zones are in different physical locations and are insulated from each other (failure of a one zone does not cause failure in another zone), the HA is not spread across a wider geographical region.

Solution

Amazon Route 53 provides DNS failover, using which a high-availability website may be developed. Route 53 provides DNS failover across AWS regions as shown in Figure 16-1. Route 53 DNS failover can be used to run applications across AWS zones or regions and configure alternate elastic load balancers to provide failover across zones or regions. Route 53 DNS failover is not a Kubernetes design pattern but makes use of the Amazon Route 53 Primary-Secondary architectural pattern.

D. Vohra, *Kubernetes Management Design Patterns*, DOI 10.1007/978-1-4842-2598-1_16

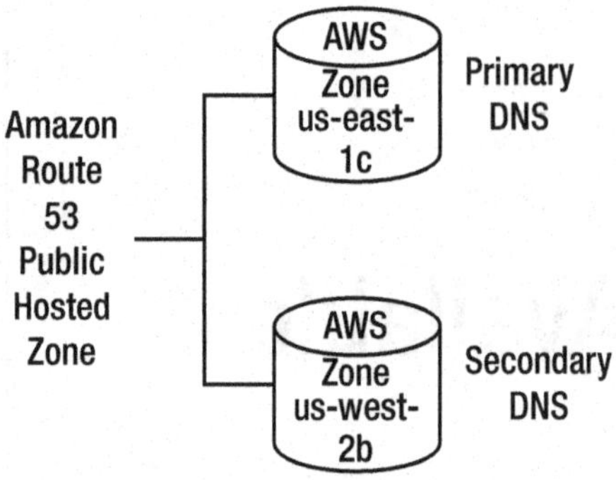

Figure 16-1. *Amazon Route 53 DNS failover*

Overview

Amazon Route 53 is a highly available and scalable cloud domain name service (DNS) connecting user requests to infrastructure running on the AWS, such as Amazon EC2 instances, load balancers, and Amazon S3 buckets. A Kubernetes cluster can be deployed using AWS CloudFormation, as discussed in Chapter 4. But the cluster developed there, using the `kube-aws` CLI tool, was a single master cluster without the provision of a failover. A highly available cluster has the tolerance for failure of a node in the cluster with built-in failover to another node in the cluster. In this chapter we shall develop a highly available Kubernetes cluster using AWS CloudFormation on CoreOS. We shall provision multiple (three) AWS CloudFormations and subsequently host an example application (hello-world) Kubernetes Service on each of the CloudFormations. We'll use a public hosted zone for an example domain to route traffic to that domain. This chapter covers the following topics.

Setting the environment

Creating CloudFormations

Configuring external DNS

Creating a Kubernetes service

Creating an AWS Route 53

Creating a hosted zone

Configuring name servers

Creating record sets

Testing high availability

Setting the Environment

The following procedure is used to create a highly available web application.

1. Create three AWS CloudFormations on CoreOS with one Kubernetes controller in each. The CloudFormations can be in the same region or multiple regions; we have used the same region in the example, as some AWS resources may not be available in all regions and availability zones. Add an A record for each of the controller IPs to the Domain `oramagsearch.com` (the URL used in the chapter, but the domain name will be different for different users).
2. Log in to each CoreOS controller instance. Create a Kubernetes service for an example application (hello-world) exposed on an elastic load balancer. With one Elastic Load Balancer exposed on each CloudFormation, three public DNS are available.
3. Create an AWS Route 53 with the two DNS configured for failover.
4. Create an AWS public hosted zone for an example domain such as the domain `oramagsearch.com` (the domain name would be different for different users).
5. Add name servers assigned to the Public Hosted Zone to the `oramagsearch.com` domain registrar.
6. Create two alias resource record sets pointing to two different elastic load balancers. The record sets are configured for failover, with one being the primary and the other being the secondary in the Failover configuration.

Create a single EC2 instance with Amazon Linux AMI. The instance is used to launch the three CloudFormations, and SSH log in to each of the controllers to create a Kubernetes service.

Creating CloudFormations

SSH Login into the Amazon Linux instance from three different Linux shells on the local machine.

```
ssh -i docker.pem ec2-user@ec2-54-242-131-243.compute-1.amazonaws.com
```

As discussed in Chapter 3, the procedure to create an AWS CloudFormation is as follows:

1. Install `Kube-aws` (required to be installed only once for the Amazon Linux instance)
2. Set up Cluster Parameters such as creating an EC2 key pair, KMS key, and External DNS name. The same EC2 key pair (`kubernetes-coreos`) and External DNS name (`oramagsearch.com`) are used for each CloudFormation.
3. Create an Asset Directory for a Cluster CloudFormation (a different directory for each of the CloudFormations).
4. Initialize the cluster CloudFormation.
5. Render the contents of the Asset Directory.
6. Customize the cluster to create three worker nodes instead of one.
7. Validate the CloudFormation stack.
8. Launch the cluster CloudFormation.

A typical command to create an EC2 key pair is as follows:

```
aws ec2 create-key-pair --key-name kubernetes-coreos --query 'KeyMaterial' --output text >
kubernetes-coreos.pem
chmod 400 kubernetes-coreos.pem
```

The command to create a KMS key is as follows:

```
aws kms --region=us-east-1 create-key --description="kube-aws assets"
```

Copy the `KeyMetadata.Arn` string and use it to initialize a CloudFormation stack. For example, a cluster called `kubernetes-coreos-cluster-1` with the asset directory as `kube-coreos-cluster-1` is initialized as follows:

```
 mkdir kube-coreos-cluster-1
cd kube-coreos-cluster-1
kube-aws init --cluster-name=kubernetes-coreos-cluster-1 --external-dns-name=ORAMAGSEARCH.
COM --region=us-east-1  --availability-zone=us-east-1c  --key-name=kubernetes-coreos  --kms-
key-arn="arn:aws:kms:us-east-1:xxxxxxxxxx:key/xxxxxxxxxxxxxxxxxxx"
```

The commands to render the contents of an assets directory, validate a CloudFormation stack, and launch a CloudFormation stack are as follows:

```
kube-aws render
kube-aws validate
kube-aws up
```

Next, launch into the controller instance for each of the Kubernetes clusters. The Public IP of a controller may be obtained from the EC2 Console as shown in Figure 16-2.

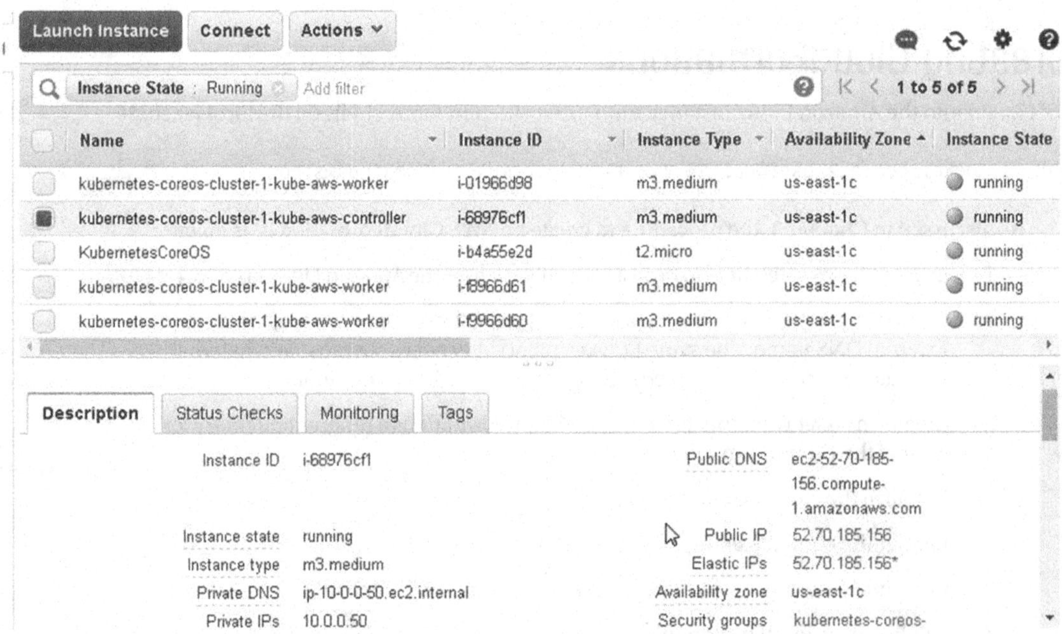

***Figure 16-2.** CloudFormation for Kubernetes cluster*

SSH log in using the EC2 key pair:

```
ssh -i "kubernetes-coreos.pem"  core@52.70.185.156
```

The CoreOS command prompt should be displayed.
Install the kubectl binaries and list the nodes:

```
sudo wget https://storage.googleapis.com/kubernetes-release/release/v1.3.0/bin/linux/
amd64/./kubectl
sudo chmod +x ./kubectl
./kubectl get nodes
```

The single master node and the three worker nodes in a cluster should be listed, as shown in Figure 16-3.

```
core@ip-10-0-0-50 ~ $ sudo wget https://storage.googleapis.com/kubernetes-releas
e/release/v1.3.0/bin/linux/amd64/./kubectl
--2016-08-06 22:19:48--  https://storage.googleapis.com/kubernetes-release/relea
se/v1.3.0/bin/linux/amd64/kubectl
Resolving storage.googleapis.com... 209.85.144.128, 2607:f8b0:400d:c06::80
Connecting to storage.googleapis.com|209.85.144.128|:443... connected.
HTTP request sent, awaiting response... 200 OK
Length: 56515944 (54M) [application/octet-stream]
Saving to: 'kubectl'

kubectl              100%[===================>]  53.90M  63.8MB/s    in 0.8s

2016-08-06 22:19:49 (63.8 MB/s) - 'kubectl' saved [56515944/56515944]

core@ip-10-0-0-50 ~ $ sudo chmod +x ./kubectl
core@ip-10-0-0-50 ~ $ ./kubectl get nodes
NAME                          STATUS                     AGE
ip-10-0-0-132.ec2.internal    Ready                      2m
ip-10-0-0-133.ec2.internal    Ready                      2m
ip-10-0-0-134.ec2.internal    Ready                      2m
ip-10-0-0-50.ec2.internal     Ready,SchedulingDisabled   2m
core@ip-10-0-0-50 ~ $
```

Figure 16-3. *Listing nodes in a Kubernetes cluster*

Similarly, log in to the second controller instance as shown in Figure 16-4.

```
[ec2-user@ip-10-0-0-224 ~]$ ssh -i "kubernetes-coreos.pem"  core@52.207.18.45
The authenticity of host '52.207.18.45 (52.207.18.45)' can't be established.
ECDSA key fingerprint is 59:f2:dd:8f:d6:19:7b:19:40:f5:5e:0d:75:8d:fb:34.
Are you sure you want to continue connecting (yes/no)? yes
Warning: Permanently added '52.207.18.45' (ECDSA) to the list of known hosts.
CoreOS stable (1068.8.0)
Last login: Sat Aug  6 22:40:14 2016 from 54.198.174.131
Update Strategy: No Reboots
core@ip-10-0-0-50 ~ $
```

Figure 16-4. *SSH logging into second controller instance*

List the cluster nodes as shown in Figure 16-5.

```
core@ip-10-0-0-50 ~ $ ./kubectl get nodes
NAME                          STATUS                     AGE
ip-10-0-0-110.ec2.internal    Ready                      2m
ip-10-0-0-111.ec2.internal    Ready                      2m
ip-10-0-0-112.ec2.internal    Ready                      2m
ip-10-0-0-50.ec2.internal     Ready,SchedulingDisabled   2m
core@ip-10-0-0-50 ~ $ ▌
```

Figure 16-5. *Nodes for second Kubernetes cluster*

And similarly, SSH log in to the third controller instance as shown in Figure 16-6.

```
[ec2-user@ip-10-0-0-224 ~]$ ssh -i "kubernetes-coreos.pem"  core@52.204.178.21
The authenticity of host '52.204.178.21 (52.204.178.21)' can't be established.
ECDSA key fingerprint is 5e:69:e6:da:f0:d5:c7:4d:b2:1c:96:55:a9:f3:f5:b3.
Are you sure you want to continue connecting (yes/no)? yes
Warning: Permanently added '52.204.178.21' (ECDSA) to the list of known hosts.
CoreOS stable (1068.8.0)
Last login: Sat Aug  6 22:54:13 2016 from 54.198.174.131
Update Strategy: No Reboots
core@ip-10-0-0-50 ~ $ ▌
```

Figure 16-6. *SSH logging into third controller instance*

List the cluster nodes as shown in Figure 16-7.

```
core@ip-10-0-0-50 ~ $ ./kubectl get nodes
core@ip-10-0-0-50 ~ $ ./kubectl get nodes
NAME                          STATUS                     AGE
ip-10-0-0-189.ec2.internal    Ready                      1m
ip-10-0-0-190.ec2.internal    Ready                      1m
ip-10-0-0-191.ec2.internal    Ready                      1m
ip-10-0-0-50.ec2.internal     Ready,SchedulingDisabled   1m
core@ip-10-0-0-50 ~ $ ▌
```

Figure 16-7. *Nodes for thirdKubernetes cluster*

When the three CloudFormations have been started, in all three controllers should be running in the EC2 Console, with each controller managing three worker nodes as shown in Figure 16-8.

Figure 16-8. *EC2 instances for three CloudFormations for Kubernetes clusters*

Configuring External DNS

Next, add an A record for each of the controller instances to the `oramagsearch.com` (the domain name would be different for different users) domain zone file as shown in Figure 16-9.

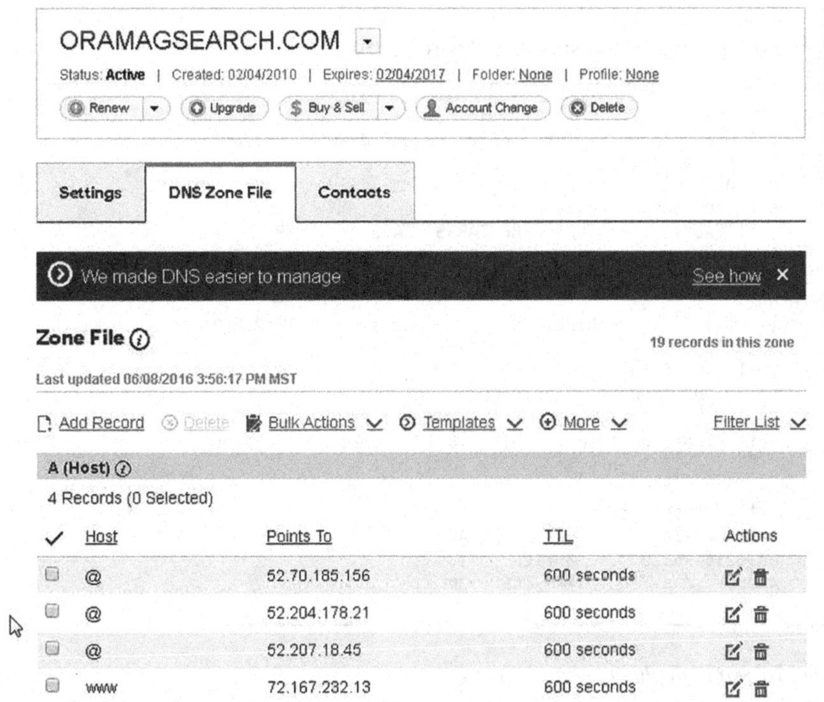

Figure 16-9. *Adding A records for controller instances*

Creating a Kubernetes Service

In this section we shall create a `hello-world` application and expose the application as a service of type LoadBalancer on each of the three Kubernetes clusters. As a result, three elastic load balancers each exposing the `hello-world` service should be available.

SSH log in to each of the controller instances and after verifying that the cluster nodes are being listed create an application with the `tutum/hello-world` Docker image.

```
kubectl -s http://localhost:8080 run hello-world --image=tutum/hello-world --replicas=2
--port=8
```

List the cluster-wide pods:

```
kubectl get pods -o wide
```

List the deployments:

```
kubectl get deployments
```

Subsequently, expose the deployment as a service of type LoadBalancer:

```
kubectl expose deployment hello-world--port=80 --type=LoadBalancer
```

List the services:

```
kubectl get services
```

The output from the preceding commands is shown in Figure 16-10.

```
core@ip-10-0-0-50 ~ $ ./kubectl -s http://localhost:8080 run hello-world --image
=tutum/hello-world --replicas=2 --port=80
deployment "hello-world" created
core@ip-10-0-0-50 ~ $ ./kubectl get pods -o wide
NAME                           READY     STATUS    RESTARTS   AGE       IP
    NODE
hello-world-3739649373-fz010   1/1       Running   0          33s       10.2.43.
3   ip-10-0-0-191.ec2.internal
hello-world-3739649373-xbrvl   1/1       Running   0          33s       10.2.6.2
    ip-10-0-0-190.ec2.internal
core@ip-10-0-0-50 ~ $ ./kubectl get deployments
NAME          DESIRED   CURRENT   UP-TO-DATE   AVAILABLE   AGE
hello-world   2         2         2            2           1m
core@ip-10-0-0-50 ~ $ ./kubectl expose deployment hello-world --port=80 --type=L
oadBalancer
service "hello-world" exposed
core@ip-10-0-0-50 ~ $ ./kubectl get services
NAME          CLUSTER-IP   EXTERNAL-IP         PORT(S)   AGE
hello-world   10.3.0.66    a91023d495c29...    80/TCP    10s
kubernetes    10.3.0.1     <none>              443/TCP   3m
core@ip-10-0-0-50 ~ $
```

Figure 16-10. *Creating a `hello-world` deployment and service*

Describe the service:

```
kubectl describe svc hello-world
```

The service details, including the `LoadBalancer Ingress`, are listed as shown in Figure 16-11.

```
core@ip-10-0-0-50 ~ $ ./kubectl describe svc hello-world
Name:                   hello-world
Namespace:              default
Labels:                 run=hello-world
Selector:               run=hello-world
Type:                   LoadBalancer
IP:                     10.3.0.251
LoadBalancer Ingress:   a26d378025c2411e691100aa20bff3c6-791280703.us-east-1.elb
.amazonaws.com
Port:                   <unset> 80/TCP
NodePort:               <unset> 32330/TCP
Endpoints:              10.2.47.2:80,10.2.84.3:80
Session Affinity:       None
Events:
  FirstSeen     LastSeen        Count   From                    SubobjectPath  T
ype             Reason                  Message
  ---------     --------        -----   ----                    -------------  -
------- ------                  -------
  43s           43s             1       {service-controller }                  N
ormal           CreatingLoadBalancer    Creating load balancer
  41s           41s             1       {service-controller }                  N
ormal           CreatedLoadBalancer     Created load balancer

core@ip-10-0-0-50 ~ $
```

Figure 16-11. *Describing the `hello-world` service*

The elastic load balancer should also be listed in the EC2 Console ➤ LOAD BALANCING ➤ Load Balancers display. The Public DNS name of the load balancer is obtained from the EC2 Console as shown in Figure 16-12.

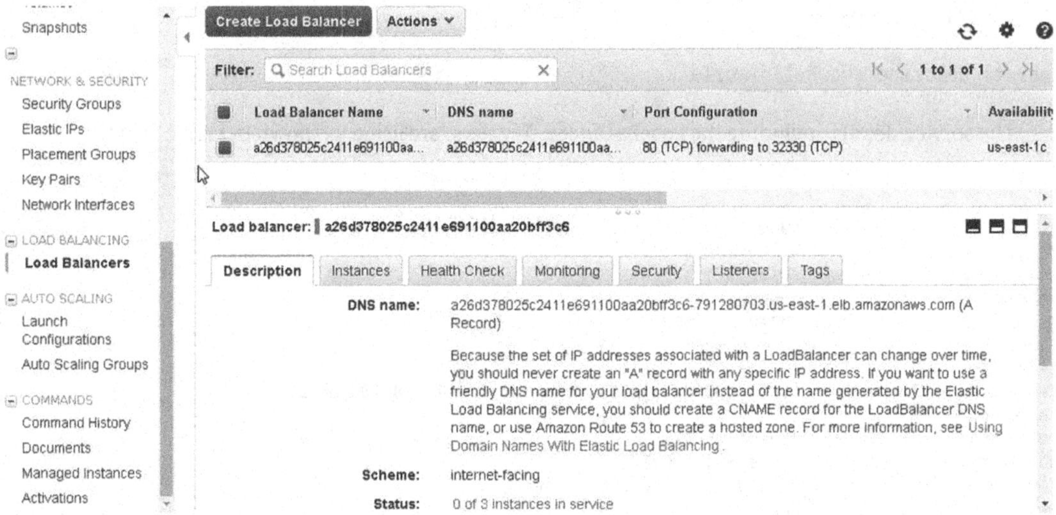

Figure 16-12. *LoadBalancer for a service*

The Instances tab lists the EC2 instances being load-balanced by the load balancer. Initially the Status may be OutOfService as shown in Figure 16-13.

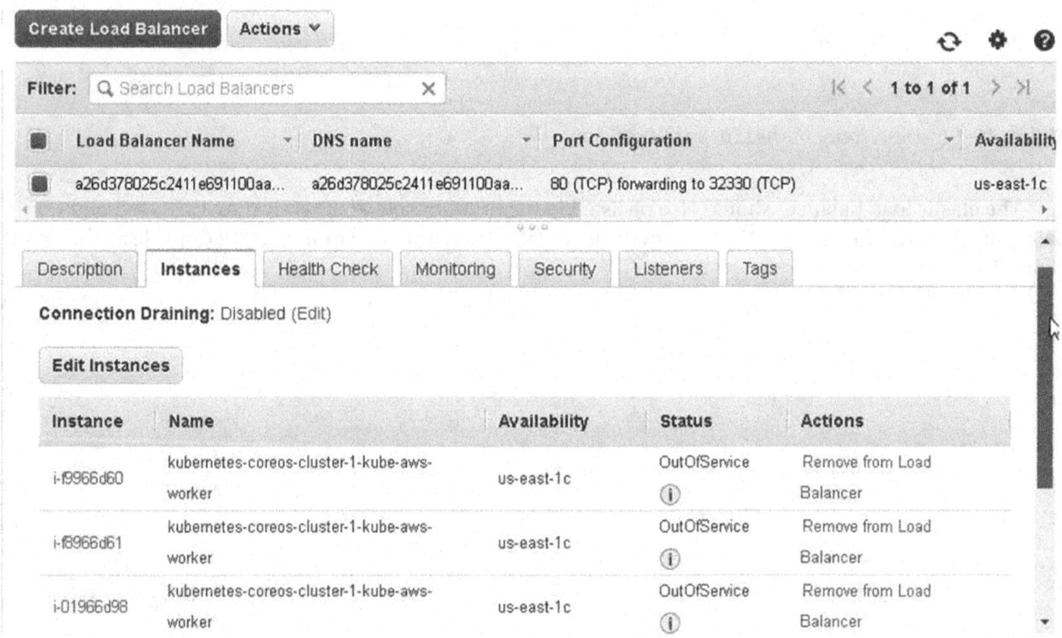

Figure 16-13. *Initially the instances in the LoadBalancer may be OutOfService*

After about a minute, the Status should become InService as shown in Figure 16-14.

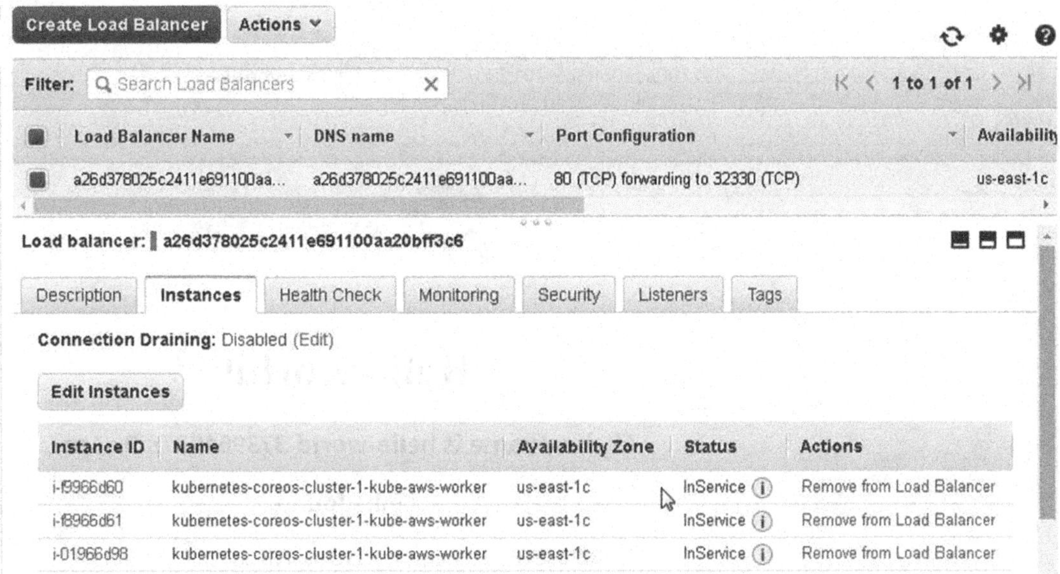

Figure 16-14. *LoadBalancer instances InService*

The Listeners tab should list the load balancer listener as shown in Figure 16-15.

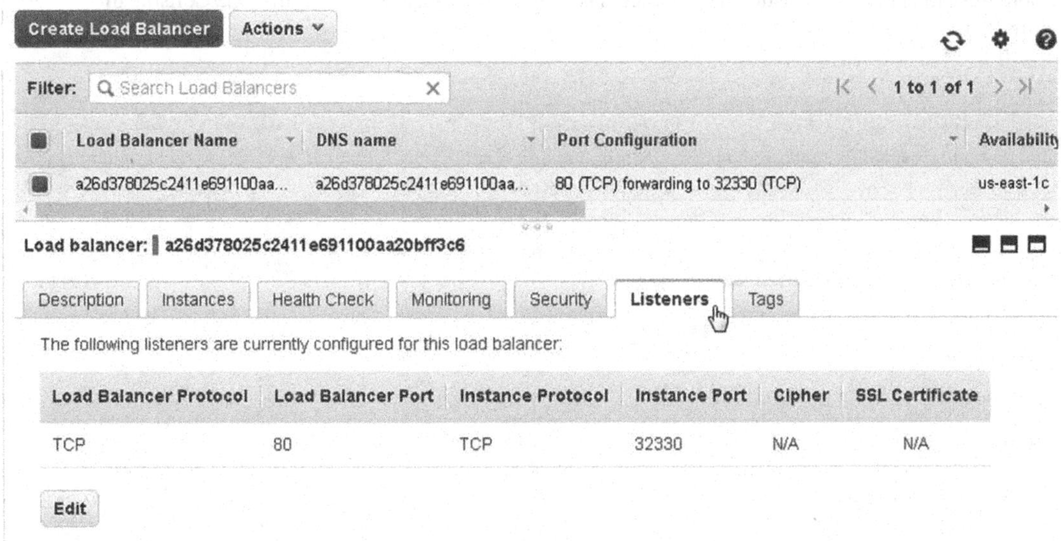

Figure 16-15. *Listeners for LoadBalancer*

Invoke the Public DNS name in a web browser. The `hello-world` application output should be displayed as shown in Figure 16-16.

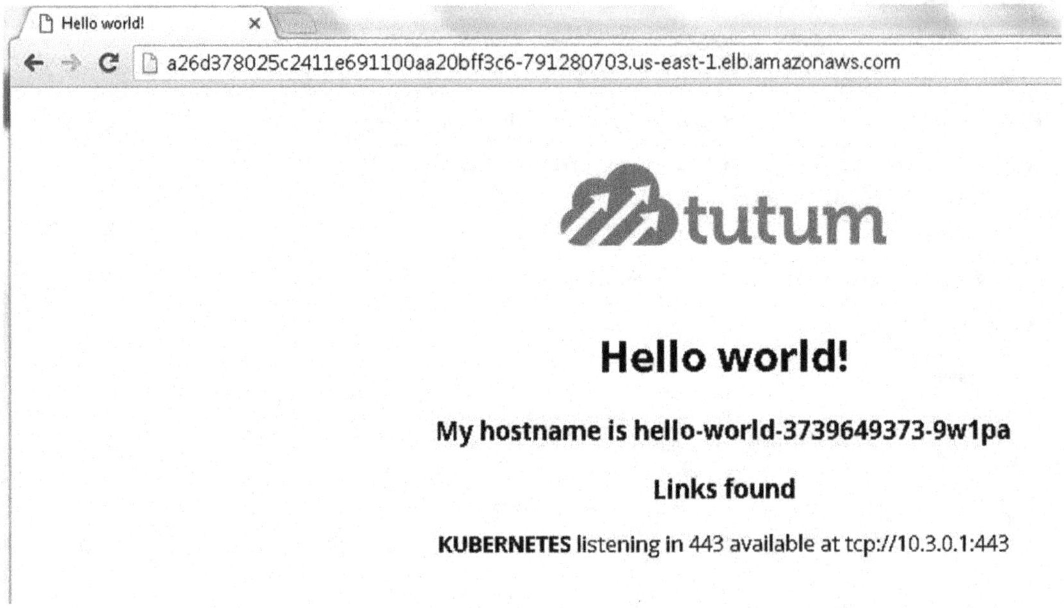

Figure 16-16. *Invoking the public DNS in a browser*

When the Kubernetes service `hello-world` of type `LoadBalancer` has been created in each of the Kubernetes clusters, three elastic load balancers should be created as shown in the EC2 Console in Figure 16-17.

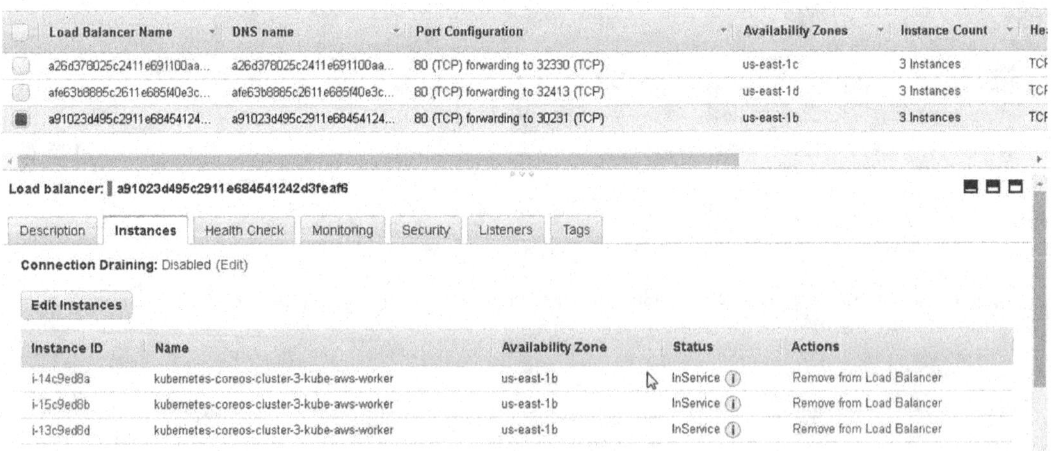

Figure 16-17. *Three LoadBalancers, one for each CloudFormation*

The Public DNS name for each of the ELBs should display the result for the `hello-world` application as shown in Figure 16-18.

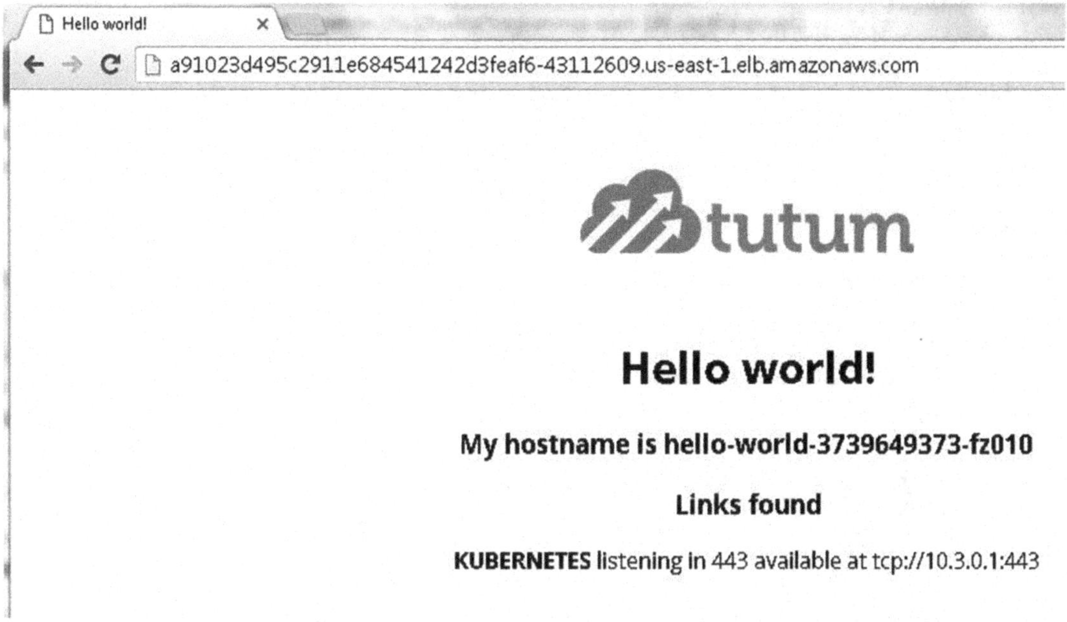

***Figure 16-18.** Invoking the public DNS for another Elastic Load Balancer*

Creating an AWS Route 53 Service

In this section we shall create an AWS Route 53 service to route user requests to the `oramagsearch.com` domain to the elastic load balancers, more specifically the public DNS name of the ELBs. We shall create two resource record sets, pointing to two different ELBs configured for failover, with one of the ELBs being the primary resource record set and another being the secondary record set. When the `oramagsearch.com` domain is invoked in a web browser, the AWS Route 53 service routes the request to the primary resource record set. If the primary record set becomes unavailable, the service routes the user request to the secondary record set, in effect providing high availability of the Hello World web application on the `oramagsearch.com` domain.

To create an AWS Route 53 service, select Route 53 in AWS Services as shown in Figure 16-19.

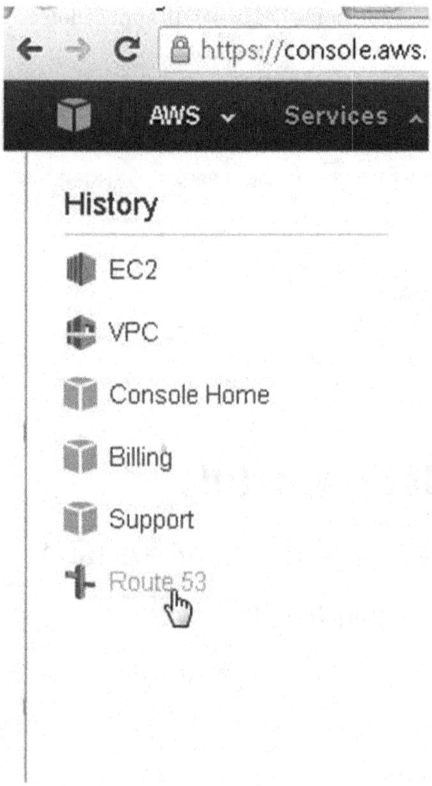

Figure 16-19. *Selecting the Route 53 service*

Creating a Hosted Zone

To create a hosted zone, select Hosted Zones in the margin and click Create Hosted Zone as shown in Figure 16-20.

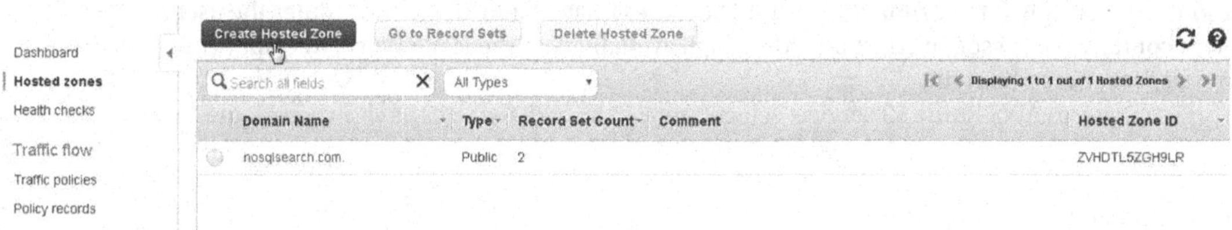

Figure 16-20. *Creating a hosted zone*

In the Create Hosted Zone dialog, specify a Domain Name (`oramagsearch.com`). The domain name must be registered with the user. Select Public Hosted Zone as the type, as shown in Figure 16-21.

Figure 16-21. *Configuring a hosted zone*

A new public hosted zone is created. The name servers for the hosted zone are also assigned, as shown in Figure 16-22.

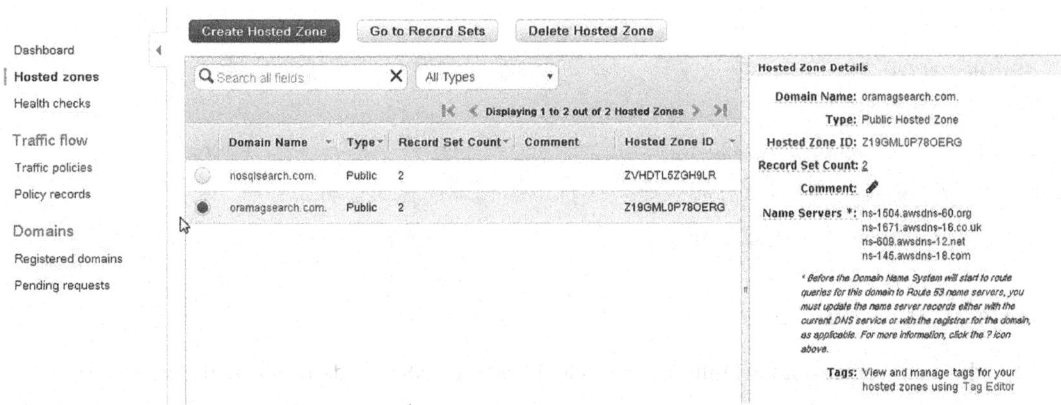

Figure 16-22. *A new public hosted zone*

Configuring Name Servers on a Domain Name

Next, we need to update the name server records for the domain `oramagsearch.com` with the domain registrar so that the Domain Name System is able to route requests for the domain to Route 53 name servers. Copy the Route 53 name servers as shown in Figure 16-23.

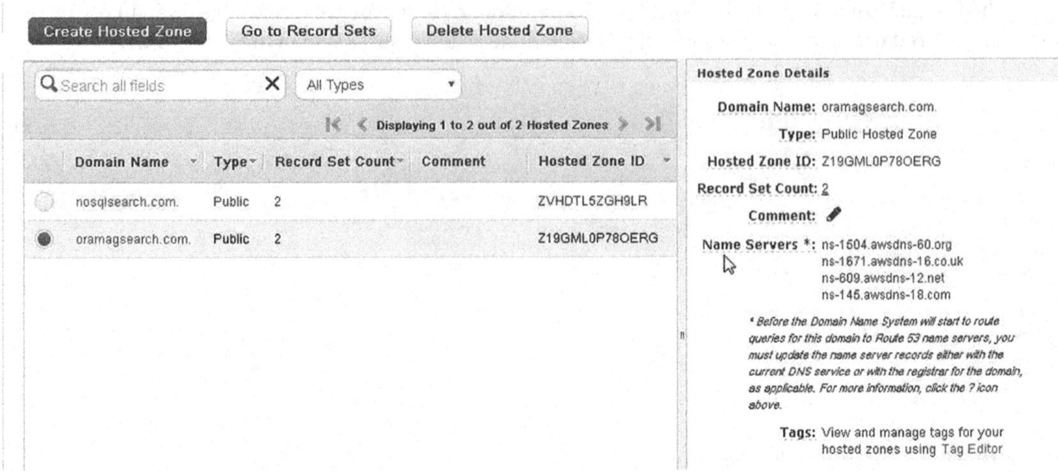

Figure 16-23. *Route 53 name servers*

The default name server records for a domain are typically provided by the domain registrar as shown in Figure 16-24.

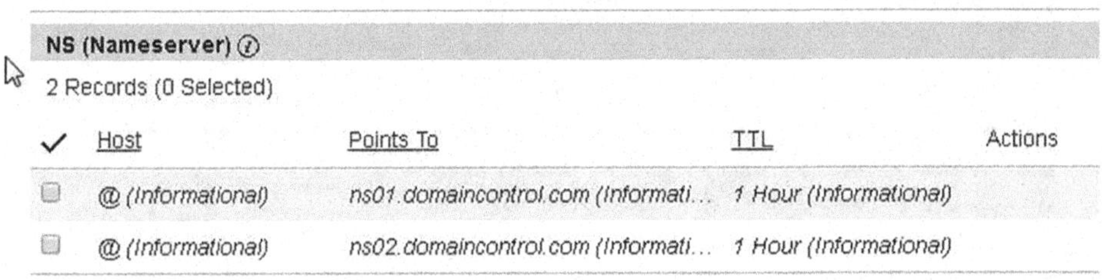

NS (Nameserver)
2 Records (0 Selected)
Host
Points To
TTL
Actions
@ (Informational) ns01.domaincontrol.com (Informati… 1 Hour (Informational)
@ (Informational) ns02.domaincontrol.com (Informati… 1 Hour (Informational)

Figure 16-24. *Domain nameservers*

Add the name servers for the Route 53 service to the domain NS records as shown in Figure 16-25.

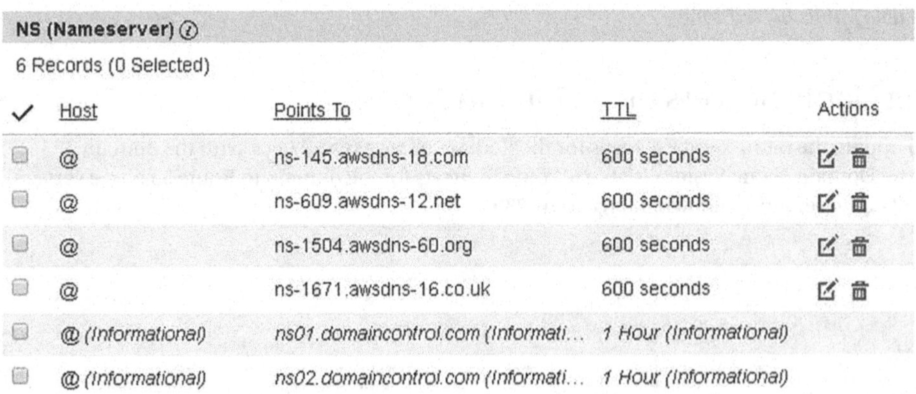

NS (Nameserver)
6 Records (0 Selected)
Host
Points To
TTL
Actions
@ ns-145.awsdns-18.com 600 seconds
@ ns-609.awsdns-12.net 600 seconds
@ ns-1504.awsdns-60.org 600 seconds
@ ns-1671.awsdns-16.co.uk 600 seconds
@ (Informational) ns01.domaincontrol.com (Informati… 1 Hour (Informational)
@ (Informational) ns02.domaincontrol.com (Informati… 1 Hour (Informational)

Figure 16-25. *Adding name servers for Route 53 to DNS record*

Next, select the default name servers provided by the domain registrar as shown in Figure 16-26.

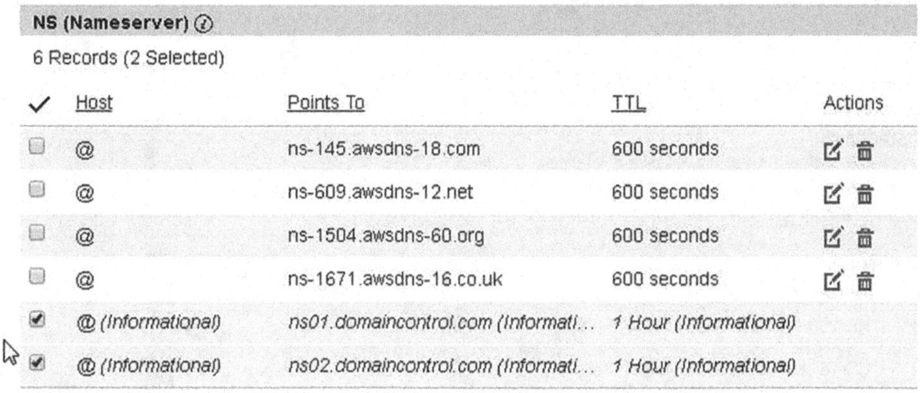

Figure 16-26. Selecting default name servers on domain

Click on Delete to delete the default name servers as shown in Figure 16-27.

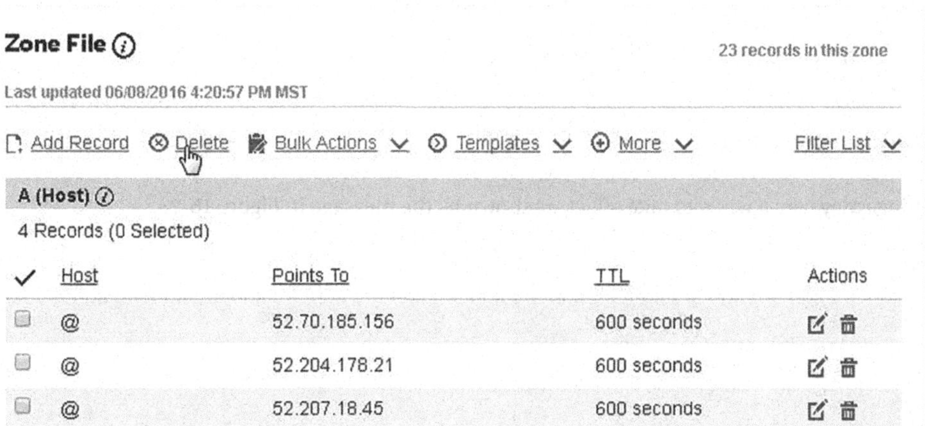

Figure 16-27. Deleting default name servers

Save the custom name server settings as shown in Figure 16-28.

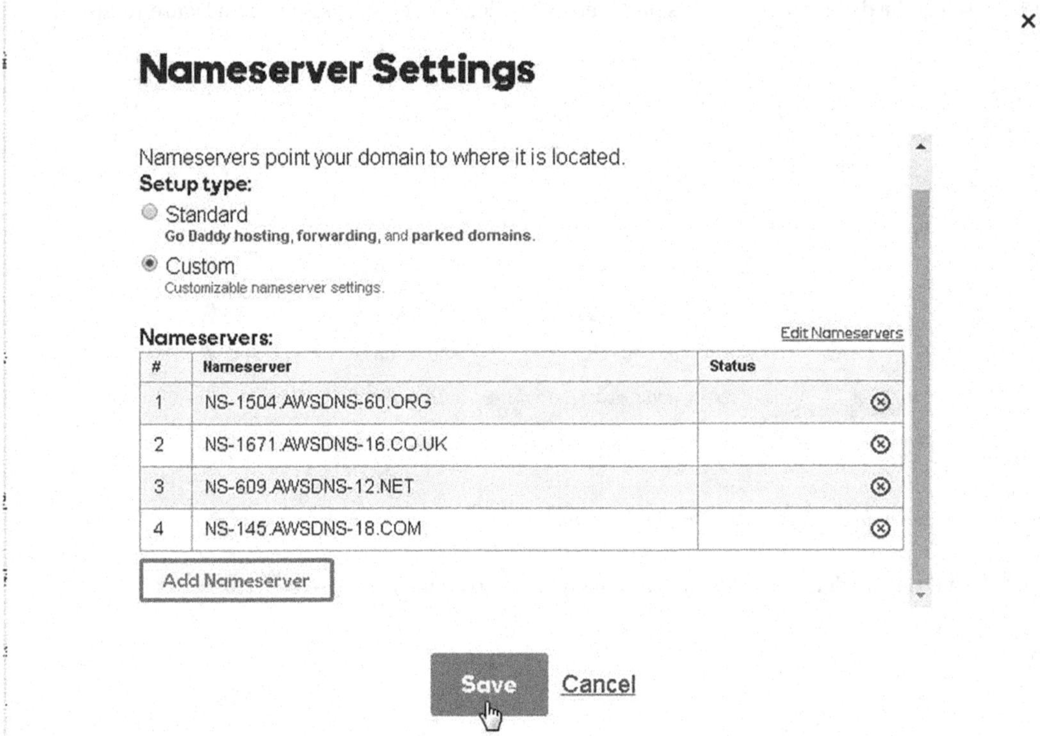

Figure 16-28. *Domain name servers*

The new settings may take a while to take effect, as shown by the message in Figure 16-29.

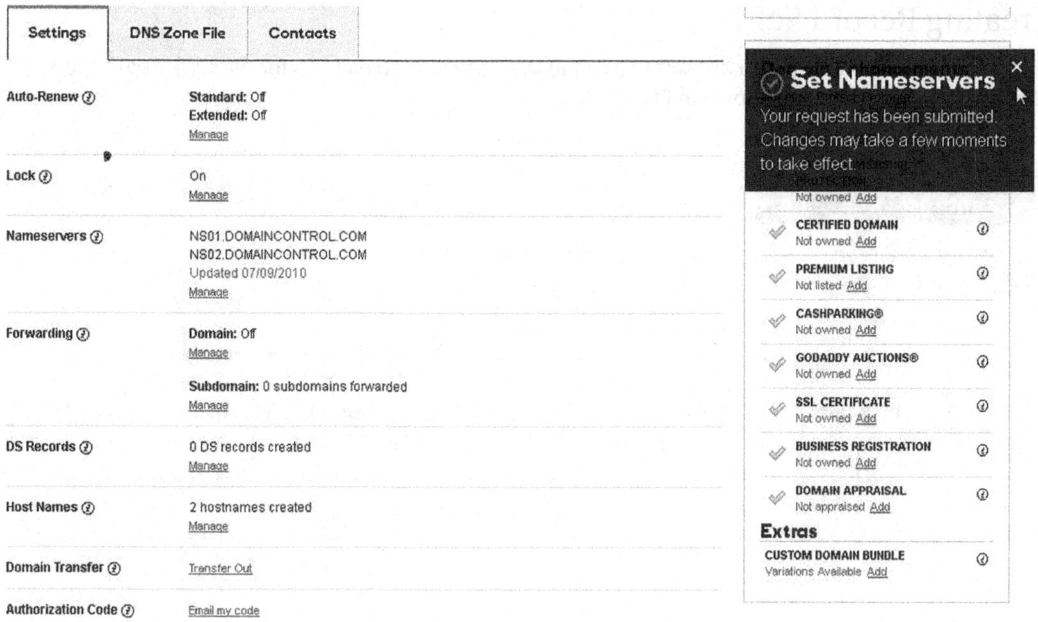

Figure 16-29. *Updating domain nameservers can take a while*

When the new name server records have taken effect, the NS records should indicate the same as shown in Figure 16-30.

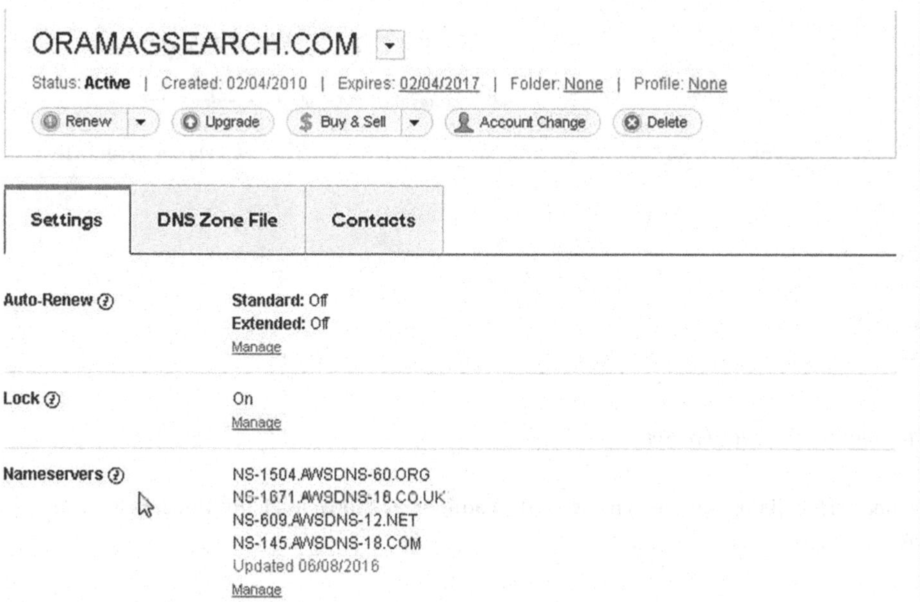

Figure 16-30. *Configured domain nameservers*

Creating Record Sets

Next, we shall create resource record sets to point to the elastic load balancers for the `hello-world` service. Click on Go to Record Sets as shown in Figure 16-31.

Figure 16-31. *Start creating a record set by clicking Go To Record Sets*

Then click on Create Record Set as shown in Figure 16-32.

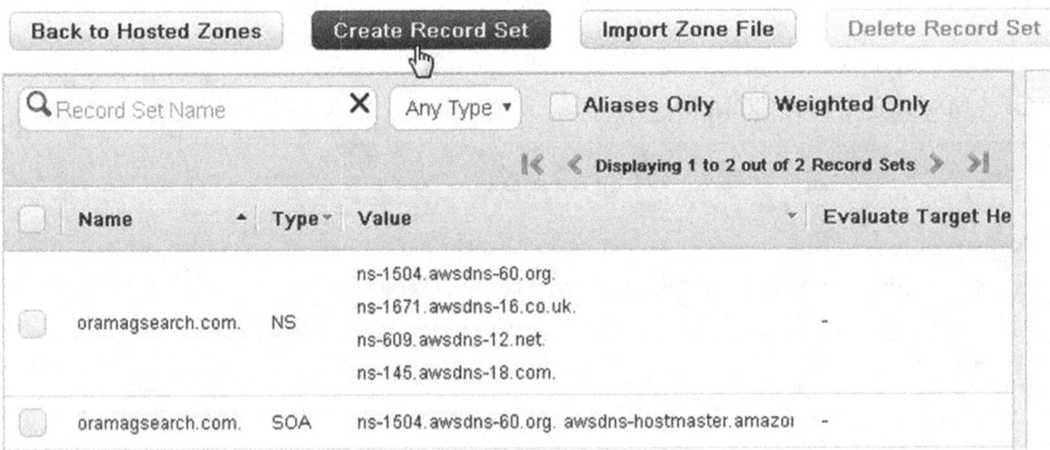

Figure 16-32. *Clicking on Create Record Set*

In the Create Record Set dialog, set the Type as A - IPv4 address as shown in Figure 16-33. Select the Alias radio button.

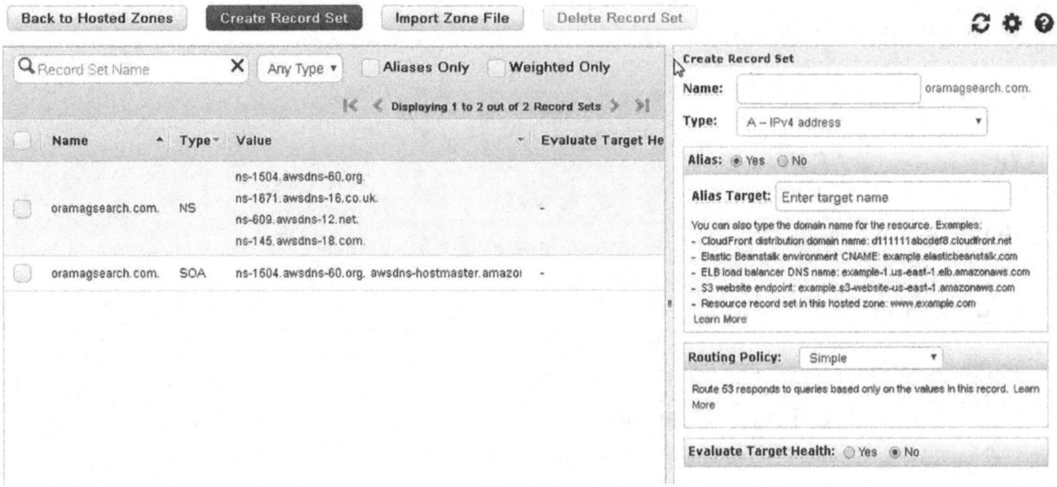

Figure 16-33. *Setting the Type in the Create Record Set dialog*

Click in the Alias Target field to display the drop-down for the targets. Select one of the ELB Load Balancers, assuming that all the ELB Load Balancers are for the `hello-world` service as shown in Figure 16-34.

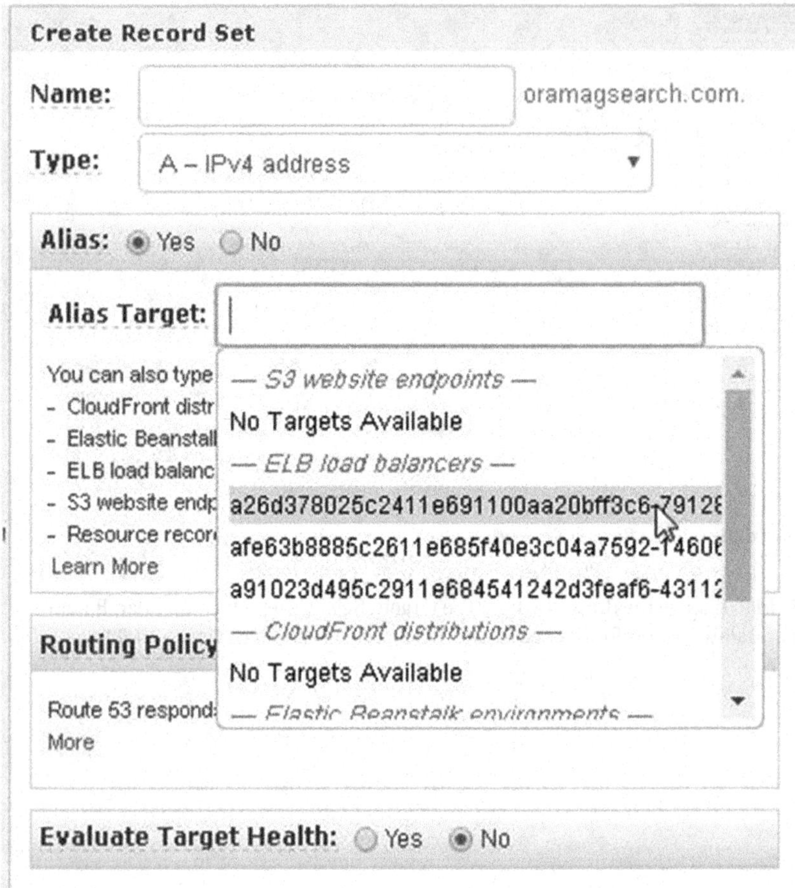

Figure 16-34. *Selecting one of the ELB Load Balancers as alias target*

For Routing Policy, select Failover as shown in Figure 16-35.

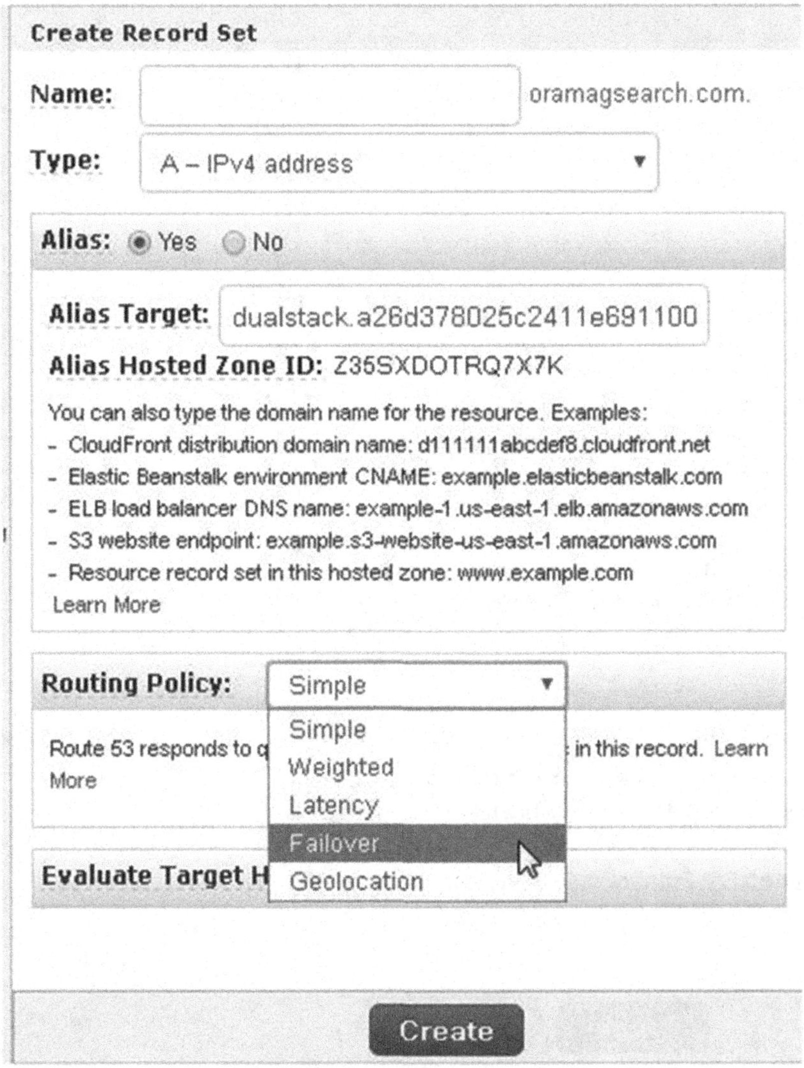

Figure 16-35. Selecting Failover as the Routing Policy

For Failover Record Type, select Primary as shown in Figure 16-36.

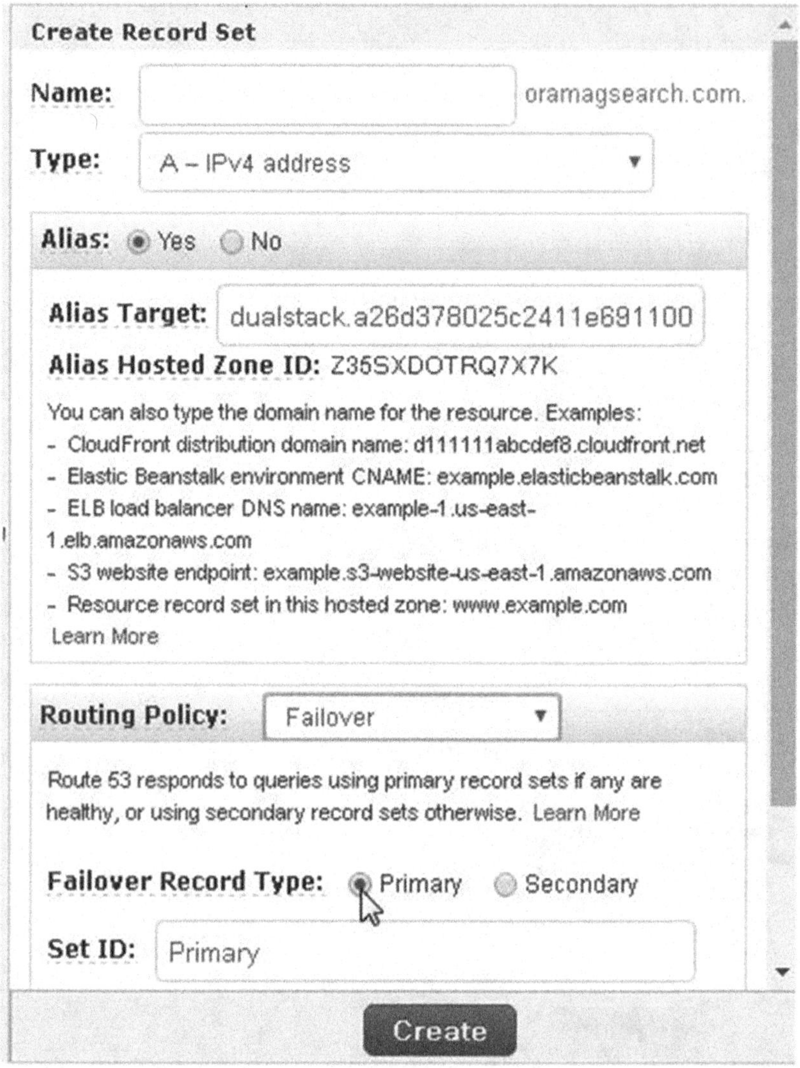

Figure 16-36. *Setting the Failover Record Type as Primary*

For Evaluate Target Health, select Yes. For Associate with Health Check, select No. Click on Create as shown in Figure 16-37.

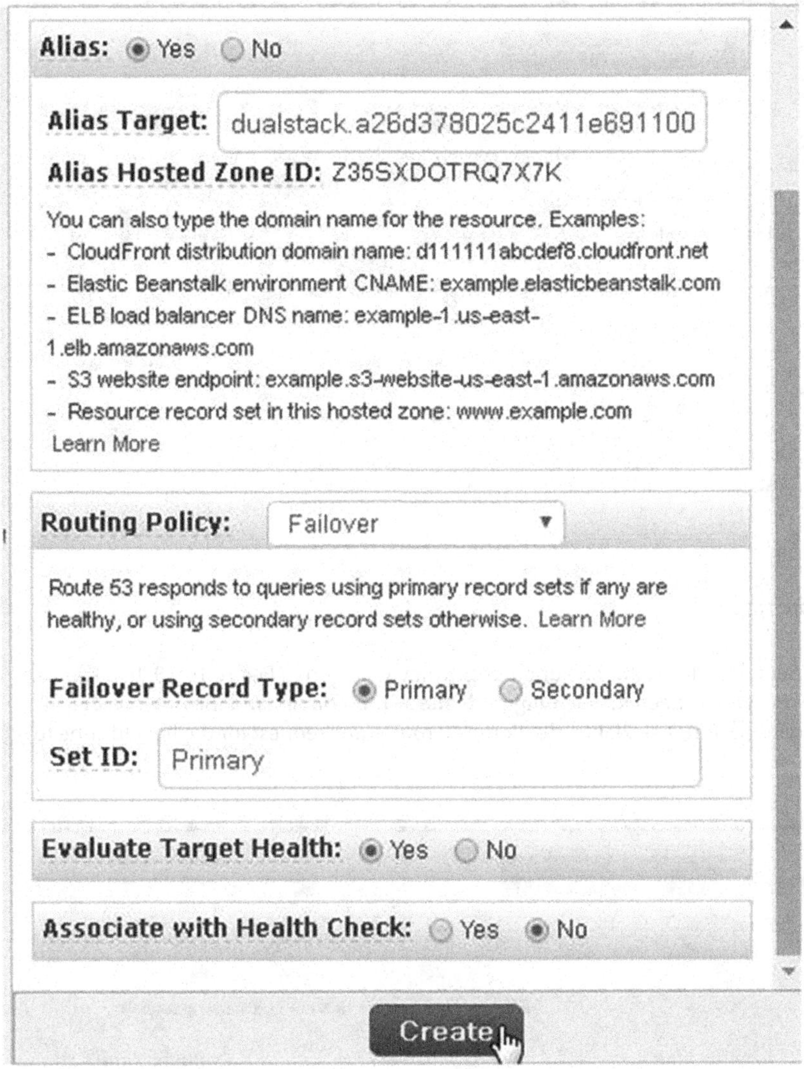

Figure 16-37. *Creating a record set*

A new resource record set is added as shown in Figure 16-38.

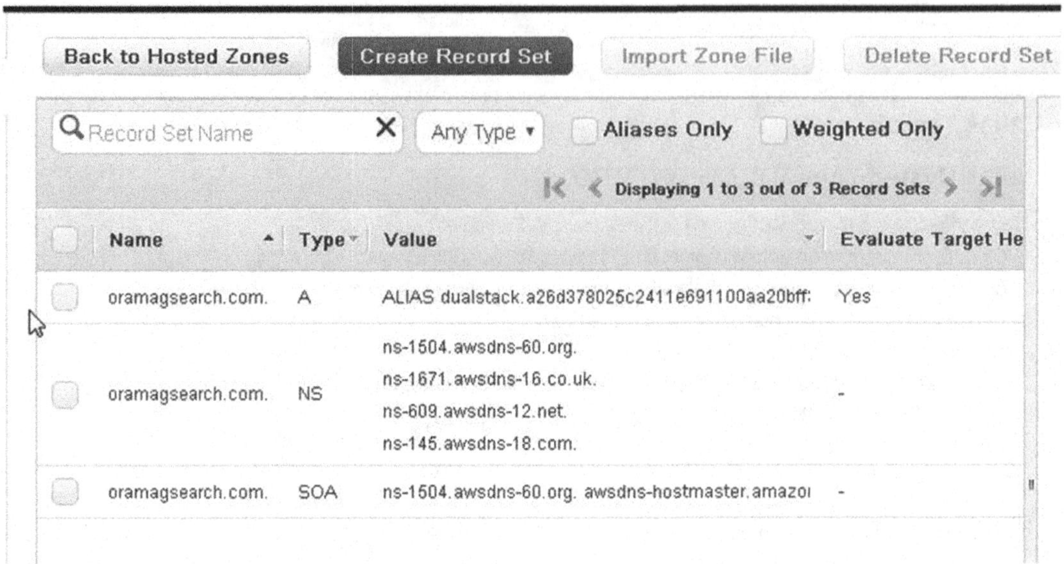

Figure 16-38. *Resource record set*

Click on Create Record Set to create another resource record set as shown in Figure 16-39. In a Failover routing policy, two resource record sets need to be configured, one as the primary and the other as the secondary. If the primary record set is not available, the Route 53 routes any request for the hosted zone to the secondary record set.

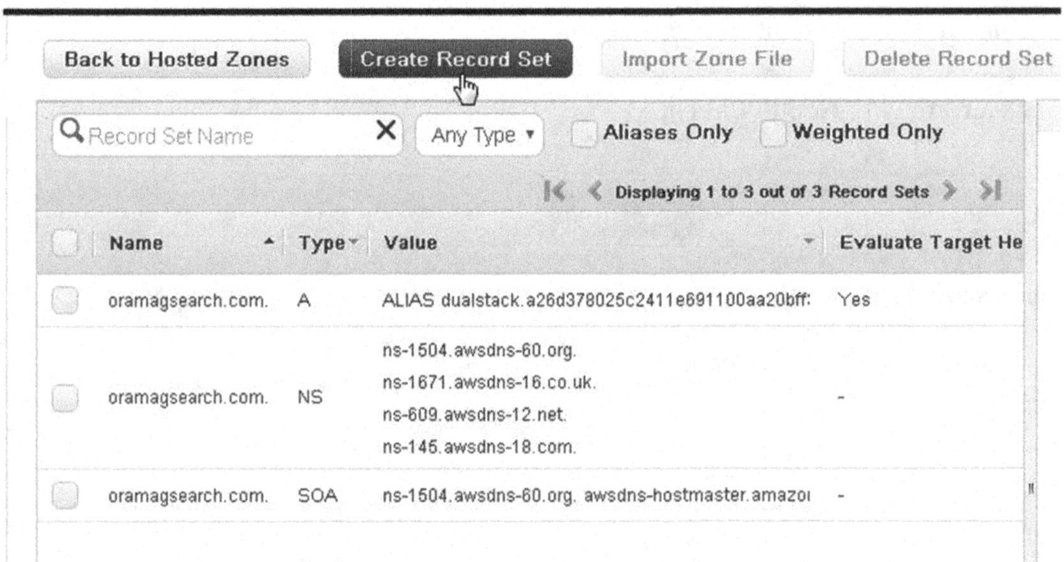

Figure 16-39. *Clicking on Create Record Set to create another record set*

In Create Record Set, set the Type as A -IPv4 address and the Alias as Yes. For Alias Target select a different ELB Load Balancer as shown in Figure 16-40.

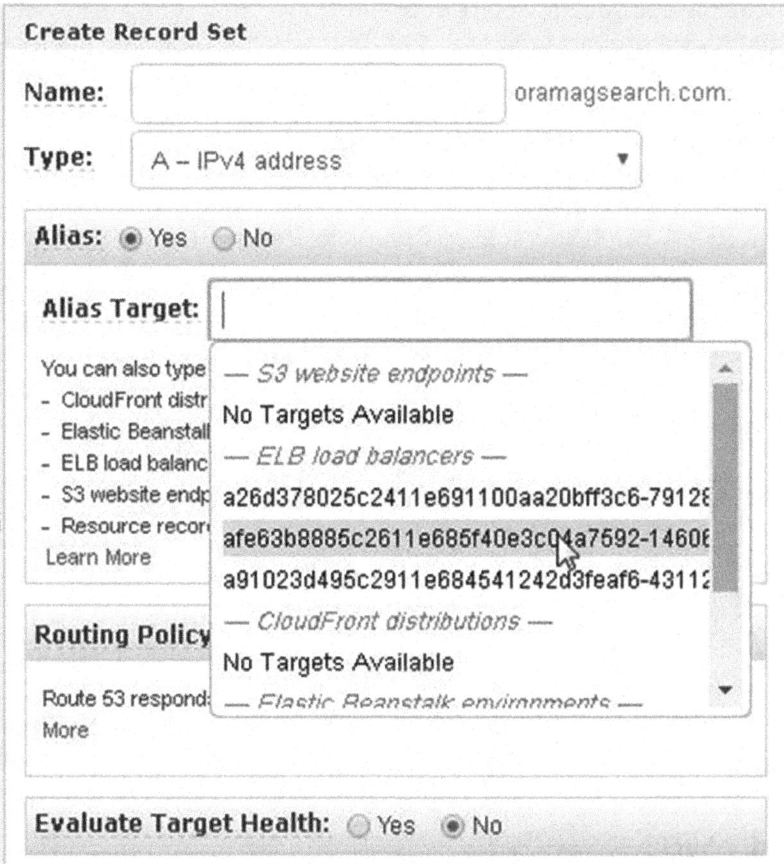

Figure 16-40. *Configuring the record set*

Set the Routing Policy as Failover. Select Secondary as the Failover Record Type. Set Evaluate Target Health as Yes and Associate with Health Check as No. Click on Create as shown in Figure 16-41.

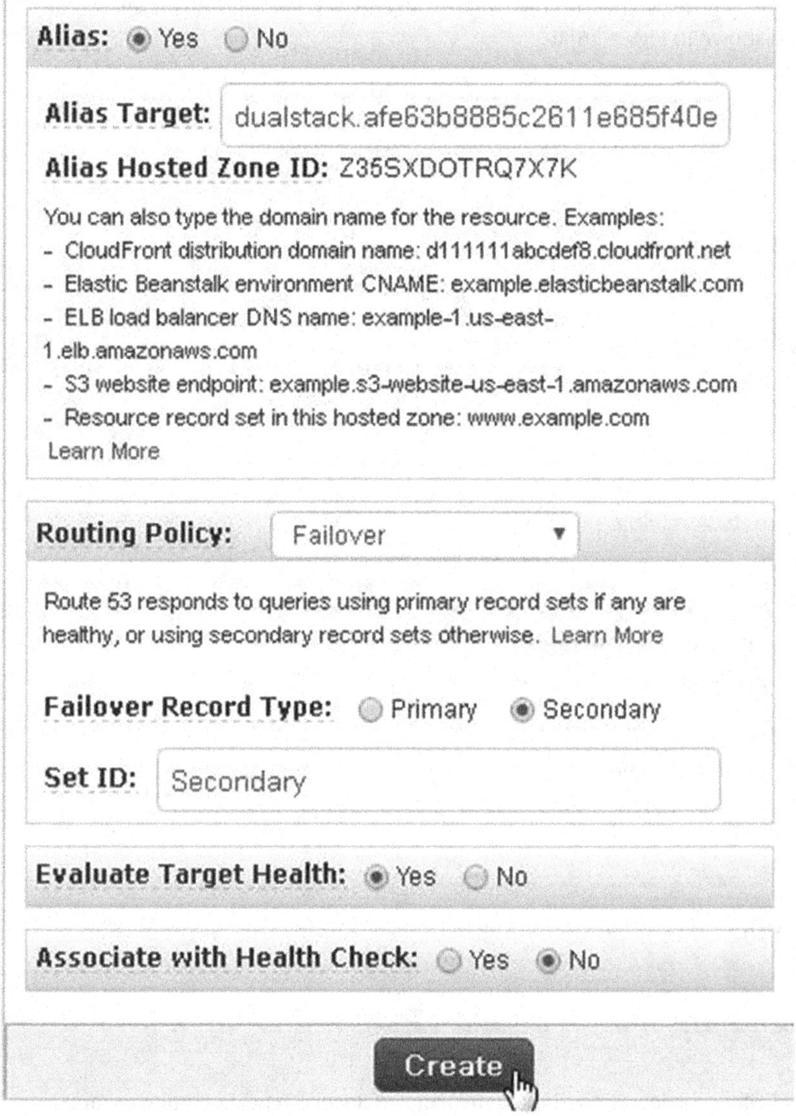

Figure 16-41. *Creating a second record set*

A second resource record set is added, as shown in Figure 16-42.

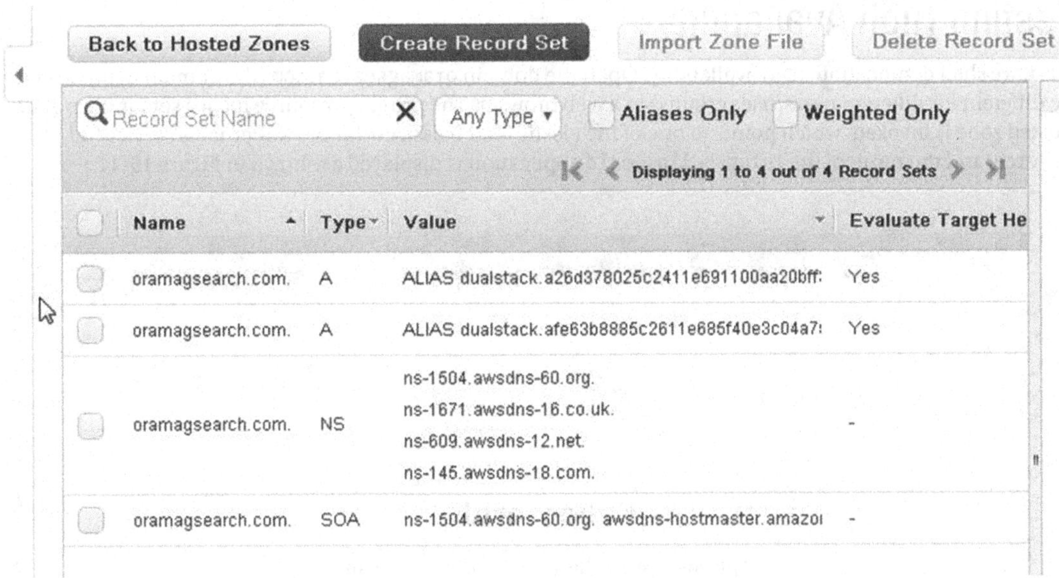

Figure 16-42. A second resource record set

The Public Hosted Zone for the `oramagsearch.com` (domain name would be different for different users) domain should list the Record Set Count as 4 instead of 2 to start with, as shown in Figure 16-43.

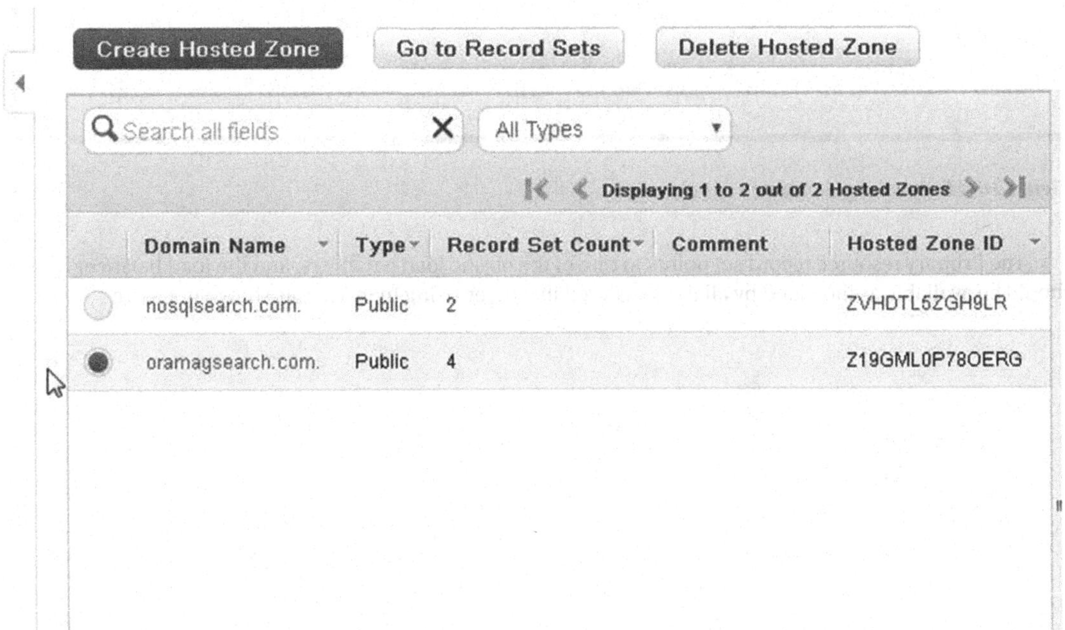

Figure 16-43. Public hosted zone with four record sets

Testing High Availability

Next, we shall demonstrate high availability. Open the domain `oramagsearch.com` (the domain name would be different for different users/user groups) in a web browser. The primary resource record set for the public hosted zone is invoked, which points to one of the elastic load balancers for the Kubernetes service `hello-service`, and the result of the `tutum/hello-world` application is displayed as shown in Figure 16-44.

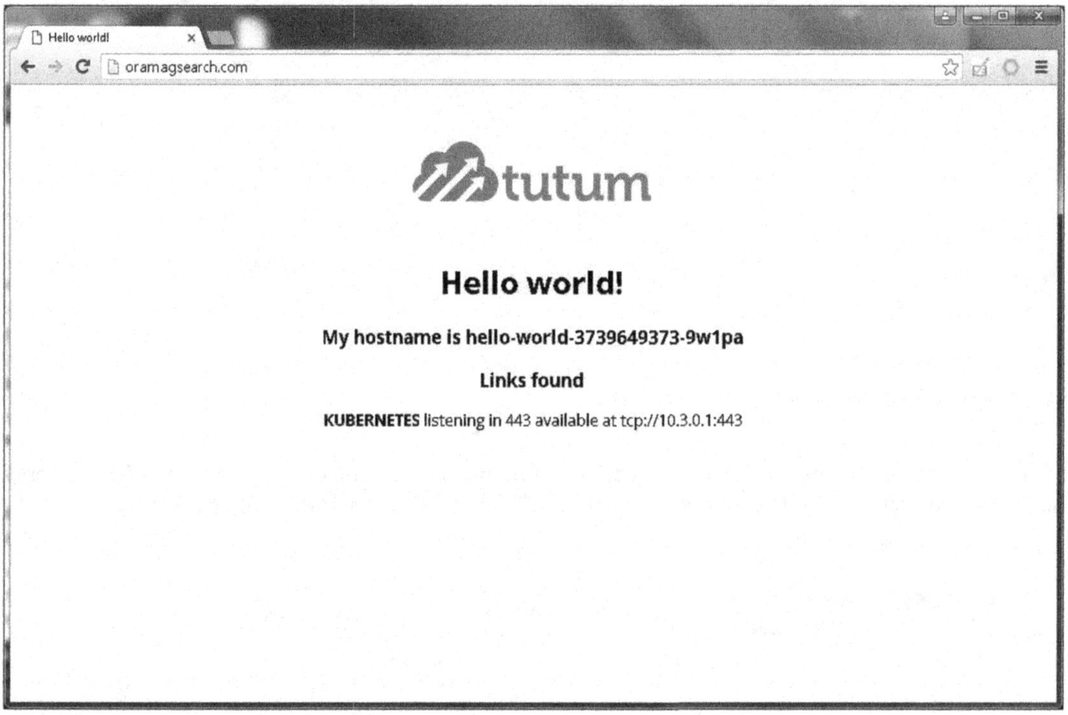

Figure 16-44. *Invoking domain in browser*

The Primary resource record set points to one of the elastic load balancers, and the load balancer should be available as indicated by all the registered instances being InService, as shown in Figure 16-45.

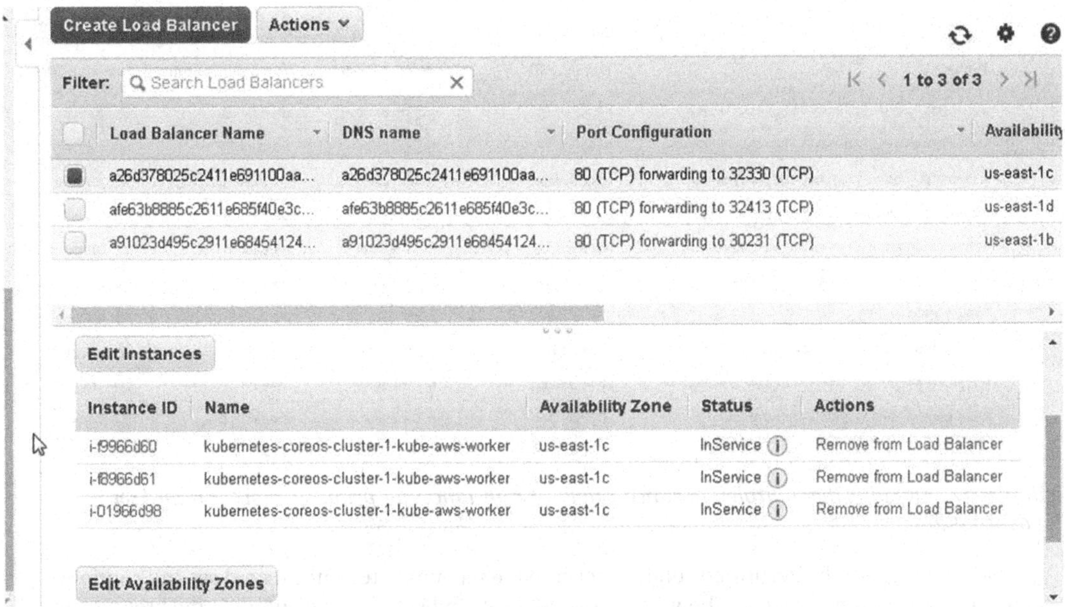

Figure 16-45. *LoadBalancer for primary resource record set with all instances inService*

To demonstrate high availability, stop the controller for the Kubernetes cluster exposing the elastic load balancer pointed to by the primary resource record set, as shown in Figure 16-46.

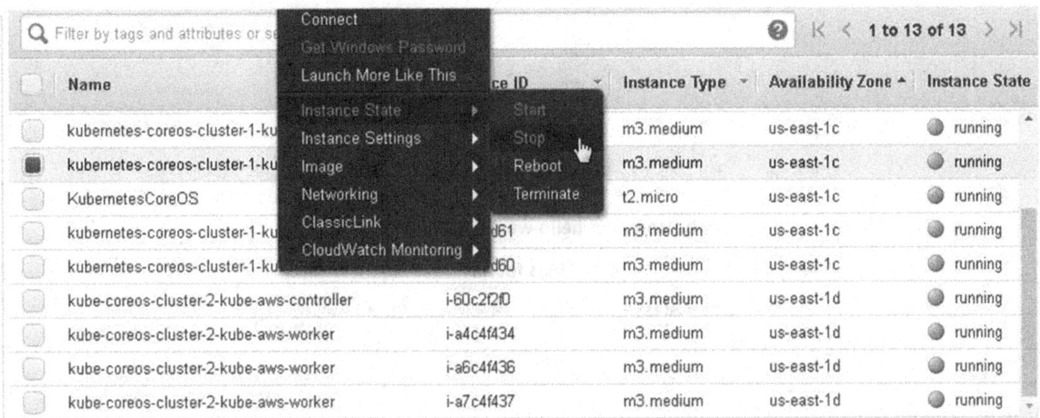

Figure 16-46. *Stopping the controller instance for the cluster exposing the ELB pointed to by the primary resource record set*

The controller instance and the worker node instances should be stopped, as shown in Figure 16-47, in effect making the elastic load balancer for the primary resource record set unavailable. If the hosted zone had just one resource record set without the Failover routing configured, the `oramagsearch.com` domain would become unavailable.

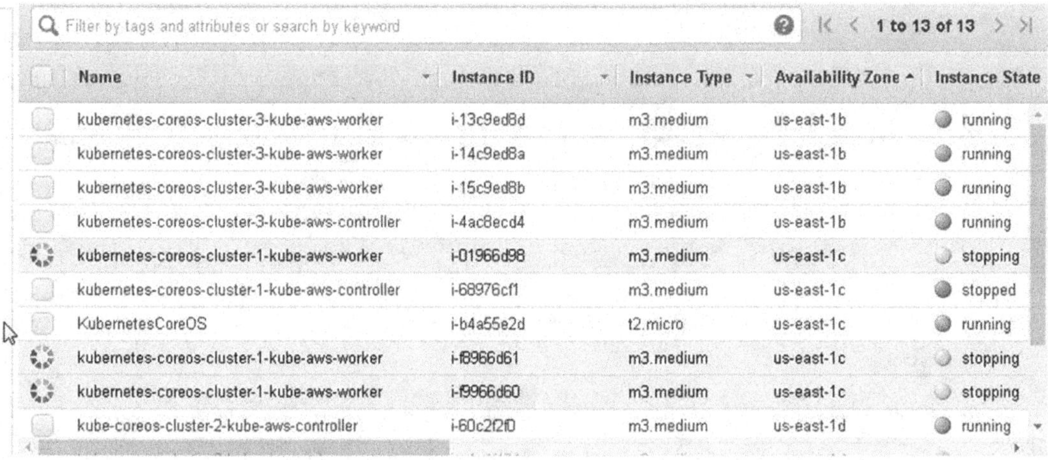

***Figure 16-47.** Stopping the controller instance and worker instances for primary resource record set CloudFormation*

But the `oramagsearch.com` hosted zone fails over to the secondary resource record set and continues to serve the `hello-world` service, as shown in Figure 16-48. As indicated by the output in the browser, the hostname has changed (the hostname could also change due to the service distributing traffic between Pods on the same deployment) but the service continues to be available.

***Figure 16-48.** The `oramagsearch.com` hosted zone fails over to the secondary resource record set and continues to serve*

When the primary resource record set becomes unavailable and the user request is routed to the secondary record set, in effect the service is being served by one record set and is thus not highly available any more. To make the service highly available, we need to either make the primary record set point to a different elastic load balancer or delete and create a new record set. Taking the second approach, select the primary resource record set and click Delete Record Set as shown in Figure 16-49.

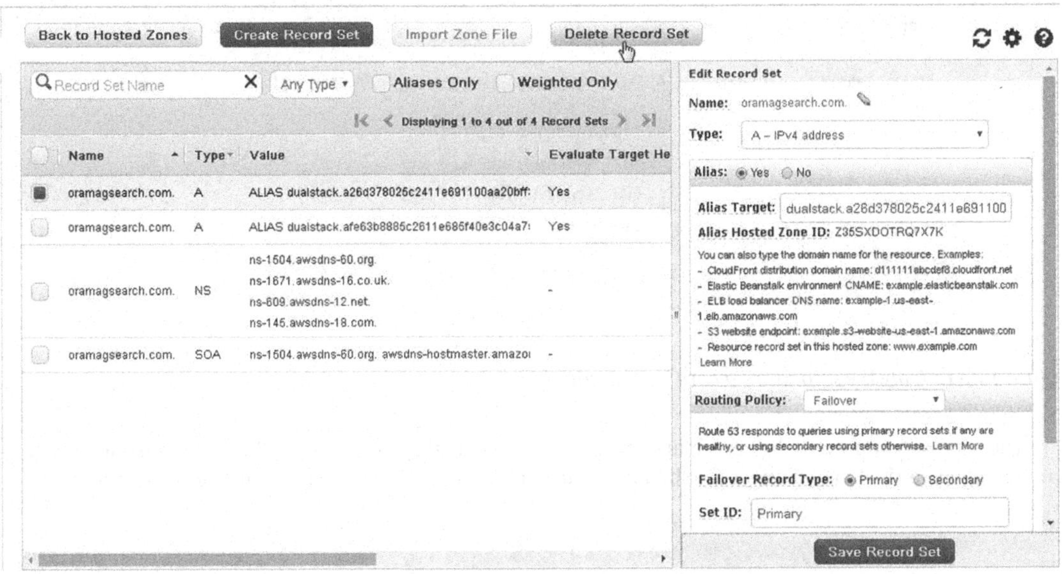

Figure 16-49. *Deleting the primary resource record set*

Click on Confirm in the Confirmation dialog as shown in Figure 16-50.

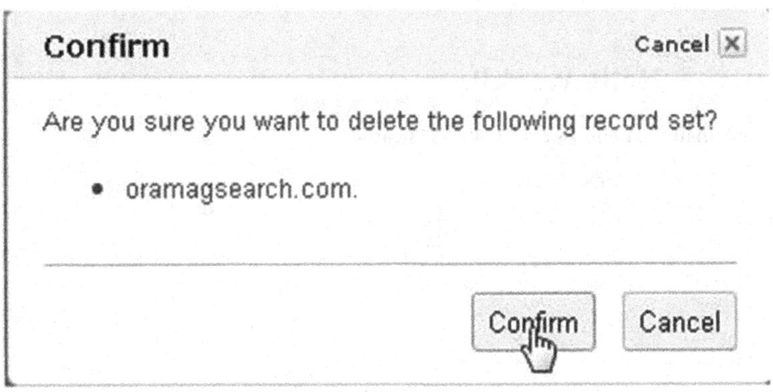

Figure 16-50. *Confirmation dialog*

Only the secondary record set is available to route user requests to, as shown in Figure 16-51.

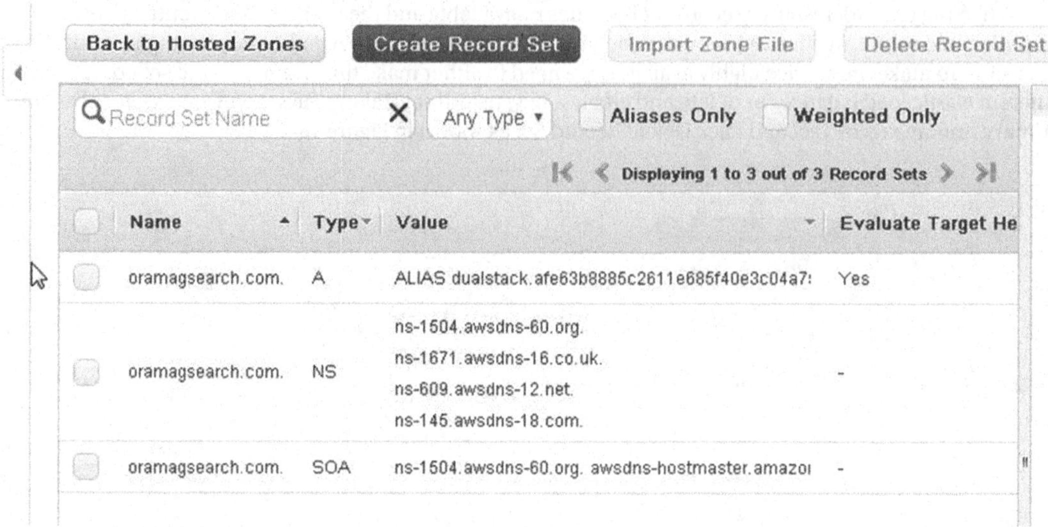

Figure 16-51. *Only the secondary record set is available*

The service continues to be served at `oramagsearch.com` as shown in Figure 16-52. The hostname may have changed, as the load balancer also balances the load between the two replicas in the deployment.

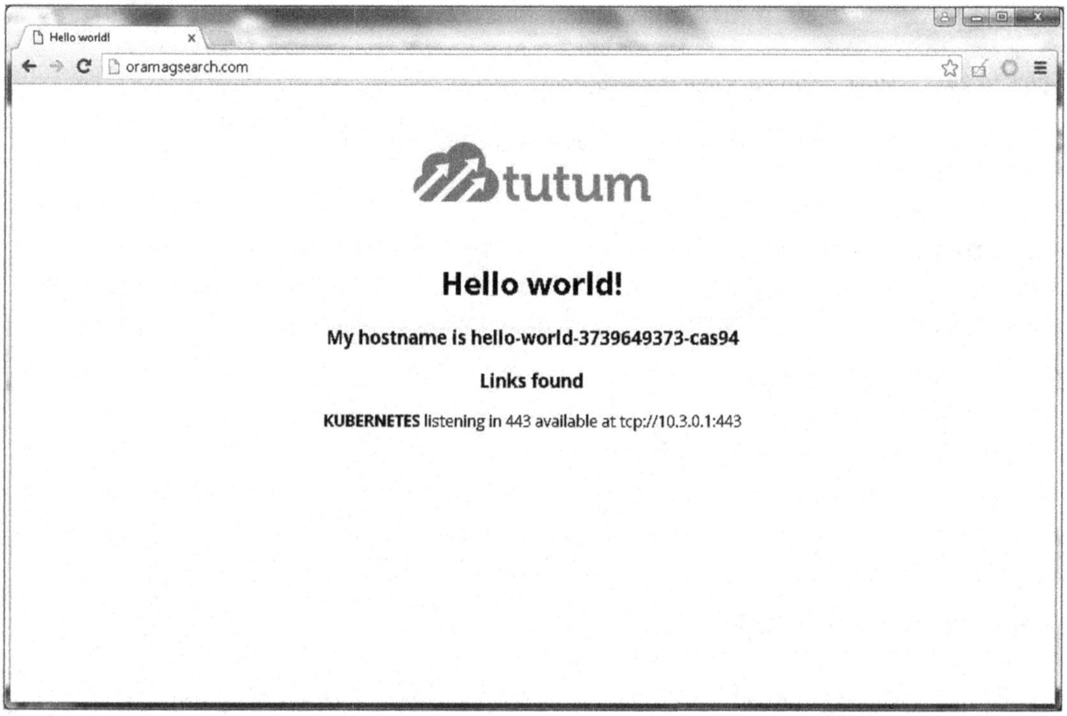

Figure 16-52. *Hosted zone served by secondary record set*

To add a primary resource record set, click on Create Record Set as shown in Figure 16-53. In the Create Record Set dialog set the Type as A - IPv4 address. Set Alias as Yes and select the third elastic load balancer in Alias Target.

Figure 16-53. Adding back a primary resource record set

Set the Routing Policy as Failover and the Failover Record Type as Primary. With other settings the same as when the Primary/Secondary record set was created, click on Create as shown in Figure 16-54.

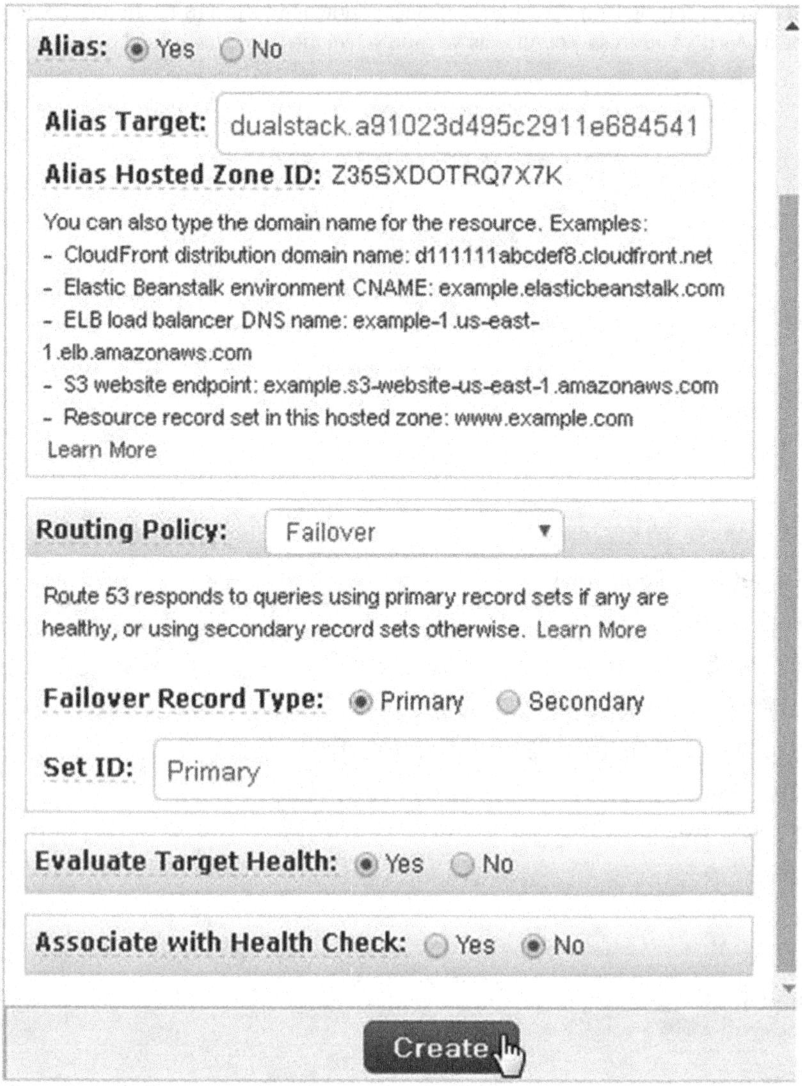

Figure 16-54. *Creating a primary resource record set*

A Primary Record Set is added as shown in Figure 16-55.

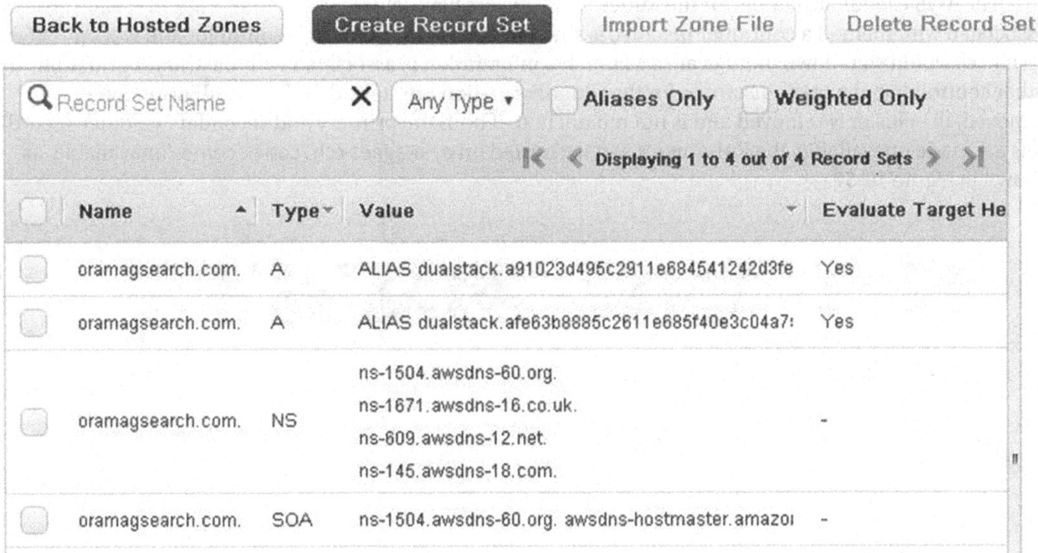

Figure 16-55. *A new primary resource record set*

The web browser request is routed to the primary resource record set, as shown in Figure 16-56.

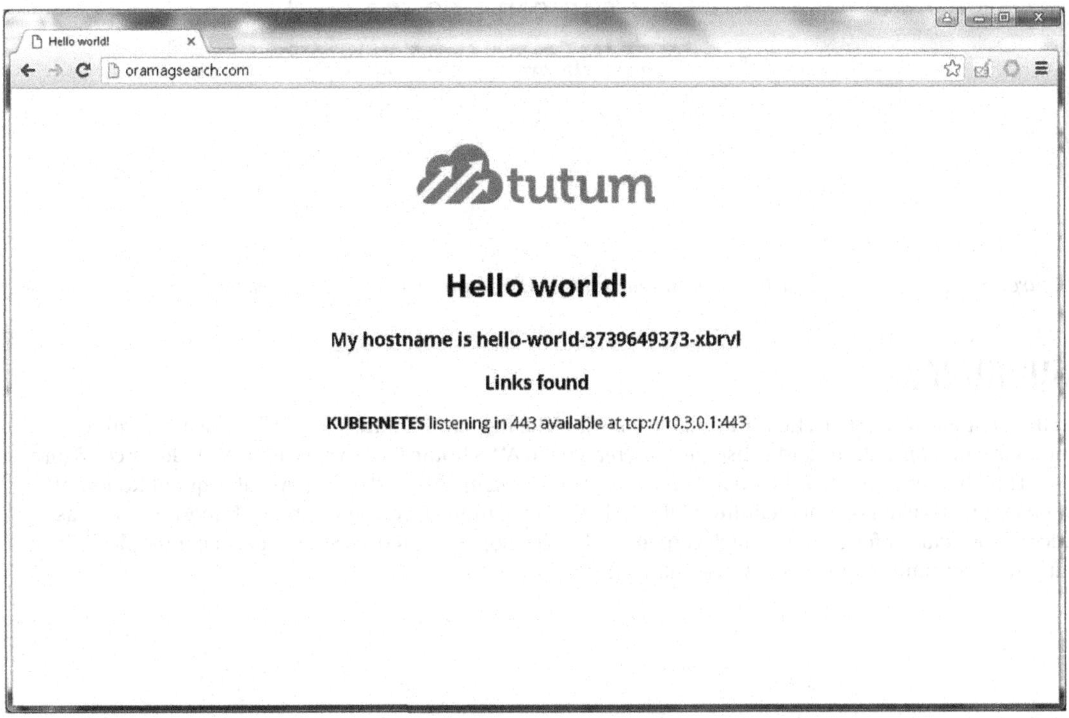

Figure 16-56. *Hosted zone served the new primary resource record set*

The AWS CloudFormations for the Kubernetes clusters have launch configurations and scaling groups associated with them. If a controller instance is shut down directly, at first the controller and worker instances would shut down; but because a launch configuration is associated with the CloudFormation, other controller and worker instances for the CloudFormation are started. If the CloudFormation is removed, the cluster is removed and is not relaunched. If both the primary and secondary resource record sets are made unavailable, the Kubernetes service hosted on `oramagsearch.com` becomes unavailable, as shown in Figure 16-57.

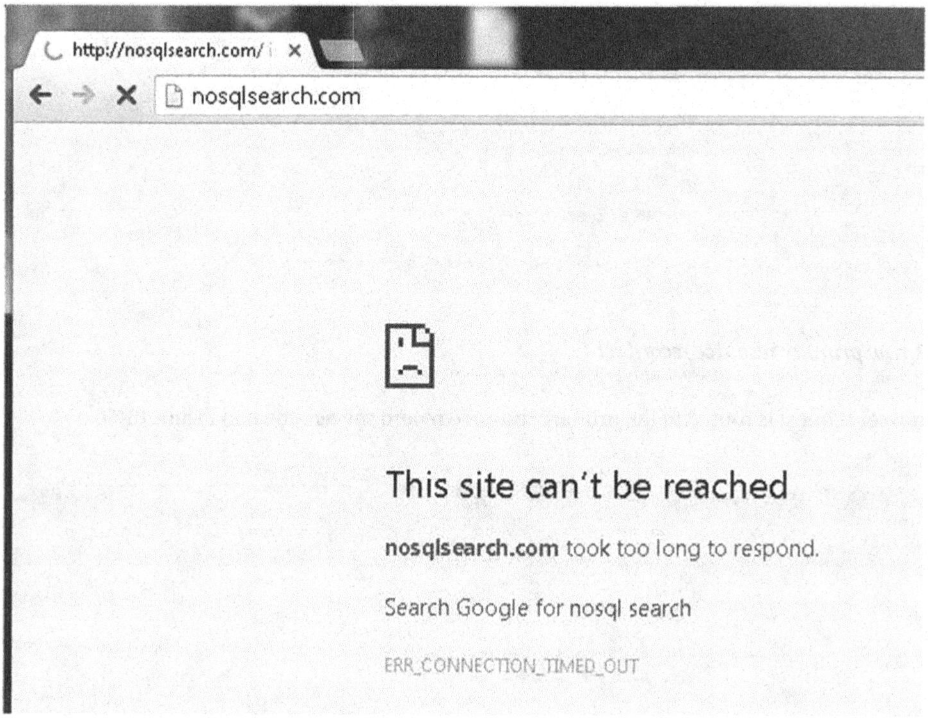

Figure 16-57. *The hosted zone becomes unreachable if all resource record sets are deleted*

Summary

In this chapter we created a highly available website. The high availability is made feasible by creating multiple cloud formations and subsequently creating an AWS Route 53 service with DNS failover configured.

This chapter concludes the book *Kubernetes Management Design Patterns*. As subsequent Kubernetes versions are developed, other features will be added. At the time of writing this book, Kubernetes 1.3 has added cross-cluster federation, which can be used to develop federated services that span multiple clusters, thus providing another form of high availability.

Index

D. Vohra, *Kubernetes Management Design Patterns*, DOI 10.1007/978-1-4842-2598-1

D

E

F

G

H

I, J

K

S

T

U

V

W, X, Y, Z

Printed in the United States
By Bookmasters